COMMERCIAL LAW IN SCOTLAND

COMMERCIAL LAW IN SCOTLAND

3rd Edition

Professor Fraser Davidson, LLB, PhD
Professor of Law, University of Stirling

Professor Laura J. Macgregor, LLB, LLM, Dip LP
Professor of Commercial Contract Law, University of Edinburgh

Assisted by

Denis J. Garrity, LLB (Hons), Dip LP
Advocate, Terra Firma Chambers, Edinburgh

W. GREEN

 THOMSON REUTERS

First edition 2003 by Fraser Davidson and Laura J. Macgregor
Second edition 2008 by Fraser Davidson and Laura J. Macgregor

Published in 2014 by W. Green, 21 Alva Street,
Edinburgh EH2 4PS
Part of Thomson Reuters (Professional) UK Limited
(Registered in England & Wales, Company No 1679046.
Registered Office and address for service: Aldgate House, 33 Aldgate High Street,
London EC3N 1DL)

www.legal-solutions.co.uk

Typeset by LBJ Typesetting Ltd of Kingsclere
Printed and bound in Great Britain by Ashford Colour Press, Gosport, Hants

No natural forests were destroyed to make this product;
only farmed timber was used and replanted

A CIP catalogue record for this book is available from the British Library.

ISBN 978–0–414–01831–0

Thomson Reuters and the Thomson Reuters logo are
trademarks of Thomson Reuters.

© 2014 Thomson Reuters (Professional) UK Limited

DEDICATION

Fraser dedicates this book to Harry.

Laura and Denis dedicate this book to Alexander and James.

INTRODUCTION TO THE THIRD EDITION

In writing this third edition our aim has remained unchanged. The book is designed to support an under-graduate course in commercial law studied as part of an LLB degree. The Law Society of Scotland's requirements have changed since publication of previous editions and this explains, for example, the absence from this edition of a chapter on negotiable instruments.

Publication of this third edition has allowed us to incorporate many new developments which have taken place in the six years since publication of the last edition. Particular developments are noted below in the context of each chapter. In some areas, because of the way in which the UK and Scottish Governments have chosen to legislate, the law has become more rather than less complicated. Two areas in particular illustrate this point: sale and bankruptcy. As was explored in the second edition, the Sale of Goods Act 1979 was amended in 2002 in order to implement the UK's responsibilities under European law.[1] A new part was added to the Act in order to introduce remedies available only to consumers. It was unclear, however, how those remedies interacted with the remedies otherwise available to all buyers which pre-dated the changes to the Act. In other words, the Act was not amended in an integrated way. This third edition comments on two further sets of regulations introducing changes to consumers' rights relating to sale.[2] The end result is that, where the issue is a consumer one, the Act must be read in conjunction with two separate sets of regulations. Sale is no longer dominated by a codifying statute. Rather, the legislation is fragmented and difficult to understand. This is a major chal-lenge to the law student or indeed the practitioner or academic. At the time of going to print a new Consumer Rights Bill is making its way through the UK legislative process. This may simplify the law at least in relation to consumer purchases. In this book we have sought to analyse this fragmented legal landscape carefully—over-simplification would be misleading and counter-productive.

As regards bankruptcy, the last edition explained how the Bankruptcy (Scotland) Act 1985 had been subject to major amendment via the Bankruptcy and Diligence etc. (Scotland) Act 2007. Since then the 1985 Act has been further amended by Part 2 of the Home Owner and Debtor Protection (Scotland) Act 2010, which amendments are examined in this edition. Yet more importantly, the Bankruptcy and Debt Advice (Scotland) Act 2014 aims to make a number of significant amendments. However, the intention is to follow this measure with consolidating legislation. That legislation, which would include the changes effected by the 2014 Act, would then only come into force some time in 2015. We might there-fore have waited for a further year before bringing out this edition, so that the new regime could be accurately described. However, since the appearance of this edition has already been delayed by the imminence of this legislation, it has been decided to make reference to the changes effected by the 2014 Act, even though they will not yet be in force when the edition first appears. Thus the current law is set out alongside the law as it is intended to be. We hope readers find this useful. The passages dealing with the changes to be effected by the 2014 Act are italicised for ease of identification.

The following paragraphs summarise the main changes which have been made to each chapter in this new edition:

---

[1] The Sale and Supply of Goods to Consumers Regulations (SI 2002/3045), implementing Directive 99/44/EC of the European Parliament and of the Council on certain aspects of the sale of consumer goods and associated guarantees [1999] OJ L171, 7.7.99, p.12.

[2] Consumer Contracts (Information, Cancellation and Additional Charges) Regulations 2013 (SI 2013/3134) and Consumer Protection (Amendment) Regulations 2014 (SI 2014/870).

Sale and supply of goods

In addition to the legislative changes noted above, this edition comments on certain high profile Scottish cases. In *Macdonald v Pollock*[3] the Inner House analysed the question of what constitutes a sale in the course of a business and clarified the law relating to the buyer's inspection of goods. In *Douglas v Glenvarigill Co Ltd*[4] Lord Drummond Young provided useful guidance on the difficult issue of when the buyer loses the right to reject goods through lapse of time.

Agency

Agency law has seen significant developments in the case law concerning the agent's warranty of authority. The Inner House refused to extend the warranty provided by a solicitor in the context of a conveyancing transaction.[5] The warranty covers the fact of authority only and does not extend to issues concerning the solicitor's client, such as his identity or his title to land. In *Halifax Life Ltd v DLA Piper Scotland Ltd*[6] Lord Hodge introduced clarity concerning the legal effect of an agent acting for a non-existent principal.

Consumer credit

In the field of consumer credit we examine the various legislative changes made in order to give effect to the Consumer Credit Directive 2008 (2008/48). Moreover, 30 new cases are considered including the decision of the Supreme Court in *Durkin v DSG Retail Ltd*.[7] Yet, most importantly, we look at how many of the provisions of the Consumer Credit Act 1974 and related statutory instruments have been repealed and replaced by rules made by the Financial Conduct Authority ("FCA"), following the abolition of the Office of Fair Trading and the transfer of its functions in relation to consumer credit to the FCA.

Carriage of goods

In carriage of goods, apart from the Carriage by Air (Revision of Limits of Liability under the Montreal Convention) Order 2009,[8] the developments are all judicial, represented by cases such as *The Andra*,[9] *The Aquafaith*,[10] *The Bulk Chile*,[11] *The Limnos*,[12] *Mansel Oil Ltd v Troon Storage Tankers*,[13] and *Sylvia Shipping Co Ltd v Prague Bulk Carriers Ltd*.[14]

Cautionary obligations and other rights in security

In this chapter we have added a new paragraph on the impact of unfair contracts legislation on cautionary obligations. We consider a number of new decisions on standard securities, including that of the Supreme Court in *Royal Bank of Scotland Plc v Wilson*.[15] We also address the significant amendments made to the Conveyancing and Feudal Reform (Scotland) Act 1970 by the Home Owner and Debtor Protection (Scotland) Act 2010, as well as the details of the Applications by Creditors (Pre-Action

---

[3] [2011] CSIH 12; 2013 S.C. 22.
[4] [2010] CSOH 14; 2010 S.L.T. 634.
[5] *Cheshire Mortgage Corporation Ltd v Grandison; Blemain Finance Ltd v Balfour Manson LLP* [2012] CSIH 66; 2013 S.C. 160.
[6] [2009] CSOH 74.
[7] [2014] UKSC 21.
[8] SI 2009/3018.
[9] [2012] 2 Lloyd's Rep. 587.
[10] [2012] 2 Lloyd's Rep. 61.
[11] [2013] EWCA Civ 185.
[12] [2008] 2 Lloyd's Rep. 166.
[13] [2009] 2 Lloyd's Rep. 371.
[14] [2010] 2 Lloyd's Rep. 81.
[15] *Royal Bank of Scotland Plc v Wilson*, 2010 S.L.T. 1227.

Requirements) (Scotland) Order 2010.[16] On the intimation of assignation of a security we examine the decision of the Inner House in *Christie, Owen and Davies Plc v Campbell.*[17] We also look at Lord Hodge's views on the conceptual basis of lien in *Wilmington Trust Co v Rolls-Royce Plc,*[18] and the views of the Court of Appeal on co-caution in *Harvey v Dunbar Assets Plc.*[19]

Insurance

The Scottish Law Commission and the Law Commission for England and Wales have seen some of their joint recommendations on insurance law enacted. The Consumer Insurance (Disclosure and Representations) Act 2012 introduced the statutory concept of a "consumer insurance contract", and deals with the central topic of duty of disclosure, as well as warranties, representations and remedies for breach.

Personal insolvency

In addition to the legislative developments noted above, this edition considers the Bankruptcy (Certificate for Sequestration) (Scotland) Regulations 2010[20] and the Protected Trust Deeds (Scotland) Regulations 2013.[21] We also look at the views of Lord McEwan in *Accountant in Bankruptcy v Sneddon,*[22] Lord Hardie in *Barlow v City Plumbing Supplies Holdings Ltd,*[23] Sheriff Principal Dunlop in *Junespear Ltd v Dear,*[24] Sheriff Holligan in *Brown's Trustee, Applicant*[25] and *Accountant in Bankruptcy v Campbell,*[26] Sheriff Way in *Young v Accountant in Bankruptcy,*[27] and Sheriff Mann in *Stewart's Trustee v Stewart.*[28]

Partnership

The law concerning the liability of an incoming partner for debts which pre-date his assumption was examined by Lord Hodge in *Sim v Howat.*[29] Not only did he provide an invaluable review of the difficult and conflicting case law, but he also provided a more convincing legal analysis, no longer relying on presumptions. As one problem is resolved, however, a new one develops. A recent (albeit relatively low level) English authority suggests that members of an LLP owe no fiduciary duties to one another, and, on the facts, that the fiduciary duties they owed to the LLP itself were minimal.[30] Whether this approach will be followed in Scotland is yet to be seen. This chapter notes further statutory amendments including the enactment of the Partnerships (Prosecution) (Scotland) Act 2013.

Commercial dispute resolution

In this area the main focus is the transformation of the Scots law of arbitration effected by the Arbitration (Scotland) Act 2010, along with associated orders and the already emerging case law under the Act. The potential impact of the Courts Reform (Scotland) Bill 2014 is also considered, as are the

---

[16] SSI 2010/317.
[17] 2009 S.C. 436.
[18] [2011] CSOH 151.
[19] [2013] EWCA Civ 952.
[20] SSI 2010/397.
[21] Protected Trust Deeds (Scotland) Regulations 2013 (SSI 2013/318).
[22] [2008] CSOH 11.
[23] 2009 S.C.L.R. 350.
[24] 2008 S.L.T. (Sh. Ct) 69.
[25] 2010 S.L.T. (Sh. Ct) 45.
[26] 2012 S.L.T. (Sh. Ct) 35.
[27] 2010 S.L.T. (Sh. Ct) 37.
[28] 2012 S.L.T. (Sh. Ct) 231.
[29] [2012] CSOH 171.
[30] *F&C Alternative Investments (Holdings) Ltd v Bathelemy* [2011] EWHC 1731 (Ch); [2011] EWHC 1851 (Ch); [2012] Bus. L.R. 884; [2012] 3 W.L.R. 10; [2011] EWHC 2807 (Ch); [2012] Bus. L.R. 891. Appealed on costs only [2012] EWCA Civ 843; [2013] 1 W.L.R. 548; [2012] 4 All E.R. 1096; [2013] 1 W.L.R. 548.

Cross-Border Mediation (Scotland) Regulations 2011.[31] Attention is also paid to new case law on the operation of ombudsmen schemes, the potential unfairness of arbitration clauses, and legal obligations attaching to mediation.

The law is stated as at May 1, 2014.

Acknowledgments

As before, we must record our appreciation for the assistance we have received in producing this book. Thus much thanks must go to our colleagues Gillian Black, David Cabrelli, Janeen Carruthers, Bryan Clark, Gavin Little, Tikus Little, Hector MacQueen, Donna McKenzie-Skene, Scott Wortley, Hong-Lin Yu and Rebecca Zahn. A special mention is owed to Lorna Richardson, who provided detailed comments on several chapters. Thanks also to all at W. Green, especially Alan Bett, Philippa Blackham and Janet Campbell.

---

[31] SSI 2011/234.

CONTENTS

TABLE OF CASES

TABLE OF STATUTES

TABLE OF SCOTTISH STATUTES

TABLE OF STATUTORY INSTRUMENTS

TABLE OF SCOTTISH STATUTORY INSTRUMENTS

Chapter 1

SALE AND SUPPLY OF GOODS

INTRODUCTION

The main statutory source of the law on sale is the Sale of Goods Act 1979 ("the 1979 Act"), the **1.1** complex historical development of which is examined below. This codifying statute has been amended quite extensively. General common law principles are, however, also relevant. Sale is a contract and therefore draws some of its rules from general contractual principles. The resultant scheme of regulation is, therefore, complex. The analysis must also be drawn wider than sale alone, taking in hire, hire purchase and contracts for the supply of goods and services. If one issue were, amongst this mass of legal rules, to be highlighted as an important theme, it is the extent of consumer protection. Important protections appear, for example, in the form of the statutory implied terms contained in ss.12–15 of the 1979 Act, and the controls on contracting-out of such protections applied by the Unfair Contract Terms Act 1977 ("UCTA 1977").

The first Act to codify the law on sale of goods was the Sale of Goods Act 1893. This statute was, however, a codifying statute only insofar as it applied in England. It was only once the Bill had been before Parliament for four years that provisions extending to Scotland were finally agreed. Prior to 1893 the law of sale in Scotland and England had contained important differences. The Scots law of sale, unlike English law, is based on Roman law.[1] Thus whereas one could say that the Act codified English law, it enacted important changes to Scots law. In 1979 a further consolidating Act was passed, and it is this Act which remains the main point of reference for the law of sale in the UK today.[2]

In view of the fact that some of the provisions governing Scots law were added at a later stage, after the 1893 Act had been originally conceived, it is perhaps not surprising that some of those provisions were defective and led, later, to problems.[3] The statutory reforms which have taken place in recent years have resolved most, if not all, of the problems.

The most important statutory reform of the 1979 Act arose following joint consultation of the English and Scottish Law Commissions.[4] The joint report, published in 1987, resulted in the passing of the Sale and Supply of Goods Act 1994. This Act, more than any other, resolved the issues which had remained problematic for Scots law. In particular, it removed the English terms "condition" and "warranty" from the Scottish provisions, and extended the protections for purchasers or consumers provided by the statutory implied terms to contracts other than sale.[5] A further joint report was published in 1993[6] which led to the Sale of Goods (Amendment) Act 1995 which strengthened the purchaser's rights where he buys part of a larger bulk of goods.

More recent amendments have proved necessary in order to implement the UK's obligations under European Directives. The most significant were introduced by the Sale and Supply of Goods to Consumers Regulations 2002.[7] These regulations, which came into force on March 31, 2003, were passed in order to implement the European Directive on certain aspects of the sale of consumer goods and associated guarantees.[8] The regulations introduce several important changes to the field of consumer protection, most notably by amending the implied term as to satisfactory quality; introducing the consumer's right to the repair or replacement of goods; and regulating consumer guarantees.[9] Also relevant is the Consumer Contracts (Information, Cancellation and Additional Charges) Regulations 2013,[10] which came into force on June 13, 2014. The regulations enact further consumer protection measures, including obligations on traders to provide information and consumer's cancellation rights. Finally, the Consumer Protection (Amendment) Regulations 2014[11] amend the Consumer

---

[1] See W. Gordon, "Sale" in K.G.C. Reid and R. Zimmermann (eds), *A History of Private Law in Scotland* (Oxford: Oxford University Press, 2000), Vol.II, Ch.12.

[2] References to statutory provisions in this chapter are to the 1979 Act unless otherwise indicated. Prior to the 1979 Act the law had been amended in the Supply of Goods (Implied Terms) Act 1973.

[3] See J.J. Gow, *Mercantile and Industrial Law of Scotland* (Edinburgh: W. Green, 1964), pp.75–76.

[4] See the eventual joint report, Law Commission and Scottish Law Commission, *Report on Sale and Supply of Goods*. HMSO, 1987. Cmnd.137. Law Com. No.160; Scot. Law Com. No.104.

[5] See para.1.11.8 below.

[6] Law Commission and Scottish Law Commission, *Sale of Goods Forming Part of a Bulk*. HMSO, 1993. Law Com. No.215; Scot. Law Com. No.145.

[7] Sale and Supply of Goods to Consumers Regulations 2002 (SI 2002/3045), hereinafter "2002 Regulations".

[8] Directive 99/44/EC of the European Parliament and of the Council on certain aspects of the sale of consumer goods and associated guarantees [1999] OJ L171, 7.7.99, p.12.

[9] As is commented on, at paras 1.12.1 and 1.15 below, the changes protect consumers in sale, sale and supply of goods, hire and hire purchase.

[10] SI 2013/3134, implementing the EU Consumer Rights Directive (2001/83/EU).

[11] SI 2014/870, implementing Directive 2005/29/EC of the European Parliament and of the Council concerning unfair business-to-consumer commercial practices ([2005] OJ L149, 11.6.05, p.22).

Protection from Unfair Trading Regulations 2008[12] by providing consumers with new rights of redress in relation to either misleading actions or aggressive commercial practices. These new consumer rights of redress come into force on October 1, 2014.

One final, perhaps obvious, point which should be made is that, here, as in other areas of the law concerning consumers, the law develops slowly. This is because consumers tend not to litigate, generally lacking the funds to do so. This explains the relatively few high level decisions on significant issues, for example, the implied term on quality and fitness of goods (1979 Act s.14).

DEFINITION OF A CONTRACT OF SALE OF GOODS

The definition of a contract of sale of goods is found in s.2(1) of the 1979 Act: **1.2**

> "A contract of sale of goods is a contract by which the seller transfers or agrees to transfer the property in goods to the buyer for a money consideration, called the price."

The seller may transfer the property, i.e. the ownership, in the goods as part of the contract of sale.[13] However, the seller may agree to transfer property at some point in the future, or conclude a contract subject to a condition. In both of the latter cases the contract still falls within the definition given above and is described as an agreement to sell.[14] In a conditional contract, the condition may be either suspensive or resolutive. Where the condition is suspensive, performance of the obligation is delayed, or suspended, until the condition is purified. By contrast, where the condition is resolutive, the obligation is already in force, and purification of the condition brings the obligation to an end.[15]

Section 61(1) defines "goods" as "all corporeal moveables except money". Incorporeal property such as copyright cannot be goods, nor can heritable property. The definition continues,

> "in particular 'goods' includes emblements, industrial growing crops, and things attached to or forming part of the land which are agreed to be severed before sale or under the contract or sale; and includes an undivided share in goods".

Thus, where it was agreed that the buyer would enter the seller's land to fell and remove timber, the timber came within the latter part of the definition of goods.[16] Because ownership of land is usually from the heavens to the centre of the earth,[17] minerals tend to form part of an ordinary title to land. They can, however, be transferred, as heritable property, under a separate title.[18] However, once minerals have been extracted, there is no reason why they cannot fall within the definition of "goods".[19]

The definition of goods has proved problematic in its application to computer software. Although a disk can clearly fall within the definition, this seems to ignore the real product, which is the software supplied on the disk. Such software may be downloaded over the internet,[20] which places the contract

---

[12] SI 2008/1277. These Regulations implement the Directive noted immediately above, and also Directive 99/44/EC of the European Parliament and of the Council on certain aspects of the sale of consumer goods and associated guarantees [1999] OJ L171, 7.7.99, p. 12.

[13] See s.2(4).

[14] See s.2(5).

[15] See Hector L. MacQueen and Joe Thomson, *Contract Law in Scotland*, 3rd edn (Edinburgh: Butterworths, 2012), paras 3.61–3.70.

[16] *Munro v Liquidator of Balnagown Estates Co Ltd*, 1949 S.C. 49.

[17] *A coelo usque ad centrum.*

[18] See explanation in Robert Rennie, *Minerals and the Law of Scotland* (Welwyn Garden City: EMIS, 2001), Ch.1.

[19] However, cf. *Morgan v Russell* [1909] 1 K.B. 357, per Alverstone CJ at 365, although Walton LJ at 366 reserved judgment on whether a contract for minerals which had not been worked at the date of the contract could be a contract for the sale of goods in terms of the 1893 Act.

[20] If the material is downloaded over the internet then the Electronic Commerce (EC Directive) Regulations 2002 (SI 2002/2013) will apply. These regulations are the implementation in the UK of the Electronic Commerce Directive 2000/31/EC on certain legal aspects of information society services, in particular electronic commerce, in the Internal Market [2000] OJ L178/1. The terms of the regulations are not analysed in detail here.

outwith the 1979 Act entirely, and, importantly, denies the buyer important protections under that Act.[21] Lord Penrose has defined a contract for the supply of computer software as "a contract *sui generis*, which may involve elements of nominate contracts such as sale, but which would be inadequately understood if expressed wholly in terms of any of the nominate contracts".[22] Sir Iain Glidewell in a leading English case, *St Albans City and District Council v International Computers Ltd*,[23] indicated that while a disk fell within the definition of goods, the same could not be said of a computer program.[24] His comments were, however, obiter. The case law is, therefore, conflicting and it is not possible at present to provide any definitive answer to the question of whether software constitutes "goods".[25]

The term "goods" also includes an undivided share in the goods.[26] Section 5 further subdivides goods into "existing" and "future" goods. The former are goods owned or possessed by the seller at the time of sale, whereas the latter are goods to be manufactured or acquired by the seller after the making of the contract of sale. Clearly, the latter type of contract can only be an agreement to sell.[27] Goods may also be specific or unascertained, specific goods being goods identified and agreed upon at the time the contract is made,[28] and unascertained being neither so identified nor agreed upon. Subject to one exception, it is only possible to have an agreement to sell unascertained goods.[29] A sale transfers ownership of the property to the buyer, while an agreement to sell gives the buyer only a personal right against the seller. The distinction between sale and agreement to sell is of vital importance in a variety of contexts, chiefly insolvency, where the buyer will lose out in a contest with the seller's liquidator or trustee in bankruptcy, should there be only an agreement to sell.

OTHER TRANSACTIONS

1.3 Many contracts do not fall within the 1979 Act. Where the contract involves exchanging goods for goods, and there is no element of payment of a monetary "price" then the contract is barter and not sale.[30] Where the contract is one of part exchange, such as the common example of sale of used cars, the "price" will usually be goods plus money. The legal analysis applied to such situations has tended to be that the contract is a contract of sale.[31] However, this may have been because, at that stage, only by defining the contract as sale would the purchaser receive the protection of the statutory implied terms. Similar protections are now provided to contracts of barter through the Sale and Supply of Goods Act 1994, and so the underlying reasons for classification as sale have now disappeared (see para.1.11.8 below).

Contracts for work and materials also previously presented a problem of definition given that they involve the provision of both goods and services. Again, the question has become less important because the 1994 Act extended to consumers under such contracts the same protections from the implied terms as were previously provided only to purchasers under sale contracts.[32]

[21] Specifically the implied terms relating to description, fitness for purpose and quality at ss.12, 13 and 14, commented on below at paras 1.11.3–1.11.5.

[22] *Beta Computer Systems Europe Ltd v Adobe Computer Systems Europe Ltd*, 1996 S.L.T. 604 at 609.

[23] *St Albans City and District Council v International Computers Ltd* [1996] 4 All E.R. 481; [1997] F.S.R. 251 CA. See also the discussions in P.S. Atiyah, John N. Adams, H.L. MacQueen, *Sale of Goods*, 12th edn (Harlow: Longman, 2010), pp.75 and 243.

[24] *St Albans City and District Council v International Computers Ltd* [1996] 4 All E.R. 481 at 492–494. Sir Iain Glidewell made an attempt to protect buyers of programs even though the contract for sale of a program fell outwith the Sale of Goods Act 1979. He indicated that the same implied terms which protect the buyer under a sale of goods contract (terms as to description, fitness for purpose and quality under ss.12, 13 and 14) could be implied into a contract for sale of a program as a matter of common law. Again, this was obiter and it will be interesting to see whether his view is developed in a later case.

[25] Although see the New Zealand case of *Erris Promotions Ltd v Commissioner of Inland Revenue* [2004] 1 N.Z.L.R. 811.

[26] Inserted into the definition of "goods" in s.61(1) of the 1979 Act by the Sale of Goods (Amendment) Act 1995 s.2.

[27] See s.5(3).

[28] See s.61(1).

[29] See para.1.8 et seq. below, and in particular, para.1.8.2 on sales from an identified bulk.

[30] *Widenmeyer v Burn, Stewart & Co Ltd*, 1967 S.C. 85; *Ballantyne v Durant*, 1983 S.L.T. (Sh Ct) 38.

[31] *Sneddon v Durant*, 1982 S.L.T. (Sh Ct) 39.

[32] For an expansive analysis of the nature of such contracts see *Marjandi Ltd v Bon Accord Glass Ltd* Unreported October 15, 2007 Aberdeen Sheriff Court.

A number of other contracts pose difficulties of classification. Party A may agree to buy goods from party B on condition that B purchases goods from A. This contract, which may be described as "counter-trade" could be classed as two contracts of sale, but given that both transactions occur in the same contract, it is probably better classified as a form of barter. The contract may also be any of the following types which are subject to separate regulation: credit sale, conditional sale, hire or hire purchase.[33] Whereas the first two types could be classed as types of sale, hire purchase cannot, given that there is no obligation on the hirer to buy the goods. A case which amply illustrates the difficulties inherent in classifying transactions is *Esso Petroleum Ltd v Customs and Excise Commissioners*,[34] in which coins showing the images of members of the 1970 England World Cup team were provided as free gifts to purchasers of Esso products. Two members of the House of Lords thought that there was no contract which related to the coins, the others thought that there was a contract, although one classed it as sale and two classed it, not very helpfully, as a "collateral contract".

SALE OR SECURITY?

Section 62(4) provides that the 1979 Act does not apply to "a transaction in the form of a contract of **1.4** sale which is intended to operate by way of mortgage, pledge, charge, or other security". This section is aimed at so called "sham sales".[35] As is explored later in this book (see para.5.3.11 below), it is difficult, if not impossible, in Scots law to create a security over moveable property without taking possession of that property. Parties seek, therefore, to enter into what may look like sale, but is, in truth, an attempt to take a security over moveables without taking possession of those moveables. If A lends £2,000 to B, B can "sell" his car to A, but under an agreement that B will retain possession of the car. The idea is that A will sell the car back once repaid. There being no real intention to create a contract of sale, the car is actually being used as security for the money lent by A to B. Thus if B became bankrupt, then A could argue that the car is in fact A's property. Because s.62(4) disapplies the Act to such sham sales, the property in the goods will not pass, and the security will be ineffectual.[36]

FORMATION OF THE CONTRACT

Although generally the normal rules of conclusion of contracts apply to contracts for the sale of goods, **1.5** recently the Consumer Contracts (Information, Cancellation and Additional Charges) Regulations 2013 has imposed important consumer protection measures which apply at the point of formation. The Regulations came into force on June 13, 2014 and apply to any contracts entered into on or after that date.[37] They replaced the Consumer Protection (Distance Selling) Regulations 2000 and the Cancellation of Contracts made in a Consumer's Home or Place of Work etc. Regulations 2008,[38] and so many of the requirements they impose are not new.

The Regulations differentiate three types of contracts: contracts made on-premises; those made off-premises; and distance contracts. All three terms are defined in reg.5. The essence of a distance contract is that the contract is concluded at a distance without the simultaneous physical presence of the trader and the consumer with the exclusive use of one or more means of distance communication. Off-premises contracts are one of four types listed in reg.5. The first two concern situations in which either a contract is concluded or the consumer makes an offer in the simultaneous physical presence of both, but away from the business premises of the trader. The third type is where the contract is concluded on the trader's business premises

---

[33] See Consumer Credit Act 1974 and Supply of Goods and Services Act 1982.

[34] *Esso Petroleum Ltd v Customs and Excise Commissioners* [1976] 1 W.L.R. 1.

[35] See also the discussion of retention of title clauses at para.1.8.3 below.

[36] See examples in *Robertson v Halls Trustee* (1896) 24 R. 120; *Hepburn v Law*, 1914 S.C. 918; *Scottish Transit Trust Ltd v Scottish Land Cultivators Ltd*, 1955 S.C. 254.

[37] Consumer Contracts (Information, Cancellation and Additional Charges) Regulations 2013 ("CC (IC and AC) Regs") reg.1.

[38] CC (IC and AC) Regs reg.2.

or through distance communication immediately after the consumer was personally and individually addressed in a place which is not the business premises of the trader in the simultaneous presence of both. Finally, the fourth type is a contract concluded during an excursion organised by the trader with the aim or effect of promoting the sale of goods or services to the consumer. On-premises contracts are defined as neither distance nor off-premises contracts. A consumer is defined as an individual acting for purposes which are wholly or mainly outside that individual's trade, business, craft or profession.[39] A trader is defined as a person acting for purposes relating to that person's trade, business, craft or profession, whether acting personally or through another person acting in the trader's name or on the trader's behalf (i.e. an agent).[40]

Whichever one of the three types of contract (distance, off-premises or on-premises) is concluded, the trader is obliged to provide consumers with specific information about the transaction. The consumer will not be bound in the contract until such information is provided. Exclusions do apply. There is, for example, no obligation to provide information where the transaction is off-premises and the payment is not more than £42.[41] The type of information differs with the type of contract. Schedule 1 lists the information to be provided in respect of an on-premises contract.[42] This includes the main characteristics of the goods or service, the identity of the trader and the total price. Schedule 2 lists the information to be provided in respect of a distance and off-premises contract.[43] This includes delivery arrangements, and the trader's complaints-handling policy, if there is one, and cancellation rights. The trader must also provide the consumer with a cancellation form if a right to cancel exists (for the right to cancel see below at para.1.12.2.4).[44] Additionally, where the contract is off-premises or distance, the trader must provide the consumer with a copy of the signed contract or a confirmation of the contract within a reasonable time after conclusion of the contract.[45] A term is implied into the contract that the trader has complied with these obligations.[46]

THE PRICE

1.6 Although the price will usually be fixed in the contract of sale, it may be determined in other ways. It may be left to be fixed in a manner agreed by the contract, or may be determined by a course of dealing between the parties.[47] If neither of these possibilities is open to the parties, the buyer is bound to pay a reasonable price for the goods.[48] The 1979 Act provides that what is a reasonable price is a question of fact which depends upon the circumstances of each case.[49] It was stated in one Scottish case[50] that a reasonable price need not be the market price[51] but must be fair and just to both parties,[52] and that circumstances might require a balancing of advantages and disadvantages between the seller and buyer.[53] The parties may agree that the price is to be fixed by the valuation of a third party, and where that third party fails to do so, the contract will be avoided.[54] If one contracting party has been at fault in preventing the third party from carrying out the valuation, then the other contracting party has a right to sue him for damages.[55]

---

[39] CC (IC and AC) Regs reg.4.
[40] CC (IC and AC) Regs reg.4.
[41] CC (IC and AC) Regs reg.7(4).
[42] CC (IC and AC) Regs reg.9.
[43] CC (IC and AC) Regs regs 10 and 13.
[44] CC (IC and AC) Regs reg.10(b), the form is provided in part B of Sch.3.
[45] CC (IC and AC) Regs regs 12 and 16.
[46] CC (IC and AC) Regs reg.18.
[47] See s.8(1).
[48] See s.8(2).
[49] See s.8(3)—assuming of course that the absence of agreement on price does not indicate a fundamental lack of consensus, see *May and Butcher Ltd v R.* [1934] 2 K.B. 17 HL.
[50] *Glynwed Distribution Ltd v S Koronka & Co Ltd*, 1977 S.C. 1.
[51] *Glynwed Distribution v S Koronka & Co Ltd*, 1977 S.C. 1, per Lord Kissen at 7–8; per Lord Leechman at 11.
[52] *Glynwed Distribution v S Koronka & Co Ltd*, 1977 S.C. 1, per Lord Kissen at 8; per Lord Leechman at 11.
[53] *Glynwed Distribution v S Koronka & Co Ltd*, 1977 S.C. 1, per Lord Kissen at 8.
[54] See s.9(1).
[55] See s.9(2). See also *Essoldo v Ladbroke Group* [1976] C.L.Y. 337, where the English courts granted an injunction preventing one of the parties from obstructing the determination of the price.

TIME

If a contract provides that time is of the essence in relation to a particular matter, then late performance **1.7** by one party of that stipulation will entitle the other party to rescind. In a contract of sale, unless the terms of the contract indicate that the parties intended otherwise, stipulations as to time of payment are not of the essence.[56] Whether any other stipulation as to time is or is not of the essence is a matter of interpretation of the terms of the contract.[57] The appropriate remedy for breach of a term relating to time where time is not of the essence is damages rather than recission.

THE PASSING OF PROPERTY

The main purpose of the contract is to pass the property in goods, i.e. transfer ownership thereof from **1.8** seller to buyer. The regime which was imposed by the Sale of Goods Act 1893 in relation to passing of ownership of goods was very different from the regime under Scots common law which pre-dated this Act. At common law, the transfer of ownership required both the will or intention of the seller and delivery.[58] Under the 1979 Act the general rule is that property in goods (as ownership is described in the Act) passes when the parties intend it to pass.[59] In the case of unascertained goods, property cannot pass until the goods have been ascertained[60] although there is an exception to this rule in the case of unascertained goods which are part of an identified bulk.[61]

RULES FOR ASCERTAINING INTENTION

The parties may have made their intentions as to the passing of property clear. Where they have not, the **1.8.1** Act states that regard must be had to the terms of the contract, the conduct of the parties and the circumstances of the case.[62] However, after this process of interpretation has been completed, the parties' intentions may remain unclear. In such a case, the 1979 Act contains a number of rules which assist with the task of ascertaining intention. Such rules are only relevant where the intention of the parties is not clear. As Lord President Strathclyde explained:

> "The rules in section 18 are merely intended to be a guide in ascertaining the intention of the parties. But, if the intention of the parties is quite plain . . . then the rules of section 18 do not come into play at all."[63]

Rule 1 states:

> "Where there is an unconditional contract for the sale of specific goods in a deliverable state the property in the goods passes to the buyer when the contract is made, and it is immaterial whether the time of payment or the time of delivery, or both, be postponed."

However, this is out of step with many modern transactions, especially sales to consumers. Thus Lord Diplock stated in *RV Ward Ltd v Bignall*[64]:

---

[56] See s.10(1).
[57] See s.10(2).
[58] Stair, *Institutions*, I, 7, 8 and III, 2, 5; Erskine, *Institute*, II, 1, 18; Bankton, *Institute*, II, 1, 20; Bell, *Principles*, s.1299, and *Commentaries*, I, 177.
[59] See s.17(1).
[60] See s.16.
[61] See discussion at para.1.8.2 below.
[62] See s.17(2).
[63] *Woodburn v Andrew Motherwell Ltd*, 1917 S.C. 533 at 538.
[64] *RV Ward Ltd v Bignall* [1967] 1 Q.B. 534.

> "In modern times very little is needed to give rise to the intention that the property in specific goods is to pass only on delivery or payment."[65]

The term "unconditional contract" probably refers to a contract with no conditions relating to the passing of property rather than a contract with no conditions whatsoever.[66] A "deliverable state" means that the goods are in such a state that the buyer would, under the contract, be bound to take delivery of them.[67] In *Gowans v Bowe & Sons*[68] in a contract for the sale of potatoes it was agreed that, when the potatoes were mature, the farmer would lift them and put them into pits on the farm. When the buyer wanted the potatoes, he was to send his workmen to lift the potatoes from the pits, clean and sort them, before putting them into the buyer's bags. The farmer would then cart them to the railway station or harbour for the buyer. After the potatoes were put into pits, the seller became bankrupt. It was held that property in the potatoes had passed to the buyer. Lord Cullen explained:

> "I am unable to regard such carting as something to be done to put the goods into a deliverable state. I think that, in the ordinary working out of such a contract, the potatoes would be delivered to the buyers when lifted by them from the pits and put into their own bags. According to the intention of the parties here, the carting was, I think, only a facility for removal after delivery."[69]

Rule 2 states that:

> "Where there is a contract for the sale of specific goods and the seller is bound to do something to the goods for the purpose of putting them into a deliverable state, the property does not pass until the thing is done and the buyer has notice that it has been done."

The *Gowans* case is an example of this rule. In that case the contract was for the sale of specific goods (the whole crop of potatoes). The seller was bound to put the potatoes into pits to put them into a deliverable state, and the buyer had been made aware that the seller had completed this task.

Rule 3 states that:

> "Where there is a contract for the sale of specific goods in a deliverable state but the seller is bound to weigh, measure, test, or do some other act or thing with reference to the goods for the purpose of ascertaining the price, the property does not pass until the act or thing is done and the buyer has notice that it has been done."

In *Nanka Bruce v Commonwealth Trust Ltd*[70] a sub-buyer was to weigh the goods, and the price paid by the buyer was calculated on the basis of this weight. It was held that the sale was not conditional on the weighing of the goods. The weighing was simply to check that the weight of the goods was as represented. Property in the goods had passed prior to the weighing being carried out. Rule 3 would not have been appropriate, given that, in that case, the sub-buyer and not the seller was obliged to weigh the goods.

Rule 4 states that:

> "When goods are delivered to the buyer on approval or on sale or return or other similar terms the property in the goods passes to the buyer—
>
> (a) when he signifies his approval or acceptance to the seller or does any other act adopting the transaction;
> (b) if he does not signify his approval or acceptance to the seller but retains the goods without giving notice of rejection, then, if a time has been fixed for the return of the goods, on the expiration of that time, and, if no time has been fixed, on the expiration of a reasonable time."

---

[65] *RV Ward Ltd v Bignall* [1967] 1 Q.B. 534, per Lord Diplock at 545.
[66] But see *Varley v Whipp* [1900] 1 Q.B. 513, per Channell J at 517.
[67] See s.61(5).
[68] *Gowans v Bowe & Sons*, 1910 2 S.L.T. 17.
[69] *Gowans v Bowe & Sons*, 1910 2 S.L.T. 17, per Lord Cullen at 18.
[70] *Nanka Bruce v Commonwealth Trust Ltd* [1926] A.C. 77.

This rule, in common with the other rules, may be excluded by agreement between the parties.[71] In some cases it may be difficult to tell whether goods have, in fact, been provided by a seller to a buyer on a sale or return basis, or have been sent by a principal to an agent for the agent to sell on the principal's behalf.[72] If it is the former, the buyer is likely to be free to keep the whole proceeds of resale. Where at least a proportion of the resale price is handed by the original buyer to the original seller, the buyer retaining a proportion of the price in payment of his fee, it is likely to be regarded as the latter. The importance of the distinction is seen where the contract stipulates that the property in the goods will not pass until the seller is paid in full. Were the contract to be regarded as a sale or return contract, then the second buyer might find that he is not the owner of the goods, where the first buyer fails to pay for them. If, however, the first buyer were reselling as the original seller's agent, the second buyer would receive good title to the goods.[73]

In one case, a retailer, on being sent goods by a wholesaler in order to effect sales to customers, became the purchaser himself on pledging the goods.[74] There are indications in the judgments that the Second Division was keen to ensure that the loss would not fall on the third party pawnbroker who had no knowledge of the relationship between the wholesaler and the retailer.[75]

Property does not pass where the buyer fails to return the goods to the seller within the agreed period for reasons outwith his control, such as seizure by a creditor.[76]

Rule 5 is divided into three parts.

Part 1 provides that:

> "Where there is a contract for the sale of unascertained or future goods by description, and goods of that description and in a deliverable state are unconditionally appropriated to the contract, either by the seller with the assent of the buyer or by the buyer with the assent of the seller, the property in the goods then passes to the buyer; and the assent may be express or implied, and may be given either before or after the appropriation is made."

Because assent may be implied rather than express, it is sufficient if the buyer fails to respond to a notice from the seller that the goods are in a deliverable state and have been appropriated to the contract.[77] Express assent is not required. A useful analysis of the meaning of "unconditional appropriation" was made by Pearson J in *Carlos Federspiel & Co SA v Charles Twigg & Co Ltd*.[78] He emphasised the consensual nature of appropriation:

> "[T]he element of common intention has always to be borne in mind. A mere setting apart or selection of the seller of the goods which he expects to use in performance of the contract is not enough. If that is all, he can change his mind and use those goods in performance of some other contract and use some other goods in performance of this contract."[79]

He continued:

> "To constitute an appropriation of the goods to the contract, the parties must have had, or be reasonably supposed to have had, an intention to attach the contract irrevocably to those goods, so that those goods and no others are the subject of the sale and become the property of the buyer".[80]

He then suggested that the appropriating act was usually the last act to be carried out by the seller, although if the seller was due to carry out an "important and decisive" further act then property would

---

[71] *Weiner v Gill* [1906] 2 K.B. 574.

[72] *Weiner v Harris* [1910] 1 K.B. 285.

[73] *Weiner v Harris* [1910] 1 K.B. 285; and see paras 1.10 et seq. below, especially 1.10.1.

[74] *Bryce v Ehrmann* (1904) 7 F. 5.

[75] *Bryce v Ehrmann* (1904) 7 F. 5, per the Lord Justice Clerk Macdonald at 10; per Lord Moncreiff at 16.

[76] *Re Ferrier* [1944] Ch. 295.

[77] *Pignataro v Gilroy* [1919] 1 K.B. 459.

[78] *Carlos Federspiel & Co SA* [1957] 1 Lloyd's Rep. 240.

[79] *Carlos Federspiel & Co SA* [1957] 1 Lloyd's Rep. 240, per Pearson J at 255.

[80] *Carlos Federspiel & Co SA* [1957] 1 Lloyd's Rep. 240, per Pearson J at 255.

not usually pass until that final act had been carried out.[81] So in *Hendy Lennox (Industrial Engines) Ltd v Grahame Puttick Ltd*[82] appropriation did not occur when generators were set aside and marked with the names of individual customers. It occurred only when customers were sent invoices and delivery notes bearing the serial numbers of the generators to be delivered to them.

Appropriation must be unconditional. So, if the contract stipulates, for example, that the property will only pass when the price is paid in full, that condition will prevail.

Part 2 provides that:

> "Where in pursuance of the contract, the seller delivers the goods to the buyer or to a carrier or other bailee or custodier (whether named by the buyer or not) for the purpose of transmission to the buyer, and does not reserve the right of disposal, he is to be taken to have unconditionally appropriated the goods to the contract."

This rule is, in effect, an example of appropriation. The giving of goods to a carrier may not mean that there has been appropriation. This point is illustrated by a case where a number of orders were dispatched together to the same carrier with no indication of which goods were due to which customer.[83] The goods had not been ascertained so that property could not pass. Moreover, property will not pass if the seller reserves the right of disposal. So where goods are entrusted to a shipper under a bill of lading made out in the seller's favour, they remain at his disposal and no property passes.[84]

Part 3 was added by the Sale of Goods (Amendment) Act 1995. It states:

> "Where there is a contract for the sale of a specified quantity of unascertained goods in a deliverable state forming part of a bulk which is identified either in the contract or by subsequent agreement between the parties and the bulk is reduced to (or to less than) that quantity, then, if the buyer under that contract is the only buyer to whom goods are then due out of the bulk—
>
> (a) the remaining goods are to be taken as appropriated to that contract at the time when the bulk is so reduced; and
> (b) the property in those goods then passes to that buyer."

The effect of this part might be described as "appropriation by exhaustion".[85] Goods in a bulk are reduced to such an extent that the remaining amount is inevitably destined for one buyer alone. This is sufficient for appropriation and thus the passing of property.

SALES FROM AN IDENTIFIED BULK

1.8.2 Sections 20A and 20B contain important provisions which must be read in conjunction with s.18 (r.5(3)). The law has always proceeded on the basis that it is a logical impossibility to sell unascertained goods.[86] Thus where, for example, there was an agreement to buy part of a bulk cargo,[87] no property could pass until that bulk had been divided into the appropriate fractions, because otherwise it was impossible to say exactly which goods the buyer owned. This could cause problems in insolvency situations, since if the seller went bankrupt (or into liquidation, if a company), the buyer would lose out in a contest for the goods with a liquidator or trustee in bankruptcy. This would be the case even if the buyer had actually paid for the goods. In such a case, the liquidator or trustee would retain and resell

---

[81] *Carlos Federspiel & Co SA* [1957] 1 Lloyd's Rep. 240, per Pearson J at 255–256.

[82] *Hendy Lennox (Industrial Engines) Ltd v Grahame Puttick Ltd* [1984] 1 W.L.R. 485.

[83] *Healy v Howlett & Sons* [1917] 1 K.B. 337.

[84] See s.19(2) and paras 4.8 et seq. below.

[85] Which was previously recognised by case law: see *Karlshamns Oljefabriker A/B v Eastport Navigation Corp (The Elafi)* [1982] 1 All E.R. 208; although the Act now makes it clear that property to what remains passes, even if it was less than the amount the buyer contracted for.

[86] See s.16.

[87] As is commonplace in the commodity trades: see para.1.3, joint report by the Law Commissions, *Sale of Goods Forming Part of a Bulk*, 1993. Law Com. No.215; Scot. Law Com. No.145.

the goods, leaving the buyer to pursue a claim as an ordinary creditor.[88] Pressure from certain commodity trade associations and concern that the parties to international sale contracts might select another legal system to govern their relations led to a report on the matter by the Law Commissions, and ultimately to an attempt to provide some protection for buyers in such situations by the addition of ss.20A and 20B by the Sale of Goods (Amendment) Act 1995.

Thus, where the buyer has paid in advance for a specified quantity of goods which are part of a bulk which has been identified by the parties,[89] he acquires an undivided share in the bulk, and becomes an owner in common with the other buyers and/or the seller.[90] So, if the owner of a cargo of 3,000 tonnes of coal sells 1,000 tonnes to each of three buyers, those buyers become owners in common of that cargo. Should the owner manage only to sell 1,000 tonnes to a single buyer before becoming insolvent, then he and the buyer become owners in common of the cargo.

It is important to bear in mind that these provisions only apply where the parties do not provide otherwise.[91] Also they apply only where the parties have agreed that the goods are to be supplied from an identified bulk, i.e. a mass or collection of goods of the same kind, which are contained in a defined space or area, and is such that any goods in the bulk are interchangeable with any other goods therein of the same number or quantity.[92] That identification may occur in the contract or by subsequent agreement,[93] such as where a buyer of grain is informed after the formation of the contract that the goods will be drawn from a particular cargo (as long as this reflects the agreement of the parties). The provisions are not designed to apply where a seller receives an order to be filled from his general stock at his discretion. Nor would they apply if both parties had a specific source in mind if they did not actually agree that the goods would be drawn from that source. Moreover, they only apply when the buyer agrees to buy a specified quantity of goods from the bulk,[94] i.e. 1,000 tonnes from the bulk, but not one third or 20 per cent of the bulk. (A person purchasing a fraction or percentage of an identified bulk would acquire an undivided share of the goods, but would not be subject to the provisions of ss.20A and 20B.) Finally, they only apply when the buyer has paid for the goods or at least some of them.[95] Part payment of the price for any goods is treated as payment for a corresponding part of the goods.[96] So, if the buyer agrees to buy 1,000 tonnes of coal at £100 per tonne, and pays half the price in advance, i.e. £50,000, he is treated as having paid for 500 tonnes.

Section 20A(3) states that the size of share which the buyer has at any time is such share as the quantity he has paid for out of the bulk bears to the quantity of goods in the bulk at that time. So, if the buyer has paid for 1,000 tonnes out of a 3,000 tonne cargo, he is entitled to a one third share of the cargo. Equally, if the liquidator of the seller company has sold and removed a further 1,000 tonnes from the cargo, leaving only 2,000 tonnes, then the buyer remains entitled to 1,000 tonnes. Consequently, his share increases to one-half.[97] More importantly, should in the above scenario 1,000 tonnes have instead been stolen or destroyed, the buyer is again entitled to the 1,000 tonnes he has paid for, and thus one-half of the bulk. In other words s.20A(3) imposes the risk of any loss on the seller. On the other hand, s.20A(4) directs that if the aggregate of the shares of buyers exceeds the size of the bulk, the shares must be reduced proportionately.[98] So, if each of three buyers has bought and paid for 1,000 tonnes out of a 3,000 tonne cargo, and it transpires that there are only 2,700 tonnes in the cargo, the entitlement of each buyer, *inter se*, is reduced to 900 tonnes. This does not mean that any buyer is then contractually

---

[88] See *Re Wait* [1927] 1 Ch. 606; *Re London Wine Shippers* [1986] P.C.C. 121; but cf. *Re Stapylton Fletcher Ltd* [1994] 1 W.L.R. 1181.

[89] See s.20A(1).

[90] See s.20A(2).

[91] See s.20A(2).

[92] See s.61(1).

[93] See s.20A(1)(a), see para.4.3 of the Law Commissions' joint report for examples of situations which fall within the ambit of the provision, *Sale of Goods Forming Part of a Bulk*, 1993. Law Com. No.215; Scot. Law Com. No.145.

[94] See s.20A(1).

[95] See s.20A(1)(b).

[96] See s.20A(6).

[97] It would be possible for the amount of the bulk to increase, and for the share owned by the buyer thus to decrease, e.g. where a buyer has bought 500 gallons of oil held in a particular storage tank. At the time of entering into the contract, it contains 1,000 gallons, so his share is a half. Should another 1,000 gallons be deposited in the tank, his share would be a quarter.

[98] See s.20A(4).

entitled to only 900 tonnes. Section 20B(3)(c) provides that nothing in either s.20A or s.20B affects the right of any buyer under his contract. Each of the buyers in the above scenario retains a claim against the seller for failing to deliver the appropriate amount of goods, although such claim might, in practice, be worth very little in an insolvency situation. The aim of s.20A(4) is to achieve equity among buyers when it is practically impossible to deliver to each the amount he is due.

Ultimately, of course, a buyer will seek delivery of the goods due to him from the bulk. Where the buyer has paid for only some of the goods due to him, and some are delivered to him, it is assumed that the goods so delivered are goods for which he has paid.[99] In other words, where the buyer has ordered 2,000 tonnes of coal from the bulk, but paid only for 1,000, should 1,000 tonnes be delivered to him, it will be deemed to be the 1,000 tonnes he has paid for, and he will be precluded from arguing that he has received the other 1,000 tonnes and thus remains entitled to 1,000 tonnes from the bulk. At common law, the agreement of all common owners is required for any dealing with the property. This is clearly not practical in the current context, so any common owner is deemed to consent to:

(1) any delivery from the bulk to any other common owner of goods due to the latter under his contract[100]; and
(2) any removal or disposal by another common owner of goods which are part of the latter's share of the bulk.[101]

No cause of action accrues against anyone who acts in accordance with the above provisions, nor is there any obligation on any buyer to compensate another in respect of any shortfall in the goods received by that buyer.[102] These provisions, put crudely, operate on a "first come, first served basis". Take the scenario of three buyers who each buy and pay for 1,000 tonnes out of a 3,000 tonne cargo. One buyer takes delivery of his 1,000 tonnes, and it then transpires that there are only 2,700 tonnes in the cargo, so that the "entitlement" of each buyer was only 900 tonnes. The other buyers have no right against the first, as he was contractually entitled to the 1,000 tonnes of which he received delivery. An alternative scenario would be that one buyer buys and pays for 1,000 tonnes out of a 3,000 tonne cargo, while another agrees to buy the other 2,000 tonnes, but pays for only half. Although the latter's share in terms of s.20A is only 1,000 tonnes, he is contractually entitled to 2,000 tonnes, so that if he takes delivery of that amount, the other buyer may not complain, even if he faces a shortfall as a result.

RESERVATION OF THE RIGHT OF DISPOSAL AND RETENTION OF TITLE

1.8.3   As has been illustrated above, the governing principle in the transfer of property in goods is the intention of the parties. Section 19 permits the seller to reserve the right of disposal in the goods until certain conditions are fulfilled. Even though goods have been delivered to the buyer, the seller retains the property in the goods until those conditions are fulfilled.

A practical example of the operation of this section is the use of retention of title clauses. Such clauses permit the parties to agree that the seller will retain the property in the goods notwithstanding delivery to the buyer, until the buyer has paid the price in full. Such clauses are relatively uncontroversial in Scots law, being, in effect, a contract of sale subject to a suspensive condition.[103] However, more complex clauses known as "all sums" clauses proved to be problematic for the courts. Such clauses provide that title to the goods is reserved until all sums due by the buyer to the seller in the context of all transactions between the two parties have been paid. Such clauses were initially considered to be an attempt to create a security over corporeal moveables without possession and there-

[99] See s.20A(5).
[100] See s.20B(1)(a).
[101] See s.20B(1)(b).
[102] See s.20B(2), (3)(a).
[103] *Archivent Sales & Development Ltd v Strathclyde Regional Council*, 1985 S.L.T. 154, although in that case the retention of title clause was defeated by the operation of s.25 of the Sale of Goods Act 1979 which permits a buyer in possession to transfer the property in goods under certain conditions, see below. On sales subject to a suspensive condition, see Stair, I, 14, 4.

fore invalid.[104] Section 62(4) of the 1979 Act disapplies the Act in relation to such clauses. Eventually, the House of Lords held that such clauses were valid, considering them to be a simple application of the rules contained in s.17 and s.19(1) of the Act.[105] The buyer was not attempting to create a security without possession because he had never had the property in the goods.

However, even that decision created only a limited protection for a seller seeking payment. While such clauses allow a seller who is owed money by the buyer to assert ownership of the goods as against the buyer (or the buyer's liquidator or trustee in bankruptcy), no retention of title clause, whatever its form, allows a seller to assert ownership against a bona fide purchaser from the buyer.[106] Accordingly those drafting such clauses sought to confer a measure of protection by adding terms which provided that the proceeds of any sale of the goods by the buyer were to be held in trust for the original seller. Whilst such clauses may be effective in English law,[107] they are not effective in Scots law, Lord President Emslie commenting that "the essential ingredients of a trust are entirely lacking".[108] Another ingenious term sought to overcome the principles of accession and *specificatio* in the law of property by purporting to retain title to the goods, even where the original goods had been incorporated by the buyer into a new product or irreversibly changed in nature.[109] Since these goods would be regarded as new goods, such a term would be regarded, not as an attempt to retain ownership of goods, but as an assertion of some sort of right of ownership over goods which would not belong to the seller at common law. Given that such terms do not appear to receive effect even in England,[110] and in light of the hostility of the Scottish courts to certain forms of retention of title clauses, such a term is likely to be found invalid as an attempt to create a security without possession.[111]

THE PASSING OF RISK

The passing of the property in goods is related to the passing of risk, i.e. which party bears the risk if **1.9** the goods are damaged or destroyed. Provisions on the passing of risk are contained in s.20 of the 1979 Act. However, the 2002 Regulations recently added an important amendment to this section, providing that s.20 is, effectively, ignored where certain criteria apply.[112] The contract must be a consumer contract, and the buyer must also be a "consumer". A "consumer contract" is a contract where one party deals in the course of a business and the other party does not so deal.[113] "Consumers" are natural persons acting for purposes outside their trade, business or profession.[114] Where the contract relates to the transfer of the ownership or possession of goods, the goods must also be of a type "ordinarily supplied for private use or consumption".[115] Following the amendments enacted by the 2002 Regulations, this latter limitation does not apply where the consumer is an individual[116]: the goods remain at the seller's risk until they are delivered to the consumer. There is therefore a blanket consumer protection rule on the passing of risk in what might be called "pure" consumer situations.[117] Similarly,

---

[104] *Deutz Engines Ltd v Terex Ltd*, 1984 S.L.T. 273. For the rule against the creation of securities over corporeal moveables without possession, see W.M. Gloag and J.M. Irvine, *The Law of Rights in Security* (Edinburgh: W. Green, 1897), pp.188–189 and see discussion at paras 5.3.1.1 et seq. below.

[105] *Armour v Thyssen Edelstahlwerke AG*, 1990 S.L.T. 891.

[106] See discussion of sales by buyers in possession in para.1.10.3 below.

[107] *Aluminium Industrie Vaasen BV v Romalpa Aluminium Ltd* [1976] 1 W.L.R. 676.

[108] *Clark Taylor & Co Ltd v Quality Site Development (Edinburgh) Ltd*, 1981 S.C. 111, per Lord President Emslie at 116. If the essential requirements of a trust had been present in the wording of the contract, the answer may well have been different.

[109] *Deutz Engines Ltd v Terex Ltd*, 1984 S.L.T. 273, per Lord Ross at 274–275.

[110] See *Re Peachdart Ltd* [1984] 1 Ch. 131.

[111] See *Deutz Engines Ltd v Terex Ltd*, 1984 S.L.T.273; but cf. *Zahnrad Fabrik Passau GmbH v Terex Ltd*, 1986 S.L.T. 84.

[112] 2002 Regulations reg.4(2) adding new s.20(4) to the 1979 Act.

[113] Unfair Contract Terms Act 1977 ("UCTA 1977") s.25(1).

[114] 2002 Regulations reg.2.

[115] UCTA 1977 s.25(1).

[116] 2002 Regulations reg.14 inserting new s.25(1A) into the Unfair Contract Terms Act 1977.

[117] See also a similar amendment made to s.32, which deals with the effect of delivery to a carrier. Section 32(1) provides that where the seller is authorised or required to send the goods to the buyer, delivery of goods to the carrier is deemed to be delivery

where the Consumer Contracts (Information, Cancellation and Additional Charges) Regulations 2013 apply in any sales contract, the goods remain at the trader's risk until they come into the physical possession of the consumer or a person identified by the consumer to take possession of the goods.[118]

Outside those "pure" consumer situations, unless the parties agree otherwise, the general rule is that the owner of the goods bears the risk of their damage or deterioration, in other words, the risk passes when the property (in the sense of ownership) passes. Thus s.20(1) stipulates:

> "Unless otherwise agreed, the goods remain at the seller's risk until the property in them is transferred to the buyer, but when the property in them is transferred to the buyer the goods are at the buyer's risk whether delivery has been made or not."

Importantly, therefore, risk does not depend upon actual possession of the goods.

The rule in s.20(1) is subject to two further exceptions. Firstly, if delivery has been delayed through the fault of either party, the goods are at that party's risk as regards any loss which might not have occurred but for that fault.[119] An example of this rule in operation can be found in *Demby Hamilton & Co Ltd v Barden*[120] where the buyer delayed in providing instructions as to the delivery of apple juice in casks. When the apple juice went "off", the buyer was held to bear the risk of deterioration even though property in the goods remained with the seller. Secondly, nothing in s.20 affects the duties of either party as a custodier of the goods of the other party.[121] So the party in possession will remain liable for loss deriving from his negligence or that of his servants.

Certain of the provisions of the Act dealing with destruction of the goods follow the common law of contract. The Act provides that where there is a contract for the sale of specific goods and, without the seller's knowledge, they have perished at the time the contract is made, the contract is void.[122] A similar rule applies in a contract for the sale of specific goods where, without the fault of either party, the goods perish after the contract is entered into but before the risk passes to the buyer. The contract is again void.[123] It may not be easy to establish whether goods have perished. In *Asfar v Blundell*,[124] a vessel carrying dates was sunk during the course of a voyage. The defendant argued that there had been no change in nature of the dates, they "were still dates, composed of stone, skin, flesh" even though they had been impregnated with sewage and had begun to ferment. Lord Esher MR stated that goods have perished if they are so changed in their nature "as to become an unmerchantable thing . . . which no buyer would buy and no honest seller would sell".[125] In this case the dates had undoubtedly changed in nature and become unmerchantable,[126] and so it was held that no freight was payable. If the goods which are the subject of the contract have, in fact, never existed, then the contract will always have been void, and will not be rendered void only by the operation of ss.6 and 7. The seller may be liable in damages for representing to the buyer that the goods exist.[127]

It was seen that s.20 is subject to the contrary agreement of the parties, and parties will commonly contract so as to ensure that the risk is borne by the party in possession, irrespective of ownership. So, for example, if a seller is successful in inserting a retention of title clause into the contract, he would almost invariably also include a term to the effect that the goods are at the buyer's risk, as soon as the latter acquires possession. By contrast ss.6 and 7 are not expressed to be subject to contrary agreement, so that it does not seem open to the parties to place the goods at either's risk, where ss.6 or 7 would

---

of goods to the buyer. The 2002 Regulations reg.4(3) adds a new s.32(4) to the 1979 Act. Its effect is that where the contract is a consumer contract and the buyer is a "pure" consumer, s.32 does not apply, and delivery of goods by the seller to the carrier is not deemed to be delivery to the buyer.

[118] CC (IC and AC) Regs reg.43(2).

[119] See s.20(2).

[120] *Demby Hamilton & Co Ltd v Barden* [1949] 1 All E.R. 435.

[121] See s.20(3).

[122] See s.6.

[123] See s.7.

[124] *Asfar v Blundell* [1896] 1 Q.B. 123.

[125] *Asfar v Blundell* [1896] 1 Q.B. 123, per Lord Esher MR at 128.

[126] For discussion of the term "merchantable", the forerunner to the current standard of "satisfactory" in relation to quality of goods in s.14(2), see para.1.11.5.1 below.

[127] *McRae v Commonwealth Disposals Commission* (1951) 84 C.L.R. 377.

render the contract void. It is implicit in all that has been said so far that if the goods are at the buyer's risk when destroyed, then he remains liable for the price, while if they are destroyed while at the seller's risk, then (subject to s.7) he remains liable to fulfill the contract.

The interaction of the buyer's right to reject[128] and the passing of risk is also a complex issue. The passing of risk may be subject to the buyer's right to reject where the goods turn out to be defective or otherwise disconform to contract. It has been suggested that, even if the property has passed to the buyer, the risk always remains with the seller where the buyer has a right to reject, presumably subject to an obligation on the part of the buyer to take reasonable care of the goods while they are in his possession.[129]

SALES BY A NON-OWNER

Having discussed how the property in goods passes, it is appropriate to consider whether ownership of **1.10** goods may be transferred where they are sold by a non-owner. Section 21(1) states that

> "where goods are sold by a person who is not their owner, and who does not sell them under the authority or with the consent of the owner, the buyer acquires no better title to the goods than the seller had, unless the owner of the goods is by his conduct precluded from denying the seller's authority to sell."

This is an expression of the rule *nemo dat quod non habet*, or that no one can pass a better title than that which he had. The exception to this rule, i.e. the latter part which prevents the owner from denying the seller's authority to sell, is difficult to analyse. It resembles personal bar, or what is known as estoppel in English law. However, doubts have been expressed in English law as to whether it is in fact based on estoppel, in particular because it is not limited to the usual type of estoppel which prevents the true owner from denying the seller's authority to sell, but, in addition, has the effect of permitting ownership of goods to pass. In particular, Lord Devlin commented:

> "We doubt whether this principle . . . ought really to be regarded as part of the law of estoppel. At any rate it differs from what is sometimes called 'equitable estoppel' in this vital respect, that the effect of its application is to transfer a real title and not merely a metaphorical title by estoppel."[130]

It may be that the exception can be explained by reference to the apparent authority of an agent,[131] a concept which is also based on personal bar.[132] Section 21(1) contains no reference to good faith on the part of the buyer, and can be contrasted in this respect with the sections having a similar effect, ss.24 and 25 commented on at paras 1.10.2 and 1.10.3 below. Despite this omission it is suggested that good faith is indeed relevant in the context of s.21(1).[133]

Further exceptions to the *nemo dat* rule exist, and, in common with the exception discussed above, they may rest upon the principle of apparent authority. The logic behind these exceptions was explained by Lord Denning as follows:

---

[128] See para.1.12.2 below.

[129] See Atiyah, Adams, and MacQueen, *Sale of Goods*, 12th edn (2010), pp.345–46, citing *Head v Tatersall* (1870) L.R. 7 Ex. 7 as authority for this proposition. Some support for this view is perhaps to be found in a Scottish case decided after the passing of the Act: see *Kinnear v Brodie* (1901) 8 S.L.T. 475.

[130] *Eastern Distributors Ltd v Goldring* [1957] 2 Q.B. 600, per Lord Devlin at 611.

[131] See para.2.4.2 below.

[132] *Eastern Distributors Ltd v Goldring* [1957] 2 Q.B. 600, per Lord Devlin at 611; see paras 27–28, Scottish Law Commission, *Corporeal Moveables: Protection of the Onerous Bona Fide Acquirer of Another's Property*. HMSO, 1976. Scot. Law Com. Memorandum No.27.

[133] Section 21(1) is an application of the agency concept, apparent authority. In order for the third party to benefit from the protection of this agency concept, the third party must act reasonably, see para.2.4.2.2 below.

"In the development of our law, two principles have striven for mastery. The first is for the protection of property: no one can give a better title than he himself possesses. The second is for the protection of commercial transactions: the person who takes in good faith and for value without notice should get a good title. The first principle has held sway for a long time, but it has been modified by the common law itself and by statute so as to meet the needs of our own times."[134]

Further exceptions to the general rule are considered below.

SALE BY A MERCANTILE AGENT

1.10.1 The Factors Act 1889 s.2(1) provides:

"Where a mercantile agent is, with the consent of the owner, in possession of goods or of the documents of title to goods, any sale, pledge, or other disposition of the goods, made by him when acting in the ordinary course of business of a mercantile agent, shall . . . be as valid as if he were expressly authorised by the owner of the goods to make the same; provided that the person taking under the disposition acts in good faith, and has not at the time of the disposition notice that the person making the disposition has not authority to make the same."[135]

One may have assumed that if the mercantile agent had tricked the principal into leaving the goods with him, then that would prevent the operation of this section. However, the focus of the section is the consent of the owner to the agent's possession. In *Pearson v Rose & Young*[136] the Court of Appeal held that the fact that the agent had obtained the registration book for the car subsequently sold by him by larceny was not important. The only question was whether the goods were in his possession with the consent of the owner. Lord Denning explained that consent may be provided for different purposes:

"That means that the owner must consent to the agent having them for a purpose which is in some way or other connected with his business as a mercantile agent. It may not actually be for sale. It may be for display or to get offers, or merely to put in his showroom; but there must be a consent to something of that kind before the owner can be deprived of his goods."[137]

In other words, if an individual entrusts his car to a car dealer for the purpose of finding out what sort of offers might be made on it, any unsuspecting individual to whom the dealer sells the vehicle obtains a good title, even if the dealer tricked the owner into giving up possession. However, if the owner had given the dealer the car merely to be repaired, the dealer could not give a good title to a bona fide purchaser, as he does not have the goods in his capacity as a mercantile agent.

According to the Factors Act 1889, a mercantile agent is someone

"having in the customary course of his business as such agent authority either to sell goods or to consign goods for the purpose of sale, or to buy goods, or to raise money on the security of goods."[138]

In other words, a mercantile agent is someone who customarily sells goods in the course of a business. So a car hire company was not a mercantile agent where it occasionally sold cars from its fleet.[139]

---

[134] *Bishopsgate Motor Finance Corporation Ltd v Transport Brakes Ltd* [1949] 1 K.B. 322, per Lord Denning at 336–337.

[135] For further details on mercantile agents see para.2.3.2 below. This Act was applied to Scotland by the Factors (Scotland) Act 1890.

[136] *Pearson v Rose & Young* [1951] 1 K.B. 275.

[137] *Pearson v Rose & Young* [1951] 1 K.B. 275, per Lord Denning at 288.

[138] See s.1(1); see also s.26 of the 1979 Act. For a recent unsuccessful attempt to invoke this definition see *Fadallah v Pollack* [2013] EWHC 3159 (QB) at [35].

[139] *Belvoir Finance Ltd v Harold G Cole Ltd* [1969] 1 W.L.R. 1877.

SALE BY A SELLER IN POSSESSION

Section 24 of the Act provides that:

1.10.2

"Where a person having sold goods continues or is in possession of the goods, or of the documents of title to the goods, the delivery or transfer by that person, or by a mercantile agent acting for him, of the goods or documents of title under any sale, pledge, or other disposition thereof, to any person receiving the same in good faith and without notice of the previous sale, has the same effect as if the person making the delivery or transfer were expressly authorised by the owner of the goods to make the same."[140]

The requirement for continuity of possession has been interpreted as continuity of physical possession only. It does not matter if the legal nature of the seller's possession has changed in nature, i.e. if the seller becomes an agent or custodier for the buyer.[141] The seller's continued possession of the goods may even be wrongful[142]—unlike s.2(1) of the Factors Act 1889 there is no requirement in this section that the possession be with the consent of the owner. So someone who has sold goods, but who instead of delivering them to the buyer, purports to sell them again to a bona fide purchaser, gives a good title to the latter. But someone who sold goods, yielded possession to the buyer, and thereafter recovered possession, e.g. by hiring the goods from the buyer, would no longer be a seller in possession, and so would not be able to confer a good title if he purported to sell the goods.[143]

The word "disposition" is interpreted widely. In *Worcester Works Finance Ltd v Cooden Engineering Co Ltd*[144] it was interpreted as including the repossession by the original owner from the seller in possession with that seller's consent. Seizure of the goods against the seller's will does not, however, amount to a disposition within the meaning of the section.[145] The case of *Michael Gerson (Leasing) Ltd v Wilkinson*[146] contains an unusual interpretation of the idea of the "delivery or transfer" which the seller in possession makes to the buyer in terms of s.24. A company, E, sold goods under a sale and leaseback arrangement to a finance company, MG, but without ever delivering them to MG. In other words E sold the goods to MG, which then leased them to E, E remaining in possession at all times. E then purported to enter a similar sale and leaseback arrangement in relation to some of the same goods (known as the Sch.3 goods) to another finance company, State. In neither case were the goods actually delivered to either of the finance companies. State then sold the Sch.3 goods to another company, Sagebush. The Court of Appeal found that E was a seller in possession in terms of s.24, and that there had been a constructive delivery of the Sch.3 goods from E to State, followed by an immediate redelivery to E as a hirer. State therefore obtained good title to the Sch.3 goods under s.24, and could resell them to Sagebush.

SALE BY A BUYER IN POSSESSION

Section 25(1) provides that:

1.10.3

"Where a person having bought or agreed to buy goods obtains, with the consent of the seller, possession of the goods or the documents of title to the goods, the delivery or transfer by that person, or by a mercantile agent acting for him, of the goods or documents of title, under any sale, pledge or other disposition thereof, to any person receiving the same in good faith and without

---

[140] See also s.8 of the Factors Act 1889.

[141] *Pacific Motor Auctions Proprietary Ltd v Motor Credits (Hire Finance) Ltd* [1965] A.C. 867; *Worcester Works Finance Ltd v Cooden Engineering Co Ltd* [1972] 1 Q.B. 210.

[142] *Worcester Works Finance Ltd v Cooden Engineering Co Ltd* [1972] 1 Q.B. 210.

[143] *Fadallah v Pollak* [2013] EWHC 3159, per Judge Richard Seymour, discussing (at [45] to [46]) *Pacific Motor Auctions Pty Ltd v Motor Credits (Hire Finance) Ltd* [1965] A.C. 867.

[144] *Worcester Works Finance Ltd v Cooden Engineering Co Ltd* [1972] 1 Q.B. 210.

[145] See *Forsythe International (UK) Ltd v Silver Shipping Co Ltd and Petroglobe International Ltd (The Saetta)* [1994] 1 All E.R. 851.

[146] *Michael Gerson (Leasing) Ltd v Wilkinson* [2000] 3 W.L.R. 1645.

notice of any lien or other right of the original seller in respect of the goods, has the same effect as if the person making the delivery or transfer were a mercantile agent in possession of the goods or documents of title with the consent of the owner."[147]

This provision may often defeat retention of title clauses.[148] Even though such a clause may ordinarily be effective to retain ownership of the goods in the seller, s.25(1) allows a buyer in possession to confer a good title on a bona fide purchaser. Section 25(2) specifically provides that a buyer under a conditional sale agreement (see para.3.1.2.2 below) is not a person who has bought or agreed to buy goods for the purposes of this section. A buyer under a sale or return contract is similarly not within the ambit of the section.[149] So if property in the goods has not already passed to a buyer under a sale or return contract, he cannot confer a good title on a bona fide purchaser, hence the discussion in para.1.8.1 above of the importance of determining whether an individual has really taken goods on sale or return or is selling them as the seller's agent. Buyers from individuals who have taken goods on sale or return will often be protected because such individuals fall within the definition of mercantile agents.

Just as *Michael Gerson (Leasing) Ltd v Wilkinson*[150] is illustrative of the wide interpretation given by the courts to terms such as "possession" and "delivery" in the context of s.24, so *Four Point Garage Ltd v Carter*[151] is illustrative of the same approach to cases falling within s.25. The defendant agreed to buy a car from a dealer, F, and paid the full purchase price without taking possession of the car. F did not have the car, but intended to purchase it from the plaintiff, also a car dealer. F asked the plaintiff to deliver the car direct to the defendant, so that at no time did F take possession of the car. The plaintiff delivered the car to the defendant, but thought that he was leasing it to the defendant. The defendant thought that the car had been delivered to him by F. F then went into liquidation without paying the plaintiff. The plaintiff brought an action against the defendant claiming that the car had remained in his ownership. It was held that, through the operation of s.25, the defendant had obtained good title to the car. F had acted as a buyer in possession, even though he had at no time actually been in possession of the car. Simon Brown J explained his reasoning on this point as follows:

"There appears no possible good reason to differentiate under the statute between a case where, as here, the plaintiff sellers themselves deliver direct to the sub-purchaser and a case where . . . instead, the seller delivers to his buyer, who then forthwith delivers on to the sub-purchaser. Often no doubt the precise arrangement would depend on no more than the geographical inter-relationship of the three parties."[152]

Clearly, the protection of the buyer acting in good faith, the defendant here, is a high priority. The result also ignores the requirement in s.25 that there be delivery or transfer of the goods by the buyer in possession. In the case, F, the buyer "in possession" did not actually deliver the goods to the defendant. As is characteristic of the operation of s.25, F, the buyer in possession, does not have good title to the goods, but is nevertheless able to pass good title to a buyer in good faith.

The buyer in possession must have the seller's consent to his possession, but it does not matter if the consent is subsequently withdrawn and the original contract is rescinded.[153] However, s.25 cannot operate to pass good title where the original seller had no title to the goods whatsoever. Thus where goods are stolen from A by B and B sells to C, who then sells to D, D does not obtain a good title, and D cannot claim that C is a buyer in possession with the consent of the seller.[154] In the opinion of Lord Goff, the original Factors Acts sought to give

---

[147] See also s.9 of the Factors Act 1889, applied to Scotland by the Factors (Scotland) Act 1890.

[148] Discussed at para.1.8.3 above.

[149] *Weiner v Harris* [1910] 1 K.B. 285.

[150] *Michael Gerson (Leasing) Ltd v Wilkinson* [2000] 3 W.L.R. 1645.

[151] *Four Point Garage Ltd v Carter* [1985] 3 All E.R. 12. This case also indicates that s.25 may defeat a retention of title clause, as also occurred in *Archivent Sales & Development Ltd v Strathclyde Regional Council*, 1985 S.L.T. 154.

[152] *Four Point Garage Ltd v Carter* [1985] 3 All E.R. 12, per Simon Brown J at 15.

[153] *Newtons of Wembley v Williams* [1965] 1 Q.B. 560.

[154] *National Employers Mutual General Insurance Association Ltd v Jones* [1990] 1 A.C. 24.

"protection to those who had dealt in good faith with factors or agents, to whom goods, or documents of title to goods, had been entrusted, to the extent that the rights of such persons should . . . override those of the owner who had so entrusted the goods or documents to the factor or agent".[155]

The Acts did not seek to

"enable a factor or agent, entrusted with goods by a thief or a purchaser from a thief, to give a good title to a bona fide purchaser from him, overriding the title of the true owner".[156]

SALES OF MOTOR VEHICLES SUBJECT TO HIRE PURCHASE OR CONDITIONAL SALE AGREEMENTS

As stated above, s.25 is explicitly stated not to apply to conditional sale agreements.[157] Similarly, it **1.10.4** cannot apply to sales by the hirer under a hire purchase agreement[158] given that he has not bought or agreed to buy the goods. However, such legal niceties tend not to be appreciated by most individuals who "buy" goods under conditional sale or hire purchase agreements, and who regard themselves as the owner of the goods. Normally, this has little practical consequence, as these goods are not often resold. The major exception to this practice is, of course, cars, which are routinely resold. Under the 1979 Act, an unsuspecting purchaser of a car which the seller held on hire purchase found that he had no title. Because this was a distressingly frequent occurrence, the situation was addressed by ss.27–29 of the Hire-Purchase Act 1964. These sections apply to a party who has hired a motor vehicle under a hire purchase agreement, or holds it under a conditional sale agreement and has not yet become the owner of the vehicle. Where that party makes a disposition[159] of the motor vehicle to a private purchaser acting in good faith and without notice of the relevant hire or conditional sale agreement, the disposition is valid.[160] The provisions aim to protect private but not trade purchasers.[161] It makes no difference that the motor vehicle may have passed through the hands of several trade purchasers before reaching the private purchaser.[162] However, the first private purchaser to acquire the motor vehicle must do so in good faith. If he does not, then no subsequent purchaser can acquire good title to it.[163]

It might be added that someone who buys a vehicle from an individual who is hiring it under a contract of lease, rather than a contract of hire purchase, cannot be given a good title.[164]

SALE UNDER A VOIDABLE TITLE

Section 23 reflects the common law rule that where a seller has a voidable title to goods, but it has not **1.10.5** been avoided at the time of sale, the buyer obtains a good title provided he acts in good faith and without notice of the defect in title.[165] It should be noted, however, that even after the buyer's title has

---

[155] *National Employers Mutual General Insurance Association Ltd v Jones* [1990] 1 A.C. 24, per Lord Goff at 58.

[156] *National Employers Mutual General Insurance Association Ltd v Jones* [1990] 1 A.C. 24, per Lord Goff at 59.

[157] See s.25(2).

[158] See para.3.1.2.1 below.

[159] "Disposition" is defined in s.29(1) and includes "any sale or contract of sale (including a conditional sale agreement), any . . . hiring under a hire-purchase agreement and any transfer of the property of goods in pursuance of a provision in that behalf contained in a hire-purchase agreement".

[160] See s.27(2).

[161] See the discussion in *GE Capital Bank Ltd v Rushton* [2005] EWCA Civ 1556; [2006] 1 W.L.R. 899 on what constitutes a private purchaser.

[162] See s.27(3) and see the English House of Lords case, *Shogun Finance Ltd v Hudson* [2003] UKHL 62; [2004] All E.R. 215 in which the House held that there must be a valid hire purchase agreement.

[163] See s.27(4).

[164] *Mitchell v Heys & Sons* (1894) 21 R. 600.

[165] See *MacLeod v Kerr*, 1965 S.L.T. 358.

been avoided, the buyer in possession may be able to pass good title under s.25.[166] It must be doubted whether this is the case if the contract is void ab initio.[167]

THE SELLER'S DUTIES

1.11

DELIVERY

1.11.1 The seller must deliver the goods and the buyer must accept and pay for them.[168] The word "delivery" is not used here in the sense of physical delivery, but rather "voluntary transfer of possession".[169] Thus, whether the buyer must collect the goods from the seller or the seller must send them to the buyer is a matter of interpretation of the terms of the contract.[170] In the absence of any provision to the contrary, the place of delivery is the seller's place of business, or, if he has none, his residence, but if the contract is for the sale of specific goods which the parties knew to be in some other place at the time the contract was made, that place is the place of delivery.[171] Where the seller is obliged to deliver the goods to the buyer in terms of the contract but there is no stipulation as to time, they must be sent within a reasonable time,[172] and delivery must be made at a reasonable hour.[173] Where the Consumer Contracts (Information, Cancellation and Additional Charges) Regulations 2013 apply, unless the contract contains an agreed time, for any sales contract, goods must be delivered without undue delay and in any event not more than 30 days after the day on which the contract is entered into.[174]

It has been stated that "in ordinary commercial contracts for the sale of goods the rule clearly is that time is prima facie of the essence with respect to delivery".[175] Breach of the obligation of delivery on the part of the seller would therefore give the buyer the right to rescind. The buyer may, however, lose that right if, after the due date for delivery, the buyer continues to press for delivery.[176] The buyer in this position may stipulate a new time for delivery so that time can again be of the essence provided that the period stipulated is reasonable.[177]

DELIVERY OF THE WRONG QUANTITY

1.11.2 Where the seller delivers goods which are less than the agreed amount, the buyer may reject them or keep them, paying at the contract rate.[178] Where he delivers more than the agreed amount of goods the buyer may reject them all, or reject only the excess, or keep them all, paying at the contract rate.[179] In either case the buyer may not reject the whole of the goods delivered unless the shortfall or excess is material.[180] Each of the rules on delivery of the wrong quantity may be varied by the parties by agreement.[181]

---

[166] *Newtons of Wembley v Williams* [1965] 1 Q.B. 560.
[167] *Morrisson v Robertson* (1908) 15 S.L.T. 697.
[168] See s.27.
[169] See s.61(1).
[170] See s.29(1).
[171] See s.29(2).
[172] See s.29(3).
[173] See s.29(5).
[174] CC (IC and AC) Regs reg.42(3).
[175] *Hartley v Hymans* [1920] 3 K.B. 475, per McCardie J at 484.
[176] *Hartley v Hymans* [1920] 3 K.B. 475; *Charles Rickards Ltd v Oppenheim* [1950] 1 K.B. 616.
[177] *Charles Rickards Ltd v Oppenheim* [1950] 1 K.B. 616.
[178] See s.30(1).
[179] See s.30(2), (3).
[180] See s.30(2D).
[181] See s.30(5).

DUTY TO PASS GOOD TITLE

Section 12(1) provides that it is an implied term of the contract of sale that the seller has a right to **1.11.3** sell the goods, and, in the case of an agreement to sell, that he will have such a right at the time when the property is to pass. Lack of a right to sell does not necessarily mean that the seller does not own the goods. In *Niblett v Confectioners Materials Co Ltd*[182] the seller did not have a right to sell because the goods infringed a third party's trademark. This case must be contrasted with *Microbeads AC v Vinhurst Road Markings Ltd*,[183] in which the goods which were the subject of the contract of sale again infringed a patent. However, that patent had been granted after the time of sale. Therefore, because at the time of sale there was no patent to infringe, there was no concomitant breach of the seller's duty under this section.

The buyer's remedy for breach of s.12(1) is rejection of the goods and return of the price. This remedy constitutes a significant protective measure for the buyer, and this is illustrated by cases such as *Warman v Southern Counties Car Finance Corporation Ltd*.[184] In this case the hirer exercised his remedy of rejection of a car. He was found entitled not only to the return of his instalment payments, but also the costs of insuring it, repairing it, and defending an action by the true owner. The party who had hired the car to him was held not entitled to claim anything for the hire of the car during the period in which the hirer had the use of it.

Butterworth v Kingsway Motors Ltd[185] is a further example of the buyer's right to rescind due to breach of the implied term contained in s.12(1). It is perhaps of greater interest for its analysis of the transfer of title to a car sold in breach of a hire purchase contract. R sold the car while she held it on hire purchase, mistakenly believing that she had the right to do so. Ownership of the car, however, remained with the hire company.[186] However, she continued to make the hire payments when they became due. The car was then sold several times until R eventually discovered that she had had no right to sell it. The eventual buyer, B, rescinded the contract because of the breach by his immediate seller, K, of s.12(1) and obtained the return of the price. However, when R made the last payment due, title to the car vested in her, and, according to the court, perfected all of the other titles of parties who had bought and sold the car subsequent to the sale by her. The car eventually vested in K. The court left open the question whether B would have been entitled to rescind had K's title to the car been perfected prior to the raising of the action for reduction by B. The wider question is, given that the Act recognises a number of situations in which a party who has no right to sell goods can nonetheless confer a good title on a bona fide purchaser,[187] whether the buyer may rescind the contract under s.12(1) even though the true owner of the goods cannot impugn his title. It is submitted that since there is still a clear breach of s.12(1) in such situations, the buyer may indeed rescind.

In *McDonald v Provan (of Scotland Street) Ltd*[188] the seller unsuccessfully sought to use the doctrine of *specificatio* to avoid the duties imposed on him by s.12(1). F had welded together two halves of different cars, one-half being part of a stolen car. He had then sold the car to P who acted in good faith, and who then sold it to M, before it was removed by the police. P argued that, applying the doctrine of *specificatio*, the new car constituted an entirely new entity, and the right of property in it vested in the party who had constructed it, namely F. In rejecting this argument, Lord President Clyde commented:

> "The doctrine which the defenders seek to invoke is an equitable doctrine, not a strict rule of law
> . . . and the doctrine can only be invoked where there is complete *bona fides* on the part of the
> manufacturer . . . The result is that the defenders never did acquire an exclusive right of property

---

[182] *Niblett v Confectioners Materials Co Ltd* [1921] 3 K.B. 387.

[183] *Microbeads AC v Vinhurst Road Markings Ltd* [1975] 1 W.L.R. 218.

[184] *Warman v Southern Counties Car Finance Corporation Ltd* [1949] 2 K.B. 576. Note that this case was decided under the equivalent provisions of the hire purchase legislation. See also *Rowland v Divall* [1923] 2 K.B. 500.

[185] *Butterworth v Kingsway Motors Ltd* [1954] 2 All E.R. 694.

[186] This case was decided before the enactment of the Hire Purchase Act 1964.

[187] See para.1.10 above.

[188] *McDonald v Provan (of Scotland Street) Ltd*, 1960 S.L.T. 231.

in the composite vehicle and were thus not in the position of having an unqualified right to sell it to the pursuer. If so, they would be in breach of s.12(1)".[189]

The companion of s.12(1) is s.12(2), under which the seller impliedly promises that the goods are free, and will remain free until the time when the property is to pass, from any charge or incumbrance not disclosed or known to the buyer before the contract is made, and also that the buyer will enjoy quiet possession of the goods.[190] The seller does not, under s.12(2), provide an absolute guarantee of the buyer's position against every disturbance which might occur, as there is no breach of the duty under this section where a third party wrongfully disturbs the buyer's possession.[191] The operation of s.12(2) is illustrated by the *Microbeads* case, considered above. It was noted that there was no breach of s.12(1) where the goods infringed a patent, because that patent had not been granted at the time of sale, so that at the time of sale the seller did have a right to sell the goods. Nonetheless, the fact that the buyer could not use the goods because of the patent meant that he could not enjoy quiet possession of the goods, so that there was indeed a breach of s.12(2).[192]

DUTY TO PROVIDE GOODS OF CORRECT DESCRIPTION

1.11.4 Where goods are sold by description, there is an implied term under s.13 that the goods will correspond with their description. Obviously, all generic sales will be by sales by description, e.g. where a buyer orders a ton of potatoes. Yet, according to Lord Wright, the class of goods sold by description is a wide one:

> "There is a sale by description even though the buyer is buying something displayed before him on the counter; a thing is sold by description, though it is specific, so long as it is sold not merely as the specific thing, but as a thing corresponding to a description, e.g. woollen undergarments, a hot water bottle, a second-hand reaping machine . . .".[193]

Online sales will also constitute sales by description.

Section 13 specifically provides that the sale is not prevented from being a sale by description "by reason only that, being exposed for sale or hire, they are selected by the buyer". The description may not be in words but could be in images or numbers. In *Beale v Taylor*[194] a car was advertised for sale as "Herald convertible, white, 1961, twin carbs, £190". When he saw the car, the buyer checked the metallic disc on the back of the car which read "1200", reaffirming his view that the car was the first model of the "1200" to come out in 1961. The car was, in fact, made up of parts of two different models welded together. He successfully established that this was a sale by description, even though that "description" was the year and model number of the car in the advert and affixed to the back of the car.

Lord Diplock defined the characteristics which form part of the description in *Ashington Piggeries v Christopher Hill Ltd*[195]:

> "[D]escription is confined to those words in the contract which were intended by the parties to identify the kind of goods to be supplied. It is open to the parties to use a description as broad or as narrow as they choose. But ultimately the test is whether the buyer could fairly and reasonably

---

[189] *McDonald v Provan (of Scotland Street) Ltd*, 1960 S.L.T. 231 at 232.

[190] The cases discussed in the context of s.12(1): *Niblett v Confectioners Materials Co Ltd* [1921] 3 K.B. 387; *Microbeads AC v Vinhurst Road Markings Ltd* [1975] 1 W.L.R. 218; and *McDonald v Provan (of Scotland Street) Ltd*, 1960 S.L.T. 231; each contain discussions of potential breaches of s.12(2). For a case (on unusual facts) concerning breach of the duty under s.12(2)(b), to give to the buyer quiet possession, see *Rubicon Computer Systems Ltd v United Paints Ltd* (2000) 2 T.C.L.R. 453 and the other cases cited therein decided on the basis of this subsection.

[191] *Empresa Exportadora De Azucar (CUBAZUCAR) v Industria Azucarera Nacional SA (IANSA) (The Playa Larga)* [1983] 2 Lloyd's Rep. 171.

[192] See also *Rubicon Computer Systems Ltd v United Paints Ltd* [2002] T.C.L.R. 453 CA, where it was held to be a breach of s.12(2) when the suppliers of a computer system installed a feature which allowed them to lock the buyers out of the system.

[193] *Grant v Australian Knitting Mills Ltd* [1936] A.C. 85 at 100.

[194] *Beale v Taylor* [1967] 1 W.L.R. 1193 CA.

[195] *Ashington Piggeries v Christopher Hill Ltd* [1972] A.C. 441 at 503–504.

refuse to accept the physical goods proffered to him on the ground that their failure to correspond with that part of what was said about them in the contract makes them goods of a different kind from those he agreed to buy. The key to s.13 is identification."

Where the buyer is buying a motor vehicle it may be difficult to determine which of its characteristics need to conform to a generic description. In *Brewer v Mann* the car was described by the car dealer as a "1930 Bentley Speed Six".[196] It transpired that the original 1936 engine had been replaced by an earlier 1927 one. Brewer, who had taken the car on hire purchase, ceased payments and the car was repossessed. She sued the dealer, the company for whom he worked and the finance company with whom she had concluded her finance agreement. At first instance it was held that, in order to conform to description, the car required to have its original engine. The Court of Appeal overturned this decision, criticising the test as too strict. If a buyer wanted an original engine, then he should negotiate for one: "it does not come for free."[197] The car conformed to this description provided the chassis number was incorporated into the car.[198]

The goods may be defective, and yet still conform to description. In the above case the plaintiffs sold feedstuff to the defendants who were mink breeders. The feedstuff caused the death of thousands of mink because an ingredient, Norwegian herring meal, contained a toxic agent. The contract under which the herring meal was supplied provided that it was sold as "fair, average quality". It was held that this was not part of the description. The fact that it was contaminated was not a breach of s.13—herring meal was still herring meal, even if it was poisonous. Similarly in *Border Harvesters Ltd v Edwards Engineering (Perth) Ltd*[199] it was held that there was no breach of s.13 when a grain dryer failed to achieve its stated capacity, i.e. did not achieve the desired quality, Lord Kincraig noting:

> "What was contracted for was described as a Kamas dryer; what was supplied was a Kamas dryer. What the dryer was capable of doing was . . . not part of the description."[200]

There is some confusion as to whether the buyer must prove that he actually relied on the description before a breach of s.13 can be established.[201] To require actual reliance is, perhaps, to state the position too forcefully. Weaker formulations of the test were offered in *Harlingdon & Leinster Enterprises Ltd v Hull Fine Art Ltd*.[202] A painting was advertised as being by Gabriele Munter. An employee of the seller made it clear to a potential buyer that the seller knew nothing about the artist, whereas the buyers were dealers in German expressionist art and had examined the painting. After the purchase, when the painting turned out to be a forgery, the buyer tried, unsuccessfully, to establish a breach of s.13. Lord Justice Nourse explained:

> "It is suggested that the significance which some of these authorities attribute to the buyer's reliance on the description is misconceived. I think that that criticism is theoretically correct. In theory it is no doubt possible for a description of goods which is not relied on by the buyer to become an essential term of a contract for their sale. But in practice it is very difficult, and perhaps impossible, to think of facts where that would be so. The description must have a sufficient influence in the sale to become an essential term of the contract and the correlative of influence is reliance. Indeed, reliance by the buyer is the natural index of a sale by description."[203]

---

[196] [2010] EWHC 2444; [2012] EWCA Civ 246; [2012] RTR 28; [2012] EWHC 2633.

[197] [2012] EWCA Civ 246; [2012] RTR 28 at [296].

[198] [2012] EWCA Civ 246; [2012] RTR 28 at [304].

[199] *Border Harvesters Ltd v Edwards Engineering (Perth) Ltd*, 1985 S.L.T. 128.

[200] *Border Harvesters Ltd v Edwards Engineering (Perth) Ltd*, 1985 S.L.T. 128 at 131. See also *Manchester Liners Ltd v Rea Ltd* [1922] 2 A.C. 74, per Lord Dunedin at 80, relied on by Lord Kincraig in the *Border Harvesters* case.

[201] *Joseph Travers & Son v Longel Ltd* (1948) 64 T.L.R. 150 suggests that this is the case.

[202] *Harlingdon & Leinster Enterprises Ltd v Hull Fine Art Ltd* [1991] 1 Q.B. 564.

[203] *Harlingdon & Leinster Enterprises Ltd v Hull Fine Art Ltd* [1990] 3 W.L.R. 13, per Nourse LJ at 21 and 18. The use of "essential term" is ambiguous: he may have been referring to a "condition" in English law, breach of which permits the buyer to rescind, as opposed to a warranty, breach of which enables the purchaser to use the remedy of damages only, see ss.11(3) and 60. Following the amendments made by the 1994 Act, the terms "condition" and "warranty" are not relevant to Scots law. The test in Scotland is whether or not the breach is material, in which case the buyer can rescind, or non-material, in which case the buyer is limited to claiming damages only, see s.15B.

Alternatively, Slade LJ indicated that it must be possible "to impute to the parties . . . a common intention that it shall be a term of the contract that the goods will correspond with the description".[204] Such tests will undoubtedly be difficult to apply. The ambiguity present here is unfortunate. If actual reliance is a requirement then this might dilute the protection afforded to the buyer by this important section.

DUTY TO SUPPLY GOODS OF THE REQUISITE QUALITY AND FITNESS

1.11.5 Under s.14, where the goods are sold in the course of a business, the goods must be of satisfactory quality and fit for the buyer's purpose.[205] The expression "in the course of a business" has a wide meaning. The sale of the entire stock of a business was held to be a sale in the course of a business,[206] and the outcome of *Stevenson v Rogers*[207] suggests that it will only be purely private sales which fall outwith this definition. The Court of Appeal relied on the fact that this section had been amended,[208] explaining "the requirement for regularity of dealing, or indeed any dealing, in the goods was removed".[209] Thus the sale of a fishing boat, the main asset of a fishing business, was held to be a sale in the course of a business. The Inner House recently confirmed, in a case on very similar facts, that the approach of the Court of Appeal in *Stevenson v Rodgers* was the correct one.[210]

The requirement that the goods must be sold in the course of a business means that the implied terms do not apply to purely private sales.[211] Yet the terms implied under s.14 also apply where the person selling in the course of a business is acting as an agent for a private individual, unless the buyer is aware that the principal is not acting in the course of a business or reasonable steps have been taken to bring this fact to the buyer's attention prior to the conclusion of the contract.[212] In *Boyter v Thomson*[213] it was held that this section applied whether the principal was disclosed or undisclosed.[214] In a situation where the principal is undisclosed when the contract is concluded, once the buyer is aware of the principal's identity, the buyer must elect to sue either principal or agent.[215]

Goods supplied under the contract include packaging and instructions. In *Geddling v Marsh*[216] the plaintiff was injured when a bottle containing mineral water exploded. The seller was held to be in breach of s.14 even though the explosion was caused by a defect in the bottle, rather than the mineral water itself, and the bottle was returnable. In *Wormell v RHM Agricultural (East) Ltd*[217] the seller was found to be in breach of s.14 where defective instructions on tins of weedkiller rendered an otherwise effective product virtually useless.

According to the English courts, the terms implied under s.14 can extend to any foreign object supplied with the goods. In *Wilson v Rickett, Cockerell & Co*[218] the plaintiff had bought a consignment of coal from the defendant. Damage was caused to the plaintiff's house when a detonator which had been mistakenly included with the consignment exploded. The Court of Appeal rejected the argument that the goods supplied under the contract (coal) were of excellent quality and that the detonator was not supplied under the contract at all. Lord Denning stated:

---

[204] *Harlingdon & Leinster Enterprises Ltd v Hull Fine Art Ltd* [1990] 3 W.L.R. 13, per Slade LJ at 30.

[205] See s.14(2), (3).

[206] *Buchanan-Jardine v Hamilink*, 1983 S.L.T. 149.

[207] *Stevenson v Rogers* [1999] 1 All E.R. 613.

[208] See Sale of Goods Act (Implied Terms) Act 1973 s.3, which eventually became Sale of Goods Act 1979 s.14(2).

[209] *Stevenson v Rogers* [1999] 1 All E.R. 613 CA, per Potter LJ at 623.

[210] *Macdonald v Pollock* [2011] CSIH 12; 2013 S.C. 22. Noted by W.C.H. Ervine, "Clarifying the Sale of Goods Act", 2012 S.L.T. 187.

[211] This is confirmed by s.14(1), which indicates that, except as provided for by the Act, there is no implied term about the quality or fitness of goods. There may, of course, be express terms.

[212] See s.14(5).

[213] *Boyter v Thomson*, 1995 S.L.T. 875.

[214] See para.2.7.4 below.

[215] See para.2.7.4 below.

[216] *Geddling v Marsh* [1920] 1 K.B. 668.

[217] *Wormell v RHM Agricultural (East) Ltd* [1986] 1 All E.R. 769.

[218] *Wilson v Rickett, Cockerell & Co* [1954] 1 Q.B. 598.

"[T]he section refers to the 'goods supplied under a contract of sale'. In my opinion that means the goods delivered in purported pursuance of the contract. The section applies to all goods so delivered, whether they conform to the contract or not".[219]

However, this decision is contrary to an earlier Scottish authority on almost exactly the same facts, *Duke v Jackson*.[220] Subsequent Scottish cases have sought to distinguish *Duke*,[221] and, in view of the convincing criticism which it received from the Court of Appeal in *Wilson v Rickett, Cockerell & Co*, *Duke* is unlikely to be treated as authoritative in the future.

Merely because goods meet the standard stipulated in the contract does not preclude them from failing to measure up to the statutory implied terms.[222]

The meaning of "satisfactory quality"

Before examining the implied term as to satisfactory quality,[223] its several limitations should be noted. **1.11.5.1** It does not apply to any defect which is specifically drawn to the buyer's attention before the contract is made.[224] Nor does it apply where the buyer examines the goods before the contract is made, to any defect which that examination ought to reveal.[225] The 1973 amendments clarified an ambiguity relating to the buyer's examination of goods. Older authority suggested that the implied term might not apply where the buyer carried out a cursory examination, where the defect would have been revealed had the examination been carried out properly.[226] The wording of the above provision was amended from "such" examination to "that" examination. The implied term is therefore only excluded in respect of defects which would have been revealed by the type of examination that was actually carried out.[227] Clearly, the end result is better protection for the buyer.

The 1893 Act referred to "merchantable" rather than "satisfactory quality", although that term was not defined in the Act. A large body of case law grew up around the term, and this undoubtedly helped frame the eventual statutory definition. The first attempt to define "merchantable quality" occurred in the Supply of Goods (Implied Terms) Act 1973 which provided that goods were of merchantable quality

"if they are as fit for the purpose or purposes for which goods of that kind are commonly bought as is reasonable to expect having regard to any description applied to them, the price (if relevant) and all the other relevant circumstances".[228]

The Law Commissions in their joint report[229] made several criticisms of the term "merchantable". It was thought to be out-of-date, and inappropriate in a consumer context. The focus on fitness for purpose did not take into account many aspects which were important to consumers such as appearance and finish and freedom from minor defects. Finally, the definition did not include durability or safety of the goods, characteristics which are obviously important.

Satisfactory quality is elaborated upon in s.14(2A). Goods are of satisfactory quality

---

[219] *Wilson v Rickett, Cockerell & Co* [1954] 1 Q.B. 598 at 607.

[220] *Duke v Jackson*, 1921 S.C. 362.

[221] *Fitzpatrick v Barr*, 1948 S.L.T. (Sh Ct) 5.

[222] *Britvic Soft Drinks Ltd v Messer UK Ltd* [2002] 3 All E.R. (Comm) 321 CA: soft drinks met the appropriate British Safety Standard specified in the contract, but contained benzene, and so could not be sold on to the public. Thus they were neither satisfactory in terms of s.14(2), nor fit for their purpose in terms of s.14(3). See also *Lowe v W Machell Joinery Ltd* [2011] EWCA Civ 798; 138 Con. L.R. 48.

[223] See W.C.H. Ervine, "Satisfactory quality: what does it mean?" [2004] J.B.L. 684.

[224] See s.14(2C)(a).

[225] See s.14(2C)(b).

[226] *Thornett & Fehr v Beers & Son* [1919] 1 K.B. 486.

[227] *Macdonald v Pollock* [2011] CSIH 12; 2013 S.C. 22, noted by W.C.H. Ervine, "Clarifying the Sale of Goods Act", 2012 S.L.T. 187.

[228] Section 7(2) inserted a new s.62(1A) into the 1893 Act.

[229] Law Commission and Scottish Law Commission, *Report on Sale and Supply of Goods*, 1987. Cmnd.137.

"if they meet the standard that a reasonable person would regard as satisfactory, taking account of the description of the goods, the price (if relevant) and all the other relevant circumstances."

Satisfactory quality is considered from the standpoint of the hypothetical reasonable person: that standard does not import expertise.[230] It will also vary according to the nature of the goods and who is likely to use them, for example, where the goods are a soft toy, the court will consider how a toddler would handle those goods.[231] Quality is specifically stated to include the state and condition of goods, and the following (among others) are, in appropriate cases, aspects of the quality of goods: fitness for all the purposes for which goods of the kind in question are commonly supplied; appearance and finish; freedom from minor defects; safety and durability.[232] The 2002 Regulations added a new "relevant circumstance" to this list, namely, public statements on the specific characteristics of the goods made about them by the seller, the producer or his representative, particularly in advertising or on labelling where the contract is a consumer contract.[233] The "relevant circumstances" are commented on below, but, for the moment, it should be noted that not all of these aspects will be relevant in every case—the section states that they are aspects of the quality of goods "in appropriate cases". Satisfactory quality is a relative concept, and goods of moderate or even poor quality will be satisfactory in certain circumstances.

Views are mixed on whether "satisfactory" quality is preferable to "merchantable" quality. The new concept clearly resolved certain ambiguities. However, the word "satisfactory" does not denote a very high standard in normal English usage, and may even be close to "mediocre". The Law Commissions' initial suggestion of "acceptable" quality was dropped. Framing a definition which applies to all of the diverse consumer and commercial sales may be an impossible task. This view is perhaps endorsed by Rougier J:

"Any attempt to forge some exhaustive, positive and specific definition of such a term, applicable in all cases, would soon be put to mockery by some new undreamt of set of circumstances."[234]

Case law interpreting the definition, rather than the definition itself, is of key importance. The types of goods which the courts have applied the definition to are many and varied.[235] Although opinion on this point is mixed, it is thought that the courts may consider older case law on "merchantable quality" as an aid to interpretation of "satisfactory quality".[236] Certain questions remain open. *Shine v General Guarantee Corporation*[237] suggested that merchantable quality included not only the condition of the goods but also the reasonable expectations of the buyer. The buyer, a second hand car enthusiast, succeeded in proving that the car he had bought was not merchantable because it had been immersed in water for over 24 hours and had been written off by its insurers. It is not clear whether satisfactory quality includes such reasonable expectations.

Aspects of the quality of goods

Fitness for all common purposes

1.11.5.2 Older authority suggested that goods were of merchantable quality if they were fit for any of the common purposes of such goods.[238] The 1994 amendments refer to all common purposes, which is a much higher standard for the seller to attain. This is a significant improvement on the previous position.

---

[230] *Clegg v Andersson* [2003] EWCA Civ 320; [2003] 2 Lloyd's Rep. 32, per Hale LJ at [73].

[231] *Jewson Ltd v Boyhan* [2005] 1 Lloyd's Rep. 505.

[232] See s.14(2B)(a)–(e).

[233] Regulation 3 inserting new s.14(2D)–(2F) to the 1979 Act.

[234] *Bernstein v Pamson Motors (Golders Green) Ltd* [1987] 2 All E.R. 220, per Rougier J at 222.

[235] One unusual example is *Bon Accord Granite v Buchan*, 2005 G.W.D. 28–531, in which the goods were a gravestone.

[236] See the summary of the opposing views in W.C.H. Ervine, "Satisfactory quality: what does it mean?" [2004] J.B.L. 684, 689–690.

[237] *Shine v General Guarantee Corporation* [1988] 1 All E.R. 911.

[238] *M/S Aswan Engineering Establishment Co Ltd v Lupdine Ltd* [1987] 1 W.L.R. 1.

If brand new goods are not fit for one of the purposes for which they are usually supplied, then the seller must make this fact known to the buyer.[239]

Section 14(3) also concerns fitness for purpose, although it covers the situation where the goods are required for some particular purpose made known to the seller, whereas s.14(2) concerns fitness for ordinary purposes. If the buyer's purpose is an uncommon one, he may be able to fall back on the protection in s.14(3).

Appearance and finish

This issue arose most frequently in relation to new cars. One can contrast Mustill LJ in *Rogers v Parish (Scarborough) Ltd*[240] who considered that the quality of a new car includes "pride in the vehicle's outward and interior appearance" with Rougier J in *Bernstein v Pamson Motors (Golders Green) Ltd* who considered that whereas the buyer of a Rolls Royce would not "tolerate the slightest blemish on its exterior paintwork; the purchaser of a motor car very much at the humbler end of the range might be less fastidious".[241] Because appearance and finish are now specifically incorporated in the definition, this issue should no longer be subject to doubt.[242] All buyers are entitled to expect that goods meet a satisfactory standard of appearance and finish.

Freedom from minor defects

The inclusion of this issue in the definition effectively reverses an infamous Scottish case, *Millars of Falkirk v Turpie*.[243] The sellers of a car had failed several times to rectify several minor defects. The purchaser, Mr Turpie, sought to reject the goods, arguing that they were not of merchantable quality. The sellers refused to accept his rejection and brought an action for the price. It was held that because the fault was a comparatively minor one which could have been cured at the cost of £25, the new car was of merchantable quality. Lord President Emslie indicated that such defects were to be expected in new cars. This was a common judicial view at that time. Similar sentiments were expressed by Rougier J in *Bernstein v Pamson Motors (Golders Green) Ltd*[244] where he stated that the buyer of a new car "must put up with a certain amount of teething troubles and have them rectified", adding by way of explanation "no system of mass production can ever be perfect."[245]

Although one would have thought that the reference within s.14(2B)(c) to freedom from minor defects would have removed any doubt whatsoever on this point, this seems not to be the case. In *Lamarra v Capital Bank Plc*[246] a hirer had entered into a hire purchase contract in relation to a Range Rover which proved to have a number of minor defects: the navigation disc was missing; the front wheels were not correctly balanced causing excessive tyre wear; there was road-related noise emanating from the transmission or drive system; there was a scratch on the ashtray cover; there was a misalignment of the glove box; and the paintwork on parts of the roof was poorly finished. The buyer was protected by the same implied term relating to quality of goods as applies in cases of sale because of the importation of these standards into hire purchase contracts in terms of s.10 of the Supply of Goods (Implied Terms) Act 1973. At first instance the sheriff rejected the pursuer's argument that the goods were not of satisfactory quality, failing entirely to take into account the reference in the 1979 Act to freedom from minor defects. The sheriff clearly considered it to be significant that the hirer would have recourse to a manufacturer's guarantee. Thankfully, the sheriff's approach was rejected by an Extra Division of the Inner House. It was held that the sheriff had been wrong in law to ignore the provisions

---

[239] See para.3.36, Law Commission and Scottish Law Commission, *Report on Sale and Supply of Goods*, 1987. Cmnd.137.

[240] *Rogers v Parish (Scarborough) Ltd* [1987] Q.B. 933, per Mustill LJ at 944.

[241] *Bernstein v Pamson Motors (Golders Green) Ltd* [1987] 2 All E.R. 220, per Rougier J at 228.

[242] Appearance and finish was also at issue in the case of *Lamarra v Capital Bank Plc* [2006] CSIH 49; 2006 S.L.T. 1053, commented on in more detail under "Freedom from minor defects" below.

[243] *Millars of Falkirk v Turpie*, 1976 S.L.T. (Notes) 66.

[244] *Bernstein v Pamson Motors (Golders Green) Ltd* [1987] 2 All E.R. 220.

[245] *Bernstein v Pamson Motors (Golders Green) Ltd* [1987] 2 All E.R. 220, per Rougier J at 228–229.

[246] *Lamarra v Capital Bank Plc* [2006] CSIH 49; 2006 S.L.T. 1053. For comment see P. Hood, "An unsatisfactory hire-purchase", 2007 Edin. L.R. 421.

on freedom from minor defects. The court is "required to put itself in the position of a reasonable person and ask itself whether, in the state in which it was shown to be when it was delivered, this Range Rover was of satisfactory quality for such a vehicle."[247]

The Extra Division also rather resoundingly rejected the sheriff's emphasis of the role of the warranty. In their view, it could not fall within the description "all the other relevant circumstances" in s.10(2A) of the Supply of Goods (Implied Terms) Act 1973 which fell to be taken into account in assessing what the reasonable person would consider to be satisfactory. This reference is only to the circumstances which "have a bearing upon the quality of the goods in question".[248] A warranty is

> "concerned with the provision of remedial action within a limited period after delivery . . . [B]ecause the issue of whether the quality of the goods is satisfactory requires to be judged at the time of delivery, the warranty can have no bearing upon that matter."[249]

It was not even clear whether the purchaser in the case would have had the benefit of the warranty, given that warranties are usually issued to the first purchaser of the goods, which in this case was the defender.[250] Finally, referring to the sheriff's emphasis of the unreasonableness of the buyer's attitude, the Extra Division indicated that the reasonableness or otherwise of the buyer's conduct cannot be relevant to the determination of satisfactory quality.[251]

Hopefully the "anti-consumer" approach typified by *Millars of Falkirk v Turpie*[252] has finally been laid to rest. Given that the Inner House in *Lamarra* confirmed that satisfactory quality did not imply "perfection" in the goods concerned,[253] there may yet be room for doubt.

Safety

In contrast to the original wording of s.14, the amended wording now refers to safety. This important issue should be relatively simple to assess. Goods safe in themselves may be rendered unsafe by inadequate or misleading instructions,[254] or because they are delivered with the wrong delivery note, creating an erroneous impression as to the goods actually delivered.[255]

Durability

Certain dicta suggested that durability was an aspect of merchantability.[256] This issue is now put beyond doubt by the inclusion of this characteristic as part of satisfactory quality. The buyer must show that the goods were not durable at the time of supply by the seller, although it will usually not be possible to do so until some time after the initial supply. If goods break down soon after they have been purchased this will be a factor which the courts will take into account in assessing durability.[257] However, the courts will also look at factors such as the frequency of use to which the goods were put, and any mistreatment of the goods. Price and description are also relevant to this assessment.

---

[247] *Lamarra v Capital Bank Plc* [2006] CSIH 49; 2006 S.L.T. 1053 at [50].

[248] *Lamarra v Capital Bank Plc* [2006] CSIH 49; 2006 S.L.T. 1053 at [62].

[249] *Lamarra v Capital Bank Plc* [2006] CSIH 49; 2006 S.L.T. 1053 at [62].

[250] *Lamarra v Capital Bank Plc* [2006] CSIH 49; 2006 S.L.T. 1053 at [65].

[251] *Lamarra v Capital Bank Plc* [2006] CSIH 49; 2006 S.L.T. 1053 at [71]–[72].

[252] *Millars of Falkirk v Turpie*, 1976 S.L.T. (Notes) 66.

[253] *Lamarra v Capital Bank Plc* [2006] CSIH 49; 2006 S.L.T. 1053 at [61]. The type of goods may yet be relevant, in the sense of whether they are "top of the range"—the purchaser of the yacht in *Clegg v Andersson* was entitled to expect it to be "perfect or nearly so" [2003] EWCA Civ 320, per Lady Hale at [73].

[254] *Wormell v RHM Agricultural (East) Ltd* [1986] 1 All E.R. 769; reversed on another point on appeal [1987] 3 All E.R. 75.

[255] In *Albright & Wilson UK Ltd v Biachem Ltd* [2001] EWCA Civ 301; [2001] 2 All E.R. (Comm) 537, chemicals were delivered with the wrong delivery note. Because of the misleading impression this gave, the chemicals were mixed with others causing a serious explosion. Although the decision was reversed in part in the House of Lords, there was no discussion in the House of this particular point, see [2002] UKHL 37; [2002] 2 All E.R. (Comm) 753.

[256] See Lord Diplock in *Lambert v Lewis* [1982] A.C. 225 at 276.

[257] See also in this context the protection provided to the consumer in terms of s.48A. This provides that any lack of conformity of goods which becomes apparent within six months of delivery of the goods to the consumer is deemed to have existed at the date of delivery; see para.1.12.1 below.

In *Thain v Anniesland Trade Centre*[258] the buyer purchased for £2,995 a five-year-old Renault 19 which had done about 80,000 miles. The car developed a gearbox fault after two weeks of running which was so serious that the car had to be written-off. The court held that it was sufficient if the car was fit for its initial use, and that durability was not a quality reasonably to be expected of a second hand car. The low price and high mileage were key issues in deciding what would be satisfactory to a buyer.

In most cases where the goods are found not to be of satisfactory quality because they are not durable, the buyer has the right to damages only, given that the right to rescind will probably have been lost due to lapse of time.

Public statements

The relevant circumstance added by the 2002 Regulations is public statements on the specific characteristics of the goods made about them by the seller, the producer or his representative, particularly in advertising or on labelling.[259] It applies only where the contract is a consumer contract.[260] "The producer" is given a wide definition to catch

> "the manufacturer of goods, the importer of goods into the European Economic Area or any person purporting to be a producer by placing his name, trade mark or other distinctive sign on the goods."[261]

The seller can escape this type of liability if he can show that, at the time the contract was made, he was unaware, and could not reasonably have been aware, of the statement; before the contract was made, the statement had been withdrawn in public; or the decision to buy the goods could not have been influenced by the statement.[262] The list of relevant circumstances is not, as has already been stated, an exclusive one, and public statements may still be relevant even though they do not fall within the terms of this new provision.[263]

Implied term as to fitness for purpose

As explained above, fitness for all common purposes is one of the factors to be taken into account under s.14(2A) in assessing whether the goods are of satisfactory quality. However, a separate implied term as to fitness for purpose exists in s.14(3). Where the buyer, expressly or by implication, makes known to the seller any particular purpose for which the goods are being bought, the goods must be reasonably fit for that purpose whether or not that is a purpose for which such goods are commonly supplied. However, the buyer will not have access to this remedy where the circumstances show that he has not relied, or that it was unreasonable for him to rely, on the seller's skill or judgment.

1.11.5.3

There is no duty on the buyer to make known an obvious purpose. Lord Wright explained in *Grant v Australian Knitting Mills Ltd*:

> "There is no need to specify the particular purpose for which the buyer requires the goods which is nonetheless the particular purpose, because it is the only purpose for which anyone would ordinarily want the goods."[264]

By contrast, if the goods have a number of purposes, in order to rely on s.14(3), the buyer will have to make known to the seller the particular purpose for which he, the buyer, will be using the goods.[265] The

---

[258] *Thain v Anniesland Trade Centre*, 1997 S.L.T. (Sh Ct) 102.

[259] A public statement which is false would also be likely to contravene the Consumer Protection from Unfair Trading Regulations 2008 which came into force on May 26, 2008.

[260] 2002 Regulations reg.3 inserting new s.14(2D)–(2F) to the 1979 Act.

[261] 2002 Regulations reg.6 inserting new definitions into 1979 Act s.61(1). This definition contains similarities to the description of the party liable under the Consumer Protection Act 1987 in the context of defective products; see Consumer Protection Act 1987 s.2(2)(b).

[262] 2002 Regulations reg.3(2E)(a)–(c).

[263] 2002 Regulations reg.3(2F).

[264] *Grant v Australian Knitting Mills Ltd* [1936] A.C. 85, per Lord Wright at 99.

[265] *Flynn v Scott*, 1949 S.C. 442.

relationship with s.14(2) should be borne in mind: if the purpose for which the goods are used is a common purpose then the buyer will be able to argue that the goods are not of satisfactory quality in terms of s.14(2). As such, this section is aimed at "sub-standard goods".[266] By contrast, "it is the function of s.14(3) not s.14(2) to impose a particular obligation tailored to the particular circumstances of the case".[267] Where the buyer intends to use the goods for an unusual or extraordinary purpose and fails to make this known to the seller, he will probably fail under both s.14(2) and (3).[268]

Jewson Ltd v Boyhan is a good example of the kinds of difficulties faced by a buyer in order successfully to rely on s.14(3).[269] The defender, a property developer, had approached Jewsons, a hardware store, in order to purchase boilers for one of his developments, the conversion of a building into flats. The development was not a success, and the defender attributed the poor sales of the flats to very poor energy ratings of the boilers. It was held that the defender did not, in fact, rely on Jewson's expertise, nor would it have been reasonable for him to have done so. He did not inform them of the particular characteristics of the flats to be sold, nor was there any discussion of the merits of different types of boilers which could have been installed.[270]

The goods may also appear to be unfit for their purpose, and yet it may be proved that this is due, not to a defect in the goods, but rather to some idiosyncrasy or abnormal feature of the buyer or the buyer's business. Should that be the case, there will be no breach of s.14(3). In order to rely on s.14(3) the buyer must make the seller aware of the idiosyncrasy. So, for example, a buyer was unsuccessful in proving that a Harris tweed coat was unmerchantable where she contracted dermatitis through wearing it, because it was proved that her skin was abnormally sensitive, and the coat would not have injured the skin of a normal person.[271]

As stated above, s.14(3) cannot be successfully used where the seller can show that the buyer has not relied, or it would not have been reasonable for him to rely, on the seller's skill and judgment. The onus lies on the seller to prove that the buyer has not relied, or it was unreasonable for him to rely,[272] and, generally, reliance will be presumed. As Lord Wright commented in *Grant v Australian Knitting Mills*:

> "The reliance will seldom be express: it will usually arise by implication from the circumstances: thus to take a case like that in question, of a purchase from a retailer, the reliance will be in general inferred from the fact that a buyer goes to the shop in the confidence that the tradesman has selected his stock with skill and judgment . . .".[273]

If the buyer knows that the seller has no choice as to the goods sold, there may be no reliance, for example, where the seller is only permitted to sell one type of beer from a pub and the buyer is aware of this fact.[274] The buyer may similarly fail to prove reliance where the buyer has greater expertise in the market in question than the seller. Nevertheless, even where the seller is manufacturing goods to the buyer's directions, the buyer may still be relying on the seller to carry out the process competently.[275] A defect may be discovered by the buyer through an examination prior to the contract being concluded. In such a case, a claim under s.14(2) is ruled out due to the buyer's awareness of the defect. However, a claim under s.14(3) might be possible. Although one might have thought that, in such a case, the buyer is not relying on the seller's skill and judgment, he may be relying on the seller to rectify the defect.[276] Otherwise, pre-contractual knowledge of a defect will mean that the buyer does not rely on the seller's skill and judgment, unless perhaps the seller advises the buyer that the goods will still be fit for their purpose despite the defect.

---

[266] *Jewson Ltd v Boyhan* [2003] EWCA Civ 1030; [2005] 1 Lloyd's Rep. 505, per Sedley LJ at [77].

[267] *Jewson Ltd v Boyhan* [2005] 1 Lloyd's Rep. 505, per Sedley LJ at [77].

[268] *B S Brown & Son Ltd v Craiks Ltd*, 1970 S.C. (HL) 51.

[269] *Jewson Ltd v Boyhan* [2003] EWCA Civ 1030; [2005] 1 Lloyd's Rep. 505

[270] *Jewson Ltd v Boyhan* [2003] EWCA Civ 1030; [2005] 1 Lloyd's Rep. 505, per Clarke LJ at [61].

[271] *Griffiths v Peter Conway Ltd* [1939] 1 All E.R. 685. See also *Slater v Finning Ltd*, 1996 S.L.T. (HL) 916.

[272] *BSS Group Plc v Makers (UK) Ltd (t/a Allied Services)* [2011] EWCA Civ 809; [2011] T.C.L.R. 7, per Rimer LJ at [41].

[273] *Grant v Australian Knitting Mills* [1936] A.C. 85 at 99.

[274] *Wren v Holt* [1903] 1 K.B. 610.

[275] *Ashington Piggeries v Christopher Hill Ltd* [1972] A.C. 441.

[276] *R&B Customs Brokers Ltd v UDT Ltd* [1988] 1 W.L.R. 321.

IMPLIED TERMS IN SALES BY SAMPLE

Under s.15 there is an implied term that:

1.11.6

(1) the bulk will correspond with the sample in quality[277];
(2) the buyer will have a reasonable opportunity of comparing the bulk with the sample[278]; and
(3) the bulk will be free from any defect making the goods unsatisfactory which would not be apparent on a reasonable examination of the sample.[279]

A sale is by sample where there is an express or implied term in the contract to that effect.[280]

ATTEMPTS TO EXCLUDE LIABILITY UNDER THE IMPLIED TERMS

Generally, it is not open to the seller to argue that he could not have discovered the defect. Liability for **1.11.7** breach of the implied terms is absolute in this respect.[281] The Unfair Contract Terms Act 1977 prevents the seller from excluding the duties imposed on him to pass good title under s.12.[282] This obligation applies regardless of the type of contract at issue, i.e. whether or not it is a consumer contract.

Turning to the other implied terms, i.e. those in s.13 (conformity with description), s.14 (quality or fitness) and s.15 (sale by sample), the ability to exclude such terms depends upon whether the contract is a consumer contract or not, using the definition of consumer contract contained in s.25(1) of the Unfair Contract Terms Act 1977, as amended by the 2002 Regulations.[283] If the contract is a consumer contract, the attempt to exclude the duties of the seller is void.[284] In all other cases, the attempt to exclude will be subject to a fair and reasonableness test.[285] The onus of proving that the contract is not a consumer contract rests on the party who claims that it is not, i.e. the party trying to exclude liability. The changes which the 2002 Regulations made to the definition of a consumer must be borne in mind here.[286] Previously, where the contract related to the transfer of ownership or possession of goods, a contract would only be a consumer contract where the goods were of a type ordinarily supplied for private use or consumption. As a result, attempts to exclude the implied terms in sale of goods cases in relation to a consumer would only be automatically void where the goods were of this nature. Where goods were supplied to a consumer but were of a type normally supplied for use in a business, the lesser test of whether it was fair and reasonable to incorporate the exclusion clause applied. Following the 2002 amendments, this limitation is disapplied where the consumer is an individual. Individuals are now protected, and attempts to exclude the implied terms are automatically void, regardless of the individual's intended purpose for the goods purchased. Where the consumer is not an individual, the position remains unchanged: for attempts to exclude the implied terms to be void, where the contract is for the transfer of ownership or possession of goods, the goods must still be of a type ordinarily supplied for private use and consumption. If the goods are not of this nature, the attempt to exclude the implied term is subject to the lower test of whether it was fair and reasonable to incorporate the exclusionary term. It should be recalled, however, that this relates only to attempts to exclude the implied terms in ss.13–15. Attempts to exclude the implied term relating to the passing of good title in s.12 are always void, regardless of the characteristics of the buyer.

The 2002 Regulations also made relevant amendments where goods are purchased at auctions. The more stringent test for exclusion clauses, i.e. the one which imposes the sanction of voidness, does not

---

[277] See s.15(2)(a).
[278] See ss.14(2C)(c) and 15.
[279] See s.15(2)(c).
[280] See s.15(1).
[281] *Frost v Aylesbury Dairy Co Ltd* [1905] 1 K.B. 608.
[282] UCTA 1977 s.20(1)(a).
[283] See the discussion of this definition at para.1.9 above.
[284] UCTA 1977 s.20(2)(i).
[285] UCTA 1977 s.20(2)(ii); and see *Britvic Soft Drinks Ltd v Messer UK Ltd* [2002] 3 All E.R. (Comm) 321 CA.
[286] See the discussion of this definition at para.1.9 above.

apply where the consumer buys second hand goods sold by public auction at which individuals have the opportunity of attending in person or where the buyer is not an individual and the goods are sold by auction or competitive tender.[287] The lesser test of whether it was fair and reasonable to incorporate the exclusion clause is applicable in such situations.

Where the "fair and reasonableness" test applies, the onus of proving that the exclusion was fair and reasonable lies on the party who so contends.[288] Guidelines for the court to use in applying the fair and reasonable test are contained in Sch.2 to the Act. The guidelines are specifically stated to apply to contracts of sale and supply of goods.[289] Relevant factors include the relative bargaining strengths of the parties, whether the term was customary in the trade and whether there were alternative means of meeting the buyer's requirements.

1.11.8 IMPLIED TERMS IN OTHER CONTRACTS

The protections in general terms

1.11.8.1 Thus far, the discussion in this chapter has been limited to sale contracts only. There are, however, many other types of contracts in which consumers are involved in which they require a similar degree of protection. Important protections are found in the Supply of Goods and Services Act 1982. This Act, which originally did not apply to Scotland, was extended to Scotland by virtue of the Sale and Supply of Goods Act 1994.[290] The protections fall into two parts. The first part includes contracts for the transfer of property in goods other than sale, hire purchase and donation. Effectively this class would contain contracts of barter and contracts for the supply of work and materials. The definition of a contract for the "transfer of goods" is "a contract under which one person transfers or agrees to transfer to another the property in goods, other than an excepted contract".[291] Excepted contracts, to which the provisions do not apply, are sale and hire purchase. Such contracts are already protected by other statutes.[292] The fact that services are provided in addition to goods and the nature of the consideration are both irrelevant—the contract remains a contract for the transfer of goods.[293] The protections contained in the second part of the Act relate to contracts of hire.[294] A contract of hire is "a contract under which one person ('the supplier') hires or agrees to hire goods to another, other than an excepted contract". Hire purchase is an excepted contract. For both parts the actual protections are very similar to the protective regime of the implied terms within the Sale of Goods Act 1979, applying to sale contracts.[295]

The consumer's remedies

1.11.8.2 Protective rules similar to those found in ss.12–15 of the Sale of Goods Act 1979 are applied to cases of hire purchase by the Supply of Goods (Implied Terms) Act 1973. However, in Scotland, the same protections were not available in other consumer contracts. This contrasted with the position under English law where similar protections were available by virtue of the Supply of Goods and Services Act 1982, an Act which did not apply to Scotland. This anomaly was resolved in 1994.[296] Where the contract is a consumer contract,[297] the same statutory implied terms apply in contracts of barter,

---

[287] 2002 Regulations reg.14 inserting new s.25(1B) into UCTA 1977 s.25(1).

[288] UCTA 1977 ss.20(2), 24 and 25, as amended by the Act 1979 s.63(1) and Sch.2 paras 21, 22.

[289] Although they may be taken into account in contexts wider than simply sale and supply of goods, see *Farrans Construction Ltd v Ready Mixed Concrete (Scotland) Ltd* CA244/01 2004 G.W.D. 13–283, per Lord Drummond Young at [53].

[290] See s.6 and Sch.1.

[291] See s.11A(1).

[292] In sale the buyer is already protected by the implied terms in the 1979 Act, and in hire purchase the hirer is protected by the Supply of Goods (Implied Terms) Act 1973.

[293] See s.11A(3).

[294] See s.11G.

[295] See ss.11B–11F for contracts for the transfer of goods and ss.11H–11K for hire.

[296] The Sale and Supply of Goods Act 1994 inserted a new Pt 1A (ss.11B–11K) into the Supply of Goods and Services Act 1982.

[297] "Consumer contract" is defined by reference to s.25(1) of UCTA 1977 commented on below.

contracts for the provision of work and materials, and contracts of hire as they do in the context of sale.[298]

The amendments recently enacted by the 2002 Regulations to the implied terms in the context of sale have similarly been applied to other consumer contracts. Thus, provisions similar to those governing the seller's liability for public statements have been applied to contracts for the transfer of goods,[299] contracts of hire[300] and contracts of hire purchase,[301] in all cases only where the contract is a consumer contract.[302]

The general scheme of remedies visible in the context of contracts of sale, namely the ability to rescind for a material breach and the ability to claim damages for a non-material breach,[303] was also applied to contracts for the transfer of goods by the 1994 Act.[304] It is not surprising, therefore, to see that the new hierarchy of remedies contained in the 2002 Regulations including repair and replacement has been applied to contracts for the transfer of goods[305] in the same way as it has to contracts of sale. The same pattern of remedies depending upon whether or not the breach was material was not extended to contracts of hire by the 1994 Act. The Law Commissions considered that the protections offered by Scots common law were sufficient. As a result, the amendments contained in the 2002 Regulations providing the consumer with a right to repair or replacement do not apply in cases of hire or hire purchase.

As is the case in contracts of sale, the implied terms in the context of contracts other than sale rely on the definition of "consumer contract" found in the Unfair Contract Terms Act 1977, as amended by the 2002 Regulations, commented on above.[306]

Attempts to exclude the statutory implied terms

The discussion in this part assumes that the exclusionary term in question has been incorporated into the contract, a factor which is governed by common law principles.   **1.11.8.3**

As stated above, the Unfair Contract Terms Act 1977 controls attempts to exclude the implied terms. As anticipated above[307] it is impossible to exclude the duties imposed on the seller to pass good title under s.12.[308] This is regardless of the type of contract at issue, i.e. whether or not it is a consumer contract.

In relation to the other implied terms, i.e. those in s.13 (conformity with description), s.14 (quality or fitness) and s.15 (sale by sample), the ability to exclude such terms depends upon whether the contract is a consumer contract or not. The definition of "consumer contract" is that contained in the Unfair Contract Terms Act 1977 as amended by the 2002 Regulations.[309] If the contract is a consumer contract, the attempt to exclude the duties of the seller is void.[310] In all other cases, the attempt to exclude will be subject to a fair and reasonableness test.[311]

The same regime applies to attempts to exclude the implied terms in contracts for the transfer of goods and contracts of hire,[312] and hire purchase.[313] Section 21 of the Unfair Contract Terms Act 1977

---

[298] "Satisfactory quality" is confusingly defined for both contracts for the transfer of goods and contracts of hire, necessitating reading s.11J(3), the interpretation section, and Sch.2 para.6(10) together.

[299] 2002 Regulations reg.8 inserting new s.11D(3A)–(3C) and (10) into the Sale and Supply of Goods Act 1982.

[300] 2002 Regulations reg.11 inserting new s.11J(3A)–(3C) and (10) into the Sale and Supply of Goods Act 1982.

[301] 2002 Regulations reg.13 inserting new s.10(2D)–(2F) and (8) into the Supply of Goods (Implied Terms) Act 1973.

[302] "Consumer contract" is defined by reference to s.25(1) of UCTA 1977: see new s.11M(5) and s.11J(10) referring to s.11F(3) of the 1982 Act and s.12A(3) of the Supply of Goods (Implied Terms) Act 1973.

[303] 1979 Act s.15B.

[304] Sale and Supply of Goods Act 1982 s.11F.

[305] 2002 Regulations reg.9 inserting new Pt 1B ss.11M–11S into the Sale and Supply of Goods Act 1982. The new scheme of remedies is discussed at para.1.12.1 below.

[306] See the discussion of this definition at para.1.9 above.

[307] See para.1.11.7 above.

[308] UCTA 1977 s.20(1)(a).

[309] See the discussion of this definition at para.1.9 above.

[310] UCTA 1977 s.20(2)(i).

[311] UCTA 1977 s.20(2)(ii).

[312] Supply of Goods and Services Act 1982 ss.11B–11K.

[313] Supply of Goods (Implied Terms) Act 1973 ss.8–11, although a right to reduction of the price was already provided in Scots law in terms of the Contract (Scotland) Act 1997 s.3.

provides that in all cases the implied term relating to title cannot be excluded, and the other implied terms cannot be excluded in consumer contracts,[314] although in other contracts they can be excluded subject to the reasonableness test.

THE BUYER'S REMEDIES

1.12 The 2002 Regulations overhauled the entire scheme of remedies available to the consumer. Previously, where the goods did not conform to the contract, the buyer's only remedies were a right to damages in the case of a breach by the seller of any term of the contract, and the right to rescind and reject the goods if the breach was material.[315] Additional protection was provided where the contract was a consumer contract, in that any breach by the seller of any of the implied terms under ss.13–15 was deemed to be a material breach.[316] New remedies were added in 2002 applying only where the buyer is a consumer, referred to in this part as the "consumer remedies". Broadly, the consumer has the right to have the goods repaired, replaced, the price reduced[317] and a further right to rescind.[318] Despite limited authority to the contrary, Scots law did not previously contain a right of repair or replacement.[319] The consumer remedies take the form of a new Pt 5A of the Act, headed: "Additional Rights of Buyers in Consumer Cases".[320] This serves to stress the point that these consumer remedies exist *in addition to* the pre-existing remedies of rejection and damages afforded to all buyers under s.15B(1).[321]

THE CONSUMER REMEDIES IN GENERAL

1.12.1 The consumer remedies apply only where the contract is a consumer contract, and the consumer is a "pure" consumer, in the sense that he is a natural person acting for purposes which are outside his trade, business or profession.[322] They arise where the goods do not conform to the contract at the time of delivery,[323] and lack of conformity is defined as the existence of a breach of an express term of the contract or one of the implied terms in ss.13, 14 or 15.[324]

Although, in principle, the relevant time for assessing conformity is the time of delivery, the regulations contain an extended meaning for the word "delivery". The protections extend to any goods which do not conform within the period of six months after delivery.[325] This provision is known as a "reversed burden of proof". Any lack of conformity which becomes apparent within six months of delivery is

---

[314] See the discussion of this definition at para.1.9 above.

[315] See s.15B(1).

[316] See s.15B(2).

[317] A right to reduction of the price was already provided in Scots law in terms of the Contract (Scotland) Act 1997 s.3.

[318] Regulations reg.5 which inserts a new Pt 5A to the 1979 Act.

[319] *Lindley Catering Investments v Hibernian FC Ltd*, 1975 S.L.T. (Notes) 56; *Strathclyde Regional Council v Border Engineering Contractors Ltd*, 1998 S.L.T. 175; and see the interesting discussion in the unreported sheriff court case, *Magnet Ltd v John B Cape t/a Briggate Investments Ltd* A85/06 Unreported July 19, 2007 Cupar Sheriff Court. The Scottish Law Commission indicated relatively recently that they favoured the existing pattern of remedies and would not favour the introduction of a right to cure as the primary remedy: see para.7.21, Scottish Law Commission, *Report on Remedies for Breach of Contract*. The Stationery Office, 1999; Scot. Law Com. No.174. The right to rescind is, of course, already available under s.15B(1)(b) of the 1979 Act.

[320] See W.C.H. Ervine, "The Sale and Supply of Goods to Consumers Regulations 2002", 2003 S.L.T. (News) 67 and M. Hogg, "The consumer's right to rescind under the Sale of Goods Act: a tale of two remedies", 2003 S.L.T. (News) 277.

[321] The independence of these two regimes was reasserted recently in *Lowe v W Machell Joinery Ltd* [2011] EWCA Civ 798; 138 Cons L R 48, per Lloyd LJ at [52]. The consumer is not obliged to opt for repair or replacement. He may continue to rely on his original rights in s.15B(1).

[322] 2002 Regulations reg.5, inserting new s.48A into the 1979 Act, and reg.2. The definition is slightly wider than that which appears in Directive 99/44 ("purposes which are outside his trade, business or profession"). This wider definition is consistent with Directive 93/13/EEC on unfair terms in consumer contracts [1993] OJ L95/29.

[323] See s.48A(1)(b).

[324] See s.48F.

[325] See s.48A(3).

deemed to have existed at the date of delivery. The seller requires to prove otherwise by establishing either that the goods did conform at the date of delivery or that the extension is incompatible with the nature of the goods or the nature of the lack of conformity.[326] So, for example, the provision will not apply in the case of goods which are not in their nature durable. The reversed burden of proof does not apply to the buyer's existing right to damages or rescission under s.15B(1) of the 1979 Act.

The right of repair or replacement in detail

The buyer has the right to have the goods repaired or replaced by the seller,[327] and the seller must repair **1.12.1.1** or replace within a reasonable time but without causing significant inconvenience to the buyer.[328] A new definition of "repair" is inserted into the 1979 Act, namely, to bring the goods into conformity with the contract.[329] Necessary costs must be borne by the seller, including labour, materials and postage.[330] The seller can, however, escape these remedies in certain situations: firstly, where the remedy is impossible; secondly, where the grant of one remedy, e.g. repair, would be disproportionate in comparison to the other, e.g. replacement; and, thirdly, where either remedy would be disproportionate to the other remedies introduced into the Act by the 2002 Regulations, namely reduction in price, or rescission.[331] The issue of whether the remedy is "disproportionate" depends on whether the costs are unreasonable, taking into account the value which the goods would have had if they had conformed to the contract, the significance of the lack of conformity and whether the other remedy could be effected without significant inconvenience to the buyer.[332] The Act now indicates that the nature and purpose for which the goods were acquired are both relevant to the assessment of what amounts to a reasonable time or significant inconvenience.[333] It can be appreciated from this that although it is for the buyer to indicate in the first instance the remedy he would prefer, protections are available to the seller when that remedy is inappropriate. So in relation to many (if not most) low cost goods, it would not be open to the buyer to insist on repair, because the cost of that course of action may well be significantly greater than that of replacement.

It is open to the buyer to apply to the court for an order of specific implement requiring the seller to repair or replace.[334] The court also has a wide power to order payment of damages or repayment of the price.[335]

The right of reduction of the purchase price and rescission in detail

The rights of reduction of the purchase price or rescission are subsidiary rights. They are only avail- **1.12.1.2** able[336] if the buyer is unable to require the seller to repair or replace on grounds of impossibility, disproportion of the remedy sought,[337] or failure by the seller to repair or replace within a reasonable time and without significant inconvenience to the buyer as detailed above.[338]

Where the buyer is seeking to rescind the contract, the court may order that any reimbursement that the buyer obtains be reduced to take account of the period during which he has been able to use the goods since the time of delivery.[339] This may be contrasted with the right to rescind the contract under s.15B(1), where the buyer is entitled to recover the price without any similar reduction. As is the case

---

[326] See s.48A(4).
[327] See s.48B(1)(a) and (b).
[328] See s.48B(2)(a).
[329] See s.61(1).
[330] See s.48B(2)(b).
[331] See s.48B(3).
[332] See s.48B(4).
[333] See s.48B(5).
[334] See s.48E(2).
[335] See s.48E(6).
[336] See s.48C(2).
[337] See s.48B(3).
[338] See s.48B(2).
[339] See s.48E(5).

with repair or replacement, the court has a wide power to order payment of damages or repayment of the price.[340]

Assessment of the consumer remedies

1.12.1.3 The 2002 Regulations constitute an important change to the buyer's remedies. Ultimately, the consumer wants the goods that he paid for, and the right to repair or replacement ensures that this goal is achieved. The fact that the consumer remedies exist in addition to the buyer's rights under s.15B(1) was not made particularly clear when the Sale of Goods Act was amended in 2002. Happily, the courts have stepped into the breach. In *Clegg v Andersson* it was stated that

> "the buyer does not have to act reasonably in choosing rejection rather than damages or cure, and the fact that the remedy of rejection may be thought to be disproportionate by some is irrelevant."[341]

It seems beyond doubt that the buyer should retain his primary right to reject and recover the purchase price. Repair or replacement may not be the consumer's first choice for several reasons. They may involve delay and administrative problems. The relationship between the seller and the buyer may have completely broken down, in which case the buyer may emphatically not want a repair to be carried out. It should be recalled, however, that if the buyer does require the seller to repair or replace the goods, he may not rescind the contract and reject the goods under s.15B(1) until he has given the seller a reasonable time to effect that replacement or repair.[342]

THE RIGHT TO REJECT, AND LOSS OF THE SAME

1.12.2 The buyer's right to reject is perhaps the most important weapon in his armoury. A clear rejection will not be rendered equivocal by later activities, for example an indication from the buyer's solicitor that damages rather than rejection are being claimed.[343] It may be relatively difficult to persuade the court that a buyer has, in the circumstances, accepted the goods and lost the right to reject. Acceptance has this effect by virtue of s.35(1) of the 1979 Act and may be deemed to have occurred where the buyer expressly intimates acceptance; or does an act inconsistent with the seller's ownership; or retains the goods for a reasonable period of time without intimating rejection. This section is however subject to the buyer's right to examine the goods under s.35(2). A buyer who has not previously examined the goods is not deemed to have accepted them until he has had a reasonable opportunity of examining them to ascertain that they are in conformity with the contract (or in the case of a sale by sample, of comparing the bulk with the sample).

Acts inconsistent with ownership of the seller

1.12.2.1 *Clegg v Andersson* is a good illustration of the manner in which the court will assess whether the buyer has carried out acts which are inconsistent with ownership remaining in the seller.[344] In the case, the buyer of a yacht requested further information on the manner in which defects in the yacht could be rectified in circumstances where the sellers accepted that some sort of remedial work was required on the yacht. In the Court of Appeal, the sellers based their argument that the buyer had accepted the goods on several facts, inter alia the buyer's decision to insure the yacht; attempting to register the yacht in the buyer's name; an intention to move the yacht to a different port; and the leaving of personal effects on the yacht. None of these actions were, in the opinion of the court, indicative of acceptance of the goods in the circumstances. According to Hale LJ:

---

[340] See s.48E(6).

[341] *Clegg v Andersson* [2003] EWCA Civ 320; [2003] 2 Lloyd's Rep. 32, per Hale LJ at [74], and see also *Lowe v W Machell Joinery Ltd* [2011] EWCA Civ 798; 138 Con. L.R. 48, per Lloyd LJ at [52].

[342] See s.48D.

[343] As was the case in *Macdonald v Pollock* [2010] CSIH 12; 2013 S.C. 22.

[344] *Clegg v Andersson* [2003] EWCA Civ 320; [2003] 2 Lloyd's Rep. 32.

"[I]f a buyer is seeking information which the seller has agreed to supply which will enable the buyer to make a properly informed choice between acceptance, rejection or cure, and if cure in what way, he cannot have lost the right to reject."[345]

Lady Justice Hale's judgment is notable in particular for her emphasis of the irrelevance in this context of the reasonableness or otherwise of the buyer's conduct in his choice of remedy: "He does not require to act reasonably in choosing rejection rather than damages or cure. He can reject for whatever reason he chooses."[346]

The buyer's "reasonable opportunity" to examine goods

Where the buyer neglects to examine the goods at the proper time and only examines them much later, he will be deemed to have accepted them.[347] However, the decision in the case of *Truk (UK) Ltd v Tokakidis GmbH*[348] suggests that the courts may treat the buyer leniently when it comes to assessing what is a reasonable period within which to reject. In that case goods were delivered to the buyers in June, and it was only when a further prospective buyer became interested in the goods that the unsatisfactory nature of the goods came to light. Further discussions took place between the original seller and buyer, and it was only in March of the next year that the goods were rejected. In holding that rejection had taken place within a reasonable time, Judge Raymond Jack commented:

1.12.2.2

"[W]here goods are sold for resale, a reasonable time in which to intimate rejection should usually be the time actually taken to resell the goods together with an additional period in which they can be inspected and tried out by the sub-purchaser."[349]

Judge Jack also emphasised that what is a reasonable period depends on the circumstances of the case and may involve a balancing of the opposing interests of the buyer and seller.[350]

Special protection is provided to consumers by s.35(3) which states that the buyer cannot lose the right of examination of the goods under s.35(2) by agreement, waiver or otherwise. Thus, the common practice of forcing the buyer on delivery of goods to sign an "acceptance note" (indicating that the goods have been accepted in good condition) before the buyer has had an opportunity to examine the goods does not exclude the buyer's right of examination where the buyer is a consumer.[351] The corollary of this is that a buyer who is not a consumer can exclude his rights in this way. However, the seller would have to show that it is fair and reasonable to exclude the buyer's rights in terms of UCTA 1977.

Section 35(4) provides that the buyer is deemed to have accepted the goods when, after the lapse of a reasonable time, he retains the goods without intimating to the seller that he has rejected them. Section 35(5) specifically states that, in assessing this issue, the question of whether the buyer has had a reasonable opportunity of examining the goods to ascertain whether they are in conformity with the contract is material. It is difficult to give guidance on what will constitute acceptance through lapse of reasonable time. It is essentially a question of fact, and conflicting case law exists,[352] particularly in

---

[345] *Clegg v Andersson* [2003] EWCA Civ 320; [2003] 2 Lloyd's Rep. 32 at [75].

[346] *Clegg v Andersson* [2003] EWCA Civ 320; [2003] 2 Lloyd's Rep. 32 at [74].

[347] *Pini & Co v Smith & Co* (1895) 22 R. 699.

[348] *Truk (UK) Ltd v Tokakidis GmbH* [2000] 1 Lloyd's Rep. 543.

[349] *Truk (UK) Ltd v Tokakidis GmbH* [2000] 1 Lloyd's Rep. 543, per Raymond Jack J at 551.

[350] *Truk (UK) Ltd v Tokakidis GmbH* [2000] 1 Lloyd's Rep. 543, per Raymond Jack J at 550.

[351] For an example of a non-consumer contract where an acceptance note had the effect of barring the buyer from subsequently rejecting the goods, see *Mechans Ltd v Highland Marine Charters*, 1964 S.L.T. 27.

[352] See *Burrell v Harding's Executrix*, 1931 S.L.T. 76, where a buyer purchased a reredos which he understood, because of an innocent misrepresentation by the seller, dated from the 15th century. More than two years later the buyer was held entitled to reject when he discovered that part of it was a modern copy. Compare *Leaf v International Galleries* [1950] 2 K.B. 86, where the buyer had bought a painting which he understood, due to a misrepresentation by the seller, was a Constable. The buyer was found not entitled to rescind five years later. These cases may be complicated by the fact that the relationship between rescission for breach under the 1979 Act and rescission for innocent misrepresentation has not been fully analysed by the Scottish courts: see Atiyah, Adams, and MacQueen, *Sale of Goods*, 12th edn (2010), p.528, fn.2.

relation to the rejection of defective cars.[353] Much depends on the nature of the goods, in other words, how complex those goods are and how easily one can determine whether they are defective. The decision in *Truk* suggests that the concept of a reasonable time may be significantly extended if it is reasonable for the buyer to delay testing the functioning of goods. The period cannot be extended indefinitely, however. In *Douglas v Glenvarigill Co Ltd*,[354] a case which concerned the purchase of a car, the defects did not manifest themselves until approximately 15 months after purchase, at which time the buyer purported to reject. Lord Drummond Young held that, in the case of a latent defect, time begins to run for the purposes of s.35(4) as soon as the goods are delivered and that 15 months was "simply too long a period for rejection".[355] Reaching this conclusion "with some regret",[356] he had considered whether the period should start to run from the point at which the defects manifested themselves. He rejected this for several reasons, including "commercial closure . . . to permit the seller in particular, but also the buyer to some extent, to arrange his affairs on the basis that the goods have been effectively sold."[357]

Any attempt within a consumer contract to stipulate a period within which the buyer must reject goods would be regarded as an attempt to restrict the buyer's rights and would be void in terms of UCTA 1977.[358] In a non-consumer contract case, such a clause would be subject to the reasonableness test.[359]

The impact of repair on the buyer's right to reject

1.12.2.3   In terms of s.35(6), the buyer is not deemed to have accepted the goods merely because he asks for, or agrees to, their repair by the seller, nor where the goods are delivered to another purchaser under a sub-sale or other disposition. The "reasonable time" after which the buyer is deemed to have accepted the goods is suspended while the goods are being repaired.[360] The impact of the repair of goods on the right to reject was considered in the Scottish House of Lords case, *J&H Ritchie v Lloyd Ltd*.[361] The pursuers carried on a farming business and bought a combination seed drill and power harrow from the defenders in March 1999. They began to use the drill the following month. A day after it was put into operation, the pursuers noticed that a vibration was coming from part of the drive chain of the harrow. They stopped using the equipment the following day. The harrow was taken to the defenders' premises for inspection. The defenders discovered that two bearings were missing, and obtained replacement bearings. At this stage there was an unusual turn of events in that the defenders, without checking their proposed course of action with the pursuers, repaired the goods. The pursuers were then informed that a repair had been carried out. When the pursuers asked for details of the repair, the defenders refused this request and also refused to provide them with a copy of an engineer's report. Nevertheless, the pursuers were able, through discussions with the repairer, to discover the general nature of the defect and the repair. They were concerned at the possibility that, while the goods were being used and before the defect had been identified, the defect might have harmed other parts of the machine. These concerns

---

[353] See *Bernstein v Pamson Motors (Golders Green) Ltd* [1987] 2 All E.R. 220, where the buyer retained the car for three weeks and covered 140 miles. This was thought by Rougier J to be too long a period to allow the buyer to reject. Compare *Rogers v Parish (Scarborough) Ltd* [1987] Q.B. 933, where the buyer was found entitled to reject even though he had retained the car for six months and covered 5,500 miles. See also the recent case *Douglas v Glenvarigill Co Ltd*, 2010 S.L.T. 634, commented on in the text above.

[354] [2010] CSOH 14; 2010 S.L.T. 634.

[355] [2010] CSOH 14; 2010 S.L.T. 634 at [35].

[356] [2010] CSOH 14; 2010 S.L.T. 634 at [36].

[357] [2010] CSOH 14; 2010 S.L.T. 634 at [34].

[358] See s.20(2)(a)(i).

[359] See s.20(2)(a)(ii). For an example of a clause in a non-consumer which failed the reasonableness test see *RW Green Ltd v Cade Bros Farms* [1978] 1 Lloyd's Rep. 602.

[360] *Douglas v Glenvarigill* [2010] CSOH 14; 2010 S.L.T. 634. The reasonable time is also suspended while the parties are discussing the possibility of repair, *Clegg v Andersson* [2003] EWCA Civ 320; [2003] 2 Lloyd's Rep. 32, applied in *Fiat Auto Financial Services Ltd v Connelly*, 2007 S.L.T. (Sh Ct) 111.

[361] *J&H Ritchie v Lloyd Ltd* [2007] UKHL 9; 2007 S.L.T. 377. For comment see P. Hood, "A stitch in time? Repairs and rejection in Sale of Goods", 2008 Edin. L.R. 316; J. Thomson, "A simple case? *J&H Ritchie Ltd v Lloyd Ltd*, 2007 S.L.T. 377", 2007 J.R. 241.

are understandable: this was a "complex piece of power operated agricultural machinery".[362] Their concerns were perhaps compounded by the fact that the machine would not now be used until the following spring. There would therefore be a long delay before they knew whether the machine as a whole had been damaged because the bearings had been omitted. These factors led the pursuers to reject the goods. The sellers argued that the buyers were not entitled to reject the goods, and were bound to accept and pay for them under s.27.

The House of Lords unanimously decided in favour of the pursuers. Lords Rodger and Hope gave the principal speeches. Although both used the mechanism of an implied term in order to find for the pursuers, their reasoning differs. Lord Hope, emphasising the silence of the 1979 Act on this point and the absence of the express agreement of the parties, found that a term was to be implied into the contract of sale. The content of such a term would be determined by the circumstances of the case.[363] He conceded that there are cases

> "where the nature of the defect, and exactly what needs to be done to correct it, and at what expense to the seller, are immediately obvious to both parties. It may then be said that a buyer who, having been equipped with all that knowledge, allows the seller to incur the expense of repair is under an implied obligation to accept and pay for the goods once the repair has been carried out."[364]

In such a case, the buyer will no longer have the right to reject the goods. However, in cases such as this one the term to be implied was to the effect that the buyer would retain the right to elect either to reject or accept the goods until such point as he had been provided with the information he needed "to make an informed choice".[365] The defenders' refusal to inform the pursuers of the nature of the defect constituted a breach of this implied duty.

Lord Rodger's approach differed in that he found that the repair of the goods was governed by another contract, quite separate from the contract for sale of goods. This was an agreement to deliver the machine for repairs to be carried out, and it was into this separate contract, gratuitous in nature,[366] that a term was to be implied that,

> "so long as the respondents were duly performing their obligations under it, the appellants were not to exercise their right to rescind the contract of sale . . . if . . . the respondents eventually repaired the equipment to the proper standard and duly made it available to the appellants, the appellants would not be entitled to rescind the contract of sale and reject the equipment because of the original breach."[367]

The "inspection and repair" contract was breached when the defenders refused to supply the information required by the pursuers.

The judgment in *Ritchie* makes a positive contribution to the law by filling what was a lacuna—although the 1979 Act indicates that the buyer does not lose his right to reject the goods simply by agreeing to a repair, the Act does not cover what happens once the repair has been carried out. This is not surprising—although the 1979 Act is a "statutory code"[368] it cannot cover every eventuality. The most obvious and useful mechanism to solve the problem was an implied term. Lord Hope's approach is to be preferred. Lord Rodger perhaps complicated matters by introducing a separate contract. Both Law Lords stressed the fact-sensitive nature of this type of case. Clearly, it will be difficult to predict the manner in which cases involving a similar legal issue will be decided in the future.

---

[362] *J&H Ritchie v Lloyd Ltd* [2007] UKHL 9; 2007 S.L.T. 377, per Lord Hope at [18].

[363] *J&H Ritchie v Lloyd Ltd* [2007] UKHL 9; 2007 S.L.T. 377 at [15]. This being the case, the term is a term implied in fact and not in law.

[364] *J&H Ritchie v Lloyd Ltd* [2007] UKHL 9; 2007 S.L.T. 377 at [15].

[365] *J&H Ritchie v Lloyd Ltd* [2007] UKHL 9; 2007 S.L.T. 377 at [16].

[366] Professor Thomson has pointed out that whilst the gratuitous nature of the contract is not problematic in Scots law, it may prove problematic in English law due to the lack of consideration, "A simple case? *J&H Ritchie Ltd v Lloyd Ltd*", 2007 S.L.T. 377; 2007 J.R. 241, 246.

[367] *J&H Ritchie v Lloyd Ltd* [2007] UKHL 9; 2007 S.L.T. 377 at [34].

[368] *J&H Ritchie v Lloyd Ltd* [2007] UKHL 9; 2007 S.L.T. 377. Lord Rodger stated at [13]: "The problem is not capable of being solved satisfactorily by a statutory code"; see also Lord Hope at [15].

Instead of requiring the seller to repair goods, if the buyer attempts to repair them himself, or to have them repaired without reference to the seller, then this would probably constitute an act inconsistent with the seller's ownership thereby excluding the right of rejection.

There is no necessary connection between the passing of property (see para.1.8 above) and the question of whether the goods have been accepted. Property in goods may pass to the buyer long before he actually sees them. Obviously, if they turn out to be defective, he may reject them. Equally, where there is a retention of title clause in the contract, the buyer may have been using the goods for a significant period of time without being their owner. In such circumstances, he would be deemed to have accepted them.

Cancellation Rights

1.12.2.4 The buyer has certain statutory cancellation rights which exist in UK law because of the requirement to incorporate EU Directives into UK law. Two types of cancellation rights are commented on here: (1) the consumer's rights under the Consumer Contracts (Information, Cancellation and Additional Charges) Regulations 2013; and (2) the consumer's rights under the Consumer Protection from Unfair Trading Regulations 2008.[369]

The Consumer Contracts (Information, Cancellation and Additional Charges) Regulations 2013

1.12.2.4.1 The trader's obligations to supply the consumer with information at the point of formation of the contract, imposed by the Consumer Contracts (Information, Cancellation and Additional Charges) Regulations 2013, have already been referred to.[370] This legislation also provides the consumer with cancellation rights. The consumer has the right to cancel a distance or off-premises contract without giving any reasons or incurring any costs other than those specified.[371] The cancellation period differs according to whether the contract is, on the one hand, a service contract or contract for the supply of digital content which is not available in a tangible medium or, on the other hand, a sales contract. In the former case the cancellation period ends at the end of 14 days after the day on which the contract is entered into.[372] In the latter case the cancellation period ends at the end of 14 days after the day on which the goods come into the physical possession of the consumer or any person other than a carrier identified by the consumer to take possession of them.[373] If the trader fails to comply with his information requirements already described,[374] then the cancellation period may be extended by up to 12 months.[375] Where the consumer has exercised a right to cancel, the trader must pay a refund without undue delay[376] and in any event by 14 days after the day on which the trader is informed of the consumer's decision to cancel.[377] If the contract is a sales contract, and the trader has not offered to collect the goods, the time is the end of 14 days after either the day on which the trader receives the goods back, or if earlier, the day on which the consumer supplies evidence of having sent the goods back.[378] After cancellation of a sales contract, the costs of returning the goods must be borne by the consumer unless the trader has agreed to bear those costs or the trader has failed to comply with his information duties described above.[379] The consumer is not required to bear any cost of collecting goods unless the trader

---

[369] SI 2008/1277, hereinafter the "2008 Regulations". These Regulations implement Directive 2005/29/EC of the European Parliament and of the Council concerning unfair business-to-consumer commercial practices ([2005] OJ L149, 11.6.2005, p. 22).

[370] See para.1.5.

[371] See CC (IC and AC) Regs reg.29 and the costs specified therein.

[372] CC (IC and AC) Regs reg.30(2).

[373] CC (IC and AC) Regs reg.30(3).

[374] See para.1.5.

[375] CC (IC and AC) Regs reg.31.

[376] CC (IC and AC) Regs reg.34(4).

[377] CC (IC and AC) Regs reg.34(6).

[378] CC (IC and AC) Regs reg.34(5).

[379] CC (IC and AC) Regs reg.35(5).

has offered to collect the goods and the consumer has agreed to bear the costs of the trader doing so.[380] Failure to comply with the requirement to provide notice of cancellation rights in the context of an off-premises contract results in criminal sanctions.[381]

The Consumer Protection from Unfair Trading Regulations 2008

The 2008 Regulations sought to tackle so-called unfair commercial practices, insofar as they take place **1.12.2.4.2** in a business to consumer situation. These regulations tackled issues such as misleading advertisements, high pressure selling, and misleading and dishonest mailings to consumers. Whereas the 2008 Regulations lacked a strong enforcement mechanism for individual consumers, this has now been remedied through amendments to the 2008 Regulations enacted by the Consumer Protection (Amendment) Regulations 2014. The 2014 Regulations have added a new Part 4A to the 2008 Regulations, entitled Consumers' Rights to Redress.[382] The 2014 Regulations, and thus the new Consumer Rights to Redress, come into force on October 1, 2014, applying to contracts entered into, or payments made, on or after that date.[383]

A "consumer" in this context means an individual acting for purposes that are wholly or mainly outside that individual's business.[384] A "business" includes (a) a trade, craft or profession; and (b) the activities of any government departments or local or public authority.[385] A "trader" means a person acting for purposes relating to that person's business, whether acting personally or through another person acting in the trader's name or on the trader's behalf (i.e. acting through an agent).[386] "Product" means goods, a service, digital content, immoveable property, rights or obligations.[387] A trader who demands payment from a consumer in full or partial settlement of the consumer's liabilities or purported liabilities to the trader is treated for the purposes of the Regulations as offering to supply a product to the consumer.[388] "Goods" here mean any tangible moveable items, including water, gas and electricity if and only if they are put up for sale in a limited volume or set quantity.[389]

Regulation 3 of the 2008 Regulations contains a general prohibition against unfair commercial practices.[390] A commercial practice is "unfair" if it "contravenes the requirements of professional diligence" and "it materially distorts or is likely to materially distort the economic behaviour of the average consumer with regard to the product."[391] "Professional diligence" is defined as "the standard of special skill and care which a trader may reasonably be expected to exercise towards consumers which is commensurate with either (a) honest market practice in the trader's field of activity, or (b) the general principle of good faith in the trader's field of activity.[392]

In addition to this general prohibition against unfair commercial practices in reg.3, the 2008 Regulations contain more specific provisions combating aggressive practices, misleading action, misleading omissions and banned practices,[393] all commented on in the paragraphs that follow.

Schedule 1 lists banned practices, in other words a blacklist of particular practices which are always unfair. Thirty one practices are listed, clearly too many to comment on here. Examples include spurious claims to belong to a trade organisation or code of conduct, or baiting consumers through adverts of products which are not actually sold.

---

[380] CC (IC and AC) Regs reg.35(8) as amended by the Consumer Protection (Amendment) Regulations 2014 (SI 2014/870) reg.9(2).

[381] CC (IC and AC) Regs reg.19.

[382] SI 2014/870, hereinafter the "2014 Regulations".

[383] 2014 Regulations reg.1(2).

[384] 2008 Regulations reg.2, as amended by 2014 Regulations reg.2(3).

[385] 2008 Regulations reg.2, as amended by 2014 Regulations reg.2(2).

[386] 2008 Regulations reg.2, as amended by 2014 Regulations reg.2(7).

[387] 2008 Regulations reg.2, as amended by 2014 Regulations reg.2(6).

[388] 2008 Regulations reg.2, as amended by 2014 Regulations reg.2(9), inserting new reg.2(1A) and (1B) into the 2008 Regulations.

[389] 2008 Regulations reg.2, as amended by the 2014 Regulations reg.2(5).

[390] 2008 Regulations reg.3(1).

[391] 2008 Regulations regs 3(3)(a) and (b).

[392] 2008 Regulations reg.2(1).

[393] 2008 Regulations reg.3(4).

Misleading actions are covered in reg.5 and occur when a practice misleads because it contains false information, or if its overall presentation deceives or is likely to deceive the average consumer and causes him to take a transactional decision[394] he would not otherwise have taken.[395] Such deception must relate to one of 11 elements[396]: the existence or nature of the product; the main characteristics; the extent of the trader's commitments; the motives for the commercial practice; the nature of the sales process; any statement or symbol relating to direct or indirect sponsorship or approval of the trader or the product; the price or the manner in which the price is calculated; the existence of a specific price advantage; the need for a service, part, replacement or repair; the nature, attributes, and rights of the trader; and the consumer's rights or the risks he may face. Alternatively, it might concern marketing of the product (including comparative advertising) which creates confusion with any products, trade marks, trade names or other distinguishing marks of a competitor.[397] Finally, it might concern a failure by a trader to comply with a commitment in a code of conduct which the trader has undertaken to comply with and the commitment is a firm one capable of being verified rather than being aspirational.[398]

Misleading omissions are covered in reg.6. A practice may be misleading because it omits or hides material information, or provides it in a manner which is unclear, unintelligible, ambiguous or untimely or it fails to identify its commercial intent, unless this is already apparent from the context. It must also be proved that, as a result, it causes or is likely to cause the average consumer to take a transactional decision he would not have taken otherwise.

A commercial practice is aggressive if, in its factual context, taking account of all of its features and circumstances it significantly impairs or is likely significantly to impair the average consumer's freedom of choice or conduct in relation to the product concerned through the use of harassment, coercion or undue influence and it thereby causes or is likely to cause him to take a transactional decision he would not have taken otherwise.[399] Regulation 7, in addition to setting out this definition, specifies the factors which will impact on the presence of harassment, coercion or undue influence, for example the timing, location, nature and persistence of the practice.[400]

Moving now to the Consumers' Rights to Redress added by the 2014 Regulations as a new Part 4A to the 2008 Regulations, they are available only under specific conditions. The transaction must be one of three types: where a consumer enters in to a contract with a trader for the sale or supply of a product by the trader (a "business to consumer contract"); where the consumer enters into a contract with a trader for the sale of goods to the trader (a "consumer to business contract"); or where the consumer makes a payment to the trader for the supply of a product (a "consumer payment").[401] The trader must have engaged in a prohibited practice.[402] This is defined as either misleading actions under reg.5, or aggressive practices under reg.7, both of the 2008 Regulations.[403] Thus the Consumers' Rights to Redress only apply in relation to some of the practices tackled by the 2008 Regulations—misleading actions or aggressive practices, but not banned practices or misleading omissions. The latter two practices will be subject to other enforcement methods not involving individual consumer actions in court, and so are not commented on here. The prohibited practice must be a significant factor in the consumer's decision to enter into the contract or make the payment.[404]

Where the consumer has been subject to misleading actions or aggressive practices, the consumer may "unwind" a business to consumer contract.[405] In order to do so, he must indicate to the trader

---

[394] For the meaning of this see 2008 Regulations reg.27B(2).

[395] 2008 Regulations reg.5(2).

[396] 2008 Regulations reg.5(4).

[397] 2008 Regulations reg.5(3)(a).

[398] 2008 Regulations reg.5(3)(b).

[399] 2008 Regulations reg.7(1).

[400] 2008 Regulations reg.7(2).

[401] 2008 Regulations reg.27A.

[402] 2008 Regulations reg.27A(4)(a).

[403] 2008 Regulations reg.27B.

[404] 2008 Regulations reg.27A(6).

[405] 2008 Regulations reg.27E. The consumer may also unwind a consumer to business transaction, see 2008 Regulations reg.27G.

that he rejects the product within 90 days, beginning with the later of the day on which the consumer enters into the contract and the "relevant day". The "relevant day" can be one of several possibilities depending on the type of transaction: the day on which (a) the goods are first delivered, (b) the performance of the service begins, (c) the digital content is first supplied, (d) the lease begins, or (e) the right is first exercisable.[406] Separate provisions govern "mixed contracts", i.e. contracts involving the sale or supply of more than one of goods, a service, digital content, immoveable property or rights.[407] The product can only be rejected if it remains capable of being rejected, i.e. the goods or digital content must not have not been fully consumed, the service must not have been fully performed, the lease must not have expired or the right must not have been fully exercised.[408] Where the consumer exercises his right to unwind the contract, the contract comes to an end, releasing the parties from their obligations, the trader must provide the consumer with a refund, and the consumer must make the goods available for collection by the trader.[409]

The 2014 Regulations also contain provisions allowing the consumer to opt for a discount, available in business to consumer transactions only (i.e. not consumer to business ones). The consumer has this right in business to consumer contracts where he has made one or more payments for the products or one or more payments have not been made, and the consumer has not exercised his right to unwind.[410] The relevant regulation contains a formula for calculation of the discount. Broadly, it contains tariffs which apply depending upon the seriousness of the prohibited practice. If it is more than minor, the discount is 25 per cent, for significant 50 per cent, for serious 75 per cent, and for very serious 100 per cent.[411] The seriousness is assessed by reference to the behaviour of the person who engaged in the practice, the impact of the practice on the consumer, and the time that has elapsed since the prohibited practice took place.[412] If the consumer paid in excess of £5,000 for the product, then the discount he receives will be the difference in value between the market price of the product and the amount he paid.[413]

The 2014 Regulations also added new provisions concerning the consumer's right to damages in either business to consumer or consumer to business transactions.[414]

It will be recalled that a trader who demands payment from a consumer in full or partial settlement of the consumer's liabilities or purported liabilities to the trader is treated for the purposes of the Regulations as offering to supply a product to the consumer.[415] The 2014 Regulations has introduced rights to unwind such transactions[416] and rights to claim damages in relation to such transactions.[417] The right to damages has been introduced for consumer payments for any other types of products.

The consumer has the ability to bring an action under Part 4A in either the Court of Session or the sheriff court.[418] The 2014 Regulations have also added a section which ensures that the consumer is not, through the use of both the Consumers' Rights to Redress in Part 4A and other statutory provisions, over-compensated.[419]

---

[406] 2008 Regulations reg.27E(4)(a) to (e).
[407] 2008 Regulations reg.27E(5) and (6).
[408] 2008 Regulations reg.27E(8).
[409] 2008 Regulations reg.27F(1).
[410] 2008 Regulations reg.27I(1).
[411] 2008 Regulations reg.27I(4).
[412] 2008 Regulations reg.27I(5).
[413] 2008 Regulations reg.27I(6).
[414] 2008 Regulations reg.27J.
[415] 2008 Regulations reg.2, as amended by the 2014 Regulations reg.2(9), inserting new reg.2(1A) and (1B) into the 2008 Regulations.
[416] 2008 Regulations reg.27H.
[417] 2008 Regulations reg.27J.
[418] 2008 Regulations reg.27K.
[419] 2008 Regulations reg.27L. Consequential amendments are made which ensure that the consumer is not overcompensated where the prohibited practice constitutes a misrepresentation, see 2014 Regulations reg.8.

RIGHT OF PARTIAL REJECTION

1.12.3 Under s.35A, unless, as a matter of interpretation of the contract, the parties have a contrary intention, the buyer has four options where some or all of the goods do not conform to the contract. The buyer may:

(1) accept all the goods;
(2) reject all the goods;
(3) reject only the disconforming goods;
(4) reject some of the disconforming goods.

Where the contract is a contract by instalments, the same right of partial rejection is conferred in respect of each instalment.[420] The buyer's rights in this respect are subject to an important qualification: acceptance of any of the goods in a commercial unit is deemed to be acceptance of all the goods in that unit.[421] A commercial unit is a unit the division of which would seriously impair the value of the goods or the character of the unit, e.g. a pair of shoes or a set of encyclopaedias.

THE BUYER'S PERSONAL REMEDIES

1.12.4 A buyer may have a right to claim damages from the seller. Sometimes he will be able to exercise this alongside the remedy of rejection. Sometimes it will be his only remedy, because the breach is not of an order that would give him the right to reject, or where he or she has lost that right through accepting the goods, or where rejection is not practically possible because no goods were delivered in the first place.

Damages for non-delivery

1.12.4.1 Where the seller wrongfully neglects or refuses to deliver the goods to the buyer, the buyer may maintain an action against the seller for damages for non-delivery.[422] The measure of damages is the estimated loss directly and naturally arising, in the ordinary course of events, from the seller's breach,[423] and where there is an available market for the goods, prima facie, the measure is the difference between the contract and market prices at the time when they ought to have been delivered, or if no time was fixed, at the time of refusal to deliver.[424] The operation of this formula is seen in *Williams Bros Ltd v Agius*[425] where the buyer of coal was awarded damages reflecting the difference between the contract price of 16s 3d per ton and the market price of 23s 6d per ton, even though the buyer had contracted to resell the coal at 19s per ton, the House of Lords reasoning that he would have to buy at the market price in order to fulfil his own contract. A buyer will, of course, be subject to the normal contractual duty to mitigate his loss, which in the case of an anticipatory breach may oblige him to acquire replacement goods without delay.[426] However, he is not bound, in mitigation, to accept the seller's offer of goods of an alternative make.[427]

---

[420] See s.35A(2).

[421] See s.35(7).

[422] See s.51(1).

[423] See ss.51(2), 53A(1).

[424] See s.51(3).

[425] *Williams Bros Ltd v Agius* [1914] A.C. 510.

[426] See, e.g. *Kaines (UK) Ltd v Osterreichische Warrenhandelgesellschaft* [1993] 2 Lloyd's Rep. 1 CA, where in a highly volatile market damages were calculated on the basis that the buyer should have bought alternative goods as soon as the seller indicated that he would not perform, rather than reflecting the difference between the contract price and the (much higher) market price at the scheduled date of delivery.

[427] See *Allen v W Burns Tractors Ltd*, 1985 S.L.T. 252, where the buyer's damages reflected the higher cost of obtaining from a different source the goods he had ordered.

Damages for defective goods

Once again, the measure of damages is the estimated loss directly and naturally arising, in the ordinary **1.12.4.2** course of events, from the seller's breach.[428] Where defective goods are rejected, the buyer will, prima facie, be entitled to damages calculated on the basis that the goods have not been delivered. Where the buyer elects to retain defective goods the measure of damages will, prima facie, be the difference between the value of the goods at the time of delivery and their value had the contract been fulfilled.[429] If defective goods cause the buyer physical injury[430] or damage to his property,[431] damages should reflect this fact, while in certain cases consumers have even been successful in recovering damages for inconvenience or distress.[432] Claims for loss of profit may be allowable, if these should have been within the contemplation of the parties.[433] It has also been held that where the goods were acquired for resale to the public, damages could include the cost of recalling defective goods.[434]

THE BUYER'S RIGHT TO SPECIFIC IMPLEMENT

Where there is a contract to deliver specific or ascertained goods, and these have not been delivered, **1.12.5** s.52 allows the buyer to ask the court to order that the contract be performed specifically. This provision is stated to be supplementary to the right of specific implement in Scotland.[435] Theoretically, therefore, as the remedy of specific implement is a general right in respect of breach of contract,[436] that remedy should be available on a wider basis than conceded by s.52, i.e. in respect of unascertained goods. Nonetheless, since the courts have traditionally asserted a discretion to withhold the remedy in appropriate circumstances,[437] this remains a purely theoretical possibility, because even where the goods are ascertained the courts will decline to award implement where the buyer can obtain replacement goods on the open market.[438]

THE BUYER'S DUTIES

Needless to say, the buyer has duties in addition to rights under the contract.   **1.13**

TO PAY FOR THE GOODS

The buyer must accept and pay for the goods in accordance with the contract of sale.[439] Although the **1.13.1** parties may vary this rule by agreement, delivery of the goods and payment of the price are stated to be concurrent conditions:

---

[428] See s.53A(1).

[429] See s.53A(2).

[430] *Godley v Perry* [1960] 1 W.L.R. 9.

[431] *Wilson v Rickett Cockerell & Co Ltd* [1954] 1 Q.B. 598.

[432] *Bernstein v Pamson Motors (Golders Green) Ltd* [1978] 2 All E.R. 220.

[433] See, e.g. *George Mitchell (Chesterhall) Ltd v Finney Lock Seeds Ltd* [1983] 2 A.C. 803.

[434] *Britvic Soft Drinks Ltd v Messer UK Ltd* [2002] 3 All E.R. (Comm) 321 CA.

[435] See s.52(4).

[436] *Stewart v Kennedy (No. 1)* (1890) 17 R. (HL) 1.

[437] *Moore v Paterson* (1881) 9 R. 337, per Lord Shand at 351.

[438] *Union Electric Co v Holman & Co*, 1913 S.C. 954, per Lord President Dunedin at 958. See analysis by L. Macgregor, "Specific Implement in Scots Law" in J. Smits, D. Haas and G. Hesen (eds), *Specific Performance in Contract Law: National and Other Perspectives* (Antwerp: Intersentia, 2008), pp.77–79.

[439] See s.27.

"[T]he seller must be ready and willing to give possession of the goods to the buyer in exchange for the price and the buyer must be ready and willing to pay the price in exchange for possession of the goods."[440]

As noted above,[441] time is not usually of the essence in contracts of sale, and so the seller will not have the right to rescind if payment is not made timeously. However, the contract of sale may expressly confer on the seller the right of resale where the buyer has failed to pay timeously (or otherwise defaults).[442] If the seller, having reserved this right, actually sells the goods, the original contract of sale is rescinded, although this is subject to the seller's right to claim damages against the original buyer.[443] In two other situations the unpaid seller has a right of resale: firstly, where the goods are perishable; and, secondly, where the seller has given notice to the buyer of his intention to resell.[444] Although the Act does not specifically address the effect of resale in the latter two situations, it has been held that resale has the effect of rescinding the original contract of sale, and the seller is entitled to any profit on resale.[445]

TO TAKE DELIVERY

1.13.2 The buyer is obliged to take delivery of the goods within a reasonable time,[446] although failure to do so will not usually justify rescission unless the failure or refusal amounts to a repudiation of the contract.[447] Where the goods are perishable, it is assumed that time is of the essence, and a failure to take delivery will justify the seller's rescission and resale.[448] If the buyer has been requested to take delivery but fails to do so within a reasonable time of the request, he is liable for any loss caused by such failure and also for a reasonable charge for the care and custody of the goods.[449]

TO ACCEPT THE GOODS

1.13.3 The buyer has a duty to accept the goods.[450] Wrongful rejection entitles the seller to rescind.

THE SELLER'S REMEDIES

1.14 The seller, of course, has certain personal remedies where the buyer defaults—the right to sue for the price of the goods and/or damages. But where a seller has not been paid, he may be able to exercise certain remedies based on his possession of the goods.

THE POSSESSORY REMEDIES OF THE UNPAID SELLER

1.14.1 For the purposes of the protections contained under s.39, the seller is "unpaid" where the whole of the price has not been paid or tendered[451] (so that a seller is unpaid if any of the price is outstanding), or when a bill of exchange or other negotiable instrument has been received as conditional payment and

---

[440] See s.28.
[441] See para.1.7 above.
[442] See s.48(4).
[443] See s.48(4).
[444] See s.48(3).
[445] *RV Ward Ltd v Bignall* [1967] 1 Q.B. 534.
[446] See s.37(1).
[447] See s.37(2). For an example of a case where the time of delivery was held to be of the essence of the contract, see *Shaw v Waddell & Son* (1900) 2 F. 1070.
[448] *Sharp v Christmas* (1892) 8 T.L.R. 687.
[449] See s.37(1).
[450] See s.27.
[451] See s.38(1)(a).

it has been dishonoured.[452] An unpaid seller has three rights which are exerciseable even though property in the goods has passed to the buyer:

(1) a lien on the goods or right to retain them while he is in possession of the goods;
(2) where the buyer is insolvent, a right to stop the goods in transit after he has given up possession of them;
(3) a right of resale.[453]

Lien

Section 41(1) sets out three situations in which the unpaid seller is able to exercise his right of lien, i.e. **1.14.1.1** his right to retain possession until paid:

(1) where the goods have been sold without any stipulation as to credit; in other words, where it has not been agreed that the buyer should be permitted a certain period within which to make payment;
(2) where the goods have been sold on credit but the term of credit has expired; e.g. where the buyer has been given two months to pay, but has not done so at the end of this period;
(3) where the buyer becomes insolvent,[454] i.e. where he has ceased to pay his debts in the ordinary course of business, or cannot pay his debts as they become due.[455] In this case the right can be exercised even where the contract allows the buyer a period of credit. The Act takes the view that the seller should not be obliged to yield the goods to a buyer who is unable to pay.

The Act lays stress on continuity of possession rather than the character of possession, because even if the seller is in possession of the goods as the buyer's custodier or agent, the right remains exerciseable.[456] Where part delivery has been made, the right may be exercised over the remainder, unless the circumstances indicate an agreement to waive the right over the remainder.[457]

The seller's lien may be lost in the following circumstances:

(1) when the seller delivers the goods to a carrier or custodier for the purpose of transmission to the buyer without reserving the right of disposal of the goods; thus if the seller gives the goods to a haulier to be sent to the buyer, or to a warehouseman to be held for the buyer, the right is lost. The same is true if he ships them to the buyer under a bill of lading (see para.4.8 below) made out in the buyer's favour. Yet if that bill of lading is made out in his own favour, he is regarded as having retained a right of disposal, and so may still exercise the right of lien;
(2) when the buyer or his agent lawfully obtains possession of the goods;
(3) by waiver.[458]

If the seller relinquishes possession, then the right of lien is lost for good. It cannot be resurrected by the seller regaining possession.[459] A buyer who has rejected the goods cannot claim to be an unpaid seller for the purpose of exercising a right to retain the goods until the price is returned.[460]

Stoppage in transit

Where the buyer is insolvent, an unpaid seller who has relinquished possession can stop the goods in **1.14.1.2** transit, resuming possession until the buyer pays the price.[461] This right can only be exercised as long

---

[452] See s.38(1)(b).
[453] See s.39(1)(a)–(c).
[454] See s.41(1)(a)–(c).
[455] See s.61(4).
[456] See s.41(2).
[457] See s.42.
[458] See s.43.
[459] *London Scottish Transport Ltd v Tyres (Scotland) Ltd*, 1957 S.L.T. (Sh Ct) 48; *Hostess Mobile Catering v Archibald Scott Ltd*, 1981 S.L.T. (Notes) 125.
[460] *JL Lyons & Co Ltd v May and Baker Ltd* [1923] 1 K.B. 685.
[461] See s.44.

as the goods are in transit, so it is important to be able to determine how long the transit lasts. The Act states that goods are in transit from the time they are delivered to a carrier or custodier for transmission to the buyer, until the buyer or his agent takes delivery of them.[462] Obviously, if a carrier is the buyer's agent, then the goods are effectively in the hands of the buyer and there is no transit.[463] If the buyer (or agent) obtains delivery before the goods arrive at their appointed destination, the transit is at an end.[464] If, after the goods have arrived at their appointed destination, the carrier or custodier acknowledges to the buyer (or agent) that he holds the goods on his behalf, the transit is at an end, and it does not matter that a further destination has been indicated by the buyer.[465] However, if the buyer rejects the goods and the carrier or custodier continues in possession, the transit continues, even though the seller has refused to have the goods back.[466] Where the carrier or custodier wrongfully refuses to deliver the goods to the buyer or the buyer's agent, the transit is at an end.[467] Finally, where part delivery has been made, the remainder of the goods may be stopped in transit, unless the circumstances indicate an agreement to give up possession of all the goods.[468]

Stoppage in transit may be effected either by the seller retaking actual possession of the goods or by the giving of appropriate instructions to the carrier or custodier.[469] If the goods are in the physical possession of the employee of the carrier or custodier, and the instructions are given to the carrier, they must be given in sufficient time to allow the carrier to communicate them to the employee to prevent delivery to the buyer.[470] When the goods have been stopped in transit, they must be redelivered to, or according to the directions of, the seller, who bears the expenses of redelivery.[471] If proper instructions are not given, the carrier will not be responsible for the consequences. Indeed, if the unpaid seller refuses to take delivery of the goods or to give directions for their delivery, and refuses to pay freight due to the carrier, he will be liable to the carrier in damages equivalent to the amount of freight.[472] On the other hand, if the carrier ignores timeous instructions to halt delivery, and delivers the goods to the buyer, he will be liable in damages to the seller.[473]

Effect of resale by the buyer

1.14.1.3 What if the buyer, against whom either of the possessory remedies is sought to be exercised, turns out to have resold the goods? The answer is that the rights of lien and stoppage are effectual against a sub-buyer unless the seller assented to the resale.[474]

In the context of his discussion of s.47(1) in *Mordaunt Bros v British Oil & Cake Mills Ltd*,[475] Pickford J observed:

> "[T]he assent which affects the unpaid seller's right of lien must be such an assent as in the circumstances shews that the seller intends to renounce his rights against the goods. It is not enough to shew that the fact of a sub-contract has been brought to his notice and that he has assented to it merely in the sense of acknowledging the receipt of the information . . . The assent . . . means an assent given in such circumstances as shew that the unpaid seller intends that the sub-contract shall be carried out irrespective of the terms of the original contract."[476]

---

[462] See s.45(1).

[463] See s.45(5) which indicates that when the goods are delivered to a ship chartered by the buyer, it is a question of fact whether they are in the master's possession as a carrier, or as the buyer's agent.

[464] See s.45(2).

[465] See s.45(3).

[466] See s.45(4): it seems likely that this provision prevails over s.45(3).

[467] See s.45(6).

[468] See s.45(7). For an example of an unsuccessful attempt to argue that the sellers had agreed to give up possession of all the goods, see *Mechan & Sons Ltd v North Eastern Ry Co*, 1911 S.C. 1348.

[469] See s.46(1).

[470] See s.46(3).

[471] See s.46(4).

[472] *Booth Steamship Co Ltd v Cargo Fleet Iron Co Ltd* [1916] 2 K.B. 570.

[473] *Mechan & Sons Ltd v North Eastern Ry Co*, 1911 S.C. 1348.

[474] See s.47(1).

[475] *Mordaunt Bros v British Oil & Cake Mills Ltd* [1910] 2 K.B. 502.

[476] *Mordaunt Bros v British Oil & Cake Mills Ltd* [1910] 2 K.B. 502, per Pickford LJ at 507.

It was also stated that the assent might be more easily inferred where the transaction entered into with the sub-buyer is for specific as opposed to unascertained goods.[477] The seller has been held to have assented to a sub-sale where he was aware that the price was to be paid by the buyer to him from the proceeds of the sub-sale.[478]

The principle in s.47(1) is subject to the specific exception that where a document of title has been transferred to a buyer, and the buyer transfers the document to a person who takes it in good faith and for value, then if a sale has been entered into between buyer and sub-buyer, the seller's right of lien or stoppage in transit is defeated,[479] and if a pledge or disposition other than a sale is entered into, the seller's right of lien or stoppage in transit can only be exercised subject to the rights of the pledgee, e.g. pawnbroker, or transferee.[480] So if goods are shipped, and a copy of the bill of lading (see para.4.8 below) is sent to the buyer, the transference of this bill of lading to the sub-buyer will allow him to demand possession of the goods from the original seller.[481]

Seller's right of resale

Although the exercise of the seller's rights of lien or stoppage in transit does not automatically rescind the contract,[482] resale by a seller who has exercised these rights will confer a good title on the buyer.[483] Additionally, the seller is given an express power of resale where the goods are perishable or where he gives notice of his intention to resell, and the price is not paid or tendered within a reasonable time.[484] The seller may also recover damages from the buyer for any loss occasioned by the breach of contract.[485] Where the seller has expressly reserved the right of resale in case of the buyer's default, and the buyer does, in fact, default, the resale is treated as an implied rescission of the contract and the seller may have a claim for damages.[486] This means that the seller is selling his own goods in the resale and is therefore entitled to retain any profit on the resale.[487]

1.14.1.4

THE SELLER'S PERSONAL REMEDIES

Apart from remedies based on possession of the goods, a seller confronted with a breach of contract by the buyer has certain personal remedies against the buyer, namely, to sue for the price and to sue for damages. The advantage of being entitled to sue for the price is that the seller is under no obligation to mitigate his loss by looking for a new buyer.

1.14.2

Action for the price

The seller may sue for the price:

1.14.2.1

- where the property has passed and the buyer wrongfully neglects or refuses to pay.[488] However, the seller cannot claim where the property in the goods has not passed due to the wrongful act of the buyer[489];

---

[477] *Mordaunt Bros v British Oil & Cake Mills Ltd* [1910] 2 K.B. 502, per Pickford LJ at 507. See also *DF Mount Ltd v Jay & Jay (Provisions) Co Ltd* [1960] 1 Q.B. 159, per Salmon J at 168.
[478] *DF Mount Ltd v Jay & Jay (Provisions) Co Ltd* [1960] 1 Q.B. 159.
[479] See s.47(2)(a).
[480] See s.47(2)(b).
[481] See *Cahn v Pocketts Bristol Channel Steam Packet Co Ltd* [1899] 1 Q.B. 643.
[482] See s.48(1).
[483] See s.48(2).
[484] See s.48(3).
[485] See s.48(3).
[486] See s.48(4).
[487] *RV Ward Ltd v Bignall* [1967] 1 Q.B. 534.
[488] See s.49(1).
[489] *Colley v Overseas Exporters* [1921] 3 K.B. 302.

- where the price is payable on a day certain irrespective of delivery, and the buyer wrongfully neglects or refuses to pay, whether or not the property has passed or goods have been appropriated to the contract.[490]

The day certain rule is something of an anomaly, in that it allows the seller to claim the price, even when no property has passed. The meaning of a "day certain" is ambiguous. Obviously it can be a specific date, but the authorities indicate that a date fixed by reference to some future or contingent event is not a day certain. So in one case where payment was to be made on submission of an invoice, this was not payment on a day certain,[491] whereas in another a contract which provided for payment of specific instalments on completion of stages of the work, this was stated to be payment on a day certain.[492] It would seem inequitable that a seller who rescinds the contract in response to failure to pay on a day certain should be able to claim the price without delivering the goods, yet such is the logic of an English decision of the House of Lords,[493] although it appears that Scots law might prevent such a result.[494]

Damages for non-acceptance

1.14.2.2 Where the buyer wrongfully neglects or refuses to accept and pay for the goods, the seller can sue for damages for non-acceptance.[495] This may be the seller's only remedy, but where the property in the goods has passed, the seller may choose to sue for damages, rather than exercising his option of suing for the price. The measure of damages is the estimated loss directly and naturally arising in the ordinary course of events from the buyer's breach of contract.[496] Where there is an available market for the goods, the measure will be the difference between the market price and the current price when the goods ought to have been accepted, or if no time was fixed for acceptance, at the time of refusal to accept.[497]

The seller may recover damages even if it seems that, looking at the transaction as a whole, the seller has not made a loss. In one case, following breach by the buyer, the seller had been able to sell the goods for more than the contract price.[498] Nevertheless, the seller was awarded the difference between the contract and the market price at the date of breach. The following statement was approved in the case:

"[T]he seller cannot recover from the buyer the loss below the market price at the date of the breach if the market falls, nor is he liable to the purchaser for the profit if the market rises."[499]

On the other hand, if the contract price and the market price at the time of breach are identical, and the goods can be readily resold at that price, then the seller may only receive nominal damages.[500] Where supply exceeds demand the seller will usually be entitled to the profit lost on the sale.[501] Lord Justice Jenkins explains matters in *Charter v Sullivan*[502] as follows:

"The number of sales he can effect, and consequently the amount of profit he makes, will be governed . . . either by the number of cars he is able to obtain from the manufacturers, or by the number of purchasers he is able to find. In the former case demand exceeds supply, so that the

---

[490] See s.49(2).

[491] *Henderson & Keay Ltd v AM Carmichael Ltd*, 1956 S.L.T. (Notes) 58.

[492] *Workman Clark & Co v Lloyd Brazileno* [1908] 1 K.B. 968, although the case contains very little discussion of s.49(2) of the Act.

[493] *Hyundai Heavy Industries Co Ltd v Papadopoulos* [1980] 1 W.L.R. 1129.

[494] See *Lloyds Bank Plc v Bamberger*, 1993 S.C. 570, per Lord Justice Clerk Ross at 573F–G.

[495] See s.50(1).

[496] See s.50(2).

[497] See s.50(3).

[498] *Campbell Mostyn (Provisions) Ltd v Barnett Trading Co* [1954] 1 Lloyd's Rep. 65.

[499] *AKAS Jamal v Moolla Dawood Sons & Co* [1916] 1 A.C. 175 at 179, approved by Somervell LJ in *Campbell Mostyn (Provisions) Ltd v Barnett Trading Co* [1954] 1 Lloyd's Rep. 65 at 68.

[500] *Charter v Sullivan* [1957] 2 Q.B. 117.

[501] *WL Thompson Ltd v Robinson (Gunmakers) Ltd* [1955] Ch. 177.

[502] *Charter v Sullivan* [1957] 2 Q.B. 117.

default of one purchaser involves him in no loss, for he sells the same number of cars as he would have sold if that purchaser had not defaulted. In the latter case supply exceeds demand, so that the default of one purchaser may be said to have lost him one sale."[503]

CONSUMER GUARANTEES

Although this is not strictly speaking related to the contract of sale of goods, it would be remiss not to **1.15** point out that the 2002 Regulations contain new protections for consumers in relation to guarantees.[504] The consumer guarantee is defined as

> "any undertaking to a consumer by a person acting in the course of his business, given without extra charge, to reimburse the price paid or to replace, repair or handle consumer goods in any way if they do not meet the specifications set out in the guarantee statement or in the relevant advertising."[505]

"Consumer" is given the normal definition supplied by the 2002 Regulations, a natural person contracting for purposes which are outside his trade, business or profession.[506] A guarantee is further defined in s.15(1) as a contractual obligation owed by the guarantor under the conditions which are set out in the guarantee itself and also in any associated advertising. This contrasts with the position under Scots law where guarantees could be classed as promises or unilateral obligations.[507] Where goods are supplied with a guarantee, the guarantee takes effect when the goods are delivered.[508] Certain minimum standards are set, including the fact that the guarantee must be in plain, intelligible language[509] and must be in English where the goods are offered within the UK.[510] It must include essential particulars such as the duration and territorial scope together with the name and address of the guarantor.[511] Where the consumer requests a copy of the guarantee it must be provided to him within a reasonable time,[512] and this particular provision binds not only the guarantor but any person who offers the goods which are the subject of the guarantee for sale or supply.[513] The consumer also has the right to apply for an order of specific implement in relation to certain of his rights under this section.[514]

It is common for consumers in the UK to be offered an extended warranty relating to consumer goods. Such extended warranties, purchased by the consumer, apply for perhaps two to five years, and are generally expensive. Retailers encourage consumers to buy them by indicating that they provide the consumer with the comfort of knowing that their goods will be automatically replaced should they break down within the warranty period. Such extended warranties have always been controversial given that, in buying such a warranty, in effect, the consumer is paying for protections which he or she probably already possesses under the implied terms of the 1979 Act. In conformity with the terms of the original Directive, such warranties are not covered by the 2002 Regulations because guarantees are defined as being "given without extra charge".[515] Such warranties remain problematic being essentially valueless, replicating protections already present in legislation. The fact they fall outwith the protection of the 2002 Regulations is also a matter of concern.

---

[503] *Charter v Sullivan* [1957] 2 Q.B. 117, per Jenkins LJ at 124–125.

[504] 2002 Regulations reg.15.

[505] 2002 Regulations reg.2. See also reg.15(1) which provides that the guarantee is a contractual obligation owed by the guarantor under the conditions which are set out in the guarantee itself and also in any associated advertising.

[506] 2002 Regulations reg.2.

[507] See M. Hogg, "Scottish Law and the European Consumer Sales Directive", 2001 E.R.P.L. 337, 349.

[508] 2002 Regulations reg.15(1).

[509] 2002 Regulations reg.15(2).

[510] 2002 Regulations reg.15(5).

[511] 2002 Regulations reg.15(2).

[512] 2002 Regulations reg.15(3).

[513] 2002 Regulations reg.15(4).

[514] In relation to rights under 2002 Regulations reg.15(2), (4) or (5).

[515] 2002 Regulations reg.2.

Chapter 2

AGENCY

2.1   # INTRODUCTORY ISSUES

GENERAL[1]

2.1.1 An agent has been described as

> "a person who has authority to act for and on behalf of another (called the principal) in contracting legal relations with third parties; and the agent representing the principal creates, alters, or discharges legal obligations of a contractual nature between the latter and third parties."[2]

Not all of the aspects of agency can be included in a short definition, but this definition encapsulates the essence of agency which is the ability to create and discharge legal relations for another party. In exchange for payment of a fee, the principal is able to benefit from the agent's expertise in negotiating contracts. The principal may appoint an agent who is based in a foreign country, allowing the principal to make use of the specialised knowledge of local market conditions which the agent possesses. The international aspect of agency is of key importance, particularly since the enactment of the 1986 Commercial Agents Directive,[3] implemented in Great Britain by the Commercial Agents (Council Directive) Regulations 1993.[4] The Directive aims to protect commercial agents, and its impact on the Scots law of agency has been extensive.

The extent of the agent's authority is an important issue. If the agent exceeds his authority then he is unable validly to act for his principal. For example, any contract which an unauthorised agent purports to conclude on behalf of his principal will not be valid. That contract may become valid where the principal successfully ratifies. The third party may also have a remedy through the operation of apparent authority. Both these legal ideas are explored later in this chapter. As a general rule, however, unauthorised agents cannot validly act on behalf of their principals.

The manner in which the agent acts is important. The form of the contract entered into will often depend upon the amount of information which was imparted to the third party by the agent during negotiations. Issues such as whether the agent made it clear to the third party that he was acting for a principal, and whether that principal was named by the agent, can be determinative of the contractual relationships formed, as is explored later in this chapter.

AGENCY AND MANDATE

2.1.2 Mandate differs from agency in that mandate is a gratuitous contract. In mandate, terminology is often confusing.[5] The mandant is the equivalent of the principal and the mandatory the equivalent of the agent. Many of the mandatory's rights and duties are similar to those of the agent in agency.

CAPACITY

2.1.3 The extent to which an agent and a principal must have capacity to contract is an area which is subject to a surprising amount of doubt. Given that the agent is acting as the extended arm of the principal, the principal should not be able to enlarge his contractual capacity by employing an agent. A principal who

---

[1] The issues covered in this chapter are examined in more detail in L. Macgregor, *The Law of Agency in Scotland* (Edinburgh: W. Green, 2013).

[2] T.B. Smith, *A Short Commentary on the Law of Scotland* (Edinburgh: W. Green, 1962), p.774, citing J.E. De Villiers and J.C. Macintosh, *The Law of Agency in South Africa*, 2nd edn (Cape Town: Juta, 1956), p.16.

[3] Directive 86/653/EEC on the co-ordination of the laws of Member States relating to self-employed commercial agents [1986] OJ L382/17.

[4] Commercial Agents (Council Directive) Regulations 1993 (SI 1993/3053), amended by Commercial Agents (Council Directive) (Amendment) Regulations 1993 (SI 1993/3173) and Commercial Agents (Council Directive) (Amendment) Regulations 1998 (SI 1998/2868).

[5] Macgregor, *The Law of Agency in Scotland* (2013) at para.4–10.

has no contractual capacity will lack the ability to appoint an agent, and will not be personally bound by contracts which the agent purports to enter into on his or her behalf.

The contractual capacity of the agent is a more difficult issue. His lack of capacity is not a significant issue in the course of his actions on behalf of the principal. He acts, in a sense, as a conduit of rights, or as the mechanism through which the principal can enter into contract with third parties. His lack of capacity does not threaten the formation of such contracts. His lack of capacity would, however, be a significant problem where another party sought to argue that a contract had indeed been formed between agent and third party. This can occur, for example, where the agent acts on behalf of an undisclosed principal, as is explored below.[6]

CONSTITUTION

2.1.4 The principal and agent may have entered into an actual written contract, and indeed, where the Commercial Agents (Council Directive) Regulations 1993 apply, either party has the right to receive from the other, on request, a signed written document setting out the terms of the agency contract including any terms subsequently agreed.[7] In cases not governed by the regulations, a written agreement is not required, an oral agency agreement being sufficient.

In most cases the principal and agent will indeed have entered into a written contract. Regardless of whether the agency contract is formed orally or in writing, actual offer and acceptance is not required. Rather, it may arise simply through the agent beginning to act on the principal's behalf with the principal's consent.[8]

Because very few formalities are required in order to constitute the agency relationship, the concept of agency is sometimes applied to provide a solution to problems in other areas of the law. Recent examples include the reliance on what was described as "ad hoc agency" in order to avoid unfair results which would otherwise be caused by strict adherence to the doctrine of the separate legal personality of companies.[9]

THE COMMERCIAL AGENTS (COUNCIL DIRECTIVE) REGULATIONS 1993

2.2

INTRODUCTION

2.2.1 The Commercial Agents Directive 1986[10] was implemented in Great Britain[11] by the Commercial Agents (Council Directive) Regulations 1993.[12] The regulations took effect from January 1, 1994 and apply to all agency agreements in force as from that date. They apply to the activities of commercial agents taking place in Great Britain, regardless of the nationality of that agent.[13] The aim of the Directive

---

[6] See para.2.7.4 below.

[7] Commercial Agents (Council Directive) Regulations 1993 (SI 1993/3053) reg.13.

[8] *Gilmour v Clark* (1853) 15 D. 478; *Wright v Baird* (1868) 6 S.L.R. 95; *Bank of Scotland v Dominion Bank (Toronto)* (1891) 18 R. (HL) 21.

[9] See the judgments of Lord Drummond Young in *Whitbread Group Plc v Goldapple Ltd (No.2)*, 2005 S.L.T. 281; *Laurence McIntosh Ltd v Balfour Beatty Group Ltd* [2006] CSOH 197; *John Stirling (t/a M & S Contracts) v Westminster Properties Scotland Ltd* [2007] CSOH 117; [2007] B.L.R. 537. The concept of ad hoc agency as used in these cases is analysed in L. Macgregor and N. Whitty, "Payment of another's debt, unjustified enrichment and ad hoc agency" in (2011) Edin. L.R. 57.

[10] Directive 86/653.

[11] The phrase "Great Britain" is used here to denote England, Wales and Scotland. For Northern Ireland, see the Commercial Agents (Council Directive) Regulations (Northern Ireland) 1993 (SR 1993/483), effective from January 13, 1994.

[12] Commercial Agents (Council Directive) Regulations 1993 (SI 1993/3053), as amended.

[13] See reg.1(2). For an analysis of the application of the regulations in international private law see Macgregor, *The Law of Agency in Scotland* (2013) paras 9–04—9–07.

is visible in its source, art.117 of the Treaty of Rome, which refers to the "need to promote improved working conditions and an improved standard of living for workers". Relevant too is the preamble to the Directive which refers to the harmonisation of conditions for commercial agents to ensure their uniform protection throughout the European Union.[14]

The regulations are intensely protective of the commercial agent. This contrasts with the tradition of agency law in Scotland and England, where the principal is often identified as the party in the relationship requiring protection, in particular because of the tendency of agents to enter into contracts in excess of their authority. Not surprisingly, the application of the regulations in the Scottish and English courts has been fraught with difficulty. Even now, when the regulations have been in force for more than 20 years, problems continue, for example in the context of when the activities of an agent can be considered "secondary"[15] or the calculation of compensation.[16]

The regulations are further complicated by the fact that certain of them can be excluded by the contracting parties, whereas others are mandatory. Each individual regulation must be checked to ascertain its status in this respect.

2.2.2 DEFINITION OF A COMMERCIAL AGENT

General aspects

2.2.2.1 A commercial agent is defined in the regulations as follows:

> "A self-employed intermediary who has continuing authority to negotiate the sale or purchase of goods on behalf of another person (the 'principal'), or to negotiate and conclude the sale or purchase of goods on behalf of and in the name of that principal."[17]

A commercial agent may be an individual, a company or a partnership.[18] The definition refers to the sale or purchase of goods, thus excluding from its ambit agents who provide services.[19] The commercial agent must have "continuing authority" which also excludes those agents carrying out one-off transactions on behalf of their principals. Given that the commercial agent must act in the name of the principal,[20] where the agent acts on behalf of an undisclosed principal, a situation which is possible in the UK but not in the rest of the European Union, the regulations will not apply.[21]

Although this point is not specifically addressed in the definition, case law has indicated that an agent will only fall within the definition of a commercial agent where he has a direct contractual relationship with the principal.[22]

"Negotiate"

2.2.2.2 Only commercial agents who "negotiate" fall within the definition of a commercial agent. The exact meaning of this word has been considered in English case law. In *Parks v Esso Petroleum Co Ltd*[23] Morritt LJ relied on the Oxford English Dictionary meaning of "negotiate", in order to exclude from the definition of a commercial agent an agent who managed a petrol station. In his view:

---

[14] Directive 86/653 preamble.
[15] See para.2.2.2.4 below.
[16] See para.2.9.4 below.
[17] See reg.2(1) ("commercial agent").
[18] See *AMB Imballaggi Plastici Srl v Paciflex Ltd* [1999] 2 All E.R. (Comm) 249.
[19] Whilst this may appear to be a simple distinction in theory, it may be a difficult one to make in the context of contracts comprising a mixture of goods and services, see *Marjandi Ltd v Bon Accord Glass Ltd* Unreported October 15, 2007 Aberdeen Sheriff Court, per Sheriff Tierney.
[20] *Sagal v Atelier Bunz GmbH* [2009] EWCA Civ 700; [2008] 2 CLC 850.
[21] See the discussion of the undisclosed principal in para.2.7 below.
[22] *Light v Ty Europe Ltd* [2003] EWCA Civ 1238; [2003] Eu. L.R. 858 (overturning *Light v Ty Europe Ltd* [2003] EWHC 174 QB; [2003] 1 All E.R. (Comm) 568).
[23] *Parks v Esso Petroleum Co Ltd* [1999] 1 C.M.L.R. 455 Ch D; [2000] E.C.C. 45; [2000] Eu. L.R. 25; (1999) 18 Tr. L.R. 232 CA.

"This definition does not require a process of bargaining in the sense of invitation to treat, offer, counter-offer and finally acceptance, more colloquially known as haggle. But equally it does require more than the self-service by the customer followed by payment in the shop of the price showed on the pump."[24]

At least one more recent case suggests that a more lenient approach is appropriate. In *PJ Pipe & Valve Co Ltd v Audco India*, taking a purposive approach, i.e. looking to the aim of the Directive, Mr Justice Fulford opined that

"the question of whether the agent actually participates in discussions on price or commercial terms has less relevance than whether the agent is retained to develop goodwill in his principal's business."[25]

Exclusions

Certain types of business are expressly excluded from the definition of a commercial agent, namely: **2.2.2.3**

(1) an officer of a company or association who is empowered to enter into commitments binding on that company or association[26];
(2) a partner acting on behalf of his firm[27];
(3) a person acting as an insolvency practitioner[28];
(4) a commercial agent whose activities are unpaid (a mandatory in Scots law)[29];
(5) a commercial agent acting on commodity exchanges or in the commodity market[30]; and
(6) Crown Agents for Overseas Governments and Administrations, as set up under the Crown Agents Act 1979, or its subsidiaries.[31]

"Secondary"

The regulations do not apply where the agent's activities are classed "secondary".[32] The definition of **2.2.2.4** secondary, an issue left to the discretion of the individual Member States, has proved problematic in the UK.[33] In particular, this issue has been interpreted in a different way in the Scottish and English courts.[34] An issue which remains ambiguous is the nature of the comparison being carried out, in other words, it is not clear what the agent's activities as a commercial agent are to be compared against to arrive at the conclusion that they are "secondary". Some English cases suggest that the agent's activities as a commercial agent should be compared with the other non-agency activities he may have with a principal.[35] However, the DTI suggested that the comparison should be made with the rest of the agent's non-agency activities.[36] Scots cases have adopted yet another approach. In the leading case of *Gailey v Environmental Waste Controls*, Lord Drummond Young gave a wide meaning to "secondary", rejecting the view that it involves a simple numerical comparison between the agent's activities as a commercial agent and his activities in other fields.[37] His approach has, however, been described as incorrect by the

---

[24] *Parks v Esso Petroleum Co Ltd* (1999) 18 Tr. L.R. 232 CA at 238.
[25] *PJ Pipe and Valve Co v Audco India Ltd* [2005] EWHC 1904 QB at [149].
[26] See reg.2(1)(i).
[27] See reg.2(1)(ii).
[28] See reg.2(1)(iii).
[29] See reg.2(2)(a).
[30] See reg.2(2)(b).
[31] See reg.2(2)(c).
[32] See reg.2(3), (4).
[33] For a more detailed analysis of this question see Macgregor, *The Law of Agency in Scotland* (2013) paras 9–13—9–15.
[34] See the discussion by S. Saintier and J. Scholes, *Commercial Agents and the Law* (London: LLP, 2005), pp.45–51.
[35] See *Tamarind International Ltd v Eastern Natural Gas (Retail) Ltd* [2000] Eu. L.R. 708, per Morison J.
[36] DTI Guidance Notes.
[37] See, in particular, the judgment of in *Gailey v Environmental Waste Controls* [2004] Eu. L.R. 423, per Lord Drummond Young at [26].

leading authors in this field in English law.[38] Before analysing the Scottish approach in more detail, it is helpful to consider the provisions themselves.

The provisions are contained in reg.2(3) and (4) and para.2 of the Schedule. The normal activities of a commercial agent are defined, indicating by implication what is secondary. Those activities are the sale and purchase of goods,[39] where transactions are normally individually negotiated and concluded on a commercial basis,[40] and procuring a transaction on one occasion is likely to lead to further transactions in those goods with that customer, or to transactions with customers in the same geographical area.[41] After this general definition has been applied, reference must be made to indications and counter-indications contained in the Schedule. The process was recently described as follows:

> "They are considered secondary if it can be reasonably taken that the primary purpose of the arrangement is other than as set out in paragraph 2, applying the indications and counter-indications as set out respectively in paragraphs 3 and 4 of the schedule."[42]

Paragraph 3 contains the indications—the factors which suggest that the situation falls within para.2. These activities are part of a commercial agent's normal activities:

(1) the principal is the manufacturer, importer or distributor of the goods;
(2) the goods are specifically identified with the principal in the market in question rather than, or to a greater extent than, with another person;
(3) the agent devotes substantially the whole of his time to representative activities (whether for one principal or for a number of principals whose interests are not conflicting);
(4) the goods are not normally available in the market in question other than by means of the agent;
(5) the arrangement is described as commercial agency.[43]

Paragraph 4 contains the counter-indications: the factors which suggest that the situation does not fall within para.2. These activities suggest that the agent is unlikely to be a commercial agent:

(1) promotional material is supplied direct to potential customers;
(2) persons are granted agencies without reference to existing agents in a particular area or in relation to a particular group;
(3) customers normally select goods for themselves and merely place their order through the agent.[44]

The legislative provisions are undoubtedly ambiguous, a fact borne out by the difficulties experienced in the Scottish courts.[45] Perhaps the main difficulty is that they are not drafted in the way in which a UK Act of Parliament would be drafted. They contain broad ideas and do not seek to cover all possibilities.[46] Whether the courts should adopt a purposive approach to the interpretation of "secondary" is a controversial question, Lord Drummond Young having answered this question in the negative in *Gailey* on the basis that Member States have complete discretion on the definition of "secondary".[47] The current approach of the Scottish courts can be summarised as follows: the focus should lie on the

---

[38] Saintier and Scholes, *Commercial Agents and the Law* (2005), p.49.
[39] See Sch. para.2(a).
[40] See Sch. para.2(b)(i).
[41] See Sch. para.2(b)(ii).
[42] *Marjandi Ltd v Bon Accord Glass Ltd* Unreported October 15, 2007 Aberdeen Sheriff Court, per Sheriff Tierney.
[43] See Sch. para.3(a)–(e).
[44] See Sch. para.4(a)–(c). The regulations also contain a presumption that the activities of mail order catalogue agents for consumer goods and consumer credit agents do not fall within para.2 and are therefore secondary, Sch. para.5.
[45] See the problems experienced in *Gailey v Environmental Waste Controls* [2004] Eu. L.R. 423; *McAdam v Boxpak Ltd*, 2006 S.L.T. 217.
[46] See for example the sheriff's comments in *McAdam v Boxpak Ltd*, quoted by Lord Abernethy in the Inner House 2006 S.L.T. 217 at [7] and [8].
[47] *Gailey v Environmental Waste Controls* [2004] Eu. L.R. 423 at [30].

purpose of the arrangement between principal and agent at its inception.[48] An essential question is whether the agent was engaged to develop goodwill in the principal's business.[49] If the answer to this question is yes, then the agent's role is not likely to be secondary, and he is likely to fall within the definition of a commercial agent. In general, the difference of interpretation of this concept in Scotland and England is a matter for concern, particularly given that the broad interpretation given to "secondary" by the Scottish courts acts to decrease the number of agents brought within the protective ambit of the regulations.[50]

THE AGENT'S AUTHORITY

As stated above, the extent of the agent's authority has an important impact on the success of the aim **2.3** of agency: generally the constitution of a contractual relationship between principal and third party. Ideally, the extent will be spelled out in the contract between principal and agent. The agent's authority may, however, be implied. The implication of authority arises in different ways. It may arise because it is necessary to carry out the object of the agency agreement, because it is incidental to it, or because it is customary in the particular trade in question. It may be implied in the sense that it is *usual*, meaning that it arises as an implication from the post the agent holds, e.g. a solicitor benefits from the authority which it would be usual for someone in that profession to have.[51] Case law may assist in the determination of whether any particular action is or is not within an agent's implied authority.[52] For example a solicitor has implied authority to order a search for incumbrances in conveyancing transactions,[53] but not to enter into a contract on behalf of a client,[54] nor to obtain an overdraft facility for that client.[55]

GENERAL AND SPECIAL AGENTS

A general agent is an agent who is employed to carry out all of the business of a particular principal, or **2.3.1** at least, all of the business of the principal of a particular kind. The special agent, by contrast, is employed to carry out one particular transaction. Although this issue is not entirely free from doubt, a solicitor appears to be a general agent.[56] The distinction between general and special agents is an important one given that it shapes the type of implied authority which that agent has.[57] If the agent is a general agent, the third party may assume that that agent has all the powers which an agent of that type would usually possess. If the agent is a special agent, his implied powers will only be such as are necessary to carry out the single transaction which he has been appointed to carry out.

---

[48] *McAdam v Boxpak Ltd*, 2006 S.L.T. 217 at [20], although Saintier and Scholes suggest that the test should be a continuing one; see Saintier and Scholes, *Commercial Agents and the Law* (2005), p.47.

[49] *McAdam v Boxpak Ltd*, 2006 S.L.T. 217 at [20]–[21], applied in *Marjandi Ltd v Bon Accord Glass Ltd* Unreported October 15, 2007 Aberdeen Sheriff Court, per Sheriff Tierney at [68].

[50] Goodwill having been identified as a key issue by the Scottish courts, an agent will not be considered a commercial agent unless he has been engaged to increase the principal's goodwill. Saintier and Scholes, *Commercial Agents and the Law* (2005), p.49, have argued that goodwill, although a central issue in the context of the termination provisions, is not the key issue here. The effect of this emphasis is to narrow the class of agents considered to be commercial agents to those who are engaged with the specific purpose of increasing the principal's goodwill. The alternative approach, in terms of which the activities of the agent as a commercial agent are simply compared with his other activities, will not have a similar limiting effect.

[51] "Usual" authority is an expression which has different meanings in English law, see Macgregor, *The Law of Agency in Scotland* (2013) paras 11–16—11–17.

[52] Macgregor, *The Law of Agency in Scotland* (2013) paras 5–14—5–23.

[53] *Fearn v Gordon and Craig* (1893) 20 R. 352.

[54] *Danish Dairy Co v Gillespie*, 1922 S.C. 656, per Lord President Clyde at 665; per Lord Skerrington at 667; and per Lord Cullen at 671.

[55] *Commercial Bank of Scotland v Biggar*, 1958 S.L.T. (Notes) 46.

[56] See Macgregor, *The Law of Agency in Scotland* (2013) para.5–03. See, however, Bell, *Principles*, s.219(7) who classes a solicitor as a special agent.

[57] See the explanation given by Lord Young in *Morrison v Statter* (1885) 12 R. 1152 at 1154.

MERCANTILE AGENTS

2.3.2 The term "commercial agent" is likely to denote an agent falling within the ambit of the Commercial Agents (Council Directive) Regulations 1993.[58] Although the scope of the regulations is wide, many agents are not governed by the regulations, for example those dealing in services, not goods.

Historically, agents were sometimes described as either "factors" or "brokers". The distinction between factors and brokers was important: a factor was usually entrusted with possession of goods, and sold the goods in his own name.[59] By contrast, a broker did not usually take possession of goods, nor sell goods in his own name, and acted more as an intermediary.[60] This distinction is less important in a modern context, although it continues to be visible in some areas: auctioneers are classed as factors, whereas stockbrokers and insurance brokers are, not surprisingly, brokers. The word "factor" is used to describe those involved in factoring of heritable property or debt factoring.[61]

The term "mercantile agent" acquired a specific meaning through the operation of the Factors Acts.[62] A mercantile agent is defined as an agent who "in the customary course of business" has "authority either to sell goods, or to consign goods for the purpose of sale, or to buy goods, or to raise money on the security of goods."[63] Such an agent, through the operation of the Act, has the ability to pass title to the principal's goods, where the principal has not consented and would not have consented to the agent's particular transaction. The relevant section stipulates that where the mercantile agent is in possession of goods or documents of title with the consent of the owner, any sale, pledge or other disposition of the goods made by him when acting in the ordinary course of business, is as valid as if he were expressly authorised by the owner of the goods to make the same.[64] As a result, the third party transacting with the mercantile agent need have few concerns over the agent's lack of authority. There are certain qualifications, however. The third party must act in good faith, and must not have notice of the agent's lack of authority.[65]

A bona fide purchaser of goods can benefit from protections which are similar to those available under the Factors Acts under the Sale of Goods Act 1979. Section 24 tackles the situation where a seller, although having sold goods, is left in possession of the goods or documents of title for the goods after the sale with the consent of the owner. Although in possession of the goods, he does not possess, nor can he pass, good title to those goods. Through the application of s.24, however, the sale is treated as though the seller in possession were an agent of the actual seller. In effect, therefore, the bona fide third party gets good title. Section 25 applies a similar scheme to the situation where a buyer, having bought or agreed to buy goods, is in possession of goods after a sale with the consent of the owner. In both cases, the protections apply additionally in the case where the bona fide purchaser bought from a mercantile agent acting for the seller or buyer in possession.[66]

DEL CREDERE AGENCY

2.3.3 When an agent contracts on behalf of a principal, he does not normally provide the principal with a guarantee of the solvency of the third party with whom the agent contracts (on the principal's behalf). If such a guarantee is, in fact, given, the agency is known as *del credere* agency.[67] The agent will, of course, charge a fee for the provision of this extra service. As with other types of agency, the agency

---

[58] Commercial Agents (Council Directive) Regulations 1993 (SI 1993/3053), as amended.

[59] *Cunningham v Lee* (1874) 2 R. 83 at 87, per Lord President Inglis.

[60] *Cunningham v Lee* (1874) 2 R. 83 at 87, per Lord President Inglis.

[61] On debt factoring see E. McKendrick (ed) *Goode on Commercial Law*, 4th edn (London: Penguin, 2010), pp.788–876.

[62] See Factors Act 1889 s.2(1) applied to Scotland by the Factors (Scotland) Act 1890. See also the discussion at para.1.10.1 above.

[63] Factors Act 1889 s.1(1).

[64] Factors Act 1889 s.2(1).

[65] Factors Act 1889 s.2(1).

[66] See paras 1.10.2 and 1.10.3 above.

[67] *Lloyds Executors v Wright* (1870) 7 S.L.R. 216.

relationship may be created expressly or by implication.[68] Aside from the provision of the guarantee, in other respects *del credere* agency operates in the same way as any normal agency relationship.

AGENT ACTING OUTSIDE HIS AUTHORITY

The operation of the Factors Acts, explained above, is one example of an agent who, despite his lack of **2.4** authority, has the ability to enter into valid contracts on the principal's behalf. The aim of these provisions is clearly protection of the third party from abuses by the agent of his authority. Other concepts of the law of agency have a similar protective effect towards third parties. The two most important are ratification and ostensible or apparent authority.

RATIFICATION

Where an agent has purported to enter into a contract in excess of his authority, no contract will be **2.4.1** formed between principal and third party. It may, however, be possible for the principal to ratify the agent's actings. Valid ratification creates a direct contractual relationship between the principal and the third party which is effective from the moment when the agent purported to enter into the contract on the principal's behalf. Ratification is a unilateral act on the part of the principal, and can be either express or implied from the principal's conduct.[69] It may operate in different ways: it may validate a particular transaction which the agent purported to conclude in excess of his authority, or where the "agent" was not an agent at all, but purported to act for a specific principal.[70] Ratification in this latter case, in effect, creates the agency relationship.

Ratification is retrospective in effect: once the principal has ratified, a contractual relationship is deemed to exist between principal and third party from the moment the agent purported to enter into the contract on the principal's behalf, as though the agent had been fully authorised at that time. The retrospective nature of ratification can be problematic in practice. In particular, it leads to difficult results where the third party attempts to withdraw from the "contract"[71] after it has been concluded by the unauthorised agent but before ratification. In English law, the case of *Bolton Partners v Lambert* suggests that the retrospective effect of ratification renders the third party's attempt to withdraw ineffective.[72] This point remains undecided in Scotland. Although *Bolton* has been discussed in two Scottish cases, in neither case was the court willing to indicate whether *Bolton* would be followed in Scotland.[73]

Ratification is subject to stringent requirements, all of which must be fulfilled before it can be effective. These requirements are considered below.

Principal in existence

The principal must be in existence at the time the agent entered into the contract with the third party on **2.4.1.1** the principal's behalf. Thus, where a promoter enters into a contract on behalf of a company which has

---

[68] *Lloyds Executors v Wright* (1870) 7 S.L.R. 216; *Steins Assignees v Brown* (1828) 7 S. 47.

[69] *Ballantine v Stevenson* (1881) 8 R. 959; *Barnetson v Petersen* (1902) 5 F. 86.

[70] See J.J. Gow, *Mercantile and Industrial Law of Scotland* (Edinburgh: W Green, 1964), pp.517, 520; *Alexander Ward & Co Ltd v Samyang Navigation Co Ltd*, 1975 S.C. (HL) 26; 1975 S.L.T. 126.

[71] It is not, in fact, a contract given that the unauthorised agent cannot create contractual relations between principal and third party.

[72] *Bolton Partners v Lambert* (1889) 41 Ch. D. 295; *Bedford Insurance Co v Instituto de Resseguros do Brasil* [1985] Q.B. 966, per Parker LJ at 981; *Presentaciones Musicales v Secunda* [1994] Ch. 271. Although the authorities on this point are English, there is no reason to suspect that a different result would be reached in Scots law.

[73] *Licenses Insurance Corp & Guarantee Fund v Shearer* [1906] 14 S.L.T. 345 and *Goodall v Bilsland*, 1909 S.C. 1152.

not yet been incorporated, the company is not bound. Rather, the promoter is personally liable, and the acts of the promoter cannot be ratified.[74]

Principal must have legal capacity

2.4.1.2 The principal must have had legal capacity both at the time the agent entered into the contract, and at the time of ratification.[75] He must have legal capacity at the time the agent purports to enter into the contract as a result of the retrospective nature of ratification. Because he is treated as being bound in a contract with the third party from the moment the agent purported to enter into it on his behalf, he must have possessed contractual capacity at that time. Although there is no specific Scottish authority on this point, it is likely that the principal must also have legal capacity when he ratifies. This is because ratification is a juristic act which must be carried out by a party with legal capacity.

The requirement of legal capacity of the principal was, at one time, highly relevant in a company law context. Previously, contracts entered into by directors or other agents for the company which were outside the company's objects clause could not be ratified by the shareholders.[76] In such circumstances, neither the third party nor the company would be bound. Under the existing law, matters are more complex. It is crucial to draw a distinction between contracts which are entered into between third parties and the company in circumstances where (i) the directors or the company have exceeded or abused the company's constitutional powers; and (ii) the directors have exceeded or abused their own constitutional powers. With regard to the capacity of the company, i.e. (i), it is now provided that the company has the capacity to enter into a contract or that such capacity can be assumed.[77] As a result, as regards third parties and the company, the contract is binding. However, internally, where the directors have abused the powers of the company, the actions of the director may only be ratified by the company by special resolution.[78] Moreover, any relief from liability incurred by the director may be authorised by special resolution.[79]

Where a third party deals with a company in good faith, the power of the directors to bind the company, i.e. (ii) above, is deemed to be free of any limitation under the company's constitution. This will include limitations imposed by the objects clause.[80] In such circumstances, the company and the third party will be bound by the contract where the directors have exceeded their powers. Internally, the shareholders may ratify the director's abuse of their constitutional powers by ordinary resolution.[81] Where a director exceeds or abuses his powers, he will also be in breach of his statutory duty to observe the company's constitution.[82] An ordinary resolution of the shareholders may also absolve the director of such a breach.[83] Where an ordinary resolution is passed, the court must refuse an aggrieved shareholder leave to raise derivative proceedings, in terms of which the shareholder could argue that the director's breach of the constitution (i) has caused the company loss; or (ii) has resulted in a gain in the hands of the director which should be restored to the company.[84]

Some of the case law in this area is not easy to rationalise. In *Alexander Ward & Co Ltd v Samyang Navigation Co Ltd*,[85] a Scottish House of Lords case, solicitors raised an action for debt at a time when

---

[74] Companies Act 2006 s.51(1). The Companies Act provisions effectively gave statutory form to the pre-existing common law: see *Tinnevelly Sugar Refining Co Ltd v Mirrlees, Watson & Yaryan* (1894) 21 R. 1009; *Kelner v Baxter* (1866) L.R. 2 C.P. 174; *Cumming v Quartzag Ltd*, 1980 S.C. 276.

[75] *Boston Deep Sea Fishing and Ice Co Ltd v Farnham* [1957] W.L.R. 1051.

[76] For an illustration see *Ashbury Ry Carriage and Iron Co Ltd v Riche* (1875) L.R. 7 H.L. 653.

[77] Companies Act 2006 s.39(1).

[78] Companies Act 1985 s.35(3). Whether and how the shareholders are to ratify the actions of a director where they have exceeded or abused the company's powers is not dealt with in the Companies Act 2006, so the law remains unclear. A special resolution is a resolution of the shareholders passed by a majority of not less than 75 per cent (Companies Act 2006 s.283(1)).

[79] Companies Act 1985 s.35(3).

[80] Companies Act 2006 s.40(1).

[81] *Bamford v Bamford* [1970] Ch. 212. An ordinary resolution is a resolution of the shareholders passed by simple majority, i.e. 50 per cent (Companies Act 2006 s.282(1)).

[82] Companies Act 2006 s.171(1)(a).

[83] Companies Act 2006 s.239(1).

[84] Companies Act 2006 s.268(1)(c)(ii).

[85] *Alexander Ward & Co Ltd v Samyang Navigation Co Ltd*, 1975 S.C. (HL) 26. See the discussion of this case in *Thomas Dagg & Sons Ltd v Dickensian Property Co Ltd* A174/01 Unreported January 19, 2005.

no directors were in office. The question before the court was whether the company acting through liquidators could ratify the raising of the action. It was held that the company was a competent principal at the time of raising of the action, and ratification was possible. Lord Hailsham explained that because the company was competent either to appoint directors or authorise proceedings in general meeting at the time at which the solicitors raised the action, then it followed that it was a competent principal, even if it had not carried out either of these steps at the relevant time.[86]

Agent must enter transaction as an agent

In cases where ratification by the principal, in effect, "creates" the agency relationship, the agent must enter into the contract with the third party as an agent and not on his own account.[87] Whether the "agent" has named the principal in this situation is not important—it is sufficient simply for the "agent" to make it clear that he acts for an unidentified principal.[88] **2.4.1.3**

This rule can be illustrated by a famous English case, *Keighley, Maxsted & Co v Durant*.[89] The agent had received authority from the principal to buy corn subject to a maximum price. The agent was unable to buy at that price, and bought at a higher price, intending the transaction to be a joint speculation by the principal and him. After the transaction, the agent informed the principal of the purchase, and the principal, happy with the agent's actings, purported to ratify the contract. When the agent failed to take delivery of the goods, the principal was sued by the seller. The principal was found not liable for failing to take delivery of the goods because he was not a party to the contract. Because the agent had not intended to enter into the contract purely in a representative capacity, ratification was not possible. A contractual relationship had been formed only between seller and agent.

Although *Keighley* is highly authoritative, there is a Scottish case earlier in date which conflicts with it. In *Lockhart v Moodie & Co*[90] A and B had entered into a joint venture agreement for the purchase of yarn. A authorised B to buy yarn at a maximum price of 1s 11d per spindle. B purchased yarn at a greater price, 1s 14d, buying in his own name and not disclosing to the seller any involvement on the part of A. B became bankrupt and the seller sued A for the sums due. The First Division found A liable, but only to the extent of the approved price. The result could be explained on the basis that the principal is the joint venture[91] and that ratification is carried out by that joint venture, a view which is consistent with the opinion of Lord President Inglis in the case.[92] Nevertheless, the case remains something of an anomaly. It was not discussed in *Keighley*, and seems not to have been subsequently referred to in any Scottish case. The influential Scottish writer, Gloag, suggested that the Scottish courts are more likely to follow *Keighley*.[93]

Time limits

If the act which requires to be ratified is subject to a time limit, then the principal must ratify within that time limit. Thus in *Goodall v Bilsland*[94] the agent, a solicitor, was authorised to object to the renewal of a license at the licensing court. He was unsuccessful and appealed to the Licensing Appeal Court, but without first obtaining his principal's authority to raise the appeal. Although the principal later ratified his actions, this occurred after the expiry of the time limit within which the appeal had to be raised. Ratification was held to be ineffective. **2.4.1.4**

---

[86] *Alexander Ward & Co Ltd v Samyang Navigation Co Ltd*, 1975 S.C. (HL) 26 at 47.

[87] *Weir v Dunlop & Co* (1861) 23 D. 1293; *Reid's Trustees v Watson's Trustees* (1896) 23 R. 636.

[88] The implications of acting for a disclosed and named principal, a disclosed and unnamed principal, and an undisclosed principal are considered at para.2.7. below.

[89] *Keighley, Maxsted & Co v Durant* [1901] A.C. 240.

[90] *Lockhart v Moodie & Co* (1877) 4 R. 859.

[91] A joint venture is a type of partnership which is formed for one specific purpose, see para.8.2.1 below.

[92] *Lockhart v Moodie & Co* (1877) 4 R. 859 at 866.

[93] W.M. Gloag, *Law of Contract*, 2nd edn (Edinburgh: W. Green, 1929), p.143.

[94] *Goodall v Bilsland*, 1909 S.C. 1152. See also the English cases of *Bird v Brown* (1850) 19 L.J. Ex. 154 and *Dibbins v Dibbins* [1896] 2 Ch. 348.

The scope and justification of this particular requirement are not clear. For example, it is not known which types of acts it applies to, for example contracts or other juristic acts, nor is it clear whether it applies to all time limits or only those which are legally binding. In English law it has been suggested that a time limit is only relevant where it is essential to the validity of an act that it should be done within that time.[95]

Contract must not be void or illegal

2.4.1.5 If the contract which was entered into by the agent on the principal's behalf is affected by illegality, or is void, then ratification will have no effect.[96] The contract remains invalid.

The principal must make an informed choice

2.4.1.6 As already noted, the principal can be deemed to have ratified through his conduct. Before such an inference may be made, he must be aware of all the relevant facts. In *Forman & Co Proprietary Ltd v The Liddesdale*[97] an agent was authorised to instruct repairs to a ship which had been damaged when it was stranded. The agent instructed repairs which went beyond mere "stranding damage" and amounted to refurbishment of the ship. After the repairs had been carried out, the principal used the ship. It was held that simple acceptance and use of the repaired ship did not amount to ratification of the agent's actions.

Protection of other parties

2.4.1.7 Ratification may operate in a manner which is arguably prejudicial to the interests of the third party, for example if, following *Bolton Partners v Lambert*,[98] he is prevented from withdrawing from a contract by the principal's subsequent ratification. Other parties too may find that their rights are affected by ratification. Thus far Scots law, unlike English law,[99] has not seen the development of a general rule preventing the operation of ratification where it would unfairly prejudice the rights of other parties. It seems beyond doubt that a Scottish court would apply such protections in practice. It could choose to follow English law on this point, although a better solution would be to develop the idea as it was expressed in the works of the Scottish institutional writers, Erskine and Bell.[100]

2.4.2 OSTENSIBLE/APPARENT AUTHORITY

General

2.4.2.1 An agent acting outside his authority fails to bind his principal in a contract with the third party. Where ratification operates, the contract between principal and third party may be validated. However, there are other ways in which a third party may be protected from the actions of unauthorised agents. Another legal concept, ostensible or apparent authority, may be available to the third party.[101] Apparent authority prevents the principal from acting inconsistently by first giving the third party the impression that the agent is properly authorised, and then subsequently seeking to deny the agent's authority. As such,

---

[95] P.G. Watts and F.M.B. Reynolds, *Bowstead and Reynolds on Agency*, 19th edn (London: Sweet & Maxwell, 2010), para.2–089.

[96] *Bedford Insurance Co Ltd v Instituto de Resseguros do Brasil* [1985] Q.B. 966, per Parker LJ at 986.

[97] *Forman & Co Proprietary Ltd v Liddesdale (The Liddesdale)* [1900] A.C. 190.

[98] *Bolton Partners v Lambert* (1889) 41 Ch. D. 295

[99] *Smith v Henniker-Major & Co* [2003] EWCA Civ 762; [2003] Ch. 182, per Robert Walker LJ at 71; and *Owners of the Borvigilant v Owners of the Romina G* [2003] EWCA Civ 935; [2003] 2 Lloyd's Rep. 520, per Clarke LJ at [70]. Similar protections exist under O. Lando and H. Beale (eds), *Principles of European Contract Law* ("PECL"), Pts I and II (1999), Pt III (2004) (The Hague/London/Boston: Kluwer Law International), see Art 3:207(2).

[100] Erskine, *Institute*, III, 3, 49 and Bell, *Commentaries*, I, 141.

[101] For discussion of apparent authority in Scots law see D. Busch and L. Macgregor, "Apparent authority in Scots law: Some International Perspectives", 2007 Edin. L.R. 349.

apparent authority is a type of personal bar.[102] The following definition of apparent authority, taken from an English case, has proved highly authoritative in Scots law:

> ". . . a legal relationship between the principal and the contractor created by a representation, made by the principal to the contractor intended to be and in fact acted on by the contractor, that the agent has authority to enter on behalf of the principal into a contract of a kind within the scope of the 'apparent authority' so as to render the principal liable to perform any obligations imposed on him by such a contract."[103]

If the third party is successful in his attempt to prove the existence of apparent authority, then the agent's lack of authority is not "cured". The agent remains unauthorised, and the so called "contract" between principal and third party is not validated. Rather, if the third party raises an action against the principal, the principal will be prevented from pleading the agent's lack of authority in the context of that action. In this way the third party can recover damages from the principal representing his loss in not having the anticipated contract with the principal.

Requirements

Apparent authority is subject to a number of requirements. The principal must create the impression of **2.4.2.2** authority either through his words or conduct. This requirement is interpreted widely, encompassing not only positive conduct on the part of the principal but also failure to act where he is subject to a duty to act.[104] There must be a causal link between that action or inaction and the third party's belief, in other words the third party must believe that the agent is authorised as a direct result of the principal's conduct. It follows, therefore, that if the third party actually knows that the agent is not authorised, even in the face of conduct of the principal suggesting otherwise, then apparent authority cannot arise.[105] Finally, the third party must have relied on that representation and have suffered loss through that reliance.

The Scottish case law on apparent authority is unhelpful and it is not surprising that English cases (such as *Freeman & Lockyer v Buckhurst Park Properties (Mangal)*) have been relied upon in the Scottish courts.[106] One of the leading Scottish cases is *International Sponge Importers Ltd v Watt*[107] in which Cohen, a commercial traveller, was authorised to sell sponges on behalf of International Sponge Importers Ltd. Cohen often called upon a firm of saddlers, Watt & Co, to sell sponges. The usual method of payment for the sponges was for Watt to make out a cheque in the name of the principal company and send it direct to that company. On certain occasions in the past, Cohen had collected cheques from Watt made out to the company. In the past Cohen had also induced Watt to pay by providing cheques made out in Cohen's name and handed directly to him, or in cash. Cohen absconded, owing sums to his principal company. The principal was unsuccessful both in the Court of Session and the House of Lords where it was held that he could not recover, having failed to object to the unauthorised methods of collection of payment previously used by the agent.[108] The decision is, however, a difficult one because the evidence of the acquiescence on the part of the principal to the unauthorised methods used in the past is weak.

---

[102] For recent confirmation that ostensible authority is a form of personal bar, see *Bank of Scotland v Brunswick Developments (1987) Ltd (No.2)*, 1997 S.C. 226, per Lord President Rodger at 243.

[103] *Freeman & Lockyer v Buckhurst Park Properties (Mangal) Ltd* [1964] Q.B. 480, per Diplock LJ at 503, whose speech was approved by Lord President Hope in the Scottish case of *Dornier GmbH v Cannon*, 1991 S.C. 310 at 314.

[104] See Lord Diplock in *Freeman & Lockyer v Buckhurst Park Properties (Mangal) Ltd* [1964] 2 Q.B. 480 at 503, approved by Lord President Hope in *Dornier GmbH v Cannon*, 1991 S.C. 310 at 314; and by Lord Macfadyen in *John Davidson (Pipes) Ltd v First Engineering Ltd*, 2001 S.C.L.R. 73 at 78.

[105] *Colvin v Dixon* (1867) 5 M. 603.

[106] *Freeman & Lockyer v Buckhurst Park Properties (Mangal) Ltd* [1964] Q.B. 480.

[107] *International Sponge Importers Ltd v Andrew Watt & Sons*, 1911 S.C. (HL) 57.

[108] See *International Sponge Importers Ltd v Andrew Watt & Sons*, 1911 S.C. (HL) 57, per Lord Low (Second Division) at 65; per Lord Chancellor, Lord Loreburn (HL) at 67.

The case is also an apt illustration of the possible confusion which exists between implied authority and apparent authority.[109] It could, of course, be part and parcel of the normal powers of a commercial traveller to accept cheques made out in his principal's name. It is, however, unlikely that it would extend to accepting cash. In cases of this type, the focus of attention should lie on the third party's reasonable perceptions of the situation and the manner in which those were created. Where those perceptions were created by the principal, and provided that all the necessary requirements are fulfilled, the third party will have a claim against the principal on the basis of apparent authority.

Scope

2.4.2.3 Apparent authority is likely to arise in certain factual situations, for example where the agent was previously fully authorised, but the agent's authority has ceased. If that agent continues to act as though he was authorised, then apparent authority may arise. Because of this possibility, it is important for a principal to inform existing customers that the agent's authority or employment has ceased. The principal may inform clients by using a circular or advertisement. If all customers are informed, then apparent authority cannot arise. This requirement is given statutory form for partnerships in the Partnership Act 1890.[110] This assumes, of course, that the third party has not become aware of the limitation of the agent's authority through other means. If the third party is indeed already aware of the cessation of the agent's authority, then the principal's failure to inform him is irrelevant—apparent authority will not arise.[111]

Generally apparent authority arises where the agent is a general rather than a special agent. Third parties may reasonably assume from the status of general agent that the agent has the wide powers usual for that type of agent. As a result, the third party's belief in the agent's authority is likely to be considered reasonable. Special agents, by contrast, do not possess general powers. Thus a third party could not argue that his impression of the extent of authority was reasonable, and thus apparent authority could not arise.

Recent developments—a "representation" by the agent?

2.4.2.4 As already stated, the requirement of conduct on the part of the principal is interpreted widely in the context of an apparent authority case. This being the case, it is sometimes difficult to tell whether the third party was relying on the principal's conduct (and thus has a relevant claim for apparent authority) or was, rather, relying on the agent's actions (in which case he will not). Some writers have indeed advocated the extension of apparent authority to cases in which the impression of authority has been created by the agent, and not the principal.[112] Although this development was rejected in the House of Lords case of *Armagas v Mundogas SA*,[113] the Court of Appeal came close to recognising the development in the key case of *First Energy (UK) Ltd v Hungarian International Bank Ltd*.[114] In this case the agent, Jamison, was a senior manager in charge of the Manchester office of HIB, the principal. Jamison had been negotiating with First Energy, and sought to arrange finance for them. First Energy was aware that Jamison was not authorised to grant the finance arrangement on his own. Jamison nevertheless indicated that he would contact his principal and obtain the necessary authority. After a short delay he confirmed to First Energy that he now possessed the necessary authority and confirmed the finance facility in a letter signed by him alone. The bank later sought to repudiate the transaction on the basis of Jamison's lack of authority. The Court of Appeal held that, although Jamison did not have the authority to grant the loan facility, he did have apparent authority to communicate to First Energy that

---

[109] See the judgment of Lord Ardwall: *International Sponge Importers Ltd v Andrew Watt & Sons*, 1911 S.C. (HL) 57 at 67.
[110] Partnership Act 1890 s.36.
[111] *North of Scotland Banking Corp v Behn Möller & Co* (1881) 8 R. 423 at 429.
[112] I. Brown, "The agent's apparent authority: paradigm or paradox?" [1995] J.B.L. 360. Arguably the Scottish case of *Smith v Scott & Best* (1881) 18 S.L.R. 355 comes close to recognition of apparent authority on the basis of conduct by the agent, not the principal.
[113] *Armagas v Mundogas SA* [1986] A.C. 717.
[114] *First Energy (UK) Ltd v Hungarian International Bank Ltd* [1993] 2 Lloyd's Rep. 194; with comment by F.M.B. Reynolds at (1993) 110 L.Q.R. 21.

head office approval of the loan had been obtained. The court held that the bank was bound by Jamison's actions.

The judges in the Court of Appeal approached the facts of the case in different ways. Lord Justices Steyn and Nourse took a practical approach, indicating that it would be unreasonable for a third party such as First Energy to bear the burden of establishing the extent of the agent's authority.[115] Lord Justice Steyn identified two types of apparent authority. The first is the apparent authority to enter into the loan facility. This Jamison did not have. It would have required a representation[116] on the part of the principal which was lacking, and would also have been impossible as a result of First Energy's actual knowledge of Jamison's lack of authority. The second is the apparent authority to make representations to clients on behalf of the principal. Such representations could encompass communicating head office approval. Lord Justice Steyn indicated that this apparent authority to make representations arose from the position in which Jamison had been placed: he had been "clothed with ostensible authority to communicate that head office approval had been given".[117]

Lord Justice Steyn also classified ostensible authority as a type of implied or usual authority. In his view, there are two meanings of "usual authority":

> "First, it sometimes means that the agent had implied actual authority to perform acts necessarily incidental to the performance of the agency. Secondly, it sometimes means that the principal's conduct in clothing the agent with the trappings of authority was such as to induce a third party to rely on the existence of the agency . . .".[118]

Thus, on the facts before him, Jamison had possessed the second type of usual authority.

It is difficult to state the principles of the English law of apparent authority in the aftermath of the *First Energy* case. As a Court of Appeal case, *First Energy* cannot "overrule" the binding House of Lords authority of *Armagas v Mundogas SA*.[119] *First Energy* has received little attention from the Scottish courts. Whilst it remains the case that the representation must not come from the agent himself, Lord Justice Steyn's approach in *First Energy* removes much of the rigour from that exclusion. Clarification of the rules in this area is certainly required.

THE AGENT'S DUTIES/PRINCIPAL'S RIGHTS 2.5

DUTY TO FOLLOW INSTRUCTIONS

The agent is under a common law duty to perform the contract of agency according to its terms. The **2.5.1** principal's instructions must be clear, and the agent will not be liable for any losses caused as a result of the ambiguity of the instructions.[120] Under the Commercial Agents (Council Directive) Regulations 1993, the commercial agent is under a similar duty to "comply with reasonable instructions given by [the] principal".[121] If the agent acts in such a way as to breach his express instructions then he will be liable to the principal for any loss caused.[122]

---

[115] *First Energy (UK) Ltd v Hungarian International Bank Ltd* [1993] 2 Lloyd's Rep. 194, per Steyn LJ at 200 and 203; per Nourse LJ at 208.

[116] In English law, the word "representation" is used to describe the action or inaction on the part of the principal required in order to prove apparent authority. In Scots law the relevant phrase is "inconsistent conduct", see generally Busch and Macgregor, "Apparent authority in Scots law: Some International Perspectives", 2007 Edin. L.R. 349.

[117] *First Energy (UK) Ltd v Hungarian International Bank Ltd* [1993] 2 Lloyd's Rep. 194 at 204.

[118] *First Energy (UK) Ltd v Hungarian International Bank Ltd* [1993] 2 Lloyd's Rep. 194, per Steyn LJ at 201.

[119] [1986] A.C. 717.

[120] *Ireland v Livingston* (1872) L.R. 5 H.L. 395.

[121] Commercial Agents (Council Directive) Regulations 1993 (SI 1993/3053) reg.3(2)(c).

[122] *Gilmour v Clark* (1853) 15 D. 478; *Wright v Baird* (1868) 6 S.L.R. 95; *Bank of Scotland v Dominion Bank (Toronto)* (1891) 18 R. (H.L.) 21.

If the principal does not provide express instructions, the agent may still be bound to comply with duties which are usual in the particular trade in which the agent is working.[123]

DUTY OF SKILL AND CARE

2.5.2 The agent has a duty to perform the agency contract with skill and care, although the extent of this duty may vary. The institutional writers Erskine and Bell equated the agent's duty with that of " a prudent man in managing his own affairs".[124] Where the agent is a professional person his duty is that of a reasonably competent and careful member of that profession.[125] The agent's duty may vary depending upon a variety of other factors such as the custom in the particular trade, any course of prior dealings between the parties, and the particular circumstances of the case.[126]

If the agent breaches his duty of skill and care, the principal may claim damages for breach of contract,[127] although in the context of such an action the court may take into account any relevant conduct of the principal such as the giving of defective instructions.[128] If the agent's duty is framed in an extremely broad manner such as to amount to an absolute discretion, the agent may not be liable in damages to the principal for defective performance except perhaps where he has completely failed to exercise the discretion or acted in a wholly unreasonable manner.[129]

DUTY TO KEEP ACCOUNTS

2.5.3 Although the agent is under a duty to keep accounts, such accounts need not be written. The course of the relationship between the agent and the principal may indicate that a verbal accounting only is required.[130]

2.5.4 AGENT'S FIDUCIARY DUTY/THE REQUIREMENTS OF GOOD FAITH

Fiduciary duties

2.5.4.1 The agent is subject to fiduciary duties which characterise agency as a relationship involving trust and good faith. Bell's explanation of the duty sets a high standard:

> "An agent is bound to maintain the most entire good faith, and make the fullest disclosure of all facts and circumstances concerning the principal's business."[131]

English case law has been highly influential in this area, particularly the case, *Bristol and West Building Society v Mothew*[132] in which the agent's duty to show loyalty to his principal was identified as a key idea in this context.

---

[123] Bell, *Commentaries*, I, 517.

[124] Bell, *Commentaries*, I, 516; Bell, *Principles*, s.221; Erskine, *Institute*, III, 3, 37.

[125] *Cooke v Falconers Representatives* (1850) 13 D. 157, per Lord Fullerton at 172; *Beattie v Furness-Houlder Insurance (Northern) Ltd*, 1976 S.L.T. (Notes) 60. In the case of solicitors, see the analysis by R. Rennie, *Solicitors' Negligence* (Edinburgh: Law Society of Scotland; Butterworths, 1997), paras 3.02 et seq.

[126] *Hastie v Campbell* (1857) 19 D. 557, per Lord President McNeill at 561; per Lord Curriehill at 564, 565; *Alexander Turnbull & Co Ltd v Cruikshank and Fairweather* (1905) 7 F. 791.

[127] *Salvesen & Co v Rederi Aktiebolaget Nordstjernan* (1905) 7 F. (HL) 101.

[128] *Mackenzie v Blakeney* (1879) 6 R. 1329.

[129] *Glasgow West Housing Association v Siddique*, 1998 S.L.T. 1081.

[130] *Russell v Cleland* (1885) 23 S.L.R. 211.

[131] Bell, *Principles*, s.222.

[132] [1988] Ch 1.

An agent who accepted secret commission would be in breach of this duty.[133]

The Commercial Agents (Council Directive) Regulations 1993 impose on commercial agents a duty to look after the interests of the principal and act dutifully and in good faith.[134] Although three particular aspects of the duty to act in good faith are detailed in the regulations, these do not form an exhaustive list of the agent's duties in this respect. The commercial agent must:

"(1) make proper efforts to negotiate and, where appropriate, conclude the transactions he is instructed to take care of[135];

(2) communicate to his principal all the necessary information available to him[136]; and

(3) comply with all reasonable instructions given by his principal."[137]

Duty to account

One of the most important aspects of the agent's fiduciary duty is the duty to account to the principal **2.5.4.2** for all benefits received by the agent in the course of performance of the principal's business.[138] This would include any secret commission that the agent has received and has not disclosed to the principal.[139] For this duty to arise, the sums received must have been received in the course of the agency business and not as a result of any other business carried out by the agent.[140] The duty extends to benefits other than money, including anything over and above the agent's agreed remuneration.[141] The duty is insufficiently wide to prevent the agent from working for another principal in addition to the original principal.[142] Such a "non-competition" clause cannot be implied into the agency contract and would require to be inserted as an express term.[143]

A breach of this duty by the agent results not in an action of damages on the part of the principal, but rather in an action of account, reckoning and payment.[144] If the principal is successful in such an action, the agent must pay to the principal the gain which he has made in breach of the duty. This differs from an action of damages where the principal's damages would be measured by reference to the principal's loss. Given that the character of the action is disgorgement of gains, the agent must actually have made a gain or profit from breach.[145] In addition to raising an action of account, reckoning and payment against the agent, the principal may have the right to rescind the contract with the third party if the agent and the third party colluded to defraud him.[146]

---

[133] See the recent example in English law of *Daraydan Holdings Ltd v Solland International Ltd* [2004] EWHC 622 (Ch); [2004] 3 W.L.R. 1106.

[134] Commercial Agents (Council Directive) Regulations 1993 (SI 1993/3053) reg.3(1).

[135] See reg.3(2)(a).

[136] See reg.3(2)(b).

[137] See reg.3(2)(c).

[138] *Neilson v Skinner & Co* (1890) 17 R. 1243, per Lord Young at 1251; *Trans Barvil Agencies (UK) Ltd v John S Baird & Co Ltd*, 1988 S.C. 222, per Lord McCluskey at 227.

[139] *Imageview Management Ltd v Kelvin Jack* [2009] EWCA Civ 63 [6]; [2009] All E.R. 666 and see comment by L. Macgregor, "An agent's fiduciary duties: modern law placed in historical context" in 2010 Edin. L.R. 121.

[140] *Manners v Raeburn and Verel* (1884) 11 R. 899; *Lothian v Jenolite Ltd*, 1969 S.C. 111, per Lord Walker at 125.

[141] *Trans Barvil Agencies (UK) Ltd v John S. Baird & Co Ltd*, 1988 S.C. 222, per Lord McCluskey at 231.

[142] *Lothian v Jenolite Ltd*, 1969 S.C. 111. See also *Rossetti Marketing Ltd v Diamond Sofa Co Ltd* [2011] EWHC 2482; [2012] 1 All E.R. (Comm) 18; [2012] EWHC 354; [2012] EWCA Civ 1021; [2013] 1 All E.R. (Comm) 308 and comment by L. Macgregor, "100 per cent body and soul: an agent's ability to act for a competitor of his principal", 2013 Edin. L.R. 71.

[143] *Lothian v Jenolite Ltd*, 1969 S.C. 111, per Lord Wheatley at 123. An express term had been inserted into the agency contract in *Alexander Graham & Co v United Turkey Red Co Ltd*, 1922 S.C. 533.

[144] *Sao Paolo Alpargatas SA v Standard Chartered Bank Ltd*, 1985 S.L.T. 433; *Trans Barvil Agencies (UK) Ltd v John S Baird & Co Ltd*, 1988 S.C. 222, per Lord McCluskey at 231.

[145] *Sao Paolo Alpargatas SA v Standard Chartered Bank Ltd*, 1985 S.L.T. 433; see also, at 438, Lord Grieve's approval of a dictum from Lord Upjohn in *Boardman v Phipps* [1966] 3 W.L.R. 1009 at 1070 where he sets out a four stage test to be used in analysing whether the agent has a duty to account.

[146] *Huntingdon Copper and Sulphur Co Ltd v Henderson* (1877) 4 R. 294, per the Lord Ordinary (Lord Young) at 302.

Duty not to disclose confidential information

2.5.4.3 The agent is under a duty not to disclose or make use of any confidential information concerning the principal's business which has come to the agent's knowledge through performance of the agency contract. This duty may not necessarily end with termination of the agency relationship.[147]

Transactions between principal and agent

2.5.4.4 The agent is under a duty not to enter into any transactions with the principal which would allow the agent to make a profit at the principal's expense.[148] This duty may be part of a wider duty on the agent not to enter into situations in which the agent's interests conflict with the principal's.[149] There are many illustrations of this rule in the context of solicitor/client relationships. Where a solicitor arranges the sale of property belonging to his client, but fails to disclose that the solicitor himself is the buyer, then this would constitute a breach of the duty.[150] This occurred in *McPherson's Trustees v Watt*,[151] in which a solicitor acted for his client, trustees, in the sale of four houses. Unknown to the trustees, the solicitor proposed to buy two of the houses himself, and arranged for the remaining two to be sold to his brother. Lord Blackburn explained the conflict of interest as follows:

> "The mere fact that the agent was in circumstances which made it his duty to give his client advice puts him in such a position that, being the purchaser himself, he cannot give disinterested advice—his own interests coming in contact with his client's, that mere fact authorises the client to set aside the contract if he chooses so to do."[152]

Even if the solicitor discloses, and obtains the client's agreement to his role as a buyer, this may still constitute a breach of the duty.[153] In such a situation, the solicitor may also be in breach of his duty to provide the client with independent advice. Perhaps somewhat surprisingly, it was held in a more recent Scottish case that there may be nothing to prevent an agent from buying property from his client where the purchase takes place after his relationship with the client has ended.[154]

If the agent was instructed to buy goods from a third party on the principal's behalf but, instead of doing so, sells goods to his principal keeping his identity as seller secret, the principal may choose to rescind the contract and claim from the agent any profit which the agent made through the transaction.[155]

Duty not to delegate

2.5.4.5 It is perhaps misleading to state that the agent is under a duty not to delegate any work which he is required to carry out in the performance of the agency contract. The duty is subject to numerous exceptions and it is probably more accurate to state the reverse: that the agent has the right to delegate except in particular circumstances. The duty not to delegate was originally an application of the general rule of contract law which provides that where *delectus personae* is present, i.e. where the agent has been chosen to carry out work because of special skill which he possesses, then the choice of that agent excludes performance by another.[156] The institutional writers Stair and Erskine indicated that the agent

---

[147] *Liverpool Victoria Legal Friendly Society v Houston* (1900) 3 F. 42. See the conflicting case of *Earl of Crawford v Paton*, 1911 S.C. 1017, although in this case the information may not have been confidential, see Lord Dundas at 1026 and Lord Salvesen at 1028.

[148] *Cunningham v Lee* (1874) 2 R. 83, per Lord Ardmillan at 89.

[149] *Huntingdon Copper and Sulphur Co Ltd v Henderson* (1877) 4 R. 294, per Lord Mure at 307; per Lord Young at 299.

[150] *Cleland v Morrison* (1878) 6 R. 156; *Rigg's Executrix v Urquhart* (1902) 10 S.L.T. 503.

[151] *McPherson's Trustees v Watt* (1877) 5 R. (HL) 9.

[152] *McPherson's Trustees v Watt* (1877) 5 R. (H.L.) 9 at 21.

[153] *Cleland v Morrison* (1878) 6 R. 156, per Lord Young at 172.

[154] *Connolly v Brown* [2006] CSOH 187; 2007 S.L.T. 778.

[155] Bell, *Principles*, s.222.

[156] William W. McBryde, *The Law of Contract in Scotland*, 3rd edn (Edinburgh: W. Green, 2007), paras 12–36, 12–37, 12–40, 12–41.

could delegate where the agent's task was one which did not involve any particular skill.[157] It is always open to the parties to stipulate expressly in the agency contract that certain tasks may or may not be delegated.

As in many parts of the law of agency, the custom of a particular trade has an impact on whether the agent has the ability to delegate. The agent may be required to carry out a task which is clearly outside his expertise. In such a situation the agent has the implied power to delegate such a task in order to perform the agency contract properly.[158] An example of the operation of this rule is the solicitor's ability to instruct local agents where the original solicitor's case is being heard in a different part of Scotland.[159] The original solicitor has the implied power to delegate.

The contractual structure which is created following delegation is an issue which is not clear in Scots law. Delegation may have one of two effects: the new agent may completely replace the original agent and enter into a direct contractual relationship with the principal; or the new agent may enter into a contract with the original agent, creating a chain of contracts joining principal, original agent and new agent. The former situation is more correctly described as novation[160] and the latter as subcontracting. Whether novation or subcontracting has occurred will depend upon the interpretation of both the original agency contract and the agreement between the original agent and new agent, and also the particular facts and circumstances. For example, if the principal has consented to the arrangement then it is more likely that novation rather than subcontracting has occurred.[161] This follows because novation leads to more serious consequences for the principal and therefore requires the principal's consent. The original agent is removed from the contractual structure entirely, leaving the principal more financially exposed.

Relief

The agent has a duty to relieve the principal from his liability where the agent has entered into a **2.5.4.6** contract in excess of his authority. An example of this can be found in *Milne v Ritchie*[162] where the agent had instructed builders to build a house for the principal but had agreed a price which was in excess of that authorised by the principal. Although the principal was bound to pay to the builders the agreed price, the principal had a right of action against the agent allowing him to recover the amount by which the actual price exceeded the authorised price.[163]

AGENT'S RIGHTS/PRINCIPAL'S DUTIES **2.6**

PRINCIPAL'S DUTIES **2.6.1**

Commercial Agents (Council Directive) Regulations 1993

As is the case with the agent vis-à-vis the principal, the principal owes a general duty of good faith **2.6.1.1** towards his agent in terms of the Commercial Agents (Council Directive) Regulations 1993.[164] The principal's duty is drafted in much the same manner as the agent's duty, namely it includes non-exclusive examples of the operation of that duty. These examples are considered in the paragraphs which follow.

---

[157] Stair, *Institutions*, I, 12, 7; Erskine, *Institute*, III, 3, 34.
[158] Erskine, *Institute*, III, 3, 34; Bell, *Commentaries*, I, 517.
[159] *Robertson v Foulds* (1860) 22 D. 714.
[160] McBryde, *Contract*, 3rd edn (2007), paras 25–21, 25–26.
[161] For a more detailed discussion of this problem, see Macgregor, *The Law of Agency in Scotland* (2013) paras 7–15—7–27.
[162] *Milne v Ritchie* (1882) 10 R. 365.
[163] *Milne v Ritchie* (1882) 10 R. 365, per Lord Young at 366.
[164] Commercial Agents (Council Directive) Regulations 1993 (SI 1993/3053), as amended.

The principal must provide the commercial agent with the necessary documentation relating to the goods concerned[165] and obtain for the commercial agent the information necessary for the agent's performance of the agency contract.[166] The principal must also

> "notify his commercial agent within a reasonable time once he anticipates that the volume of commercial transactions will be significantly lower than that which the commercial agent could normally have expected."[167]

The latter duty, which is an onerous one, deserves specific comment. It forces the principal to monitor the relevant market closely and thus may run counter to the commercial realities of the situation in the UK. Local agents are often employed in a particular country where the principal has no commercial presence. In such a case the agent is more likely to have greater knowledge of local market conditions than the principal, and thus is better placed to predict a reduction in the volume of transactions.

The principal must advise the commercial agent within a reasonable time whether he accepts or refuses a transaction which the commercial agent has procured for the principal, and of any non-execution by the principal of a transaction arranged by the commercial agent.[168] Generally, when the agent enters into a contract on the principal's behalf, the principal is contractually bound to the third party from that moment in time. However, the definition of a commercial agent also anticipates that an agent may be authorised only to negotiate, not to conclude contracts on the principal's behalf. Bearing in mind this possibility, this duty on the part of the principal can be understood.

2.6.2 AGENT'S RIGHTS

Remuneration and commission at common law

2.6.2.1 The agency contract will usually contain an express right to remuneration. The agent's remuneration may be calculated on the basis of commission on sales concluded by him. The contract may, however, be silent on the issue, in which case there is a rebuttable presumption in favour of remuneration where the work carried out forms the agent's livelihood.[169] The courts will consider evidence from the particular trade in order to establish the rate of remuneration, although such evidence may equally indicate that no remuneration is payable. Where the agent is not a professional person, that agent's remuneration may be due on a *quantum meruit* basis.[170]

The agent's right to commission will usually be expressly stipulated in the agency contract. Even if it is so stipulated, it may be no easy matter to apply the contractual provisions to the situation at hand. Where the agent's role is to find a contracting party for the principal, the problematic issue is usually whether the eventual contract between principal and third party has been entered into as a direct result of the agent's efforts or whether the principal and third party would have entered into a contract in any event, without the agent's intervention. As a general rule, the agent's entitlement to commission arises where the transaction was "brought about, or materially contributed to" by the actings of the agent.[171] The principal may also be under a duty not to act to "frustrate" payment of the agent's commission, for example, by entering into a contract with another party expressly to avoid making payment of commission to the agent.[172]

---

[165] See reg.4(2).

[166] See reg.4(2)(b).

[167] See reg.4(2)(b).

[168] See reg.4(3).

[169] *Mackersy's Executors v St Giles Cathedral Managing Board* (1904) 12 S.L.T. 391; *Campbell v Campbell's Executors* (1910) 47 S.L.R. 837.

[170] *Robb v Kinnear's Trustees* (1825) 4 S. 108; *Kennedy v Glass* (1890) 17 R. 1085.

[171] *Walker, Fraser & Steele v Fraser's Trustees*, 1910 S.C. 222, per Lord Dundas at 229, applied in *G2 Legal v Adie Hunter*, 2006 S.L.T. (Sh Ct) 63. See also *AR Brett & Co Ltd v Bow's Emporium Ltd*, 1928 S.C. (HL) 19, per Lord Shaw at 20; *Robertson v Burrell* (1899) 6 S.L.T. 368; *Douglas Goodfellow and Partners v Gordon*, 1987 S.C.L.R. 684.

[172] *Dudley Bros & Co v Barnet*, 1937 S.C. 632.

Remuneration and commission under the Commercial Agents (Council Directive) Regulations 1993

The regulations provide the commercial agent with a right to remuneration where the agency contract **2.6.2.2** is silent. The commercial agent is entitled to

> "the remuneration that commercial agents appointed for the goods forming the subject of his agency contract are customarily allowed in the place where he carries on his activities and, if there is no such customary practice, a commercial agent shall be entitled to reasonable remuneration taking into account all aspects of the transaction."[173]

The regulations also contain detailed provisions which protect the commercial agent's right to commission. He is entitled to commission on transactions concluded during the period covered by the agency contract:

> "(1) where the transaction has been concluded as a result of his action[174]; or
> (2) where the transaction is concluded with a third party whom he has previously acquired as a customer for transactions of the same kind."[175]

Commission may also be payable where the commercial agent

> "has an exclusive right to a specific geographical area or to a specific group of customers and where the transaction has been entered into with a customer belonging to that area or group."[176]

Even after termination of the commercial agency contract the agent may have the right to commission where a transaction is "mainly attributable to his efforts"[177] during the agency contract and the transaction is entered into within a reasonable time after termination or if the order of the third party reached the principal or the commercial agent before the agency contract terminated.[178] The commercial agent's right to commission is not, however, unqualified. It is not due where the transaction will not be executed for a reason for which the "principal is not to blame".[179] The choice of the word "blame" here is an unusual one for UK lawyers unused to the attribution of blame in a contractual context. Presumably the effect is that commission will not be due where the principal is not in breach. It does not, however, cover situations of frustration, which are dealt with in another part of the regulations.[180]

Continuation of the principal's business

Where the agent is remunerated by commission only, his continued remuneration depends upon the **2.6.2.3** continuation of the principal's business. Although there is little case law on this issue in Scotland, the English courts have considered whether it is possible to imply a term into the agency contract binding the principal to continue his business so as to secure the agent's right to commission. It has been found that, as a general rule, no such term can be implied.[181] Despite the force of this general rule, the agency contract may be framed in such a way that the natural interpretation is that the principal has undertaken a binding obligation to continue his business.[182]

---

[173] Commercial Agents (Council Directive) Regulations 1993 (SI 1993/3053), as amended, reg.6(1).
[174] See reg.7(1)(a).
[175] See reg.7(1)(b).
[176] See reg.7(2).
[177] See reg.8(a).
[178] See reg.9.
[179] See reg.11(1)(b).
[180] See reg.16.
[181] *Patmore v Cannon* (1892) 19 R. 1004; *State of California (SS) Co Ltd v Moore* (1895) 22 R. 562; *Rhodes v Forwood* (1876) 1 App. Cas. 256; *Gardner v Findlay* (1892) 30 S.L.R. 248, per Lord Low at 250; *L French & Co v Leeston Shipping Co Ltd* [1922] 1 A.C. 451.
[182] *Turner v Goldsmith* [1891] 1 Q.B. 544 CA; *Reigate v Union Manufacturing Co (Ramsbottom) Ltd* [1918] 1 K.B. 592.

Reimbursement, relief and lien

2.6.2.4 The agent has a right to be reimbursed by the principal for all expenses which he has incurred in the proper performance of the agency contract.[183] If the sums were expended by the agent in a course of action which constituted improper rather than proper performance of the agency contract, then the sums will not be recoverable. An example of improper performance is contained in *Tomlinson v Scottish Amalgamated Silks Liquidator*.[184] The agent, a company director, was unsuccessful in his attempt to recover his expenses for defending an action for fraud. Such expenses were not part of the proper performance of the agency contract. Indeed, had the charge been found relevant, the director would have been acting wholly contrary to his duties as an agent.

The agent is entitled to relief from any liabilities which have accrued as part of the proper performance by him of the agency contract.[185] As with reimbursement, the right to relief can be lost if the agent has acted in a manner which is contrary to his obligations under the agency contract, for example by seeking to defraud or conceal material facts from the principal.[186] The right to relief has also been qualified by the custom of a particular trade.[187]

The agent has a lien, or right to retain the principal's goods in his possession, as security against payment of his commission or remuneration. The lien may be general or special: a general lien allows the agent to retain goods in security of any transaction carried out by the agent on the principal's behalf, not necessarily a transaction involving the goods retained, whereas a special lien allows the agent only to retain goods which are the subject of the transaction out of which the debt concerned has arisen. Commercial or mercantile agents,[188] solicitors[189] and stockbrokers[190] are able to exercise general liens, which enable them to retain the principal's goods against payment of the general balance due by the principal. Accountants possess only the more limited special lien.[191]

CONTRACTS WITH THIRD PARTIES

2.7 The aim of an agency transaction is usually to create a contractual relationship between the principal and the third party. However, in certain circumstances, this relationship will not be created. Instead, a contract may be formed between the agent and the third party or indeed no contract may be formed. In identifying the contracting parties, in an agency context as in any other context, the courts must look to the intentions of the parties. It has often been stated that, in order to decide this issue, one must ascertain whether the third party intended to give "credit" to the principal or to the agent.[192] In other words, was the third party relying on the financial standing of the principal or the agent when entering into the contract? If he was relying on the principal's "credit", then a contract is formed between third party and principal; if he was relying on the agent's "credit" then a contract is formed between third party and agent. In order to identify the contractual relationships which have been formed, it is also relevant to consider the information which the agent disclosed to the third party at the moment of formation of the contract. Three particular types of situation can be identified:

---

[183] *Drummond v Cairns* (1852) 14 D. 611; *Marshall Wilson Dean and Turnbull v Feymac Properties Ltd*, 1996 G.W.D. 22–1247.

[184] *Tomlinson v Scottish Amalgamated Silks Liquidator*, 1935 S.C. (HL) 1.

[185] *Stevenson v Duncan* (1842) 5 D. 167.

[186] *Robinson v Middleton* (1859) 21 D. 1089.

[187] *Dinesmann & Co v Mair & Co*, 1912 1 S.L.T. 217.

[188] *Sibbald v Gibson and Clark* (1852) 15 D. 217, per Lord Justice Clerk Hope at 221.

[189] *Drummond v Muirhead and Guthrie Smith* (1900) 2 F. 585.

[190] *Glendinning v John D Hope & Co*, 1911 S.C. (HL) 73.

[191] *Findlay (Liquidator of Scottish Workmens Assurance Co Ltd) v Waddell*, 1910 S.C. 670.

[192] Bell, *Principles*, s.224A; Bell, *Commentaries*, I, 541, Lord McLaren's note; *Carsewell v Scott & Stephenson* (1839) 1 D. 1215; *Miller v Mitchell* (1860) 22 D. 833, per Lord Neaves at 846; per Lord Ivory at 849, 850.

(1) where the agent acts for a disclosed and named principal;
(2) where the agent acts for a disclosed but unnamed principal; and
(3) where the agent acts for an undisclosed principal.

Each situation is considered below.

AGENT ACTS FOR A DISCLOSED AND NAMED PRINCIPAL

Where the agent discloses to the third party both the fact of agency and the identity of the principal, the **2.7.1** general rule is that the contract is formed between third party and principal. The agent will not incur personal liability in any contract with the third party.[193] Even where the principal is not expressly named, but the third party could, with relative ease, identify the principal, the contract is still formed between the principal and the third party.[194] However, this general rule of non-liability for the agent can be rebutted by evidence to the contrary. Such evidence may exist as a matter of custom, i.e. the custom of the particular trade may indicate both that the contract is concluded between agent and principal and that the agent accepts personal liability.[195]

WRITTEN CONTRACTS

Where a written contract has been entered into, there is a presumption to the effect that the party who **2.7.2** signs the contract intends to accept personal liability under it. This presumption is difficult to rebut and, applied to an agency context, the onus lies on the agent to prove that he did not intend to accept personal liability.[196] The strength of this presumption is illustrated by cases in which attempts to overturn it failed even though the third party was aware that the agent was acting in a representative capacity[197] or where the terms of the contract were consistent with the agent acting in a representative capacity, but he signed it without qualifying his signature.[198]

It is not only the agent's method of signature which is relevant, however. The court must interpret the contract as a whole in the circumstances in which it was made.[199] In one of the leading Scottish cases, the agent, a sales manager for two companies, sought to employ a sub-agent.[200] He sent a letter on the headed notepaper of one of the companies confirming the arrangements, which he signed using his personal signature. The court held that the agent had failed to discharge the onus that he, having personally signed the contract, and not the company, was bound by it.

Even if the agent adds a description of the capacity in which he is signing the contract after his signature, this may be insufficient to rebut the presumption of personal liability. It has been held that where a director and secretary signed a contract adding the designations "director" and "secretary" and the name of the company after their signatures, this was insufficient to rebut the presumption.[201] The designations were merely descriptive of the agents' roles. Instead, the agent must make his representative

---

[193] *Miller v Mitchell* (1860) 22 D. 833; *Fenwick v Macdonald, Fraser & Co Ltd* (1904) 6 F. 850; *Stone and Rolfe Ltd v Kimber Coal Co Ltd*, 1926 S.C. (HL) 45; *Groenius BV v Smith*, 2003 S.L.T. 80, per Lord Clarke at 87.

[194] *Armour v TL Duff & Co*, 1912 S.C. 120, per Lord Guthrie at 124, discussed in *Smith v Strathclyde Passenger Transport Executive*, 2003 S.L.T. (Sh Ct) 97.

[195] For example, solicitors grant letters of obligation in conveyancing transactions where it is customary for certain of the obligations to be personal obligations binding the solicitor rather than the client: *Johnstone v Little*, 1960 S.L.T. 129 OH; cf. *Digby Brown & Co v Lyall*, 1995 S.L.T. 932; or stockbrokers who deal with one another as principals even though they are clearly acting in a representative capacity, *Maffett v Stewart* (1887) 14 R. 506.

[196] *Stewart v Shannessy* (1900) 2 F. 1288.

[197] *Lindsay v Craig*, 1919 S.C. 139; *Gibb v Cunningham and Robertson*, 1925 S.L.T. 608; *Muirhead v Gribben*, 1983 S.L.T. (Sh Ct) 102.

[198] *Brown v Sutherland* (1875) 2 R. 615.

[199] *Brebner v Henderson*, 1925 S.C. 643, per Lord President Clyde at 645, 647; *Stone and Rolfe v Kimber Coal Co Ltd*, 1926 S.C. (HL) 45; *Crimin v Cairnbay*, 2004 G.W.D. 28–587.

[200] *Stewart v Shannessy* (1900) 2 F. 1288.

[201] *Brebner v Henderson*, 1925 S.C. 643; although cf. *McLean v Stuart*, 1970 S.L.T. (Notes) 77.

capacity clear, for example by adding "as agent for and on behalf of" or "per procuration". The operation of this rule in statutory form can be found in the Bills of Exchange Act 1882 insofar as it applies to the drawer, indorser or acceptor of a bill.[202]

Where the agent is acting on behalf of an unincorporated association which has no legal capacity, even words clearly indicating that he does not intend to undertake personal liability will be insufficient to avoid liability on his part.[203] This is an example of the rule discussed above that the principal must have legal capacity for agency to operate successfully.[204]

AGENT ACTS FOR A DISCLOSED BUT UNNAMED PRINCIPAL

2.7.3 In this type of situation the agent makes the fact that he is acting in a representative capacity clear, but fails to name his principal. There is, unfortunately, very little authority on this issue in Scots law and, consequently, much confusion.[205] The identity of the contracting parties may be established by applying the rule outlined above, namely, ascertaining whose credit or financial reputation the third party was relying on when he entered into the contract.[206] Alternatively, the issue may be resolved using the doctrine of election. The third party may have alternative actions against principal and agent, and must elect which of the two to hold liable.[207] The cases discussed below are perhaps the only clear examples of these two solutions in Scots law.

In *Lamont Nisbett & Co v Hamilton*[208] the agents were managing owners of a ship who instructed insurance brokers to insure the ship. When the agents went into liquidation, the insurance brokers brought an action against the owners of the ship for payment of insurance premiums. The insurance brokers were unsuccessful. The court held that they had, all along, taken the agents as their contracting parties. Lord President Dunedin reached this result by asking who the third party, the pursuers, gave credit to, and concluding that it was to the agents.[209] The insurance brokers were aware that the agents were acting in a representative capacity. The name of the principal, the owner of the ship could easily have been ascertained from the Register of Owners.[210]

In *Ferrier v Dods* an auctioneer had been instructed to sell a horse. The auctioneer was acting in a representative capacity, but the name of the principal was not disclosed. The buyer was unhappy with the quality of the horse, and considered that the seller was in breach of the warranty which he had been given to the effect that the horse was sound. After the auction, once he had found out the identity of the seller, the buyer returned the horse to the seller. It was held that the buyer would have been entitled to sue either the principal or the agent, but that, having returned the horse to the principal, he had elected to hold the principal liable as his debtor. The opinions in the case focus mainly on the issue of election, and not on whose credit the purchaser looked to when he made the purchase.

The position is clearer where the agent refuses to identify his unnamed principal. The agent will be personally liable. *Gibb v Cunningham and Robertson* provides an example of the operation of this rule.[211] A solicitor refused to name his clients, and was therefore found liable to implement a contract which he had concluded on their behalf.

---

[202] Bills of Exchange Act 1882 s.26(1).

[203] For example a church congregation in *McMeekin v Easton* (1889) 16 R. 363; and unincorporated clubs in *Thomson v Victoria Eighty Club* (1905) 43 S.L.R. 628 and *Cromarty Leasing Ltd v Turnbull*, 1988 S.L.T. (Sh Ct) 62.

[204] See para.2.1.3. above.

[205] See the comments of Lord Prosser in *P & M Sinclair v Bamber Gray Partnership*, 1987 S.L.T. 674 at 676.

[206] *Lamont Nisbet & Co v Hamilton*, 1907 S.C. 628; and see the discussion by the Inner House in *Ruddy v Monte Marco* [2008] CSIH 47, 2008 S.C. 667.

[207] *Ferrier v Dods* (1865) 3 M. 561.

[208] *Lamont Nisbett & Co v Hamilton*, 1907 S.C. 628.

[209] *Lamont Nisbett & Co v Hamilton*, 1907 S.C. 628, per Lord President Dunedin at 635, 636.

[210] See *Armour v TL Duff & Co*, 1912 S.C. 120.

[211] *Gibb v Cunningham and Robertson*, 1925 S.L.T. 608. This case could also be explained on the basis that it is an application of the presumption that the signatory of a written contract is personally bound by it.

AGENT ACTS FOR AN UNDISCLOSED PRINCIPAL

In this situation the agent is acting in a representative capacity, but this fact is entirely concealed from **2.7.4** the third party. That third party, unaware of the existence of a principal, considers that he has concluded a contract with the person with whom he is dealing (i.e. the agent). He will have no reason to suspect that that person is an agent. After the third party has concluded a contract, and during the "life" of that contract, the principal may disclose his existence and, provided that the agent has acted within his authority,[212] may sue the third party direct. The third party may also choose to sue the principal rather than the agent once the principal is disclosed. Liability is, however, alternative and not joint and several. Lord Young explained alternative liability as follows:

> ". . . if a person really acting for another goes into the market and buys as if for himself, he binds himself, but if the party from whom he buys finds out his true position then he can treat him as an agent only. He cannot have two principals to deal with, and no double remedy is allowed."[213]

The doctrine of the undisclosed principal is undoubtedly conceptually difficult. It seems to contradict important rules of the law of contract. Where it operates, the third party can be held to have concluded a contract with a party who is a complete stranger to him. It is difficult to see how *consensus in idem* can be achieved in such circumstances, even taking the law of contract's usual objective stance. Although attempts have been made to explain the legal basis of the concept none of these is convincing.[214] The concept is generally justified by reference solely to its commercial utility.[215]

Once the principal is disclosed, the third party must elect to sue either the agent or the principal.[216] Election can be express, or can be inferred from conduct.[217] Once the third party has elected, his election is final.[218] Although this point is not entirely free from doubt. Where the pursuer institutes proceedings against the relevant party but those proceedings do not progress as far as the obtaining of a decree, then an election has not taken place.[219] Only if decree has been obtained has election occurred. However, receiving a dividend on bankruptcy has been held to be the equivalent of pursuing a party to judgment and therefore the equivalent of decree.[220]

It is not always possible for the principal to act as an undisclosed principal. He may be prevented from doing so where, as a matter of interpretation of the contract which the so-called agent has concluded with the third party, the possibility of another contracting party is excluded. This may occur in several ways: the contract may contain a clause indicating that the named contracting party is the sole contracting party[221]; the definition of the contracting party may exclude an undisclosed principal by implication; or the existence of an undisclosed principal may be excluded as a matter of interpretation of the contract as a whole.[222] Importantly, however, the mere identification of a particular person as the contracting party will not without more exclude the possibility of an undisclosed principal's intervention.[223] The essential question is whether the third party has indicated an unwillingness to contract with a different party, and that question will be answered by reference to the terms of the

---

[212] *Hutton v Bulloch* (1874) L.R. 9 Q.B. 572.

[213] *Meier & Co v Küchenmeister* (1881) 8 R. 642, per Lord Young at 646.

[214] See, e.g. N. Seavey, "The Rationale of Agency" (1920) Yale L.J. 859; W. Muller-Freienfels, "The Undisclosed Principal" (1953) 16 M.L.R. 299; R. Barnett, "Squaring Undisclosed Agency with Contract Theory" (1987) 75 Calif. L.R. 1969.

[215] P.G. Watts and F.M.B. Reynolds, *Bowstead and Reynolds on Agency*, 19th edn (London: Sweet & Maxwell, 2010), para.8–071.

[216] *Bennett v Inveresk Paper Co* (1891) 18 R. 975, per Lord McLaren at 983; *Laidlaw v Griffin*, 1968 S.L.T. 278.

[217] *Ferrier v Dods* (1865) 3 M. 561, the facts of which are discussed above. Election was inferred from the buyer's conduct of returning the horse to the seller.

[218] *David Logan & Son Ltd v Schuldt* (1903) 10 S.L.T. 598; *British Bata Shoe Co v Double M Shah Ltd*, 1980 S.C. 311.

[219] *Meier & Co v Küchenmeister* (1881) 8 R. 642; *Black v Girdwood* (1885) 13 R. 243, although this case concerned a partnership and liability was thus joint and several and not alternative; *Craig & Co v Blackater*, 1923 S.C. 472.

[220] *David Logan & Son Ltd v Schuldt* (1903) 10 S.L.T. 598.

[221] *United Kingdom Mutual Steamship Assurance Association v Nevill* (1887) 19 Q.B.D 110; *JH Rayner (Mincing Lane) Ltd v Department of Trade and Industry* [1990] 2 A.C. 418, per Lord Oliver at 516.

[222] *Humble v Hunter* (1842) 12 Q.B. 310; *JA Salton & Co v Clydesdale Bank Ltd* (1889) 1 F. 110.

[223] *Talbot Underwriting Ltd v Nausch, Hogan & Murray Inc (The Jascon 5)* [2006] EWCA Civ 889; [2006] 2 Lloyd's Rep. 195, per Moore-Bick LJ at [27].

particular contract, interpreted in accordance with its surrounding circumstances.[224] Additionally, in the normal case, a third party's willingness to contract with someone other than his immediate contracting party is assumed. This point was explained by Diplock LJ in the leading English case of *Teheran-Europe Co Ltd v ST Belton (Tractors) Ltd* as follows:

> "In the case of an ordinary commercial contract such willingness of the other party may be assumed by the agent unless either the other party manifests his unwillingness or there are other circumstances which should lead the agent to realize that the other party was not so willing."[225]

It is possible that an undisclosed principal may be prevented from intervening on a contract where his concealment is carried out with the express purpose of deceiving the third party. The parameters of this exception are, however, unclear. The case usually referred to as authority for this proposition is *Said v Butt*.[226] In this case a theatre critic instructed an agent to buy a ticket for the first night of a theatre performance. He was unable to purchase a ticket himself because he knew that the managing director of the theatre would not sell a ticket to him personally. He had, in the past, criticised the managing director of the theatre. When he arrived at the theatre on the night of the performance, he was refused admission. It was held that the principal could not enforce this contract. The reasoning used by the judges is far from clear. Much of the discussion is based on the law of error rather than agency principles. The impact of the case should not, therefore, be overemphasised. The facts were very special, possibly unique, given that the performance in question was a "first night" performance, attendance at which might be akin to "invitation only". In many cases the identity of the contracting parties will not be a significant issue. If that is the case, then the third party can have no objection to the intervention of an undisclosed principal. It is only in cases where the identity of the other contracting party is significant, for example where the third party selected the agent as a contracting party because of that agent's particular skill, that the undisclosed principal can be prevented from intervening on the contract.

WHERE THE AGENT EXCEEDS HIS AUTHORITY

2.8 If the agent has exceeded his authority, and the principal cannot ratify the agent's actions, then no contract is formed between principal and third party. There are a number of ways in which an agent can be personally bound with a third party in contract. This may occur simply because the parties intended it to occur. It may also occur where the agent has acted for a non-existent principal. The issue of contractual intention is a key one in this context. The cases already referred to in which an agent acted for unincorporated associations or clubs,[227] are, in effect, cases in which an agent acted for a non-existent principal. Focusing on contractual intentions in those cases, all parties must have been aware that the principal had no legal capacity. One can infer from that that all parties must have intended the agent to be personally bound. On the facts this may not be the case, however. In *Halifax Life Ltd v DLA Piper Scotland Ltd*[228] a solicitor, acting on behalf of a consortium, negotiated missives for the sale of property. After missives were concluded it transpired that the consortium did not exist. In the context of an action against the solicitor's firm for implement of the missives, Lord Hodge emphasised that no party in the transaction could have intended the solicitor to be personally bound. It was held that he was not a party to the contract and could not be required to implement it. The third party is not, however, left with no action against the non-performing agent. Rather, he can raise an action of breach of warranty

---

[224] *Talbot Underwriting Ltd v Nausch, Hogan & Murray Inc (The Jascon 5)* [2006] EWCA Civ 889; [2006] 2 Lloyd's Rep. 195, per Moore-Bick LJ at [34].

[225] *Teheran-Europe Co Ltd v ST Belton (Tractors) Ltd* [1968] 2 Q.B. 545 at 555, quoted with approval by Moore-Bick LJ in *Talbot Underwriting Ltd v Nausch, Hogan & Murray Inc (The Jascon 5)* [2006] EWCA Civ 889; [2006] 2 Lloyd's Rep. 195 at [24]. See also *Rolls Royce Power Engineering Plc v Ricardo Consulting Engineers Ltd* [2003] EWHC 2871; [2004] 2 All E.R. (Comm) 129, especially [55]–[58].

[226] *Said v Butt* [1920] 3 K.B. 497. *Dyster v Randall & Sons* [1926] Ch 932.

[227] See para.2.7.2 above and the cases cited in footnote 203.

[228] [2009] CSOH 74, and see comment by L. Macgregor, "Acting on behalf of a non-existent principal", 2010 Edin. L.R. 92.

of authority against the agent.[229] Until recently, Scottish case law contained very few examples of this action. There may be many reasons for this, and one possible reason is that the agent is less likely to be strong financially. This makes the principal a more attractive "target" for the third party.

The action for breach of warranty of authority is contractual in nature.[230] Its exact basis is unclear, but it may be that it rests on an implied contract between agent and third party. As part of this contract the agent warrants to the third party that he is properly authorised. There is, of course, no actual contract between agent and third party, and so this implied contract is a legal fiction.[231] Because of the contractual nature of this action, fault on the part of the agent is irrelevant: the agent is liable for breach of the warranty even if he honestly believed that he was fully authorised. The measure of damages is the loss which the third party has suffered as a result of not having the principal as a contracting party.[232] The agent's misrepresentation must have actually caused the loss. The third party will not, therefore, be able to recover damages where he already knew that the agent was not authorised and did not rely on the agent's misrepresentation.[233] Given that damages seek to value what the third party has lost through not having a contract with the principal, if that contract would in any event have been a losing bargain, the third party has suffered no loss as a result of the agent's breach of warranty and can recover no damages.[234]

In recent Scottish cases attempts were made to extend the ambit of the warranty of authority as it applies to a solicitor representing a client in a conveyancing transaction.[235] The factual scenarios in the cases were similar, and can be illustrated using a fictitious example. Mr Smith lives at 100 Albion Avenue. A fraudster, Jones, pretends to be Mr Smith and produces utility bills for 100 Albion Avenue (which are stolen or forgeries). Jones induces the lender to lend to him, agreeing to grant a standard security over 100 Albion Avenue to secure the loan. Jones does not, of course, own the property, and the standard security is invalid. Jones disappears, leaving the lender out of pocket. Jones was represented by a solicitor who was also taken in by this deception. The lender (the third party using agency language) raises an action against Jones' solicitor (the agent), arguing that the solicitor has breached his warranty of authority causing the lender loss, and that compensation is due. The question then becomes what the solicitor's warranty covers. It is clear that the solicitor warrants that his client (Jones) has authorised him, but does he also warrant that his client is who he says he is, or does in fact hold title to 100 Albion Avenue? The Inner House in a judgment delivered by Lord Clarke answered this question with an emphatic "no", explaining:

> "We are of the clear view that there are no reasons in principle or practice, for extending the somewhat limited scope and nature of the implied warranty of agents in the way in which the reclaimers' submissions in the present case contended for."[236]

It is now clear that the agent's warranty of authority is limited in scope, covering only the fact that the agent has been authorised by his principal. It does not cover any other issues relating to the principal.

Generally, claims for breach of warranty of authority are raised in contract. It is possible, however, for the third party to recover damages which are delictual in nature where the agent has acted either negligently or fraudulently in misrepresenting his authority.[237]

---

[229] In *Halifax v DLA Piper* Lord Hodge suggested that such an action could be raised.

[230] *Anderson v Croall & Sons* (1903) 6 F. 153.

[231] See Gloag, p.155

[232] *Anderson v Croall & Sons* (1903) 6 F. 153.

[233] *Royal Bank Scotland v Skinner*, 1931 S.L.T. 382.

[234] *Irving v Burns*, 1915 S.C. 260.

[235] *Frank Houlgate Investment Co Ltd v Biggart Baillie LLP* [2009] CSOH 165; 2010 S.L.T. 527; [2011] CSOH 160; 2012 S.L.T. 265; [2013] CSOH 80; 2013 S.L.T. 993; *Cheshire Mortgage Corporation Ltd v Grandison; Blemain Finance Ltd v Balfour & Manson LLP* [2011] CSOH 157; 2012 S.L.T. 672; [2012] CSIH 66; 2013 S.C. 160. For comment on the latter see L. Macgregor, "The Agent's Warranty of Authority: Thus Far But No Further", 2013 Edin. L.R. 398.

[236] *Cheshire Mortgage Corporation Ltd v Grandison; Blemain Finance Ltd v Balfour & Manson LLP* [2012] CSIH 66; 2013 S.C. 160.

[237] See Gloag, p.154. Although there appear to be no Scottish cases, it is thought that Scots law would use the same basis as is used in English law, *Hedley Byrne & Co Ltd v Heller & Partners Ltd* [1964] A.C. 465.

In one case it was argued that the principal had a similar action for breach of warranty of authority against the agent.[238] Although the principal successfully recovered damages from his agent in this particular case, recovery was not on the basis of breach of warranty of authority. The principal's remedy against the agent in this type of situation is an action for breach of the agency contract. The warranty of authority is given only by the agent to the third party, and so only the third party can make use of this particular action.

2.9   TERMINATION OF THE AGENCY CONTRACT

TERMINATION UNDER THE COMMERCIAL AGENTS (COUNCIL DIRECTIVE) REGULATIONS 1993

2.9.1 Minimum periods of notice of termination are imposed by the Commercial Agents (Council Directive) Regulations 1993. These requirements apply to both parties. Either agent or principal must provide one month's notice in the first year of the agency contract; two months in the second year; and three months thereafter.[239]

The regulations contain rights on the part of the agent to receive either "compensation" or "indemnity"[240] on termination of the agency contract.[241] This part of the regulations has proved to be by far the most controversial part, and has given rise to conflicting case law in Scotland and England.

INDEMNITY AND COMPENSATION IN GENERAL

2.9.2 The contracting parties cannot, by agreement, avoid payment of compensation or indemnity. If the contract is silent on the issue of which of the two types of payment is due to the agent, then compensation and not indemnity is payable.[242] By contrast, the indemnity provisions must be expressly opted into in the agency contract.[243] The commercial agent's rights can be time-barred. He must notify the principal within a year of termination of the agency contract if he wishes to pursue his entitlement.[244]

The commercial agent's rights to either indemnity or compensation are excluded in certain situations. The agent has no right to a payment where the principal terminated the agency contract as a result of the commercial agent's breach or default caused by frustration of contract.[245] Nor is payment due where the commercial agent himself has terminated the agency contract although termination may be justified in two separate situations: firstly, where the principal is in breach of the agency contract[246]; and secondly where termination occurs due to the "age,[247] infirmity or illness of the agent in consequence of which he cannot reasonably be required to continue his activities".[248] Finally, payment is

---

[238] *Salvesen & Co v Rederi Aktiebolaget Nordstjernan* (1905) 7 F. (HL) 101.

[239] Commercial Agents (Council Directive) Regulations 1993 (SI 1993/3053) reg.15(2)(a)–(c).

[240] The words "indemnity" and "compensation" have, under the regulations, a meaning which is entirely different from (any of) their usual meanings in Scots law.

[241] See regs 17 and 18.

[242] See reg.17(2). This was the case in one of the leading Scottish cases, *King v Tunnock Ltd*, 2000 S.C. 424.

[243] See reg.17(2). An attempt by the principal through contractual drafting to award the commercial agent either compensation or indemnity, whichever is the lower, was recently held impermissible and inconsistent with the regulations. The practical effect was that the parties had not properly opted for indemnity and compensation was payable, see *Charles Shearman (t/a Charles Shearman Agencies) v Hunter Boot Limited* [2014] EWHC 47 (QB).

[244] See reg.17(9).

[245] See reg.18(a) read in conjunction with reg.16.

[246] reg.18(b)(i).

[247] Although see *Frape v Emerco International Ltd*, 2002 S.L.T. 371, where compensation was payable where the contract "terminated" on the agent's 65th birthday, as agreed in the contract.

[248] reg.18(b)(ii).

excluded where the commercial agent has assigned his rights and duties under the agency contract to another person, with the consent of the principal.[249]

THE INDEMNITY PROVISIONS

The commercial agent's right to indemnity seeks to secure for him the benefit of the work which he has **2.9.3** carried out prior to termination which would otherwise accrue to the principal.[250] His entitlement arises,

"if and to the extent that:

(1) he or she has brought the principal new customers or has significantly increased the volume of business with existing customers and the principal continues to derive benefits from the business with such customers; and

(2) the payment of this indemnity is equitable having regard to all the circumstances and, in particular, the commission lost by the commercial agent on the business transacted with such customers."[251]

Payment of indemnity is, in contrast to payment of compensation, subject to a limit of one year's commission based on the average of either the last five years of the agency, or, if the agency has lasted less than five years, the annual average over the period of the agency.[252] The fact that indemnity is subject to a limit may make the indemnity option more attractive to a principal than compensation, particularly given the uncertainty over the method of valuation of compensation, described in more detail immediately below.

In contrast to the compensation provisions, there has been very little litigation on the indemnity provisions.[253]

THE COMPENSATION PROVISIONS

The compensation provisions seek to compensate the commercial agent for the damage he suffers as a **2.9.4** result of termination of his relationship with the principal. Such damage is

"deemed to occur particularly when the termination takes place in either or both of the following circumstances, namely circumstances which—

(1) deprive the commercial agent of the commission which proper performance of the agency contract would have procured for him whilst providing his principal with substantial benefits linked to the activities of the commercial agent; or

(2) have not enabled the commercial agent to amortize the costs and expenses that he has incurred in the performance of the agency contract on the advice of his principal."[254]

These circumstances are merely examples, not an exhaustive list, of the situations in which the agent will be entitled to compensation.[255] "Termination" is interpreted widely, compensation remaining payable where the contract comes to an end on its natural expiry.[256] It is payable, for example where the agreed date of termination of the contract was the agent's 65th birthday.[257]

---

[249] reg.18(c).

[250] See reg.17(3). *Moore v Piretta PTA Ltd* [1999] 1 All E.R. 174.

[251] reg.17(3).

[252] reg.17(4).

[253] See *Moore v Piretta PTA Ltd* [1999] 1 All E.R. 174 and *Hardie Polymers Ltd v Polymerland Ltd*, 2002 S.C.L.R. 64. In the latter case, the issue was whether the contract, properly interpreted, opted for either compensation or indemnity.

[254] reg.17(7)(a), (b).

[255] See *King v T Tunnock Ltd*, 1996 S.C.L.R. 742, later overturned: see *King v T Tunnock Ltd*, 2000 S.C. 424, although not on this particular issue.

[256] *Whitehead v Jenks & Cattell Engineering Ltd* [1999] Eu. L.R. 827; *Frape v Emerco International Ltd*, 2002 S.L.T. 371; *Light v Ty Europe Ltd* [2003] 1 All E.R. (Comm) 568.

[257] *Frape v Emerco International Ltd*, 2002 S.L.T. 371.

The method of calculation of compensation has proved highly controversial. Until recently, the leading case in Scots law was *King v T Tunnock Ltd*.[258] This case is now arguably inconsistent with a subsequent English House of Lords case, *Lonsdale v Howard & Hallam Ltd*.[259] Because this area remains subject to uncertainty full discussion of *King v Tunnock* is provided here. Mr King had been employed since 1962 by Tunnocks as an agent selling Tunnock's bakery and confectionery products. His family had had a long-standing connection with the company, his father having worked for Tunnocks before him. In 1994, Tunnocks closed their bakery section, and terminated the agency relationship with Mr King. There was no written agency agreement and Mr King was given no payment in lieu of notice, nor payment of indemnity or compensation. An Extra Division of the Inner House found that Mr King was entitled to compensation.

The controversial part of the judgment lies in the use by the Inner House of principles of French law as a guide to calculation of the amount of compensation. The source of the compensation provisions is, of course, the original Directive which the British regulations implemented. It is acknowledged, however, that the Directive "borrowed" the concept of compensation from French law.[260] The Inner House was referred to the established practice in France of awarding the agent two years' loss of average gross commission.[261] Their Lordships then used this French judicial custom to assist in their assessment of Mr King's compensation, although they noted that, "even in France the two year rule is only a benchmark and can be varied at the discretion of the judge".[262] Several factors in Mr King's case supported his claim for a relatively high amount of commission, for example the long duration of the agency relationship and the high level of commission which had been generated by it. Their Lordships awarded him £27,144 which represented two year's gross commission.

The approach taken by the Inner House in *King v Tunnock* was subject to criticism in later English cases, in almost all of which the agent was awarded much less than two years' gross commission.[263] *Lonsdale v Howard & Hallam Ltd*[264] provided the House of Lords with a much-needed opportunity to clarify the law.[265] Lord Hoffmann, who delivered the principal speech in the case,[266] explained that the agent's entitlement to compensation arises because, at the moment of termination, the agent in effect "hands back" the goodwill in the principal's business which that agent helped to create.[267] Although Lord Hoffmann considered the approach of French law to valuation of compensation, he suggested that such comparisons were not helpful because of the difference in trading conditions between the UK (where agents do not tend to sell their agencies to other agents) and France (where a market in agencies exists). Finally, relying on the case of *Honeyvem Informazioni Commerciali Srl v Mariella De Zotti*,[268] decided by the European Court of Justice, he indicated that the national court enjoys a margin of discretion in relation to calculation of compensation.[269] Lord Hoffmann's emphasis of the declining nature of the principal's business had a significant reducing effect on the level of the agent's compensation. The agent was awarded the minimal amount of £5,000, Lord Hoffmann even indicating that the trial judge at first instance could not have been faulted if he had, instead, refused to award any compensation.

As a decision by the House of Lords on a piece of legislation which affects Scotland and England in the same manner, *Lonsdale v Howard & Hallam Ltd*[270] should be treated as highly persuasive, if not

---

[258] *King v T Tunnock Ltd*, 1996 S.C.L.R. 742, reversed in *King v T Tunnock Ltd*, 2000 S.C. 424.

[259] *Lonsdale v Howard & Hallam Ltd* [2007] UKHL 32; [2007] 1 W.L.R. 2055.

[260] See Watts and Reynolds, *Bowstead and Reynolds on Agency*, 19th edn (2010), para.11–046.

[261] *King v T Tunnock Ltd*, 2000 S.C. 424 at 430.

[262] *King v T Tunnock Ltd*, 2000 S.C. 424 at 439.

[263] *Barrett McKenzie v Escada (UK) Ltd* [2001] All E.R. (D) 78; *Ingmar GB Ltd v Eaton Leonard Inc* [2001] All E.R. (D) 448 QB; *Tigana Ltd v Decoro Ltd* [2003] EWHC 23 QB; *Vick v Vogle-Gapes* [2006] EWHC 1665 QB.

[264] *Lonsdale v Howard & Hallam Ltd* [2007] UKHL 32; [2007] 1 W.L.R. 2055.

[265] For comment on this case see L. Macgregor, "Compensation for Commercial Agents: An End to Plucking Figures From the Air?", 2008 Edin. L.R. 86.

[266] The decision was unanimous, Lords Bingham, Carswell, Neuberger, and (importantly for those considering this area from a Scottish perspective) Lord Rodger concurring.

[267] *Lonsdale v Howard & Hallam Ltd* [2007] UKHL 32; [2007] 1 W.L.R. 2055 at [9].

[268] *Honyvem Informazioni Commerciali Srl v Mariella De Zotti* [2006] E.C.R. 1–2879 at [34]–[36].

[269] Although that case concerned payment of indemnity, not compensation.

[270] *Lonsdale v Howard & Hallam Ltd* [2007] UKHL 32; [2007] 1 W.L.R. 2055.

binding, in the Scottish courts in future cases. The more lenient approach of the Inner House in *King v Tunnock* is probably no longer possible in the Scottish courts. This marks, in effect, a significant reduction of the compensation payable to commercial agents where, at the time of termination of the contract, the principal's business is in decline. This, it is suggested, is an unsatisfactory result, contrary to the highly protective aim of the Directive.

TERMINATION AT COMMON LAW

The agency relationship may terminate by agreement or simply on the expiry of the period of time **2.9.5** stipulated for performance.[271] The contract may also terminate because the purpose for which it was entered into comes to an end.[272] If the parties have not expressly agreed a date of termination or formula for calculating the same, then the courts will ascertain the date of termination as a matter of interpretation of the agency contract as a whole.[273]

The principal may decide to revoke the agency contract,[274] although the right to revoke may be excluded as a matter of interpretation of the contract.[275] Where the principal does revoke, he must relieve the agent of any losses suffered by him where revocation occurs before the agent has completed ongoing transactions.[276] An attempt by the principal to revoke where that is not within his power may lead to liability to the agent in damages, again as a matter of interpretation of the agency contract.[277] The agent may have the right to payment of commission on termination.

The agent may also have the ability unilaterally to revoke the agency contract. He may be liable to the principal in damages where, for example, he delays in informing the principal of his revocation[278] or renounces at a critical time.[279]

The contract between principal and agent involves *delectus personae*,[280] and, as a result, the death of either principal[281] or agent[282] terminates that contract. This does not mean, however, that the agent's authority immediately terminates. His authority continues in order to allow him to finalise any transactions which he was in the course of conducting on behalf of the principal.[283] It is thought that the agent's powers are limited to completing existing transactions and not commencing new transactions.[284]

FRUSTRATION OF THE AGENCY CONTRACT

The agency contract, like any other contract, may be frustrated by the occurrence of unexpected events. **2.9.6** Following frustration, both parties will be released from performance of their future obligations under the contract, although rights which have accrued prior to frustration are enforceable by the parties. The cessation of the principal's business will frustrate the agency contract given that the very purpose for which the agency relationship was created has ceased. The courts are very reluctant to imply a term into

---

[271] *Brenan v Campbell's Trustees* (1898) 25 R. 423; *Ferguson and Lillie v Stephen* (1864) 2 M. 804.

[272] *Price & Co v Tennent* (1844) 6 D. 659; *Black v Cullen* (1853) 15 D. 646.

[273] *Stevenson v North British Ry Co* (1905) 7 F. 1106.

[274] *Walker v Somerville* (1837) 16 S. 217; *Douglas Goodfellow and Partners v Gordon*, 1987 S.C.L.R. 684.

[275] *Galbraith and Moorhead v Arethusa Ship Co Ltd* (1896) 23 R. 1011.

[276] Erskine, *Institute*, III, 3, 40.

[277] *Galbraith and Moorhead v Arethusa Ship Co Ltd* (1896) 23 R. 1011.

[278] Erskine, *Institute*, III, 3, 40.

[279] Erskine, *Institute*, III, 3, 40.

[280] See para.2.5.4.5 above.

[281] *Pollok v Paterson*, December 10, 1811 F.C. 369, per Lord Meadowbank at 376; *Kennedy v Kennedy* (1843) 6 D. 40; *Lord Advocate v Chung*, 1995 S.C. 32.

[282] Erskine, *Institute*, III, 3, 40.

[283] See *Campbell v Anderson* (1829) 3 W. & S. 384; *Pollok v Paterson*, December 10, 1811 F.C. 369, per Lord Meadowbank at 376; although cf. *Kennedy v Kennedy* (1843) 6 D. 40.

[284] See the discussion of this same point in the context of partnership at para.8.5.3 below.

the agency contract binding the principal to continue with his particular business.[285] Although the principal may, following such termination, be liable to the agent in damages for losses suffered in the context of ongoing transactions,[286] no damages will be payable for the agent's expenditure made in anticipation of the continuation of the contract.[287]

Frustration of the agency contract can also be caused by impossibility of performance[288] or supervening illegality.[289] The sequestration or liquidation of the principal[290] or agent or mental incapacity[291] of either will have a similar effect.

---

[285] *SS State of California Co Ltd v Moore* (1895) 22 R. 562, per Lord Adam at 567; per Lord McLaren at 567.

[286] Erskine, *Institute*, III, 3, 40.

[287] *London, Leith, Edinburgh and Glasgow Shipping Co v Ferguson* (1850) 13 D. 51; *Patmore & Co v B Cannon & Co Ltd* (1892) 19 R. 1004.

[288] *Rhodes v Forwood* (1876) 1 App. Cas. 256.

[289] *Hugh Stevenson & Sons Ltd v AG für Cartonnagen-Industrie* [1918] A.C. 239.

[290] *SS State of California Co Ltd v Moore* (1895) 22 R. 562.

[291] *Pollok v Paterson*, December 10, 1811 F.C. 369 at 375, per Lord Meadowbank at 377.

Chapter 3

CONSUMER CREDIT

This chapter will mainly concern itself with an examination of the Consumer Credit Act 1974. However, it may be useful to begin with an examination of how credit may be provided and the legal nature of those arrangements.

TYPES OF CREDIT

3.1 The idea of credit may seem superficially simple, but there is a variety of types of credit and a variety of ways to classify the giving of credit. However, a relatively simple classification is the distinction between lender credit and vendor credit.

LENDER CREDIT

3.1.1 Lender credit is quite straightforward. Essentially it involves one party lending money to another. This can take the form of a loan from a financial institution, typically a bank or building society. Loans may be at fixed rates with standard monthly repayments, but can easily feature variable rates and repayments. Bank overdrafts are also a form of loan, the amount and the rate of interest typically fluctuating, and the borrower not generally being committed to make fixed repayments. Some arrangements can have features of both devices, such as where a debtor makes regular repayments on an amount owed, but is then permitted to extend his borrowing up to an agreed (often the original) figure—revolving credit. Prior to the passing of the Consumer Credit Act 1974, the making of loans was governed by the Moneylenders Acts, but as banks and building societies were exempted from that legislation, many loans were governed purely by the common law. As will be seen, assuming that they meet the prerequisites for the application of the Act, all such forms of credit now fall within the scope of the Consumer Credit Act 1974.

Sometimes the loan is secured. This might be through a simple guarantee. Alternatively, the borrower might assign his right to a payment from a third party, e.g. under a life assurance policy. Or he might pledge an item of moveable property, as where goods are pawned.[1] Or he might grant a standard security over heritable property; what might be called a mortgage by the layperson (see para.5.3.6 below). While certain types of security were governed by detailed legislation, such as the Pawnbrokers Acts, others again were governed, more or less exclusively, by the common law. As will be seen, generally if the basic transaction is governed by the Consumer Credit Act 1974 so too is any associated security transaction.

VENDOR CREDIT

3.1.2 While a loan may obviously be used to purchase goods, and indeed the borrower may be formally restricted by the terms of the agreement to use it for that purpose, vendor credit is credit actually supplied by the seller (or owner) of goods to the buyer (or hirer) to finance the transaction between them. It takes various forms.

Hire purchase

3.1.2.1 The reason why reference had to be made in the previous paragraph to hirers and owners is because of the contract of hire purchase, which is probably the most common form of vendor credit. Essentially, such an agreement sees the debtor making payments for the "hire" of the goods, with an option but not an obligation to purchase the goods either on paying the final instalment, or on paying a further sum. That sum can be purely nominal and usually is. In *Close Asset Finance v Care Graphics Machinery Ltd*[2] a "hirer" was bound to make payments in respect of goods, amounting to several million pounds

---

[1] There is a detailed and complex regime dealing with pawn under ss.114–122 of the Consumer Credit Act 1974. It will not be addressed in this Chapter, but rather in the Chapter on rights in security: see para.5.3.2 below.
[2] *Close Asset Finance v Care Graphics Machinery Ltd* [2000] C.C.L.R. 43.

over a number of years. Thereafter, it had an option to purchase the goods for £50. It was argued that this was a sale agreement, since no reasonable person would fail to exercise the option clause. It was held that as the hirer was not legally obliged to buy the goods, the contract could not be one of sale and must be a contract of hire purchase. It might be added that the most common form of hire purchase transaction involves a trader selling goods to a finance company, which then "sells" them to the debtor on hire purchase. The debtor then has no direct contractual relationship with the trader, although it is possible that the trader might be bound by any promises made to the debtor, or be delictually liable to him, whether for misrepresentations or otherwise.[3] The distinction between hire purchase and simple hire is, of course, that under the latter contract there is no intention to sell the goods and the hirer has no option to purchase. It is, however, not uncommon for certain hire contracts to extend over the economic life of the goods and to involve hire charges which are the equivalent of the sale price of the goods and the charge which might be levied for credit. Even before the passing of the Consumer Credit Act 1974, hire purchase was the subject of detailed legislative control, while hire was essentially governed by the common law. Now, both are addressed by the Act.

Credit sale and conditional sale agreements

A conditional sale agreement is simply a contract of sale where the passing of the property is subject to **3.1.2.2** a suspensive condition, typically the payment of the final instalment of the price. A credit sale agreement may often appear identical in that both types of transaction see the price paid in instalments, but the critical difference is that in a credit sale, although the goods are sold on credit, property in them usually passes immediately the contract is made. The crucial difference between credit or conditional sale and hire purchase is that in the former the buyer is bound to purchase the goods. So in *John G Murdoch & Co Ltd v Greig*,[4] where the contract referred to hire payments, the fact that the "hirer" was bound to purchase the goods meant that the contract was one of sale. Similarly, in *Forthright Finance v Carlyle*[5] a "hire-purchase" agreement bound the "hirer" to make a number of payments. After he had made the final payment he would become the owner of the goods, unless he exercised an option not to receive title to the goods. Lord Justice Phillips opined[6]:

> "This contract has all the ingredients of a conditional sale agreement. The option not to take title, which one would only expect to be exercised in the most unusual of circumstances does not affect the true nature of the agreement."

Although both credit and conditional sale agreements are contracts for the sale of goods, they are dealt with differently by the Consumer Credit Act 1974. Despite being conceptually quite distinct, conditional sale is mainly regulated alongside hire purchase, as was the case under the more recent hire purchase statutes. While credit sale did receive some limited acknowledgment under that legislation, it is not specifically recognised by the Consumer Credit Act 1974, although it would normally be regarded as a debtor-creditor-supplier agreement under that Act (see para.3.3.3.3 below).

OTHER FORMS OF CREDIT

3.1.3

Cheque trading

This involves a voucher purchased by a customer from a cheque trader, which allows the former to **3.1.3.1** purchase goods to that value from any shop prepared to accept the cheque. The most well known form of cheque trading in Scotland involves cheques issued by the Provident Clothing and Supply Co. When the customer uses the cheque to buy goods, he is charged the cash price, and the amount is marked on the back of the cheque, allowing him to spend the rest of the cheque elsewhere. The cheque trader then

---

[3] *Andrews v Hopkinson* [1957] 1 Q.B. 229.
[4] *John G Murdoch & Co Ltd v Greig* (1889) 16 R. 396.
[5] *Forthright Finance v Carlyle* [1997] 4 All E.R. 90.
[6] *Forthright Finance v Carlyle* [1997] 4 All E.R. 90 at 97b.

reimburses the retailer, typically subject to a discount. The customer pays off the amount of the cheque in instalments (traditionally weekly, but often now monthly), the total of these instalments amounting to rather more than the amount of the cheque, the difference thus representing interest paid on the amount borrowed. While the exact legal nature of cheque trading has never been determined by the higher courts, it resembles a form of money lending (and thus now potentially subject to the Consumer Credit Act 1974), and this is the view taken of it by an English county court.[7] The transaction between customer and retailer is certainly nothing more than a simple contract of sale.[8]

Credit cards

3.1.3.2 Credit cards are, of course, extremely widely used. They have certain affinities with cheque trading in that the card issued by the credit card company to a customer may then be used to purchase goods or services from any business prepared to accept the card. When a card is used to acquire goods or services, the customer signs a voucher permitting the business to claim payment from the credit card company. On presentation of the voucher, the credit card company then pays the business for the goods or services—usually subject to a discount—and recovers the full amount from the customer. Some credit cards require the customer to repay the whole amount incurred on a card during a particular period at the end of that period, e.g. American Express cards. Most cards, however, while permitting such repayment, allow customers to use the card up to a pre-arranged limit, and to repay as much or as little as the customer wishes (subject to a specified minimum payment) during each period. Interest is, of course, charged on the outstanding balance. The network of relationships described above is often slightly more complex in that businesses are often recruited for credit card companies by third parties known as merchant acquirers. Merchant acquirers may then make payments on behalf of the company and levy a charge thereon.

The legal nature of credit card transactions was considered in *Re Charge Card Services*.[9] The Court of Appeal held that there were three essential contracts involved in the use of a credit card. These were:

(1) the contract between credit card company and the retailer by virtue of which the retailer agrees to accept payment via the card and the credit card company agrees to pay the retailer for the goods or services purchased (usually subject to a discount);

(2) the contract between credit card company and the cardholder whereby the latter is issued with the card which enables him to purchase goods, and agrees to pay the company the price he was charged for those goods (plus interest if necessary); and

(3) the contract between the retailer and the cardholder whereby the former sells goods and services to the latter on the basis that payment via the card was accepted in substitution for payment by cash.

This means that the retailer[10] "must . . . be taken to have accepted the company's obligation to pay in place of liability on the customer to pay [the retailer] direct."

Thus the cardholder's obligation to the retailer is entirely discharged by tendering the card in payment, and does not revive if the credit card company fails to pay the retailer. Equally, the cardholder is liable to pay the credit card company, whether or not the company pays the retailer. It seems to follow from the above analysis that, if the card is used in circumstances where the company is under no obligation to pay, e.g. where a credit limit has been exceeded, the use of the card does not discharge the customer's obligation to pay the retailer. It is then an interesting question whether he would be liable to pay the full amount for the goods or services, or the discounted amount the retailer expected to receive from the credit card company. The status of credit card transactions under the Consumer Credit Act 1974 is considered in detail below (see para.3.6.3.1).

---

[7] *Premier Clothing Co Ltd v Hillcoat*, reported at para.4.1.64, Committee on Consumer Credit, *Report of the Committee on Consumer Credit* (HMSO, 1971), Cmnd.4596.

[8] *Davies v Commissioners of Customs and Excise* [1975] 1 W.L.R. 204.

[9] *Re Charge Card Services (No.2)* [1989] Ch. 497.

[10] *Re Charge Card Services (No.2)* [1989] Ch. 497, per Sir Nicholas Browne-Wilkinson V.C. at 513H–514A.

It might be added that payment for goods and services via a debit card involves immediate payment from the customer's bank account through an electronic transfer of funds. There is no substitution of a right of payment by the customer by a right of payment by the bank. Depending on the state of the customer's bank account, such transactions may or may not involve the granting of credit by the bank to the customer. In the *Charge Card* case it was unsuccessfully argued that payment by credit card was analogous to payment by cheque, as it was common ground that payment by cheque or any other bill of exchange was conditional, the buyer's liability remaining if the cheque were not honoured.[11] Where payment by cheque is accompanied by the use of a cheque guarantee card, then the holder of that card has authority from the bank to make an offer to the retailer, which if acted upon, creates contractual relations between the bank and the retailer.[12] If the conditions relating to the use of the card are observed, the bank undertakes to meet the sum for which the cheque is drawn, whether or not its customer has sufficient funds in his account. This is not however a contract of guarantee (cautionary obligation), but rather an independent contract between bank and customer.[13] Nonetheless, even where a guarantee card is used, it is probable that payment by cheque remains conditional and does not discharge the buyer's liability if, despite the use of the card, the cheque is dishonoured.[14] In other words, use of a cheque guarantee card does not substitute a right of payment by the bank for a right of payment by the customer. Instead it adds a parallel right of payment by the bank.

Retailers' revolving credit

Some retailers operate a system whereby the customer makes regular fixed payments (usually monthly) **3.1.3.3** allowing him to obtain goods or services from the retailer on credit up to a specified multiple of his payments. For example, a customer who is bound to pay £50 per month might be allowed 10 times that amount, i.e. £500, in credit at any one time. As each payment is made, the customer is permitted to obtain goods or services provided the credit limit is not exceeded. Interest would usually be charged on the amount of credit outstanding at the end of each month. The legal nature of such arrangements is undecided. They are not direct cash loans, as the amount of credit is dependent upon the value of the goods or services obtained. They are certainly not hire purchase transactions. There is, however, some support that they amount to a series of credit sales[15] and thus potentially subject to the Act.

INTRODUCTION TO THE ACT—THE CROWTHER REPORT

The law of consumer credit has until recently been largely comprehended by the Consumer Credit Act **3.1.4** 1974, and in many important respects still is. However, as will be seen below, many of the provisions of the Act have been repealed and replaced by rules made by the Financial Conduct Authority ("FCA"). While the FCA rules are generally very similar in effect to the provisions of the Act and related statutory instruments which they replace, they have already imposed extra requirements not found in the previous legislation.[16] For example, there are additional rules in relation to high-cost, short-term credit, i.e. unsecured loans which are designed to be repaid inside 12 months or less, where the APR is at least 100 per cent (popularly known as payday loans). The number of times which such loans can be 'rolled over', i.e. a further loan taken out to pay off an existing loan, is to be capped at two.[17] Additionally, where the

---

[11] *Re Charge Card Services (No.2)* [1989] Ch. 497 at 511D–E; and see *McLaren's Trs v Argylls Ltd*, 1915 2 S.L.T. 241.

[12] See Evans LJ in *First Sport Ltd v Barclays Bank Plc* [1993] 3 All E.R. 789 at 794e.

[13] Lord Justice Evans in *First Sport Ltd v Barclays Bank Plc* [1993] 3 All E.R. 789 at 795d opines: "The bank's undertaking that the payment of the cheque is 'guaranteed' does not mean that its contract with the payee, when the offer is accepted, is strictly a contract of guarantee. It is a separate and independent obligation which is not dependent in any way upon default by the customer . . . in performance of any obligation which he incurs. To this extent, the commonly used description of such cards as 'cheque guarantee cards' is strictly a misnomer."

[14] *Re Charge Card Services* [1987] Ch. 150, per Millett J at 166C.

[15] See *NG Napier Ltd v Patterson*, 1959 J.C. 48; and authorities cited at para.4.1.64, *Report of the Committee on Consumer Credit* (HMSO, 1971), Cmnd.4596.

[16] See FCA, *Detailed rules for the FCA regime for consumer credit* (February 2014), para.1.4.

[17] FCA, *Detailed rules for the FCA regime for consumer credit* (February 2014), p.48.

debtor has granted a continuous payment authority, i.e. authorised the creditor to take payments of any amount the latter wishes at any time from his debit or credit card, the number of failed attempts to recover the amount of a payday loan via this method is limited to two.[18] Moreover, the FCA intends to consult in the summer on proposals to cap the cost of high-cost, short-term credit.[19] The FCA indeed is charged[20] with a review of the remaining provisions of the Act with a view to seeing whether their repeal is also possible. Thus the treatment of this area in the next edition of this work may be radically different.

The genesis of the 1974 Act lies in the 1971 *Report of the Committee on Consumer Credit*[21]—the Crowther Report. The report found that the then existing law relating to credit transactions was seriously defective, inter alia, because:

- transactions were regulated according to historical legal form rather than their substance and function;
- the law was excessively technical; and
- the law failed to distinguish between consumer and commercial transactions, and conferred inadequate protection upon consumers.

The committee felt that piecemeal reform of the law would not be adequate. Instead it recommended repeal of the great mass of existing legislation and its replacement by two Acts. One would be designed to harmonise the treatment of all forms of consumer credit, strengthening the position of the consumer and creating effective enforcement mechanisms. The other would restructure the general law of credit and security. The government, however, was not convinced of the necessity of the latter measure,[22] and pressed ahead only with the former recommendation. The result was the Consumer Credit Act 1974. Although the Act creates the general framework for the regulation of consumer credit, much of the substance of that regulation takes the form of the detailed provisions of statutory instruments, reference to which will be made where appropriate. It might be added that the DTI announced a review of the Act in 2001. There followed a number of consultation documents[23] laying out possible routes to reform and ultimately a White Paper, *Fair, Clear and Competitive—The Consumer Credit Market in the 21st Century*,[24] providing a blueprint for reform. Most of the proposals contained in the White Paper have since received legislative effect, either in the form of statutory instruments or through the medium of the Consumer Credit Act 2006. That Act effected substantial amendments to the 1974 Act. Further amendments resulted from EU initiatives. The Unfair Commercial Practices Directive (2005/29) aimed to establish an elaborate consumer protection regime, which would overlap in certain respects with the regime created by the 1974 Act. While the Directive did not permit Member States to maintain national provisions which exceeded its scope of protection, one exception under Article 3.2 related to provisions governing contracts. This meant that the parallel protections under the 1974 Act would continue to operate. However, the imposition of criminal sanctions went beyond the scope of that exclusion. Accordingly, the Consumer Protection from Unfair Trading Regulations 2008,[25] which implement the Directive, repealed a number of provisions of the 1974 Act which created criminal offences, albeit that much of that behaviour would continue to be criminal under the Regulations. The EU then issued the Consumer Credit Directive 2008 (2008/48) with a view towards achieving greater harmony across Member States in this area of law. This was sought to be implemented by the Consumer Credit (EU Directive) Regulations 2010,[26] amending the 1974 Act in relation to agreements entered into on or after February 1, 2011. For the sake of simplicity, it is the new regime which will be described.

---

[18] FCA, *Detailed rules for the FCA regime for consumer credit* (February 2014), pp.52–55.

[19] FCA, *Detailed rules for the FCA regime for consumer credit* (February 2014), para.1.5.

[20] By Part V of the Financial Services and Markets Act (Regulated Activities) Amendment Order 2014 (SI 2014/366).

[21] *Report of the Committee on Consumer Credit* (HMSO, 1971), Cmnd.4596.

[22] See para.14, *Reform of the Law of Consumer Credit* (HMSO, 1973), Cmnd.5427.

[23] e.g. Department of Trade and Industry, *A Consultation Document on the Licensing Regime under the Consumer Credit Act 1974*. DTI, 2002. Department of Trade and Industry, *Tackling Loan Sharks and More!* DTI, 2003.

[24] *Department of Trade and Industry, Fair, Clear and Competitive—The Consumer Credit Market in the 21st Century* (The Stationery Office, 2003), Cm.6040.

[25] Unfair Trading Regulations 2008 (SI 2008/1277).

[26] Consumer Credit (EU Directive) Regulations 2010 (SI 2010/1010).

Introduction

The impact of legislation designed to protect consumers is considerably enhanced by the creation of **3.2.1** effective enforcement machinery. Large parts of the pre-Act regime depended entirely upon individual consumers for enforcement. Money lending and pawnbroking featured licensing systems, but these were largely ineffective because of the decentralised nature of these systems and the lack of a single authority responsible for enforcement. Thus responsibility for the overall administration and enforcement of the 1974 Act and associated regulations was that of the Office of Fair Trading ("OFT"), with enforcement at local level being the responsibility of weights and measures authorities. However that responsibility is being transferred from the OFT to the Financial Conduct Authority ("FCA") with a view to ensuring that a single body has responsibility for the regulation of all forms of financial services.[27] The OFT was abolished by s.26(3) of the Enterprise and Regulatory Reform Act 2013.

One of the main controls created by the 1974 Act was a comprehensive licensing system operated by the OFT. This, however, has been replaced by making any activity which previously required a licence a regulated activity under s.22 of the Financial Services and Markets Act,[28] thus falling within the authorisation regime of the FCA.[29] Thus Part III of the 1974 Act is entirely repealed.[30] It is not proposed to examine the new regime, since it addresses the conduct of business rather than the regulation of individual credit transactions.

THE CONCEPTUAL STRUCTURE OF CONSUMER CREDIT— REGULATED AGREEMENTS
3.3

Introduction

As well as providing for the overall control of the credit industry through the now abolished licensing **3.3.1** system, the Act looks to regulate individual credit transactions. It was anticipated that the Act would regulate all forms of consumer credit, but, as will be seen, there are certain forms which fall outwith the scope of the Act. Moreover, the original Act comprehended certain agreements although no consumer was involved, given that it defined an individual so as to include a business so long as it was not a body corporate. It was anticipated that the 2006 Act might alter this so as to define the term individual as referring only to an actual physical person, but instead the new definition indicates that the term "individual" includes:

(1) a partnership consisting of two or three persons not all of whom are bodies corporate; and

(2) an unincorporated body of persons which does not consist entirely of bodies corporate and is not a partnership.

Category (1) obviously contemplates a small firm, while category (2) would include a social or sporting club. Nonetheless, the latter category could conceivably include an association comprised of a number of large companies together with one actual person.

---

[27] Financial Services Act 2012 s.7 amended the Financial Services and Markets Act 2000 so that the FCA has responsibility for regulating the provision of credit and hire and the operation of credit reference and credit advice services: see s.22(1A) and Sch.2, paras 23–24H of the 2000 Act. See also s.107 of the 2010 Act.

[28] Financial Services Act 2012 ss.107–108.

[29] One of the bodies created by the Financial Services Act 2012 to replace the Financial Services Authority. It is the new conduct of business authority: see *A New Approach to Financial Regulation*, Cm 8268, Ch.4. See also Ch.1 of the Financial Services and Markets Act 2000.

[30] See Financial Services and Markets Act 2000 (Regulated Activities) (Amendment) (No.2) Order 2013 (SI 2013/1881); Financial Services and Markets Act (Regulated Activities) Amendment Order 2014 (SI 2014/366).

Such bodies are still regarded as deserving of the protections conferred by the Act, and it should be recalled throughout this discussion of the Act that the term "individual" has this particular meaning.

In essence, the Act applies to all regulated agreements entered into by "individuals". These are consumer credit agreements, consumer hire agreements and exempt agreements.

CONSUMER CREDIT AGREEMENT

3.3.2 A consumer credit agreement is an agreement by which the creditor provides the debtor with credit of any amount.[31] Credit is defined by s.9(1) as including "a cash loan or any other form of financial accommodation". This means that not only loans but hire purchase, credit sale and conditional agreements fall within the definition. Hire purchase agreements indeed are specifically included.[32] However, in *Joyce v Barlow*[33] it was said that a deferment of payment in the absence of a contractual right to defer was a mere indulgence and not a financial accommodation amounting to credit. In *Office of Fair Trading v Ashbourne Management Services Ltd*[34] the OFT argued that a contract whereby an individual paid for gym membership on a monthly basis involved the provision of credit. Rejecting that (admittedly, fairly extraordinary) argument, Kitchen J[35] drew a distinction between "cases in which a liability or obligation to pay is incurred or, but for the payment terms, would have been incurred at the outset, and is discharged in instalments . . . [and] cases in which payment falls due in stages as the contact is performed." It may be added that a creditor includes the assignee of a creditor, who may thus enforce the agreement, but is subject to the various duties imposed on a creditor by the Act.[36]

Prior to the 2006 amendments, if the credit exceeded £25,000, the agreement would not be regulated by the Act. It was thus vital to determine the amount of credit provided, so that it was necessary to differentiate between the actual credit provided and what the debtor was charged for credit. Although it is no longer necessary to ascertain the amount of credit for this purpose, the question of what the debtor was charged for credit remains of vital importance in a variety of contexts such as the provisions relating to the form of agreements, interest chargeable on default, and rebates on early settlement. Thus the Act continues to state that in calculating the amount of credit supplied, the total charge for credit is not taken into account.[37] The meaning of the total charge for credit has always been prescribed by regulations of some complexity. These were originally the Consumer Credit (Total Charge for Credit) Regulations 1980,[38] which were then largely supplanted by the Consumer Credit (Total Charge for Credit) Regulations 2010,[39] which implement art.19 of and Annex 1 to the Consumer Credit Directive. However, both are now entirely supplanted by the Financial Services and Markets Act 2000 (Regulated Activities) Order 2001,[40] supplemented by FCA Rules.

TYPES OF CREDIT AGREEMENT

3.3.3 The Act subdivides credit agreement into a variety of types.

---

[31] See s.8(1).

[32] See s.9(3).

[33] *Joyce v Barlow*, 1999 C.L. February 262.

[34] *Office of Fair Trading v Ashbourne Management Services Ltd* [2011] EWHC 1237 (Ch).

[35] *Office of Fair Trading v Ashbourne Management Services Ltd* [2011] EWHC 1237 (Ch) at [95].

[36] See *Jones v Link Financial Ltd* [2013] 1 W.L.R. 693; especially Hamblen J at [28]–[36].

[37] See s.9(4). This provision goes on to state that an item which is part of the total charge for credit shall not be treated as credit, merely because time is allowed for its payment. See *Humberclyde Finance Ltd v Thompson* [1997] C.C.L.R. 23; *Griffiths v Welcome Financial Services* [2007] C.C.L.R. 3.

[38] Consumer Credit (Total Charge for Credit) Regulations 1980 (SI 1980/51) as amended.

[39] Consumer Credit (Total Charge for Credit) Regulations 2010 (SI 2010/1011).

[40] See SI 2001/544 art.60M.

Fixed sum and running account credit

Fixed sum credit means precisely that—the amount of credit is established and does not vary.[41] A loan **3.3.3.1** would be one example—so would a hire purchase agreement. Running account credit allows the debtor to obtain, from time to time, cash, goods or services from the creditor or a third party.[42] Examples would be an overdraft, a store card or a credit card.

The reasons why a distinction is drawn between fixed sum and running account credit are, firstly, the criteria as to whether an agreement is exempt vary according to which category it occupies, and secondly, the prescribed form of the agreements will differ.

Restricted and unrestricted use credit

This distinction is made in line with the recommendation of the Crowther Committee that credit should **3.3.3.2** be dealt with according to the purpose it serves, rather than its legal form. It is particularly helpful in distinguishing between debtor-creditor and debtor-creditor-supplier agreements, and in working out whether an ancillary agreement qualifies as a linked transaction under the Act. A restricted use credit agreement under s.11(1) involves the credit being used to finance a specific transaction between the debtor and either the creditor or another person (the supplier). A typical example of this would be a hire purchase agreement. An unrestricted use credit agreement under s.11(2) sees the debtor free to use the credit as he wishes. A good example of this would be an overdraft. In terms of s.11(3), an agreement which provides that credit must be used for a specific purpose will still count as an unrestricted use credit agreement if the credit is provided in such a way as to leave the debtor free to use it as he chooses (albeit in breach of contract). Essentially, when the credit is intended to finance a transaction with a supplier, the funds must be transferred directly to the supplier if the agreement is to be seen as a restricted use credit agreement.

Debtor-creditor agreements and debtor-creditor-supplier agreements

Every credit agreement must be either a debtor-creditor agreement or a debtor-creditor-supplier agree- **3.3.3.3** ment. The Act is interested in agreements where there is a business connection between the creditor and the supplier, taking the view (see para.3.6.3 below) that the fate of the credit and supply contracts should be to some degree intertwined. These are debtor-creditor-supplier agreements. Debtor-creditor-supplier agreements may involve only two parties, such as where the supplier of goods and services also makes available the credit.[43] One example would be a store card. Another would be a hire purchase agreement where the trader sells the goods to the finance company, which then supplies both the goods and credit to the debtor. Alternatively, three parties may be involved, as where a restricted use credit agreement is used to finance a transaction between the debtor and supplier under existing arrangements or in contemplation of future arrangements between the creditor and the supplier.[44] Cheque trading (see para.3.1.3.1 above) provides an example of this. Another example would be the use of a credit card, whereby the card issuer has arranged with the supplier that it will furnish the credit to finance the purchase of goods and services. Use of a debit card ordinarily creates neither a debtor-creditor agreement nor a debtor-creditor-supplier agreement, as no credit is normally granted. If a customer is permitted to draw on an overdraft via a debit card, the purchase of goods or services with this facility on the face of it would create a debtor-creditor-supplier agreement. However, the Act specifically prevents this outcome,[45] and the use of the card as described creates a simple debtor-creditor

---

[41] See s.10(1)(b).

[42] See s.10(1)(a). If a person looks to obtain credit in order to purchase particular goods or services, and is persuaded to take out a store card to finance the transaction, then while it may appear that this is a form of fixed sum credit, the view has been taken that this is simply the first instance of drawing on a running account credit facility—*Goshawk Dedicated (No.2) v Bank of Scotland* [2006] 2 All E.R. 610.

[43] See s.12(a).

[44] See s.12(b).

[45] See s.187(3A).

agreement. Use of a credit card simply to obtain money also creates a debtor-creditor agreement. The same is true when a debit card is used to obtain money by drawing on an overdraft facility. If the money is obtained from a retailer through a "cash back" facility, that retailer is simply to be regarded as the lender's agent, and not a party to the transaction.

An unrestricted use credit agreement made by the creditor under pre-existing arrangements with the supplier, in the knowledge that the credit is to be used to finance a transaction between the debtor and the supplier, also falls to be regarded as a debtor-creditor-supplier agreement. So if, for example, you need a loan to buy a car and the dealer sends you round to a finance company with which he has an understanding, the loan being made in the knowledge that it will be used to purchase the car sets up a debtor-creditor-supplier agreement, even though there is no formal restriction on the use of the money. The crucial element is the connection between the creditor and supplier. If a creditor lends a debtor money to acquire a car, then it does not matter that the creditor is aware of the purpose of the loan or even of the identity of the supplier, if there is no arrangement between the creditor and supplier. This is a debtor-creditor agreement, not a debtor-creditor-supplier agreement.[46]

CONSUMER HIRE AGREEMENTS

3.3.4 Under s.15 this is an agreement whereby an "individual" (see para.3.3.1 above) hires goods, and: (1) is not a hire purchase agreement; and (2) is capable of subsisting more than three months. The first condition is designed to draw a distinction between hire proper and hire purchase, which is in essence a form of credit and is regulated in a different way under the Act. The second condition is designed to exclude short-term hire, such as daily or weekly vehicle rental. It may be noted that an agreement for an indefinite period or for a definite period of, say, a year does not cease to fall within the condition merely because either party is entitled to terminate at any time. Equally, an agreement which stipulates a hire period of three months, but which allows for the option of renewal, also falls within the condition. In both cases the agreement is capable of subsisting more than three months.[47] A contract under which an individual makes equipment available in his premises for the use of his customers and, in return for a commission, passes on to the owner of the equipment the money which his customers pay for using it, is not a consumer hire agreement.[48]

CREDIT HIRE AGREEMENTS

3.3.5 This is not a category of agreement recognised by the Act, but a strange hybrid emerging from commercial practice. Typically, such agreements arise where a motorist whose car has been disabled in an accident is permitted to hire a replacement for the period during which his own car is out of commission. The hire charges do not have to be paid until the conclusion of an action for damages against the other motorist, which the lessor is given the right to pursue in the motorist's name. The lessor then looks to deduct the cost of its services from damages recovered on behalf of the motorist. In *Dimond v Lovell*[49] it was contended that such arrangements did not involve the provision of credit. According to Lord Hoffmann,[50] the argument of the company was that the

---

[46] See s.13.

[47] But see *Burdis v Livsey* [2002] 3 W.L.R. 762 CA.

[48] *TRM Copy Centres UK Ltd v Lanwall Services Ltd* [2009] 1 W.L.R. 1375.

[49] *Dimond v Lovell* [2000] 2 All E.R. 897 HL.

[50] *Dimond v Lovell* [2000] 2 All E.R. 897 at 903g–h. He also points out the advantages of this sort of arrangement from a consumer's point of view at 910b–c: "By virtue of her contract, she obtained not only the use of the car but additional benefits as well. She was relieved of the necessity of laying out the money to pay for the car. She was relieved of the trouble and anxiety of pursuing a claim . . . She was relieved of the risk of having to bear the irrecoverable costs of successful litigation and the risk . . . of having to bear the expense of unsuccessful litigation." However, companies do not render those extra services free. A charge for them is typically built into the cost of hire. It was the view of their Lordships that the cost of those extra services were not recoverable from the other party. Damages under this head would be limited to an amount equivalent to the bare cost of hiring a replacement car.

"services provided to D were not only the use of the car but also the pursuit of her claim. If one treats these obligations as forming part of an entire contract, [the company] could not recover any part of the consideration unless it had not only allowed D the use of the car, but also brought the claim for damages to a conclusion. Only at this point would [the company] become entitled to payment and therefore the provision for 'credit' was not really credit at all. Payment was not postponed beyond the date at which it would in any event have first become payable."

Yet this argument foundered on the fact that the company had a right but not a duty to pursue the claim. Accordingly, in allowing D to defer payment until damages had been obtained from L, the company was indeed providing her with credit. Thus such an agreement may amount to a consumer credit agreement, and possibly also a consumer hire agreement under the Act.

EXEMPT AGREEMENTS

Under s.16 and associated orders, certain types of agreement which would otherwise be regulated **3.3.6** agreements used to be excluded from the scope of the Act. Now s.16 is repealed, but the same broad categories of exempt agreement are reconstituted under the Financial Services and Markets Act 2000 (Regulated Activities) Order 2001,[51] supplemented in certain cases by FCA Rules. The categories include:

- certain types of consumer hire agreement where the consumer leases metering equipment from a public telecommunications operator or gas, electricity or water authorities;
- certain types of consumer credit agreement where the creditor is either a local authority or a specified organisation or an organisation of a specified description, e.g. certain specified building societies, friendly societies, insurance companies, charities, trade unions and land improvement companies, and the agreement is secured by a heritable security. This exemption would tend to exclude most mortgages and other loans secured on land;
- fixed sum debtor-creditor-supplier agreements (other than hire purchase or credit sale agreements or those secured by pledge, i.e. pawn) where the number of payments to be made by the debtor is four or fewer, those payments are made within a period of 12 months beginning with the date of agreement and the credit is provided without interest or any other charges;
- debtor-creditor-supplier agreements financing the purchase of land where the number of payments to be made by the debtor is four or fewer, and the credit is provided without interest or any other charges;
- debtor-creditor-supplier agreements for running account credit where the credit has to be repaid in full by a single repayment in respect of a period not exceeding three months and there are either no charges or only insignificant charges payable for the credit, e.g. certain types of charge card where the debtor is required to repay the amount of credit in full at the end of each month;
- debtor-creditor agreements where the cost of credit is low, i.e. where the rate of interest does not exceed the higher of 13 per cent or 1 per cent above the base rate of the major banks in operation 28 days before the date on which the agreement was made. It would be extremely rare for a commercial lender to make such a low cost loan, but this exception would embrace the practice of certain businesses of making loans to employees on very favourable terms; and
- consumer credit agreements connected with foreign trade.

The same fate is suffered by the categories of exempt agreement created by s.16A (high net worth debtors and hirers), s.16B (the business exemption) and s.16C (the investment property exemption). The first two categories are considered in detail in the previous edition of this work (see paras 3.3.6.1,

---

[51] See SI 2001/544 arts 60D, 60H, 60O and 60Q.

3.3.6.2). The third category is designed to ensure that buy to let mortgages did not fall within the Act following the removal of the £25,000 ceiling.

SMALL AGREEMENTS

3.3.7 The Act continues to apply to regulated agreements no matter how small the sum involved. However, it is recognised that it would be unduly burdensome to require creditors to comply with all the provisions of the Act where small sums are involved. Accordingly, the provisions of the Act relating to formalities and cancellation rights (see paras 3.5.7, 3.5.10 below) do not apply to small agreements. These are regulated consumer credit or consumer hire agreements where the credit given or hire payments do not exceed £50.[52] But a conditional sale or hire purchase agreement can never be a small agreement.[53] Nor can any agreement which is secured otherwise than by a guarantee or indemnity.[54] Again, if a transaction which involves credit in excess of £50 is split into two or more agreements, these cannot be small agreements.[55]

NON-COMMERCIAL AGREEMENTS

3.3.8 The provisions of the Act relating to formalities and cancellation rights (see paras 3.5.7, 3.5.10 below) similarly do not apply to non-commercial agreements. These are regulated consumer credit or consumer hire agreements not made by the creditor/owner in the course of a business carried on by him. This provision is directed towards the situation where a private individual provides credit, such as loans between friends or family.[56] Yet the word "business" was interpreted in *Hare v Schurek*[57] as referring to a consumer credit or consumer hire business, despite the plain words of the Act suggesting no such restriction. Thus a hire purchase agreement entered into in the course of a car dealing business was treated as a non-commercial agreement.

MULTIPLE AGREEMENTS

3.3.9 These are either agreements which are divided into different parts falling under different categories under the Act, or an agreement which is indivisible but the terms of which place it in more than one category.[58] As regards the former type the principle to be followed is that each part is to be treated as a separate agreement and dealt with accordingly, while an agreement of the latter type must be treated as falling into each category. An example of the former type is a contract between bank and customer which operates under significantly different provisions depending on whether or not the customer is overdrawn. Where the customer is not overdrawn, no credit is being given and thus the agreement is not regulated by the Act at all. Where he is, it is clearly a regulated debtor-creditor agreement. Another example is that of credit hire agreements (see para.3.3.5 above), which can be both consumer hire and consumer credit agreements. An example of the latter type is the issue of a credit card which also allows cash to be drawn. If used in this way, it clearly creates a debtor-creditor relationship, while if used as a credit card it creates a debtor-creditor-supplier relationship. The agreement falls into both categories and is regulated accordingly.

---

[52] See s.17(1).
[53] See s.17(1).
[54] See s.17(1).
[55] See s.17(3).
[56] In *Khodari v Tamimi* [2009] EWCA 1109; ad hoc loans which a bank manager made from his own pocket to a customer of the bank were held not to be made in the course of a business carried on by him.
[57] *Hare v Schurek* [1993] C.C.L.R. 47.
[58] See s.18.

LINKED TRANSACTIONS

The Act acknowledges that when a regulated agreement is entered into, it may be accompanied by **3.3.10** certain ancillary agreements, e.g. when a television is hired or bought on credit, the consumer may be persuaded to enter into a maintenance contract or a contract insuring the set against damage. The view the Act takes is that where such agreements are clearly linked to the main contract then any rights enjoyed under the main agreement in relation to withdrawal, cancellation or early settlement equally apply to the main agreement. A linked transaction is entered into by the debtor or hirer (or a relative) and any other party. To qualify as a linked transaction in terms of s.19 it must:

(1) be a transaction entered into in compliance with the main agreement, e.g. if it is a condition of obtaining a loan that the customer takes out ill health or unemployment insurance; or

(2) be financed by a debtor-creditor-supplier agreement involving three parties, e.g. if a car dealer sends the consumer along to a finance company to obtain a loan to purchase a car, the contract for the sale of the car is a linked transaction (similarly if a credit card is used to buy goods, the sale contract is a linked transaction); or

(3) be a transaction initiated by:

    (a) the creditor or owner or his associate;

    (b) a person who in the negotiation of the transaction is represented by a credit broker who is also a negotiator in antecedent negotiations for the principal agreement;

    (c) a person who, at the time the transaction is initiated, knows that the principal agreement has been made or contemplates that it might be made and that person initiated it by suggesting it to the debtor or hirer (or his relative), who enters into it:

        (i) to induce the creditor or owner to enter into the principal agreement; or

        (ii) for another purpose related to the principal agreement; or

        (iii) where the principal agreement is a restricted use credit agreement for a purpose related to a transaction financed or to be financed by the principal agreement.

The types of situation which fall within category (3) include the situation where the creditor or dealer simply persuades the debtor to enter into a maintenance contract, or where the creditor simply refuses to enter into the main agreement unless the debtor enters into a maintenance contract (without making it a formal condition of the former contract that the debtor enters the latter).[59]

It may be noted that any agreement for the provision of a security, e.g. a guarantee, cannot be a linked transaction.[60]

SEEKING BUSINESS/SEEKING CREDIT

Having introduced the conceptual framework employed by the Act, before proceeding to examine how **3.4** the Act controls the operation of regulated agreements, it is useful to consider how the Act safeguards the consumer at the pre-contractual stage, through controls on advertising, quotations and canvassing. Some attention will also be paid to safeguards for individuals seeking credit.

---

[59] But in *Goshawk Dedicated (No.2) v Bank of Scotland* [2006] 2 All E.R. 610, Ferris J assumed (at [82]) that the Act would only apply if it was the party to the ancillary contract who persuaded the debtor to enter into it. This is surely erroneous.
[60] See s.19(1).

RECOVERING FEES FROM CREDIT BROKERS

3.4.1 Consumers may approach credit brokers seeking an introduction to a source of credit. The Act aims to offer some protection against the possibility of a credit broker charging a substantial fee for seeking to obtain credit, while aware that the consumer is unlikely to receive credit. So where the consumer wants to make a consumer credit or consumer hire agreement, or a credit agreement to finance the purchase of a house, or a credit agreement secured on land, if the credit broker's introduction does not lead to a relevant agreement within six months thereof, the consumer cannot be liable to pay the broker a fee or commission in excess of £5. If he has already paid, he is entitled to recover any sum in excess of £5.[61]

CREDIT INTERMEDIARIES

3.4.2 The provisions regulating credit intermediaries under s.160A of the Act are repealed since such matters fall with FCA Rules.

CREDIT REFERENCE AGENCIES

3.4.3 It is very important for those involved in the business of giving credit to know whether a potential customer is a good risk. Thus organisations have emerged specialising in collecting information regarding the credit histories of individuals, which information they will sell to credit givers. These are credit reference agencies. The difficulty for the consumer is that he can be refused credit essentially because of the information supplied by one of these agencies, without ever discovering that this is the case. Thus, under s.157(A1), when a creditor decides not to proceed with a regulated agreement (other than an agreement secured on land or a consumer hire agreement[62]) on the basis of information obtained from a credit reference agency, he must when informing the debtor of the decision advise the debtor that the decision has been reached on the basis of information from a credit reference agency and provide the debtor with its particulars, including[63] its name, address and telephone number. It can be seen that the information must be provided automatically when a credit reference agency has been instrumental in an individual being refused credit. In any other case s.157(1) states that a creditor, owner or negotiator must, within seven working days of receiving a written request from the consumer, supply the name and address of any credit reference agency from which information had been sought about his financial standing.[64] Naturally, a creditor or owner in this context would include prospective creditors or owners. This obligation does not apply to any request made more than 28 days after the termination of negotiations.[65] It is an offence to fail to comply with ss.157(A1) or 157(1).[66] However, information need not be disclosed under s.157 if disclosure would contravene the Data Protection Act 1998; is prohibited by an EU obligation; would, or would be likely to, prejudice the prevention or detection of crime, the apprehension or prosecution of offenders, or the administration of justice; or would create or would be likely to create a serious risk that any person would be subject to violence or intimidation.[67]

A consumer which is a firm or unincorporated body can under s.158 then make a written request to a credit reference agency to provide a copy of any file it holds on the firm or body, at the same time tendering a fee of £2. Assuming the agency has been provided with such particulars as it may reasonably require in order to identify the file, it must respond within seven working days, even if it is only

---

[61] See s.155.

[62] See s.157(4).

[63] These are the minimum details which must be provided, but a creditor may choose to provide further details, such as an email address.

[64] See also the Consumer Credit (Credit Reference Agency) Regulations 2000 (SI 2000/290).

[65] See s.157(2).

[66] See s.157(3).

[67] See s.157(2A).

to indicate that it does not hold a file on the consumer.[68] A "file" means any information kept about the consumer by the agency, however stored, and reduced to a transcript in plain English if not stored in plain English.[69] Along with the file the credit reference agency must provide a statement indicating the consumer's right under s.159 to have wrong and prejudicial information corrected or removed from the file.[70] Failure to comply with any provision of s.158 is an offence.[71] A consumer who is an individual has similar rights under the more general terms of s.7 of the Data Protection Act 1998.

When the right[72] to have wrong and prejudicial information corrected or removed from the file is exercised, the credit reference agency must, within 28 days of receiving the relevant notice from the consumer, inform him that it either has made the appropriate corrections or deletions or has taken no action, and give him a copy of any amended entry.[73] Within 28 days of being so notified (or if not notified, within 28 days of the expiry of the period during which he should have been notified), a consumer, unless he has been informed that the incorrect entry has been deleted, may serve a further notice requiring it to add to the file an accompanying notice of correction (not exceeding 200 words).[74] This means that the consumer can suggest his own correction if the agency declines to amend, or makes an amendment with which he disagrees. The idea is that the agency would then have to include a copy of the consumer's amendment when supplying information including or based on the challenged entry.

The agency then has a further 28 days to indicate that it intends to comply.[75] However, if it appears to the agency that it would be improper to publish such amendment because it is incorrect, defamatory, frivolous, scandalous, or otherwise unsuitable, then it may refer the matter to the relevant authority, who may make such an order as it thinks fit.[76] The consumer may also make such a reference should the agency fail to respond within the 28-day period.[77] The relevant authority will be the FCA where the consumer is a firm or unincorporated body, but otherwise will be the Information Commissioner.[78] It is an offence to fail to comply with such an order.[79]

ADVERTISING

3.4.4 The controls formerly imposed by ss.43 to 47 of the Act and associated orders are now removed and replaced by the provisions of the FCA's financial promotion regime.[80]

QUOTATIONS

3.4.5 Section 52 used to authorise the making of regulations regarding the form and content of any document by which a person who carries on a consumer credit or consumer hire business, gives prospective customers information about the terms on which he is prepared to do business, and requiring such persons to provide quotations to individuals who seek them. Detailed regulations were indeed made, but s.52 and related orders have been repealed and such matters will now be addressed by FCA rules.

---

[68] See s.158(1); Consumer Credit (Credit Reference Agency) Regulations 2000 (SI 2000/290).
[69] See s.158(5).
[70] See s.158(2).
[71] See s.158(4).
[72] Under s.159(1).
[73] See s.159(2).
[74] See s.159(3).
[75] See s.159(4).
[76] See s.159(5)(b).
[77] See s.159(5)(a).
[78] See s.159(8).
[79] See s.159(6).
[80] See Financial Services and Markets Act 2000 (Financial Promotion) Order 2005 (SI 2005/1529), although s.46 had previously been replaced by the Consumer Protection from Unfair Trading Regulations 2008 (SI 2008/1277).

CANVASSING

3.4.6 The Act seeks to prohibit the doorstep peddling of loans. Thus canvassing debtor-creditor agreements off trade premises is a criminal offence.[81] Canvassing signifies soliciting a consumer to enter a regulated agreement by making oral representations during a visit which was not previously arranged.[82] Indeed even if the visit was arranged an offence is still committed if the request was not in writing and signed by (or on behalf of) the person making it.[83] Trade premises mean the business premises, not only those of the creditor, but also a supplier, the canvasser or even the debtor.[84] So no offence is committed if the representative of a finance company visits the debtor's shop to persuade him to borrow money. Nor is an offence committed if a debtor is persuaded to enter into an agreement off trade premises where the canvasser had not visited for that purpose, e.g. where a loan is agreed as the result of a chance encounter at a social event.[85] As a result of a determination by the Director General of Fair Trading it is not an offence for a representative of a bank to canvass off trade premises in order to persuade a customer to accept an overdraft on his current account. Obviously, it is not a criminal offence to canvass debtor-creditor-supplier agreements such as hire purchase agreements. Finally, it is a criminal offence to canvass off trade premises the services of a credit broker, debt adjuster or debt counsellor.[86]

CIRCULARS TO MINORS

3.4.7 By virtue of s.50, it is an offence to send, with a view to financial gain, to a person under 18 a document inviting him to borrow money, obtain goods or services on credit, hire goods or even apply for information about any of these things. However, if a circular which happens to be sent to a minor indicates that the particular facility is not open to anyone below 18, then it does not invite that minor to obtain the facility.[87] It has also been held that, if a sender can show that applications from minors were refused as a matter of policy, any such communication would not be sent to a minor "with a view to financial gain", and thus no offence is committed where the minor receives such a document.[88]

UNSOLICITED CREDIT TOKENS AND CREDIT CARD CHEQUES

3.4.8 The provisions relating to unsolicited credit tokens under s.51 and to credit card cheques under ss.51A and 51B are replaced by FCA Rules to largely the same effect.

3.5   # ENTERING INTO AGREEMENTS

INTRODUCTION

3.5.1 Regulated agreements are contracts and thus to some extent are entered into in the same way as any other contract. So in *Brophy v HFC Bank*[89] filling in an application form for a credit card was treated as an offer to enter into a contract, which would be accepted by the creditor counter-signing the form

---

[81] See s.49(1).
[82] See s.48(1).
[83] See s.49(2).
[84] See s.48(2).
[85] See s.48(1)(a).
[86] See s.154.
[87] *Alliance & Leicester Building Society v Babbs* [1993] C.C.L.R. 77.
[88] *Alliance & Leicester Building Society v Babbs* [1993] C.C.L.R. 77.
[89] *Brophy v HFC Bank* [2011] E.C.C. 14.

and creating an executed agreement in terms of s.61 (see para.3.5.7). The argument that the application was a mere invitation to treat was rejected since the form made it clear that it contained a request for credit and that the applicant should not sign it unless he was willing to be bound by the terms and conditions set out therein. Nor was the situation caught by s.59, which renders void agreements which purport to bind a person to enter into a prospective regulated agreement, e.g. an agreement for the sale of goods under which the buyer agrees to enter into a credit agreement in order to enable him to pay the price. That section did not apply to an offer to enter into an agreement.

Moreover, Pt V of the Act sets up a number of protections for individuals who might enter into consumer credit agreements. However, there are certain types of agreement which are excluded from the provisions of Pt V. These are:

(1) non-commercial agreements[90] (see para.3.3.8 above), although the provisions relating to antecedent negotiations (see para.3.5.6 below) do apply here[91];

(2) agreements which meet all of the following criteria[92]; being:

    (a) a small agreement (see para.3.3.7 above);
    (b) for restricted use credit; and
    (c) a debtor-creditor-supplier agreement.

An example would be a credit sale agreement where the amount of credit does not exceed £50. Once again the provisions relating to antecedent negotiations apply here, as do the regulations on disclosure of information (see para.3.5.2) and the provisions relating to withdrawal from agreements (see para.3.5.9).[93]

There is also an exclusion which only applies where the FCA permits it. It may be made subject to such conditions as the FCA thinks fit, and only where it considers the exclusion not to be against the interests of debtors.[94] This is a debtor-creditor agreement to finance the making of such payments arising on, or connected with the death of a person as may be prescribed.[95] However, a number of provisions do apply in this context—the regulations on disclosure of information and the form and content of agreements (see para.3.5.7), the provisions relating to antecedent negotiations, adequate explanations, assessment of creditworthiness, copies of draft agreements, the signing of agreements, the duty to supply a copy of executed agreements (see para.3.5.8), and withdrawal from agreements.[96]

There used to be a similar exclusion relating to a debtor-creditor agreement enabling the debtor to overdraw on current account. However, the FCA plays no role regarding exclusions regarding overdrafts, and more of the provisions of Part V apply to overdrafts, depending on what sort of overdraft is involved. The Act speaks of authorised non-business overdraft agreements. These are agreements when the overdraft is authorised in advance, which are not entered into wholly or predominantly for the purposes of the debtor's business (if any), and under which the credit must be repaid on demand or within three months. If an agreement would be an authorised non-business overdraft agreement but for the fact that the credit is not repayable on demand or within three months, then all the provisions mentioned in regard to the previous exclusion apply.[97] If an agreement *is* an authorised non-business overdraft agreement, then all those provisions, except those relating to adequate explanations, the signing of the agreement and withdrawal, apply.[98] If an agreement is an authorised business overdraft agreement, then only the regulations on the form and content of agreements and the provisions relating to antecedent negotiations, assessment of creditworthiness, and the duty to supply a copy of executed agreements,

[90] See s.74(1)(a).
[91] See s.74(1A).
[92] See s.74(1)(d).
[93] See s.74(2).
[94] See s.74(3).
[95] See s.74(1)(c).
[96] See s.74(1F).
[97] See s.74(1D).
[98] See s.74(1C).

apply.[99] In relation to any other overdraft agreement only the provisions relating to antecedent negotiations apply.[100]

The provisions of Pt V are examined in the succeeding paragraphs.

PRE-CONTRACTUAL INFORMATION

3.5.2 The Consumer Credit (Disclosure of Information) Regulations 2010[101] demand that any prospective creditor must disclose certain information to a prospective debtor. The regulations do not apply to certain agreements[102]:

- an agreement to which s.58 (opportunity for withdrawal from prospective land mortgage, see para.3.5.8) applies;
- an authorised non-business overdraft agreement which is for credit which exceeds £60,260 or is secured on land;
- any other agreement for credit exceeding £60,260;
- any other agreement secured on land;
- an agreement entered into by the debtor wholly or predominantly for the purposes of his business.

In the last three cases the Consumer Credit (Disclosure of Information) Regulations 2004[103] or where applicable the Financial Services (Distance Marketing) Regulations 2004[104] (see para.3.5.11) continue to apply. However, the creditor may choose to provide information as directed by the 2010 Regulations as opposed to either set of 2004 Regulations.[105] Failure to comply with the regulations means that the agreement can only be enforced by the creditor via an order of the court[106] (see para.3.8.2 below).

The sort of information which must be disclosed depends on how the agreement is to be entered into. However, apart from special cases, in good time[107] before the agreement is made, the creditor must disclose to the debtor in the prescribed manner the standard pre-contract credit information.[108] This comprises[109]:

(1)   the type of credit;
(2)   the identity and geographical address of the creditor and, where applicable, of the credit intermediary,
(3)   the total amount of credit to be provided and the conditions for drawing on it[110];
(4)   the duration or minimum duration of the agreement or a statement that the agreement has no fixed or minimum duration;

---

[99] See s.74(1B).

[100] See s.74(1E).

[101] SI 2010/1013. These regulations implement arts 5.1 to 5.5, and art.6.4 of the Consumer Credit Directive and arts 3.1 to 3.3 and 5.2 of Directive 2002/65/EC concerning the distance marketing of consumer financial services.

[102] See reg.2.

[103] SI 2004/1481. These are discussed in the previous edition of this work.

[104] SI 2004/2095.

[105] See reg.2(4)–(5).

[106] See s.55(2). This goes on to provide that a retaking of the goods or land to which the agreement relates amounts to enforcement.

[107] That phrase is not defined and the Department for Business Innovation and Skills, *Guidance on the Regulations Implementing the Consumer Credit Directive* (2010), para.9.4 indicates that its meaning "will depend on the precise circumstances of the transaction", but continues (para.9.5) that the debtor "must be given adequate opportunity to consider the pre-contractual information (and any accompanying explanation) before being invited to sign the credit agreement".

[108] See reg.3(2); unless that information has already been disclosed to the debtor by a credit intermediary in the prescribed manner: reg.3(3).

[109] See reg.3(4).

[110] In the case of running-account credit, the total amount of credit may be an indication of how the credit limit will be determined where it is not practicable to express the limit as a sum of money.

(5) in the case of credit in the form of deferred payment for specific goods, services or land, or a linked credit agreement, a description of the goods, etc., the cash price of each and the total cash price;

(6) the rate of interest charged, any conditions applicable thereto, any reference rate (e.g. Bank of England lending rate) on which that rate is based and any information on any changes to the rate (including the periods that the rate applies, and any conditions or procedure applicable to changing it)[111];

(7) the APR and the total amount payable under the agreement illustrated (if not known) by way of a representative example[112] mentioning all the assumptions used in order to calculate that rate and amount;

(8) the amount (expressed as a sum of money), number (if applicable) and frequency of repayments to be made by the debtor and, where appropriate, the order in which repayments will be allocated to different outstanding balances charged at different rates of interest[113];

(9) any charges for maintaining an account recording both payment transactions and draw downs (i.e. money going in or out), unless the opening of an account is optional, and any charge payable for using a method of payment in respect of payment transactions or draw downs (e.g. direct debit charges);

(10) any other charges and the conditions under which they may be changed;

(11) if applicable, a statement that fees will be payable by the debtor to a notary on conclusion of the agreement;

(12) any obligation to enter into an ancillary contract such as an insurance contract, where the conclusion of such a contract is compulsory in order to obtain the credit or to obtain it on the terms and conditions marketed;

(13) the rate of interest applicable in the case of late payments, the arrangements for its adjustment, and any default charges;

(14) a warning regarding the consequences of missing payments (e.g. possible legal proceedings, repossession of debtor's home);

(15) any security to be provided by or on behalf of the debtor;

(16) the existence or absence of a right of withdrawal;

(17) the debtor's right of early repayment under s.94, and where applicable, information concerning the creditor's right to compensation and the way in which that compensation will be determined;

(18) the requirement to inform a debtor under s.157A(1) a decision not to proceed with a prospective agreement has been reached on the basis of information from a credit reference agency and of the particulars of that agency,

(19) the debtor's right under s.55C to be supplied on request with a free copy of the draft agreement except where the creditor is at the time of the request unwilling to make the agreement, or the agreement is in an excluded category or is a pawn agreement,

(20) if applicable, the period of time during which the creditor is bound by the above information.

---

[111] Where different rates of interest are charged in different circumstances the creditor must provide this information in respect of each rate.

[112] For this purpose, where the debtor has informed the creditor or credit intermediary of one or more components of his preferred credit, such as the duration of the agreement or the total amount of credit, and where the creditor would in principle agree to offer credit on such terms, the creditor or credit intermediary must take those components into account when calculating the representative APR and the total amount payable. In the case of running-account credit, where the credit limit is not known at the date on which the pre-contract credit information is disclosed, the total amount of credit is to be assumed to be £1,200 or in a case where credit is to be provided subject to a maximum credit limit of less than £1,200, an amount equal to that maximum limit: reg.3(5).

[113] In the case of running-account credit, the amount of each repayment is to be expressed as (a) a sum of money; (b) a specified proportion of a specified amount; (c) a combination of (a) or (b); or (d) where the amount of any repayment cannot be expressed in accordance with (a), (b) or (c), a statement indicating the manner in which the amount will be determined.

A different approach is taken to agreements[114] made by telephone. If the agreement is a distance contract,[115] then the full range of information mentioned in the previous paragraph must be provided before the agreement is entered into, and this may be done orally.[116] However, the debtor may explicitly consent to a narrower range of information being disclosed.[117] If that happens the creditor must state that the full range of information can be made available on request, indicating the nature of that information.[118] The information to be disclosed is[119]:

- the identity of the person on the phone and his link with the creditor;
- a description of the main characteristics of the credit agreement which includes the information mentioned under headings 3 to 8 in the previous paragraph;
- the total price to be paid for the credit including all taxes paid via the creditor or, if an exact price cannot be indicated, the basis for its calculation enabling the debtor to verify it;
- notice of the possibility that other taxes or costs may exist that are not paid via or imposed by the creditor;
- whether or not there is a right to withdraw under s.66A, or a right to cancel under reg.9 of the Financial Services (Distance Marketing) Regulations 2004[120] and, where there is a right to cancel, its duration and the conditions for exercising it, including information on the amount which the consumer may be required to pay under reg.13, as well as the consequences of not exercising that right.

Where the agreement is not a distance contract, e.g. where although the contract is made by phone there were previous face to face discussions between the parties, then the creditor need only supply a description of the main characteristics of the credit agreement which includes the information mentioned under headings 3 to 8 in the previous paragraph.[121] It is important to add that in relation to all agreements made by telephone, whether distance contracts or not, the creditor must disclose to the debtor in the prescribed manner the full standard pre-contract credit information *immediately after* the agreement is made.[122] This may allow the debtor to reflect upon the agreement and consider whether he wishes to withdraw even before he receives a copy of the agreement.

If an agreement[123] is made at the debtor's request, using a means of distance communication other than telephone which does not enable the provision before the agreement is made of the pre-contract credit information, the creditor must disclose to the debtor in the prescribed manner the full standard pre-contract credit information immediately after the agreement is made.[124]

Where a distance contract is entered into by the debtor wholly or predominantly for the purposes of his business, while the creditor may choose to meet the requirements of whichever of regs 3, 4 or 5 applies in that case, he is regarded as complying with those regulations by disclosing the relevant information immediately after the agreement is entered into.[125] It is also the case that, while in regard to a distance contract to which reg.3, 4 or 5 applies, the creditor must ensure that the information provided to the debtor includes the contractual terms and conditions (including details of contractual obligations

---

[114] Other than authorised non-business overdraft agreements: reg.4(1).

[115] A distance contract is an agreement made under an organised distance sales or service-provision scheme run by or on behalf of the creditor who, for the purpose of that agreement, makes exclusive use of one or more means of distance communication up to and including the time at which the agreement is made. A means of distance communication is any means which may be used for the making of an agreement without the simultaneous physical presence of the parties. Thus contracts where all negotiations, etc. take place exclusively via telephone or e-mail or a combination thereof are distance contracts: reg.1(2).

[116] See reg.4(2).

[117] See reg.4(2).

[118] See reg.4(2).

[119] See reg.4(2).

[120] SI 2004/2095.

[121] See reg.4(3).

[122] See reg.4(4).

[123] Other than an authorised non-business overdraft agreement: reg.5(1).

[124] See reg.5(2).

[125] See reg.6.

arising under the applicable law, i.e. terms implied by law). This requirement does not apply to a contract entered into by the debtor wholly or predominantly for the purposes of his business.[126]

While the standard pre-contract credit information must be provided in relation to pawn agreements, if the debtor is not a new customer, the creditor need only inform him in good time before the agreement is made of his right to receive that information, free of charge, on request.[127] In other words such a debtor need only be provided with the information if he asks for it. In this context the debtor is a new customer if he has not entered into a pawn agreement with the creditor in the three years preceding the start of the negotiations antecedent to the agreement.[128]

As regards information being disclosed in the prescribed manner, this means by way of the Standard European Credit Information Form, which is laid out in Sch.1 of the Regulations.[129] That form must be in writing, and capable of being removed by the debtor.[130] Any additional information provided by the creditor must be in a separate document to the form.[131] Yet where the agreement is a multiple agreement, the information in respect of each part may be provided in the same form, provided that information that is not common to each part of the agreement is disclosed separately within the relevant section of the form and it is clear which information relates to which part.[132]

The Regulations deal somewhat differently with authorised non-business overdraft agreements. (There is no requirement regarding pre-contractual information with regard to business overdraft agreements.) Thus, in good time before the agreement is made the creditor must disclose certain information to the debtor in the prescribed[133] manner.[134] To some extent this information overlaps with the standard pre-contract credit information mentioned above, i.e. in relation to the information mentioned under headings 1, 2, 6, 7 13, 18 and 20. Otherwise it comprises[135]:

- the total amount of credit;
- the duration of the agreement;
- the conditions and procedure for terminating the agreement;
- where applicable, an indication that the debtor may be requested to repay the amount of credit in full on demand at any time;
- the charges, other than the rates of interest, payable by the debtor under the agreement (and the conditions under which they charges may be varied).

However, the full set of information described above does not necessarily have to be given if[136]:

- the agreement is made by telephone (whether or not it is a distance contract);
- the agreement is made at the debtor's request using a means of distance communication, other than a telephone, which does not enable the provision of the relevant information before the agreement is made;
- the agreement does not come within either of the above categories but the debtor requests that the overdraft be made available immediately.

If the agreement is made by telephone and is a distance contract, then the full set of information must be given before the agreement is made unless the debtor explicitly consents to more limited

---

[126] See reg.7.
[127] See reg.9.
[128] See reg.1(6).
[129] See reg.8(1).
[130] See reg.8(2).
[131] See reg.8(4).
[132] See reg.8(5).
[133] In this context this means that the creditor may either employ the European Consumer Credit Information form set out in Sch.3, ensuring that any information contained in the form is clear and easily legible, or else simply disclose the information in writing so that all information is equally prominent: see reg.11.
[134] See reg.10(2).
[135] See reg.10(3).
[136] See reg.10(4).

information.[137] This is all but identical to the the narrower range of information to be disclosed under reg.4(2), discussed above.[138] Where the agreement is made by telephone and is not a distance contract, the approach is practically identical to that taken by reg.4(3), discussed above.[139] The same applies if the agreement falls under the third of the above bullet points.[140] In all the above cases the information can be provided orally. If in a situation falling under the first or third of the above bullet points a current account is held in joint names, disclosure need only be made to one debtor, provided that each has consented to this.[141] If the agreement falls under the second of the above bullet points, then there is no requirement to provide pre-contractual information.

PRE-CONTRACTUAL EXPLANATIONS AND ADVICE

3.5.3 The provisions of s.55A relating to the creditor providing the debtor with an adequate explanation of certain matters in order to place him in a position enabling him to assess whether the agreement is adapted to his needs and his financial situation, and with relevant advice, are replaced by FCA rules to similar effect.

Assessment of creditworthiness

3.5.4 The provisions of s.55B demanding that, before making a regulated consumer credit agreement or significantly increasing the amount of credit to be provided or a credit limit for running-account credit under an existing regulated consumer credit agreement, the creditor must undertake an assessment of the debtor's creditworthiness, are replaced by FCA rules to similar effect.

Copy of draft agreement

3.5.5 Before the agreement is actually entered into, if the debtor so requests, the creditor must give him without delay a copy of the prospective agreement or such of its terms as have then been reduced to writing.[142] The creditor need not do so if he is unwilling to proceed with the agreement.[143] Failure to provide a copy is a breach of statutory duty,[144] although it may prove difficult to prove that loss resulted from such a breach.

ANTECEDENT NEGOTIATIONS

3.5.6 The Act impinges on pre-contractual negotiations through the concept of antecedent negotiations. These are[145] any negotiations with the debtor or hirer conducted by:

    (1) the creditor or owner; or

---

[137] See reg.10(5A). It is also the case in relation to distance contracts a creditor must ensure that the information he provides regarding the contractual obligations which would arise if the contract were concluded, accurately reflects the contractual obligations which would arise under the applicable law: see reg.10(7).

[138] See reg.10(5).

[139] See reg.10(6).

[140] See reg.10(8).

[141] See reg.10(9).

[142] Section 55C(1). Section 55C looks to give effect to art.6.6 of the Consumer Credit Directive 2008, 48/EC.

[143] Section 55C(2). Nor does the provision apply to an agreement secured on land, or pawn agreements, nor where the amount of credit exceeds £60,260, nor where the debtor enters into it in the course of his business: s.55C(4). If the agreement contains a declaration by the debtor that he has entered into the agreement wholly or predominantly for the purposes of a business carried on or intended to be carried on by him, that will be presumed to be the case unless, when the agreement is entered into, the creditor (or any person who has acted for him in connection with entering into the agreement) knows or has reasonable cause to suspect that this is not in fact the case: s.55C(5).

[144] Section 55C(3).

[145] See s.56(1).

(2) a credit broker who supplies the creditor with goods to be supplied to the debtor under a debtor-creditor-supplier agreement involving two parties, e.g. when an individual looks to buy furniture from a shop on hire purchase, and the shop sells the furniture to the finance company which then enters into a hire purchase agreement with the individual; or

(3) the supplier in a debtor-creditor-supplier agreement involving three parties, e.g. the store from which goods are bought using a credit card.

Negotiations begin when the negotiator and the debtor first enter into communication, including communication by advertisement, and include all representations made by the negotiator to the debtor and any other dealings between them.[146] The point of all of this is that in categories (2) or (3) above the negotiator is treated as acting both for himself and as the creditor's agent, i.e. the creditor is liable for the negotiator's misrepresentations, etc.[147] The Act seeks to preclude any attempt to avoid this, in that an agreement is void to the extent that it purports to make the negotiator the debtor's agent, or to relieve the creditor of liability for the negotiator's acts or omissions.[148] As regards (2) the agency only extends to representations "in relation to the goods sold or proposed to be sold" by the dealer to the creditor. This is an important qualification. In *UDT v Whitfield*[149] W was interested in acquiring a new car on hire purchase, although he already had a car on hire purchase. The car dealer offered him a trade in allowance which would be more than sufficient to pay the outstanding balance in relation to the existing hire purchase agreement, and undertook to clear off that balance. The remaining amount owed on the new car was to be financed by hire purchase agreement with UDT. In the event, the dealer failed to clear off the balance under the first agreement. W argued that UDT was liable for the dealer's failure to fulfill this obligation. The county court agreed, taking the view that as far as W was concerned, the purchase of the new car, the trade in agreement and the undertaking to pay off the outstanding sum on the old car were a single transaction. Thus the promise to pay off the outstanding sum could be regarded as a representation "in relation to the goods sold". However, in *Powell v Lloyds Bowmaker Ltd*,[150] which featured very similar facts, that reasoning was explicitly rejected. The sheriff insisted that "the goods sold" meant only the new car, so that the finance company could not be liable for any representation made by the dealer as regards paying the sum outstanding on the car being traded in. The Court of Appeal has since ruled that *Whitfield* is correct and *Powell* is wrong.[151]

FORM AND CONTENT OF AGREEMENTS

Regulations made under s.60 prescribe the form and content of any agreement. These used to be the **3.5.7** Consumer Credit (Agreement) Regulations 1983[152] but these have largely been supplanted by the Consumer Credit (Agreement) Regulations 2010,[153] which implement art.10 of the Consumer Credit Directive. However, the 2010 Regulations do not apply to certain types of agreement[154] unless pre-contract credit information has been disclosed in compliance with the Consumer Credit (Disclosure of Information) Regulations 2010[155] (see para.3.5.2). In other words, if the creditor follows the 2010 regime in relation to pre-contractual disclosure, even otherwise excluded agreements are subject to the 2010 version of the Agreement Regulations. The excluded types are: an agreement under which the

---

[146] See s.56(4).

[147] The courts were reluctant to find an agency relationship in such situations at common law, even when the dealer played a significant role in arranging the contract: see *Branwhite v Worcester Works Finance Ltd* [1969] 1 A.C. 552.

[148] See s.56(3).

[149] *UDT v Whitfield* [1987] C.C.L.R. 60. Should the goods be sold by the dealer to a third party, e.g. a credit broker, who in turn sells them on to the creditor, then the conditions prescribed by the Act are not met and the creditor is not made liable under s.56 for anything said or done by the dealer: *Black Horse Ltd v Langford* [2007] C.C.L.R. 5.

[150] *Powell v Lloyds Bowmaker Ltd*, 1996 S.L.T. (Sh Ct) 117.

[151] *Forthright Finance Ltd v Ingate* [1997] 4 All E.R. 99.

[152] SI 1983/1553.

[153] SI 2010/1014.

[154] See reg.2(2).

[155] SI 2010/1013, see r.2(5).

creditor provides the debtor with credit which exceeds £60,260; an agreement entered into by the debtor wholly or predominantly for the purposes of his business; and an agreement secured on land other than an agreement to which s.58 (opportunity for withdrawal from prospective land mortgage, see para.3.5.8) applies.[156] All these excluded agreements will continue to be subject to the 1983 Regulations. Agreements to which s.58 apply will also continue to be subject to the 1983 Regulations unless the creditor chooses to comply with the 2010 Regulations.[157] The approach adopted by the 1983 Regulations is described in the previous edition of this work. The current edition will concentrate on the 2010 Regulations.

In terms of the form and content of agreements, while separate provision is made for pawn agreements where a pawn-receipt is given which is not separate from any document embodying the agreement[158] and for authorised overdraft agreements,[159] the documents embodying an agreement must otherwise contain the information specified in Sch.1. Some of that information must appear in relation to all agreements, while certain information need only appear in relation certain types of agreement.[160] The information must be presented in a clear and concise manner[161] and for information to be clear the wording, apart from any signature, must be easily legible and of a colour readily distinguishable from the background.[162] Such documents must also contain statements of the protection and remedies available to debtors under the Act as indicated in Sch.2,[163] and details of any security provided in relation to the agreement by the debtor.[164] Where documents embody both the principal agreement and a subsidiary agreement which finances the premium under a payment protection insurance policy, or a contract of shortfall insurance, or a contract of insurance relating to the guarantee of goods supplied under the principal agreement, the creditor has the option of including only the information and statements of protection, and remedies that apply to the principal agreement.[165]

In terms of s.61(1) an agreement is not properly executed, and thus cannot be enforced by the creditor except if the court so orders, unless:

---

[156] See reg.2(3).

[157] See reg.2(1A).

[158] See reg.6. The receipt must state the names of the parties and the nature of the agreement, contain a statement indicating that an article has been taken in pawn and a description of the article, and include a notice in the form laid out in Sch.3 dealing with the debtor's right to redeem the article and the consequences if he does not.

[159] See reg.8. Thus the following information shall be specified in writing in a clear and concise manner: the type of credit; the identities and geographical addresses of the creditor, debtor and any credit intermediary involved; the duration of the agreement; the credit limit and the conditions governing its drawdown; the rate of interest charged, any conditions applicable thereto, any reference rate on which it is based and any information on changes to the rate (including the periods that it applies, and any conditions or procedure applicable to changing it) where different rates of interest are charged in different circumstances the information must be provided in respect of each rate; the total charge for credit, calculated at the time the agreement is made, mentioning all the assumptions used in order to calculate it (but not in the case of an authorised business overdraft agreement, or an authorised non-business overdraft agreement secured on land); an indication that the debtor may be requested to repay the amount of credit in full on demand at any time; and the charges payable by the debtor under the agreement (and the conditions under which they may be varied). The requirement for the information to be clear includes a requirement that the wording is easily legible and of a colour which is readily distinguishable from the background medium upon which the information is displayed.

[160] See reg.3(1). There are 33 headings in Sch.1, so it is nor proposed to lay out all the required information here. However, certain information which is prescribed in terms of s.61(1) is discussed below. Otherwise, the information which is required includes such matters as a statement of the legal nature of the agreement, e.g. "hire purchase agreement", details of the parties, the duration, how the credit is provided, the total charge for credit, the APR, the total amount payable, details of certain fees and charges, and details of certain rights under the Act.

[161] See reg.3(2). The Department for Business Innovation and Skills, *Guidance on the Regulations Implementing the Consumer Credit Directive* (2010), para.10.7 states that information is unlikely to be clear and concise if set out in different documents or "interspered to such an extent that parts of the information are unlikely to be read or have an impact."

[162] See reg.3(3).

[163] See reg.3(4).

[164] See reg.3(5).

[165] See reg.3(6)–(7).

- a document in prescribed form, containing all prescribed terms and conforming to the Regulations is signed in the prescribed manner by both the debtor or hirer and by or on behalf of the creditor or owner[166]; and
- the document embodies all the terms of the agreement, other than implied terms[167]; and
- the document is, when presented or sent to the debtor or hirer for signature, in such a state that its terms are readily legible.[168]

If any term is not legibly presented, then not only is there a breach of s.61, but the term might not be enforceable under the Unfair Terms in Consumer Contracts Regulations 1999. Indeed, even if all the requirements of the Act are complied with, a term might not be enforceable under the regulations merely because it is expressed in language which, though perfectly clear to a lawyer, is not plain and intelligible to a layperson.[169] The prescribed terms in this context[170] are the amount of credit or the credit limit,[171] the rate of interest (including any conditions governing the application of the rate, the period during which it applies and the conditions and procedure for changing it), and the number (if applicable) and frequency of repayments to be made by the debtor. It can be appreciated that, while s.61(1)(a) only demands that the prescribed terms appear, s.61(1)(b) then insists that the document contains all express terms of the agreement. As regards the document being signed[172] in the prescribed manner, that document shall contain a space indicated for the purpose of the debtor's signature,[173] e.g. a signature box. The document shall be signed by the debtor[174] in the indicated space and the date of signature shall be inserted in that space.[175] It shall also be signed by or on behalf of the creditor and the date of the signature inserted, but there is no need to have a particular space for that signature and date.[176] That being said, except where an agreement is cancellable (see para.3.5.10), the date on which the unexecuted agreement becomes executed (i.e. when both signatures appear) may be inserted, and then that is the only date which need be inserted.[177] If a later agreement modifies the agreement, but any information required by Sch.1 or reg.8 is not changed, it is sufficient that a statement in the modifying agreement clearly indicates that the information in the earlier agreement remains unchanged.[178] Such a statement must be contained in the document which is signed by the debtor[179] unless the modifying agreement is an authorised overdraft agreement.[180] If the key information is changed in any respect, the requirements of the Regulations must be met.

COPIES OF THE AGREEMENT

Where an agreement has been made, s.61A insists that the creditor must give the debtor a copy of the **3.5.8** agreement and any other document referred to therein[181] unless the debtor already has a copy of the

---

[166] See s.61(1)(a).

[167] See s.61(1)(b).

[168] See s.61(1)(a).

[169] See Unfair Terms in Consumer Contracts Regulations 1999 (SI 1999/2083) reg.7.

[170] See reg.4(1).

[171] This limit may be expressed as a sum of money; a statement that it will be determined by the creditor from time to time and that notice of it will be given by the creditor to the debtor; a sum of money together with a statement that the creditor may vary the limit to such sum as he may from time to time determine and that notice of it will be given by the creditor to the debtor; or, in a case not falling within the above heads, either a statement indicating the manner in which the limit will be determined and that notice of it will be given by the creditor to the debtor, or a statement indicating that there is no limit: see Sch.1 para.7. See also *Napier v HFC Bank Ltd*, 2010 S.L.T. (Sh Ct) 174; *Brophy v HFC Bank* [2011] E.C.C. 14.

[172] For electronic signatures see reg.4(5).

[173] See reg.4(2).

[174] Or by or on behalf of the debtor in the case of a partnership or an unincorporated body.

[175] See reg.4(3)(a).

[176] See reg.4(3)(b).

[177] See reg.4(3)(c).

[178] See reg.5(2).

[179] See reg.5(3).

[180] See reg.5(3A).

[181] See s.61A(1).

unexecuted agreement and this is in identical terms.[182] In this latter case the creditor must inform the debtor in writing when the agreement has been executed, indicating that it is in identical terms to the agreement of which the debtor has a copy, and telling the debtor he has the right to a copy of the executed agreement if he so requests within 14 days of receiving such information.[183] The creditor must respond to such a request without delay.[184] Any failure to meet the above requirements means that the agreement is not properly executed.[185]

Section 61A does not apply to copies of overdraft agreements which are the subject of separate provision under s.61B. This states that, when an authorised[186] overdraft agreement has been made, a document containing its terms must be given to the debtor. This document must be provided before or at the time the agreement is made.[187] However, in certain cases the document must be provided immediately after the agreement is made. These are when authorised non-business (see para.3.5.1) overdraft agreements are made by telephone or by some other means of distance communication which does not enable the provision of pre-contractual information before the agreement is made, or where authorised non-business overdraft is requested with immediate effect.[188] Yet where the full extent of pre-contractual information required by the Consumer Credit (Disclosure of Information) Regulations 2010[189] (see para.3.5.2) has been supplied to the debtor, the document may be provided some time after the agreement is made.[190] Should the above requirements not be observed, a court order is required to enforce the agreement against the debtor.[191] The standard approach of the Act in such a context is to provide that the agreement is not properly executed, which has much the same effect, and it is not clear why this was not followed in relation to s.61B.

Nor does s.61A apply to a cancellable agreement[192] (see para.3.5.10) nor to an agreement secured on land, nor where the amount of credit exceeds £60,260, nor where the debtor enters into it in the course of his business.[193] Yet in these latter three cases if the creditor or a credit intermediary has opted to disclose the pre-contractual information required by reg.3(2) of the Consumer Credit (Disclosure of Information) Regulations 2010 (see para.3.5.2) then s.61A will apply after all.[194] Otherwise, agreements in these three categories are governed by ss.62 to 63, which used to apply to all regulated agreements prior to the advent of ss.61A and 61B. In such cases if the creditor or owner has already signed the agreement when the debtor or hirer signs, the latter must receive a copy of the agreement there and then.[195] If the creditor or owner has not signed, then as well as the debtor or hirer receiving a copy on signing the agreement, he is entitled to receive a second copy within seven days of the creditor or owner signing.[196] Copies of credit token agreements need not be sent within seven days, as long as they are supplied before or at the same time as the credit token.[197] In addition the debtor or hirer can always demand a further copy of the agreement at any time during its currency on payment of a fee of £2.[198] Special rules apply where a prospective regulated agreement is to be secured on land. These rules do not apply to bridging loan agreements or restricted use credit agreements to finance the purchase of the land, i.e. ordinary mortgages.[199] The rules therefore are directed towards second mortgages, and seek

---

[182] See s.61A(2).
[183] See s.61A(3).
[184] See s.61A(4).
[185] See s.61A(5).
[186] These are overdrafts which have been agreed in advance of the debtor overdrawing.
[187] See s.61B(1).
[188] See s.61B(2)(b)–(c).
[189] (SI 2010/1013).
[190] See s.61B(2)(a).
[191] See s.61B(3).
[192] See s.61A(6)(a).
[193] See s.61A(6)(b).
[194] See s.61A(6)(b).
[195] See s.63(1).
[196] See ss.62(1), 63(2)–(3). It may be sent by post or transmitted electronically in certain circumstances: see para.3.5.11 below and s.176A.
[197] See s.63(4).
[198] See ss.77–79.
[199] See s.58(2).

to ensure that the debtor is not pressurised into entering them without a chance to reflect on the transaction. In such cases, the prospective debtor must receive a copy of the unexecuted agreement, containing a notice indicating his right to withdraw and how it may be exercised.[200] This copy is for him to consider rather than sign, and at least seven days must elapse before he is sent a copy to sign.[201] During the intervening period the creditor must not approach him in any way, unless the debtor specifically so requests.[202] The creditor must continue to refrain from contact for a further seven days after this copy is sent for signature, or until the debtor has signed and returned it if this is earlier.[203] The right to receive this copy to consider is in addition to the normal rights to receive copies under ss.62 and 63 (see above).

WITHDRAWAL

Under s.57 the debtor or hirer has always had the right to withdraw from a prospective agreement. This remains the case. Thus where the creditor or owner has not signed when the debtor or hirer signs, the latter is entitled to withdraw at any time before the former signs. This may be done by notice to any of the following[204]: **3.5.9**

- the creditor or owner;
- any credit broker or supplier who was the negotiator in antecedent negotiations; or
- anyone who in the course of a business negotiated on behalf of the debtor or hirer.

Notice may be given orally or in writing and no particular form is required as long as the intention to withdraw is communicated. Withdrawal has the same effect as cancellation (see para.3.5.10 below).

However, under s.66A debtors now have a general right to withdraw from a regulated consumer credit agreement once it has actually been made by giving oral[205] or written[206] notice to the creditor.[207] Notice must be given within 14 days of the latest of the following[208]:

- the day when the agreement was made;
- when the creditor is obliged to inform the debtor of the credit limit, the day when that is first done;
- the day when the debtor gets a copy of the agreement or notice under s.61A (see previous paragraph);
- the day when the debtor gets a copy of the agreement under s.63 (see previous paragraph).

Withdrawal means that the agreement is treated as if it had never been entered into[209] and the same is true of any ancillary service contract, such as a payment protection policy.[210] However, the debtor must repay any credit supplied with accrued interest at the rate provided for by the agreement[211] and must

---

[200] See s.58(1).

[201] See s.61(2)(b). It may be sent by post or transmitted electronically in certain circumstances: see para.3.5.11 below and s.176A.

[202] See s.61(2)(c).

[203] See s.61(3).

[204] See s.57.

[205] Oral notice must be given in a manner specified in the agreement: s.66A(4).

[206] Written notice sent by fax or electronically must be sent to the number or electronic address specified for the purpose in the agreement, and is then regarded as having been received by the creditor at the time it is sent: s.66A(5). Where written notice is given in any other form, it must be sent by post to, or left at, the postal address specified for the purpose in the agreement, and is then to be regarded as having been received by the creditor at the time of posting: s.66A(6).

[207] See s.66A(1).

[208] See s.66A(2)–(3).

[209] See s.66A(7)(a).

[210] See s.66A(7)(b), (13). The creditor must without delay notify any third party of the fact that the debtor has withdrawn from the agreement: s.66A(8).

[211] See s.66A(9)(a).

do so within 30 days of withdrawing, after which time it may be recovered by the creditor as a debt.[212] But the debtor is not liable to pay to the creditor any compensation, fees or charges except any non-returnable charges paid by the creditor to a public administrative body.[213] Where the agreement is one of conditional or credit-sale or hire-purchase, and the debtor withdraws from the agreement under this section after the credit has been provided, but pays the sum payable under s.66A(9)(a) in full, title to the goods is to pass to him on the same terms as would have applied had he not withdrawn.[214] This provision does not apply to an agreement secured on land, nor to a mortgage or bridging loan, nor where the amount of credit exceeds £60,260.[215]

CANCELLATION

3.5.10 Certain agreements may also be cancelled. The practical importance of the provisions relating to cancellation is much diminished by the advent of s.66A, especially, since there is now no right to cancel if there is a right to withdraw under s.66A.[216] Subject to that major qualification, however, under s.67(1) a regulated agreement may be cancelled if two conditions are met:

(1) Oral representations by the negotiator (or his representative) must have been made in the presence[217] of the debtor in the course of antecedent negotiations.

A representation will be any statement which might be capable of inducing the debtor to enter into the agreement, although it is not necessary that these representations should actually have induced the agreement or have been intended to do so.[218] Essentially what is involved is some degree of pre-contractual interaction. The question of who counts as a negotiator is discussed under the heading of antecedent negotiations (see para.3.5.6 above). If goods are purchased from a finance company on hire purchase, then the dealer would be a negotiator. However, a company which hires goods cannot be a negotiator.[219]

(2) The agreement must have been signed by the debtor or hirer other than on the trade premises of the creditor or owner, or the negotiator, or any party to a linked transaction (other than the debtor or hirer or any relative).

This condition tends to restrict the category of agreements which are cancellable. Basically, it is aimed at giving an individual a period of reflection when they are persuaded to enter into an agreement during a visit to their home. However, it must be remembered that the emphasis of the provision is on where the agreement is signed. If after considerable pressure during a home visit, an individual agrees to enter into an agreement, but the agreement is actually signed on trade premises, the agreement is not cancellable. Yet, if an individual goes to the creditor's premises in search of credit, but for whatever reason the agreement is signed in that individual's home, it is cancellable.

There are cases which are excepted from the cancellation provisions. These are agreements exempted from the provisions of Pt V by s.74 (see para.3.3.6 above) plus agreements secured on land, agreements where credit is restricted to the purchase of land, and bridging loans in connection with the purchase of land.[220] These latter cases are exempt because the policy of the Act is not to allow agreements related to land to be cancellable, because of the legal complications which cancellation might create in such circumstances. However, it might be remembered that in certain such cases the prospective debtor

---

[212] See s.66A(10).
[213] See s.66A(9)(b).
[214] See s.66A(11).
[215] See s.66A(14).
[216] See s.67(2).
[217] See *Rankine v MBNA Europe Ltd* [2007] C.T.L.C. 241.
[218] *Moorgate Services v Kabir* [1995] C.C.L.R. 74 CA.
[219] *Lloyds Bowmaker Leasing Ltd v McDonald* [1993] C.C.L.R. 65.
[220] See s.67.

is permitted a period of uninfluenced reflection before entering into the agreement (see para.3.5.7 above).

Where an agreement is cancellable, s.64 demands that every copy of the agreement must contain a notice in the prescribed form, indicating the right to cancel, how and when it may be exercised, and the name and address of a person to whom notice of cancellation may be sent. If a second copy of the agreement is not required (see para.3.5.8 above), a separate notice detailing the cancellation information must be posted within seven days of the agreement being made.[221]

Mechanics and effect of cancellation

3.5.10.1 The receipt of the above notice or the second copy is important for the exercise of the right to cancel under s.69. Cancellation may be effected at any time within the cooling off period, which runs from the point at which the debtor or hirer signs the agreement until five days after the receipt of the second copy or notice. Notice of cancellation, which must be in writing, but need not be in any particular form as long as it effectively communicates its intention, may be sent to anyone to whom a notice of withdrawal might have been sent, or to anyone specified in the agreement. If notice is posted, then it is deemed to be served at the date of posting, and if sent electronically[222] it is deemed to be served at the time of transmission, even if it never arrives.[223]

Subject to certain exceptions, a notice of cancellation will cancel the agreement and any linked transaction, and will withdraw any offer to enter into a linked transaction.[224] Any sum paid under the agreement or a linked transaction will be repaid, and any sum payable ceases to be so.[225] A debtor or hirer has under s.70(2) a lien (see para.5.4.1 below) for any sums to be repaid on any goods in his possession under the cancelled agreement. Otherwise, s.72 dictates that any goods held must be returned, although the debtor or hirer need not take the initiative in doing so. Rather, he can hand them over at his own premises, having received a written request to do so, although he is bound to take care of them in the meantime.[226] Moreover, the debtor or hirer need not return perishable goods, goods supplied in an emergency, or goods which are consumed or incorporated in something else prior to cancellation at all.[227] Obviously, he will be unable to return services supplied prior to cancellation. Clearly, in certain cases the effect of cancellation is that the trader will lose out financially. This is mitigated to some degree by the Act providing that where goods have been supplied in an emergency, or are incorporated in something else prior to cancellation, the debtor must still pay the cash price for them despite cancellation.[228] Within 10 days of cancellation the creditor or owner must return to the debtor or hirer any goods given in part exchange or pay a sum equivalent to the part exchange allowance.[229] The Act also guards against the possibility that a debtor might be able to keep the amount of a loan simply by cancelling the loan agreement. So if the agreement is not a debtor-creditor-supplier agreement for restricted use credit, e.g. a hire purchase agreement, then if the credit has already been supplied when it is cancelled, the agreement continues in force so far as it relates to the repayment of credit and the payment of interest.[230] Nonetheless, no interest is payable on any sum repaid within a month of service of the notice of cancellation, or (if repayment was to be in instalments) before the date when the first

---

[221] This may be sent by post or transmitted electronically in certain circumstances: see s.176A.

[222] A document is regarded as electronically transmitted in terms of s.176A if: (a) the person to whom it is transmitted has agreed that it may be delivered to him by being transmitted to a particular electronic address in a particular electronic form; (b) it is so transmitted; and (c) the form in which it is transmitted allows the addressee to store the information for an appropriate period in a way which allows that information to be reproduced without change. Save under s.69 a document so transmitted shall unless the contrary is proved, be treated as having been delivered on the next working day: s.176A(2).

[223] See s.69(7).

[224] See s.69(1)(c).

[225] See s.70(1).

[226] See s.72(3)–(5).

[227] See s.72(9).

[228] See s.69(2).

[229] See s.73.

[230] See s.71(1).

instalment was due.[231] Moreover, where repayment is to be in instalments, the debtor is not liable to make any repayment unless he receives a written request from the creditor in a form prescribed by regulations, stating the amounts of the remaining instalments.[232]

DISTANCE MARKETING

3.5.11 The regulation of distance marketing of financial products occurs under the Financial Services (Distance Marketing) Regulations 2004.[233] Such products include credit agreements, so that the protections afforded by these regulations overlap with, i.e. are additional to, those provided by the Act. Such protections relate to consumers. A consumer for these purposes is defined as an individual not acting for the purposes of any business he may carry on,[234] a definition obviously narrower than that of "individual" under the Act (see para.3.3.1 above). The regulations relate to contracts where the supplier of the credit has made exclusive use of distance communication up to and including the time at which the contract is concluded.[235] Prior to conclusion of the contract the consumer must be provided with a great deal of prescribed information, including such matters as a description of the main characteristics of the financial service, the arrangements of payment and performance, and details of any cancellation or termination rights.[236] Moreover such information must be provided to the consumer in paper prior to her/him being bound,[237] along with all the terms and conditions of the contract.[238] The consumer has the right to cancel the contract by giving notice within 14 days of the conclusion of the contract or of the supply in paper form of such information as is described above, if this is later.[239] There are a number of exceptions to the right to cancellation,[240] but these generally do not apply where there has been a failure to supply the required information in paper form.[241] Cancellation also serves to cancel certain types of secondary contract related to the agreement.[242] Where fraudulent use has been made of a debit, credit or store card in order to make a payment in connection with a distance contract, the card holder is entitled to recover that sum.[243]

PROPER EXECUTION OF THE AGREEMENT

3.5.12 Under s.65 a regulated agreement which is not properly executed cannot be enforced against the debtor or hirer without the permission of the court (see para.3.8.2 below). Retaking possession of goods or land to which the agreement relates is specifically stated to amount to enforcement.[244] Thus a creditor or owner who might otherwise be entitled to recover goods or land, requires the assistance of the court to do so where the agreement is not properly executed. No restriction is placed on the right of the debtor or hirer to enforce an agreement which is not properly executed. To be properly executed the document embodying the agreement:

(1)   must be in prescribed form and contain all prescribed terms;

---

[231] See s.71(2).

[232] See s.71(3); Consumer Credit (Repayment of Credit on Cancellation) Regulations 1983 (SI 1983/1559).

[233] Financial Services (Distance Marketing) Regulations 2004 (SI 2004/2095).

[234] See reg.2(1).

[235] See reg.2(1).

[236] See reg.7 and Sch.1.

[237] Or immediately after the conclusion of the contract if it was concluded at the consumer's request using a means of distance communication which did not allow it to be sent prior to conclusion.

[238] See reg.8

[239] See regs 9–10.

[240] Such as a contract where the consumer's obligation to repay credit is secured by a legal mortgage on land: reg.11(1)(d); or a restricted use credit agreement to finance the purchase of land or an existing building, or an agreement for a bridging loan for such purposes: reg.11(1)(g).

[241] See reg.11(2).

[242] See reg.12.

[243] See reg.14.

[244] See s.65(2).

(2) must be signed as prescribed by the parties;

(3) must be legible;

(4) must contain all the terms of the agreement, apart from implied terms; and

(5) if the agreement is cancellable, must contain the prescribed information regarding cancellation rights and their exercise.

Moreover all copies of the agreement must have been supplied as required.[245]

SECURITY

Often a creditor or owner will be reluctant to enter a credit or hire transaction without the benefit of **3.5.13** some kind of security. Where security is provided by or at the request of a debtor or hirer, it is governed by the Act. Otherwise, where the security is provided without reference to the debtor or hirer, e.g. where a finance company insists that a dealer agrees to indemnify it against loss before it is prepared to buy goods from the dealer to sell to a debtor on hire purchase, the security does not fall within the scope of the Act. Where a security is governed by the Act, then if the regulated agreement is not enforceable, neither is the security,[246] although of course the fact that a security is not enforceable would not of itself affect the enforceability of the regulated agreement. Moreover, the security agreement must be in writing and signed by or on behalf of the surety[247] (the provider of the security). It must comply in form and content with the Consumer Credit (Guarantees and Indemnities) Regulations 1983,[248] and in particular must contain all express terms in legible form.[249] A copy of the security agreement and the regulated agreement and any other document referred to in the latter must be given to the surety at the time the security is provided, although if the security is provided before the regulated agreement is entered into, a copy of the latter (and any other document referred to therein) must be provided within seven days of it being made.[250] Failure to comply with any of these formalities means that the security is improperly executed and thus may only be enforced by court order (see para.3.8.2 below).

MATTERS ARISING DURING THE COURSE OF THE AGREEMENT

3.6

RIGHTS TO INFORMATION

Certain information must be produced automatically. It has always been the case under a running **3.6.1** account credit agreement that the creditor must provide the debtor with statements showing the state of the account at regular intervals of not more than 12 months. Equally, if the agreement provides for the making of payments by the debtor or the charging against him of interest or any other sum in relation to specified periods, then he must be given information as to the state of the account at the end of each such period, provided there has been any movement during that period.[251] Thus, for example, if the debtor is charged interest on his account on a monthly basis, then he must be given a statement showing

---

[245] See ss.61–64.

[246] See s.113.

[247] See s.105(1), (4)(a).

[248] Consumer Credit (Guarantees and Indemnities) Regulations 1983 (SI 1983/1556); and see s.105(2)–(3).

[249] See s.105(4)(b)–(c).

[250] See s.105(4)(d), (5)(a), (b).

[251] See s.78(4)–(5). For the period within which such information may be provided and the detail of what must be provided see, respectively, the Consumer Credit (Prescribed Periods for Giving Information) Regulations 1983 (SI 1983/1569) and the Consumer Credit (Running-Account Credit Information) Regulations 1983 (SI 1983/1570). The Consumer Credit (Information Requirements and Duration of Licences and Charges) Regulations 2007 (SI 2007/1167) regs 13–18 and Sch.2 now indicate additional forms of wording which statements must contain.

how the account has been affected at the end of each month, unless no interest was charged in a particular month. The power now exists for regulations to be made requiring any such statement to contain
information about the consequences of the debtor failing to make required payments or minimum
payments.[252] It is also the case that debtors under fixed sum credit agreements must also receive without
charge[253] statements at intervals of no more than a year.[254] The statements must relate to consecutive
periods,[255] the first beginning with either the day on which the agreement is made, or the day the first
movement occurs on the debtor's account.[256] Each statement must be given to the debtor within 30 days
of the end of the period to which it relates.[257] The form and detailed content of these statements is
prescribed by statutory instrument.[258] No information need be provided however under a non-
commercial agreement or a small agreement, nor where there is no sum payable by the debtor under the
agreement and no sum will become payable,[259] nor where the holder of a current account overdraws on
the account without a pre-arranged overdraft or exceeds a pre-arranged overdraft limit.[260] While there
appears to be no sanction for failing to provide the necessary statements in relation to running account
credit agreements, such failure in relation to fixed sum credit agreements render the creditor unable to
enforce the agreement during the period of default, while the debtor is not liable to pay any sum of
interest calculated by reference to that period, i.e. interest cannot be charged while the creditor is in
default.[261] Nor can the debtor be liable for any default charges payable during that period or payable in
respect of a breach occurring during that period.[262] Unlike statements provided on request (see below),
statements provided automatically are not binding on the creditor.[263]

In order to give effect to art.11 of the Consumer Credit Directive, s.78A now requires in most cases
that the creditor inform the borrower of any variation in the rate of interest. But it does not apply to an
agreement secured on land or where the holder of a current account overdraws on the account without
a pre-arranged overdraft or exceeds a pre-arranged overdraft limit.[264] Generally, s.78A provides that,
where the rate of interest charged is to be varied, the creditor must inform the debtor in writing of
certain matters before the variation can take effect.[265] Those matters are the variation, the amount[266] (if
different) of any payments to be made after it has effect and, if the number or frequency of payments
changes as a result of the variation, the new number or frequency.[267] However, that obligation does not
arise where all of the following conditions apply—the agreement provides firstly that the creditor is to
inform the debtor in writing periodically of such matters at such times as may be provided for in the
agreement, and secondly that the rate of interest is to vary according to a reference rate (e.g. the Bank
of England base rate), the reference rate is publicly available, information about the reference rate is
available on the premises of the creditor, and the variation results from a change to the reference rate.[268]
Furthermore, in the case of overdraft agreements it is only necessary to give notice if the interest rate
or charges actually increase.[269]

---

[252] See s.78(4A).
[253] See s.77A(3).
[254] See s.77A(1), (1C). A period of a year which expires on a non-working day may be regarded as expiring on the next working
day: s.77A(1D).
[255] See s.77A(1A).
[256] See s.77A(1B).
[257] See s.77A(1E).
[258] See the Consumer Credit (Information Requirements and Duration of Licences and Charges) Regulations 2007 (SI
2007/1167) regs 3–12 and Sch.1.
[259] See s.77A(4), (8).
[260] See s.77A(9). This situation is instead addressed by s.74B: see below.
[261] See s.77A(6)(a)–(b).
[262] See s.77A(6)(c).
[263] See s.172(1).
[264] See s.78A(6).
[265] See s.78A(1).
[266] Expressed as a sum of money where practicable.
[267] See s.78A(3).
[268] See s.78A(2).
[269] See s.78A(4)–(5).

Moreover, certain information need only be provided on request. Thus at any time during the currency of a regulated agreement, a debtor or hirer has the right to request from the creditor or owner a copy of the agreement[270] and a statement of the account between them. This statement will include, in the case of a fixed sum credit agreement, information as to the amount already paid, the amount which has become payable but is as yet unpaid (including the various amounts comprised in that total sum, and the date each fell due), and the total sum which will become payable (again detailing the various amounts comprised in that total sum and the date each will fall due).[271] In the case of a running account credit agreement, this statement will include information as to the state of the account, any amount currently payable, and the amounts (assuming the debtor does not draw further on the account) which will later become payable (including the dates these fall due).[272] In the case of a consumer hire agreement, this statement will include information as to the amount which has become payable but is as yet unpaid (again including the various amounts comprised in that total sum and the date each fell due).[273] Parallel provisions exist to confer on a person providing a security under a regulated agreement a copy of the agreement, a copy of the security agreement and a statement of the account.[274] In all the above cases the request must be in writing and a fee of £1 must be paid, but none of the above provisions apply to a non-commercial agreement (see para.3.3.8 above). In addition, the debtor under a regulated consumer credit agreement (whether non-commercial or not) may make a written request (in this case without having to pay a fee) for a statement of the amount required to pay off the entire debt, which statement should show how that amount is arrived at.[275] In this case a rebate will be due for early settlement (see para.3.7.1 below).

If the creditor or owner does not respond accurately to any such request as is mentioned in the previous paragraph within 12 days of receiving it, then he is not entitled to enforce the agreement (or the security agreement where the request comes from a person providing security) while he remains in default.[276] He is, however, bound by any statement supplied, so that if the figure quoted is too low, e.g. where the creditor tells the debtor that £1,000 is required to settle the debt when the figure should really be £10,000, then the debtor may rely upon that information.[277] This is subject to the power of the court to offer such relief from the operation of the rule as may be just.[278] It may also be noted that the English courts have held creditors to be bound by statements provided to debtors other than under these statutory provisions, as a result of the doctrine of estoppel.[279] It may be that a debtor in Scotland may be able similarly to rely on the principle of personal bar.

It is now also the case that s.77B allows debtors under fixed sum agreements to request certain information. There is a degree of overlap between this provision and s.77, but this is explicable on the basis that s.77B is inserted to comply with art.10.3 of the Consumer Credit Directive. This section applies to a regulated consumer credit agreement which is for fixed-sum credit, is of fixed duration, and where the credit is repayable in instalments.[280] However, it does not apply to an agreement secured on land, a pawn agreement, an agreement under which the creditor provides the debtor with credit which exceeds £60,260, or an agreement entered into by the debtor wholly or predominantly for the purpose of his business.[281] Where the debtor so requests, the creditor must, as soon as reasonably practicable, give to

---

[270] *Carey v HSBC Bank Plc* [2009] CL.T.C. 103; establishes (at [54]) that when a creditor is asked to supply a copy of the agreement it need not be an exact copy, but may be reconstituted from other sources, such as standard forms. Nor need it comply with the requirements as to form which applied to the creation of the original agreement: see [63]. Nonetheless, it must be a copy of the original agreement, embodying the original terms, and not the terms as they have been varied, otherwise the creditor is in default: see *Phoenix Recoveries (UK) Ltd v Kotecha* [2011] E.C.C. 15.

[271] See s.77.

[272] See s.78.

[273] See s.79.

[274] See ss.107–109.

[275] See s.97 and Consumer Credit (Settlement Information) Regulations 1983 (SI 1983/1564).

[276] See ss.77(4)(a), 78(6)(a), 97(3)(a), 107–109. But it does not amount to enforcement to inform a credit reference agency that the debtor has ceased repayments: *McGuffick v Royal Bank of Scotland Plc* [2010] 1 All E.R. 634.

[277] See s.172(1)–(2).

[278] See s.172(3).

[279] See, e.g. *Lombard North Central v Stobart* [1990] C.C.L.R. 53.

[280] See s.77B(1).

[281] See s.77B(9).

the debtor free of charge[282] a statement in writing, which includes a table showing the details of each instalment owing under the agreement as at the date of the request.[283] Such details must include the date on which the instalment is due, the amount of the instalment, any conditions relating to its payment, and a breakdown showing how much of the instalment is made up of capital repayment, interest payment and other charges.[284] Where the rate of interest is variable or the charges under the agreement may be varied, the statement must also indicate clearly and concisely that the information in the table is valid only until the rate of interest or charges are varied.[285] A breach of s.77B is merely actionable as a breach of statutory duty and carries no other consequences.[286]

IMPLIED TERMS

3.6.2 A regulated agreement may also be a contract of sale of goods and thus subject to the implied terms as to title and quality. Almost identical terms to those implied under ss.12–15 of the Sale of Goods Act 1979 are implied in contracts of hire purchase under ss.8–11 of the Supply of Goods (Implied Terms) Act 1973 and in contracts of hire under ss.7–10 of the Supply of Goods and Services Act 1982. It should be noted, however, that remedies under contracts of hire continue to be governed by the common law.

CONNECTED LENDER LIABILITY

3.6.3 Often traders and finance houses are very closely connected. Thus, although the common law would see supply contracts and credit contracts as entirely independent, the Act takes the view that in certain circumstances breach of the former should have consequences for the creditor.[287] Accordingly, s.75 provides that, if a debtor under a debtor-creditor-supplier agreement involving three parties, which is made under or in contemplation of arrangements between the supplier and creditor, has in relation to a transaction financed by the agreement a claim against the supplier in respect of a misrepresentation or breach of contract, he shall have a like claim against the creditor. In other words, in a three party debtor-creditor-supplier transaction the creditor is jointly and severally liable with the supplier for the latter's misrepresentation and breach of contract.

There are certain exceptions to this provision. It does not apply to a non-commercial agreement,[288] nor to a claim which relates to any single item to which the supplier has attached a cash price not exceeding £100 or more than £30,000.[289] So if a connected lender provides a loan to allow an individual to purchase a number of items of electrical equipment, while the creditor will be jointly and severally liable with the supplier should a cooker malfunction, if a kettle priced at £70 malfunctions, then a claim cannot be brought against the creditor. This is so even if the claim against the supplier greatly exceeds £100, as where the kettle explodes causing the buyer severe injury. Most recently, s.75 has been amended so that it does not apply to running account credit agreements, which are not secured on land, where the debtor requires to pay off the credit in full at intervals of three month or less.[290] This ensures that charge cards such as AMEX under which credit is provided, but where the account must typically be settled in full each month, do not fall within the scope of s.75.

The precise effect of s.75 has been a matter for debate for some years. In *UDT v Taylor*[291] it was suggested that where a seller was in breach of the *supply* contract, s.75 put the creditor in breach of the

---

[282] See s.77B(7).

[283] See s.77B(2)–(3). Such a request may be made at any time that the agreement is in force unless a previous request has been made less than a month before and has been complied with: s.77B(6).

[284] See s.77B(4).

[285] See s.77B(5).

[286] See s.77B(8).

[287] For the rationale, see para.6.6.22 et seq.; Report of the Committee on Consumer Credit (HMSO, 1971), Cmnd.4596.

[288] See s.75(3)(a).

[289] See s.75(3)(b).

[290] See s.75(3)(c).

[291] *UDT v Taylor*, 1980 S.L.T (Sh Ct) 28; followed by *Forward Trust Ltd v Homsby* [1995] C.C.L.R. 574. Contrast the views of Morritt LJ in *Jarrett v Barclays Bank Plc* [1999] Q.B. 1 at 15G.

credit contract, so that if the debtor could rescind the former contract, he would also be able to rescind the latter contract. That seemed to fly in the face of the terms of s.75, which clearly make a creditor jointly and severally liable with the supplier for the latter's breach of contract. That this was the correct construction was confirmed by the Inner House in *Durkin v DSG Retail Ltd.*[292] Yet the Supreme Court in that case,[293] while agreeing with that analysis,[294] contrived to find a way in which the debtor could indeed rescind the credit contract. Lord Hodge with whom the rest of the court agreed, observed[295]:

> "It is inherent in a debtor-creditor-supplier agreement . . . which is also tied into a specific supply transaction, that if the supply transaction which it financed is in effect brought to an end by the debtor's acceptance of the supplier's repudiatory breach of contract, the debtor must repay the borrowed funds which he recovers from the supplier. In my view, in order to reflect that reality, the law implies a term into such a credit agreement that it is conditional upon the survival of the supply agreement. The debtor on rejecting the goods and thereby rescinding the supply agreement for breach of contract may also rescind the credit agreement by invoking this condition. As the debtor has no right to retain or use for other purposes funds lent for the specific transaction, the creditor also may rescind the credit agreement."

In other words, in order to give proper effect to the policy behind s.75, it is necessary to imply into the credit contract a term allowing either party to rescind if the supply cotract is rescinded.

In *Renton v Hendersons Garage (Nairn) and UDT*[296] s.75 was wrongly applied to a two party debtor-creditor-supplier transaction, where the finance company purchased a vehicle from the supplier and itself sold it on a conditional sale basis to the debtor. Yet the practical outcome was identical, given that the debtor was in a direct contractual relationship with the finance company regarding the sale of the car.

Section 75 is now supplemented by s.75A. This gives a debtor under a linked credit agreement[297] a claim against the creditor in respect of a breach of contract by the supplier.[298] A linked credit agreement serves exclusively to finance an agreement for the supply of specific goods or services where the creditor uses the services of the supplier in connection with the preparation or making of the credit agreement or where the specific goods or services are explicitly specified in the credit agreement.[299] The section does not apply where the debtor enters into the agreement in the course of a business.[300] Nor does it apply where the cash value of the goods or services is £30,000 or the credit exceeds £60,260.[301] It can be appreciated that s.75A would tend to be invoked where a debtor cannot rely on s.75, because the item purchased has a cash price of more than £30,000. Section 75A gives effect to art.15.2 of the Consumer Credit Directive 2008, and one option would have been to replace s.75 with s.75A. However, because in certain respects the protection afforded by s.75A is narrower than that afforded by s.75, it was decided to retain s.75 and apply s.75A only where s.75 would not apply.[302] In

---

[292] *Durkin v DSG Retail Ltd*, 2010 S.C.L.R. 692. Of course, given that the creditor shares liability for breach of the supply contract, the question whether the cost of credit can be recovered might appear to be a difficult one, as it would not seem to be a head of damages for breach of the supply contract, unless it could be argued that the loss flowed directly from the supplier's breach of contract. Yet the Inner House opined (at [59]) that the debtor in such circumstances "can also seek to recover damages from his supplier and from his creditor, to compensate him for any loss he has already incurred, or is liable to incur, by reason of his obligations under the credit agreement to make payments to the creditor." This has become a largely academic issue now that the Supreme Court has confirmed that the debtor is indeed entitled to rescind the credit contract.

[293] *Durkin v DSG Retail Ltd* [2014] UKSC 21.

[294] *Durkin v DSG Retail Ltd* [2014] UKSC 21 at [19]–[21].

[295] *Durkin v DSG Retail Ltd* [2014] UKSC 21 at [26].

[296] *Renton v Hendersons Garage (Nairn) and UDT* [1994] C.C.L.R.29. See also *Porter v General Guarantee Corporation* [1982] C.C.L.R. 1.

[297] Except an agreement secured on land: see s.75A(8).

[298] See s.75A(1).

[299] See s.75A(5).

[300] See s.75A(6)(c).

[301] See s.75A(6)(a)–(b).

[302] See the Department for Business Innovation and Skills, *Guidance on the Regulations Implementing the Consumer Credit Directive* (2010), para.13.3.

terms of s.75A being narrower, before a claim can be made under that provision, any of the following conditions must be satisfied[303]:

- that the supplier cannot be traced;
- that the debtor has contacted the supplier but has received no response;
- that the supplier is insolvent;
- that the debtor has taken reasonable steps to pursue his claim against the supplier but has not obtained satisfaction.

In this context "reasonable steps" need not include litigation, while a debtor obtains satisfaction where he accepts a replacement product or service or other compensation from the supplier in settlement of his claim.[304] It can thus be seen that, while under s.75 the creditor shares the supplier's liability, so that the debtor can choose to proceed against either or both, the debtor can only pursue the creditor where he has done his best to obtain redress from the supplier or where seeking such redress is pointless. Moreover, s.75A only applies where the credit is clearly tied to the transaction concerned. Thus while it would apply to a three party hire purchase agreement or where the supplier directly introduces the debtor to the creditor, it would not apply to a credit card transaction.[305] Finally, s.75A applies only to breach of contract claims, and does not extend, as s.75 does, to misrepresentation claims.

Credit cards and connected lender liability

3.6.3.1 It had been argued by the credit card industry that credit card transactions would not fall within s.75 as, inter alia, a fourth party is involved—a "merchant acquirer" who recruits retailers willing to accept the card, and may well also pay their accounts, obtaining payment in return from the card issuer. However, the Court of Appeal has held that this situation still involves an "arrangement" between the supplier and creditor,[306] and the House of Lords refused permission to appeal on this point,[307] so that s.75 applies to credit card transactions. An argument that s.75 did not apply in relation to credit card purchases made abroad was rejected in the same case, and the decision of the Court of Appeal was upheld by the House of Lords.[308] The Act specifically prevents payments by debit card being subject to s.75.[309] The Act only applies to regulated agreements made on or after July 1, 1977. Thus it is argued that, if the credit card agreement was entered into before that date, s.75 will not apply, and it does not matter how often a "new" card has been issued. At the same time, if that agreement has been varied by agreement of the parties after July 1, 1977, then it is treated as having been terminated and a new agreement made.[310] Accordingly, s.75 should then apply. An alternative argument is that a debtor-creditor-supplier agreement is created not when the credit card agreement is entered into, but each time the card is actually

---

[303] See s.75A(2).

[304] See s.75A(3)–(4).

[305] See the Department for Business Innovation and Skills, *Guidance on the Regulations Implementing the Consumer Credit Directive* (2010), para.13.4.

[306] *Office of Fair Trading v Lloyds TSB Bank Plc* [2007] Q.B. 1; see especially [55]–[64]. See also *Dalglish v National Westminster Bank Plc*, 2001 S.L.T. (Sh Ct) 124.

[307] See Lord Mance in *Office of Fair Trading v Lloyds TSB Bank Plc* [2007] UKHL 48 at [24]. But see Bisping, "The Case Against s.75 of the Consumer Credit Act 1974 in Credit Card Transactions", 2011 J.B.L. 457.

[308] Their Lordships agreed that although legislation is essentially territorial in application, that principle was not disturbed by applying s.75 to UK credit agreements where the credit is granted in respect of overseas transactions. The Act cannot impose liability on foreign suppliers, but it certainly can impose liability on UK credit card providers; see Lord Hoffmann at [4]. Nonetheless, it is accepted that neither s.75(2) (which entitles the creditor to be indemnified by the supplier for loss suffered in satisfying his liability under s.75(1)), nor s.75(5) (which entitles the creditor to have the supplier made a party to the proceedings) can apply to foreign suppliers: see Lord Hoffmann at [6]. Equally, it is recognised that the provisions of the Act (ss.67–73), relating to cancellation of linked transactions where the main agreement is cancelled, cannot effectively cancel a linked transaction which takes the form of the purchase via credit card of goods or services overseas, since that contract will be governed by the appropriate foreign law. See Lord Mance at [40]–[44]. It is in any case highly unlikely that a contract between a credit card provider and a credit user would ever be entered into in a way which would make it cancellable—see para.3.5.10 above—so that this is an issue which should not arise in practice.

[309] See s.187(3A).

[310] See s.82(2).

used, so that all credit card transactions are subject to s.75, no matter when the credit card agreement was entered into. Those companies which entered into agreements before the key date have indicated that they will voluntarily accept s.75 liability, but only to the extent of the credit used on that particular purchase. A final question attending the use of credit cards is what is the position under s.75 in respect of a transaction entered into by an authorised user of the card, e.g. the spouse or child of the cardholder? The simple answer would appear to be that as the cardholder bears liability in such transactions, the user would be regarded as their agent, so that s.75 would apply straightforwardly.

MISUSE OF CREDIT CARDS

3.6.4 On the subject of credit cards, the Act seeks to offer some protection for consumers against the misuse of credit tokens. Thus under s.66 the debtor cannot be liable for any unauthorised use of a credit token unless he has either signed it (or a receipt for it), or used it. Once it has been thus accepted, if it is misused by a person in possession with the debtor's consent, the latter is liable for all loss.[311] If it is accidentally lost or stolen, s.84(1) restricts the debtor's liability to £50. The debtor is not in any case liable for any loss arising after the creditor has been given notice that it is lost, stolen or otherwise liable to misuse.[312] A credit token agreement must therefore contain the name, address and telephone number of a person to whom notice of loss must be given, and if it fails to do so the debtor will not be liable for the creditor's loss.[313]

TERMINATION AND DEFAULT

3.7

EARLY DISCHARGE BY THE DEBTOR

3.7.1 A regulated agreement may be terminated early by the debtor serving notice on the creditor and making full payment of the amount due.[314] The debtor would be entitled to demand a statement of the amount required to pay off the entire debt (see para.3.6.1 above). If an agreement is thus terminated it will also terminate the liability of the debtor (or his relative) under a linked transaction other than a contract of insurance or guarantee.[315] It may be added that in implementation of art.16.1 of the Consumer Credit Directive a right to make early payment of only part of the amount due is conferred, as long as the agreement is not secured on land.[316] To exercise this right, the debtor must give notice to the creditor.[317] If the notice is not accompanied by the relevant payment, it must be made no later than 28 days after the notice is received by the creditor or such later date as may be specified in the notice.[318] Such a right might be exercised on more than one occasion.[319]

A debtor who makes part payment may, at the same time or subsequently, request the creditor to give him a statement concerning the effect of the payment on his indebtedness, and the creditor must provide the statement within seven working days after the creditor receives the request.[320] The statement shall be in writing and shall contain the following particulars[321]:

---

[311] See s.84(2).
[312] See s.84(3).
[313] See Consumer Credit (Credit Token Agreements) Regulations 1983 (SI 1983/1555).
[314] See s.94(1).
[315] See s.96.
[316] See s.94(3).
[317] See s.94(4)(a).
[318] See s.94(4)(b)–(c).
[319] See the Department for Business Innovation and Skills, *Guidance on the Regulations Implementing the Consumer Credit Directive* (2010), para.14.1.
[320] See s.97A(1).
[321] See s.97A(2).

- a description of the agreement sufficient to identify it;
- the name, postal address and, where appropriate, any other address of the creditor and the debtor;
- where the creditor is claiming compensation for early payment (see below), the amount and the method used to determine it;
- the amount of any rebate to which the debtor is entitled under the agreement, or under the Act (see below) where that is higher;
- where the amount of the rebate under the Act is given, a statement indicating that this amount has been calculated having regard to the applicable regulations;
- where the debtor is not entitled to any rebate, a statement to this effect;
- any change to the number, timing or amount of repayments to be made under the agreement, or the duration of the agreement, which results from the partial discharge of the debt; and
- the amount of the remaining debt at the date of the statement.

No specific penalty is provided for failure to comply with this provision.

Whether early payment is made of the whole or only part of the amount due, the debtor will be entitled to a rebate on the charge for credit, calculated according to a complex formula.[322] However, in certain circumstances a creditor may be allowed to claim compensation for costs incurred as a result of full or partial early payment. The right does not apply where the agreement is secured on land and only applies where the agreement provides for the rate of interest on the credit to be fixed for a period of time and the repayment is made during that period.[323] Thus there is no such right if the rate can be varied for the creditor, and if there is an initial fixed rate period, the right can only be exercised during that period. Obviously if the rate is fixed for the duration of the agreement, the right is always available. Neither does the right apply to an agreement enabling the debtor to overdraw on a current account, nor where the amount paid is paid from the proceeds of a contract of payment protection insurance.[324] Moreover, the right may only be exercised where the amount paid exceeds £8,000 or, where more than one such payment is made in any 12 month period, the total of those payments exceeds £8,000.[325] If all the above conditions are met, the creditor may claim an amount equal to the cost he has incurred as a result only of the early payment.[326] However, the amount claimed must be fair, objectively justified,[327] and must not exceed whichever is the lower of certain sums,[328] i.e.:

- 1 per cent of the amount repaid if the agreement had more than a year to run, or 0.5 per cent of the amount repaid if the agreement had less than a year to run; or
- the total amount of interest that would have been paid by the debtor had the repayment not been made.

TERMINATION OF OPEN-END CONSUMER CREDIT AGREEMENTS

3.7.2 The debtor may at any time terminate, free of charge, an open-end consumer credit agreement (i.e. an agreement of no fixed duration), subject to any period of notice provided for by the agreement.[329] The

---

[322] See s.95. That formula is prescribed by the Consumer Credit (Early Settlement) Regulations 2004 (SI 2004/1483).

[323] See s.95A(1). Section 95A implements the remainder of art.16 of the Consumer Credit Directive.

[324] See s.95A(2)(b)–(c).

[325] See s.95A(2)(a). This means that if a repayment of £9,000 is made compensation can be claimed in respect of the whole of that sum, whereas if during a period of several months four payments of £2,000 are made, followed by a payment of £1,000, compensation can be claimed in respect of only the last payment: see the Department for Business Innovation and Skills, *Guidance on the Regulations Implementing the Consumer Credit Directive* (2010), para.14.21.

[326] See s.95A(2).

[327] See s.95A(3)(a)–(b). No further guidance is given regarding the meaning of these criteria. The Department for Business Innovation and Skills, *Guidance on the Regulations Implementing the Consumer Credit Directive* (2010), para.14.22 states that "[t]he creditor will need to ensure that he can demonstrate, if challenged that the compensation is fair and objectively justified in the circumstances".

[328] See s.95A(3)(c)–(4).

[329] See s.98A(1). Section 98A implements art.13 of the Consumer Credit Directive.

agreement cannot require such notice to be more than one month, and it need not be in writing unless the creditor so requires.[330] Where such an agreement provides for termination of the agreement by the creditor, the debtor must be given at least two months notice, or such longer period as the agreement may provide.[331] Where such an agreement provides for termination or suspension[332] by the creditor of the debtor's right to draw on credit, to have that effect the creditor must serve a notice on the debtor giving objectively justified reasons for the termination or suspension.[333] Such notice must be served before the termination or suspension or, if that is not practicable, immediately afterwards.[334] Examples of objectively justified reasons given by the provision are reasons relating to the unauthorised or fraudulent use of credit, or a significantly increased risk of the debtor being unable to repay the credit,[335] but other examples may exist. The provision does not affect any right of the debtor or creditor to terminate an agreement for breach of contract.[336] The provision does not apply to overdrafts or agreements secured on land.[337]

TERMINATION OF CONSUMER HIRE AGREEMENT BY HIRER

While it may commonly be assumed that a hirer will hire goods for as long as he requires them, the **3.7.3** agreement may bind him to a certain minimum period of hire. It is possible for this period to be extremely lengthy, and there had been signs over the years that certain businesses were committing hirers to arrangements which would see the latter pay at least as much as they might expect to pay if they were acquiring the goods on hire purchase. In such cases, hirers would obviously never become the owners of these goods, nor enjoy any of the protections of the hire purchase legislation.[338] Accordingly, by virtue of s.101, however long the contractual period of hire may be, a hirer under a regulated consumer hire agreement may terminate the agreement if it has been running for at least 18 months. The hirer must give notice equivalent to the shorter of three months and the period between hire payments. The right does not apply to agreements:

(1) which require the hirer to pay more than £1,500 per annum;
(2) where the hirer hires the goods for business purposes, and he selects goods which the owner then acquires from another at his request; or
(3) where the hirer requires the goods to hire to another in the course of business.

These exceptions reflect the fact that the right is designed to protect consumer rather than business hirers and are designed to meet the concerns of commercial equipment leasing companies. It may also be noted that on application by a person carrying on a consumer hire business, the OFT, if it thinks it would be in the interest of hirers to do so, can direct that the section will not apply to consumer hire agreements made by the applicant,[339] while the OFT may also issue a general notice disapplying s.101 to agreements of a particular description,[340] i.e. confer a blanket exemption to certain types of agreement.

---

[330] See s.98A(2).

[331] See s.98A(3).

[332] Declining a transaction because it would mean that a credit limit is exceeded would not amount to suspension: see the Department for Business Innovation and Skills, *Guidance on the Regulations Implementing the Consumer Credit Directive* (2010), para.15.8.

[333] See s.98A(4).

[334] See s.98A(4)(a). But notice need not be given if it is prohibited by an EU obligation, or would, or would be likely to, prejudice the prevention or detection of crime, the apprehension or prosecution of offenders, or the administration of justice: see s.98A(6). So if notice might tip off someone suspected of terrorism, fraud or money laundering, it would be inappropriate to give it: see the Department for Business Innovation and Skills, *Guidance on the Regulations Implementing the Consumer Credit Directive* (2010), para.15.8. It is still required however, that the reasons for not giving a notice are objectively justifiable.

[335] See s.98A(6).

[336] See s.98A(7).

[337] See s.98A(8).

[338] *Galbraith v Mitchenall Estates Ltd* [1965] 2 Q.B. 473.

[339] See s.101(8).

[340] See s.101(8A).

TERMINATION OF HIRE PURCHASE AND CONDITIONAL SALE AGREEMENTS

3.7.4 A debtor under such an agreement may terminate it and return the goods at any time before the final payment falls due by giving notice to the person authorised to receive payments under the agreement.[341] The debtor remains liable for all payments due prior to termination. He must also bring his payments up to half the total price, assuming that he has not already crossed this threshold. The agreement may stipulate a lesser but not a greater sum, while the court can itself order payment of a lesser sum, if it considers that sufficient to compensate the creditor, although it cannot relieve the debtor of existing liability.[342] The amount payable may be increased if the debtor has failed to take reasonable care of the goods. It should be noted that the cap imposed by s.100 does not apply when the creditor rather than the debtor terminates the agreement when entitled to do so.[343]

This right may assist a debtor who faces the prospect of default due to financial difficulties. Yet often such debtors cannot take advantage of it, as agreements commonly contain accelerated payments clauses. These indicate that, if the debtor defaults on any payment, all payments to be made under the agreement (including of course the final payment) immediately become due. Such clauses would be penal in nature unless they offer the debtor some rebate for early settlement, but as they invariably do, thus far they have been held to be effective.[344] Even so, such a clause must now surely be challengeable, where the debtor is a consumer, under the Unfair Terms in Consumer Contracts Regulations 1999.[345] It may be pointed out that, despite its terms, such a clause cannot have immediate effect, as the creditor will require to serve a default notice (see para.3.7.7 below) before becoming entitled to an accelerated payment. Indeed, even on the expiry of the period allowed to remedy the default, the debtor may escape the effect of the clause by seeking a time order (see para.3.8.3 below). If, however, the clause does operate, the debtor will be entitled to claim either the rebate for early settlement allowed by the Act (see para.3.7.1 above) or the rebate allowed by the clause, whichever is more advantageous.

It may further be observed that where hire purchase and conditional sale agreements fall outwith the scope of the Act,[346] it is not uncommon to find minimum payments clauses, which commit debtors to paying very substantial sums where they elect to terminate the agreement. Because such sums, which very often are far in excess of any loss the creditor can suffer as a result of the termination, are payable upon the occurrence of a specified event, rather than upon a breach of contract, they cannot be considered to be penalties.[347] This has led Lord Denning to remark[348]:

> "Let no one mistake the injustice of this. It means that equity commits itself to this absurd paradox: it will grant relief to a man who breaks his contract, but will penalise the man who keeps it."

In turn this has led to the courts at times treating what appears to be a straightforward notice of termination as an indication of a debtor's intention to default, thus allowing them to consider whether such payments were indeed penalties.[349] It must also now be questioned whether such clauses would be valid in terms of the Unfair Terms in Consumer Contracts Regulations 1999.

---

[341] See s.99.

[342] See s.100(3).

[343] *First Response Finance Ltd v Donnelly* [2007] C.C.L.R. 4. So when the debtor wrongfully sold a car which he had on hire purchase, the creditor was held to be entitled, on exercising its contractual right to terminate, to recover a sum equivalent to the remaining payments under the agreement, less the amount which it obtained when it resold the car. The argument does not appear to have been entertained that damages should be calculated on the basis that, had the contract been performed, the contract breaker would have chosen the least onerous mode of performance, so that the debtor should be assumed to have been prepared to exercise his right to terminate.

[344] *Wadham Stringer Finance Ltd v Meaney* [1981] 1 W.L.R. 39.

[345] Unfair Terms in Consumer Contracts Regulations 1999 (SI 1999/2083) Sch.2 para.1(e); and see OFT, *Unfair Contract Terms Bulletin*, No.3, p.12.

[346] A fairly unusual circumstance now that financial limits are largely removed, but still possible.

[347] *EFT Commercial Ltd v Security Change Ltd (No.1)*, 1993 S.L.T. 128.

[348] In *Bridge v Campbell Discount Co* [1962] A.C. 600 at 626.

[349] *Bridge v Campbell Discount Co* [1962] A.C. 600 at 626.

REPOSSESSION OF GOODS UNDER HIRE PURCHASE AND CONDITIONAL SALE AGREEMENTS

Of course a debtor may simply default without seeking to terminate, and ultimately the creditor may **3.7.5** look to repossess the goods. The Act provides a limited degree of protection for a debtor who has paid a reasonable number of instalments by prescribing in s.90 that the creditor must obtain a court order to repossess the goods when the debtor is in default but has paid one-third of the total price. If the creditor seeks to repossess in breach of the Act, s.91 provides that the agreement terminates, the debtor is entirely released from liability and can indeed recover all sums already paid. In *Kassam v Chartered Trust Plc*,[350] K, having paid 40 per cent of the price of a car he had taken on hire purchase, decided he wanted to sell the car and handed it over to a car dealer. The Chartered Trust repossessed the car from the dealer without a court order. The Court of Appeal held that the provisions of ss.90–91 applied if the dealer held the car on behalf of K, but not if he held it as a party who had agreed to buy the car. Even apart from these provisions, a court order is required by s.92 if the creditor wishes to enter upon any premises to take possession of goods (this provision also applies to goods hired by a consumer). Failure to observe the provisions of s.92 allows the debtor to recover damages for a breach of statutory duty.[351] Yet none of these provisions applies if the debtor voluntarily consents to repossession.[352] Nor does s.90 apply where the creditor simply recovers goods abandoned by the debtor,[353] nor where the debtor voluntarily terminates the agreement. However, the courts are slow to find that voluntarily termination has occurred. In *UDT (Commercial) Ltd v Ennis*[354] the Court of Appeal held that a letter which stated that "I am writing to inform you that I wish to terminate my agreement with you as I find I cannot fulfill the terms stated" did not amount to a voluntary termination, as the debtor did not understand the consequences.

INFORMATION ON DEFAULT

One of the main concerns behind the amendments made by the 2006 Act was to raise the awareness of **3.7.6** debtors who were encountering problems in meeting repayments. A variety of new provisions has therefore been added to the 1974 Act.

Notice of sums in arrears

While the Act always required the creditor to serve a default notice (see para.3.7.7 below) before exer- **3.7.6.1** cising certain rights, no notice was required if the creditor merely wished to take action to recover sums owing because the debtor had fallen into arrears. Nor did the creditor require to warn the debtor of the consequences of falling into arrears. Now, however, where under a consumer hire agreement or fixed sum credit agreement[355] the debtor or hirer has (in effect)[356] fallen two payments[357] behind, under s.86B the creditor or owner must within 14 days of that condition being fulfilled give him a notice of arrears[358]

---

[350] *Kassam v Chartered Trust Plc* [1998] R.T.R. 220.

[351] See s.92(3); and see *Ahmed v Toyota Finance*, 1996 G.W.D. 27–1566. If the goods are on hire, the hirer might also seek financial relief under s.132. For a view that under the common law of Scotland a court order is always required before goods may be repossessed, whatever the circumstances, see WCH Ervine, *Consumer Law in Scotland*, 3rd edn (Edinburgh: W. Green, 2004), paras 9.146–9.149.

[352] See s.173(3).

[353] *Bentinck v Cromwell Engineering Co* [1971] 1 Q.B. 324.

[354] *UDT (Commercial) Ltd v Ennis* [1968] 1 Q.B. 54. See also *Chartered Trust v Pitcher* [1988] R.T.R. 72.

[355] Which is neither a non-commercial agreement nor a small agreement: s.86B(12).

[356] The Act in fact speaks in terms of the amount of the shortfall being no less than the sum of the last two payments he is required to have made by that time: see generally s.86B(1).

[357] If the agreement provides for payments to be made at intervals of a week or less, then the provision is only triggered when the debtor or hirer falls four payments behind: s.86B(9). In calculating the amount of the shortfall in such an instance defaults occurring more than 20 weeks before the relevant date are not taken into account: s.86B(10)–(11).

[358] See s.86B(2)(a).

in a form prescribed by statutory instrument.[359] Moreover, he must keep on giving him such notices at intervals of not more than six months until debtor or hirer ceases to be in arrears[360] or until a court judgment orders the debtor or hirer to pay sums to the creditor or owner.[361] A similar duty is imposed by s.86C in relation to running account credit agreements. The notice again requires to be given when the debtor has failed to make the last two payments due under the agreement,[362] and it must be given no later than when the next periodic statement of account is due to be given to the debtor in terms of s.78(4)[363] (see para.3.6.1 above). The other provisions are pretty much identical to s.86B, save that there is no requirement that the debtor must keep receiving notices. Given that running account credit is involved, a debtor will get another notice each time he falls a further two payments behind. If a creditor fails to give the requisite notice within the prescribed period, then he cannot enforce the agreement until the notice is given.[364] Nor may he charge any interest or levy any default sum (see below) in respect of the period during which he is not in compliance with the Act.[365]

Default sums

3.7.6.2   As a result of the 2006 amendments, a new concept is created—the default sum. This is a sum (other than interest) payable by a debtor or hirer as a result of breach, but not a sum which is simply made payable at an earlier stage because of the breach.[366] Thus the concept clearly excludes sums payable under accelerated payments clauses, but would include charges levied by the creditor as a result of the breach, e.g. administration charges, fees in respect of exceeding credit limits or failing to make timeous payment, and would probably embrace sums payable by way of liquidated damages. The Act now aims to ensure that the debtor or hirer is fully aware of the sums for which he is liable on default. Thus where a default sum becomes payable, the creditor or owner must within the prescribed period serve a notice of such default sums.[367] Such notice may be served separately or incorporated into any other statement or notice which the creditor or owner gives under the Act,[368] e.g. a default notice. If the creditor or owner is in breach of this requirement, he may not enforce the agreement until the notice is served.[369] Interest may not be charged on default sums for the first 28 days after service of the notice.[370] Moreover, the debtor or hirer may only be charged simple interest, i.e. not compound interest, on default sums.[371] Nor can the rate of interest be higher than that generally payable under the agreement.[372] In Scotland summary diligence is not competent to enforce payment of a debt due under a regulated agreement or any related security.[373]

---

[359] See s.86B(8). That notice must include a copy of the then current arrears information sheet: s.86B(6). See the Consumer Credit (Information Requirements and Duration of Licences and Charges) Regulations 2007 (SI 2007/1167) regs 19–23 and Pts 1–3 and 5 of Sch.3 for details of the information and forms of wording required.

[360] This means that no sum under the agreement, no default sum or sum of interest remains outstanding: s.86B(5).

[361] See s.86B(4).

[362] See s.86C(1); and if a court judgment has been given against the debtor in relation to the agreement, there must be no sum still to be paid thereunder: s.86C(1)(d). In other words, if the debtor has already fallen into trouble under the agreement and had a court judgment issued against him, that must have been settled before the section can apply again.

[363] See s.86C(2). See the Consumer Credit (Information Requirements and Duration of Licences and Charges) Regulations 2007 (SI 2007/1167) regs 24–26 and Pts 4 and 5 of Sch.3 for the detail of the information and forms of wording required.

[364] See s.86D(3).

[365] See s.86D(4). This now prevents the possibility of enormous sums being charged during the period of grace, as in, e.g. *London North Securities Ltd v Meadows* [2005] C.C.L.R. 7, where due to interest and default charges a debt of less than £6,000 grew to over £140,000 by the time the case was heard.

[366] See s.187A.

[367] See s.86E(1)–(2). The section does not apply to non-commercial agreements or small agreements and regulations may provide that it does not apply to default sums under a certain amount: s.86E(7)–(8). See the Consumer Credit (Information Requirements and Duration of Licences and Charges) Regulations 2007 (SI 2007/1167) regs 27–32 and Sch.4 for the detail of the information and forms of wording required.

[368] See s.86E(3).

[369] See s.86E(5).

[370] See s.86E(4); and no charge may be made for the service of the notice itself: s.86E(6).

[371] See s.86F.

[372] See s.93.

[373] See s.93A.

Information sheets

Another innovation is the concept of the information sheet, introduced by s.86A. The FCA is charged **3.7.6.3** with the task of creating an arrears information sheet and a default information sheet. Such sheets will contain information designed to help debtors or hirers who receive a notice of arrears or a default notice, and must be sent by the creditor or owner along with such notice. Regulations may make provision as to the content of such a sheet.[374]

SERVICE OF DEFAULT NOTICE

The Act does not permit the creditor immediately to enforce his rights where the debtor is in breach. **3.7.7** Thus under s.87 where the debtor is in breach the creditor must serve a default notice in prescribed form[375] before he can:

- terminate the agreement;
- demand earlier payment of any sum (as under an accelerated payment clause: see para.3.7.4 above);
- recover possession of any goods or land;
- treat any of the debtor's rights as terminated, restricted or deferred; or
- enforce any security.

By contrast, a notice need not be served before the creditor may treat the debtor's right to draw on credit, e.g. under an overdraft or credit card, as restricted. Nor need a notice be served if the creditor merely wishes to sue for sums already due. When a notice requires to be served, it must indicate:

- the nature of the breach;
- what must be done to remedy it if it is remediable, or the sum (if any) to be paid as compensation if it is not (the Act recognises the possibility of a breach being neither remediable nor compensatable); and
- the consequences of failure to remedy the defect or pay the sum.

If the notice misstates any material particular, e.g. the amount the debtor requires to pay,[376] or lacks clarity,[377] it is invalid so that the creditor may not exercise any of the rights described above. Otherwise the debtor must be given at least 14 days to take the appropriate action, and if he does so, the breach is treated as never having occurred.[378] If the debtor fails to take the appropriate action within the relevant period, then obviously the creditor can proceed to exercise the available remedies. It should be noted that s.87 does not confer any remedies on the creditor. He is simply temporarily prevented from exercising certain of those he would have under the agreement.

Non-default notice

The creditor must similarly give the debtor at least seven days notice before exercising a right to do any **3.7.7.1** of the things mentioned in the above paragraph, which right is conferred by the agreement although the debtor is not in breach.[379] This would cover the type of situation where, for example, the creditor is entitled to terminate the agreement at will, or upon the happening of a certain event. These provisions only apply to agreements which have a specified period of duration.

---

[374] See s.86A(4).

[375] See s.88(1); and see Consumer Credit (Enforcement, Default and Termination Notices) Regulations 1983 (SI 1983/1561), as amended. The notice must also include a copy of the current default information sheet under ss.86A–88(4A).

[376] *Woodchester Lease Management Services Ltd v Swain* [1999] 1 W.L.R. 263 CA.

[377] See Sheriff Deutsch in *Citifinancial Europe Plc v Rice* [2013] Hous.L.R. 23 at [11]–[12].

[378] See s.89. In *Harrison v Link Financial Ltd* [2011] ECC 26; the fact that the default notice gave the debtor under 14 days to remedy the default (as a result of having been sent by 2nd class post), was one of the factors which persuaded the court to cancel his liability to the creditor.

[379] See ss.76, 98.

3.8   # JUDICIAL CONTROL

GENERAL POWERS

3.8.1 The Act gives the sheriff considerable and flexible powers in relation to the agreement, which are generally exercised through the making of one or more of the orders created by the Act. In making these orders, the court has, under s.135, a general power to make the order conditional on a party doing specified acts, or to suspend the operation of the order for a particular period or until something is done. The court has power under s.136 to amend an agreement so as to give proper effect to any order. However, the court cannot extend the period for which a hirer is entitled to goods.[380] It has been held that s.136 does not give a court a wide power to adjust an agreement so as to amount to rewriting it, but merely power to make orders ancillary to the making of other orders.[381] Nor does the court have any power to make a "just" order, where any of the specific orders considered below cannot be made.[382]

ENFORCEMENT ORDERS

3.8.2 As has been seen (in para.3.5.7 above), when an agreement has been improperly executed, s.127 dictates that the creditor must obtain an enforcement order before he may enforce the agreement. In deciding whether it should make an order, the court must have regard to the prejudice caused by the contravention, and the degree of culpability involved.[383] If it grants the order the court may also reduce[384] or extinguish any sum payable by the debtor or hirer or any surety. It is no longer the case that there are situations where the court has no discretion to grant an order.[385]

TIME ORDERS

3.8.3 Under s.129, time orders may be sought by the debtor in two contexts: (1) where court action has been taken against him to enforce a regulated agreement; and (2) where he has been served with a default notice, non-default notice or notice of sums in arrears. Such an order may be used for two broad purposes, firstly, to give the debtor a specified period of time to remedy any breach other than non-payment, and secondly, to reschedule the time and amounts of payments, having regard to the debtor's means. There seems to be some conflict in the authorities as to whether only sums due at the

---

[380] See s.135(3).

[381] *J & J Securities v Lee* [1994] C.C.L.R. 44.

[382] *Murie McDougall Ltd v Sinclair*, 1994 S.L.T. (Sh Ct) 74.

[383] See s.127(1). If there is neither prejudice nor culpability, the court will not be slow to grant an order. As Judge Simon Brown observes in *Rankine v American Express Services Europe Ltd* [2008] C.T.L.C. 195 at [9], " It is worth remembering the context and purpose of the CCA: the Consumer Credit Act was introduced to protect the individual unsophisticated in financial affairs in contracts with unscrupulous and sophisticated financial institutions. It was not designed to help individuals in the financial services business make money out of financial institutions through exploiting its undoubted technicalities."

[384] As in *Rank Xerox v Hepple* [1994] C.C.L.R. 1.

[385] Following the repeal of ss.127(3)–(5). However that repeal only affects agreements entered into after April 6, 2007. As regards agreements entered into before that date, there will continue to be certain defects which prevent the court enforcing the agreement. So where the agreement is cancellable, it cannot be enforced if there has been any failure to supply the requisite copies and the creditor has not supplied the debtor with a copy of the executed agreement prior to the commencement of court proceedings, or a breach of the provisions as to providing notification of the right to cancel: s.127(4). Nor can the court make an order where the agreement fails to set out certain basic terms, or is not signed by the debtor. These basic terms are: a term stating how the debtor or hirer is to discharge his obligation to make payments under the agreement; a term stating any power of the creditor or owner to vary the amount payable; and a term stating (in the case of a credit agreement) the amount of credit (or the credit limit) and the rate of interest on credit. See s.127(3) and the Consumer Credit (Agreements) Regulations 1983 (SI 1983/1553) Sch. 6. The House of Lords has held that when an agreement is unenforceable, it is not open to a creditor to bring a claim against the debtor based on unjust enrichment: see Lord Hoffmann in *Dimond v Lovell* [2002] A.C. 384 at 397.

date of the order can be thus rescheduled, or all sums due under the agreement may be rescheduled.[386] In *Southern District Finance v Barnes*[387] it was suggested that, if the creditor is seeking repossession of the land held in security for a loan, he is effectively demanding payment of all sums payable under the agreement, so the whole amount may be rescheduled. Of course, where an accelerated payments clause (see para.3.7.4 above) has operated, all sums under the agreement have inevitably become due.

Although in terms of factors to be taken into account, specific reference is only made to the debtor's means, the court refused to make an order in *First National Bank Plc v Syed*[388] when there were considerable arrears, a very poor default record, and the payments which the debtor could afford would not even meet interest accrued. Similarly, in *Murie McDougall Ltd v Sinclair*[389] an order was refused when, under the proposed instalments, a loan intended to be paid off in a period of four years would have taken over 40 years to pay. It was further held that the powers of the court do not extend to varying the contractual rate of interest.

Section 130 deals with the situation where a debtor has made an offer to pay by instalments which the creditor has accepted. There a time order may be made without regard to the debtor's means, and in the case of hire purchase or conditional sale agreements may deal with sums not yet due.

It is not clear whether the power to make time orders is intended to afford the debtor only temporary relief, or to allow the court very significantly to extend the term of the agreement.[390]

INTEREST PAYABLE ON JUDGMENT DEBTS

As a result of s.130A of the Act, if a creditor or owner under a regulated agreement has obtained a court **3.8.4** judgment that the debtor or hirer shall pay a sum of money, he must serve a notice on the debtor or hirer if he wishes to recover interest on that sum.[391] Equally, he must continue to serve further notices at intervals of not more than six months.[392] The debtor or hirer is not obliged to pay interest in respect of any period before he receives such a notice,[393] and should six months elapse without a further notice being given, his obligation will cease and will not revive until a further notice is given.[394] The form and content of such notices are prescribed by statutory instrument.[395]

HIRE PURCHASE AND CONDITIONAL SALE—RETURN AND TRANSFER ORDERS

Under s.133 these can be made where, in relation to a hire purchase or conditional sale agreement, an **3.8.5** application for an enforcement or time order has been made, or the creditor has brought an action to recover possession of the goods. A return order is simply an order for the return of goods to the creditor. A transfer order is only feasible where the goods under the agreement are divisible. It transfers the title to part of the goods to the debtor, returning the remainder to the creditor. It is subject to the limitation that the amount already paid exceeds the part of the total price referable to the transferred goods by at least one-third of the unpaid balance of the total price. This can be represented algebraically by the formula $V = P - 1/3U$, V standing for the maximum value of goods which may be transferred, P standing for the amount already paid, and U standing for the amount remaining unpaid. Notwithstanding

---

[386] Cases like *J & J Securities v Lee* [1994] C.C.L.R. 44, assert the former, while cases like *Cedar Holdings v Thompson* [1993] C.C.L.R. 7, assert the latter.

[387] *Southern District Finance v Barnes* [1995] C.C.L.R. 62 CA.

[388] *First National Bank Plc v Syed* [1991] 2 All E.R. 250.

[389] *Murie McDougall Ltd v Sinclair*, 1994 S.L.T. (Sh Ct) 74.

[390] *Southern District Finance v Barnes* [1995] C.C.L.R. 62 CA; and see the view of Lord Bingham in *Director General of Fair Trading v First National Bank* [2002] 1 All E.R. 97 at 109–110.

[391] See s.130A(1)(a).

[392] See s.130A(1)(b).

[393] See s.130A(2).

[394] See s.130A(3).

[395] See the Consumer Credit (Information Requirements and Duration of Licences and Charges) Regulations 2007 (SI 2007/1167) regs 34–35 and Sch.5.

a return or transfer order, a debtor may, at any time before the goods enter the possession of the creditor, pay the unpaid balance, fulfil any other conditions (if any), and claim the goods.[396] If the debtor fails to comply with a return or transfer order, the creditor may ask the court to revoke the order and instead order the debtor to pay for the goods retained.[397]

This section is designed to give the court the option, at least in those few cases where the goods under the agreement are divisible, to ensure that the debtor who has paid significant sums under the agreement, but cannot continue with it, is not left with nothing to show for his payments. The $V = P - 1/3U$ formula ensures that the court cannot intervene unless at least one-quarter of the price has been paid, and ensures that the creditor receives some degree of compensation for disappointed expectations and the fact that he will receive back second hand goods. So, in a case where the total price of the goods[398] is £6,000, and £1,500 has been paid, the operation of the formula will prevent any transfer order being made (the amount paid, P, is £1,500, while the amount unpaid, U, is £4,500, so one-third of that figure is also £1,500). The formula also sees the amount permitted to be transferred to rise sharply, the more of the price that has been paid. So, if in the above scenario £3,000 has been paid, the maximum value of goods which might be transferred is £2,000. But if £4,500 has been repaid, the maximum value of goods which might be transferred is £4,000. In other words a 50 per cent increase in the amount paid, leads to a 100 per cent increase in the amount which might be retained. It must be emphasised that the formula is a restriction on judicial generosity. The court may not return goods to a higher value, but it may return goods to a lower value than allowed by the formula. Indeed it may be practically forced to do so, as where for example $V = £4,000$, and the goods held under the agreement are two items worth £5,000 and £1,000 respectively. It is also within the discretion of the court to decide not to make a transfer order at all. As to the question as to how value is ascribed to the goods held under the agreement, that will be done by the agreement itself, or failing that by the court.[399]

PROTECTION ORDERS

3.8.6 In terms of s.131, on the application of a creditor or owner, the court may make such order as it thinks just for the protection from damage or depreciation of his property or any property subject to a security, pending the outcome of proceedings under the Act. Such an order might restrict or prohibit the use of the property, or give directions as to its custody.

UNFAIR RELATIONSHIPS

3.8.7 One of the key amendments made under the 2006 Act was the sweeping away of the provisions whereby courts could reopen credit bargains which it found to be extortionate. Despite the extremely wide powers conferred on courts, the provisions were ultimately judged to be a disappointment since fewer than 30 cases were brought to court over their years of operation, none in Scotland, and not that many of those cases were decided in favour of consumers.[400]

Instead a new set of powers is conferred on courts where they find that the relationship between the debtor and creditor arising out of a credit agreement (or that agreement taken with any related agreement) is unfair to the debtor. A credit agreement is defined in this context as being any agreement whereby a creditor provides an individual (the debtor) with credit of any amount.[401] So these provisions apply to agreements which would otherwise be exempt, except that it is specifically provided that they

---

[396] See s.133(4).

[397] See s.133(6).

[398] Including the deposit: s.133(2); and any sum payable on the exercise of an option to purchase.

[399] See s.133(7).

[400] See Department of Trade and Industry, *Tackling Loan Sharks and More!*, 2003. The exacting nature of the test set under the former legislation was stressed by the Master of the Rolls in *Wills v Wood* (1984) 128 S.J. 222; and by Dyson LJ in *Broadwick Financial Services Ltd v Spencer* [2002] 1 All E.R. (Comm) 446.

[401] See s.140C(1).

do not apply to consumer credit agreements secured on land which are regulated by the Financial Services Authority under the Financial Services and Markets Act 2000.[402] A relationship may be unfair to the debtor because of one or more of the following:

- any of the terms of the agreement or any related agreement—this might embrace not only situations where terms are clearly oppressive, but situations where their meaning is opaque, or perhaps where technical language is not properly explained;
- the way in which the creditor has exercised or enforced any of his rights under the agreement or any related agreement—obviously covering the behaviour of the creditor under the agreement[403];
- any other thing done (or not done) by or on behalf of the creditor (either before or after the making of the agreement or any related agreement)—this might embrace such things as misleading or coercive behaviour prior to entering into the agreement or harassment once the agreement has been made.[404]

The court in deciding whether to make a determination shall have regard to all matters it thinks relevant including matters relating to the creditor and matters relating to the debtor, while it may treat anything done (or not done) by or on behalf of, or in relation to an associate or former associate of the creditor as if done (or not done) by or on behalf of, or in relation to, the creditor.

A related agreement is any agreement which is consolidated by the main agreement, or is a linked transaction in relation to the main or consolidated agreement, or is a security provided in relation to the main agreement, a consolidated agreement, or a linked transaction. A consolidated agreement is a later agreement entered into by the debtor (in whole or in part) for purposes connected with debts owed under an earlier agreement where the parties to that earlier agreement include the debtor under the later agreement and the creditor under that agreement or an associate or former associate of his. A consolidated agreement may in turn itself be consolidated. In other words, the consideration of fairness comprehends all agreements with a practical connection to the main agreement. What may be unfair is not the content of the main agreement but that of a maintenance contract (linked transaction) or guarantee (security) entered into as a result of the main agreement. Equally, it may be unfair if the creditor persuades the debtor to increase the amount of indebtedness by entering into a new agreement.

Under the old provisions relating to extortionate credit bargains specific reference was made to such factors as prevailing interest rates when the agreement was made: the debtor's age, experience, business capacity and state of health; the degree to which he was under pressure at the time of the bargain and the nature of that pressure; the degree of risk undertaken by the creditor, taking into account the value of any security; and as regards a linked transaction, the extent to which it was reasonably required for the debtor's protection or was in the creditor's interests. While such factors are no longer explicitly mentioned, it is to be anticipated that several of them may still be of significance in deciding whether a relationship is unfair. Section 140D used to state that the advice and information published by the OFT under s.229 of the Enterprise Act 2002 shall indicate how the OFT expects Pt 8 of that Act (dealing with the enforcement of certain consumer legislation) to interact with ss.140A–140C of the 1974 Act. This led to the OFT providing guidance on how it interpreted ss.140A–140C,[405] although this

---

[402] See s.140A(5).

[403] In *Re London Scottish Finance (In Administration)* [2013] C.T.L.C. 231; it was held that the fact that the debtor had made a payment after a threat by the creditor to seek enforcement was not unfair, even though the debt was prima facie unenforceable, since the creditor could indeed have sought an enforcement order. However, where a payment had been made after a similar threat when the debt was absolutely unenforceable, this was held to be unfair, so that the debtor could recover the sums paid.

[404] It would appear, however, that a breach of one of the provisions of the Act will not lead to a finding of unfairness—at least where the Act itself provides the debtor with a remedy. In *Carey v HSBC Bank Plc* [2009] CL.T.C. 103; Judge Waksman observes (at [133]) that "what the debtor is seeking to do here is to achieve a more dramatic remedy against the creditor . . . than the statute has provided . . . This is a hopeless proposition".

[405] See OFT, *Unfair Relationships* (August 2011). At para.1.9 the OFT indeed notes that "[t]he courts are not required to have regard to OFT guidance, although they may choose to do so if they consider it to be relevant in the particular case." In *Harrison v Black Horse Ltd* [2012] E.C.C. 7 the Court of Appeal (at [40]) had noted these views, without either explicitly endorsing or rejecting them. However, the clear implication was that the guidance might indeed be relevant in appropriate circumstances, and

seemed to make no obvious impression on the approach of the courts. The FCA is expected to issue similar guidance.

Where the court determines that the relationship is unfair to the debtor it has a wide variety of orders at its disposal. However, an order may only be made[406]:

- on an application made by the debtor or by a surety (the provider of security, such as a guarantee the debt will be paid) in the sheriff court for the district where the debtor or surety resides or carries on business; or
- at the instance of the debtor or by a surety in any proceedings in any court to enforce the agreement or any related agreement if the debtor and creditor are parties to those proceedings; or
- at the instance of the debtor or by a surety in any other proceedings in any court where the amount paid or payable under the agreement or any related agreement is relevant.

It can therefore be appreciated that the issue must be raised by the debtor or surety, and the court cannot make an order of its own initiative.[407] Where the debtor or a surety alleges that the relationship is unfair to the debtor, it is for the creditor to prove the contrary.[408]

Where the court determines that the relationship is unfair to the debtor, it can do one or more of the following:

- require the creditor or any associate or former associate of his to repay (in whole or in part) any sum paid by the debtor or by a surety by virtue of the agreement or any related agreement, whether that sum was paid to the creditor, the associate or former associate or to any other person. It can be appreciated that it is therefore possible for a creditor to be ordered to repay money which the debtor paid to another person, and the section makes it clear that an order may be made even though it places on the creditor (or any associate or former associate of his) a burden in respect of an advantage enjoyed by another person[409];
- require the creditor or any associate or former associate of his to do or not to do (or to cease from doing) anything specified in the order in connection with the agreement or any related agreement. This is a clearly a power of considerable width;
- reduce or discharge any sum payable by the debtor, or by a surety, by virtue of the agreement or any related agreement;
- direct the return to a surety of any property provided by him for the purposes of a security;
- otherwise set aside (in whole or in part) any duty imposed on the debtor or on a surety by virtue of the agreement or any related agreement;
- alter the terms of the agreement or any related agreement;
- direct an accounting to be made between any persons.

It can be seen that the court may effectively rewrite the agreement if it considers this to be appropriate.[410]

---

while the Court of Appeal did not refer to OFT guidance, it did take into account regulatory guidance in the form of the Financial Services Authority's Insurance Conduct of Business Rules.

[406] See s.140B(2), (4)(b), (5). Any party to such proceedings is entitled to have any person who might be the subject of such an order made a party to the proceedings: s.140B(8).

[407] Under the provisions relating to extortionate credit bargains Dillon LJ in *First National Bank Plc v Syed* [1991] 2 All E.R. 250 at 252 had suggested that the court had the power to reopen a bargain on its own initiative, but this possibility had previously been rejected in *UDT v McDowell*, 1984 S.L.T. (Sh Ct) 10.

[408] See s.140B(9). In *Bevin v Datum Finance Ltd* [2011] EWHC (Ch) 3542, Peter Smith J disagreed with a statement in the 30th edn of *Chitty on Contracts* to the effect that a debtor would have to advance some evidence of unfairness before the court would consider the issue. He insisted (at [63]) that all the debtor need do was to assert that the relationship was unfair, whereupon it would fall to the creditor to prove otherwise.

[409] See s.140B(3).

[410] Under the previous provisions an APR of 42 per cent was reduced to 21 per cent in *Prestonwell Ltd v Capon* Unreported 1987, but the fact that security was provided for the loan was thought to render a higher than usual interest rate unnecessary. By contrast, in *Ketley v Scott* [1981] I.C.R. 241 an APR of 48 per cent was regarded as acceptable, as a genuine risk was being taken by the lender, and the borrower (unlike the other case) had business experience.

There is a growing body of case law under the new provisions. A number of cases have featured payment protection insurance. The leading case is *Harrison v Black Horse Ltd*,[411] where H was sold payment protection insurance by the company at the same time as he negotiated a loan from it. The company received as commission from the insurer 87 per cent of the amount payable under the policy. Having lost before the High Court, H argued that, in the absence of an explanation, the commission was so egregious that it gave rise to a conflict of interest which it was the lender's duty to disclose, since only disclosure could have given him the opportunity to decide whether he wished to purchase a product in circumstances where the lender derived so significant a benefit from the purchase. The appeal was dismissed. While Tomlinson LJ[412] (with whom Neuberger MR and Patten LJ agreed) noted that the commission was "quite startling and there will be many who regard it as unacceptable conduct on the part of lending institutions to have profited in this way", he could not see in "the mere size of the undisclosed commission an unfairness in the relationship between lender and borrower". Importantly, the Insurance Conduct of Business Rules did not require the disclosure of the receipt of commission. Tomlinson LJ noted the "anomalous result if a lender was obliged to disclose receipt of a commission in order to escape a finding of unfairness under s.140A, but yet not obliged to disclose it pursuant to the statutorily imposed regulatory framework under which it operates." That authority was reluctantly followed in *Conlon v Black Horse Ltd*,[413] Briggs LJ opining[414] that he did not mean

> "to express any sense of comfort about the principle laid down in the *Harrison* case. If I had been free to do so, I would have regarded a visceral instinct that the relevant conduct was beyond the Pale as a persuasive starting point in the analysis whether such conduct gave rise to an unfair relationship, all the more so where . . . the standards imposed at the time by the regulatory authorities manifestly failed to prevent the abuse of point of sale single premium PPI, to an extent that it has since become a national scandal, and has been prohibited for the future".

It would appear that the courts will be slow to find an unfair relationship in large-scale commercial lending, especially where both parties have equal bargaining power. So in *Rahman v HSBC Bank Plc*[415] neither a requirement for repayment of overdraft facilities on demand, nor a provision entitling the bank to demand repayment of all monies outstanding if R defaulted on any debt (a cross-default clause), could remotely be considered unfair. Similarly, in *Paragon Mortgages v McEwan-Peters*[416] David Steel J did not regard the invocation of a term entitling the lender to repayment of a mortgage on demand to be unfair, since such terms were "commonplace in the industry", while the power had not been exercised arbitrarily. A rare example of a court finding a relationship unfair is *Patel v Patel*.[417] The parties had known each other for over 50 years and were close family friends. The debt claimed arose under a series of oral loan agreements made between 1979 and 1992, the last replacing the earlier agreements on the basis terms that interest would accrue on all outstanding sums at 20 per cent p.a. compounded monthly. The creditor sought repayment, claiming £4.5 million, which represented £207,465 as the estimated total amount outstanding in 1992, plus the accrued compound interest. The High Court decided that the relationship arising from the 1992 agreement was unfair to the debtor, taking into account the terms of the agreement and the way in which the creditor had exercised his rights under the agreement, particularly his failure to provide any further calculation after 1992 or to keep any proper record of the outstanding amount. In considering what order to make under s.140B, the

---

[411] *Harrison v Black Horse Ltd* [2012] E.C.C. 7. In *MBNA Europe Bank Ltd v Thorius* [2010] E.C.C. 8; the County Court had held the ppi agreement to be unfair under s.140A precisely because the debtor was unaware that the lender would receive commission, while in *Yates v Nemo Personal Finance* Unreported, May 14, 2010, the selling of a ppi policy was held by the County Court to be an extortionate credit bargain.

[412] *Harrison v Black Horse Ltd* [2012] E.C.C. 7 at [58].

[413] *Conlon v Black Horse Ltd* [2013] EWCA Civ 1658.

[414] *Conlon v Black Horse Ltd* [2013] EWCA Civ 1658 at [26].

[415] *Rahman v HSBC Bank Plc* [2012] EWHC 11 (Ch). In *Maple Leaf v Rouvroy* [2009] 1 Lloyd's Rep. 475; it was held that the provisions did not apply as no credit had been granted. However, Andrew Smith J indicated that there was no unfairness in any case, in part because the case involved "experienced businessmen": see para.287. See also *Deutsche Bank (Suisse) SA v Khan* [2013] EWHC 482 (Comm).

[416] *Paragon Mortgages v McEwan-Peters* [2011] EWHC (Comm) 241 at [54].

[417] *Patel v Patel* [2010] 1 All E.R. (Comm) 864.

court considered what was proportionate, having regard to the nature and degree of the unfairness, and concluded that it would not be fair to require the debtor to pay anything more than the £207,465 which was outstanding in 1992.

Where the debtor is an ordinary individual, the courts have still been slow to find unfairness even where interest rates are very high if those rates reflect what the market would generally charge in those circumstances. Thus in *Consolidated Finance Ltd v Hunter*[418] H was granted a 90 day loan to enable him to pay off his bankruptcy debts and annul his bankruptcy. A compound interest rate of 2 per cent per month during the 90-day period and 3.75 per cent thereafter was not regarded as unfair, as it represented the market rate for similar short-term bridging loans. Similarly, in *Shaw v Nine Regions Ltd*[419] making a loan at an APR of almost 342 per cent was found by Roderick Evans J not to be unfair, since such rates were standard for sub-prime loans made to borrowers who could not otherwise obtain finance. Yet in both those cases the judge stressed the fact that the borrower was aware of the details of the loan and the consequences of default, that he had not been misled by the lender in any way, and that the lender had acted properly in seeking to enforce the debt.[420] By contrast in *Barons Finance v Olubisi*[421] the fact that a sub-prime loan was made at the normal rate of interest for such a loan did not prevent the relationship being unfair where the court believed that the lender had exploited a vulnerable individual.

It may be added that certain terms which might be thought to be unfair may also be challenged under the Unfair Terms in Consumer Contracts Regulations 1999.[422] A successful challenge under the regulations would render the term unenforceable.[423] The Regulations are, of course, narrower than the unfair relationship provisions, since as Tomlinson LJ points out in *Harrison v Black Horse Ltd*[424] "it is the relationship between the parties which must be determined to be unfair, not their agreement, although it is envisaged that the terms of the agreement may themselves give rise to an unfair relationship". Thus, as noted above, the creditor's behaviour or the way in which it chooses to enforce its rights may make a relationship unfair.

FINANCIAL RELIEF FOR HIRERS

3.8.8 Under s.132, where the owner of goods recovers them through or without taking court action, the hirer may request the court to order repayment of part or all of the sums repaid, and that the obligation to pay any sums owed shall cease. If it appears to the court just to do so, having regard to the extent of the enjoyment of the goods by the hirer, it may grant such an application in whole or in part. The provision is clearly designed to allow courts to afford a hirer, who has lost the goods, some degree of relief in situations where he might have to pay practically the full cost of hire without getting the corresponding benefit. Yet the courts thus far have shown little interest in exercising this discretion. In *Automotive Financial Services Ltd v Henderson*[425] H, having agreed to lease a car for three years, returned it after six months, and ceased the monthly payments. A Ltd, as it was entitled to do under the agreement, rescinded and claimed the total of the sums due on termination of agreement. He requested relief under s.132, but relief was denied by the sheriff. The case for the defenders was that the pursuers having received six months hire payments and having resold the car, had already recouped more than the original value of the car. Therefore it was unjust that they should be able to recover the whole amount

---

[418] *Consolidated Finance Ltd v Hunter* [2010] B.P.I.R. 1322; see Judge Swan at [29]–[34].

[419] *Shaw v Nine Regions Ltd* [2010] C.T.L.C. 1.

[420] See e.g. Judge Swan in *Hunter* at [22]–[28].

[421] *Barons Finance v Olubisi* Unreported, 2010, referred to at para.3.21 of OFT, *Unfair Relationships* (August 2011).

[422] Unfair Terms in Consumer Contracts Regulations 1999 (SI 1999/2083).

[423] *Falco Finance Ltd v Gough* [1999] C.C.L.R. 16.

[424] *Harrison v Black Horse Ltd* [2012] E.C.C. 7 at [37]. While Andrew Smith J observes in *Maple Leaf v Rouvroy* [2009] 1 Lloyd's Rep. 475; at para.283 that "[t]he question of the fairness of the relationship . . . calls for a different enquiry from that required by the 1999 Regulations."

[425] *Automotive Financial Services Ltd v Henderson*, 1992 S.L.T. (Sh Ct) 63.

of the sums due on termination of agreement. It was suggested that it would be just to order payment of a lesser sum. This argument did not impress the sheriff, who observed[426]:

> "The pursuers carry out a financing operation and clearly make their money by charging sums for the hire of a vehicle which, if totaled up add up to a figure some way over the price of the vehicle if that were simply bought by the customer. To suggest that the payments made should somehow entitle the customer to relief seems to me to be an unlikely proposition unless the defenders can set out a good reason why the pursuers should be satisfied in the commercial sense with what they have received. The defenders have not attempted to do so. Looking at the matter in another way, they have not even started to suggest that the payment sought is by way of a penalty."

The sheriff was held by the sheriff principal on appeal to have properly exercised his discretion.

ADR IN CONSUMER CREDIT

While the range of rights and remedies available to consumers under the Act is undoubtedly impres- **3.9** sive, it is thought that many consumers have been deterred from enforcing their rights through finding the prospect of going to court intimidating, whether in terms of cost or otherwise. Consequently, the 2006 Act extended the jurisdiction of the Financial Ombudsman Service under the Financial Services and Markets Act 2000 to cover complaints involving licensees under the 1974 Act. Since such activities are now regulated under the 2000 Act in any case, the enabling legislation (s.226A of that Act) is no longer necessary, and has been repealed.

Prior to the coming into force of the Financial Services and Markets Act 2000 a number of different complaints handling schemes operated within the financial services industry, operating under a variety of legal regimes. These were replaced by the Financial Ombudsman Service ("FOS"). Essentially the role of FOS is to consider complaints by consumers. The Ombudsman will undertake any necessary investigation, and may require a party to provide specified information or produce specified documents.[427] If a party fails to comply with such a requirement, the Ombudsman may refer the matter to the court, and if the court finds that a party failed to comply with a requirement without reasonable excuse it may treat a party as if he were in contempt. The Ombudsman must consider the representations of the parties, and may decide to hold a hearing, but is not obliged to do so.

If the parties cannot resolve the dispute, the Ombudsman will determine the complaint according to what is fair and reasonable in all the circumstances of the case, taking into account the law, the rules of regulators, codes of practice and what he considers to be good industry practice.[428] It can thus be appreciated that the consumer's legal rights are only one of the factors bearing on that decision, fairness rather than strict legality being the key consideration. If the determination is in favour of the consumer, it may direct that the licensee takes such steps in relation to the consumer as the Ombudsman considers just[429] and appropriate (whether or not a court might order such steps),[430] and/or make a money award, subject to a maximum of £150,000.[431] Such a money award may compensate not only financial loss, but also pain and suffering, damage to reputation, or distress and inconvenience.[432] A money award might also seek to cover some or all of the costs reasonably incurred by the consumer in bringing the complaint. Although the scheme is designed to be free to the consumer,[433] so that even if the complaint is rejected

---

[426] *Automotive Financial Services Ltd v Henderson*, 1992 S.L.T. (Sh Ct) 63 at 64I–J.

[427] Financial Services and Markets Act 2000 s.231.

[428] See s.228(2).

[429] See s.232.

[430] See s.229(2B).

[431] See s.229(2A). Although that figure cannot formally be exceeded, it need not be taken into account when the Ombudsman is making another type of determination. Thus it is possible, albeit unlikely, that a consumer may be benefited to an amount exceeding £150,000 if a direction confers a financial advantage on a consumer, as where goods are ordered to be transferred to the consumer. A money award is enforceable as if it were a sheriff court decree: Sch.17 Pt 3A para.16D.

[432] See s.229(3).

[433] But the FOS will levy fees on the holders of particular kinds of standard licence to meet the costs of the scheme: s.243A.

he will not be liable to meet the costs of the respondent, the consumer may be asked to contribute towards the costs of the FOS itself if the Ombudsman believes that his conduct was improper or unreasonable or that he was responsible for unreasonable delay.[434] Although the maximum figure cannot be exceeded, if the Ombudsman considers that fair compensation requires payment of a larger amount, he may recommend that the respondent pays the consumer such amount.[435] Such a recommendation is not binding. It should also be noted that within the specific consumer credit jurisdiction, the FOS can specify the maximum amount which may be regarded as fair compensation for a particular type of loss or damage,[436] i.e. create different compensation ceilings for different types of loss. The Ombudsman will allow the consumer a certain period to indicate whether he accepts or rejects the determination.[437] If he accepts the determination, it is final and binding on both parties.[438] If he rejects it, failure to respond within the allotted period being treated as rejection,[439] both parties become free to pursue their legal remedies. It can be seen that the matter lies in the hands of the consumer. The respondent may not reject a determination. No appeal lies from a determination, although it might theoretically be subject to judicial review. Failure to comply with a determination will be reported to the FCA, who will take that behaviour into account in assessing the respondent's fitness to hold a licence.

---

[434] See s.230.
[435] See s.229(5).
[436] See s.229(4A).
[437] See s.228(4).
[438] See s.228(5).
[439] See s.228(6).

Chapter 4

CARRIAGE OF GOODS

INTRODUCTION

Goods often have to be transported considerable distances, whether at the instance of a seller or buyer **4.1** or otherwise, and a carrier is often employed to effect that transport. A contract of carriage is a contract for the hire of work and services, its essence being that the carrier is hired to carry goods safely from A to B in his own vehicle. If a seller agrees to transport goods to the buyer using his own vehicle, that is not a contract of carriage. Nor is it a contract of carriage if an individual merely hires a vehicle in order that he or his employees might collect goods he has ordered. There are three main forms of carriage, by land, sea and air, and we shall outline the main features of the legal regimes relating to each, touching also on the issues raised by multimodal transport, i.e. where two or more of the above modes have to be combined.

4.2   # CARRIAGE BY LAND

COMMON CARRIER

4.2.1 A carrier will either be a private carrier or a common carrier. A common carrier is someone who holds himself out as prepared to convey goods for anyone who chooses to contract with him.[1] He does not cease to be a common carrier just because in so holding out he places limitations on the places to which he will go[2] or the type of goods he will carry,[3] or indicates that he will carry only under particular conditions.[4] Although whether a carrier falls to be regarded as a common carrier is essentially a question of fact,[5] it has been held that removal firms are not common carriers.[6] Moreover, by virtue of statute neither railway companies,[7] nor anyone providing a "universal postal service",[8] may be regarded as common carriers. It is also the case that standard form contracts in those industries which appear to involve common carriers tend to make it clear that they contract only on the basis that the carrier is not a common carrier.[9]

Certain results flow from being a common carrier. Firstly, he is taken to be making a continuing offer to carry (subject to any limitations as described above), which is open to be accepted by anyone.[10] If he refuses to carry goods when asked, he will be liable in damages,[11] unless the refusal is justified. Such refusal may be justified if:

- there is no capacity in his vehicle(s)—he is not bound to find extra capacity just because he is approached by a customer[12];
- the goods are not tendered at an appropriate time for loading[13];
- the consignor refuses to pay the freight in advance when asked to do so[14]—if the carrier carries the goods without requesting advance payment, he may not then demand payment until the carriage is complete, and is thus liable if he refuses to continue unless paid[15];
- carriage of the goods would be dangerous for himself, his employees, his vehicle, or other goods[16]—the consignor is liable to anyone who suffers loss or injury as a result of him entrusting dangerous goods to any carrier, common or otherwise, without advising the carrier

---

[1] *Barr & Sons v Caledonian Ry Co* (1890) 18 R. 139.

[2] See Parke B in *Johnson v Midland Ry Co* (1849) 4 Exch. 367 at 373.

[3] *Dickson v Great Northern Ry Co* (1886) 18 Q.B.D. 176; *A Siohn & Co Ltd v R H Hagland & Sons (Transport) Ltd* [1976] 2 Lloyd's Rep. 428.

[4] *Great Northern Ry Co v LEP* [1922] 2 K.B. 742.

[5] *Pearcey v Player* (1883) 10 R. 564.

[6] *Pearcey v Player* (1883) 10 R. 564.

[7] Transport Act 1962 s.43(6); Railways Act 1993 s.123.

[8] Postal Services Act 2000 s.99.

[9] Thus the law relating to common carriers has little scope for application, leading to calls for the concept to be abolished: McBain, "Time to Abolish the Common Carrier?" [2005] J.B.L. 545.

[10] See Brett LJ in *Nugent v Smith* (1875) 1 C.P.D. 19 at 27.

[11] Bell, *Principles*, s.159.

[12] See Cozens-Hardy MR in *Spillers & Bakers v Great Western Ry Co (No.2)* [1911] 1 K.B. 386 at 392.

[13] See Cockburn CJ in *Garton v Bristol & Exeter Ry Co* (1861) 30 L.J.Q.B. 273 at 293.

[14] *Wyld v Pickford* (1841) 8 M. & W. 443.

[15] *Barnes v Marshall* (1852) 18 Q.B. 785.

[16] *Bamfield v Goole & Sheffield Transport Co* [1910] 2 K.B. 94.

of this.[17] It is not sufficient to label packaging as dangerous without properly advising the carrier of the nature of the danger[18];

- the goods are not adequately packed[19];
- the goods are of a nature that it is unreasonable to expect the carrier to carry, e.g. where they are of immense size[20]; or
- the goods are of a value out of all proportion to the security measures he would have to take.[21]

A common carrier is bound by any rates advertised,[22] but in any case may not charge more than reasonable freight.[23] If he does charge more than is reasonable, then an action lies for the excess,[24] although as long as he does not exceed what is reasonable he is not bound to charge everyone the same rate.[25]

The reason why a common carrier may refuse to carry goods of a value out of all proportion to the security measures he would have to take is that he is strictly liable for the loss of or damage to the goods, even though there is no negligence on his part.[26] This is obviously a principle of central importance. There are a number of exceptions to this rule of strict liability. Thus the rule does not apply when the damage results from:

- an act of God, in the sense of a natural event which the carrier could not have predicted or guarded against, e.g. a sudden flood.[27] While an accidental fire would fall into this category, statute makes not only common carriers, but also private carriers liable for such damage[28];
- an act of the Queen's enemies, in the sense of armed forces of a foreign power, rather than mere rebels or rioters[29];
- the inherent vice of the goods—this means a natural characteristic of the goods which led to their damage, as where a horse became restless and injured itself trying to escape,[30] or where wine fermented and exploded during transit.[31] Naturally, a carrier cannot escape liability if an animal suffers injury because it is imperfectly secured[32]; or
- the fault of the consignor, as where the goods are inadequately addressed[33] or packaged,[34] or where the consignor insists on stowing the goods himself and does so ineffectively.[35]

It should also be noted that, even where an exception applies, a common carrier will still be liable, if he or his employees by their negligence contributed to the loss,[36] or aggravated it once it had arisen.[37] Again these defences are not available if the carrier has deviated from the agreed route, unless the loss would have resulted even without the deviation.[38] While a common carrier will be liable for damage

---

[17] *Cramb v Caledonian Ry Co* (1892) 19 R. 954.

[18] *Cramb v Caledonian Ry Co* (1892) 19 R. 954.

[19] See Kennedy LJ in *Sutcliffe v Great Western Ry Co* [1910] 1 K.B. 478 at 503.

[20] See Bailhache J in *Date v Sheldon* (1921) 7 Ll. L. Rep. 53 at 54.

[21] *McManus v Lancashire & Yorkshire Ry Co* (1859) 28 L.J. Ex. 353.

[22] *Campbell v Ker*, February 24, 1810, F.C.

[23] *Pickford v Grand Junction Ry Co* (1841) 8 M. & W. 372.

[24] *Baxendale v London and South West Ry Co* (1866) L.R.1 Ex. 137.

[25] See Blackman J in *Great Western Ry Co v Sutton* (1866) L.R. 4 H.L. 226 at 237.

[26] Bell, *Principles*, s.235.

[27] *Makin v London & North Eastern Ry Co* [1943] K.B. 467.

[28] Mercantile Law Amendment (Scotland) Act 1856 s.17. But this provision only applies if the fire should occur in Scotland. Thus if a carrier is employed to transport goods from London to Inverness, s.17 has no application should a fire occur while the goods are still in England, but would apply if the fire broke out once the vehicle had crossed the border—see *Atlantic Computing Services (UK) Ltd v Burns Express Freight Ltd*, 2004 S.C. 365. Lord Robertson in *James Kemp (Leslie) Ltd v Robertson*, 1967 S.C. 229 at 230–231; suggests that the provision also applies to private carriers.

[29] *Curtis v Mathews* [1919] 1 K.B. 425.

[30] *Ralston v Caledonian Ry Co* (1878) 5 R. 671.

[31] *Farrar v Adams* (1711) Buller N.P. 69.

[32] *Paxton v North British Ry Co* (1870) 9 M. 50.

[33] *Hunter v Caledonian Ry Co* (1858) 20 D. 1097.

[34] *Gould v South Eastern Ry Co* [1920] 2 K.B. 186.

[35] *Rain v Glasgow & South-Western Ry Co* (1869) 7 M. 439.

[36] *Burns v Royal Hotel (St Andrews)*, 1958 S.C. 354.

[37] *Notara v Henderson* (1872) L.R. 7 Q.B. 225.

[38] *James Morrison & Co Ltd v Shaw, Savill and Albion Co Ltd* [1916] 2 K.B. 783.

caused by unjustifiable delay in carriage,[39] if the delay was unavoidable, as where it was occasioned by an accident for which the carrier was not responsible, then no liability arises.[40] Of course, if delay is foreseeable, then the carrier will still be liable, unless he has warned the consignor of the possibility of delay.[41] This might arise, for example, where the carrier is aware that probable delays on a particular route might damage perishable goods. It might be added that, where a delay does threaten perishable goods, a carrier who is unable to obtain the instructions of the consignor as to their disposal, is constituted as an agent of necessity to sell them.[42]

STATUTORY LIMITATION ON LIABILITY OF COMMON CARRIER

4.2.2 The strict liability of a common carrier at common law could clearly operate very onerously, particularly where the contents of very small packages turned out to be of immense value. Thus the Carriers Act 1830 s.1 provides that no common carrier shall be liable for loss or injury to a parcel or package containing certain types of article, the total value of which exceeds £10, unless the nature and value of such articles is declared to the carrier on delivery[43] and any increased charge is paid. The types of article covered by the Act are generally things which tend to be valuable and/or fragile, e.g. gold, silver, precious stones, timepieces or paintings.[44] To entitle the carrier to levy the increased charge, he must affix in a conspicuous part of his premises a legible notice stating the increased charge.[45] If he fails in this, he may not levy the increased charge, and is liable to refund the excess,[46] but does not forfeit the protection of the Act.[47] Where the consignor has made the requisite declaration and paid any increased charge, he is entitled to recover the value of any goods lost, plus the amount of any increased charge,[48] although the carrier may attempt to prove that the actual value of the goods is less than their declared value.[49] If the consignor has either not made the requisite declaration, or not paid any properly levied increased charge, then he may not recover the value of the items lost or damaged, although if the items consigned were a mixture of articles covered by the Act and articles outwith its scope, the carrier remains strictly liable for the loss of the latter category of goods.[50] It might be added that the carrier cannot claim the protection of the Act where the loss or damage results from the dishonesty of his employee.[51] Nor does the Act absolve an employee from any personal liability, e.g. as might arise as a result of his dishonest or negligent behaviour.[52] It is always open to a carrier to make a special contract with a consignor, excluding the effect of the Act, and perhaps either excluding or limiting any liability to that consignor.[53]

PRIVATE CARRIER

4.2.3 If a carrier is not a common carrier, then he must be a private carrier. By definition, none of the consequences of being a common carrier apply to a private carrier. Thus he does not make a standing offer to carry, and thus can decide with whom he will contract. Moreover, he is not restricted as to the terms

---

[39] *Crawford v London, Midland & Scottish Ry Co*, 1929 S.N. 66.

[40] *Anderson v North British Ry Co* (1875) 2 R. 443.

[41] *McConnachie v Great North of Scotland Ry Co* (1875) 3 R. 79.

[42] *Forth Tugs Ltd v Wilmington Trust Co*, 1985 S.C. 317.

[43] Simply indicating that the goods are valuable is not the same thing as declaring their value—see Lord Hunter in *Rusk v North British Ry Co*, 1920 2 S.L.T. 139 at 141.

[44] See s.1.

[45] See s.2.

[46] See s.3.

[47] See Lord Hunter in *Rusk v North British Ry Co*, 1920 2 S.L.T. 139 at 141.

[48] See s.7.

[49] See s.9.

[50] *Treadwin v Great Eastern Ry Co* (1868) L.R. 3 C.P. 308.

[51] See s.7.

[52] See s.8.

[53] See s.6.

on which he will contract, in particular as to the amount of freight he charges. Nor is he subject to the strict liability of the common carrier. However, he does undertake to exercise reasonable care in the exercise of the contract[54] and while it is for the consignor to prove negligence or breach of duty,[55] the fact that goods delivered to the carrier in good condition are then delivered by him in a damaged state is prima facie evidence of fault.[56]

EXCLUSION OF LIABILITY

The Unfair Contract Terms Act 1977 applies to all contracts of carriage.[57] Thus any contractual term or notice which purports to exclude or restrict liability for breach of any duty to take reasonable care or exercise reasonable skill, which duty arises in the course of a business out of a term of a contract or at common law, shall only have effect if it was fair and reasonable to incorporate it into the contract.[58] Equally, a term in a consumer or standard form contract which purports to exclude or restrict liability for breach of contract only receives effect if it was fair and reasonable to incorporate it into the contract.[59] Thus any exclusion or limitation clause in a contract with a private carrier or a special contract with a common carrier is potentially liable to being struck down by the 1977 Act. It is also the case that an exclusion clause in a standard form contract of carriage with a consumer may be struck down as unfair under the Unfair Terms in Consumer Contracts Regulations 1999.[60] Yet no legislation prevents a common carrier entering into a special contract with a consignor, which excludes his strict liability at common law. It should be pointed out, however, that a common carrier may not exclude liability by notice, only by agreement.[61] **4.2.4**

  Without going into the law as to formation of contracts, it may also be observed that an issue may sometimes arise as to whether an exclusion or limitation clause is properly incorporated into the contract.[62] Moreover, exclusion or limitation clauses are construed *contra proferentem*. Thus in a contract with a common carrier such a clause would have to make it clear whether it intended to exclude strict common law liability, liability for negligence, liability for breach of contract, or all of these things. In *Graham v Shore Porters Society*[63] when the clause simply baldly excluded liability, it was construed as excluding only strict common law liability, leaving liability for negligence or breach of contract unaffected. Again, liability for negligence will usually only be held to be excluded if the clause explicitly says so, or this is the only meaning it can reasonably bear.[64] It has been held that unjustified deviation from the agreed route prevents a carrier relying on exclusion or limitation clauses.[65] There would appear to be no logical reason why this should be so, provided the exclusion clause were sufficiently widely drawn to accommodate such a breach of contract. Yet to the argument that the question whether a party can rely on an exclusion clause to justify his own serious breach has long been acknowledged to be a matter of construction rather than principle, it might be responded that Lord Wilberforce in *Photo Productions Ltd v Securicor Transport Ltd*[66] suggested that the deviation cases were sui generis and subject to special rules.[67]

---

[54] *Boomsma v Clark & Rose*, 1983 S.L.T. (Sh Ct) 67.
[55] *Copland v Brogan*, 1916 S.C. 277.
[56] *Sutton & Co v Ciceri & Co* (1890) 17 R. (HL) 40.
[57] See s.15(2)(c).
[58] See ss.16(1)(b), 25(1).
[59] See s.17(1).
[60] Unfair Terms in Consumer Contracts Regulations 1999 (SI 1999/2083).
[61] Carriers Act 1830 s.4.
[62] *McCutcheon v MacBrayne (David) Ltd*, 1964 S.L.T. 66.
[63] *Graham v Shore Porters Society*, 1979 S.L.T. 119.
[64] *Page v London, Midland & Scottish Ry Co Ltd* [1943] 1 All E.R. 455.
[65] *Lord Polwarth v North British Ry Co*, 1908 S.C. 1275.
[66] *Photo Productions Ltd v Securicor Transport Ltd* [1980] A.C. 827 at 845F.
[67] But see Lloyd LJ in *Kenya Rys v Antares Co Pte Ltd (The Antares (No.1))* [1987] 1 Lloyd's Rep. 424 at 430.

DURATION OF LIABILITY

4.2.5 A carrier's duties operate from the point at which the goods are delivered to him[68] (or his agent or employee), until he delivers the goods to the consignee or to another carrier to continue their journey.[69] That being said, it is possible for the parties to settle the duration of carriage by agreement, e.g. by stipulating that it (and thus any duty attached thereto) terminates when the goods are delivered to the consignee's address, whether or not he is there to receive them. Where the goods are not to be delivered to the consignee's premises, as where the consignee is supposed to collect them from the carrier's local office, the consignee must be informed of their arrival and allowed a reasonable time to collect them, the carriage being deemed to continue during that period.[70] Moreover, if the consignee refuses or delays to receive the goods, or turns out not to exist, then the character of the carrier's stewardship of the goods alters to that of a mere depositary or warehouseman, thus liable only to take reasonable care of them until the consignor receives them back.[71] It does not amount to delivery simply to leave the goods at the carrier's premises,[72] nor to hand them over to his employees en route,[73] unless they have been instructed to collect them.[74] Obviously, if the carrier misdelivers the goods, he will be liable for any loss. Yet in turn he may recover the value of the goods from the person to whom they were wrongly delivered, unless he is personally barred from doing so.[75] If, on the other hand, the carrier delivers to the correct address and to an apparently authorised person, he is not liable if that person misappropriates the goods.[76]

THE CARRIER'S LIEN

4.2.6 Once the contract has been carried out, a carrier has a special lien over the goods for the freight charges under the contract,[77] but has no general lien in respect of outstanding charges under other contracts of carriage involving that consignor.[78] Yet such a general lien can be created by contract[79] and most standard form contracts will do so. It was seen in the context of sale of goods how an unpaid seller of goods who exercises the right to stop goods in transit may instruct the carrier to redeliver the goods.[80] This right yields to a carrier's special lien, so that a carrier may refuse to redeliver the goods unless the freight charges are paid. However, the right will prevail over a general lien, unless the seller was a party to the agreement creating that lien.[81] (For a general discussion of the nature of liens see para.5.4.1 below.)

INTERNATIONAL CARRIAGE

4.3 The above account, like the rest of the book, states the law as it applies to Scotland. However, without going into the intricacies of private international law, if a transaction has an international dimension, it is by no means certain that it would be governed by Scots law. We are obviously not going to consider

---

[68] *Bain v Brown* (1824) 3 S. 256.
[69] *Gilmour v Clark* (1853) 15 D. 478.
[70] *Chapman v Great Western Ry Co* (1880) 5 Q.B.D. 278, per Cockburn CJ at 281.
[71] Bell, *Principles*, s.235; *Metzenburg v Highland Ry Co* (1869) 7 M. 919.
[72] Bell, *Principles*, s.162.
[73] Bell, *Principles*, s.162.
[74] Bell, *Principles*, s.162.
[75] *Caledonian Ry Co v Harrison & Co* (1879) 7 R. 151.
[76] *British Traders Ltd v Unique Transport Ltd* [1952] 2 Lloyd's Rep. 236.
[77] *Scottish Central Ry Co v Ferguson, Rennie & Co* (1864) 2 M. 781.
[78] *Peebles & Son v Caledonian Ry Co* (1875) 2 R. 346.
[79] *Great Eastern Ry Co v Lord's Trustee* [1909] A.C. 109.
[80] Sale of Goods Act 1979 s.46(4).
[81] *United States Steel Products Co v Great Western Ry Co* [1916] 1 A.C. 189.

how various foreign systems might treat carriage of goods by land, but the UK is a party to certain international conventions which govern international carriage of goods by land, so that the principles governing most contracts of that nature are clear.

INTERNATIONAL CARRIAGE OF GOODS BY ROAD 4.4

THE GENEVA CONVENTION

The UK is a party to the Geneva Convention on Contracts for the International Carriage of Goods by **4.4.1** Road, which receives effect through the Carriage of Goods by Road Act 1965. The Convention applies to contracts of carriage of goods by road for reward where the places of uplifting and delivery are in two different countries, at least one of which is a party to the Convention.[82] Obviously, the Convention does not apply where carriage occurs wholly within the UK, and nor does it apply to carriage between the UK and the Channel Islands[83] or the Republic of Ireland.[84] There are also specific exclusions in respect of furniture removal and the carriage of mail or funeral consignments.[85] The Convention does not generally apply to multimodal transport, e.g. carriage partly by road and partly by sea.[86] Yet it does apply if goods are carried for part of the journey by some other means, as long as they never leave the vehicle, e.g. where a lorry carrying goods spends part of the journey aboard a ferry.[87] That being said, for the Convention to apply there must be an international element to the carriage of goods by road. The Convention would not apply, for example, if a lorry carried goods from Glasgow to Dover, was then placed on a ferry, and immediately unloaded on reaching France.[88] Where the Convention does apply, and loss, damage or delay occurs during carriage by the other mode of transport, then the carrier's liability will usually be determined according to the law applicable to the other mode of transport.[89] Finally, it may be observed that, although parties may not contract out of the Convention,[90] they may contract into it by invoking its terms when it would not otherwise apply.[91]

CONSIGNMENT NOTE

While the Convention says nothing about the contract's constitution, each contract must be confirmed **4.4.2** by a consignment note, signed by both parties[92]—one for each party and one to accompany the goods.[93] The note must contain key particulars and statements,[94] and should contain a description of the goods if they are dangerous.[95] The carrier will not be liable for any loss which derives from inadequacy of particulars in the note.[96] On receiving the note, the carrier must check whether statements in the note as

---

[82] See art.1(1).

[83] *Chloride Industrial Batteries Ltd v F & W Freight Ltd* [1989] 1 W.L.R. 823.

[84] See art.1(5).

[85] See art.1(4). Furniture removal typically involves assistance with the packing of the goods and their distribution at the destination. A contract does not fall within the scope of this exclusion merely because it happens to be furniture which is being carried—*Parr v Clark & Rose Ltd*, 2002 S.C.L.R. 222.

[86] But see Mance LJ in *Quantum Corp Ltd v Plane Trucking Ltd* [2002] 1 W.L.R. 2678 at [59]. See also *Datec Electronic Holdings Ltd v UPS Ltd* [2007] UKHL 23.

[87] See art.2(1).

[88] *Princes Buitoni v Hapag-Lloyd Aktiengesellschaft* [1991] 2 Lloyd's Rep. 383.

[89] See art.2(1).

[90] See art.41(1).

[91] *Princes Buitoni v Hapag-Lloyd Aktiengesellschaft* [1991] 2 Lloyd's Rep. 383.

[92] See art.4.

[93] See art.5(1).

[94] See art.6.

[95] See art.22(1).

[96] See art.7.

to such things as the condition of the goods are accurate, and if he cannot check, he must enter his reservations on the note.[97] The note is prima facie evidence of the receipt of the goods, the making of the contract and any conditions mentioned therein.[98] Failure to issue the note has no effect on the validity of the underlying contract, which continues to be subject to the Convention.[99] However, if it is not issued, or even if it fails to indicate that the carriage is subject to the provisions of the Convention, the carrier cannot rely on the limitations on his liability described below.[100]

DISPOSAL AND DELIVERY

4.4.3 The consignment note must indicate the destination of the goods and the consignee's name and address.[101] The consignor has control over the goods and may alter the place of delivery or indicate a new consignee or stop the goods in transit.[102] The only limitations on this right are that any instructions given must not divide the consignment,[103] or interfere with the carrier's undertaking or prejudice the consignors or consignees of other consignments he is carrying.[104] Otherwise, the carrier must obey any instructions given,[105] and is liable for any loss or damage resulting from his failure to do so.[106] The consignor loses control over the goods when:

- the consignee receives his copy of the consignment note[107]; or
- when the goods arrive at the designated delivery place, and the consignee produces a receipt and requires their delivery and the delivery of his copy of the consignment note[108]; or
- when the goods fail to arrive at their contractual destination, and the consignee seeks to enforce his contractual rights.[109]

If carriage or delivery is rendered impossible, the carrier must seek instructions from the party entitled to dispose of the goods.[110] If they are still in transit, he may take the steps he considers to be in that party's best interests.[111] That may mean their unloading, storage or sale. Sale is possible without instructions if[112]:

- the goods are perishable or their condition warrants sale; or
- the storage expenses would be disproportionate to the value of the goods; or
- if after a reasonable time he has not received reasonable instructions to the contrary from the party entitled to dispose of the goods.

It is that party who is entitled to the proceeds of sale.[113]

---

[97] See art.8.
[98] See art.9; but prima facie evidence can of course be rebutted: see *Ulster-Swift Ltd v Taunton Meat Haulage Ltd* [1975] 2 Lloyd's Rep. 502.
[99] See art.4.
[100] See art.7(3).
[101] See art.6(1)(d), (e).
[102] See art.12(1).
[103] See art.12(5)(c).
[104] See art.12(5)(b).
[105] See art.12(2).
[106] See art.12(7).
[107] See art.12(2).
[108] See art.13(1).
[109] See arts 12(2), 13(1).
[110] See art.14(1).
[111] See art.14(2).
[112] See art.16(3).
[113] See art.16(4).

LOSS, DAMAGE OR DELAY

The carrier is prima facie liable for any loss, damage or delay occurring during carriage.[114] Delay **4.4.4** occurs when the goods have not been delivered within the agreed time limit, or if there is none, within a reasonable time.[115] If the goods have not been delivered within 30 days of the agreed time limit or, if there is none, within 60 days of the carrier receiving the goods, they are treated as lost.[116] However, the carrier is not liable if the loss, damage or delay is caused by[117]:

- the wrongful act or neglect of the claimant;
- the claimant's instructions (if not attributable to the wrongful act or neglect of the carrier);
- the inherent vice of the goods—frozen food being carried on a refrigerated vehicle has no inherent vice, so that if it spoils due to inadequate refrigeration, this defence cannot succeed[118]; or
- circumstances which he was unable to avoid and the consequences of which he was unable to prevent, e.g. when goods are violently hijacked.[119] In deciding whether the carrier could have avoided the peril, it must be shown that he did his utmost, short of carrying precautions to unreasonable extremes. Acting as a normal prudent carrier would act is not enough.[120]

The burden of proof in relation to these exceptions lies on the carrier.[121] He is further exempted from the special risks inherent in[122]:

- carriage in open, unsheeted vehicles, when this has been expressly agreed and specified in the consignment note[123];
- absent or inadequate packing of goods liable to wastage or damage if not properly packed[124];
- the handling, loading, stowage or unloading of goods by the sender or consignee or persons acting for them[125];
- the nature of goods which particularly exposes them to loss or damage, especially through breakage, rust, decay, desiccation, leakage, wastage, or the action of moth or vermin[126]—although this exemption does not apply where the carriage is performed in a specially equipped vehicle, unless the carrier can show that it was properly chosen, maintained and employed.[127] It may be added that the fact that goods are susceptible to damage through over-freezing does not make them liable to "decay"[128];
- insufficient or inadequate marking or numbering of packages[129];
- the carriage of livestock[130]—as long as he can show he took all proper steps for their care.[131]

Where he can show that the loss or damage could be attributed to any such risk, this will be presumed to be the case,[132] and it falls to the claimant to prove otherwise.[133]

---

[114] See art.17(1).
[115] See art.19.
[116] See art.20(1).
[117] See art.17(2).
[118] *Ulster-Swift Ltd v Taunton Meat Haulage Ltd* [1975] 2 Lloyd's Rep. 502.
[119] *GL Cicatiello SRL v Anglo-European Shipping Services Ltd* [1994] 1 Lloyd's Rep. 678.
[120] *JJ Silber Ltd v Islander Trucking Ltd* [1985] 2 Lloyd's Rep. 243.
[121] See art.18.
[122] See art.17(4).
[123] See art.17(4)(a).
[124] See art.17(4)(b).
[125] See art.17(4)(c).
[126] See art.17(4)(d).
[127] See art.18(4).
[128] *W Donald & Son (Wholesale Meat Contractors) Ltd v Continental Freeze Ltd*, 1984 S.L.T. 182.
[129] See art.17(4)(e).
[130] See art.17(4)(f).
[131] See art.18(5).
[132] See art.18(2).
[133] See art.18(3).

THE LIABILITY OF THE SENDER

4.4.5 The sender of goods may also be liable to the carrier under the Convention. So he is liable for any loss, damage or expense attributable to:

- inaccuracy or inadequacy of the consignment note[134];
- defective packaging, unless apparent or known to the carrier on receipt of the goods[135];
- the absence, irregularity or inadequacy of documents or other information required to be given to the carrier for the purpose of completing customs or other formalities[136];
- the dangerous nature of the goods, unless the carrier is made aware of such danger.[137]

COMPENSATION AND LIMITS THEREON

4.4.6 If a carrier is held liable for loss of or damage to the goods, compensation is assessed by reference to their value at the place and time at which they were accepted for carriage.[138] Value is determined according to the commodity exchange price, failing which the current market price, or failing both the normal price for goods of that kind and quality.[139] Liability for loss is moreover limited to 8.33 units of account per kilo of gross weight short.[140] However, if the sender, on payment of an agreed surcharge, declares in the consignment note a specific value, it is the declared value which sets the limit of the carrier's liability.[141] The carrier must also refund the carriage charges, customs duties, and other charges in respect of carriage.[142] In the case of damage amounting to less than total destruction, compensation reflects the amount by which the goods have diminished in value, and a proportionate amount of the charges, etc. must be refunded.[143] Yet compensation for damage cannot exceed the amount payable for total loss.[144] Liability for delay is generally limited to the amount of the carriage charges.[145] Yet if the sender has fixed the amount of a special interest in delivery by stipulating it in the consignment note, the carrier may be liable up to that amount in the case of delay, damage or non-delivery, in addition to his normal liability.[146] The carrier may not avail himself of any provision excluding or limiting his liability, or shifting the burden of proof, if the loss, delay or damage was caused by his wilful misconduct, or by any default regarded as such by the law of the country in which the proceedings are held.[147] The limitation provisions apply to delictual and restitutionary as well as contractual claims,[148] and embrace all individuals for whom the carrier is responsible.[149] In terms of establishing liability, taking delivery without checking the condition of the goods, or without giving a general indication of loss or damage to the carrier, is prima facie evidence of receipt in good condition.[150] Reservations must be

---

[134] See art.7(1).

[135] See art.10.

[136] See art.11(2).

[137] See art.22(2).

[138] See art.23(1).

[139] See art.23(2).

[140] See art.23(3).

[141] See art.24.

[142] See art.23(4); and see *Sandeman Comprimar SA v Transitos y Transportes Integrales SL* [2003] 3 All E.R. 108 CA on the meaning of "other charges".

[143] *William Tatton & Co Ltd v Ferrymasters Ltd* [1974] 1 Lloyd's Rep. 203.

[144] See art.25.

[145] See art.23(5).

[146] See art.26.

[147] See art.29(1). It does not amount to wilful misconduct that a driver crashes after falling asleep, having confessed that he was feeling sleepy—*TNT Global SpA v Denfleet International Ltd* [2007] 1 C.L.C. 710. But it would be a different matter if in such circumstances he had also been aware that he had exceeded his permitted driving period, or if he had decided to continue driving after having hit the side of the road or having nodded off, per Waller LJ at [16]–[17]. See also *Datec Electronic Holdings Ltd v UPS Ltd* [2007] UKHL 23.

[148] See art.28(1).

[149] See art.28(2).

[150] See art.30(1).

intimated at the time of delivery if the loss or damage is apparent, and within seven days of delivery if it is not.[151] Where the goods are delayed, written reservation must be sent to the carrier within 21 days of delivery if compensation is to be payable.[152]

MULTIPLE CARRIERS

It may be that the sender enters into separate contracts with a number of different carriers in respect of **4.4.7** the same consignment. Yet if the main carrier himself employs one or more carriers for different stages of the journey, each becomes a party to the main contract by his acceptance of the goods and the consignment note,[153] thus each becoming responsible for the entire carriage. Where this happens, proceedings may be brought against the first and last carriers as well as the carrier responsible for the portion of the carriage wherein the loss, damage or delay occurred, or against any combination of the three.[154] In *Parr v Clark & Rose Ltd*[155] it was held that while, in terms of art.4, failure to issue a consignment note has no effect on the validity of the underlying contract, which continues to be subject to the Convention, failure to provide a succeeding carrier with the consignment note is fatal to the potential liability of that carrier under art.34.

An action can only be raised[156]:

- in the court of a contracting state agreed between the parties; or
- in the court of the country where the defender is ordinarily resident, or has his principal place of business, or where is situated the branch or agency through which the contract was made; or
- in the court of the country where the carrier received the goods; or
- in the court of the country where the goods are supposed to be delivered.

No action may be raised if an action on the same grounds between the same parties is pending in a court of one of the states described above.[157]

As between the carriers themselves, the assumption is that the carrier responsible for the loss or damage should bear the ultimate liability for compensation, and that any other carrier who has had to meet a claim may therefore seek an indemnity or contribution.[158] Where more than one carrier is responsible, they bear a proportionate share of the loss,[159] and if it is not possible to determine who is responsible, then each carrier bears a share of the loss which reflects his share of the payment for carriage.[160] A similar apportionment occurs if a carrier who was partially or wholly liable to meet a claim becomes insolvent.[161] Although the question of contribution can be dealt with as ancillary to the main action,[162] separate contribution proceedings can only be brought before the court of the country where the carrier from whom contribution is sought is ordinarily resident, or has his principal place of business, or where is situated the branch or agency through which the contract was made.[163] It should be noted that all provisions relating to indemnity or contribution are subject to contrary agreement between the carriers.[164] If the carrier from whom indemnity or contribution is claimed has had notice

---

[151] See art.30(2).
[152] See art.30(3).
[153] See art.34.
[154] See art.36.
[155] *Parr v Clark & Rose Ltd*, 2002 S.C.L.R. 222.
[156] See art.31(1).
[157] See art.31(1); and see *Andrea Merzario Ltd v Internationale Spedition Leitner Gesellschaft* [2001] 1 Lloyd's Rep. 490; but compare *Royal & Sun Alliance Insurance Plc v MK Digital FZE Cyprus Ltd* [2005] 2 Lloyd's Rep. 679.
[158] See art.37(a).
[159] See art.37(b). But see *Rosewood Trucking Ltd v Balaam* [2006] 1 Lloyd's Rep. 429.
[160] See art.37(c).
[161] See art.38.
[162] *Cummins Engine Co Ltd v Davis Freight Forwarding (Hull) Ltd* [1981] 1 W.L.R. 1363.
[163] See art.39(2).
[164] See art.40.

of the main proceedings, and has had an opportunity of entering an appearance therein, he may not dispute the validity of any payment made by the carrier seeking indemnity or contribution, if the amount of that payment was determined by the court.[165] The right to recover against another carrier may not be enforced, however, until the carrier seeking indemnity or contribution has actually made the payment.[166]

LIMITATION OF ACTIONS

4.4.8 Any action arising from the contract of carriage is time-barred after a year, or after three years if wilful misconduct is involved. The limitation period runs[167]:

- in the case of delay, damage or partial loss, from the date of delivery;
- in the case of total loss, from the 30th day after the expiry of the agreed time limit for delivery, or if there is no time limit, from the 60th day from the date when the carrier received the goods;
- in all other cases on the expiry of three months from the making of the contract.

The making of a written claim suspends the running of the period, until the carrier rejects the claim in writing.[168] The limitation period also applies to claims for indemnity or contribution as between carriers, running from the date of the final judicial decision fixing compensation, or in the absence of a judicial decision, from the actual date of payment.[169]

4.5   INTERNATIONAL CARRIAGE OF GOODS BY RAIL

INTRODUCTION TO INTERNATIONAL CARRIAGE OF GOODS BY RAIL

4.5.1 The UK is a party to the 1980 Berne Convention concerning International Carriage by Rail, as modified by the Vilnius Protocol of 1999, which has legal effect in the UK.[170] That Convention in appendix B contains the Uniform Rules concerning Contracts for the International Carriage of Goods by Rail. They apply to contracts of carriage of goods where the place of taking over the goods and the place designated for delivery are in different contracting states[171] including for this purpose certain road, canal and shipping services which are complementary to rail services.[172]

CONSIGNMENT NOTE

4.5.2 Whereas under the former regime the rules only applied if a consignment note was made out, now they apply even if the note has been lost, or does not conform to the prescribed form, or never existed.[173]

---

[165] See art.39(1).

[166] *ITT Schaub-Lorenz Vertriebgesellschaft GmbH v Birkart Johann Internationale Spedition GmbH* [1988] 1 Lloyd's Rep. 487.

[167] See art.32(1).

[168] See art.32(2).

[169] See art.39(4).

[170] Through s.103 of the Railways and Transport Safety Act 2003 and the Railways (Convention on International Carriage by Rail) Regulations 2005 (SI 2005/2092).

[171] See art.1(1). But there is now no need that the carriage occur exclusively over railway lines situated in Member States. Parties to contracts of carriage by rail where either the place of taking over or the place of delivery (but not both) is situated in a Member State may agree that the rules should apply to their contract—art.1(2).

[172] See art.1(3), (4). But any element of carriage by road must occur entirely within one state, otherwise the applicable Convention is the Convention on the International Carriage of Goods by Road.

[173] See art.6(2).

Nonetheless, the rules contemplate that a separate consignment note must be made out for each consignment, and unless otherwise agreed a consignment note may not relate to more than a single wagon load.[174] The rules prescribe in great detail the particulars which the note must contain,[175] although less detail following the 1999 amendments. The note provides prima facie evidence of the making of the contract, its contents, the taking over of the goods by the carrier,[176] and the condition of the goods.[177] A duplicate of the note should generally be produced in the event of a claim.[178] The consignor is responsible for all inaccuracies and irregularities in the note,[179] and for attaching any documents required for customs.[180] The consignor will also be responsible for the packing of the goods if that is necessary.[181] Responsibility for loading and unloading goods depends on agreement, but in the absence thereof the carrier is responsible for loading and unloading packages, while for full wagon loads the consignor is responsible for loading and the consignee for unloading.[182] The carrier is entitled to ascertain whether the conditions of carriage have been complied with and verify that the consignment is as described in the note.[183]

CARRIAGE

The transit period begins as soon as the consignee has taken over the goods,[184] and the period allowed **4.5.3** shall be agreed by the consignor and carrier.[185] Failing such agreement, for consignments of a wagon load the goods must be dispatched within 12 hours of receipt and must travel at least 400 km every 24 hours, while for consignments of less than a wagon load the goods must be dispatched within 24 hours of receipt and must travel at least 200 km every 24 hours.[186] The consignor may modify the contract of carriage by asking the carrier to discontinue carriage, or delay delivery, or deliver to a different destination or a different consignee.[187] The consignee may also modify the contract unless the consignor has indicated to the contrary in the note.[188] However, neither right of modification arises where the consignee has taken possession of the note or accepted the goods, or on the arrival of the goods at their destination has asked the carrier to hand over the note and deliver the goods.[189] Assuming that the contract has not been modified, the carrier must hand over the note and deliver the goods to the consignee at the designated place of delivery on payment of the amount due under the contract.[190] It is the equivalent of delivery to hand over the goods to customs authorities, or to deposit them with a forwarding agent or in a public warehouse.[191] If carriage has been prevented, the carrier must decide whether to alter the route or to ask the person entitled to dispose of the goods for instructions.[192] Instructions must always be sought if it is impossible to continue the carriage, and if the carrier is unable to obtain these within a reasonable time, he should take such steps as seem to him to be in the best interests of the person entitled to dispose of the goods.[193] If delivery is prevented, the carrier must

---

[174] See art.6(6).
[175] See art.7.
[176] See art.12(1).
[177] See art.12(2), (3), but see art.12(4).
[178] See art.43(3).
[179] See art.8.
[180] See art.15.
[181] See art.14.
[182] See art.13.
[183] See art.11.
[184] See art.16(4).
[185] See art.16(1).
[186] See art.16(2).
[187] See art.18(1).
[188] See art.18(3).
[189] See art.18(2), (4).
[190] See art.17(1).
[191] See art.17(2).
[192] See art.20(1).
[193] See art.20(2).

ask the consignor for instructions unless the consignor has requested in the consignment note that the goods be returned to him in such circumstances.[194] Where it is impossible to continue the carriage or delivery is prevented, the carrier may immediately unload the goods, and although he is then in charge of them, he may entrust them to a third party and is then only responsible for choosing that third party with reasonable care.[195] The carrier may sell the goods if this is justified by their perishable nature or the costs of storage in proportion to the value of the goods.[196] Otherwise he may sell them if he has not received instructions regarding their disposal within a reasonable time. The proceeds are then held at the disposal of the person entitled to the goods, subject to deduction of the carriage charges,[197] and if these are more than the proceeds of sale the consignor must pay the difference.[198] Moreover, if delivery or carriage has been prevented, and the consignor has not given instructions regarding their disposal within a reasonable time, the carrier may return the goods to him or, if justified, destroy the goods at the consignor's expense.[199]

LIABILITY OF CARRIER

4.5.4 The carrier is prima facie strictly liable for delay, damage or loss during carriage.[200] Broadly the same exemptions from liability that apply in the case of carriage by road (see para.4.4.4 above) apply also in this case. Where the goods have to be carried by sea as well as rail, then (assuming the Convention applies) the carrier may also exempt himself from liability in respect of negligent handling of the ship and other perils of the sea.[201] If goods have to be carried by road as well as rail, the Geneva Convention applies, unless it can be shown that the loss or damage could only have occurred while the goods were on the railway. It is always possible for a carrier to agree to assume a greater liability than prescribed by the Act.[202]

Subject to that, however, provisions relating to limitation of liability in respect of loss are similar to those under the Geneva Convention (see para.4.4.6 above), save that liability for loss is limited to 17 (as opposed to 8.33) units of account per kilo of gross mass short.[203] As regards liability for delay, if that delay caused actual loss or damage, compensation may not exceed four times the amount of the carriage charges, and may not in any case exceed the amount payable for a total loss.[204] Liability for damage should reflect the amount by which the goods have diminished in value.[205] The maximum compensation limits are removed if loss or damage results from an act or omission which the carrier committed either with intent to cause such loss or damage, or recklessly and with knowledge that such loss or damage would probably result.[206] Moreover, if a special interest in delivery is entered in the consignment note, further compensation up to the agreed amount may be claimed if loss can be proved.[207] The contractual carrier is always liable for the whole carriage,[208] but any substitute carrier employed by the former is subject to the rules in respect of any carriage performed by him.[209] Where both the contractual carrier and the substitute carrier are liable, that liability is joint and several.[210] Actions can only be brought in the courts of Member States designated by agreement or in the court of

---

[194] See art.21(1).
[195] See art.22(2).
[196] See art.22(3).
[197] See art.22(3).
[198] See art.22(4).
[199] See art.22(6).
[200] See art.23(1).
[201] See art.38.
[202] See art.5.
[203] See art.30(2).
[204] See art.33(1), (2).
[205] See art.32.
[206] See art.36.
[207] See art.35.
[208] See art.27(1).
[209] See art.27(2).
[210] See art.27(4).

the state where the defendant has his domicile, residence, principal place of business, or the branch which concluded the contract, or in the court of the place of delivery or where the goods were taken over by the carrier.[211] Acceptance of the goods extinguishes all rights of action, subject to the following exceptions[212]:

- where partial damage was ascertained prior to acceptance;
- where partial damage was not ascertained prior to acceptance solely due to the fault of the carrier;
- claims for delay in delivery can be made within 60 days of acceptance;
- claims for loss or damage which is not apparent are open if the carrier is asked to account for it within seven days of acceptance;
- where it can be proved that the loss or damage was caused deliberately or recklessly.

Provisions regarding limitation of actions once again resemble those under the Geneva Convention.[213]

CARRIAGE BY AIR 4.6

INTRODUCTION TO CARRIAGE BY AIR

Carriage of goods by air was initially governed by the 1929 Warsaw Convention for the Unification of **4.6.1** Certain Rules Relating to International Carriage by Air. This was successively amended by the 1955 Hague Protocol, the 1962 Guadalajara Convention and the 1975 Montreal Protocols.[214] The Warsaw Convention was then entirely supplanted by the Montreal Convention of 1999,[215] which substantially updated it. However, it will not necessarily be the case that a particular contract of carriage wil be governed by the Montreal Convention, since that would depend on the other state also having ratified that Convention. Indeed, since not all states have ratified the various amendments to the Warsaw Convention, it is possible that a contract may be governed by the original version of that Convention, or by its most current version, or by the 1955 or 1962 versions. Obviously, we cannot address each of those potential regimes, and so shall concentrate on the provisions of the Montreal Convention, which already regulates domestic carriage.[216] Given the similarity of its provisions, much of the case law under the Warsaw Convention will remain relevant.

SCOPE OF CONVENTION

Carriage is international if, under the agreement of the parties, the place of departure and the destina- **4.6.2** tion are situated within different Convention states, whether or not there is a break in the carriage, or even if they are situated within the same Convention state as long as there is an agreed stopping place in another state, whether or not that other state is a Convention state.[217] So a flight from Glasgow to London is not international, but a contract to fly goods from Glasgow to Paris via London is international, even the Glasgow to London leg. Similarly, a contract which contemplates goods being flown from London to Belfast does not involve international carriage, whereas a contract which contemplates goods being flown from London to Belfast via Dublin does. Any provision which seeks to apply a

---

[211] See art.46.
[212] See art.47.
[213] See art.48; and see para.4.4.8 above.
[214] See Carriage by Air Act 1961, as amended; Carriage by Air (Supplementary Provisions) Act 1962.
[215] Carriage by Air (Implementation of the Montreal Convention 1999) Order 2002 (SI 2002/263).
[216] Carriage by Air Acts (Application of Provisions) Order 2004 (SI 2004/1899).
[217] See art.1(2).

different law, or which seeks to alter the rules as to jurisdiction is null and void.[218] As far as jurisdiction is concerned, a pursuer may choose to raise an action against a carrier in a Convention state[219]:

- which is the domicile of the carrier; or
- which is the domicile of its principal place of business; or
- where it has a place of business through which the contract was made; or
- which is the place of destination.

No court in any other state has jurisdiction and under the Warsaw Convention English courts have been prepared to grant injunctions to prevent actions being raised in such states,[220] while if an action is raised in one of the states described above, a plea of *forum non conveniens* cannot succeed.[221] Nonetheless, despite the above rules, disputes may still be settled by arbitration, as long as the forum (as selected by the claimant) is in one of the states mentioned above.[222] The arbitrator is bound to apply the provisions of the Convention.[223]

A carriage which is to be performed by successive carriers is deemed to be a single undivided carriage if the parties regard it as a single operation.[224] It does not matter if there is more than one contract and, if the carriage as a whole is international, it does not matter if any contract(s) is (are) performed entirely within the territory of a single state.[225] Each carrier is deemed to be a contracting party insofar as the contract relates to that part of the carriage under his supervision.[226] The consignor of goods has an action against the first carrier, the person entitled to the goods has an action against the last carrier, and both have an action against the carrier who performed the leg where the destruction, loss, damage or delay occurred, the carriers being jointly and severally liable.[227]

AIR WAYBILL

4.6.3 The Convention contemplates that the consignor deliver a document known as an air waybill, although any other means which provides a record of the carriage may be substituted, in which case the consignor may request a cargo receipt.[228] Where there is more than one package being sent, the carrier may demand a separate waybill for each package, or if waybills are not being employed, the consignor may demand separate cargo receipts.[229] Each waybill must have three copies, all of which must be handed over with the goods.[230] The first copy should be marked "for the carrier", and signed by the consignor.[231] The carrier holds on to this copy. The second should be marked "for the consignee", and signed by both the consignor and the carrier.[232] This copy travels with the goods. The third should be signed by the carrier, and is given to the consignor once the goods have been accepted.[233] The waybill or cargo receipt is prima facie evidence of the conclusion of the contract, the acceptance of the goods and the conditions of carriage,[234] but failure to comply with the provisions as to such documentation does not

---

[218] See art.49.
[219] See art.33.
[220] *Deaville v Aeroflot Russian International Airlines* [1997] 2 Lloyd's Rep. 67.
[221] *Milor SRL v British Airways Plc* [1996] Q.B. 702.
[222] See art.34.
[223] See art.34.
[224] See art.1(3).
[225] See art.1(3).
[226] See art.36(1).
[227] See art.36(3).
[228] See art.4.
[229] See art.8.
[230] See art.7(1).
[231] See art.7(2).
[232] See art.7(2).
[233] See art.7(2).
[234] See art.11(1).

undermine the contract, which continues to be subject to the provisions of the Convention including the provisions as to limitation of liability.[235]

The waybill or cargo receipt must contain[236]:

- an indication of the places of departure and destination;
- if these places are within the territory of a single state, an indication of an agreed stopping place in another state; and
- an indication of the weight of the consignment.

It is the consignor's duty to ensure that the contents of the waybill, or the details he supplies for insertion in the cargo receipt are accurate, and he must indemnify the carrier against all loss arising from their incorrectness or inadequacy.[237] A similar duty is owed by the carrier to the consignor in respect of statements the carrier inserts in the cargo receipt on its own behalf.[238] The statements in the waybill relating to the number of packages and the weight, dimensions and packing of the goods are prima facie evidence of the facts stated, but those relating to the volume and condition of the goods are not, unless either these facts have been checked by the carrier in the consignor's presence, and this is stated in the waybill or cargo receipt, or the statements relate to the apparent condition of the goods.[239]

Under art.9 of the Warsaw Convention, if the carrier allowed goods to be loaded without a waybill in proper form having been completed, he was disabled from relying on the limitation of liability provisions described in the next paragraph. There is no equivalent provision in the Montreal Convention.

As well as the waybill, the consignor must furnish such information and attach to the waybill such documents as are required to meet customs and other formalities required before the goods may be delivered.[240] Again, he will be liable to the carrier in respect of any loss caused by the absence, insufficiency or irregularity of any such information or documents, unless the loss is attributable to the fault of the carrier or his servants or agents.[241]

CARRIER'S LIABILITY

The carrier is strictly liable for loss of or damage to the goods during carriage by air, i.e. during the **4.6.4** period in which the goods are in his charge, whether or not they are actually airborne.[242] He is strictly liable for damage caused by delay, unless he shows that all reasonable measures were taken to avoid the damage, or that it was impossible to take such measures.[243] Moreover, he is not liable for loss of or damage to the goods resulting from one or more of the following[244]:

- the inherent defects, quality or vice of the goods[245]; their defective packaging unless performed by him or his servants or agents;
- an act of war or armed conflict; or
- an act of a public authority in connection with the entry, exit or transit of the cargo, e.g. goods destroyed or impounded by customs officials.

The carrier may also raise the defence of contributory negligence.[246]

Although, subject to the points made above, the carrier is strictly liable, that liability is subject to a limit based on the weight of the goods, unless at the time the goods were handed over the consignor

---

[235] See art.9.
[236] See art.5.
[237] See art.10(1), (2).
[238] See art.10(3).
[239] See art.11(2).
[240] See art.16(1).
[241] See art.16(1).
[242] See art.18.
[243] See art.19.
[244] See art.18(2).
[245] See *Winchester Fruit Ltd v American Airlines Inc* [2002] 2 Lloyd's Rep. 265.
[246] See art.20.

made a special declaration of interest in delivery at the destination, and if so required, paid an extra sum.[247] In that latter case the carrier would be liable to pay up to the amount declared by the consignor, unless he were able to prove that the amount declared was actually greater than the consignor's interest in delivery at the destination.[248] If only part of the goods are lost or damaged, only the weight of the goods concerned can be taken into account in assessing compensation, unless the value of the other goods is also affected.[249] So where a machine was sent in separate packages, one of which was badly damaged, it was the weight of the machine as a whole which formed the basis for assessing compensation, as the other packages were practically worthless without the damaged section.[250] It should be added that the carrier's liability is entirely unlimited in respect of his own acts or omissions or those of his employees or agents acting in the scope of their employment, if done with intent to cause damage or done recklessly and with knowledge that damage would probably result.[251] Knowledge here means actual knowledge, rather than knowledge an individual might reasonably be expected to have.[252] If goods are stolen by the carrier's cargo loaders, then he is liable, but if a member of his flight crew perpetrates the theft, the carrier will not be liable, as dealing with cargo is not in the course of such an individual's employment.[253] It is possible for a carrier to stipulate higher limits on his liability than laid down by the Convention, or agree to unlimited liability, but any provision of the contract relieving him of liability, or attempting to impose lower limits on his liability than laid down by the Convention, will be null and void.[254] He may also waive his defences under the Convention.[255]

DISPOSITION AND DELIVERY

4.6.5 Under art.12(1) the consignor may at any time withdraw the goods, or insist they be held at any place where the plane stops, or demand their return to the place of departure, or direct that they be delivered to someone other than the consignee named in the waybill, as long as he meets the expense of any such step, and does not exercise the right in a way which prejudices the carrier or other consignors. The carrier may ignore the consignor's instructions only if what is asked is impossible, and the consignor must be informed of this forthwith.[256] If the carrier carries out the consignor's instructions without requiring the production of the copy of the air waybill or cargo receipt delivered to the latter, he will be liable for any damage thereby caused to any person lawfully in possession of that document.[257] Once the goods have reached their destination, they are then at the disposal of the consignee rather than the consignor,[258] and the carrier must notify the former of their arrival, unless the contract directs otherwise.[259] The consignee is then entitled to demand delivery of the goods on the payment of any outstanding charges and the fulfilment of any conditions in the contract.[260] Should the consignee decline to accept the goods or proves impossible to communicate with, the goods remain at the disposal of the consignor.[261]

---

[247] See art.22(3). See also the Carriage by Air (Revision of Limits of Liability under the Montreal Convention) Order 2009 (SI 2009/3018).

[248] See art.22(3).

[249] See art.22(3).

[250] *Applied Implants Technology Ltd v Lufthansa Cargo AG* [2000] 2 Lloyd's Rep. 46. The fact that the damaged part was easily replaced was said by David Steel J (at 49) to be "significant from the point of view of quantum but not limitation".

[251] See art.25(5).

[252] *Nugent v Michael Goss Aviation Ltd* [2000] 2 Lloyd's Rep. 222.

[253] *Rustenberg Platinum Mines Ltd v South African Airways* [1977] 1 Lloyd's Rep. 564.

[254] See art.26.

[255] See art.27.

[256] See art.12(2).

[257] See art.12(3).

[258] See arts 12(4), 13(1).

[259] See art.13(2).

[260] See art.13(1).

[261] See art.12(4).

MAKING CLAIMS

Where the goods are damaged, the person entitled to delivery must complain in writing to the carrier as **4.6.6** soon as the damage is discovered, and certainly within 14 days of the date of their receipt.[262] A carrier cannot be a "person entitled to delivery". Thus where the carrier with whom the consignor contracted subcontracted the actual carriage, and sent a complaint regarding damage to the goods to the actual carrier, it was held that proper notice had not been given.[263] Receipt of the goods without complaint by the person entitled to delivery is prima facie evidence that they have been delivered in good condition and in accordance with the carriage documents.[264] Damage here includes partial loss.[265] Where the goods are delayed, the complaint must be made within 21 days of them being placed at the disposal of the person entitled to delivery.[266] If these time limits are not adhered to, no claim may be made against the carrier for anything short of fraud.[267] Where the carrier admits the loss of the goods, or they have not arrived within seven days of the date when they should have arrived, the consignee is entitled to sue under the contract.[268] Loss presumably includes destruction in this context. Although no mention is made of the consignor making a claim where the goods are lost, it must be assumed that the consignor is the appropriate claimant where the goods remain in his ownership.[269] If the carriage is performed by successive carriers under one undivided carriage, the consignor may sue the first carrier in respect of loss, damage or delay, the consignee may sue the last carrier, and each may sue the carrier who was performing when the loss, damage or delay occurred, the carriers being liable jointly and severally.[270] Any right to damages under the Convention is extinguished if an action is not brought within two years of the date when the goods arrived at their destination, or ought to have arrived, or the date when the carriage actually stopped.[271]

CARRIAGE OF GOODS BY SEA

4.7

INTRODUCTION TO CARRIAGE OF GOODS BY SEA

If the carrier of goods by sea is a common carrier, then he is subject to the usual strict liability at **4.7.1** common law in largely the same way as a common carrier by road.[272] Yet it would be very rare for a shipping company to be treated as a common carrier, as almost none hold themselves out as willing to carry the goods of anyone who approaches them, and indeed almost all will explicitly contract on the basis that common law liability is limited or excluded altogether. The contract of carriage will usually take the form of either a charterparty or a bill of lading.

CHARTERPARTIES

This is a contract for the hire of the carrying capacity of a ship or some defined portion thereof, and is **4.7.2** usually resorted to when a party wishes to ship a large quantity of goods. Theoretically, the contract

---

[262] See art.31(2).
[263] *Compaq Computer Manufacturing Ltd v Circle International Ltd*, 2001 S.L.T. 368.
[264] See art.31(1).
[265] Carriage by Air Act 1961 s.4A.
[266] See art.31(2).
[267] See art.31(4).
[268] See art.13(3).
[269] Compare *Thomas Cook Group Ltd v Air Malta Co Ltd* [1997] 2 Lloyd's Rep. 399 with *Abnett v British Airways Plc* [1997] A.C. 430.
[270] See art.36(3).
[271] See art.35(1).
[272] *Woods v Burns* (1893) 20 R. 602.

may be entered into orally,[273] although invariably such contracts in modern times would be in writing, and would almost certainly adopt a standard form. Charterparties tend to take the form of either voyage charterparties, where the charterer gains the use of the vessel for a single voyage, or time charterparties, where he has the use of the vessel for a particular period of time.[274] There is also an arrangement known as a demise charterparty. Under a demise charterparty the charterer leases an entire ship for a given period of time, gaining full possession of and control over it during that period, and so may determine such matters as its route.[275] A demise charterparty is therefore not a contract of carriage at all. The charterer does not ask the shipowner to carry goods for him. Instead, by leasing the ship, he is entitled to use it for whichever purpose he chooses, including carrying cargo. Usually, though not invariably, he gains the ship unmanned and so may appoint his own crew. Yet whether he appoints his own crew or simply uses the crew provided by the shipowner, they are regarded as working for him. Thus if the ship collides with another through the negligence of the crew, he rather than the shipowner is liable,[276] while if the master signs a bill of lading (see para.4.8.1 below), he does so on behalf of the charterer rather than the shipowner, so that the charterer rather than the shipowner is liable to the holder of the bill for loss or damage to the cargo.[277] All this is very different to the position under true charterparties, which we shall now consider in detail.

4.7.3 IMPLIED TERMS IN CHARTERPARTIES

Seaworthiness

4.7.3.1 It is an implied term in every charterparty that the vessel is seaworthy, either at the time of loading,[278] or in a time charterparty from the commencement of the contract.[279] If that duty is fulfilled, the owner will not be liable for loss due to the vessel becoming unseaworthy during the voyage.[280] Seaworthiness is not an absolute concept, but depends on the circumstances of the case, including the sort of voyage which is being attempted, and the type of cargo which is being carried. Thus the standard demanded of a ship carrying goods from Scotland to Australia would not usually be the standard demanded of a ship carrying goods from Oban to Mull. Equally, while the question of whether a ship's refrigeration units are operating effectively would not bear on its seaworthiness if it were carrying iron ore, the matter would be different if it were carrying meat.[281] It has been pointed out that, for a ship to be unseaworthy, "there must be some attribute of the ship itself which threatens the safety of the cargo" so that "the fact that a hold contains cargo which threatens damage to the other cargo . . . is not an attribute of the ship and does not render the ship unseaworthy".[282] Moreover, seaworthiness does not mean unsinkability. If the ship is as fit as an ordinarily prudent owner would demand in light of the voyage to be undertaken, it meets the requirement, even if it proves unable to deal with freak conditions.[283] Essentially, the ship must be able to withstand the voyage,[284] cope with its cargo,[285] be adequately equipped,[286] have a crew which is adequate in terms of size and

---

[273] *Nordstjernan v Salvesen* (1903) 6 F. 75.

[274] See McKinnon LJ in *Sea and Land Securities v Dickinson* [1942] 2 K.B. 65 at 69. It is usually open to a shipowner to reject early redelivery of the vessel and insist on claiming the hire due: see *The Aquafaith* [2012] 2 Lloyd's Rep. 61.

[275] See Lord Bingham in *Whistler International Ltd v Kawasaki Kisen Kaisha Ltd* [2001] 1 A.C. 638 at 641.

[276] *Clarke v Scott* (1896) 23 R. 442.

[277] *Baumwoll Manfactur v Furness* [1893] A.C. 8.

[278] *Cunningham v Colvills, Lowden & Co* (1888) 16 R. 295.

[279] *Giertsen v Turnbull & Co*, 1908 S.C. 1101.

[280] *Giertsen v Turnbull & Co*, 1908 S.C. 1101.

[281] *Maori King (Cargo Owners) v Hughes* [1895] 2 Q.B. 550.

[282] *A Meredith Jones & Co Ltd v Vangemar Shipping Co Ltd* (The Apostolis) (No.1) [1997] 2 Lloyd's Rep. 241, per Phillips LJ at 258.

[283] *McFadden v Blue Star Line* [1905] 1 K.B. 697.

[284] *Steel & Craig v State Line Steamship Co* (1877) 4 R. (HL) 103.

[285] *Kopitoff v Wilson* (1876) 1 Q.B.D. 377.

[286] *Adam v J & D Morris* (1890) 18 R. 153.

competence,[287] and have sufficient fuel.[288] It has also been said that the test of seaworthiness is whether an ordinarily prudent owner would have remedied the defect had he known of it.[289] This serves to stress that a latent defect, which an owner neither knew or could have known about, can make a ship unseaworthy,[290] and it will not avail an owner to argue that he believed the vessel to be seaworthy on entirely reasonable grounds, nor even that he did all he could to make it seaworthy.[291] The onus of proving a ship is unseaworthy rests on the charterers, but will be relatively easy to discharge if the circumstances are suggestive of unseaworthiness, as where a ship breaks down very shortly after setting sail.[292] The implied term as to seaworthiness may be excluded, but only the clearest and most unambiguous of language will suffice to do so.[293]

Reasonable dispatch

It is an implied term in every charterparty that the vessel is able to embark on the voyage with reason- **4.7.3.2** able dispatch.[294] Again, this term may be excluded.[295] Alternatively, the contract may have a cancellation clause, which fixes a specific date beyond which the charterer may cancel the contract without liability if the ship has not arrived.[296]

Deviation

It is an implied term in every charterparty that the vessel shall not unjustifiably deviate from its route. **4.7.3.3** That route may be prescribed in the contract, otherwise it will be by the most direct geographical route, unless some other route is more usual.[297] It may be that there are several usual routes, in which case it would be permissible to follow any of these.[298] The term is only breached by voluntary deviation, not where deviation occurs by error.[299] The term deals with unjustifiable deviation. Deviation is justifiable in order to attempt to save life, but not in order to save property. So in *Scaramanga v Stamp*[300] it was permissible to deviate to help the crew of a ship in distress, but the owner was liable to the charterer for the loss of the cargo when the ship was itself lost in seeking to salvage the ship in distress. Deviation is also justifiable in order to protect the ship or cargo from imminent danger such as a storm,[301] or to effect necessary repairs.[302]

The contract can, of course, specifically authorise deviation, but any such term, however widely expressed, will not be construed so as to ensure the main object of the contract is defeated, so that while the calling into ports which are broadly on the route of the voyage is permissible, deviation entirely

---

[287] *State Trading Corp of India Ltd v Doyle Carriers Inc (The Jute Express)* [1991] 2 Lloyd's Rep.55; *Papera Traders Co Ltd v Hyundai Merchant Marine Co Ltd (The Eurasian Dream) (No.1)* [2002] 1 Lloyd's Rep. 719.

[288] *Park v Duncan & Son* (1898) 5 S.L.T. 280.

[289] *Gilroy, Sons & Co v Price & Co* (1892) 20 R. (HL) 1.

[290] *The Glenfruin* (1885) 10 P.D. 103.

[291] *Steel & Craig v State Line Steamship Co* (1877) 4 R. (HL) 103.

[292] *Klein v Lindsay*, 1911 S.C. (HL) 9.

[293] *Nelson Line Liverpool Ltd v James Nelson & Son Ltd* [1908] A.C. 16.

[294] *Suzuki v Beynon* (1926) 42 T.L.R. 269. So a charterer is entitled to damages for the loss of a cancelled subcharter due to breach of the obligation: see *Sylvia Shipping Co Ltd v Prague Bulk Carriers Ltd* [2010] 2 Lloyd's Rep. 81.

[295] *President of India v Hariana Overseas Corp (The Takafa)* [1990] 1 Lloyd's Rep. 536.

[296] In *Mansel Oil Ltd v Troon Storage Tankers* [2009] 2 Lloyd's Rep. 371 Longmore LJ at [1] observed that "[i]n the absence of a cancelling clause an owner would be in breach of charter for failing to deliver on the contractual date, but the charterer would not be able to treat the owner as being in repudiatory breach of contract until the delay was such as to frustrate the commercial purpose of the adventure. The length of that delay is notoriously difficult to fix with any certainty and it is, therefore, not surprising that parties . . . are ready to agree to a cancelling clause in order to avoid all arguments about whether delay in delivery is such as to frustrate the he adventure."

[297] *Reardon Smith Line Ltd v Black Sea & Baltic General Insurance Co Ltd (The India City)* [1939] A.C. 562.

[298] *Reardon Smith Line v Black Sea and Baltic General Insurance Co Ltd* [1939] A.C. 562.

[299] *Rio Tinto Co Ltd v Seed Shipping Co* (1926) 42 T.L.R. 381.

[300] *Scaramanga v Stamp* (1880) 5 C.P.D. 295.

[301] *Donaldson Bros v Little & Co* (1882) 10 R. 413; but see *Whistler International Ltd v Kawasaki Kisen Kaisha Ltd* [2001] 1 A.C. 638.

[302] *Karlshamns Oljefabriker v Monarch Steamship Co*, 1949 S.L.T. 51.

away from the route of the voyage cannot be justified.[303] It might be added that exclusion and limitation clauses do not operate in relation to losses sustained during unjustifiable deviation, unless they explicitly cover this situation.[304] Unjustifiable deviation prevents the owner claiming demurrage[305] (see para.4.7.5 below), and permits the charterer to rescind.[306]

Dangerous goods

4.7.3.4 It is an implied term in every charterparty that the charterer will not ship dangerous goods,[307] although of course there is no breach where the parties are aware that a potentially dangerous cargo is to be carried. Goods may be dangerous because of the threat they impose to the ship or the remainder of the cargo,[308] or simply because their presence might cause the ship to be detained by the authorities.[309]

LOADING

4.7.4 If the ship is not already at the loading port, the charterparty may indicate a date by which it must arrive there, and failure to adhere to this will constitute a material breach.[310] Even if no such date is stipulated, the implied term that the vessel embarks on the voyage with reasonable dispatch will place the shipowner in breach if he does not proceed to the loading port within a reasonable period of time.[311] By the same token, if no port is nominated as the loading port in the charterparty, then if the charterer does not nominate a port either within the period specified in the charterparty or within a reasonable time, he will himself commit a material breach.[312] It is suggested that the charterer is under a duty to nominate only safe ports for both loading or unloading, although this matter will usually be regulated by an express term of the contract. A safe port is one which the ship can in the normal course of events safely enter, use and depart.[313] If a ship is damaged by an abnormal event in an otherwise safe port, the charterer will not be liable.[314] A port which is physically safe may be unsafe if, for example, the ship is liable to detention by the authorities.[315] The shipowner may refuse to enter an unsafe port,[316] but he may waive the right to refuse by knowingly accepting the nomination of an unsafe port.[317] He may always claim damages if he suffers loss by entering an unsafe port,[318] unless the particular type of loss could not be foreseen.[319] Unless the contract provides otherwise, the charterer is responsible for bringing the goods to the ship,[320] and the shipowner is then responsible for its loading,[321] proper stowage[322] and unloading.[323]

---

303 *Glynn v Margetson & Co* [1893] A.C. 351.
304 *Cunard Steamship Co v Buerger* [1927] A.C. 1.
305 *United States Shipping Board v Bunge y Born Ltde Sociedad* [1925] All E.R. 173.
306 *Hain SS Co Ltd v Tate & Lyle Ltd* [1936] 2 All E.R. 597.
307 *Chandris v Isbrandtsen-Moller Co Inc* [1951] 1 K.B. 240.
308 *Ministry of Food v Lamport and Holt Line Ltd* [1952] 2 Lloyd's Rep. 371.
309 *Mitchell, Cotts & Co v Steel Bros & Co Ltd* [1916] 2 K.B. 610.
310 *Allison & Co v Jacobsen & Co* (1904) 11 S.L.T. 573.
311 See *McAndrew v Adams* (1834) 1 Bing N.C 29—failure to proceed to that port without deviation amounts to breach.
312 *Zim Israel Navigation Co Ltd v Tradax Export SA (The Timna)* [1971] 2 Lloyd's Rep. 91.
313 *Kodros Shipping Corp of Monrovia v Empresa Cubana de Fletes (The Evia)* [1983] 1 A.C. 736.
314 *The Evia* [1983] 1 A.C. 736.
315 *The Evia* [1983] 1 A.C. 736.
316 *Motor Oil Hellas (Corinth) Refineries SA v Shipping Corp of India (The Kanchenjunga)* [1990] 1 Lloyd's Rep. 391 HL.
317 *The Kanchenjunga* [1990] 1 Lloyd's Rep. 391
318 *The Kanchenjunga* [1990] 1 Lloyd's Rep. 391
319 *C-Trade of Geneva SA v Uni-Ocean Lines Pte of Singapore (The Lucille)* [1984] 1 Lloyd's Rep. 244 CA.
320 *Glengarnock Iron & Steel Co Ltd v Cooper & Co* (1895) 3 S.L.T. 36.
321 *Glengarnock Iron & Steel Co Ltd v Cooper & Co* (1895) 3 S.L.T. 36.
322 *Canadian Transport Co Ltd v Court Line Ltd* [1940] A.C. 394.
323 *Ballantyne & Co v Paton & Hendry*, 1911 2 S.L.T. 510.

LAYTIME AND DEMURRAGE

A ship is an enormously costly capital asset, and over a period of time the return on this asset will **4.7.5** depend on how many voyages can be attempted. In large measure this lies in the hands of the ship-owner, but the speed at which the ship can be loaded and unloaded often depends on the charterer. Thus the contract will usually specify periods within which the cargo must be loaded and unloaded/uplifted. Such periods are known as laytime or lay-days. The contract will usually specify sums the charterer must pay if these periods are exceeded. These sums are known as demurrage, which is essentially a form of liquidated damages for breach of contract.[324] If the contract contains no provision for laytime, then loading and unloading must be completed within a reasonable time having regard to the circum-stances.[325] So factors such as adverse weather conditions, the adequacy of cargo handling facilities, and labour shortages may bear on what is regarded as a reasonable time.[326] Where the contract does provide for laytime, then it does not matter why the laytime has been exceeded, and the charterer will be liable for demurrage however blameless he may be for the delay, unless of course the contract exempts him in certain situations, or unless the delay is actually attributable to the shipowner or persons for whose actions the shipowner is responsible.[327] If the contract does not provide for demurrage, then actual damages will be payable if the laytime is exceeded, or in the absence of laytime, if the loading and unloading is not completed within a reasonable time.[328] The same is true if demurrage is payable for a fixed period, and this period is exceeded. If the provisions as to demurrage do not specify a fixed period, then the shipowner may only claim demurrage, rather than actual damages, no matter how long the period during which the ship is detained, although if the ship is detained for an unreasonably long period, the period of demurrage may be terminated by the owner rescinding the contract and claiming damages.[329]

Depending on the terms of the contract,[330] laytime commences when the ship has arrived and is ready to load or unload, as the case may be.[331] If the charterparty indicates that the ship must dock in a particular berth in a given port, then the ship cannot be treated as having arrived until it reaches that berth, although the charterer will still be liable in damages if the ship is delayed in reaching that berth through his fault.[332] However, if the charterparty simply indicates that the ship must dock in a given port, then the ship can be treated as having arrived as soon as it reaches the port and is at the effective disposal of the charterer—as was the case in *The Johanna Oldendorff*,[333] where the ship was held to have arrived notwithstanding that she was 17 miles from her usual discharging berth. Laytime will not commence where a ship is physically ready to load or unload but loading or unloading is not practically possible, as where the ship is affected by quarantine restrictions.[334] Still, laytime will commence if lack of readiness is attributable to the charterer's fault.[335] In *The Andra*[336] it was held that the charterer could not escape an obligation to pay demurrage when the receivers of a cargo had failed to discharge it, since discharge remained the responsibility of the charterer.

---

[324] *Moor Line Ltd v Distillers Co Ltd*, 1912 1 S.L.T. 147. This was also the view advanced by Hobhouse J in *Islamic Republic of Iran Shipping Lines v Ierax Shipping Co of Panama (The Forum Craftsman)* [1991] 1 Lloyd's Rep. 81 at 87. However as Hobhouse LJ stated in *Georgian Maritime Corp v Sealand Industries (Bermuda) Ltd (The North Sea)* [1999] 1 Lloyd's Rep. 21 at 26 his view was that "this is not a concept of fault or exercise of repudiation; it is the exercise of a contractual option".

[325] *Ardan Steamship Co Ltd v Weir & Co* (1905) 13 S.L.T. 373.

[326] See variously *Carlton Steamship Co v Castle Mail Packets Co* [1898] A.C. 486; *J & A Wyllie v Harrison & Co* (1885) 13 R. 92; *Rickinson, Sons & Co v Scottish Co-operative Wholesale Society*, 1918 1 S.L.T. 329.

[327] *Aktieselkabet Dampski bet Hansa v Alexander & Sons*, 1919 2 S.L.T. 166; *Glencore Grain Ltd v Goldbeam Shipping Inc (The Mass Glory)* [2002] 2 Lloyd's Rep. 244; *Triton Navigation Ltd v Vitol SA (The Nikmary)* [2004] 1 All E.R. (Comm) 698 CA.

[328] *Moor Line Ltd v Distillers Co Ltd*, 1912 1 S.L.T. 147.

[329] *Lilly & Co v Stevenson & Co* (1895) 2 S.L.T. 434.

[330] See, e.g. *The Front Commander* [2006] 1 All E.R. (Comm) 813 CA.

[331] *Micosta SA v Shetland Islands Council*, 1986 S.L.T. 193.

[332] *Wake v Stevenson & Co* (1894) 2 S.L.T. 87.

[333] *EL Oldendorff & Co GmbH v Tradax Export SA (The Johanna Oldendorff)* [1974] A.C. 479.

[334] *John and James White v The Steamship Winchester Co* (1886) 13 R. 524.

[335] *Vergottis v Wm Cory & Son* [1926] 2 K.B. 344; and see *Glencore Grain Ltd v Flacker Shipping Ltd (The Happy Day)* [2002] 2 Lloyd's Rep. 487.

[336] *The Andra* [2012] 2 Lloyd's Rep. 587.

4.8   BILLS OF LADING

INTRODUCTION TO BILLS OF LADING

4.8.1 While charterparties are employed if a shipper requires the capacity of an entire vessel, if a smaller consignment of goods is to be sent, a device known as a bill of lading will be usually be resorted to instead. Commonly, a shipper will ascertain when a ship is sailing to the port for which the goods are destined, book space on that ship, and at the appropriate time will send them to the port of departure along with a shipping note which contains details of the goods. That note will be signed by the carrier and acts as a receipt for the shipper. The goods will then be loaded. Thereafter, the shipper will prepare a bill of lading containing details of the goods shipped, which is presented to the carrier. The carrier, checks it, amends it if necessary, and issues the bill of lading. (Alternatively, the carrier may himself prepare and issue the bill of lading from information supplied by the shipper.) The bill then serves three separate functions.[337] Firstly, it is a document of title to the goods. Thus very often it will be forwarded by air to the port of destination. If the shipper is the buyer, he will forward it to himself or his agent, so that he may claim the goods on their arrival. If he is the seller, he will forward it to the buyer, or perhaps to a bank to be given to the buyer in return for payment. Secondly, it is a receipt for the goods. Thirdly, it embodies the terms of the contract of carriage.

THE BILL AS A DOCUMENT OF TITLE

4.8.2 A bill may be made out in favour of the bearer, but almost invariably in modern times it will be made out in favour of a named person (usually the shipper) or to his order. Until the goods have been delivered to the person entitled to them,[338] constructive possession of and property in the goods may be transferred by transferring the bill—whoever has the bill may claim the goods. However, if a bill made out in favour of a named person does not contain words such as "or order", or if it contains words such as "not transferable" or "not negotiable", then it may not be transferred, and delivery may be made only to that named person.[339] A bearer bill may be transferred by simple delivery. A bill made out in favour of a named person may be transferred by indorsement.[340] If indorsement takes the form of a simple signature, then the bill becomes a bearer bill, while if the name of the person to whom possession and/ or ownership is to be transferred is added (indorsement in full), the bill is then treated as made out in his favour. That person in turn can indorse the bill, although if words such as "or order" were not added to his name, further transfer by him is prevented. As described above, a bill of lading must appear very like a negotiable instrument such as a bill of exchange, and in this context it is often useful to think of it in this way. However, there is one major difference. As Lord Devlin puts it in *Kum v Wah Tat Bank Ltd*[341]:

> "It is well settled that 'negotiable' when used in relation to a bill of lading means simply transferable. A negotiable bill of lading is not negotiable in the strict sense; it cannot, as can be done by the negotiation of a negotiable instrument, give the transferee a better title than the transferor".

Thus in *Lloyd's Bank v Bank of America*[342] the buyer of goods, having pledged them to the bank, was given a bill of lading covering them by the bank, with a view to reselling them in order to be able to

---

[337] See Lord Steyn in *JI MacWilliam Co Inc v Mediterranean Shipping Co SA (The Rafaela S)* [2005] 2 A.C. 423 at [38].

[338] *Hayman & Son v McLintock* (1907) 15 S.L.T. 63.

[339] *Henderson & Co v Comptoir D'Escompte de Paris* (1873) L.R. 5 P.C. 253. But such a bill still qualifies to be regarded as a bill of lading and a document of title—see Lord Bingham in *The Rafaela S* [2005] 2 A.C. 423 at [20].

[340] Lord Justice Bowen states in *Sanders Bros v Maclean & Co* (1883) 11 Q.B.D. 327 at 341 that "indorsement and delivery of the bill of lading operates as symbolical delivery of the cargo. Property in the goods passes by such indorsement and delivery."

[341] *Kum v Wah Tat Bank Ltd* [1971] 1 Lloyd's Rep. 439 at 446.

[342] *Lloyd's Bank v Bank of America* [1938] 2 K.B. 147.

repay the bank. In fact, he instead pledged them again to a second bank, handing over the bill of lading, and absconded with the proceeds. It was held that, as the buyer's title was defective, the second bank did not obtain a good title merely by transfer of the bill of lading.

In England, it has been held that the transfer of a bill of lading does not transfer ownership of the goods, if the parties intend otherwise, so that the transfer may simply create a pledge if that is the parties' intention.[343] In Scotland the authorities are divided between those which seem to concede this possibility, and those which insist that there can be no security without actual possession, so that transfer of the bill must transfer the property in the goods, irrespective of the parties' intention.[344]

Although the above discussion has proceeded on the basis that a single bill of lading will be employed, it is not uncommon for a set of three bills to be issued, one being retained by the shipper, one being carried by the master along with the goods, and one being sent to the person to whom they are being delivered. It is important to understand that each bill is signed, and each has the status of an original bill, rather than a copy of the original. There are advantages in this practice, e.g. if the bill is sent to the consignee by air mail, he may use the bill to pledge or resell the goods long before the goods actually arrive. However, the existence of three bills relating to the same consignment clearly carries with it the potential to cause problems. Invariably each bill contains a clause indicating that once delivery is made under one bill, the others are rendered void. Nonetheless, it is quite possible for someone who holds more than one copy of the bill to indorse different copies to different individuals. It has been held that the master of a ship has no further duty than to deliver the goods to the first person to present a bill, and that he is not obliged to insist on the presentation of all three.[345]

THE BILL AS A RECEIPT

A bill of lading is a receipt acknowledging the quantity and condition of the goods shipped.   **4.8.3**

The mate's receipt

As a bill may take some time to complete, it is not unknown for the master of the ship or the firm in **4.8.3.1** charge of loading operations to issue a document known as a mate's receipt, to cover the period between receipt of the goods and the issue of the bill of lading. In *Nippon Yusen Kaisha v Ramjiban Serowgee*,[346] Lord Wright notes:

> "A mate's receipt is not a document of title to the goods shipped. Its transfer does not pass property in the goods, nor is its possession equivalent to possession of the goods. It is not conclusive, and its statements do not bind the shipowner, as do the statements in a bill of lading signed with the master's authority. It is however, prima facie evidence of the quantity and condition of the goods received, and prima facie it is the recipient or possessor thereof who is entitled to have the bill of lading issued to him."

In *Kum v Wah Tat Bank Ltd*[347] the Privy Council acknowledged a peculiar custom of trade whereby mate's receipts were used as documents of title in the same way as bills of lading, but held that the particular mate's receipt could not be so regarded, as it bore the words "not negotiable". However, the main purpose of the document is simply to acknowledge that the goods are now held by the carrier. It will be given up when the bill of lading is produced and thereafter ceases to have any function.

---

[343] *The Kronprinsessan Margareta* [1921] 1 A.C. 486; and see the views of Mustill LJ in *Enichem Anic SpA v Ampelos Shipping Co Ltd (The Delfini)* [1990] 1 Lloyd's Rep. 252 at 268.

[344] Compare *North Western Bank Ltd v Poynter, Son and Macdonalds* (1894) 2 S.L.T. 311 with *Hamilton v Western Bank of Scotland* (1856) 19 D. 152.

[345] See *Glyn Mills, Curie & Co v East and West India Dock Co* (1882) 7 App. Cas. 591.

[346] *Nippon Yusen Kaisha v Ramjiban Serowgee* [1938] A.C. 429 at 445.

[347] *Kum v Wah Tat Bank Ltd* [1973] 1 Lloyd's Rep. 439.

Clean bills of lading

4.8.3.2 Bills of lading are either clean or claused. A bill is claused when some reservation is expressed thereon by the carrier as to the quantity or condition of the goods. Otherwise the bill will be clean.[348] It can be important for the bill to be clean, if the shipper wishes to sell the goods or raise credit upon them, and indeed many contracts make payment conditional on the delivery of a clean bill of lading. A bill is still regarded as clean even though it simply notes that the goods are in "apparent" good order or condition, or even if it states, "weight, measure, quantity, conditions, contents and value unknown", the important point being that no specific reservation is stated.[349] Moreover, the bill refers to the condition of the goods at the time of loading, so that if it is subsequently amended to note damage or destruction during the voyage, it does not cease to be clean.[350]

Receipt as to quantity

4.8.3.3 At common law the rule was that the bill of lading was prima facie evidence of the quantity of goods shipped.[351] This was only a prima facie rule, so that it could be displaced by clear evidence that the quantity stated in the bill was erroneous,[352] but such evidence did have to be very clear.[353] However, s.4 of the Carriage of Goods by Sea Act 1992 now indicates that a bill of lading which represents goods which have been shipped on board a vessel, or have been received for shipment on board a vessel, and which has been signed by the master or any other person authorised by the carrier to sign bills, is conclusive evidence of shipment or receipt. That being said, where the bill states that weight or quantity is unknown, the bill is not even prima facie evidence of the quantity of goods shipped,[354] and it may be submitted that such words would exclude the effect of s.4, as the bill does not represent the goods shipped.

Moreover, and more importantly, s.4 does not apply at all where the Hague-Visby Rules apply in terms of the Carriage of Goods by Sea Act 1971 (see para.4.8.6 below). Where the Hague-Visby Rules do apply, the shipper may demand the issue of a bill showing either the number of packages or pieces, or the quantity or weight, as the case may be, as he has furnished in writing.[355] This is then prima facie evidence of the receipt of the goods described therein.[356] This of course means that the carrier may seek to prove that the details contained in the bill are erroneous, but he may not do so when the bill has been transferred to a third party acting in good faith.[357] The effect of the rules is to prevent reliance on a "weight or quantity unknown" clause. In *The River Gurara*[358] the Court of Appeal held that, where goods were containerised, the rule related to the number of packages said to be within the containers, rather than the number of containers, even though the carrier had no way of checking what was in the containers, although he could seek to show that there was not in fact the stated number of packages in the containers.

Receipt as to condition

4.8.3.4 Almost invariably, a bill will state that the goods have been shipped "in good order and condition". This can obviously only relate to external condition, as is well illustrated by an Australian case where the goods being shipped were in a container. The statement was taken to mean that the container appeared

---

[348] See Salmon J in *British Imex Industries v Midland Bank* [1958] 1 Q.B. 542 at 551.

[349] *M Golodetz & Co Inc v Czarnikow-Rionda Co Inc (The Galatia)* [1980] 1 W.L.R. 495.

[350] *The Galatia* [1980] 1 W.L.R. 495.

[351] *Smith & Co v Bedouin Steam Navigation Co Ltd* (1895) 23 R. (HL) 1.

[352] *Craig Line Steamship Co v North British Storage and Transit Co*, 1920 2 S.L.T. 418.

[353] *Dampskibsselkabet Svendborg v Love and Stewart Ltd*, 1916 S.C. (HL) 187.

[354] *Craig Line Steamship Co Ltd v North British Storage and Transit Co* (1920) 2 S.L.T. 418.

[355] See art.3 r.3.

[356] See art.3 r.4.

[357] See art.3 r.4.

[358] *Owners of Cargo Lately Laden on Board the River Gurara v Nigerian National Shipping Line Ltd (The River Gurara)* [1998] Q.B. 610.

to be in good order and condition.[359] Unless the master qualifies the bill in some way, the use of these words will then afford prima facie evidence, as between the shipper and shipowner, that the goods were in good condition when shipped.[360] Of course, as only prima facie evidence is afforded, the shipowner is entitled to seek to prove that they were not in fact in good condition.[361] However, English authority suggests that in a contest with an indorsee of a bill acting in good faith, the shipowner will be barred from arguing that the goods were not in fact in good condition.[362] Scottish authority is to the contrary,[363] but it may be that the English position would now be preferred. Of course, if the bill is qualified, as where the master marks the bill "many bags, stained, torn and resewn", then the shipowner will be not be barred from arguing with an indorsee about the condition of the goods.[364] However, qualifications would have to be specific. Marking the bill "condition unknown" has not been treated as qualifying the statement as to good condition.[365] Where the Hague-Visby Rules apply, the shipper may demand the issue of a bill showing the apparent order and condition of the goods,[366] and such a bill is prima facie evidence of the receipt of the goods in that condition.[367] Again the carrier may not seek to prove the contrary when the bill has been transferred to a third party acting in good faith.[368]

THE BILL AS AN EMBODIMENT OF THE TERMS OF THE CONTRACT OF CARRIAGE

As the contract of carriage is normally entered into prior to the issue of a bill of lading, the bill does not **4.8.4** constitute the contract, but it does provide evidence of the fact of the contract and of its terms.[369] However, anything expressed in the bill cannot contradict the terms of the contract already agreed between the parties.[370]

TRANSMISSION OF CONTRACTUAL RIGHTS UNDER BILLS OF LADING

Although a bill has for a long time been regarded as a document of title, so that ownership of the goods **4.8.5** can be transferred by transferring the bill, the contract of carriage strictly remains between the original parties. So as a result of privity of contract, the purchaser of goods would not be able to sue if the goods were damaged or destroyed during the voyage, as the contract lay between the shipper and the carrier. This was remedied by the Bills of Lading Act 1855 which transferred the shipper's rights against the carrier to any individual who acquired property in the goods as a result of consignment or indorsement of the bill. However, this Act did not protect an indorsee who did not acquire property in the goods, or who acquired property other than through indorsement. Consequently, s.2(1) of the Carriage of Goods by Sea Act 1992 now confers the right to sue the carrier upon a lawful holder of a bill, as if he were a party to the original contract. Similar rights are conferred upon those entitled to the goods under sea waybills and ship's delivery orders (see para.4.8.8 below), and the Secretary of State has power to

---

[359] *Marbig Rexel Pty v ABC Container Line NV (The TNT Express)* [1992] 2 Lloyd's Rep. 636.

[360] *Craig and Rose v Delargy* (1879) 6 R. 1269.

[361] *Crawford and Law v Allan Line Steamship Co*, 1912 S.C. (HL) 56.

[362] *Compania Naviera Vasconzada v Churchill and Sim* [1906] 1 K.B. 237. See also Scrutton LJ in *Silver v Ocean Steamship Co Ltd* [1930] 1 K.B. 416 at 426.

[363] *Craig and Rose v Delargy* (1879) 6 R. 1269.

[364] *Canadian and Dominion Sugar Co Ltd v Canadian National (West Indies) Steamships Ltd* [1947] A.C. 46.

[365] *The Skarp* [1935] P. 134.

[366] See art.3 r.3.

[367] See art.3 r.4; and see *Owners of Cargo Lately Laden on Board the David Agmashenebeli v Owners of the David Agmashenebeli (The David Agmashenebeli)* [2003] 1 Lloyd's Rep. 92.

[368] *The David Agmashenebeli* [2003] 1 Lloyd's Rep. 92.

[369] See Lord President Clyde in *Harland and Wolff Ltd v Burns and Laird Lines*, 1931 S.C. 722 at 727–728.

[370] See Lord Goddard in *Owners of Cargo Lately Laden on Board the Ardennes v Owners of the Ardennes (The Ardennes)* [1951] 1 K.B. 55 at 59–60.

extend the Act to electronic bills of lading.[371] A holder of a bill is the named consignee in possession of the bill, or a person in possession of the bill as the result of indorsement or as a result of simple delivery in the case of a bearer bill, and he is to be treated as the lawful holder where he takes the bill in good faith.[372] In this context, an individual is in good faith where he acts honestly.[373] When the holder of the bill acquires the rights of the shipper, the shipper loses those rights,[374] but the former may exercise his rights for the latter's benefit should the latter suffer loss.[375] Just as the holder may enforce the contract as if he were an original party, he will become liable under the contract, but only if he demands or takes delivery of the goods, or makes a claim under the contract.[376] This qualification is inserted to prevent commercial lenders who become holders of bills in order to obtain a form of security being made liable on the contract. Only the current holder can be made liable. If an indorsee of a bill indorses the bill onwards he ceases to be liable.[377]

BILLS OF LADING—REGULATION OF THE TERMS OF THE CONTRACT BY THE HAGUE-VISBY RULES

4.8.6 It has long been recognised that some statutory regulation of the terms of the contract of carriage by sea under a bill of lading was necessary, to prevent shipping companies imposing draconian terms on their customers.[378]

There has been some effort to co-ordinate such efforts on an international basis to ensure uniformity of treatment. These efforts have not been wholly successful, and at the time of writing there are three major international conventions bearing on the subject—the Hague Rules, the Hague-Visby Rules and the Hamburg Rules. Maritime nations around the world will have enacted legislation based on one of these Conventions. Most recently, the Rotterdam Rules have appeared with the intention of supplanting all the other conventions, but at the time of writing, while over 20 states have signed this convention, only two of the contracting states have ratified it, and the UK is not even a party to it. Currently the UK operates on the basis of the Hague-Visby Rules as incorporated into our law by the Carriage of Goods by Sea Act 1971.[379] It is not possible to contract out of the rules.[380]

The application of the rules

4.8.6.1 The rules apply to contracts for carriage of goods by sea,[381] during the period between loading and discharge,[382] and have been held to apply while goods were briefly stored on shore during the course

---

[371] See s.1(5).

[372] See s.5(2). See *Primetrade AG v Ythan Ltd (The Ythan)* [2006] 1 All E.R. 367.

[373] *Aegean Sea Traders Corp v Repsol Petroleo SA (The Aegean Sea)* [1998] 2 Lloyd's Rep. 39.

[374] See s.2(5).

[375] See s.2(4). There may remain an independent right to sue in delict where loss is sustained through the goods being negligently given up: see *East West Corp v Dampskibsselskabet af 1912 A/S* [2002] 2 Lloyd's Rep. 535; upheld at [2003] 1 Lloyd's Rep. 239.

[376] See s.3.

[377] *Borealis AB (formerly Borealis Petrokemi AB and Statoil Petrokemi AB) v Stargas Ltd (The Berge Sisar)* [2002] 2 A.C. 205 HL.

[378] Thus according to Lord Steyn in *Effort Shipping Co Ltd v Linden Management SA* [1998] A.C. 605 at 621, the Hague-Visby Rules are "intended to rein in the unbridled freedom of contract of owners to impose terms which were so unreasonable and unjust as to exempt from almost every conceivable risk and responsibility".

[379] In *Owners of Cargo on Board the Morviken v Owners of the Hollandia (The Hollandia)* [1983] 1 A.C. 565 at 572–573, Lord Diplock opined that the rules "should receive a purposive rather than a narrow, literalistic construction, particularly where the adoption of a literalistic construction would enable the purposes of the Convention to be evaded". And Lord Bingham insisted in *The Rafaela S* [2005] 2 A.C. 423 at [7] that "[e]ffect must be given so far as possible to the international consensus expressed in the Rules and not to any divergent or inconsistent rules of national law."

[380] Whether by a choice of law clause or otherwise—see Lord Diplock in *The Hollandia* [1983] 1 A.C. 565 at 574.

[381] See art.I(b).

[382] See art.I(e).

of a voyage.[383] The contract of carriage must be covered by a bill of lading (or similar document of title).[384] Thus the rules do not apply to charterparties, but do apply to bills of lading issued in relation to a ship under charterparty.[385] They will have effect with regard to the carriage of goods between ports in two different states, if either the bill of lading is issued in a contracting state, or the carriage is from a port in a contracting state.[386] Indeed they even apply where the carriage is between ports within the UK.[387] Additionally, they can be invoked by the parties in that they have effect if the contract provides that they, or the legislation of any state giving effect to them, are to govern the contract.[388] The rules impose obligations and confer rights on the parties, as briefly described below.

Provision of seaworthy vessel by carrier

At common law, the term implied in charterparties that a seaworthy vessel must be provided is also implied in bills of lading. However, s.3 of the Carriage of Goods by Sea Act 1971 states that there is no absolute undertaking to supply a seaworthy ship. Instead the carrier before and at the beginning of the voyage is obliged to exercise due diligence[389]: **4.8.6.2**

- to make the ship seaworthy;
- to properly man, equip and supply it; and
- to make the holds, refrigerating and cool chambers, and all other parts of the ship in which goods are carried fit and safe for their reception, carriage and preservation.

The carrier will not be liable for any damage due to unseaworthiness, if he has complied with the above duties,[390] but if he is in breach of any of those duties, he may not rely on any defences or limitations on liability provided by the rules.[391] If damage has been caused by unseaworthiness, the carrier has the burden of proving that he exercised due diligence to make the ship seaworthy.[392]

Care of cargo by carrier

While common law liability for loss of or damage to cargo is strict, the Hague-Visby Rules provide substantial protection for the carrier. In the first place however, they dictate that he must "properly and carefully load, handle, stow, carry, keep, care for and discharge the cargo."[393] "Properly" means in accordance with a system which is sound, in light of the knowledge the carrier has about the goods.[394] However, the rules then provide a lengthy list of circumstances where the carrier is not liable. He may voluntarily accept liability in relation to all or any of these exceptions,[395] but may not add to the list.[396] The list is far too lengthy to set out here,[397] but it may be noted that it includes perils of the sea, and any neglect or default in the navigation and management of the ship, as well as any cause not arising from his fault or the fault of those for whom he is liable. The rules also limit the carrier's liability for loss of **4.8.6.3**

---

[383] *Mayhew Foods Ltd v Overseas Containers Ltd* [1984] 1 Lloyd's Rep. 317.

[384] See art.I(b); and see *Parsons Corp v CV Scheepvaartonderneming Happy Ranger (The Happy Ranger)* [2002] 2 Lloyd's Rep.357 CA.

[385] See art.V. But charterparties may incorporate the terms of the rules—see Thomas J in *Lauritzen Reefers v Ocean Reef Transport Ltd SA (The Bukhta Russkaya)* [1997] 2 Lloyd's Rep. 744 at 746.

[386] See art.X; and see *The Rafaela S* [2003] 2 Lloyd's Rep. 113.

[387] See s.1(3).

[388] See art.X.

[389] Hague-Visby Rules art.III r.1. The carrier has the burden of proving that due diligence was exercised—*The Happy Ranger* [2006] 1 Lloyd's Rep. 649.

[390] See art.IV r.1.

[391] *Maxine Footwear Ltd v Canadian Government Merchant Marine Ltd* [1959] A.C. 589.

[392] See art.IV r.1.

[393] See art.III r.2; but only where he has consented to carry out those tasks: see *Jindal Iron & Steel Co Ltd v Islamic Solidarity Shipping Co Jordan Inc* [2005] 1 W.L.R. 1363 HL.

[394] *Albacora SRL v Westcott and Laurance Line Ltd*, 1966 S.C. (HL) 19.

[395] See art.V.

[396] See art.III r.8; and see *Homburg Houtimport BV v Agrosin Private Ltd (The Starsin)* [2003] 2 W.L.R. 711 HL.

[397] See art.IV r.2.

or damage to the goods, according to a formula laid down therein.[398] The carrier will be discharged from any liability unless suit is brought within one year of the delivery of the goods, or of the date when they should be delivered.[399] Under Scots law, suit is synonomous with action, which is required to be commenced by summons.[400] Arresting a vessel on the dependence of an action is not the same as raising an action, and is not enough to prevent a claim being time-barred.[401]

Deviation by carrier

4.8.6.4 Any deviation in attempting to save life or property, or which is otherwise reasonable is not a breach of the rules or of the underlying contract, and the carrier is not liable for loss or damage resulting therefrom.[402] In *Stag Line Ltd v Foscolo, Mango & Co*,[403] in considering what amounted to a reasonable deviation, Lord Atkin opined:

> "The true test seems to be what departure from the contract voyage might a prudent person controlling the voyage at the time make and maintain, having in mind all the relevant circumstances existing at the time, including the terms of the contract and the interests of all parties concerned, but without obligation to consider the interests of any one as conclusive."

In that case it was held not to be reasonable to deviate in order to land engineers who had been carrying out tests on the ship, whereas in *The Daffodil B*[404] it was reasonable to deviate to have a generator repaired. An unreasonable deviation disables the carrier from relying on the defences and limitations under the rules.[405]

Carriers' rights in relation to dangerous goods

4.8.6.5 If the carrier discovers that goods of an inflammable, explosive or dangerous nature have been shipped without his consent, he may land or destroy them or render them harmless, without being liable to compensation, the shipper indeed being liable for any expenses resulting from such shipment.[406]

CHARTERPARTIES AND BILLS OF LADING

4.8.7 So far the discussion has proceeded on the basis that a shipper of goods will either charter a ship to carry the goods, or send them as consignment in a general ship, employing a bill of lading. Yet it is not uncommon for the master of a ship to issue a bill of lading to the charterer. In this case, while the bill may serve as a receipt and document of title, the contract between the parties is governed by the charterparty and not the bill.[407] However, if the bill is indorsed to a third party, then it will govern the contract with the indorsee.[408] Even though a ship is under charter, some part of the cargo may yet be carried under a bill of lading. In this context, if when the bill of lading is made out the holder is aware of the charterparty, his contract may be with the charterer, otherwise it must be with the shipowner.[409] Nonetheless, under a demise charterparty (see para.4.7.2 above), the holder of a bill always contracts

---

[398] See art.IV r.5; and see *The Limnos* [2008] 2 Lloyd's Rep. 166.
[399] See art.III r.6; and see *Trafigura Beheer BV v Golden Stavraetos Maritime Inc (The Sonia)* [2003] 1 W.L.R. 2340; but compare *Borgship Tankers Inc v Product Transport Corp Ltd (The Casco)* [2005] 1 Lloyd's Rep. 565.
[400] *RM Supplies (Inverkeithing) Ltd v EMS Trans Schiffahrisges mbH & Co*, 2003 S.L.T. 133.
[401] *RM Supplies (Inverkeithing) Ltd v EMS Trans Schiffahrisges mbH & Co*, 2003 S.L.T. 133.
[402] See art.IV r.4.
[403] *Stag Line Ltd v Foscolo, Mango & Co* [1932] A.C. 328 at 343.
[404] *Danae Shipping Corp v TPAO (The Daffodil B)* [1983] 1 Lloyd's Rep. 498.
[405] *Stag Line Ltd v Foscolo, Mango & Co* [1932] A.C. 328.
[406] See art.IV r.6.
[407] *Hill Steam Shipping Co Ltd v Hugo Stinnes Ltd*, 1941 S.L.T. 303.
[408] *Karlshamns Oljefbriker A/B v Monarch Steamship Co*, 1949 S.C. (HL) 1.
[409] *Owners of Cargo Lately Laden on Board the Rewia v Caribbean Liners (Caribtainer) Ltd (The Rewia)* [1991] 2 Lloyd's Rep. 325.

with the charterer.[410] Bills may often specify a few conditions, and then indicate "all other terms as per charterparty". That does not mean that every term in the charterparty will be incorporated into the bill. Certain clauses are obviously only intended to govern the relationship between shipowner and charterer, and so will not be incorporated.[411] Otherwise, it is really a matter of construction, as to whether a particular term is intended to be incorporated.[412] Obviously, a term which is inconsistent with an actual term of the bill cannot be incorporated.[413]

ALTERNATIVES TO BILLS OF LADING

It should not be assumed that a bill of lading will invariably be employed in those situations where it might be thought appropriate. Other documents are increasingly supplanting them. Although the status of a bill of lading as a document of title presents obvious advantages, it can carry disadvantages as well. The carrier must give possession of the goods to whoever produces the bill. Given that three copies of the bill are often made, the possibility for fraud exists. The other side of the coin is that, if the carrier delivers the bill to someone who does not produce a bill of lading, he will be liable if that person turns out not to be entitled to the goods, and it will not avail him to show that he reasonably believed that person to have a right to the goods.[414] Thus carriers are understandably reluctant to relinquish possession except on production of the bill—an attitude which may lead to frustration for the owner if the arrival of the bill is delayed. Consequently, many cargoes are carried under sea waybills, documents which may set out the terms of the contract, but which are primarily receipts. They are not documents of title and are not negotiable, so that ownership of the goods cannot be transferred by transferring the waybill. **4.8.8**

Essentially, possession of the goods should only be relinquished to the person specified in the waybill, and this should be done on proof of identity, without any need to produce the waybill. Although the terms of the Carriage of Goods by Sea Act 1992 apply to waybills the Hague-Visby Rules do not, although they may presumably be applied by agreement. It may be, however, that the holder of a bill of lading sells parts of the cargo to different individuals. To enable them to obtain possession of the goods, he would issue a number of ship's delivery orders to the carrier. Again, a ship's delivery order is not a document of title, but simply an order to the carrier to deliver particular goods to a named person. It is possible for such "documents" to take electronic form.

FREIGHT

Freight is the sum payable for carriage of goods by sea. Where goods are carried under a charterparty, or a bill of lading or otherwise, it is either calculated according to the quantity of goods carried, or a fixed sum is agreed upon, which is payable regardless of the quantity carried—so-called lump sum freight. Unless the contract stipulates to the contrary, it is only payable on delivery of the goods.[415] So failure to deliver, even if caused by events outside the carrier's control disentitles him to freight, unless it is actually the fault of the owner of the goods that they have not been delivered.[416] If the goods are damaged, or there is short delivery, then the owner of the goods is entitled to deduct an appropriate amount from the freight, unless the carrier is not liable for the loss.[417] **4.8.9**

---

[410] *Baumwoll Manafactur von Carl Scheiber v Furness* [1893] A.C. 8.

[411] *Miramar Maritime Corp v Holborn Oil Trading (The Miramar)* [1984] A.C. 676.

[412] Compare *The Phonizien* [1966] Lloyd's Rep. 150 with *Owners of the Annefield v Owners of Cargo Lately Laden on Board the Annefield (The Annefield)* [1971] P. 168: incorporation of arbitration clauses. Private international law issues may also arise in this context, see *Welex AG v Rosa Maritime Ltd (The Epsilon Rosa (No.2))* [2002] 2 Lloyd's Rep. 701.

[413] *Hill Steam Shipping Co Ltd v Hugo Stinnes Ltd*, 1941 S.L.T. 303.

[414] *Motis Exports Ltd v Dampskibsselskabet AF 1912 A/S* (No.1) [2000] 1 All E.R. (Comm) 91.

[415] *Vagres Compania Maritima SA v Nissho-Iwai American Corp (The Karin Vatis)* [1988] 2 Lloyd's Rep. 330 CA.

[416] *Gaudet v Brown* (1873) L.R. 5 P.C. 134.

[417] *Gehrckens v Love and Stewart* (1905) 12 S.L.T. 720; contrast the position in England: *Thomas v Harrowing SS Co* [1915] A.C. 58.

Liability for freight

4.8.9.1 In *The Success*,[418] Hobhouse LJ opines:

> "[C]arriage is for reward and the personal liability to pay the reward is a contractual liability . . . The personal liability is that of the person with whom the performing carrier has contracted to carry the goods. This person is normally the shipper. But the shipper may be shipping as the agent of the consignee, in which case the contract will be with the consignee . . . [T]he inclusion of the words 'freight prepaid' in a bill of lading does not of itself show that the shipper is not to be under any liability for the freight if it has not in fact been paid . . . Indeed, a request to the carrier that he issue a freight prepaid bill of lading before the freight has in fact been paid would normally imply a personal undertaking by the person making the request that it would be paid."

By virtue of s.3 of the Carriage of Goods by Sea Act 1992, liability extends to any holder of a bill of lading who demands or takes delivery from the carrier, or who makes a claim against the carrier. It has been held that taking delivery means the voluntary transfer of possession, and simply co-operating in the unloading of the cargo does not amount to taking delivery.[419] A shipowner can always demand freight from a shipper even if the terms of the charter indicate that it should be paid to some other party, provided the demand is made before the freight is actually paid to that other party.[420]

Pro rata freight

4.8.9.2 Obviously, if the goods are not delivered to the agreed destination, freight will not normally be payable. However, if the parties agree that delivery should be made at a place short of the contractual destination, or such agreement can be inferred, then freight *pro rata itineris* is payable, i.e. a proportionate amount depending on how much of the journey has actually been completed.[421] No such agreement will be inferred unless the shipowner was ready and able to complete the voyage.[422] It is not enough that the goods are accepted at the intermediate port simply because the master of the ship insisted on leaving them there.[423] It must be possible to infer that the owner of the goods has voluntarily accepted delivery at that port and relinquished his right to have the goods delivered to their original destination.[424]

Advance freight

4.8.9.3 The contract may sometimes stipulate that freight or some part thereof is payable "in advance", or at a certain point in time, or on the happening of a certain event. In England, the rule appears to be that in such cases the freight is payable even though the goods are never delivered[425] (and of course the contract may be explicit on this point).[426] There would also appear to be Scottish authority to this effect.[427] Yet it has been argued[428] that the case of *Watson & Co v Shankland*[429] is authority for the view that in Scotland the rule is that freight must be repaid where the goods are not delivered, unless the contract clearly stipulates otherwise. However, that was certainly not the basis on which the case was

---

[418] *Cho Yang Shipping Co Ltd v Coral (UK) Ltd (The Success)* [1997] 2 Lloyd's Rep. 641 at 643.
[419] *The Berge Sisar* [2001] 1 Lloyd's Rep. 663 HL.
[420] *The Bulk Chile* [2013] EWCA Civ 185.
[421] *Christy v Row* (1808) 1 Taunt 300; *Hill v Wilson* (1879) 4 C.P.D. 329.
[422] *St Enoch Shipping Co Ltd v Phosphate Mining Co* [1916] 2 K.B. 624.
[423] *Metcalfe v Britannia Ironworks Co* (1877) 2 Q.B.D. 423.
[424] *Vlierboom v Chapman* (1844) 13 L.J. Ex. 384.
[425] *Civil Service Co-operative Society v General Steam Navigation Co* [1903] 2 K.B. 756; and see Hobhouse J in *Bank of Boston Connecticut (formerly Colonial Bank) v European Grain & Shipping Ltd (The Dominique)* [1987] 1 Lloyd's Rep. 239 at 246.
[426] *Great Indian Peninsular Ry Co v Turnbull* (1885) 53 L.T. 325.
[427] *Leitch v Wilson* (1868) 7 M. 150.
[428] See *Stair Memorial Encyclopaedia of the Laws of Scotland*, Vol.21, para.659.
[429] *Watson & Co v Shankland* (1871) 10 M. 142.

ultimately decided by the House of Lords,[430] and it has since been treated as not dealing with advance freight at all, and thus as not laying down any general rule.[431]

Back freight

If the delivery of the goods at the port of unloading is prevented by something outside the shipowner's **4.8.9.4** control, e.g. the goods not being picked up, he may decide to transport them elsewhere, e.g. back to the port of unloading. All the expenses of doing so are recoverable from the shipper as "back freight".[432]

Dead freight

If under a charterparty the shipper is bound to supply a full and complete cargo, any failure to do so will **4.8.9.5** render him liable for "dead freight".[433] This is essentially a claim for damages, calculated by reference to the difference between what the shipowner has earned by carrying the cargo, and what he would have earned had the obligation been fulfilled.[434] Obviously then, no question of dead freight can arise when the contract provides for lump sum freight. The principle applies not merely where a deficient cargo is supplied, but whenever the shipper fails to supply the cargo contracted for. So where the charterparty was for the shipping of a number of tugs, but these could not be loaded because their dimensions had been misdescribed, the shipowner was held to be entitled to sail without them, and to claim dead freight in respect of them.[435]

GENERAL AVERAGE

This is an ancient principle, which entered the Digest of Justinian from the law of Rhodes,[436] and which **4.8.10** has become part of the law of practically every maritime nation. It is premised on the view that there are three interests involved in any voyage, the ship, the cargo and the freight (or shipowner, cargo owner and person entitled to claim the freight—the same individual may occupy more than one of these roles). In ordinary circumstances, if for example, the ship was damaged by bad weather, then the loss would be borne by the shipowner alone. However, if any interest suffers a sacrifice in order to save the venture as a whole, then the principle of general average dictates that the three interests together bear the cost of the sacrifice. So, where part of a ship's equipment was cut up for fuel in order to keep a pump going so that the ship and its cargo would not be lost, it was held that the principle applied.[437] There are various elements involved in the application of the principle:

- There must be a danger to the whole adventure. If only the ship or only the cargo is threatened, then the principle cannot apply. So where local inhabitants forced the captain of a beached ship to sell its cargo at much less than its value, the principle did not apply, as there was no danger to the ship.[438]
- That danger must be real, not merely apprehended, however reasonable that apprehension might be.[439]
- The sacrifice must be real and intended to save the adventure. So while the principle would apply if the master of a ship cut away a mast to save the ship and the cargo, there is no real

---

[430] See *Watson & Co v Shankland* (1873) 11 M. (HL) 51.

[431] *Peacock (Iberia) Coal Co Ltd v Olsen, Johnston & Co Ltd* (1943) 60 Sh. Ct Rep. 173.

[432] *Mossgiel Steamship Co v Stewart* (1900) 16 Sh. Ct Rep. 289.

[433] *McLean and Hope v Fleming* (1871) 9 M. (HL) 38. See also *Pentonville Shipping Ltd v Transfield Shipping Inc (The Jonny K)* [2006] 1 Lloyd's Rep. 666.

[434] *McLean and Hope v Fleming* (1871) 9 M. (HL) 38.

[435] *Raeburn and Verel v Tonnelier* (1894) 11 Sh Ct Rep. 336.

[436] See Lord Pearson in *Goulandris Bros Ltd v B Goldman & Sons Ltd* [1958] 1 Q.B. 74 at 93.

[437] *Harrison v Bank of Australia* (1872) L.R. 7 Exch. 39.

[438] *Nesbitt v Lushington* (1792) 4 Term Rep. 783.

[439] *Watson & Son Ltd v Firemans Fund Insurance Co* [1922] 2 K.B. 355.

sacrifice in cutting away a mast which has already been damaged beyond repair.[440] Equally, where a sacrifice is made as a result of an order given by the authorities, it cannot be claimed that the master intended it to save the adventure.[441]

- The danger must not be attributable to the fault of the party who is claiming contribution. So a shipowner cannot claim in respect of a sacrifice occasioned by the ship being unseaworthy.[442] That being said, if the party would not have been liable for his fault, as where such liability is contractually excluded, then a contribution can be claimed.[443]

Although it is easiest to conceive of general average in terms of the sacrifice of some part of the ship or its equipment, or the jettisoning of some part of the cargo, a claim might also be incurred in respect of vital expenditure, e.g. the cost of refloating a ship which has been driven aground.[444] The determination of general average contribution takes place at the conclusion of the voyage and under the law of the place of delivery of the cargo.[445] However, this rule, like any other relating to general average, is subject to contractual modification or exclusion, and it is commonplace to incorporate into the contract a set of rules known as the York-Antwerp Rules, which modify the above principles in certain respects.

MULTI-MODAL TRANSPORT

4.8.11 There has been a tendency to discuss carriage of goods by road, rail, air and sea, as if they were mutually exclusive, and it may indeed be that goods are covered by different contracts during the various stages of their journey. Yet, especially with the rise of containerisation, it is not uncommon for a contract with a single carrier to be entered into covering all stages of a journey. The carrier may then issue a "through" bill of lading under which he undertakes to carry goods to their destination.[446] Alternatively, he could issue a combined transport document to cover the entire journey. The legal status of such documents is unclear. It is unlikely that they are documents of title, and they may not attract the operation of the Hague-Visby Rules. Even though they may cover the whole journey, different legal regimes will apply to road, rail, sea and air elements of the carriage.[447] This means that the documents have to be very carefully designed, to deal with each aspect of the carriage, for example, invoking the Hague-Visby Rules in case they are held not to apply as a matter of course. Fortunately, sets of rules to govern multi-modal transport contracts have been designed by bodies such as the International Chamber of Commerce, which can be invoked by agreement, and which will provide a clear answer to the various questions which might arise.

---

[440] *Shepherd v Kottgen* (1877) 2 C.P.D. 585.

[441] *Athel Line Ltd v Liverpool and London War Risks Association Ltd* [1944] K.B. 87.

[442] *EB Aaby's Rederi A/S v Union of India (The Evje (No.2))* [1978] 1 Lloyd's Rep. 351 CA.

[443] *The Carron Park* (1890) 15 P.D. 203.

[444] *Kemp v Halliday* (1865) 34 L.J.Q.B. 233.

[445] *Simonds v White* (1824) 2 B. & C. 805.

[446] See, e.g. *Coli Shipping (UK) Ltd v Andrea Merzario Ltd* [2002] 1 Lloyd's Rep. 608.

[447] *Mayhew Foods Ltd v Overseas Containers Ltd* [1984] 1 Lloyd's Rep. 317; *Quantum Corp Inc v Plane Trucking Ltd* [2002] 1 W.L.R. 2678 CA.

Chapter 5

Cautionary Obligations and Other Rights in Security

INTRODUCTION

While payment for goods and services may occur on receipt, our economy operates very largely on the **5.1** basis of credit. The granting of credit, of course, involves the risk that the creditor will not be paid. Insolvency law tends to operate on the basis of equal treatment, and therefore equal misery, for creditors. But generally the law of insolvency does not disturb the rights of secured creditors. This chapter deals with the various ways someone who is owed money can, at least to some extent, be assured of receiving payment. Previous chapters have already looked at hire purchase, conditional sale and reservation of title clauses, all of which are, in one sense, rights in security. There is no need to consider these again. These are security rights over corporeal moveable property, created by contract. Contract can create security rights over incorporeal moveable property and over heritage, while certain security rights over corporeal moveable property arise by operation of law rather than by agreement. The situation where a third party guarantees a party's performance of a contractual obligation—described by Scots law as a cautionary obligation—can also be regarded as a right in security. Each will be considered below. It can be appreciated that rights in security provide creditors with some extra security beyond the personal obligation of the debtor that repayment will be made, whether by granting them some sort of right in property, or by providing a personal guarantee from a third party. No personal obligation undertaken by the debtor, however expressed, can ever create a right in security.[1]

5.2   CONTRACTUALLY CREATED RIGHTS

GENERAL DUTIES OF CREDITORS

5.2.1 Whatever the form of security, the creditor is subject to certain general duties. So, if the debt is paid, then he must restore the exact property which was provided in security, unless there is express or implied agreement to the contrary.[2] Secondly, he must not merely take care of the property, but take reasonable care to protect the interests of the debtor. Thus where a creditor held shares in a company in security, and new shares were offered to existing shareholders on very advantageous terms, he was found liable in damages to the debtor for failing to communicate that offer to the debtor.[3] He must also take into account the interests of the debtor when selling the property, and a sale may be interdicted if these interests are clearly being disregarded.[4] When selling, he is in a fiduciary position, and so may not purchase the property himself unless authorised to do so by the agreement between the parties,[5] or by statute.[6] Finally, when there are two creditors who hold a security over property belonging to the debtor, and the creditor who has priority also has a security over other property of the debtor, that creditor (known as the catholic creditor) must have regard to the interests of the other creditor (known as the secondary creditor). So, if the catholic creditor chooses to enforce only the catholic security to the prejudice of the secondary creditor, as where the sale of that property yields only sufficient funds to meet the claim of the former, rendering the latter's security worthless, the secondary creditor may demand an assignation of the security over the other property.[7] This account is premised on the catholic creditor having no interest in retaining that security. If he has such an interest, as where the property is being held as security for more than one debt, then the secondary creditor has no such rights.

5.3   RIGHTS OVER CORPOREAL MOVEABLES

PLEDGE

5.3.1 This arises when the owner of corporeal moveables places them in the hands of his creditor to be retained until the obligation is satisfied.[8] If the debt is not repaid, the creditor will be entitled to sell the

---

[1] *Graham & Co v Raeburn & Verel* (1895) 23 R. 84.
[2] *Crerar v Bank of Scotland*, 1922 S.L.T. 335 HL.
[3] *Waddell v Hutton*, 1911 1 S.L.T. 223.
[4] *Kerr v McArthur's Trustees* (1848) 11 D. 301.
[5] *Taylor v Watson* (1846) 8 D. 400.
[6] *Ferguson v Rodger* (1895) 22 R. 643.
[7] *Littlejohn v Black* (1855) 18 D. 207.
[8] Bell, *Principles*, s.203.

property and use the proceeds to pay off or reduce the debt. Pledge is not competent in relation to other forms of property.[9]

The necessity of delivery

For any right in security to be created over corporeal moveables, delivery of the property to the creditor is crucial.[10] As Lord Trayner puts it in *Pattison's Trustee v Liston*[11]: **5.3.1.1**

> "It is quite certain that an effectual security over moveables can only be effected by delivery of the subject of the security."

It is not enough that the debtor is obliged to deliver the moveables to the creditor.[12] That creates merely a personal right, rather than a real right to the moveables which would be effective against a liquidator or a trustee in bankruptcy. Nor can it be argued that the debtor holds the moveables as a trustee for the creditor.[13] Equally, sham sales whereby what are essentially security transactions are presented in the form of actual sales—as where a debtor "sells" certain goods to his creditor, but retains possession and use thereof—are not valid either as sales or as rights in security.[14] Moreover, the attempt to extend a heritable security over moveables held on the property in question will fail, due to the fact that the debtor retained possession of the moveables.[15]

Yet, while delivery is vital, it may be actual, symbolic or constructive. Actual delivery is straightforward and would embrace the handing over to the creditor of the keys to the premises where the moveables are stored.[16] However, delivery must be to the creditor qua creditor, and not in some other capacity, so that when keys were delivered to the creditor in his capacity as the debtor's agent no pledge was created.[17] Symbolic delivery occurs where the creditor is given documents of title to the moveables, as where delivery occurred when the creditor was given a bill of lading (see para.4.8.1 above) in respect of certain goods.[18] Constructive delivery occurs where the keeper of the goods is instructed by the debtor to hold them on behalf of the creditor. It is not enough for the debtor to assign possession to the creditor, if this is not intimated to the keeper.[19] Moreover, the keeper of the goods must be an independent third party and not the employee of the debtor, for then the goods effectively remain in the debtor's hands and there can be no delivery.[20] It follows that there can be no delivery simply by the debtor indicating that he henceforward holds the goods on behalf of the creditor.[21] Naturally there can be no delivery until the goods have been ascertained or have come into existence,[22] but goods may be regarded as having been constructively delivered from the point that they are ascertained or have come into existence.[23]

At common law, despite what is said regarding symbolic delivery above, certain cases, by insisting upon the creditor's possession of the property as being necessary to establish the right, seemed to

---

[9] *Christie v Ruxton* (1862) 24 D. 1182.

[10] Although the DTI consultation paper, *Security over Moveable Property in Scotland* (London: DTI, 1994) suggested the creation of a new form of security over moveables, which would have been made effective, not by possession, but by registration in a register of security interests. The security was proposed to extend to certain forms of incorporeal moveable property termed receivables, i.e. sums due in respect of goods or services rendered in the course of business.

[11] *Pattison's Trustee v Liston* (1893) 20 R. 806 at 813; see also Lord Neaves in *Moore v Gleddon* (1869) 7 M. 1016 at 1022–1021, and in *Orr's Tr. v Tullis* (1870) 8 M. 936 at 950. But if physical delivery is impossible, as in the case of underground pipes, it may be that a written assignation would be enough to give the debtor a preference, in the event of the debtor's bankruptcy—*Darling v Wilson's Trustee* (1887) 15 R. 180 at 183.

[12] *Bank of Scotland v Hutchison, Main & Co Ltd Liquidators*, 1914 1 S.L.T. 111 HL.

[13] *Bank of Scotland v Hutchison, Main & Co Ltd Liquidators*, 1914 1 S.L.T. 111 HL.

[14] *Jones & Co's Trustee v Allan* (1902) 9 S.L.T. 349; and see s.62(4) of the Sale of Goods Act 1979.

[15] *Stiven v Cowan* (1878) 15 S.L.R. 422.

[16] *West Lothian Oil Co Ltd v Mair* (1892) 20 R. 64.

[17] *Pattison's Trustee v Liston* (1893) 20 R. 806.

[18] *Hayman v McLintock*, 1907 S.C. 936.

[19] *Inglis v Robertson & Baxter* (1898) 6 S.L.T. 130 HL.

[20] *Anderson v McCall* (1866) 4 M. 765.

[21] *Boak v Megget* (1844) 6 D. 662.

[22] *Hayman & Son v McLintock* (1907) 15 S.L.T. 63.

[23] *Pochin & Co v Robinows and Marjoribanks* (1869) 7 M. 622; *Black v Incorporation of Bakers* (1867) 6 M. 136.

preclude the possibility of a pledge being created simply by documents of title to the property being pledged.[24] Nonetheless, the Factors Act 1889 allows a mercantile agent who is in possession of goods or documents of title thereto with the owner's consent, to pledge those goods by pledging documents of title thereto.[25] Similarly, s.25(1) of the Sale of Goods Act 1979 directs that where a person, who has agreed by buy goods, obtains with the seller's consent possession of the goods or documents of title thereto, any pledge by such individual (or a mercantile agent acting for him) to a person acting in good faith and without notice of the original seller's rights, will have the same effect as if the "seller" were a mercantile agent in possession of goods or documents of title thereto with the owner's consent. It seems to follow from the above that such a person can pledge the goods not merely in the normal way, but also by pledging documents of title thereto. By contrast, s.24 of that Act indicates that, where a seller of goods remains in possession of the goods or documents of title thereto, any pledge by him (or a mercantile agent acting for him) to a person acting in good faith and without notice of the previous sale has the same effect as if the person pledging the goods were expressly authorised by the owner to do so. Since in this case the seller in possession is clothed with the authority of the owner, he can validly pledge the goods, but not documents of title thereto. It is submitted that the matter is not altered by the seller in possession using a mercantile agent. It may be added that, apart from such specialities, an ostensible pledge made by someone who is not the owner of the goods, nor the properly authorised agent of the owner, cannot be effective.[26]

Obligations of the creditor

5.3.1.2 The creditor must take reasonable care of the property pledged, and will be liable for damage thereto caused by his negligence or that of his employees.[27] Otherwise, he is not liable for accidental damage to that property, unless he retains it unlawfully.[28] His right expires with loss of possession,[29] but it has been held that possession is not lost merely because he gives pledged jewellery to his family to wear.[30] In the same case it was confirmed that, while he is not entitled, unless otherwise agreed, to use the property, breach of this term will usually not warrant termination of the contract. It is submitted, however, that matters might be otherwise if that use materially reduced the value of the property. English authority has even suggested that, while it is a breach of contract for the creditor himself to pledge the goods, that breach does not justify rescission.[31] If he does use the goods, he would be in the position of a hirer, and liable to the debtor accordingly.[32] If the goods are lost when being used, then the creditor will be wholly liable.[33]

PLEDGES UNDER THE CONSUMER CREDIT ACT 1974—PAWN

5.3.2 If a debtor who is not a body corporate obtains credit by pledging an article, that constitutes a pawn under the Consumer Credit Act 1974.[34] The relevant provisions of the Act replace the old Pawnbrokers Acts. The pawnee must give the pawnor a receipt in the prescribed form in return for the article.[35] Failure to do so is an offence, as is taking an article in pawn from a person whom the pawnee knows to

---

[24] Compare *Hamilton v Western Bank of Scotland* (1856) 19 D. 152 with *North-Western Bank Ltd v Poynter, Son and Macdonalds* (1894) 2 S.L.T. 311; and see para.4.8.2 above.

[25] See ss.2, 3, and see *Inglis v Robertson & Baxter* (1898) 6 S.L.T. 130 HL, especially the views of Halsbury L.C.

[26] *Mitchell v Heys and Son* (1894) 1 S.L.T. 590.

[27] *Dominion Bank v Bank of Scotland* (1889) 16 R. 1081.

[28] *Fraser v Smith* (1899) 6 S.L.T. 335.

[29] Bell, *Principles*, s.206.

[30] *Wolifson v Harrison*, 1978 S.L.T. 95.

[31] *Donald v Suckling* (1866) L.R. 1 Q.B. 585.

[32] *Wolifson v Harrison*, 1978 S.L.T. 95.

[33] See Holt J in *Coggs v Barnard* (1703) Ld. Raym. 909 at 913.

[34] See ss.8(1), 189(1).

[35] See s.114(1); and see Consumer Credit (Pawn-Receipt) Regulations 1983 (SI 1983/1566); Consumer Credit (Agreements) (Amendment) Regulations 2004 (SI 2004/1482) reg.11.

be, or who appears to be and is, a minor.[36] A pawn is redeemable at any time within six months after it is taken, or during such longer period as is agreed by the parties.[37] If the pawn has not been redeemed by the end of this period, then it continues to be redeemable until the pawn is realised by the pawnee selling it.[38] This is subject to an exception where the credit does not exceed £75 and the redemption period is six months. In such cases property passes to the pawnee at the end of that period, and redemption is no longer possible.[39] No special charge may be made for redemption beyond the end of the redemption period, and charges for the safe keeping of the pawn cannot be levied at a higher rate beyond the end of that period.[40]

A pawn is redeemed by the pawnor surrendering the pawn receipt and paying the amount owing, although the pawnee need not deliver the pawn to the bearer of the receipt if he knows or has reasonable cause to suspect that the bearer is not the owner nor authorised by the owner to redeem it.[41] A pawnee who delivers or refuses to deliver the pawn in accordance with these provisions is not liable in delict.[42] If the person entitled to redeem has lost the pawn receipt, he may redeem the pawn by instead tendering the prescribed form of statutory declaration or, where the pawnee agrees and the credit does not exceed £75, written statement.[43] A pawnee who refuses without reasonable cause to allow redemption commits an offence.[44]

Once the end of the redemption period is reached, the pawnee may seek to sell the pawn.[45] To be entitled to do so, the pawnee must give the pawnor not less than the prescribed period of notice, indicating in that notice the asking price.[46] He must then give details of the sale, its proceeds and expenses. The net proceeds, i.e. the amount raised minus expenses, may be sufficient to discharge the debt, and any surplus should be paid to the pawnor.[47] Otherwise, the size of the debt is merely diminished.[48] If the pawnor alleges that less than the true market value was raised, the pawnee may seek to prove that reasonable care was taken to obtain the true market value. If he fails, then the proceeds of sale will be treated as if the true market value were raised.[49] In other words, if, for example, a debt of £8,000 is secured by an article worth £10,000, but the pawnor fraudulently or negligently conducts the sale so that it realises only £5,000 (minus expenses of say, £500), instead of the pawnee being treated as still owing £3,500, the article will be deemed to have fetched £10,000, and he would be regarded as being owed £1,500 by the pawnor. A very similar provision deals with the situation where the pawnor alleges that expenses of sale were unreasonably high.[50]

BONDS OF BOTTOMRY AND *RESPONDENTIA*

These securities represent exceptions to the fundamental principle that security over corporeal moveables cannot be given without possession. A bond of bottomry is granted over a ship, a bond of *respondentia* over its cargo.[51] They can only be resorted to in order to raise a sum of money, which is absolutely necessary to permit the ship to complete its voyage, and which cannot otherwise be raised. If more than one bond is granted, then priority is determined by the date at which each is granted, the later having   **5.3.3**

---

[36] See ss.114(2), 115.
[37] See s.116(1), (2).
[38] See s.116(3).
[39] See s.120(1)(a).
[40] See s.116(4).
[41] See s.117(1), (2).
[42] See s.117(3).
[43] See s.118; and see Consumer Credit (Loss of Pawn-Receipt) Regulations 1983 (SI 1983/1567). Consumer Credit (Agreements) (Amendment) Regulations 2004 (SI 2004/1482) reg.13.
[44] See s.119.
[45] See s.121(1); and see Consumer Credit (Realisation of Pawn) Regulations 1983 (SI 1983/1568).
[46] See s.121(2).
[47] See s.121(3).
[48] See s.121(4).
[49] See s.121(6).
[50] See s.121(7).
[51] See generally Bell, *Principles*, ss.452–456.

priority. The bondholder's claim has priority over ordinary creditors, but not over the wage claims of master and crew.[52] The money lent by the bondholder is lost if the ship (or cargo in the case of a bond of *respondentia*) fails to reach its destination. Such bonds can be granted by the shipowner (or cargo owner in the case of a bond of *respondentia*) or his agent, but may be granted by the master of the ship, even if not authorised to do so, if the ship is in a foreign port, is unable to proceed unless the money is raised, if that money cannot be raised on the owner's personal credit, and if the master is unable to communicate with the owner.[53] If the sum raised is not repaid on the ship/cargo's arrival at its destination, the bondholder can, on application to the court, sell the ship/cargo (both if both sorts of bonds have been granted).[54] If the master of the ship, acting as agent for its owner, grants a bond of *respondentia*, the latter will be liable to the cargo owner should the cargo be thus sold.[55] It is safe to say that the conditions under which these bonds used to be granted having passed, they are now almost unheard of.

STATUTORY MORTGAGES AND FLOATING CHARGES

5.3.4 It is also now the case that various statutes provide for the creation of rights in security over particular types of corporeal moveable property. None of these rights depend on possession. Thus the Merchant Shipping Act 1995 provides[56] for the creation of a mortgage over a registered ship, or over a share in such a ship. Such a mortgage must itself be registered (in the Register of British Shipping) to be effective.[57] More than one such mortgage may be created over a particular ship (or share), and the priority of such mortgages is determined by the order in which they are registered.[58] It is important to note, however, that such mortgages yield in terms of priority to maritime liens (see para.5.4.2.3).[59] If the debt is not paid, the mortgage holder is empowered to sell the ship, but if there are other holders with priority, then he needs either their concurrence or a court order to be able to sell.[60] In similar fashion, it is also possible to create mortgages over registered aircraft.[61]

Companies[62] (but not individuals or unincorporated bodies) may create a form of security known as a floating charge.[63] Detailed consideration thereof belongs to a text on corporate insolvency, but it presents certain interesting features. In particular, when created, a floating charge applies to all property owned by the company, whether heritable or moveable, but does not specifically attach to any item.[64] This means that property can be freely bought and sold by the company, with any property sold ceasing to be subject to the charge, and any property acquired becoming subject to the charge. This will continue to be the case until the charge is discharged by payment of the debt, or until the charge crystallises. A charge crystallises either when the company goes into liquidation,[65] or where the charge holder appoints a receiver,[66] or when an administrator files a notice with the Registrar of Companies confirming that he believes that the company has insufficient assets to enable a distribution to be made

---

[52] *The Daring* (1868) L.R. 2 Adm. 260.

[53] *Miller & Co v Potter, Wilson & Co* (1875) 3 R. 105; *Dymond v Scott* (1877) 5 R. 196.

[54] *Lucovich, Petitioner* (1885) 12 R. 1090.

[55] *Anderston Foundry Co v Law* (1869) 7 M. 836.

[56] See s.16.

[57] See Sch.1 para.7.

[58] See Sch.1 para.8.

[59] *Bankers Trust International v Todd Shipyards Corp (The Halcyon Isle)* [1981] A.C. 221.

[60] See Sch.1 para.9.

[61] Civil Aviation Act 1982 s.86 and Mortgaging of Aircraft Order 1972 (SI 1972/1268).

[62] European economic interest groupings, industrial and provident societies and limited liability partnerships may also grant floating charges—see European Economic Interest Groupings Regulations 1989 (SI 1989/638) reg.18; Limited Liability Partnerships (Scotland) Regulations 2001 (SSI 2001/128) reg.3; Industrial and Provident Societies Act 1967 s.3.

[63] Bankruptcy and Diligence etc. (Scotland) Act 2007 s.38(1). The law in this area was hitherto governed by Pt XVIII of the Companies Act 1985, which will be repealed by s.46(1) of the 2007 Act, although this will not affect the validity of existing floating charges: s.46(2). The 2007 Act amends and restates the law as regards floating charges in Scotland.

[64] See Buckley LJ in *Evans v Rival Granite Quarries* [1910] 2 K.B. 979 at 999.

[65] Bankruptcy and Diligence etc. (Scotland) Act 2007 s.38(1).

[66] Insolvency Act 1986 s.53(7).

to unsecured creditors.[67] Following reform effected by the Enterprise Act 2002, receivers can only be appointed by holders of floating charges created before September 15, 2003. Holders of certain floating charges created after that date can, however, appoint an administrator. It may be noted that the appointment of an administrator does not of itself crystallise the charge. In those cases where the holder may still appoint a receiver, this may happen either on the occurrence of the events specified by the deed creating the charge as entitling him to do so, or on the occurrence of any of a number of other events which, broadly, indicate an inability to repay the loan.[68] When a charge crystallises, the effect is to constitute the holder as a holder of a fixed security over each and every item of property, moveable or heritable, which the company then owns.[69] In other words, at that point the charge ceases to float and attaches to all the company's property[70].

A charge is created by the execution of an appropriate deed and its registration in the Register of Floating Charges.[71] That being said, the company and the person in whose favour the charge is being created may apply to have advance notice of a proposed charge registered and, as long as the actual document of charge is registered within 21 days of the registration of the notice, the charge is treated as having been created when the notice was registered.[72] More than one floating charge may be created by a company, and their priority will generally be determined by the order in which they are created, with charges which are created on the same date being ranked equally.[73] Similarly, any charge created before a particular fixed security was constituted as a real right has priority in ranking over that security.[74] The terms of the deed may determine the order of ranking of charges and fixed securities.[75] It is therefore possible for the holders of existing charges and securities to agree that a newly created charge shall have priority.[76] However, a fixed security which arises by operation of law (see para.5.4), rather than through agreement, will always have priority over a charge, whatever a ranking agreement may say.[77]

RIGHTS OVER INCORPOREAL MOVEABLES

Generally, a right in security may be created over any form of incorporeal moveable property, except **5.3.5** for alimentary rights and rights involving a substantial element of *delectus personae*.[78] So debts, shares, rights under insurance policies, copyright, patents and trade marks may all be the subject of security. There are usually two steps necessary to constitute the security. The first is the assignation of the right by the owner to the security holder. Without this no security right can be created. So where a solicitor persuaded a client to take out a life assurance policy to cover cash advances, paid all the premiums and retained the policy "in security", it was held that he had no right to the proceeds in the absence of

---

[67] Insolvency Act 1986 Sch.B1 para.115(3).

[68] Insolvency Act 1986 s.52(1).

[69] Insolvency Act 1986 s.53(7); and see *Forth & Clyde Construction Co Ltd v Trinity Timber & Plywood Co Ltd*, 1984 S.L.T. 94. Indeed, depending on how the agreement is phrased, it may extend to property coming into the company's hands after that date: *Ross v Taylor*, 1985 S.L.T. 387.

[70] That being said, it has been held that if any item of the company's heritable property has been conveyed to an individual under a disposition, it is not part of the property affected by the charge, even if the charge crystallises before the disposition is recorded in the appropriate register: *Sharp v Thomson*, 1997 S.C. (HL) 66. This decision has proved controversial, and its effect has been confined to the area of floating charges: see *Burnett's Trustee v Grainger*, 2004 S.C. (HL) 19, discussed at para.7.2.11.7.

[71] Bankruptcy and Diligence etc. (Scotland) Act 2007 s.38(3). The creation of such a register by the Keeper of the Registers of Scotland is provided for by s.37.

[72] See s.39.

[73] See s.40(2).

[74] See s.40(2).

[75] See s.41(1).

[76] But such agreement would be required: s.41(4).

[77] See s.41(2); and see *Grampian Regional Council v Drill Stem (Inspection Services) Ltd*, 1994 S.C.L.R. 36.

[78] *Paterson v Baxter* (1849) 21 S.J. 125.

assignation.[79] Assignation creates a personal right against the granter of the security,[80] but the assignee requires to intimate the assignation to the "debtor" in the relevant obligation, for example the insurance company if the security is created over rights under an insurance policy. As Lord Dunpark puts it in *Gallemos Ltd v Barratt Falkirk Ltd*[81]:

> "Intimation of an assignation to the debtor is the equivalent of delivery of a corporeal moveable and is necessary to complete the title of the assignee."

So in *Strachan v McDougle*,[82] in order to provide security for a loan made by M, S assigned to her the rights under an insurance policy on his life. Yet no valid security was created because the assignation had not been intimated to the insurance company. This meant that, while M had a personal right against S in respect of receiving the proceeds of the policy, a creditor who had done diligence on the policy had a prior claim to the proceeds.

In *Christie, Owen and Davies Plc v Campbell*[83] the Inner House decided that intimation could be achieved via the cumulative effect of more than one document. It continued[84] that

> "apart from the means of intimation provided for by the 1862 Act, the law regarding intimation is correctly stated in Wilson[85] in the following terms:
>
>> 'Generally, however, intimation can be proved *rebus ipsis et factis*. The terms must be such as to convey to the debtor that the debt has been transferred and that the transferee is asserting his claim to the debt from the debtor; the amount of the debt being assigned must be stated; general statements may not suffice; letters from the debtor to the intimator can be looked at.'
>
> There are no prescribed formalities beyond what is set out in that statement of principle. The word 'intimate' simply means to 'make known'. The means of making known to the debtor the fact of the assignation, as the authorities demonstrate, may take different forms. There is no doubt . . . that in the present case the combined effect of the receipt of the letter, invoice and the agreement by the respondents was that the fact of the assignation was made known to them clearly. There is no requirement, in our law, that the intimation must be made by one document and one document only, which must contain all the necessary information."

It also advanced the obiter view[86] that it was not necessary that the debtor should acknowledge the intimation.

Forms of assignation are provided by the Transmission of Moveable Property (Scotland) Act 1862, but these need not be followed, and indeed no particular form of words is required, as long as there is expressed a clear intention to make an immediate assignation.[87] Lack of such a clear intention, or any indication that the assignation should be made in the future, will be fatal.[88] The same Act indicates how intimation should be made, but intimation may be implied from circumstances which suggest that the "debtor" cannot be unaware of the assignation, such as where the assignee takes court action or does diligence against him based on the assignation.[89] The "debtor" may be personally barred from arguing that there has been no intimation where he has acted upon the assignation, e.g. by making payments to

[79] *Wylie's Executor v McJannet* (1901) 4 F. 195.
[80] See *Campbell's Trustees v Whyte* (1884) 11 R. 1078.
[81] *Gallemos Ltd v Barratt Falkirk Ltd*, 1990 S.L.T. 98 at 101.
[82] *Strachan v McDougle* (1835) 13 S. 954.
[83] *Christie, Owen and Davies Plc v Campbell*, 2009 S.C. 436 at [13].
[84] *Christie, Owen and Davies Plc v Campbell*, 2009 S.C. 436 at [14], but see the views of Anderson at (2009) 13 Edinburgh Law Review at 484.
[85] W.A. Wilson, *The Scottish Law of Debt*, 2nd edn (Edinburgh: W. Green, 1991), para.27.3.
[86] *Christie, Owen and Davies Plc v Campbell*, 2009 S.C. 436 at [15].
[87] *Carter v McIntosh* (1862) 24 D. 925.
[88] *Gallemos Ltd v Barratt Falkirk Ltd*, 1990 S.L.T. 98; *Bank of Scotland v Hutchison, Main & Co Ltd*, 1914 1 S.L.T. 111 HL.
[89] *Whyte v Neish* (1622) Mor. 854.

the assignee.[90] Intimation is excused where the assignee is also the "debtor".[91] The fact that intimation is highly impractical will not excuse failure to intimate. So where a company assigned the right to the uncalled capital on its shares, the fact that intimation had not been made to each individual shareholder meant that there was not a valid right in security.[92]

The assignee in enforcing his rights against the debtor stands in the shoes of the assignor—*assignatus utitur iure auctoris*. So the assignee gets no better right than the assignor, and any defence which would succeed against the latter will succeed against the former. So where a life assurance policy was void as a result of a misrepresentation by the insured, it was similarly unenforceable by his assignee.[93] Moreover, if a debt was extinguished by compensation prior to assignation, it cannot be enforced by the assignee.[94] But an assignee is not affected by a latent trust.[95]

Of course in relation to certain types of property, there is no "debtor", e.g. patent. This of course means that intimation is not possible. However, in certain cases, such as patents and trade marks, the assignation will only create a personal right against the assignor until the assignation is registered in the appropriate public register.[96] Again, the right to a share in a company can only be established by the registration of a transfer of that share in the company's own register of shareholders.[97] By contrast, there is no register in respect of copyright, so that a simple assignation would be sufficient to create a real right.[98]

HERITABLE SECURITIES

Often a debtor's most valuable property is heritage—land and buildings. Section 9(1) of the **5.3.6** Conveyancing and Feudal Reform (Scotland) Act 1970 ("the Act") created a new form of security, known as the standard security. Since 1970, the standard security is, by virtue of s.9(3) of the Act, the only competent form of heritable security for a debt. Such a security may be created over any estate or interest in land which is capable of being owned or held as a separate interest and to which a title may be recorded in the Register of Sasines.[99] So a security may be created not only on property owned by the giver of the security, but over a lesser interest such as a lease, so long as title thereto is recordable. Debt is defined by s.9(8)(c) to include not only fixed but also fluctuating amounts, as well as an obligation *ad factum praestadum*, i.e. an obligation to carry out a task, such as the completion of a building project.

A standard security must be in either of two prescribed forms, depending whether the personal obligation of repayment is included in the deed (Form A), or constituted in a separate instrument (Form B).[100] To give the holder a real as opposed to merely a personal right, the security must be properly executed and duly recorded.[101] There are standard conditions contained in Sch.3, which s.11(2) applies to every standard security. These may be varied by the parties, save for the conditions as to sale, foreclosure or redemption.[102] The conditions deal with such matters as the debtor's obligations to maintain and repair the property; to complete unfinished buildings; not to demolish or alter buildings without the creditor's consent; to pay rates, etc.; to insure the subjects and not to let the subjects without the creditor's consent. They also deal with the circumstances when the debtor is to be regarded as in default and

---

[90] *Livingston v Lindsay* (1626) Mor. 860.

[91] *Russell v Earl of Breadalbane* (1831) 5 W. & S. 256.

[92] *Liquidator of the Union Club Ltd v Edinburgh Life Assurance Co* (1906) 14 S.L.T. 314.

[93] *Scottish Widows Fund and Life Assurance Society v Buist* (1876) 3 R. 1078.

[94] *Shiells v Ferguson, Davidson & Co* (1876) 4 R. 250.

[95] *Redfearn v Ferrier and Somervail* (1813) 1 Dow 50.

[96] Patents Act 1977 ss.31–33 (Register of Patents); Trade Marks Act 1994 ss.22–24 (Register of Trade Marks).

[97] Companies Act 1985 ss.183–186; and see *Guild v Young* (1884) 22 S.L.R. 520.

[98] Copyright, Designs and Patents Act 1988 s.90.

[99] See s.9(2), (8)(b). There is an exception in that such a security cannot be created over an entailed estate, but this is of no practical consequence as all entailed estates were disentailed by s.50 of the Abolition of Feudal Tenure etc. (Scotland) Act 2000.

[100] See s.9(2) and Sch.2.

[101] See *American Express Europe Ltd v Royal Bank of Scotland (No.2)*, 1989 S.L.T. 650; and s.11(1).

[102] See s.11(3).

the creditor's rights in that case, and with the creditor's right to call up the security. These standard conditions can affect third parties in that if a debtor does grant a lease without the creditor's consent, the lease can be reduced by the creditor, unless the creditor knew at the time when the security was granted that the lessee had a real right or at least a right which could be made real.[103]

Transfer

5.3.6.1 A standard security may be transferred in whole or in part via an assignation in conformity with one of the two forms prescribed by Sch.4, and on recording the assignation the security (or the assigned part) becomes vested in the assignee as if it had been granted in his favour.[104] Except as otherwise stated therein, an assignation conveys to the assignee the benefit of any additional security for the debt, the right to recover any expenses incurred by the creditor, and the benefit of any steps the creditor took to enforce the security.[105]

Ranking

5.3.6.2 It is possible for a debtor to grant more than one standard security over the same property. The basic rule is that the security which is first recorded has priority, although it is open to the parties to regulate the order of preference by agreement.[106] Obviously, the ranking of a prior security cannot be altered without the agreement of the holder of that security. However, when a security holder receives notice of the creation of a subsequent security (or of the outright assignation or conveyance of the debtor's interest), his security is restricted to[107]:

- existing advances;
- further advances he is contractually obliged to make;
- interest on any such advances; and
- expenses and outlays reasonably incurred in exercising any power conferred by the security.

If, after receiving such notice, the creditor does make any advances that he is not contractually obliged to make, it is probable that those advances are still covered by the security, but rank behind the advances of the second security holder. Accordingly, unless the security subjects are very valuable, or the sums secured relatively small, any such further advances may only be secured in a theoretical rather than a practical sense.

Competition

5.3.6.3 The holder of a standard security may find himself in competition with the holders of other forms of security, and of creditors who have sought to do diligence on the property. Thus a creditor may seek to inhibit the debtor from alienating his heritable estate. If a debtor has been inhibited prior to his granting of the security, that security has no effect against the inhibitor, who may indeed reduce it.[108]

On the other hand, an inhibition granted after the security has no effect on the security.[109]

Generally, the insolvency of the debtor has no effect on secured creditors. So a trustee in bankruptcy, or a liquidator may sell the secured property only with the consent of the secured creditor, unless a sufficient amount is obtained to discharge the security, while an administrator or receiver must obtain that consent or else seek the authority of the court to sell.[110] In all cases, the secured creditor has

---

[103] See *Trade Development Bank v Warriner and Mason (Scotland) Ltd*, 1980 S.L.T. 223; *Trade Development Bank v David W Haig (Bellshill) Ltd; Trade Development Bank v Crittall Windows Ltd*, 1983 S.L.T. 510.

[104] See s.14(1). The assignee only obtains a real right on recording: see *Sanderson's Trustees v Ambion (Scotland) Ltd*, 1994 S.L.T. 645.

[105] See s.14(2); and see *Watson v Bogue (No.1)*, 2000 S.L.T. (Sh Ct) 125.

[106] See *Scotlife Homes (No.2) Ltd v Muir*, 1994 S.C.L.R. 791; and s.13(3)(b).

[107] See s.13(1).

[108] *Baird and Brown v Stirrat's Trustee* (1872) 10 M. 414.

[109] *Campbell's Trustees v De Lisle's Executors* (1870) 9 M. 252.

[110] See, variously, Bankruptcy (Scotland) Act 1985 s.39; Companies Act 1985 s.623(4); Insolvency Act 1986 ss.16, 61.

preference in terms of any amount realised. The relationship between fixed securities and floating charges is discussed in para.5.3.4 above.

Calling-up notice

Where the creditor wishes the debt to be paid, or in default thereof, to exercise a power of sale or any **5.3.6.4** other statutory power, he must serve a calling-up notice on the proprietor(s).[111] The debtor must be given at least two months to pay, although the debtor may agree to a shorter period of notice, or waive the right to notice altogether.[112] If the debtor does not comply with the notice, that amounts to default, permitting the creditor to exercise the statutory default powers,[113] i.e. selling, carrying out necessary repairs, entering into possession and recovering rents, letting or applying to the court for a decree of foreclosure. It used to be the case that a creditor who faced default on the part of the debtor and wished to sell the subjects would consider whether to serve a calling-up notice, a default notice, or raise an action in terms of s.24. However, the Supreme Court in *Royal Bank of Scotland Plc v Wilson*[114] held that, in all cases where the creditor sought to enforce the debt, he must serve a calling-up notice. Where a notice of default (see next paragraph) is served, s.23(3) says that the debtor or proprietor may redeem the security by giving notice at any time before an enforceable contract has been concluded for the sale of the subjects by the creditor. When a calling-up notice has been served the Act makes no reference to a power to redeem. Nonetheless, it has been held that the debtor's ordinary right to redeem under s.18 by giving two months notice is not affected by the service of a calling-up notice.[115] A calling-up notice in relation to residential property expires after five years from the date of the notice.[116]

Default

Where a debtor is in breach of some non-monetary[117] obligation arising out of the security, and that **5.3.6.5** default may be remedied, the creditor may serve a notice calling on the debtor to remedy the default within a month.[118] The debtor, if aggrieved by any requirement of the notice, has 14 days to object to the court, which may uphold the notice, or vary it, or set it aside in whole or in part.[119] Should the debtor fail to comply with the notice, then the creditor may look to sell or carry out necessary repairs, or apply to the court for a decree of foreclosure.[120] Where a notice is served, the debtor or proprietor may redeem the security by giving notice at any time before an enforceable contract has been concluded for the sale of the subjects.[121] As an alternative to serving a notice of default, the creditor may instead apply directly to the court for a warrant to exercise any of the remedies available when the debtor fails to comply with a calling-up notice (see previous paragraph).[122] This opens up a wider range of remedies than are

---

[111] See s.19, and see *Hill Samuel & Co Ltd v Haas*, 1989 S.L.T. (Sh Ct) 68. For the form of the notice, see Sch.6 Form A.

[112] See s.19(10). But if the property is to any extent used for residential purposes, the period of notice may only be shortened with the written consent of any person falling into the category of entitled resident (see next paragraph), and where the debtor is not the proprietor, of the debtor and (if the security is over a matrimonial home or a family home) of the debtor's spouse or civil partner: see s.19(10A), 19(10B).

[113] See standard conditions 9(1)(a), 10.

[114] *Royal Bank of Scotland Plc v Wilson*, 2010 S.L.T. 1227.

[115] *G Dunlop & Sons' Judicial Factor v Armstrong (No.1)*, 1994 S.L.T. 199, where the power was said to be exercisable right up to the point of the conclusion of a contract of sale, subject to liability for payment of the expenses incurred by seeking to sell.

[116] See s.19(12).

[117] This is the interpretation imposed by the Supreme Court in *Royal Bank of Scotland Plc v Wilson*, 2010 S.L.T. 1227.

[118] See standard condition 9(1)(b) and s.21. For the form of the notice, see Sch.6 Form B.

[119] See s.22.

[120] See standard conditions 10(2), (6) and (7).

[121] See s.23(3).

[122] See s.24; see standard condition 9(1)(c). Once again, if the creditor is looking to enforce the security in relation to a monetary default, the decision of the Supreme Court in *Royal Bank of Scotland Plc v Wilson*, 2010 S.L.T. 1227 insists that a calling-up notice be served. This means that there is little point in making an application to the court. The exception to this is where the property in question is used for residential purposes (see next paragraph), in which case the creditor must usually serve a calling up notice and make an application to the court. A court action for ejection in terms of s.5 of the Heritable Securities (Scotland) Act 1894 will be required for non-residential property which is occupied—this would most likely be raised after a calling-up notice has been issued and expired without payment.

available following the expiry of a notice of default.[123] Such an application is mandatory where the reason for the debtor's default is the fact that the proprietor of the subjects is insolvent.[124] Where the default is remediable and is remedied before a decree is granted, the standard security has effect as if the default had not occurred.[125] The debtor and the proprietor will usually be one and the same, but that is not necessarily the case.

Residential property

5.3.6.6 Where the standard security is over land (or a real right in land) used to any extent for residential purposes the law operates rather differently.[126] Although following the decision of the Supreme Court in *Royal Bank of Scotland Plc v Wilson*[127] a calling-up notice must be served, the creditor cannot exercise the rights to sell or to enter into possession of the security subjects where the borrower is in default without a court order to such effect[128] unless the property is unoccupied and has been voluntarily surrendered.[129] Such voluntary surrender is established when the debtor (and potentially various other individuals[130]) has, in writing, certified that he does not occupy the subjects and is not aware of them being occupied by any other person; consented to the exercise of the creditor's rights; and certified that his consent is given freely and without coercion of any kind.[131] If a court order is needed, the creditor must comply with certain pre-action requirements[132] and the court cannot grant the order unless satisfied that the creditor has complied.[133] The creditor must provide the debtor with clear information about the terms of the standard security; the amount due to in thereunder, including any arrears and charges in respect of late payment; and any other obligation under the security in respect of which the debtor is in default.[134] He must also make reasonable efforts to agree with the debtor proposals in respect of

---

[123] *Bank of Scotland v Fernand*, 1997 S.L.T. (Sh Ct) 78; but see *Skipton Building Society v Wain*, 1986 S.L.T. 96.

[124] See standard condition 9(1)(c). For what amounts to insolvency in this context, see standard condition 9(2).

[125] See s.24(9).

[126] This is because the Home Owner and Debtor Protection (Scotland) Act 2010 makes the significant amendments to the 1970 Act described below. In this it considerably improves upon the protections afforded by the Mortgage Rights (Scotland) Act 2001, which were described in the previous editions of this work. The 2001 Act is largely repealed.

[127] *Royal Bank of Scotland Plc v Wilson*, 2010 S.L.T. 1227.

[128] See s.20(2A)(b), 20(4).

[129] See s.20(2A)(a). If the property is unoccupied, it may be that it is not being used for any purpose. Thus the matter may proceed as an ordinary action, and there is no need to comply with s.23 and the pre-action requirements: *Accord Mortgages Ltd v Edwards*, 2013 S.L.T. (Sh Ct) 24. However, Sheriff Braid notes (at [10]) that the pursuers would be running the risk that it might subsequently emerge that the subjects were indeed being used for residential purposes, as the action would then be incompetent. This was followed in *Northern Rock (Asset Management) Plc v Fowlie*, 2013 S.L.T. (Sh Ct) 25. Sheriff Mann opined (at [3]) that it is important "that creditors are not allowed to raise proceedings by way of ordinary cause unless they are in a position to demonstrate that, *prima facie*, the subjects are unoccupied and thus not being used for residential purposes".

[130] Those other individuals are the proprietor of the subjects (where he is not the debtor); the non-entitled spouse or civil partner of the debtor or the proprietor of subjects which are (in whole or in part) a matrimonial or family home; a person who has occupancy rights in the subjects by virtue of an order under s.18(1) of the Matrimonial Homes (Family Protection) (Scotland) Act 1981 (occupancy rights of cohabiting couples): s.23A(2).

[131] See s.23A(1).

[132] See s.24(1C).

[133] See s.24(5)(a).

[134] See s.24A(2). Information about the terms of the security must include a description of the nature and level of any charges that may be incurred by virtue of the contract to which the security relates if the default is not remedied; and information about the amount due under the security, including any arrears and any charges in respect of late payment, must be broken down so as to show the total amount of the arrears and the total outstanding amount due, including any charges already incurred. Such information must be provided as soon as is reasonably practicable upon the debtor entering into default. See Applications by Creditors (Pre-Action Requirements) (Scotland) Order 2010 (SSI 2010/317) reg.2(4). In *Northern Rock (Asset Management) Plc v Millar*, 2012 S.L.T. (Sh Ct) 58 the information was provided to the defenders as soon as they fell into arrears. It was held that the concept of default was consistent throughout the Act and (as noted in the previous paragraph) only arose when a calling up notice had expired without compliance with the debtor. Accordingly, the information was provided prematurely, so that the pre-action requirements were not complied with, and thus the court was unable to grant the orders sought. See also *Firstplus Financial Group Plc v Pervez*, 2013 Hous. L.R. 13. In *Northern Rock (Asset Management) Plc v Doyle*, 2012 Hous. L.R. 94 Sheriff Deutsch confirmed that the requirements of the Order are mandatory, and that failure to comply with them will preclude the court from granting the orders sought.

future payments and the fulfilment of any other obligation in respect of which the debtor is in default.[135] Nor must he make an application to the court if the debtor is taking steps which are likely to result in the payment within a reasonable time of any arrears or the whole amount due to the creditor; and fulfilment within a reasonable time of any other obligation in respect of which the debtor is in default.[136] Finally, he must provide the debtor with information about sources of advice and assistance in relation to management of debt[137] and encourage the debtor to contact the local authority in whose area the subjects are situated.[138]

An application to the court is made under s.24(1B), and the court may not grant the application unless satisfied that it is reasonable in the circumstances of the case to do so.[139] In considering such an application where the debtor appears himself or is represented, the court is to have regard in particular to the following matters[140]:

- the nature of and reasons for the default;
- the ability of the debtor to fulfil within a reasonable time the obligations in respect of which he is in default;
- any action taken by the creditor to assist the debtor to fulfil those obligations;
- where appropriate, participation by the debtor in a debt payment programme approved under Part 1 of the Debt Arrangement and Attachment (Scotland) Act 2002; and
- the ability of the debtor and any other person residing at the property to secure reasonable alternative accommodation.[141]

---

[135] See s.24A(3). In complying with this requirement the creditor must make reasonable attempts to contact the debtor to discuss the default; provide the debtor with details of any proposal he is making; set out in such a way as to allow the debtor to consider the proposal; allow the debtor reasonable time to consider any such proposal; notify the debtor within a reasonable time of any decision taken to accept or reject a proposal made by the debtor; and consider the affordability of any proposal for the debtor, taking into account, (where known to the creditor) the debtor's personal and financial circumstances. He must also provide the debtor with written reasons for rejecting a proposal made by the latter within 10 working days of notification of that decision. Where the debtor fails to comply with any condition of an agreement reached in respect of any proposal and the creditor decides to apply to the court under s.24(1B) (see below), then assuming the debtor has not previously broken the agreement, the creditor must give the debtor written notice of that decision and the ground of the proposed application; must not make an application until 15 working days after the date on which the debtor is deemed to receive the notice; and must not make an application if the failure is remedied during that period. See Applications by Creditors (Pre-Action Requirements) (Scotland) Order 2010 (SSI 2010/317) reg.3. As regards the date on which the debtor is deemed to receive the notice, see reg.3(4)–(5).

[136] See s.24A(4). Such steps include providing documentary evidence to the creditor of submission of a claim to an insurer under a current payment protection policy under which there seems to be a reasonable expectation of eligibility for payment; or submission of an application by the debtor to a government run debtor support scheme, where there seems to be a reasonable expectation of being eligible for support, unless the creditor does not participate in, does not agree with any term of, or does not agree to the sale of the property in accordance with such a scheme. But the debtor cannot be seen as taking such steps if his claim or application is refused or has not been determined within a reasonable time, or he is unable to pay any amount due under the security which is not covered by the policy or support scheme. Such steps also include demonstrating that the debtor or his agent for the debtor is actively marketing the property for sale at an appropriate price in accordance with professional advice. But the debtor cannot be seen as taking such a step if he rejects a reasonable offer to purchase the property or the property has not sold within a reasonable time of being put on the market, or he refuses to provide the creditor with details of any agent acting for him or to authorise any such agent to communicate with the creditor, so the creditor cannot readily ascertain if a reasonable offer has been rejected or if the property has not sold within a reasonable time. See Applications by Creditors (Pre-Action Requirements) (Scotland) Order 2010 (SSI 2010/317) reg.4.

[137] See s.24A(5). Sources of advice and assistance include: where the security is regulated, any relevant information sheet published by the appropriate regulatory body; a citizens advice bureau or other advice organisation; and the housing department of the local authority in whose area the property is situated. See Applications by Creditors (Pre-Action Requirements) (Scotland) Order 2010 (SSI 2010/317) reg.5.

[138] See s.24A(6).

[139] See s.24(5)(b). Even if the case is undefended, the pursuer must at least aver why it is reasonable to grant the application: *Northern Rock (Asset Management) Plc v Youngson*, 2012 Hous. L.R. 100; see Sheriff Mann at [14].

[140] See s.24(6)–(7). Thus, in *Mortgages 1 Ltd v Chaudhary*, 2014 S.L.T. (Sh Ct) 35, Sheriff Principal Lockhart noted that the sheriff had been wrong simply to award a decree by default when the defender failed to appear, observing (at [8]) "he is obliged to report that he has considered the issues set out in s.24(5)-(7) and to explain fully why, in the whole circumstances, he granted decree by default."

[141] In *Bank of Scotland Plc v Gallacher*, 2013 Hous. L.R. 36 the sheriff stated in relation to the debtor's ability to secure reasonable alternative accommodation that no information had been put forward by the defender and no request had been made for time to obtain alternative accommodation. Sheriff Principal Bowen, allowing the defender's appeal noted (at [8]) that the requirement

It is also now the case that an entitled resident has a right to be heard in proceedings on an application under s.24(1B), despite not being called as a defender in the application,[142] and once again the court in determining the application is to have regard to the above matters, save that it should consider the ability of the entitled resident to fulfil within a reasonable time the obligations in respect of which the debtor is in default.[143] An entitled resident[144] is a person whose sole or main residence is the subjects, and who is:

- the proprietor of those subjects (where the proprietor is not the debtor);
- the non-entitled spouse of the debtor or proprietor of the subjects which are (in whole or in part) a matrimonial home;
- the non-entitled civil partner of the debtor or proprietor of the subjects which are (in whole or in part) a family home;
- a person living together with the debtor or the proprietor as husband and wife;
- a person living together with the debtor or the proprietor in a relationship which has the characteristics of the relationship between civil partners;
- a person who lived together with the debtor or the proprietor in a relationship described in either of the previous two paragraphs if the subjects are not the sole or main residence of the debtor or proprietor; the person lived together with the debtor or proprietor throughout the period of six months ending with the date on which the subjects ceased to be the sole or main residence of the debtor or the proprietor; and the subjects (in whole or in part) are the sole or main residence of a child[145] aged under 16 who is a child of both parties in that relationship.

Even when the court has granted a decree under s.24(1B), that decree can be recalled, thus reviving the original proceedings.[146] Application for recall may be made by the debtor (but only if he did not appear and was not represented in the original proceedings),[147] an entitled resident (but only if he has not already been involved in the proceedings)[148] or the creditor.[149] That application may be made at any time before the decree has been fully implemented.[150] No such individual can competently make more than one such application.[151] In proceedings under ss.24(1B) and 24D the debtor and any entitled resident may be represented by an approved lay representative,[152] i.e. an individual approved by a person or body prescribed by statutory instrument.[153] Any approved lay representative must throughout the proceedings satisfy the sheriff that he is a suitable person to represent the debtor or entitled resident and is authorised by the debtor or entitled resident to do so.[154]

The creditor's rights

5.3.6.7　As indicated above, the full range of rights available to the creditor on default are: carrying out necessary repairs, entering into possession and recovering rents, letting or selling the subjects, and applying to the court for a decree of foreclosure. Nothing need be said about the first of these. A creditor who

---

to have regard to "the ability of the defender to secure alternative accommodation cannot be met by a lack of information or the absence of a request for a continuation to secure accommodation", adding (at [9]) that the provision is "an important one to which more than lip service should be paid."

[142] See s.24B(1).
[143] See s.24B(2).
[144] See s.24C(1). Where the proprietor's divorced spouse occupied the subjects, she could not be regarded as an entitled resident, since she did not fall into any of the specified categories: see Lord Drummond Young in *Hoblyn v Barclays Bank Plc* [2013] CSOH 104 at [5].
[145] A child includes a stepchild and any person brought up, or treated, by both parties to the relationship as their child: s.24C(2).
[146] See s.24D(1).
[147] See s.24D(2)(b).
[148] See s.24D(2)(c).
[149] See s.24D(2)(a).
[150] See s.24D(3).
[151] See s.24D(4).
[152] See s.24E(1).
[153] See s.24E(2).
[154] See s.24E(3).

takes possession is entitled to recover any rents due from tenants, as from the date of entering into possession. He is not entitled to any arrears of rent.[155] He may indeed himself grant a lease of the whole or part of the subjects for up to seven years, or for a longer period on application to the court.[156] He also has assigned to him all rights and obligations of the proprietor under the lease or in relation to the management or maintenance of the subjects.[157] It has been held that, while an obligation to contribute to common repairs (such as where the subjects form part of a tenement) may thus be transmitted, the creditor does not inherit liability for repairs which have already been done.[158]

The most important right is undoubtedly that of sale of the subjects. It has been held that this power does not confer an unfettered discretion, and the creditor must have regard to the interests of the debtor when exercising it. In particular, if the value of the property sold is likely to exceed the debt, the creditor must account for that surplus to the debtor. Therefore, if he intends to sell in a way which will result in there being no surplus, he may be interdicted by the debtor.[159] The creditor, under s.25, may sell by private bargain or public roup, and must advertise the sale and take all reasonable steps to ensure that the price is the best that can be reasonably obtained. If the creditor fails in these duties, he may be liable in damages to the debtor, but the onus of proving such failure will be a difficult one to discharge,[160] and even proven failure will not necessarily result in an award of damages unless loss is also proven.[161] In *Dick v Clydesdale Bank Plc*[162] the creditor was alleged to have caused a loss to the debtor by advertising land for agricultural use, when it could have yielded a considerably higher price had it been sold for commercial use. This argument was rejected, as no planning permission had been granted for such use, and the creditor was not obliged to emphasise the development potential of the land. Lord Hope opined[163]:

"In the ordinary case the creditor may be regarded as having fulfilled the duties imposed upon him in regard to the marketing of the subjects, if he takes and acts upon appropriate professional advice . . . [I]t is clear that the creditor is entitled to sell the security subjects at a time of his own choosing, provide he has taken all reasonable steps to ensure that the price at which he sells is the best that can be reasonably obtained at the time . . . [He] is not to be subjected to the risk of challenge simply on the theory that the subjects may have had a greater value than was realised by the sale. What matters is the reality of the market place in which the subjects were exposed when he decided to sell."

This was, of course, a case where the debtor's argument about the property having a higher value was purely speculative. It has been acknowledged that the creditor will be liable if he sells in a way which clearly is unlikely to achieve the best price[164] The proceeds of sale will be applied in the following order of priority and any surplus is payable to the owner[165]:

- the expenses of the sale;
- sums due under prior securities being redeemed;
- the sum due under the standard security and securities of equal ranking;
- sums due under postponed securities according to their ranking.

---

[155] *UCB Bank Ltd v Hire Foulis (In Liquidation)*, 1999 S.C. 250.

[156] Conveyancing and Feudal Reform (Scotland) Act 1970 s.20(3).

[157] See s.20(5).

[158] *David Watson Property Management Ltd v Woolwich Equitable Building Society*, 1992 S.L.T. 430 HL.

[159] *Armstrong, Petitioner*, 1988 S.L.T. 255, per Lord Jauncey at 258.

[160] Compare *Royal Bank of Scotland v A and M Johnston*, 1987 G.W.D. 1–5 with *Bank of Credit v Thompson*, 1987 G.W.D. 10–341 and *Associated Displays Ltd v Turnbeam Ltd*, 1988 S.C.L.R. 220.

[161] See *Davidson v Clydesdale Bank Plc*, 2002 S.L.T. 1088, where a failure was established, in that the subjects were sought to be advertised for sale, emphasising their attractive nature and location, but making no reference to the valuable mineral deposits to be found thereon. Yet there was held to be no loss, as the working of the minerals would have reduced the amenity of the property, so that no more would have been obtained through selling the property by reference to the minerals.

[162] *Dick v Clydesdale Bank Plc*, 1991 S.C. 365.

[163] *Dick v Clydesdale Bank Plc*, 1991 S.C. 365 at 370–371.

[164] *Bisset v Standard Property Investment Plc*, 1999 G.W.D. 26–1253.

[165] See s.27.

The right of foreclosure sees the creditor who has failed to find a buyer at a price sufficient to cover the amount due, taking over ownership of the subjects. It is only available[166]:

- when the creditor has exposed the subjects for sale by public roup at a price not exceeding the sum due under the security and any security of prior or equal ranking, and has failed to find a buyer; or
- he has failed to obtain that price, but has managed to sell part of the subjects for a sum below that price.

In such circumstances, he may apply to the court for a decree of foreclosure, not earlier than two months from the date of the subjects' first exposure to sale.[167] He must lodge in court a statement setting out the amount due under the security, and satisfy the court that this amount is not less than the price at which the property has been exposed, or part of it sold.[168] The application must be served on the debtor, the proprietor (if a different person) and any other heritable creditor.[169] The court may[170]:

- allow the debtor or proprietor a period of up to three months in which to pay the amount due;
- order the exposure of the subjects at a price fixed by it—the creditor may bid in that event;
- grant the decree of foreclosure.

That decree, when duly recorded, has the effect of vesting the subjects in the creditor, disburdening them of the standard security and all postponed securities and diligences, and giving the creditor the same right as the debtor to redeem securities of prior and equal ranking.[171] In other words, the creditor takes the property free of securities of lower ranking, since the sale would not have realised enough money to have met any of these claims anyway, but the property is still affected by other securities. The debtor still owes the creditor to the extent that the debt exceeds the value at which the property is deemed to be taken over.[172] It should be remembered that foreclosure is only available when the creditor sought to sell by public roup. It is not competent when the subjects are advertised for private sale.

The effect of the Consumer Credit Act 1974

5.3.6.8 The form and content of agreements must comply with the statutory regulations[173] (see para.3.5.4 above). Moreover, s.58(1) of the 1974 Act states that, before the creditor sends an unexecuted regulated agreement to be secured on land to the debtor for his signature, the creditor must first give the debtor a copy of the unexecuted agreement, containing a notice in prescribed form indicating the debtor's right to withdraw from the agreement and how that is exercisable. Under s.58(2), the withdrawal provisions do not apply to a mortgage agreement or an agreement relating to a bridging loan. Moreover, a creditor who intends to serve a calling-up or default notice, must first serve a default notice under the 1974 Act[174] (see para.3.7.6 above).

RIGHTS IN SECURITY ARISING BY OPERATION OF LAW

5.4 Certain security rights over moveables arise by operation of law, without the need for agreement by the parties. These are essentially liens, whereby a creditor in possession of the debtor's moveable property

---

[166] See s.28(1).
[167] See s.28(1).
[168] See s.28(2).
[169] See s.28(3).
[170] See s.28(4).
[171] See s.28(6).
[172] See s.28(7).
[173] Consumer Credit (Agreements) Regulations 1983 (SI 1983/1553).
[174] See ss.87, 88.

may retain it as security for payment, and hypothecs, whereby a creditor obtains a security over the debtor's moveables without possession thereof.

LIEN

It has already been seen how an unpaid seller has, by virtue of s.39(1)(a) of the Sale of Goods Act 1979, **5.4.1** a right of lien over the goods, so long as they remain in his possession (see para.1.14.1.1 above). This right is created by statute, being unknown to the common law. The typical common law lien arises where a person who has rendered services to another is entitled to retain that other's moveables until he is paid for those services, or at least paid damages for breach of contract.[175] The right of lien is thus based on possession. So where engineers were brought in to work on a ship which remained under the control of its owners, there was no possession and hence no lien.[176] A distinction is sometimes made between true possession and mere custody. So a company secretary did not have a lien over its books and papers which were in his hands, as he held them on behalf of the company rather than them having been entrusted to him for a particular task.[177] He may have had custody of this material, but the company had never relinquished possession. Moreover possession must be conferred by the owner of the property, or at least by someone entitled to confer possession, rather than by, say, a hirer.[178] And that possession must have been obtained legitimately, not as a result of mistake or fraud.[179] The right of lien is lost when possession is lost, unless possession is lost through improper means.[180] It is further argued that the right cannot revive once possession has been lost simply by the creditor resuming possession, but this is probably only true in relation to a special lien.[181] If possession is relinquished as regards part of the goods, the right of lien can still be exercised in relation to the remainder.[182] And of course a creditor may relinquish physical custody without relinquishing legal possession, e.g. by giving custody to a third party.[183] Although the right prima facie entitles the creditor only to retain possession until payment is made, it is open to him to apply to the court for a warrant to sell the property.[184] Equally, the owner may also seek such a warrant where the creditor's retention of the property threatens his commercial interests, although the creditor has a preferential interest in the sum thus realised.[185] A lien is subject to the general equitable control of the courts, who may release the property subject to such conditions as they may determine.[186]

---

[175] *Moores Carving Machine Co v Austin* (1896) 33 S.L.R. 613; but the lien probably does not extend to the cost of storing the property while awaiting payment: *Carntyne Motors v Curran*, 1958 S.L.T (Sh Ct) 6. As regards the conceptual basis of lien, while some commentators see liens as invariably contractual (see e.g. W.M. Gloag and J.M. Irvine, *The Law of Rights in Security* (Edinburgh: W. Green & Sons, 1897), p.341), this is not necessarily so. In *Wilmington Trust Co v Rolls-Royce Plc* [2011] CSOH 151 Lord Hodge was invited to recognise an unjustified enrichment lien on the basis of the South African authority, since there was no such authority in Scots law. Lord Hodge responded (at [56]), "I do not think that it can be said that all liens in Scots law arise as an incident of contract. There are indications that historically Scots law had recognised a special lien or right of retention where the *bona fide* possessor of someone else's property has improved that property before it recognised a claim for unjustified enrichment. Such a lien . . . is nevertheless a lien which has arisen to protect a person's claim to reverse unjustified enrichment." K.G.C. Reid, *The Law of Property in Scotland* (Lexis Nexis, 1996), para.173 argues that such a lien also arises when moveable property is thus improved, Equally, A.J.M. Steven, *Pledge & Lien* (Edinburgh: Edinburgh Legal Education Trust, 2008), para.11.10 points out that a salvor's right of lien exists in the absence of a contract.

[176] *Ross and Duncan v Baxter & Co* (1885) 13 R. 185.

[177] *Barnton Hotel Co Ltd v Cook* (1899) 7 S.L.T. 131.

[178] *Lamonby v Arthur G Foulds Ltd*, 1928 S.L.T. 42.

[179] *Louson v Craik* (1842) 4 D. 1452.

[180] Bell, *Principles*, s.1415.

[181] Bell, *Principles*, s.1416; and see *Morrison v Fulwell's Trustee* (1901) 9 S.L.T. 34; *London Scottish Transport Ltd v Tyres (Scotland) Ltd*, 1957 S.L.T. (Sh Ct) 48; *Hostess Mobile Catering v Archibald Scott Ltd*, 1981 S.L.T. (Notes) 125.

[182] *Gray v Wardrop's Trustees* (1851) 13 D. 963.

[183] *Renny v Kemp* (1841) 3 D. 1134.

[184] *Gibson and Stewart v Brown & Co* (1876) 3 R. 328.

[185] *Parker v Brown & Co* (1878) 5 R. 979; where the condition of the goods was deteriorating.

[186] *Garscadden v Ardrossan Dry Dock Co*, 1910 S.C. 178.

Special liens

5.4.1.1 Liens are either general or special. The normal form of lien is the special lien, which is based on the simple premise that, if A carries out work for B on particular goods entrusted to him by B, he is entitled to retain those goods until he is paid for his services.[187] However, he is not entitled to retain other property belonging to B as security for that debt.[188] By contrast, under a general lien the creditor is entitled to retain any of the debtor's property which he holds as security for general indebtedness to him. General liens are exceptional and thus recognised only in relation to a number of long established categories,[189] although a general lien might also arise as a result of usage of a particular trade,[190] or more unusually under the express terms of a contract.[191] The most common form of special lien is that of the person who repairs goods, but it would also extend to anyone who does any work on goods, as in the case of a miller,[192] or to anyone who does work in relation to goods, as in the case of a storer[193] or carrier (see para.4.2.6 above). Indeed the right will arise in relation to property which is placed in a person's hands so that certain work can be done, even if that work is not done directly in relation to that property. So an accountant, who is given papers and other documents by his client so that a particular piece of work can be done, has a special lien over that material.[194]

General liens

5.4.1.2 It is not proposed to cover the minutiae of general liens, and in particular it is inappropriate to cover the innkeeper's lien in a work of this kind. Still, such liens are recognised as extending to solicitors, bankers and factors.

Solicitors

A Scottish solicitor[195] has a lien over all of his client's papers in his hands in order to cover the whole of the account with the client, even though the account has nothing to do with a particular document.[196] It covers all disbursements and expenses incurred on behalf of the client in the ordinary course of business as a solicitor, but does not extend to cash advances made to a client.[197] Nor does it entitle the solicitor to retain money given to him by the client for a particular purpose which has been frustrated.[198] In the insolvency of the client, the solicitor must deliver up any title deed or other document of the client, but this is without prejudice to the right of lien.[199] Similarly, the order of distribution of a bankrupt estate laid down by s.51 of the Bankruptcy (Scotland) Act 1985 is specifically expressed not to affect the right of lien.[200] The effect is to render the solicitor as a preferred creditor, although relevant authority suggests that his preference is postponed to that of outlays, remuneration and expenses of the trustee in sequestration (and probably of a petitioning creditor).[201] Again, the solicitor's security extends to the whole estate,[202] so that his claim must yield to that of any creditor who has a security over a specific item of property. Subject to these points however, the solicitor's claim would be preferred to

---

[187] *National Homecare Ltd v Belling & Co Ltd*, 1994 S.L.T. 50.
[188] *Findlay v Waddell*, 1910 1 S.L.T. 315.
[189] *Laurie v Denny's Trustee* (1853) 15 D. 404.
[190] *Strong v Philips & Co* (1878) 5 R. 770.
[191] *Anderson & Co's Trustee v Fleming* (1871) 9 M. 718.
[192] *Chase v Westmore* (1816) 5 M. & S. 180.
[193] *Laurie v Denny's Trustee* (1853) 15 D. 404.
[194] *Meikle and Wilson v Pollard* (1880) 8 R. 69.
[195] No lien extends to the account of an English solicitor, unless a Scottish solicitor has paid it or become liable for it on his client's behalf: *Liquidator of Grand Empire Theatre v Snodgrass*, 1932 S.C. (HL) 73.
[196] *Paul v Meikle* (1868) 7 M. 235.
[197] *Christie v Ruxton* (1862) 24 D. 1182.
[198] *Middlemas v Gibson*, 1910 S.C. 577.
[199] Bankruptcy (Scotland) Act 1985 s.38(4); and see s.144 of the Insolvency Act 1986 in the context of liquidation.
[200] See s.51(6)(b).
[201] *Miln's Judicial Factor v Spence's Trustee* (No.1), 1927 S.L.T. 425.
[202] *Rorie v Stevenson* (1908) 15 S.L.T. 870.

that of any unsecured creditor (see also para.7.3.8 below). It is also the case that the solicitor's claim is postponed to that of any heritable creditor, who has recorded his security.[203] The solicitor's lien, of course, cannot be claimed against a third party who has a right to the papers,[204] unless that third party's right derives from the client, but even this is subject to an exception in that if the solicitor also acts for the third party, he is barred from exercising the lien against that party, unless he had previously made the party aware that he intended to enforce the lien.[205] It has also been held that, while a solicitor who has been given papers in order to conduct a court action cannot withhold the papers if they are required for the prosecution of that action,[206] he can retain them if they are required for the initiation of an action.[207]

Bankers

A banker has "a general right to retain all unappropriated negotiable instruments belonging to the customer in [his] hands for securing his balance on the general account".[208] In other words, he has a lien over any negotiable instrument (bills of exchange including cheques, promissory notes, etc.) which the customer has lodged with him for the purpose of collecting the proceeds and crediting the customer's account. If they are lodged for some other purpose, such as for safekeeping,[209] or for the bank itself to purchase them at a discount,[210] then no lien arises.

Factors

Factors or mercantile agents have a general lien over all of their employer's property, including money, which comes into their hands in the course of their employment.[211] A mercantile agent is defined by s.1(1) of the Factors Act 1889 as someone

> "having in the customary course of his business as such agent authority either to sell goods or to consign goods for the purpose of sale, or to buy goods, or to raise money on the security of goods".

However, in this context a factor would embrace anyone who buys property, makes advances or incurs liability on behalf of the principal.[212] Thus auctioneers and stockbrokers are entitled to this lien, whereas a factor in the sense of the manager of an estate is not.[213] The lien covers not only advances made and expenses and liabilities incurred in the course of employment, but also any salary or commission due.[214] It does not cover debts which may be due to the factor in another capacity.[215]

HYPOTHEC

A hypothec is a right of security over moveables which remain in the possession of the debtor. Certain **5.4.2** security rights which can be created by contract such as aircraft mortgages, ship mortgages, bonds of bottomry and bonds of *respondentia* are in essence conventionally created hypothecs (see paras 5.3.3–5.3.4). However, hypothecs can also arise by operation of law. The types of such hypothecs

---

[203] Conveyancing (Scotland) Act 1924 s.27; Land Registration (Scotland) Act 1979 s.29(2).
[204] See, e.g. *Weir and Wilson Ltd v Turnbull and Findlay* (1911) 2 S.L.T. 78.
[205] *Gray v Graham* (1855) 2 Macq. 435.
[206] *Callman v Bell* (1793) Mor. 6255.
[207] *Yau v Ogilvie & Co*, 1985 S.L.T. 91.
[208] *Robertson's Trustee v Royal Bank of Scotland* (1890) 18 R. 12, per Lord President Inglis at 16.
[209] *Leese v Martin* (No.2) (1873) L.R. 17 Eq. 224; but see *Robertson's Trustee v Royal Bank of Scotland* (1890) 18 R. 12.
[210] *Borthwick v Bremner* (1833) 12 S. 121.
[211] Bell, *Principles*, s.1445.
[212] *Glendinning v Hope* (1911) 2 S.L.T. 161 HL.
[213] See *Miller v Hutcheson and Dixon* (1881) 8 R. 489; *Glendinning v Hope* (1911) 2 S.L.T. 161 HL, Macrae (1913) 1 S.L.T. 273.
[214] *Sibbald v Gibson* (1852) 15 D. 217.
[215] *Miller v McNair* (1852) 14 D. 955.

which are relevant in the present context, are maritime hypothecs, and those which may be claimed by landlords and solicitors.

The landlord's hypothec

5.4.2.1 At common law a landlord had a hypothec over moveables (other than money, bills or bonds)[216] on the premises, e.g. equipment and stock on business premises, to secure unpaid rent. That right still exists, but has been restricted and amended by s.208 of the Bankruptcy and Diligence etc. (Scotland) Act 2007. So while at one time the right extended to moveables on any premises, it now no longer arises in relation to property kept on agricultural land or on a croft, or in a dwellinghouse[217]—a dwellinghouse for this purpose embracing a mobile home or any other place used as a dwelling,[218] and including any other structure or building, e.g. a garage or shed, used in connection with the dwellinghouse.[219] And while at common law the hypothec extended to property which a third party had knowingly allowed to enter the premises for the tenant's use and enjoyment,[220] it now no longer arises in relation to property owned by a person other than the tenant.[221]

The hypothec used to be enforced by the landlord raising an action of sequestration for rent within three months of the end of the period in respect of which the claim was brought. The diligence of sequestration for rent is now abolished,[222] but s.208(2) clarifies the fact that the hypothec still operates as a right in security over the relevant property and ranks as such in respect of that property in any sequestration, insolvency proceedings, or other proceedings involving ranking. While at common law it would secure arrears of up to a year's rent, it now extends to all arrears of rent and subsists for as long as the rent is unpaid, although it cannot be extended to cover any rent which is not yet due, as was occasionally possible at common law.[223]

Of course, the value of the security could be significantly reduced, or perhaps even rendered worthless, if the tenant, in anticipation of the hypothec being enforced, were able to strip the premises. Thus a landlord who fears that the tenant may seek to remove certain goods, may seek to interdict removal, or seek a warrant for the return of goods which have been removed.[224] Nonetheless, such remedies are to be regarded as exceptional, and a landlord who seeks them without giving notice to the other party does so *periculo petentis*, i.e. at his own risk. Thus if such a remedy is sought without notice to the other party, and subsequently turns out to have been unnecessary, the landlord will be liable in damages.[225] Anyone who removes any of the property subject to the security will be liable to the landlord for its value, but property ceases to be subject to the security when acquired from the tenant by a third party in good faith.[226] Indeed, even when the tenant has been interdicted from disposing of items secured by the hypothec, such property ceases to be subject to the security when acquired from the tenant in good faith and for value.[227]

Solicitor's hypothec

5.4.2.2 A solicitor who has incurred costs in conducting litigation on a client's behalf has a hypothec over any expenses awarded to the client, and may move for a decree for those expenses in his own name as agent disburser. The result of this is that payment of the expenses to the client does not affect his claim, and

---

[216] Bell, *Principles*, s.1276.
[217] See s.208(3).
[218] See s.208(13). So a houseboat, caravan or even a tent could be covered.
[219] See s.208(13).
[220] *Rudman v Jay* (1908) 15 S.L.T. 853.
[221] See s.208(4). And if the property is owned in common by a tenant and third party, the right only arises to the extent of the tenant's interest in that property: s.208(7).
[222] See s.208(1).
[223] See s.208(8).
[224] *Nelmes & Co v Ewing* (1883) 11 R. 193.
[225] See, e.g. *Gray v Weir* (1891) 19 R. 25.
[226] See s.208(5)(a).
[227] See s.208(5)(b).

the claim is effectual even if the client has been sequestrated or been subject to diligence prior to it arising.[228] Should the solicitor permit the decree for expenses to be awarded in the client's name, he may still assert his right by giving notice to the other party, but in this case someone who has already done diligence on the client's estate would have a prior claim.[229] It might be thought that the creditor's right would not arise where the action is abandoned or settled by the client, but it has been held[230] that a solicitor is entitled to have himself sisted as a party to the action in order to obtain a decree for expenses:

- where a finding of expenses has already been made[231];
- where expenses follow as a necessary consequence of a previous interlocutor;
- where the parties have settled in order to defeat his claim.

At common law the hypothec only extends to expenses but, in terms of s.62(1) of the Solicitors (Scotland) Act 1980, a court can give a solicitor a charge over any property recovered by an action in order to secure his costs.

Maritime liens

Despite their designation these "liens" are really hypothecs, as they do not depend on possession of the **5.4.2.3** ship to which they attach. A maritime lien is "a privileged claim on a vessel in respect of a service done to it, or an injury caused by it".[232] The right is ultimately enforceable by the sale of the ship under the authority of the court. As far as liability for damage is concerned, the negligent handling of the ship itself must cause the damage (to property or persons) for the lien to arise.[233] Thus, where in a storm ship A ran aground because the crew of ship B cut her mooring ropes in order to avoid a collision, the owners of ship B had no lien over ship A, as "the ship" had not caused the damage.[234] As far as services are concerned, a seaman has a lien for his wages, whether or not he has a contract with the owner,[235] and if the proceeds of the sale of the ship are insufficient to discharge the claim, he has a secondary lien over the freight (see para.4.8.9), albeit not over the cargo.[236] Although this is a common law right, s.39(1) of the Merchant Shipping Act 1995 precludes a seaman from contracting out of his right to wages, while s.41 provides that the master of the vessel has the same rights and remedies for his remuneration and all disbursements or liabilities properly made or incurred by him on account of the ship as a seaman has for his wages. To be properly made, a disbursement would have to be made on the owner's behalf, within the scope of the master's authority.[237] So disbursements made on another's behalf, e.g. a charterer, would not fall within the lien.[238] Those who effect repairs and supply necessaries to a ship have a lien if this is done in a foreign port, but they have no lien if such things are done in a port within the UK.[239] A salvor has a lien,[240] and indeed would have a lien properly so called if he retained actual possession of the ship.[241] A maritime lien has priority over a ship mortgage and a

---

[228] See *Black v Kennedy* (1825) 4 S. 124; *Hunter v Pearson* (1835) 13 S. 495; *Pollard v Galloway and Nivison* (1881) 9 R. 21.

[229] *Stephen v Smith* (1830) 8 S. 847.

[230] *McLean v Auchinvole* (1824) 3 S. 190.

[231] As in *Ammon v Tod* (1912) 1 S.L.T. 118, where decree, including expenses, had been given in favour of the client, but the other party had appealed, and the parties had then settled.

[232] *The Ripon City* [1897] P. 226, per Gorel Barnes J at 242.

[233] *The Veritas* [1901] P. 304.

[234] *Currie v McKnight* (1896) 4 S.L.T. 161 HL.

[235] *Morgan v Steamship Castlegate and the Freight Due for the Transportation of the Cargo Lately Laden on Board (The Castelgate)* [1893] A.C. 38.

[236] *The Mary Ann* (1845) 9 Jur. 94. Someone who is claiming for damage done similarly has a secondary claim to the freight: *The Willem III* (1871) 3 A. & E. 487.

[237] *The Castlegate* [1893] A.C. 38.

[238] *The Castlegate* [1893] A.C. 38.

[239] *Clydesdale Bank Ltd v Walker and Bain*, 1925 S.L.T. 676. Indeed *Constant v Christensen* (1912) 2 S.L.T. 62 insists that there is no lien for necessaries even if supplied in a foreign port.

[240] *The Bold Buccleugh* (1851) 7 Moo. P.C.C. 267.

[241] *Mackenzie v Steam Herring Fleet Ltd* (1903) 10 S.L.T. 734.

subsequent possessory lien, but defers to an existing possessory lien.[242] Often a number of individuals will hold a maritime lien over a ship. Generally, the last person to render a service has priority over other holders of maritime liens.[243] However, a lien in respect of damage done by the ship will have priority over all other liens,[244] save for subsequent salvage liens.[245] This means that prior salvage liens defer to damage liens, but they will otherwise be preferred to all other liens.[246] Liens for wages are preferred to liens for a master's disbursements.[247]

CAUTIONARY OBLIGATIONS

5.5

INTRODUCTION

5.5.1 There are three parties involved in cautionry—the cautioner, the creditor and the principal debtor. In a cautionary obligation the cautioner promises the creditor that, if the principal debtor fails to pay a certain sum or fulfil a certain obligation (the principal debt), then he (the cautioner) will pay or fulfil. In other words, cautionry is a form of guarantee. It is thus a form of security for a creditor, albeit taking the form of a right against a person (the cautioner) rather than a right in property

NATURE OF CAUTIONARY OBLIGATIONS

5.5.2 It may help to understand the nature of cautionry if it can be contrasted with other obligations to which it bears some similarity. So a representation as to credit, which is an assurance made by A to B that C is creditworthy (perhaps up to a certain defined limit) in order that C can obtain money, credit or goods from B, is not a cautionary obligation as long as A does not bind himself to pay any debt incurred by C.[248] Similarly, a letter of comfort whereby A indicates to B that it is his policy to ensure that any obligation undertaken by C is discharged, but falls short of accepting any legal obligation to perform that obligation, is certainly not a cautionary obligation.[249]

Third party pledge

5.5.2.1 The arrangements considered above do not amount to cautionry because they fall short of offering any guarantee of performance. One might regard property being pledged by a third party as security for the repayment of a debt as not amounting to a cautionary obligation for a more fundamental reason—the fact that it is a property based security, rather than the undertaking of a personal obligation of

---

[242] See *Shipping Controller (The War Bahadur) v The Athena (The Athena)* (1923) 14 Ll. L. Rep. 515 HL; *The Russland* [1924] P 55.

[243] *The Lyrma (No.2)* [1978] 2 Lloyd's Rep. 30.

[244] *Currie v McKnight* (1896) 4 S.L.T. 161 HL.

[245] *The Inna* [1938] P. 148.

[246] *The Lyrma (No.2)* [1978] 2 Lloyd's Rep. 30.

[247] *The Mons* [1932] P. 109.

[248] See *Park v Gould* (1851) 13 D. 1049. If such a representation turned out to be false, then any contract which it induced, e.g. a cautionary obligation induced by the creditor's statement as to the debtor's financial standing, would be voidable: *Royal Bank of Scotland v Greenshields*, 1914 1 S.L.T. 74. Again, if it were negligently made, it might render the maker delictually liable, should the other party rely on it: *Hedley Byrne & Co v Heller* [1964] A.C. 465.

[249] See *Kleinwort Benson v Malaysia Mining Corporation Bhd* [1989] 1 W.L.R. 379 CA, where a statement by a parent company to a creditor of its subsidiary to the effect that it was its policy to ensure that the subsidiary was in a position to meet its liabilities was held not to impose any legal liability. However compare *Chemco Leasing SpA v Rediffusion Plc* [1987] 1 F.T.L.R. 201; *Re Atlantic Computers Plc* [1995] B.C.C. 696.

performance.[250] Yet it was decided in *Hewitt v Williamson*[251] that the granting of the standard security for the debts of a third party could be a cautionary obligation. This was not a proper cautionary obligation, however, but a cautionary obligation in a broad sense, which was not subject to certain basic rules pertaining to cautionary obligations, e.g. the rule that the cautioner is freed by any material alteration in the obligation between the creditor and principal debtor to which he does not consent (see para.5.6.2.2 below). Indeed, Lord Macfadyen admitted that he would not have regarded the granting of the security as a cautionary obligation at all, but for the decision in *Smith v Bank of Scotland*,[252] in which the House of Lords treated just such an arrangement as a cautionary obligation. It has been pointed out[253] that, although it is not apparent from the report in *Smith*, Mrs Smith had undertaken personal liability for her husband's debts, and was thus a cautioner, the granting of the standard security being thus intended to secure not her husband's debts but the cautionary obligation. So there is no need, as a result of *Smith*, to treat third party pledges as cautionary obligations. Nonetheless, subsequent cases[254] have continued to do so, with the result that it is difficult to insist that they are not cautionary obligations, whether this makes theoretical sense or not. Still, such pledges should be treated as cautionary obligations only in the sense that the creditor is subject to the duty of good faith as elaborated in *Smith* (see para.5.5.6 below). Otherwise they should not be regarded as cautionary obligations, and in particular, the "cautioner" should not be regarded as providing a personal guarantee of the debt.

Accessory obligation

One other way of distinguishing cautionry from other similar obligations is that a cautionary obligation **5.5.2.2** is an accessory rather than an independent obligation in that it always requires the presence of a principal debt. As Lord Justice Clerk Ross puts it in *City of Glasgow District Council v Excess Insurance Co Ltd*[255]:

> "The obligation of a cautioner is not an independent obligation, but is essentially conditional in its nature, being properly exigible only on the failure of the principal debtor to pay at the maturity of his obligation."

It is thus the absence of a principal debt which distinguishes cautionry from contracts such as insurance and indemnity. So in *Milne v Kidd*[256] an obligation to purchase shares if they did not reach a certain price was held to be a contract of indemnity rather than caution. Equally, in the English case of *Sutton & Co v Grey*[257] G had contracted that he would have one-half of any commission earned as a result of introducing clients to S & Co, and in return would bear one-half of any loss sustained through such clients. It was held that this was a contract of indemnity rather than guarantee, Lord Esher MR observing:

> "The test is whether the defendant is interested in the transaction . . . or whether he is totally unconnected with it. If he is totally unconnected with it, except by means of his promise to pay the loss, the contract is a guarantee; if he is not totally unconnected with the transaction, but is to derive some benefit from it, the contract is one of indemnity."

---

[250] So in *Braithwaite v Bank of Scotland*, 1999 S.L.T. 25, Lord Hamilton opined (at 30C–D) that, "a cautionary obligation is one in which A grants to C a personal obligation to make payment to C in the event of the default of B to make such payment. Such an obligation is to be distinguished from that in which identified or identifiable property is made available by A to C, whether in the form of real security or otherwise, against the failure of B to pay his debts to C . . . Arrangements ancillary to the granting of real security over identified or identifiable property or made for similar purposes in relation to such property are likewise to be so distinguished."

[251] *Hewit v Williamson*, 1998 S.C.L.R. 601.

[252] *Smith v Bank of Scotland*, 1997 S.L.T. 1061. And Lord Hamilton in *Braithwaite v Bank of Scotland*, 1999 S.L.T. 25 suggested (at 30B) that as a result of Smith, "the concept of cautioner and cautionry may be invoked in relation to any circumstance in which A exposes himself or his property in security of the debts of B to C".

[253] In Professor Gretton's perceptive commentary on *Hewitt v Williamson*, 1998 S.C.L.R. 601 at 616–618.

[254] e.g. *Forsyth v Royal Bank of Scotland*, 2000 S.L.T. 1295; *Royal Bank of Scotland v Clark*, 2000 S.C.L.R. 193.

[255] *City of Glasgow District Council v Excess Insurance Co Ltd*, 1986 S.L.T. 585 at 588G.

[256] *Milne v Kidd* (1869) 8 M. 250. It is sometimes difficult in practice to determine whether a particular contract is intended to be an indemnity or a guarantee: see *Heald v O'Connor* [1971] 1 W.L.R. 497.

[257] *Sutton & Co v Grey* [1894] 1 Q.B. 285 at 288.

Again, if party A orders goods for party B on the understanding that A will pay for them, that is not cautionry, since A is undertaking the primary obligation, rather than guaranteeing an obligation undertaken by B. As Lord President Robertson says in *Stevenson's Trustee v Campbell & Sons*[258]:

> "If two come to a shop and one buys and the other . . . says, 'Let him have the goods, I will be your paymaster' . . . this is an undertaking as for himself and he shall be intended to be the very buyer."

The same might be said of delegation, where instead of A guaranteeing B's obligation to C, C consents to A taking over responsibility for performance of that obligation.[259]

Indeed, even if the function of a contractual arrangement is to guarantee the performance of another contract, if the obligation under that arrangement is independent in form, it will not be regarded as a cautionary obligation. This is the position with the various arrangements which have emerged in modern times whereby a party secures performance of a contract by agreeing with a bank (typically for a consideration) that the bank will make a payment if the party entitled to performance indicates that the other party to the contract has defaulted. These arrangements are styled performance bonds, performance guarantees or demand guarantees. Lord Justice Potter explains the legal position in *Cargill International SA v Bangladesh Sugar and Food Industries Corporation*[260]:

> "Such a bond is a guarantee of performance. That is not to say that it is a guarantee in the sense that it has all the normal incidents of a contract of surety; it is of course a contract of primary liability as far as the bank which gives it is concerned."

They are not regarded as guarantees, since they are usually payable if certain conditions are met, irrespective of whether default in the contract "guaranteed" can be established. Lord Denning MR remarks that a bank which gives a performance bond[261]

> "must honour it according to its terms. It is not concerned in the least with the relations between the supplier and the customer; nor with the question whether the supplier has performed his contractual obligation or not; nor with the question whether the supplier is in default or not."

As will be seen (see para.5.6.1), the nature of cautionry as an accessory obligation generally has the effect that if the principal debt is unenforceable, then so too is the cautionary obligation.[262] The validity of an independent obligation on the other hand, will not usually be affected by the invalidity of another contract. An illustration is provided by the English case of *Yeoman Credit Ltd v Latter*.[263] A finance company agreed to sell a car to a young person on hire purchase. L agreed to cover the company against loss under the contract. When the young person defaulted, L argued that because of the way loss was defined under his (L's) contract with the finance company it was in essence a guarantee. Accordingly, as the main contract was invalid due to the young person's lack of capacity, the guarantee was also invalid. The Court of Appeal, however, held that the contract was an indemnity, and thus unaffected by the potential invalidity of the young person's contract with the finance company.

---

[258] *Stevenson's Trustee v Campbell & Sons* (1896) 23 R. 711 at 714.

[259] *Morrison v Harkness* (1870) 9 M. 35.

[260] *Cargill International SA v Bangladesh Sugar and Food Industries Corporation* [1998] 1 W.L.R. 461 at 468G.

[261] *Edward Owen Engineering Ltd v Barclays Bank International Ltd* [1978] Q.B. 159 at 171. It would appear that if liability under a performance bond is made contingent upon failure of the party in the main contract to perform—the interpretation which tends to be imposed on such arrangements by the Scottish courts—then the bond will nonetheless be regarded as a cautionary obligation. See *City of Glasgow District Council v Excess Insurance Co Ltd*, 1986 S.L.T 585; *Royal Bank of Scotland Ltd v Dinwoodie*, 1987 S.L.T 82; *Trafalgar House Construction (Regions) Ltd v General Surety and Guarantee Ltd* [1995] 3 All E.R. 737 HL.

[262] However, see *Swan v Bank of Scotland* (1835) 2 Sh. & Macl. 67 HL; *Garrard v James* [1925] Ch. 616.

[263] *Yeoman Credit Ltd v Latter* [1961] 1 W.L.R. 828. It should be noted, however, that a very similar result was reached in *Stevenson v Adair* (1872) 10 M. 919, where a cautionary obligation was enforced despite the lack of capacity of the principal debtor, since the cautioner was aware of the lack of capacity when entering into the obligation. This seeming exception to the principle that if the principal debt is unenforceable, then so too is the cautionary obligation, is explicable in terms of personal bar. In *Yeoman* the fact that Latter was aware of the lack of capacity was one of the factors which helped the court reach the conclusion that the contract was intended to be one of indemnity rather than guarantee.

CONSTITUTION AND FORM

A cautionary obligation can be formed in the same way as any other contract. In particular, a general **5.5.3** offer to enter into a cautionary obligation is valid and can be enforced by anyone who acts on it. Thus in *Fortune v Young*[264] Y gave F a letter indicating that he would guarantee the repayment of any money advanced to F, up to a certain sum. The Inner House held that this guarantee could be enforced by any person who chose to lend money to F. Equally, where an offer to provide caution has been made to an individual, it is possible to constitute the obligation simply by acting on that offer.[265]

The creation of a cautionary obligation may be complicated by the fact that there are to be co-cautioners. Where it is intended that there should be more than one cautioner, the assumption is that each enters into the obligation on the basis that either all become cautioners for the whole sum or none. Thus in *Scottish Provincial Insurance Co v Pringle*[266] money was lent only on condition that repayment be guaranteed by four individuals. Three of the four signed the document, but the principal debtor forged the signature of the fourth. It was held that none of the co-cautioners was bound. Lord Wood noted[267]:

> "The subscription of any one was *per se* of no binding efficacy. It was only by the combination of the subscriptions of all, that the subscription of each could come to be of obligatory force."

Similarly, in *Ellesmere Brewery Co v Cooper*,[268] where one of four guarantors added the words "£25 only" to his signature, this was held to release all the guarantors from any obligation. It may however be that this is primarily a matter of construction. In *Harvey v Dunbar Assets plc*[269] it was held that the principle cannot apply if the actual terms of the guarantee provide otherwise. On appeal[270] Gloster LJ observed[271]:

> "an analysis of the relevant authorities shows that, whether a signatory to a guarantee has assumed liability under the document, in circumstances where other contemplated security has not been obtained, is essentially one of construction of the relevant guarantee . . . The authorities do not establish some absolute rule, or enshrined principle that . . . if an intended surety [cautioner] does not sign, the other intended sureties are not bound. It all depends on the construction of the guarantee. The principle of suretyship, which is engaged, is that a surety is entitled to contribution from every co-surety and to the benefit of every security held by the creditor in respect of the debt. If the surety is to be deprived of that right, the guarantee must so provide."

However, the appeal was allowed, as the Court of Appeal did not believe that the words of the guarantee did exclude that right. Gloster LJ continued[272]:

> "the authorities clearly demonstrate that, if the form of the document, on its face, shows that it is intended to be a joint composite guarantee, contained in a single document, which assumes that it will be signed by all the sureties named as such in the document, then, certainly as a starting point in the construction exercise, the guarantee will be regarded as subject to the condition that the signatures of all sureties are necessary for its validity, and that liability as a guarantor will only be imposed on any individual signatory if all the named sureties do indeed sign."

---

[264] *Fortune v Young*, 1918 S.C. 1.

[265] *Wallace v Gibson* (1895) 22 R. (HL) 56.

[266] *Scottish Provincial Insurance Co v Pringle* (1858) 20 D. 465. See also *Paterson v Bonar* (1844) 6 D. 987. But this is not the rule in judicial cautionry, i.e. caution required in relation to court proceedings: *Simpson v Fleming* (1860) 22 D. 679.

[267] *Scottish Provincial Insurance Co v Pringle* (1858) 20 D. 465 at 471.

[268] *Ellesmere Brewery Co v Cooper* [1896] 1 Q.B. 75.

[269] See *Harvey v Dunbar Assets plc* [2012] EWHC 2890 (Ch).

[270] *Harvey v Dunbar Assets plc* [2013] EWCA Civ 952.

[271] *Harvey v Dunbar Assets plc* [2013] EWCA Civ 952 at [22].

[272] *Harvey v Dunbar Assets plc* [2013] EWCA Civ 952 at [23].

Following the repeal of the Mercantile Law Amendment (Scotland) Act 1856 s.6 there is no longer any requirement that cautionary obligations should be in writing,[273] unless a cautionary obligation is a gratuitous unilateral obligation not undertaken in the course of a business—as many will be. In this case by virtue of s.1(2)(a)(ii) of the Requirements of Writing (Scotland) Act 1995 the obligation would require to be in writing and subscribed by the cautioner. If these requirements of form were not met, the obligation would still be valid if the creditor has acted (or refrained from acting) in reliance on the obligation with the knowledge and acquiescence of the cautioner, been affected to a material extent as a result of such action, and would be adversely affected to a material extent if the obligation were invalid.[274]

It should also be noted that if security for a regulated agreement under the Consumer Credit Act 1974 is provided in the form of a guarantee or indemnity, such guarantee or indemnity must be in writing,[275] and properly executed. This means that it must be in the form prescribed by regulations,[276] must embody all the terms of the security,[277] and must be signed by the guarantor,[278] who must get a copy of both the regulated agreement and the security agreement.[279] If the agreement is not in writing or is not properly executed, it cannot be enforced except by order of the court.[280]

If someone signs in a representative capacity a document constituting a cautionary obligation, the courts will be slow to assume that he intends to undertake personal liability.[281]

PROPER AND IMPROPER CAUTIONRY

5.5.4 Proper cautionry arises where the fact that the cautioner is bound as cautioner appears clearly on the face of the deed by which they are bound.[282] In improper cautionry the principal debtor and cautioner appear to be bound jointly as co-debtors, although their true relationship can either be discerned from a closer reading of the deed,[283] or the creditor is otherwise aware that one party acts in reality as cautioner.[284] Where two parties appear to be bound jointly as co-debtors, and the creditor is not aware that, as between themselves, the parties have agreed that one is the principal debtor and one is his cautioner, that is not a cautionary obligation. Thus, whatever the rights of those individuals *inter se*, the cautioner is not entitled to the rights of a cautioner vis-à-vis the creditor.[285]

The point of the distinction was that, although an improper cautioner, once that relationship was established to exist, was entitled to all the normal rights of a cautioner,[286] only a proper cautioner was entitled to the benefit of discussion and the benefit of division.[287] The benefit of discussion allowed the cautioner to insist that, in the event of default, the creditor should first take all reasonable steps to enforce the debt against the principal debtor, including obtaining a decree against the debtor and doing diligence thereon, before proceeding against the cautioner. However, that right was removed by s.8 of

---

[273] Although that provision will continue to apply to cautionary obligations entered into before August 1, 1995. For an account of its effect, see E.A. Marshall, *Scots Mercantile Law*, 3rd edn (Edinburgh: W. Green, 1997), para.8.42.

[274] Requirements of Writing (Scotland) Act 1995 s.1(3)–(5).

[275] Consumer Credit Act 1974 s.105(1).

[276] See s.105(4)(a); Consumer Credit (Guarantees and Indemnities) Regulations 1983 (SI 1983/1556).

[277] See s.105(4)(b).

[278] Consumer Credit (Guarantees and Indemnities) Regulations 1983 (SI 1983/1556) reg.4.

[279] See ss.105(4)(d), (5).

[280] See s.105(7).

[281] *Montgomery Litho Ltd v Maxwell*, 1999 S.L.T. 1431.

[282] Bell, *Principles*, s.247.

[283] As in *Paterson v Bonar* (1844) 6 D. 987, where, despite the parties appearing to be jointly and severally liable to a bank under a credit account, the fact that only one party could operate the account showed that the others were cautioners. And in *Scottish Provincial Insurance Co v Pringle* (1858) 20 D. 465, despite several persons accepting joint and several liability for a loan, the fact that one had assigned a life assurance policy to pay the debt on his death indicated that he was the true debtor, and the others cautioners.

[284] *Jackson v McIver* (1875) 2 R. 882.

[285] *Union Bank of Scotland v McMurray* (1870) 7 S.L.R. 596.

[286] *Mackenzie v Macartney* (1831) 5 W. & S. 504 HL.

[287] Bell, *Commentaries*, I, 365.

the Mercantile Law Amendment (Scotland) Act 1856, unless it is expressly provided for "in the instrument of caution". Thus, failing such provision, a creditor need not pursue the debtor before enforcing the cautionary obligation against the cautioner.[288] The debtor simply needs to default in order that the creditor can seek to enforce the cautionary obligation against the cautioner. Section 8 speaks of "payment of the debt", thus raising the possibility that it does not apply where the principal debt is an obligation of performance, so that the benefit of discussion would still be available in such a case.[289] The benefit of division dictates that each co-cautioner is only liable for his pro rata share of the debt (not counting insolvent cautioners), and cannot be asked to pay unless all co-cautioners are similarly asked.[290] In improper cautionry each cautioner is jointly and severally liable with the principal debtor for the entire sum.[291]

EFFECT OF MISREPRESENTATION, ETC.   5.5.5

By the creditor

As a cautionary obligation is a contract, if it is induced by the creditor's misrepresentation, undue influ- 5.5.5.1
ence or force and fear, or by facility and circumvention, it is rendered void or voidable as appropriate.[292] Equally, a cautionary obligation may be rendered void by essential error.[293] *Royal Bank of Scotland v Ranken*[294] makes it clear that any misrepresentation must be material, and also induce the cautioner to enter into the obligation. Thus in that case, where one cautioner was actually aware of the true position, he remained bound, whereas another cautioner who was misled was entitled to avoid the obligation. Nonetheless, it remains the case that a creditor is under no duty to disclose material facts of which the cautioner may be ignorant.[295] Yet there is a duty of disclosure if the circumstances of the arrangement between the debtor and the creditor are unusual, and not what the cautioner would expect.[296] Lord Clyde indicates in *Smith v Bank of Scotland*[297] that the duty of disclosure extended to "some fact in the relationship between the creditor and the debtor which is material to the risk and . . . would not be expected to exist".

Moreover, if the creditor does volunteer any information, whether spontaneously or in answer to a question, he must give a full and fair representation of the situation. The contract may be avoided if he misleads the cautioner by revealing only part of the true situation.[298] Equally, he must disclose the true

---

[288] *Morrison v Harkness* (1870) 9 M. 35; *Sheldon and Ackhoff v Milligan* (1907) 14 S.L.T. 703; *Scottish Metropolitan Property v Christie*, 1987 S.L.T. (Sh Ct) 18.

[289] See *Johannesburg Municipal Council v D Stewart & Co* (1902) Ltd, 1909 S.C. 860; but see the views of Lord Shaw in 1909 S.C. (HL) 53 at 57.

[290] Bell, *Principles*, ss.62, 267; but see *McArthur v Scott* (1836) 15 S. 270.

[291] *Richmond v Graham* (1847) 9 D. 633.

[292] See *Smith v Bank of Scotland* (1829) 7 S. 244; *Forbes v Forbes's Trustees (No.2)*, 1957 S.L.T. 346; *Sutherland v WM Low & Co* (1901) 9 S.L.T. 91.

[293] *Bennie's Trustees v Couper* (1890) 17 R. 782.

[294] *Royal Bank of Scotland v Ranken* (1844) 6 D. 1418, see especially Lord Jeffrey at 1437.

[295] *Young v Clydesdale Bank* (1889) 17 R. 231.

[296] See *Hamilton v Watson* (1845) 4 Bell's App. 67, especially Lord Campbell at 103.

[297] *Smith v Bank of Scotland*, 1997 S.L.T. 1061 at 1065J. In *Royal Bank of Scotland v Etridge (No.2)* [2001] 4 All E.R. 449; Lord Scott (at [346]–[350]) discusses the case of *Bank of Scotland v Bennett*. Mrs Bennett as guarantor was entitled on paying the debt to the benefit of any security which the bank held over the debt. However, the bank did not mention that the practical value of a major security it held was much diminished because of a ranking agreement it had with another creditor. Lord Scott stated that this ranking agreement should have been disclosed. On the other hand, in *North Shore Ventures Ltd v Anstead Holdings Inc* [2012] Ch 31; the Court of Appeal held (reversing the decision at first instance) that the fact that the owner of the creditor was being investigated in relation to alleged embezzlement was not an unusual feature of the contractual relationship between the creditor and the debtor and thus did not have to be disclosed. While the matter was no doubt relevant, Morritt C observed that to hold that it had to be disclosed would have been to impose a general duty of disclosure on a creditor, a step which had always been resisted in this context: see [25]–[32].

[298] *Falconer v North of Scotland Banking Co* (1863) 1 M. 704; and see Lord Clyde in *Smith v Bank of Scotland*, 1997 S.L.T. 1061 at 1065L.

position if he becomes aware that the cautioner is labouring under a material misapprehension.[299] It is submitted that the creditor is not entitled to decline to answer, if asked a specific question by the cautioner.[300]

By the debtor

5.5.5.2 As long as the principal debtor is not acting as the creditor's agent,[301] the traditional approach of Scots law has been to insist that the debtor's misrepresentation or undue influence does not affect the validity of the cautionary obligation, unless the creditor is aware of that misrepresentation, etc.[302] However, as Lord Clyde has pointed out in *Smith v Bank of Scotland*,[303] "the rule is not absolute". So, while the normal rule applies in relation to a fraudulent misrepresentation, where fraud is involved, the creditor cannot enforce the obligation unless he has given valuable consideration, e.g. lent the debtor money on the strength of the obligation.[304] Moreover, Lord Clyde cites with approval English authority to the effect that a creditor will not be entitled to enforce the cautionary obligation, even if unaware of the debtor's fraud, if a reasonable person would have suspected that fraud had occurred.[305] More general contractual principles would render void a cautionary obligation induced by force and fear exercised by the debtor.[306] It is also the case that where the creditor is in breach of the duty of good faith, he will be unable to enforce the obligation if the debtor has been guilty of misrepresentation, etc. The duty of good faith will be considered in the next paragraph.

THE DUTY OF GOOD FAITH

5.5.6 The facts of *Smith v Bank of Scotland* appeared unexceptional. Mrs Smith claimed that she had been induced to guarantee her husband's business debts as a result of his misrepresentation and undue influence. However, as these vitiating factors were unknown to the creditor, the law would have seemed clearly to indicate that the validity of the cautionary obligation could not be challenged. Yet in practically identical circumstances in England the guarantee would have been unenforceable because of the doctrine of constructive notice as explained by the House of Lords in *Barclays Bank Plc v O'Brien*.[307] This indicates that, in circumstances where the creditor is aware that the surety (cautioner) reposes trust and confidence in the debtor in financial matters, the creditor will be put on his inquiry, and fixed with constructive notice of the debtor's misrepresentation and undue influence unless the creditor took reasonable steps to ensure that the surety's agreement had been properly obtained (see para.5.5.6.1). In other words, the creditor will be regarded as aware of any such misrepresentation or undue influence. This, of course, was not the law of Scotland, as was recognised by the Inner House in *Smith*.[308]

Yet, in the House of Lords, Lord Clyde indicated that he had[309]

> "not been persuaded that there are sufficiently cogent grounds for refusing the extension to Scotland of the development which has been achieved in England by the decision in *Barclays Bank plc v O'Brien*."

---

[299] *Royal Bank of Scotland v Greenshields* (1914) 1 S.L.T. 74; and see Lord Clyde in *Smith v Bank of Scotland*, 1997 S.L.T. 1061 at 1065L–1066A.

[300] *Young v Clydesdale Bank* (1889) 17 R. 231, per Lord Shand at 244; *Royal Bank of Scotland v Greenshields* (1914) 1 S.L.T. 74, per Lord McKenzie at 75; but cf. *Wallace's Factor v McKissock* (1898) 25 R. 642, per Lord McLaren at 653.

[301] In which case the fraud, etc. is attributable to the creditor: see *Mair v Rio Grande Rubber Estates Ltd*, 1913 S.L.T. 166 HL.

[302] *Young v Clydesdale Bank* (1889) 17 R. 231.

[303] *Smith v Bank of Scotland*, 1997 S.L.T. 1061 at 1065I.

[304] *Clydesdale Bank v Paul* (1877) 4 R. 626, per Lord Shand at 628–629.

[305] *Smith v Bank of Scotland*, 1997 S.L.T. 1061 at 1065J–K; the English case is *Owen and Gutch v Homan* (1853) 4 H.L.C. 997, especially the views of Lord Cranworth LC at 1035–1036.

[306] *Trustee Savings Bank v Balloch*, 1983 S.L.T. 240.

[307] *Barclays Bank Plc v O'Brien* [1994] 1 A.C. 180.

[308] *Smith v Bank of Scotland*, 1996 S.L.T. 392.

[309] *Smith v Bank of Scotland*, 1997 S.L.T. 1061 at 1067K.

It is clear then that a major change was to be effected in the law for reasons of policy. However, while it was one thing to import the result in the *O'Brien* case, importing the principle on which it rested would be more problematic; constructive notice being derived from the English law of equity and having no proper counterpart in Scots law. Lord Clyde therefore preferred to rest the decision on the principle of good faith, which he saw as underpinning the examples, considered in the previous paragraph, of situations where the creditor is disabled from enforcing the obligation.[310] It is, of course, the case that many specific rules might be said to be rooted in a broad concept such as good faith, but it is not usually open for parties seeking relief to refer generally to "good faith" or "equity" or "justice". Lord Clyde therefore required to provide some practical content to the doctrine of good faith in this context. Thus where "the circumstances of the case are such as to lead a reasonable man to believe that, owing to the personal relationship between the debtor and proposed cautioner, the latter's consent may not be fully informed or freely given", the creditor must "warn the potential cautioner of the consequences of entering into the proposed cautionary obligation and advise him or her to take independent advice".[311] If the creditor fails in this duty, he is not in good faith.

It was not clear from Lord Clyde's speech whether any failure to act in good faith disabled the creditor from enforcing the obligation, whether or not the debtor had acted wrongfully. However, subsequent cases have made it clear that the cautioner would require to prove not only a breach of good faith by the creditor, but also an actionable wrong by the debtor, before the cautionary obligation may be impugned.[312] It has also been said that the duty does not apply if the cautioner does not undertake the obligation gratuitously.[313] Subsequent cases have also clarified the range of relationships where the duty of good faith imposes an obligation on the creditor to warn and advise the potential cautioner. So these include not only husband and wife, but also parent and child—at least where the parent is the cautioner.[314] Moreover

> "the rule can apply even in circumstances where the person who is in a close personal relationship with the cautioner is not himself the borrower, provided he has an interest to use the personal relationship to prevail upon the cautioner to agree to act as such, and the existence of that relationship is known to the creditor. Thus in *Smith* the actual principal debtor appears to have been a firm of which the pursuer's husband was a partner, rather than the pursuer's husband as an individual."[315]

Further, while the principle will not normally arise where a shareholder or director is asked to guarantee a company's debts, it can arise if, for example, a son persuades his mother to guarantee the debts of a company in which she holds shares and which he runs.[316] Given the intention to assimilate Scots law to that of England in this area, English decisions are presumably also instructive in this context. Thus *O'Brien* itself tells us that the principle extends to every case "where there is an emotional relationship between cohabitees" (whether heterosexual or homosexual), or wherever the "surety reposes trust and confidence in the principal debtor in relation to his financial affairs", as long as the creditor is aware of such facts.[317] So it has been applied in the case of a non-cohabiting couple, who enjoyed "a stable sexual and emotional relationship of long standing",[318] while in another English case it was applied where an employee was persuaded to guarantee the debts of her employer's business.[319] Nonetheless, if the obligation secured is for the cautioner's benefit as much as that of the debtor, then the duty of

---

[310] *Smith v Bank of Scotland*, 1997 S.L.T. 1061 at 1066B.

[311] *Smith v Bank of Scotland*, 1997 S.L.T. 1061 at 1068F–I.

[312] See *Braithwaite v Bank of Scotland*, 1999 S.L.T. 25 at 33B–C; *Wright v Cotias Investments Inc*, 2000 S.C.L.R. 324 at 332E–F. It has also been said that the debtor's mere failure to explain the nature of the obligation to the cautioner is not a wrong: *Thomson v Royal Bank of Scotland (No.3)*, 2003 S.C.L.R. 964 at 994B; Lord Justice Clerk Gill in *Wilson v Bank of Scotland*, 2004 S.C. 153 at [26].

[313] *Wilson v Bank of Scotland*, 2004 S.C. 153, per Lord Justice Clerk Gill at [24].

[314] *Wright v Cotias Investments Inc*, 2000 S.C.L.R. 324.

[315] *Wright v Cotias Investments Inc*, 2000 S.C.L.R. 324, per Lord McFadyen at 335C.

[316] *Wright v Cotias Investments Inc*, 2000 S.C.L.R. 324.

[317] *Barclays Bank Plc v O'Brien* [1994] 1 A.C. 180, per Lord Browne-Wilkinson at 198c–f.

[318] *Massey v Midland Bank Plc* [1995] 1 All E.R. 929, per Steyn LJ at 933c–d.

[319] *Credit Lyonnais Bank Nederland N V v Burch* [1997] 1 All E.R. 144.

good faith does not arise. So, if a mother has a substantial interest in the company which is run by her son,[320] there is no need to advise or warn her. Nor is there any duty of good faith owed where a husband and wife jointly guarantee a loan made to both of them.[321]

The duty of good faith—independent legal advice

5.5.6.1 In practice, institutional lenders have proved reluctant to assume the responsibility of explaining in detail to potential cautioners the implications of entering into the transaction, and instead have refused to proceed until they have confirmation that any potential cautioner is legally advised.[322] It has indeed been held that the creditor's duty of good faith is discharged if it appears that the potential cautioner has independent legal advice. Thus in *Forsyth v Royal Bank of Scotland*[323] Lord Macfadyen opined that if the cautioner had her own legal advisor, the bank need take no steps at all to advise her, observing:

> "The creditor is entitled to assume that a granter of a standard security who has the benefit of a solicitor acting for her will thereby have the benefit of separate advice, and that advice will cover at least all the ground which he would, in the absence of a solicitor have had to cover in order to preserve his good faith. Since he is entitled to make that assumption, the creditor is not in breach of the requirements of good faith if he does nothing himself to advise or warn the granter of the security."

Moreover, if the solicitor also acts for the bank, it is for the solicitor to decide whether a conflict of interest precludes him advising the cautioner. If so, it is for the solicitor and not the bank to advise her to seek independent advice, and the bank is entitled to assume that this has been done.[324] The focus of the law is on the creditor's behaviour. So if he believes on reasonable grounds that a cautioner has received independent advice, he does not fail to act in good faith by taking no further steps.[325] On the other hand, if the situation was not clear, the bank could not be in good faith unless it inquired further.[326] It has also been held[327] that, where a solicitor, although advising the bank, also believed himself to be acting for the cautioners, that belief could be imputed to the bank as his principal, thus ensuring that the bank acted in good faith. It was further held that the bank was not in breach of duty to a cautioner, simply because her co-cautioner (in this case her husband) failed to pass on the advice he received from the solicitor.

Since *O'Brien* the House of Lords in England[328] has insisted that it is for the bank to satisfy itself that a potential guarantor has been properly advised. This means that the bank should ask the potential guarantor for the name of the solicitor advising her or him, and indicate that it will require written confirmation that the solicitor has explained the nature of the obligation and its practical implications before proceeding with the obligation. The bank should not proceed with the obligation without this confirmation. Their Lordships added that, where the bank did not want to assume the responsibility of explaining the debtor's financial affairs to the potential guarantor, it would have to supply the solicitor acting for her with the financial information necessary for that purpose, and will require the debtor's consent to reveal that information. If that consent were not forthcoming, again the bank should not proceed with the obligation. This seems to go a lot further than the duty of good faith as interpreted in

---

[320] As was the case in *Wright v Cotias Investments Inc*, 2000 S.C.L.R. 324.

[321] *Ahmed v Clydesdale Bank Plc*, 2001 S.L.T. 423.

[322] This has been judicially recognised, see *Royal Bank of Scotland v Etridge (No.2)* [2001] 4 All E.R. 449, per Lord Clyde at 478g.

[323] *Forsyth v Royal Bank of Scotland*, 2000 S.C.L.R. 61 at 75C.

[324] *Forsyth v Royal Bank of Scotland*, 2000 S.C.L.R. 61 at 75D.

[325] *Broadway v Clydesdale Bank Plc (No.1)*, 2000 G.W.D. 19–763.

[326] *Broadway v Clydesdale Bank Plc (No.1)*, 2000 G.W.D. 19–763. And see *Thomson v Royal Bank of Scotland (No.3)*, 2003 S.C.L.R. 964 at 996E–F.

[327] *Broadway v Clydesdale Bank Plc (No.2)*, 2001 G.W.D. 14–552. But a solicitor's knowledge will not be attributed to the bank where he deliberately misrepresents the position to the bank: see *Thomson v Royal Bank of Scotland (No.3)*, 2003 S.C.L.R. 964.

[328] *Royal Bank of Scotland v Etridge (No.2)* [2001] 4 All E.R. 449.

the Scots courts, and indeed the Inner House has confirmed that the decision is not to be regarded as having altered the law of Scotland.[329]

A cautioner therefore has no remedy, unless the debtor has committed anactionable wrong against the cautioner, and a break of the duty of good faith has arisen because the creditor has neither explained the implications of entering into the transaction in detail to the cautioner, not urged the cautioner to seek independent legal advice. It is, therefore, not surprising that, since *Smith*, no cautioner has successfully argued that there has been a breach of the duty of good faith until this year.[330]

EXTENT OF THE CAUTIONER'S LIABILITY

Cautionary obligations must be construed *contra proferentem*, the *proferens* in this case being the **5.5.7** creditor.[331] Thus while the court will try to ascertain the true intention of the parties, and this may involve taking into account general commercial practice,[332] the extent of the cautioner's knowledge,[333] "the factual matrix and in particular the transactional context of the guarantee",[334] and reading the obligation as a whole,[335] any ambiguities will be resolved in favour of the cautioner.[336] So in *Harmer & Co v Gibb*[337] the cautioner guaranteed payment for all goods "as you may from time to time sell and deliver to M . . . up to a value of £200." This was held to impose upon the cautioner a liability to ensure payment for up to £200's worth of goods, and not a liability for the total amount owed by the debtor, subject to a limit of £200. The debtor owed £300 and the creditor held a security over the debt to the value of £120. Had the latter construction prevailed, the cautioner would have been liable for the whole amount of the debt, minus the security (£300 – £120 = £180). But under the former construction he was liable for only £200, minus the proportion of the security which the amount guaranteed bore to the whole debt. In other words, since he had guaranteed two-thirds of the debt, he was entitled to two-thirds of the security (£120 × 2/3 = £80). So his ultimate liability was £200 – £80 = £120.

Similarly, where a cautioner guarantees all advances to be made to a particular debtor, up to a given limit, then unless the contrary is clearly expressed, the obligation will be interpreted as not extending to any advance made subsequent to the limit being reached, rather than guaranteeing the entire debt subject to a stated maximum limit of liability.[338] Two consequences follow from the former interpretation. Firstly, any payment made by the debtor to the creditor once the limit is reached goes towards reducing the cautioner's ultimate liability (see para.5.6.1.4 below).[339] Secondly, once the cautioner has paid the creditor the amount guaranteed, he can seek to recover from a bankrupt debtor's estate. The reasoning behind this is that, as he has paid in full that part of the debt he has undertaken to guarantee, his obligation to the creditor is fully discharged (see para.5.6.1.4 below). Were the alternative interpretation to be applied, the cautioner would not be regarded as having discharged his obligation until the

---

[329] *Clydesdale Bank Plc v Black*, 2002 S.C.L.R. 857, see especially Lord Marnoch at 872D–873A; Lord Sutherland observes at 876C: "I do not consider that any inference can be drawn from what Lord Clyde said in either *Smith* or *Etridge* that he was of the opinion that in Scotland there was or should be a duty to investigate how far the written warnings and advice had been seen, understood and followed up by a guarantor and thereby 'satisfy' themselves that all was well." See also Lord Justice Clerk Gill in *Wilson v Bank of Scotland*, 2004 S.C. 153 at [54].

[330] All the key criteria being met in *Cooper v Bank of Scotland Plc* [2014] CSOH 16; Lord Tyre granted partial reduction of the standard security granted by Mrs Cooper to the bank.

[331] *Aitken's Trustees v Bank of Scotland*, 1945 S.L.T. 84, per Lord Justice Clerk Cooper at 89.

[332] *Calder & Co v Cruikshank's Trustee* (1889) 17 R. 74.

[333] *Bank of Scotland v Wright* [1991] B.C.L.C. 244.

[334] *Waydale Ltd v DHL Holdings (UK) Ltd (No.2)*, 2001 S.L.T. 207, per Lord Hamilton at 232A.

[335] *Huewind Ltd v Clydesdale Bank Plc*, 1996 S.L.T. 369 at 372.

[336] *Baird v Corbett* (1835) 14 S. 41 at 47; *Tennant & Co v Bunten* (1859) 21 D. 631, per Lord Cowan at 634.

[337] *Harmer & Co v Gibb* (1911) 2 S.L.T. 211.

[338] *Bank of Scotland v MacLeod*, 1986 S.L.T. 504. It is possible that the obligation will take the form of a guarantee of any advances made to the debtor, once a certain figure has been exceeded. Again this could be subject to a limit. So if the cautioner guarantees advances over £800,000, subject to a maximum liability of £1 million, that guarantee is not effective until £800,000 is advanced, and the limit of his liability is reached once £1,800,000 has been advanced: *Huewind Ltd v Clydesdale Bank Plc*, 1996 S.L.T. 369.

[339] *Cuthill v Strachan* (1894) 1 S.L.T. 527.

principal debt is paid in full. Accordingly, the cautioner would not be entitled to seek to recover from the debtor unless the creditor had received full payment.[340]

Finally, the cautioner's liability can never exceed that of the principal debtor. This was shown in *Jackson v McIver*,[341] where M had lent the debtor £300, taking in return a blank promissory note signed by the debtor and J. When the debtor defaulted, J having become bankrupt, M sought to fill in the note for £2,000, hoping that if that sum were claimed from J's estate, the dividend would yield £300. It was held that, as J was effectively guaranteeing the repayment of £300, he was a cautioner, so that the maximum M could claim from his estate was £300. Lord Gifford stated[342]:

> "Cautionry is an accessory obligation, and the accessory can never be bound for more than the principal. Cautioners in a cash credit bond . . . can never be liable for more than the balance due by the principal, although the bond *ex facie* may be for a much larger amount."

It should be noted that the above principle is qualified to the extent that the cautioner will additionally be liable for any expenses reasonably incurred in seeking to enforce the principal debt against the debtor.[343]

THE RIGHTS OF CAUTIONERS

5.5.8 We have already observed that certain rights (benefits of division and discussion, see para.5.5.4 above) derive from proper cautionry. What other rights do cautioners have?

Relief

5.5.8.1 A cautioner is entitled to call on the principal debtor to relieve him of liability, even if the debt is not yet due.[344] Moreover, when the debt is due, he may demand that the debtor pays it.[345] Alternatively, he may himself pay the principal debt as soon as it falls due.[346] When the cautioner has paid the principal debt, then he is entitled to recover the amount paid, including any expenses he has incurred, from the principal debtor:

> "Cautioners on making payment of the debt, or any portion of the debt, have a right to relief and indemnification against the principal debtor to the full extent to which they have been answerable for him. This right of relief . . . arises *de iure* without any formal assignation by the creditor."[347]

The right of relief prescribes after five years from the date of payment of the debt.[348] Additionally, where the debtor is insolvent, and the cautioner has properly paid the debt or is liable to do so, he may retain any property of the debtor as may be in his hands, and may plead compensation in respect of any money debt he owes the debtor.[349]

Where there is more than one cautioner, unless each is bound only for a specific part of the debt,[350] any who has paid more than his share may seek relief to that extent from the other cautioner(s).[351] In

---

[340] *Harvie's Trustees v Bank of Scotland* (1885) 12 R. 1141.

[341] *Jackson v McIver* (1875) 2 R. 882.

[342] *Jackson v McIver* (1875) 2 R. 882 at 885.

[343] *Struthers v Dykes* (1847) 9 D. 1437.

[344] *Doig v Lawrie* (1903) 10 S.L.T. 523; assuming this is not inconsistent with the terms of the cautionary obligation, see Lord Kinnear in *Roughead v White*, 1913 1 S.L.T. 23 at 27.

[345] *Cunningham v Montgomerie* (1879) 6 R. 1333.

[346] *Gray v Thompson* (1847) 10 D. 145. A cautioner seeking relief, having paid the debt before it is due, might be met by the plea that there was no reasonable obligation or necessity to pay it: *Owen v Bryson* (1833) 12 S. 130.

[347] *Smithy's Place Ltd v Blackadder*, 1991 S.LT 790, per Lord Cameron at 795C–E.

[348] *Smithy's Place Ltd v Blackadder*, 1991 S.LT 790.

[349] *McPherson v Wright* (1885) 12 R. 942.

[350] In which case no relief arises: see *Morgan v Smart* (1872) 10 M. 610.

[351] *Marshall & Co v Pennycook* (1908) 15 S.L.T. 581. It does not matter that the cautioners were bound in different deeds, or were originally unaware of each other's existence; *McPhersons v Haggarts* (1881) 9 R. 306; *Union Bank of Scotland v Taylor*, 1925 S.L.T. 583, especially Lord President Clyde at 586. However, no right of relief is owed to a cautioner who has paid the debt

deciding the amount of such relief insolvent cautioners are not counted. Thus in *Buchanan v Main*,[352] where two out of five co-cautioners were insolvent, when two other cautioners had paid the principal debt, they were entitled to require the fifth cautioner to contribute one-third of the debt. This of course presupposes that the cautioners are each bound equally. Yet what might happen if, for example, two cautioners guaranteed repayment of an overdraft, one subject to a limit of £5,000, the other subject to a limit of £10,000, and the overdraft stands at £3,000 when one of the obligations is enforced? The Scottish cases have not really addressed this point, but English authority witnesses the application of either the maximum liability[353] or independent liability[354] approaches. The former insists that the ratio of liability is determined by the maximum liability each cautioner might have under his obligation. As this is £10,000 and £5,000 respectively, it is clear that these cautioners must always bear any liability in the ratio of 2:1, and this ratio must apply whatever the overall liability may be. The independent liability approach determines the ratio by asking what liability would each cautioner bear, if he alone guaranteed the obligation. In the above scenario, each cautioner would be liable for £3,000, so that they should therefore bear that liability equally. However, if the sum due were £7,500, then as the first cautioner would be liable for the whole of that sum, and the liability of the second would be restricted to £5,000, the proportion in which they should share that liability among themselves would be 75/50, or 3:2. Therefore if the first cautioner paid £7,500, he would be entitled to recover two-fifths of that—£3,000—from the other.

Assignation

Where the cautioner has paid the principal debt in full, he can demand from the creditor an assignation **5.5.8.2** of the debt, as well as any security for it, or diligence done on it.[355] Such security must have been granted by the debtor. The right does not extend to securities granted to the creditor by third parties.[356] If the creditor holds the security over two debts, then he is entitled to retain it despite the cautioner paying the principal debt if the other debt is unpaid,[357] unless the second debt is incurred subsequent to the cautioner paying the principal debt.[358]

Sharing in securities

All cautioners are entitled to share any security granted by the debtor to a co-cautioner, even if that **5.5.8.3** security is granted after the cautionary obligations have been undertaken,[359] unless they have agreed that they should not have the benefit of that security.[360] The principle does not apply to securities granted by a third party.[361] There is also authority for the view that the principle may not apply when co-cautioners have limited the amount for which they are liable, but this seems to depend on them being regarded as having guaranteed separate, specific sums[362]—a relatively unusual construction.

Ranking in bankruptcy

If the principal debtor is bankrupt, and the creditor is paid in full by the cautioner, then the cautioner is **5.5.8.4** entitled to rank on the principal debtor's estate for the amount paid. However, if the creditor has ranked upon the principal debtor's estate, and then obtained payment of the remainder of the debt from the

---

when there was no obligation or necessity to do so: *Henderson v Paul* (1867) 5 M. 628.

[352] *Buchanan v Main* (1900) 3 F. 215.
[353] *Ellesmere Brewery Co v Cooper* [1896] 1 Q.B. 75.
[354] *American Surety of New York v Wrightson* (1910) T.L.R. 603.
[355] *Ewart v Latta* (1863) 1 M. 905.
[356] *Gordon's Trustees v Young* (1910) 1 S.L.T. 134.
[357] *Sligo v Menzies* (1840) 2 D. 1478.
[358] *Fleming v Burgess* (1867) 5 M. 856.
[359] *Steel v Dixon* (1881) 17 Ch.D. 825.
[360] *Hamilton & Co v Freeth* (1889) 16 R. 1022.
[361] *Scott v Young*, 1909 1 S.L.T. 47.
[362] *Lawrie v Stewart* (1823) 2 S. 327. See also *Morgan v Smart* (1872) 10 M. 610.

cautioner, the cautioner has no right to a ranking because of the rule that the same debt cannot be ranked twice on the bankrupt estate.[363] Where some limit is placed on the amount guaranteed, much will depend on the construction imposed on the obligation. Where the cautioner is seen as having guaranteed the whole of the obligation, albeit subject to a maximum liability, then the cautioner is not entitled to rank, and remains liable (up to his limit) to the creditor for any shortfall after the latter has ranked.[364] On the other hand, if the cautioner is regarded as having guaranteed a specific part of the principal debt, then payment up to the limit will entitle the cautioner to rank for that amount. Alternatively, if the creditor has already ranked on the debtor's estate and obtained a dividend, the cautioner is entitled to deduct the amount of that dividend from the amount otherwise owed to the creditor. So in *Veitch v National Bank of Scotland*[365] V had imposed a limit of £1,500 on his guarantee. Ultimately, the amount of the principal debt was around £6,000, while the dividend saw creditors being paid £2 for every £3 they were owed, so that the creditor received around £4,000, thus leaving £2,000 still owing. It was held that the debt should be regarded as, in effect, two debts—£1,500 which was covered by the guarantee, and £4,500 which was not. The £4,000 paid by way of dividend could be regarded as paying two-thirds of both debts, i.e. £1,000 of the £1,500 guaranteed, and £3,000 of the £4,500 not guaranteed. Therefore since £1,000 of the £1,500 guaranteed had already been repaid by way of dividend, the cautioner's liability was limited to £500, even though the creditor was still owed £2,000.

It has also been held[366] that, if the cautioner pays the amount for which he is liable before the debtor becomes insolvent, the creditor is limited to ranking for the amount remaining unpaid, leaving the cautioner to rank for the amount he has paid. It would be open to the creditor to prevent this result by drawing up the obligation so as to make it clear that, whenever the cautioner pays, only the creditor is entitled to rank on the debtor's estate, the cautioner being precluded from ranking.

5.6   TERMINATION OF THE CAUTIONARY OBLIGATION

TERMINATION BY EXTINCTION OF THE PRINCIPAL DEBT

5.6.1 The accessory nature of the cautionary obligation is reflected by the fact that the extinction of the principal debt necessarily entails the extinction of the cautionary obligation.[367] There are several ways in which this may occur.

Discharge of the principal debtor

5.6.1.1 If the creditor releases the principal debtor from his obligation without the cautioner's consent, the latter is in turn released from his obligation.[368] Thus in *Aitken's Trustees v Bank of Scotland*[369] a father guaranteed his son's overdraft to the extent of £500. When the overdraft reached £2,000 the bank sued the son for repayment. He repaid £1,500, and confident that the remaining £500 was covered by the guarantee, the bank allowed a decree of *absolvitor* to be pronounced against him. This was held to be tantamount to discharging the debtor, and the cautioner was released from liability.

---

[363] *McKinnon v Monkhouse* (1881) 9 R. 393.

[364] *Harvie's Trustee v Bank of Scotland* (1885) 12 R. 1141.

[365] *Veitch v National Bank of Scotland* (1907) 14 S.L.T. 800.

[366] In *McKinnon's Trustee v Bank of Scotland* (1915) 1 S.L.T. 182.

[367] Similarly, if the obligation being secured no longer exists, neither can a standard security: *Albatown Ltd v Credential Group Ltd*, 2001 G.W.D. 27–1102.

[368] It follows that if the cautioner's consent to discharge is obtained, then he is not released, and that consent may be expressed through a term in the contract, or given at the time of discharge, or even thereafter: *Fleming v Wilson* (1823) 2 S. 296; *Wright's Trustees v Hamilton's Trustees* (1834) 12 S. 692.

[369] *Aitken's Trustees v Bank of Scotland*, 1945 S.L.T. 84.

There are two exceptions to the above rule. One is statutory.[370] The other arises where the creditor simply agrees not to sue the principal debtor, while expressly reserving his remedies against the cautioner—a *pactum de non petendo*.[371] In this situation, however, the cautioner's right of relief against the principal debtor is preserved. The creditor's arrangement with the debtor may be expressed in terms of an absolute discharge, and yet be construed as a *pactum de non petendo*, as long as his remedies against the cautioner are reserved.[372]

Novation, etc.

The cautioner is discharged by novation, i.e. where the existing principal debt is extinguished and a **5.6.1.2** new one substituted.[373] The same result flows from the substitution of a new principal debtor. However, in *De Montfort Insurance Co Plc v Lafferty*,[374] De Montfort acted as cautioner for an obligation owed to L by a local authority. Later, under what was termed a deed of novation, L released the local authority from that obligation, which was transferred to a company. However, L could still demand payment from the local authority of any sum not paid by the company. Lord Penrose[375] took the view that the contention that the deed of novation created a new agreement did not reflect the reality of the transaction. Nothing about the transaction was altered, and in particular the principal debtor was not released from any obligation unless that obligation were performed by another. Accordingly, the granting of the deed of novation did not release De Montfort. Moreover, while an offer to guarantee any transaction the debtor might enter into with A cannot generally be taken up by B,[376] the assignation of an existing principal debt to a new creditor will not usually release the cautioner.[377]

Compensation

A plea of compensation can be taken by the cautioner if, when the creditor seeks to have the cautioner **5.6.1.3** pay the principal debt, he owes money to either the cautioner or the debtor.[378] Alternatively, if the creditor pleads the debt guaranteed in compensation for a debt or debts due by him to the principal debtor, that will extinguish the cautionary obligation.[379]

The rule in Clayton's case

That rule[380] is that in the case of a current account between debtor and creditor, in the absence of appro- **5.6.1.4** priation, the earliest credit item is set against the earliest debit item. So in *Deeley v Lloyds Bank Ltd*[381] D guaranteed X's overdraft. When the overdraft reached £1,000 D intimated that he would not guarantee any further advances. The overdraft continued to run for some time, with X paying in significant sums of money, but also withdrawing ever larger sums. When the bank eventually sought to enforce the guarantee, the overdraft stood at several thousand pounds. However, D was held not to be liable, since as soon as X had paid sums amounting to £1,000 into the account, the guarantee was extin-

---

[370] Thus under s.60(1) of the Bankruptcy (Scotland) Act 1985, a cautioner will not be freed by the debtor's discharge under the Act, nor by the creditor voting for, or assenting to, or not opposing such discharge, or any composition (see para.7.3.5 below).

[371] See, e.g. *Muir v Crawford* (1875) 2 R. (HL) 148, where it was also noted that the cautioner does not need to be informed of a pactum de non petendo.

[372] *Aitken's Trustees v Bank of Scotland*, 1945 S.L.T. 84, per Lord Justice Clerk Cooper at 90.

[373] *Commercial Bank of Tasmania v Jones* [1893] A.C. 313. But the acceptance of additional obligations by the debtor is not novation, and thus will not release the cautioner, as long as the original obligation remains enforceable; *Hay and Kyd v Powrie* (1886) 13 R. 777.

[374] *De Montfort Insurance Co Plc v Lafferty*, 1998 S.L.T. 535.

[375] *De Montfort Insurance Co Plc v Lafferty*, 1998 S.L.T. 535 at 538F.

[376] See, e.g. *Bowie v Watson* (1840) 2 D. 1061.

[377] *Waydale Ltd v DHL Holdings (UK) Ltd (No.2)*, 2001 S.L.T. 207.

[378] *Bechervaise v Lewis* (1872) L.R. 7 C.P. 372.

[379] See Lord Ormidale in *Hannay & Son's Trustee v Armstrong Bros & Co* (1875) 2 R. 399 at 414.

[380] As expressed in *Devaynes v Noble, Claytons Case* (1816) 1 Mer. 572.

[381] *Deeley v Lloyds Bank Ltd* [1912] A.C. 756. For Scottish illustrations of the principle see *Royal Bank of Scotland v Christie* (1839) 1 D. 745; *Cuthill v Strachan* (1894) 21 R. 549.

guished. Yet as noted above, the principle only applies in relation to current accounts, and only where payments are not appropriated. While current accounts are not entirely confined to the banking industry,[382] normal trading accounts between businesses, or between tradesmen and their customers, are not regarded as current accounts, even if advances are sometimes made thereunder.[383] It is always open to the debtor to indicate how he wishes a payment to be applied,[384] and in the absence of any such indication, the creditor is entitled to make that decision.[385] So it is only where neither the debtor nor creditor has made any appropriation that there is room for the rule to operate.[386] The creditor may always preclude the operation of the rule by a term in the contract, while in practice this situation is avoided by the creditor closing the existing account once the obligation is withdrawn, and opening a new account.

Prescription

5.6.1.5 If the principal debt prescribes, then the cautionary obligation should also fall.

TERMINATION BY THE ACTIONS OF THE CREDITOR

5.6.2 The cautionary obligation can similarly be extinguished by certain behaviour on the part of the creditor. The recognised categories thereof are considered below, and of course on the application of basic contractual principles a cautioner may always be released by the creditor's failure to comply with a specific undertaking of the cautionary obligation.[387] Whether the creditor owes a more general duty to the cautioner is doubtful. Certainly, Lord Ross, observes in *Lord Advocate v Maritime Fruit Carriers Ltd*[388]:

> "I am not prepared to hold that a creditor in Scotland owes no duty to act reasonably in a question with a guarantor".

Equally, Lord Low[389] suggests that if, during the currency of a continuing obligation, circumstances come to the attention of the creditor which materially affect the risk which the cautioner has undertaken, and which would have dissuaded the cautioner from undertaking that risk, the creditor is bound to communicate these to the cautioner. Moreover, Lord Salvesen[390] suggests that the principle which demands that the creditor under a guarantee of fidelity disclose to the cautioner material information regarding the employee whose fidelity is guaranteed, probably also applies to the case of a bank

> "making further advances to the credit of a secured account after knowledge that the person to whom the advances were made had become insolvent or had been guilty of dishonesty. Such a proceeding might well be characterised as unfair dealing towards the cautioner, sufficient to free him from responsibility for advances made after the debtor's misconduct had been disclosed to the bank."

Apart from the fact that the last case is extrapolating from a duty of disclosure under what is essentially a contract of insurance, the problem with the views expressed in all of these cases is that they are essentially obiter. Moreover, the attempt to create some sort of general duty of the creditor to act fairly or

---

[382] See the unusual case of *McKinlay v Wilson* (1885) 13 R. 210.
[383] *Hay & Co v Torbet* (1908) 15 S.L.T. 627; *Dougall v Lornie* (1899) 7 S.L.T. 145.
[384] As in *Buchanan v Main* (1900) 8 S.L.T. 297.
[385] *Jackson v Nicoll* (1870) 8 M. 408. So it is therefore open for a creditor to appropriate a payment to an unsecured debt rather than a secured debt: *Anderson v North of Scotland and Town and County Bank* (1909) 2 S.L.T. 262.
[386] *Westminster Bank Ltd v Cond* (1940) 46 Com. Cas. 60.
[387] See *Clydebank and District Water Trustees v Fidelity and Deposit Co of Maryland* (1915) 2 S.L.T. 357 HL.
[388] *Lord Advocate v Maritime Fruit Carriers Ltd*, 1983 S.L.T. 357 at 360.
[389] *Britania Steamship Insurance Association Ltd v Duff*, 1909 2 S.L.T. 193 at 195.
[390] *Bank of Scotland v Morrison*, 1911 1 S.L.T. 153 at 156; speaking of *Snaddon v London, Edinburgh and Glasgow Assurance Co Ltd* (1902) 10 S.L.T. 410.

reasonably runs into the difficulty that this seems to be at odds with the way in which the relationship between the creditor and cautioner has developed in the cases as a whole. The law has tended to recognise very specific duties owed by the creditor to the cautioner, and even the recently established duty of good faith operates within defined limits, and has a specific content (see para.5.5.6).

What are the categories of case where the creditor's behaviour is recognised as releasing the cautioner?

Giving time

This occurs where the creditor legally disables himself from demanding immediate payment when the **5.6.2.1** principal debt falls due. Simply failing to press for immediate payment is not "giving time" in this technical sense.[391] An example of giving time is provided by the case of *C & A Johnstone v Duthie*,[392] where the fact that the creditor had accepted payment from the debtor in the form of two bills of exchange payable three months from their date was held to have released the cautioner. Lord Kinnear noted[393]:

> "The reason why the giving of time discharges the cautioner is because he is thereby deprived of the chance of considering whether he will have recourse to his remedy against the principal debtor or not, and because it is then out of his power to operate the same remedy against him as he would have had under the original contract."

The case further confirmed that it was not necessary to show actual harm to the cautioner for this result to follow, nor indeed would proof of actual benefit to the cautioner through giving time constitute a defence. However, as Lord President Inglis points out in *Calder & Co v Cruikshank's Trustee*[394]:

> "There is a broad distinction taken in all cases between the guarantee of a particular debt of a certain amount, to be paid at a certain time, and a general guarantee for the price of goods sold or for money advanced or the like. In the former case if a creditor innovates or alters the relation of debtor and creditor in any essential point, he liberates the cautioner. In the latter case that result by no means follows."

In particular, to quote Lord Justice Clerk Moncrieff in *Stewart, Moir and Muir v Brown*[395]:

> "[The cautioner] necessarily, by the generality of the obligation, leaves the principal debtor and creditor free to arrange the details of their transactions as they think fit, provided these are not at variance with the ordinary custom of merchants."

It may be added that a cautioner will not be released if he has consented to time being given,[396] or if the creditor has expressly reserved his rights against him.[397]

Alteration of principal debt

Any alteration of the contract between the creditor and principal debtor without the cautioner's consent **5.6.2.2** will release the latter. So in *NG Napier Ltd v Crosbie*[398] an agreed increase of the amount of the debtor's weekly repayment liberated the cautioner from the obligation. Lord Guthrie observed[399]:

---

[391] *Hamilton's Executor v Bank of Scotland*, 1913 1 S.L.T. 296.

[392] *C & A Johnstone v Duthie* (1892) 19 R. 624.

[393] *C & A Johnstone v Duthie* (1892) 19 R. 624 at 629.

[394] *Calder & Co v Cruikshank's Trustee* (1889) 17 R. 74 at 80.

[395] *Stewart, Moir and Muir v Brown* (1871) 9 M. 763 at 766.

[396] *Hamilton's Executor v Bank of Scotland*, 1913 1 S.L.T. 296.

[397] As the cautioner will be entitled to enforce the debt against the debtor; see *Muir v Crawford* (1875) 2 R. (HL) 148; *Huewind v Clydesdale Bank Plc*, 1996 S.L.T. 369.

[398] *NG Napier Ltd v Crosbie*, 1964 S.L.T. 185.

[399] *NG Napier Ltd v Crosbie*, 1964 S.L.T. 185 at 138.

"The rule of law is well settled that if a creditor agrees with the principal debtor to a material alteration of the contract without the consent of the cautioner, the cautioner is discharged . . . The rule is founded on equitable considerations. If a cautioner has accepted liability for another's obligations under a contract, it would be unjust that he should be held bound if the effect of an alteration of the creditor's agreement with the principal debtor would be to increase the amount of his liability or to modify to his prejudice the conditions of his liability."

As this principle operates on the basis that the cautioner should not be bound to guarantee an obligation other than that to which he agreed, if the alteration of the contract between the creditor and principal debtor occurs before the cautionary obligation is entered into, it can obviously have no effect on that obligation.[400] The excerpt from the judgment of Lord President Inglis in *Calder & Co v Cruikshank's Trustee*,[401] quoted in the section on giving time (above), might tend to suggest that the principle does not apply in cases of general guarantees. However, the better view is that it does apply so as to ensure that the cautioner does not end up guaranteeing something quite different from that which he has undertaken but, given the nature of the guarantee, it is impossible to predict the precise content of what is covered by the guarantee.

Obviously, if the cautioner has agreed to guarantee the debt of the principal debtor on the basis that it is fixed at or will not exceed a certain sum, he will be released if that sum is exceeded. It has also been argued that, where the cautioner has fixed a limit on the amount guaranteed, he should be released if the creditor advances sums beyond that limit. The basis of this argument is that, although the cautioner is protected by the limit, he is prejudiced by the creditor continuing to lend money beyond that guaranteed, as the bigger the debt, the more likely it is that the debtor will default. This argument has been rejected, however.[402]

Discharging a co-cautioner

5.6.2.3   It goes without saying that one mode of termination is by the creditor formally discharging the cautioner, but the Mercantile Law Amendment (Scotland) Act 1856 s.9 states:

"Where two or more parties become bound as cautioners . . . any discharge granted by the creditor . . . to any one of such cautioners, without the consent of the other cautioners, shall be deemed and taken to be a discharge granted to all the cautioners; but nothing herein contained shall be deemed to extend to the case of a cautioner consenting to the discharge of a co-cautioner who may have become bankrupt."

However, the above only applies where the co-cautioners are jointly liable, not where they have each guaranteed repayment of a separate sum. So in *Morgan v Smart*,[403] a debt of £105 was guaranteed by B and S, B to the extent of £70 and S to the extent of £35. It was held that the discharge of B did not affect the liability of S. It is probably the case that the principle does not apply where the creditor in discharging a co-cautioner expressly reserves his rights against the cautioner.[404] The last clause of s.9 appears to make little sense. What is meant by saying that the provision does not apply if a cautioner agrees to the discharge of a bankrupt co-cautioner? The answer is that the drafters probably intended to use the word "creditor" instead of "cautioner", i.e. to provide that a cautioner is not released where the creditor discharges a co-cautioner who is bankrupt.

Giving up securities

5.6.2.4   Given that a cautioner who pays the debt is entitled to the assignation of any security held by the creditor over the debt, a creditor who voluntarily gives up any such security releases the cautioner to

---

[400] *Hewit v Williamson*, 1999 S.L.T. 313.
[401] *Calder & Co v Cruikshank's Trustee* (1889) 17 R. 74 at 80.
[402] *Bank of Scotland v MacLeod*, 1986 S.L.T. 504; *Huewind Ltd v Clydesdale Bank Plc*, 1995 S.L.T. 392.
[403] *Morgan v Smart* (1872) 10 M. 610.
[404] This is certainly so in England—*Thompson v Lack* (1846) 3 C.B. 540—and has obiter support in Scotland: *Morton's Trustees v Robertson's Judicial Factor* (1892) 20 R. 72, per Lord McLaren at 78.

the extent of the value of that security.[405] It had been thought that the same applied where the creditor fails to make a security effectual,[406] but in *Bank of Ireland v Morton*[407] the First Division suggests that in the supposed authority to that effect the creditor was under a contractual duty to make the security effectual. Lord President Cullen, delivering the opinion of the court, noted[408]:

> "The decisions . . . suggest that whether it is incumbent on a creditor to complete a particular security depends on the express and implied terms of the contract between the creditor and cautioner. However, even if that duty arises as a matter of law, it must . . . be subject to the terms of the contract."

Thus the duty was excluded by the terms of the contract in question. In the ordinary case, the fact that the cautioner obtains only partial release reflects the extent to which the cautioner is prejudiced by the creditor's conduct. If, however, the creditor has agreed with the cautioner to retain or have recourse to a particular security, its release amounts to a breach of contract, entirely liberating the cautioner.[409] It remains an open question in Scotland whether the creditor in realising a security owes a duty of care to the cautioner, so as to minimise the latter's liability.[410]

TERMINATION BY THE CAUTIONER

Clearly, where a cautioner guarantees a specific transaction, he cannot withdraw from it on his own **5.6.3** initiative. Nor may he withdraw from a continuing guarantee, to which he has committed himself for a specified period, before the end of that period.[411] Yet, if a guarantee is of a continuing nature, with no time limit expressed, the cautioner is entitled at any time to inform the creditor that he will not guarantee future advances.[412] The cautioner may then give reasonable notice to the principal debtor to oblige the latter to obtain the cautioner's discharge by the creditor (usually by paying all sums due under the guarantee).[413]

TERMINATION BY OPERATION OF LAW   **5.6.4**

Under the contract

If the obligation is granted for a specific transaction or for a specific period of time, then the completion **5.6.4.1** of that transaction or the expiry of that period without any failure by the debtor will terminate the obligation, and the cautioner will not be taken to have guaranteed any further advances by the creditor.[414]

Death

If the contract does not provide otherwise, the death of either the principal debtor or creditor releases **5.6.4.2** the cautioner in respect of any debt not then due, but he remains liable for existing debts. Thus in

---

[405] *Sligo v Menzies* (1840) 2 D. 1478.

[406] *Fleming v Thomson* (1826) 2 W. & S. 277.

[407] *Bank of Ireland v Morton (No.2)*, 2003 S.C. 257.

[408] *Bank of Ireland v Morton (No.2)*, 2003 S.C. 257 at [18].

[409] *Drummond v Rannie* (1836) 14 S. 437.

[410] See *LA v Maritime Fruit Carriers Co Ltd*, 1983 S.L.T. 357 There is authority for that view in England: see *Standard Chartered Bank Ltd v Walker* [1982] 1 W.L.R 1410 CA. But cf. *Downsview Nominees Ltd v First City Corp* [1993] A.C. 295. The English cases however indicate that the creditor is entitled to accord primacy to his own interests in realising the security (see *China and South Sea Bank Ltd v Tan* [1990] 1 A.C. 536 PC), and assuming he takes care to obtain a reasonable price when doing so, he cannot be challenged on the basis that it would have been more advantageous to the guarantor to have realised at a different time (see *AIB Finance Ltd v Debtors* [1998] 2 All E.R. 929).

[411] *Spence v Brownlee* (1834) 13 S. 199.

[412] *Buchanan v Main* (1900) 8 S.L.T. 297.

[413] See *Doig v Lawrie* (1903) 10 S.L.T. 523.

[414] *Scott v Mitchell* (1866) 4 M. 551.

Woodfield Finance Trust (Glasgow) Ltd v Morgan[415] M guaranteed the payments by P on a 139 week TV rental contract. After 65 weeks P died owing several weeks arrears. The creditor pursued M for the arrears and for the remaining payments under the contract. M was held liable for the arrears, but not for any sum due after P's death.

On the other hand, the death of a cautioner has no effect on his liability. So if he has guaranteed repayment of a specific debt, his estate will be liable to carry out that obligation. Indeed, if a continuing guarantee is for a definite period, then the cautioner's estate remains liable for sums advanced after his death up to the date of expiry of that guarantee. If such a guarantee is for an indefinite period, it will remain in force until his representatives intimate that it is withdrawn.[416] The problems which this rule may create can be exacerbated by the fact that the creditor is under no duty to inform the representatives of the existence of the obligation. So in *British Linen Co v Monteith*[417] a creditor was entitled to enforce a guarantee against representatives 14 years after the death of the cautioner. Lord Deas stated[418]:

> "It is said there is great hardship in holding representatives liable who may never have heard of the obligation. It may be so. But who is to blame for this? The granter of the obligation, who left no trace of it in his repositories? or the bank officers who may or may not have heard of his death? I think that the duty lies on the debtor, who binds his representatives, to keep them informed that he has done so, rather than upon the creditor, who receives and relies on the obligation."

Yet there are suggestions[419] that a creditor who is aware that such representatives are ignorant of the obligation, but nonetheless allows them to dispose of the estate, may be personally barred from enforcing the obligation.

Change in the constitution of a firm

5.6.4.3 The Partnership Act 1890 s.18 states:

> "A continuing guaranty or cautionary obligation given either to a firm or to a third person in respect of the transactions of a firm is, in the absence of any agreement to the contrary, revoked as to future transactions by any change in the constitution of the firm to which, or of the firm in respect of the transactions of which, the guaranty or obligation was given."

This would embrace not only the assumption of a new partner, and the retirement of an existing partner, but also the incorporation of the firm as a company,[420] so that conversion into a limited liability partnership should arguably have the same effect.

Prescription

5.6.4.4 A cautionary obligation may prescribe if no relevant claim nor acknowledgment of the existence of the obligation has been made within five years of it becoming enforceable.[421] The crucial question is when the obligation becomes enforceable. Normally, it will become enforceable on default by the debtor, so that failure to act on the obligation within five years of that default will see the obligation prescribe.[422]

---

[415] *Woodfield Finance Trust (Glasgow) Ltd v Morgan*, 1958 S.L.T. (Sh Ct) 14.

[416] Or possibly only until the representatives advise the creditor of the death. Certainly in England notification of the death has been enough to terminate the obligation without any need to intimate that the guarantee is withdrawn: see *Coulthart v Clementson* (1879) 5 Q.B.D. 42.

[417] *British Linen Co v Monteith* (1858) 20 D. 557.

[418] *British Linen Co v Monteith* (1858) 20 D. 557 at 562.

[419] *Caledonian Banking Co v Kennedy's Trustees* (1870) 8 M. 862, per Lord Justice Clerk Moncrieff at 868.

[420] See respectively, *Spiers v Houston's Executors* (1829) 3 W. & S. 392; *Royal Bank of Scotland v Christie* (1841) 2 Rob. 118; *Hay & Co v Torbet* (1908) 15 S.L.T. 627.

[421] See Prescription and Limitation (Scotland) Act 1973 s.6(1)–(3) and Sch.1 para.1(g), Sch.2 para.2; *Royal Bank of Scotland v Brown*, 1983 S.L.T. 122.

[422] See *City of Glasgow District Council v Excess Insurance Co Ltd*, 1986 S.L.T. 585, especially Lord Justice Clerk Ross at 588G.

But much depends on the terms of the obligation itself. In *Royal Bank of Scotland v Brown*[423] the cautioners undertook to pay "on demand" all sums due by a company to the bank. The bank had made a claim in the company's liquidation in 1969, but had failed to recover anything. It was not until 1974 that payment was demanded from the cautioners, and not until 1979 that an action was raised to enforce the cautionary obligation. It was argued that, as the obligation became enforceable in 1969 it must have prescribed. It was held, however, that the words "on demand" in the obligation meant that the obligation did not become enforceable until a demand for payment was made. No such demand had been made until 1974, so that the prescriptive period had not yet run out by the time the action was raised.

CAUTIONARY OBLIGATIONS AND UNFAIR CONTRACTS LEGISLATION

The final matter to be addressed is the extent to which cautionary obligations are subject to unfair **5.7** contracts legislation. In *United Trust Bank Ltd v Dohil*[424] Judge Picken assumed that a guarantee was potentially subject to the Unfair Contract Terms Act 1977. It might be wondered how that Act might apply to a guarantee, since its primary effect is to subject exclusion and limitation clauses in consumer or standard form contracts to a test of fairness and reasonableness (see para.4.2.4). However, the clause in question bound a guarantor to accept the creditor's assessment of the sum owed, and Judge Picken felt able to regard this as a form of exclusion clause, since the Court of Appeal had so regarded a conclusive evidence clause in *Axa Sun Life Services Plc v Campbell Martin*,[425] although this was not a guarantee case. Yet even if this reasoning is followed, there may still be an obstacle to the Act applying to cautionary obligations. Part II of the Act, which applies to Scotland, takes a rather different approach to Pt I, which applies to England. Whereas Pt I applies to all contracts, subject to specified exceptions, Pt II only applies to the contracts it enumerates. Cautionary obligations are not among the enumerated contracts, unless they are regarded as a contract relating to services in terms of s.15(2)(c).

There is also English authority on the applicability of the Unfair Terms in Consumer Contracts Regulations 1999 (see para.6.12 for the general effect of the Regulations). Regulation 4(1) provides that "[t]hese Regulations apply in relation to unfair terms in contracts concluded between a seller or a supplier and a consumer". At first glance then, the Regulations would not seem to apply to cautionry for the simple reason that the creditor is not selling anything nor supplying any service to the cautioner. Any service provided is provided by the cautioner to the creditor. This was indeed the view taken by Judge Kershaw in *Bank of Scotland v Singh*[426] where he observed[427] that "all the contractual benefit flows one way and all the contractual burden falls the other". This was followed by Judge Price in *Manches LLP v Freer*[428] and Judge Bompas in *Williamson v Governor of the Bank of Scotland.*[429] However, Field J took a different approach in *Barclays Bank Plc v Kufner.*[430] He noted that, in *Bayerische Hypothetken-und Wechselbank AG v Dietzinger*,[431] the European Court of Justice took the view a bank guarantee granted by a consumer to secure the overdraft of a third party could fall within the scope of EC Directive 85/577 (protecting consumers in respect of contracts negotiated away from business premises) as long as the third party was also a consumer. Since the definition of "consumer"

---

[423] *Royal Bank of Scotland v Brown*, 1983 S.L.T. 122.

[424] *United Trust Bank Ltd v Dohil* [2011] 2 All E.R. 765 at [19]. The issue was the fairness of a clause binding a guarantor to accept the creditor's assessment of the sum owed.

[425] *Axa Sun Life Services Plc v Campbell Martin* [2011] 2 Lloyd's Rep 1. See Stanley Burnton LJ at [72]–[74] and Rix LJ at [108].

[426] *Bank of Scotland v Singh* Unreported, June 17, 2005 (QB) at [86].

[427] *Bank of Scotland v Singh* Unreported, June 17, 2005 (QB) at [90].

[428] *Manches LLP v Freer* [2006] EWHC 991 (QB) at [25].

[429] *Williamson v Governor of the Bank of Scotland* [2006] EWHC 1289 (Ch) at [46].

[430] *Barclays Bank Plc v Kufner* [2009] 1 All E.R. (Comm) 1. See [25]–[28].

[431] *Bayerische Hypothetken-und Wechselbank AG v Dietzinger* [1998] 1 W.L.R 1035. See [18]–[23].

under the 1985 Directive is practically identical to that contained in EC Directive 93/13 on Unfair Terms the Consumer Contracts, and indeed the definition in reg.3(1) of the Regulations (which of course seek to give effect to the latter Directive)—a natural person acting for purposes which can be regarded as outside his trade or profession—it seemed to make sense that the concept be accorded the same meaning under both Directives and hence under the Regulations. Accordingly, the Regulations could apply to a bank guarantee "at least where the guarantor and the principal debtor each entered into their respective contracts as natural persons and were not acting in the course of their trade or profession". This approach was then followed by David Richards J in *Royal Bank of Scotland v Chandra*,[432] and by Judge Picken in the *Dohil*[433] case. Since the relevant criteria were not met in any of these cases, the Regulations were held not to apply, so that the views of the judges are, strictly, obiter. However, the reasoning appears persuasive. Finally, it may be added that in *Paragon Mortgages v McEwan-Peters*[434] David Steel J accepted that guarantees were not subject to the unfair relationships provisions of the Consumer Credit Act 1974, as, unlike the loans they supported, they did not involve the grant of credit.

---

[432] *Royal Bank of Scotland v Chandra* [2010] 1 Lloyd's Rep 677 at [102].
[433] *United Trust Bank Ltd v Dohil* [2011] 2 All E.R. 765 at [73].
[434] *Paragon Mortgages v McEwan-Peters* [2011] EWHC (Comm) 241 at [53].

Chapter 6

INSURANCE

INTRODUCTION

Insurance allows parties, whether consumers or businesses, to anticipate the risk of particular events **6.1** and protect themselves from the financial consequences of the occurrence of such an event or events. In effect, the insured is "buying" a right to financial compensation should the insured-risk event occur. This is important in business and commerce, where the assessment and management of risk is a significant part of business and continuity planning. Upon receiving a request for insurance cover, the insurer can decide whether to provide cover and, if so, set an appropriate premium, or cost of the policy, for the insured. In order to do so, the insurer must have access to all the information that might have a bearing on an insured risk occurring. This fact explains why a major focus of insurance law is the insured's duty to disclose material facts to the insurer.

The nature of the relationship between an insurer and an insured is contractual, and much of "insurance law" is applied contract law. Other branches of commercial law are also important, for example, the law of agency insofar as it applies to insurance intermediaries. In addition to these general rules, there is, however, a body of law that has developed to govern insurance contracts. Perhaps the most significant of these legal rules is the classification of an insurance contract as a contract uberrima fides, or involving the utmost good faith.[1] The consequences flowing from this classification are explored in detail below.[2]

Insurance law has been built up through case law, industry practice, a complex regulatory framework and, in particular, the application and interpretation of the Marine Insurance Act 1906. The 1906 Act was and remains central to insurance law, as it codified the previous common law for all insurance contracts, not only marine insurance. There is also now the Consumer Insurance (Disclosure and Representations) Act 2012. Until the 2012 Act, there was no statutory distinction between consumer and business insurance contracts.[3] The 2012 Act came into force on April 6, 2013, and introduced the statutory concept of a "consumer insurance contract".[4] The Act is not retrospective, and so applies to consumer insurance contracts entered into (or renewed) subsequent to that date.[5] The key provisions covered by the Act relate to the duty of disclosure, warranties and representations, and remedies available for any "qualifying misrepresentation". It is not open to parties to contract out of the relevant provisions of the Act to the detriment of the consumer.[6] Each topic is dealt with at the appropriate point in the chapter below, bearing in mind that the pre-existing law continues to apply to (a) business insurance contracts, and (b) all "consumer insurance contracts" entered into prior to April 6, 2013.

Insurance law generally has been the subject of wide-ranging proposals for reform, following a number of joint projects by the Scottish Law Commission and the Law Commission of England and Wales. The Consumer Insurance (Disclosure and Representations) Act 2012 is the first enactment based on those proposals, and it is expected that more will follow.

The regulatory regime that applies to the insurance industry is complex. The focus of this chapter is the law governing the contract of insurance itself, and a detailed examination of the regulatory regime is outwith its scope.[7] It should be borne in mind, however, that the regulatory regime may operate to temper certain aspects of the law that appear harsh. The Insurance: Conduct of Business Sourcebook ("ICOBS") promoted by the Financial Conduct Authority is a key example of this, and certain aspects of that will be examined below.

DEFINITIONS

6.2 The following definition of the contract of insurance was provided by Channell J in *Prudential Insurance v Inland Revenue Commissioners*[8]:

> "It must be a contract whereby for some consideration, usually but not necessarily for periodical payments called premiums, you secure to yourself some benefit, usually but not necessarily the payment of a sum of money, upon the happening of some event . . . [T]he event should be one

---

[1] *Life Association of Scotland v Foster* (1873) 11 M. 351, per Lord President Inglis at 359. The application of this principle to "consumer insurance contracts" is now restricted by virtue of s.2(4) of the Consumer Insurance (Disclosure and Representations) Act 2012.

[2] See the analysis of the duty of disclosure in para.6.5 below.

[3] A separate body of consumer protections had developed, however; for example, self-regulation and industry practice, as well as legislation targeting unfair contract terms generally.

[4] Consumer Insurance (Disclosure and Representations) Act 2012 s.1.

[5] Although certain related changes to the Insurance: Conduct of Business Sourcebook ("ICOBS") apply to pre–2012 Act consumer insurance contracts—see paras 6.5.2.9 and 6.6.4 below.

[6] Consumer Insurance (Disclosure and Representations) Act 2012 s.10.

[7] Details of the regulation of insurance can be obtained from one of the main textbooks on insurance law, for example, J. Birds, *Birds' Modern Insurance Law*, 9th edn (London: Sweet & Maxwell, 2013).

[8] *Prudential Insurance v Inland Revenue Commissioners* [1904] 2 K.B. 658 at 663; see also *Digital Satellite Warranty Cover Ltd, Re* [2011] EWCA Civ 1413 regarding insurance being the "principal object" of the contract.

which involves some amount of uncertainty. There must be either uncertainty whether the event will ever happen or not, or if the event is one which must happen at some time there must be uncertainty as to the time at which it will happen."

To this general definition must now be added the definition of a "consumer insurance contract". Section 1 of the Consumer Insurance (Disclosure and Representations) Act 2012 defines this as

"a contract of insurance between (a) an individual who enters into the contract wholly or mainly for purposes unrelated to the individual's trade, business or profession, and (b) a person who carries on the business of insurance and who becomes a party to the contract by way of that business".

TYPES OF INSURANCE

The principles of insurance differ according to the type of insurance taken out by the insured. In indem- **6.3** nity insurance, the insured is indemnified for his loss, but never more than fully indemnified.[9] In the case of life assurance, however, an agreed payment (which might have little bearing on any financial "loss" occurring at the time of the death) is paid by the insurer in the event of death occurring during the currency of the policy. This chapter will, in the main, concentrate on general principles of insurance law, rather than aspects specific to particular types of policy. However, where there are important differences between life and indemnity insurance, the differences will be highlighted.

Indemnity insurance may be first party or third party. First party insurance covers the insured against damage to his property, and an example of this would be a home contents insurance policy. Third party insurance, as the term suggests, covers the insured's liability to a third party. The difference between first and third party insurance can be illustrated by considering motor insurance. The insured may take out first party insurance to cover personal injury to himself and property damage in the form of damage to his car. He must also take out third party insurance against his liability for property damage or personal injury caused to another road user.[10] Such insurance will only cover the insured where he is legally liable to the third party. Before the insurer under such a policy would make any payment, the injured party would have to establish that the insured was delictually liable.

INSURABLE INTEREST

The concept of insurable interest is notoriously difficult to define. One of the leading English texts **6.4** contains the following definition:

"Insurable interest may be described loosely as the assured's pecuniary interest in the subject-matter of the insurance arising from a relationship with it recognised in law."[11]

In the leading judgment in the English Court of Appeal case, *Feasey v Sun Life Assurance Co of Canada*, Waller LJ indicated that the context and terms of the policy itself are highly significant to the determination of the insurable interest.[12] He held:

---

[9] See the definition provided by Brett LJ in *Castellain v Preston* (1883) 11 Q.B.D. 380 at 386.

[10] Road Traffic Act 1988 ss.145(3)(a), 143(1).

[11] J. Birds, B. Lynch and S. Milnes (eds), *MacGillivray on Insurance Law*, 12th edn (London: Sweet & Maxwell, 2012), para.1–13. See also Bell, *Principles*, s.457, and the analysis of various definitions by Waller LJ in *Feasey v Sun Life Assurance Co of Canada* [2003] EWCA Civ 885 at [64]–[71].

[12] *Feasey v Sun Life Assurance Co of Canada* [2003] EWCA Civ 885 at [71], [80]; [2003] 2 All E.R. (Comm) 587; [2004] 1 C.L.C. 237; [2003] Lloyd's Rep 1 R. 637.

"(1) It is from the terms of the policy that the subject of insurance must be ascertained; (2) It is from all the surrounding circumstances that the nature of an insured's insurable interest must [be] discovered; (3) There is no hard and fast rule that because the nature of an insurable interest relates to a liability to compensate for loss, that insurable interest could only be covered by a liability policy rather than a policy insuring property or life or indeed properties or lives; (4) The question whether a policy embraces the insurable interest intended to be recovered is a question of [contractual] construction. The subject or terms of the policy may be so specific as to force a court to hold that the policy has failed to cover the insurable interest, but a court will be reluctant so to hold. (5) It is not a requirement of property insurance that the insured must have a 'legal or equitable' interest in the property as those terms might normally be understood. It is sufficient for a sub-contractor to have a contract that relates to the property and a potential liability for damage to the property to have an insurable interest in the property. It is sufficient under section 5 of the Marine Insurance Act for a person interested in a marine adventure to stand in a 'legal or equitable relation to the adventure.' That is intended to be a broad concept".

The requirement of insurable interest was originally introduced to prevent persons using insurance policies for the purposes of gaming or wagering. It was thought to be contrary to public policy to permit a person to take out insurance over the life of another person where the insured had no financial interest in the life assured. Although insurable interest is a common law requirement, it is also present in certain insurance statutes, as explored below.

It is not surprising to find courts going to considerable lengths in order to find that an insurable interest exists. If the insured has no insurable interest, then the insurance contract is treated as an illegal contract, and the insured may be prevented from recovering the premiums that he has paid.[13] The words of the Master of the Rolls, Lord Brett, expressed in 1884 remain equally relevant today: "[I]t is the duty of a Court always to lean in favour of an insurable interest, if possible".[14]

He continued,

"for it seems to me that after underwriters have received the premium, the objection that there was no insurable interest is often, as nearly as possible, a technical objection, and one which has no real merit, certainly not as between the assured and the insurer."[15]

Feasey v Sun Life Assurance Co of Canada contains a wide-ranging (and at times controversial) analysis of insurable interest.[16] In *Feasey*, the insured had changed its insurance arrangements at the instigation of the insurer.[17] Nevertheless, it was the insurer who later raised the plea of no insurable interest in relation to the new arrangements. The policy was one that covered the insured's members in respect of their legal liabilities for personal injury or death occurring to persons who were either employees of the member or who came on board the members' vessels. Before the change of the insured's policy took place, the policy was, in effect, one of liability insurance, i.e. insurance covering potential legal liabilities. The change in arrangements meant that the policy resembled a first party insurance policy, which sought to insure the lives of the injured persons themselves. However, the insured clearly did not have the type of insurable interest in the lives of those injured that would normally be sufficient to satisfy the requirements of insurable interest in the context of life assurance. Although the majority held that an insurable interest did, in fact, exist, they did so only by defining insurable interest in a novel manner.[18] In many respects the dissenting judgment of Ward LJ is more persuasive.

Life insurance is usually treated separately from indemnity and marine insurance, and this distinction is followed in the paragraphs that follow. Nevertheless, all three judges in *Feasey* suggested that

---

[13] For Scots law on the availability of unjustified enrichment remedies in the context of an illegal contract, see L. J. Macgregor, "Illegal Contracts and Unjustified Enrichment", 2000 Edin. L.R. 19.

[14] *Stock v Inglis* [1884] 12 Q.B.D. 564 at 571.

[15] *Stock v Inglis* [1884] 12 Q.B.D. 564 at 571.

[16] *Feasey v Sun Life Assurance Co of Canada* [2003] EWCA Civ 885.

[17] The change was, in fact, necessary due to changes in Lloyd's rules regarding liability insurance.

[18] In effect, Waller and Dyson LJJ applied a new, four part, categorisation of the subject matter of insurance policies, finding that the insurance policy in question fell into the fourth category of policies, "in which the court has recognised interests which are not even strictly pecuniary", per Waller LJ at [90].

the categories ought to be aligned. The situation remains uncertain, given that *Feasey* was decided at Court of Appeal and not House of Lords level, and has not yet been discussed either in the Outer or Inner House in Scotland.

LIFE ASSURANCE

Although an insurable interest is a requirement in terms of the Life Assurance Act 1774,[19] that Act **6.4.1** provides no definition of the concept:

> "[No] insurance shall be made by any person or persons, bodies politick or corporate, on the life or lives of any person or persons or on any other event or events whatsoever, wherein the person or persons for whose use, benefit, or on whose account such policy or policies shall be made, shall have no interest, or by way of gaming or wagering".[20]

The Act limits the insured's recovery to "the amount of value of the interest of the insured in such life or lives".[21] This implies that the insured can recover only his financial interest in the life assured.

It is assumed that an insured has an insurable interest in his own life,[22] and in the life of his or her spouse/civil partner.[23] The effect of the Married Women's Policies of Assurance (Scotland) Act 1880 should be noted here. This Act, which also now applies to civil partners,[24] permits a married woman to take out a policy on the life of her husband for her own benefit.[25] It also provides that where a husband or wife takes out a life policy on his or her own life for the benefit of his or her spouse or children (or both) the policy is deemed to be held by the insured in trust for the spouse or children.[26] Parents owe to their children an obligation of aliment,[27] and, as a result, children have an insurable interest in the lives of their parents. Children have no corresponding obligation to aliment their parents, and so parents have no insurable interest in the lives of their children. Outwith these defined classes of relationship, the insured would have to possess a financial interest in the life insured to have an insurable interest.[28]

The 1774 Act is ambiguous as to the point in time at which the insurable interest must exist in the life assured.[29] This issue was considered in what remains a highly significant case, *Dalby v India & London Life Assurance Co*.[30] In this case, four policies of insurance, worth a total of £3,000, had been taken out with the plaintiff's company, Anchor Life, over the life of the Duke of Cambridge. Anchor Life then reinsured[31] the policies with the defendant insurance company. The insured then cancelled the policies, but Anchor maintained the reinsurance policy in place. When the Duke died, Dalby claimed under the reinsurance policy. The defendants argued that the plaintiff's insurable interest in the Duke's life had ceased when the insured had cancelled the policies. However, it was held that it was sufficient if the insurable interest existed at the time at which the insurance contract was entered into, and there

---

[19] The term "assurance" is sometimes used where the policy holder insures his life as opposed to any other interest, the holder being referred to as the "assured". These terms are not used in this Chapter, where all references are to "insurance" and the "insured".

[20] Life Assurance Act 1774 s.1.

[21] Life Assurance Act 1774 s.3.

[22] *Griffiths v Fleming* [1909] 1 K.B. 805, per Farwell LJ at 821.

[23] *Wight v Brown* (1845) 11 D. 459; also Civil Partnership Act 2004 s.253. This right does not extend to engaged couples nor to cohabitees.

[24] Civil Partnership Act 2004 s.132.

[25] Married Women's Policies of Assurance (Scotland) Act 1880 s.1.

[26] Married Women's Policies of Assurance (Scotland) Act 1880 s.2, as amended by the Married Women's Policies of Assurance (Scotland) Amendment Act 1980 s.1. There is no requirement that the policy be delivered or intimated to the beneficiaries.

[27] See Family Law (Scotland) Act 1985 s.1(1)(c).

[28] Where the employer has a financial interest in the life of an employee, the employer may also have an insurable interest in that life: see *Turnbull & Co v Scottish Provident Institution* (1896) 34 S.L.R. 146.

[29] See ss.1 and 3.

[30] *Dalby v India & London Life Assurance Co* (1854) 15 C.B. 365.

[31] Insurer A may enter into a contract of insurance with insured B. Reinsurance occurs where insurer A insures the risk which it has undertaken in terms of that policy with a different insurer, insurer C.

was no requirement that it continue in existence until the time of the loss.[32] Parker B indicated that to hold otherwise would mean that an insured would pay a fixed premium during the course of the insurance policy, but the amount of his eventual claim would be uncertain, depending upon a recalculation of his insurable interest at the time of the death of the life assured.[33] As is explored immediately below, the same question, i.e. the time at which insurable interest must exist, receives a different answer in the context of indemnity insurance.

INDEMNITY INSURANCE

6.4.2 Although this point is not clear from the terms of the Act itself, case law suggests that the 1774 Act does not apply to indemnity insurance.[34] Nevertheless, it is quite clear that the insured in indemnity insurance must have an insurable interest as a result of the operation of Scots common law.[35] This rule also follows logically from the nature of indemnity insurance, given that the insured must have suffered a financial loss in order to have a valid claim. The insurable interest must exist at the date of the loss, and it is probably the case that it must exist at the time of entering into the insurance contract.[36]

Care must be taken in identifying the insured's financial interest in the event insured against. In *Fehilly v General Accident Fire and Life Assurance Corp Ltd*[37] a tenant had sought to insure its interest in the subjects of let, a ballroom in Stirling. When the building was destroyed by fire, the tenants sought to recover from the insurer the value of the building at the time of destruction. The tenant failed in its attempt to recover the full value of the building, on the basis that it did not have an insurable interest in the full value of the building. This was because, in terms of the repair clause of the lease, the tenant was only obliged to maintain the subjects in the condition in which they were in when the lease was entered into, and not fully to reinstate the building in the event of it being destroyed.[38] The tenant's insurable interest was limited to the market value of the lease.

The insured must have an insurable interest in any heritable property which he seeks to insure. Where the insured has a right to the property that is less than outright ownership, care must be taken to ensure that he actually has a sufficient insurable interest. Problems have occurred due to the distinction made between the legal personality of a limited company and that of its shareholders.[39] In *Cowan v Jeffrey Associates*[40] Mr Cowan, the director and sole shareholder of a company, had signed personal guarantees covering the company's indebtedness, and was owed a substantial amount of money by the company, through a loan and for work which he had carried out on the company's behalf. The company owned the business premises. He decided to purchase those premises from the company (i.e. in his own name). As part of his plans, he insured the premises against fire. He entered into the insurance contract at a time when no contract had been entered into for the purchase of the premises; Mr Cowan was simply a prospective purchaser. It can be seen, therefore, that, although Mr Cowan had no contractual or other right to the premises, he had a great deal to lose should they be destroyed. When the premises were, in fact, destroyed by fire, he claimed under the insurance policy. The defenders argued that he had no insurable interest and refused to meet his claim. Lord Hamilton followed pre-existing House of Lords authority[41] to find that the pursuer had no insurable interest. He was clearly dissatisfied with the authorities, and noted that they had

---

[32] This point was confirmed in *Feasey v Sun Life Assurance Co of Canada* [2003] EWCA Civ 885, per Waller LJ at [73]; [2003] 2 All E.R. (Comm) 587; [2004] 1 C.L.C. 237; [2003] Lloyd's Rep 1 R. 637.

[33] *Dalby v India & London Life Assurance Co* (1854) 15 C.B. 365 at 403.

[34] *Mark Rowlands v Berni Inns Ltd* [1985] Q.B. 211, per Kerr LJ at 227; *Siu Yin Kwan v Eastern Insurance Ltd* [1994] 2 A.C. 199, per Lord Lloyd at 211.

[35] Bell, *Principles*, s.457.

[36] See the Law Commission and The Scottish law Commission, *Insurance Contract Law*, Issues Paper 4 (Insurable Interest), January 2008 para.5.20.

[37] *Fehilly v General Accident Fire and Life Assurance Corp Ltd*, 1982 S.C. 163.

[38] *Fehilly v General Accident Fire and Life Assurance Corp Ltd*, 1982 S.C. 163, per Lord Cowie at 169–170.

[39] *Salomon v Salomon & Co* [1897] A.C. 22.

[40] *Cowan v Jeffrey Associates*, 1998 S.C.L.R. 619.

[41] In particular, *Macaura v Northern Assurance Co Ltd* [1925] A.C. 619, a decision of the House of Lords in a Northern Irish appeal.

not been followed in Canada where a wider test has been adopted. Under the Canadian version of the test, which depends upon the insured's "factual expectancy", where the insured has a "moral certainty"[42] of profit or loss, then this is sufficient to provide him with an insurable interest.

Problems may also arise due to the manner in which partnerships take title to heritable property. In *Arif v Excess Insurance Group Ltd*[43] it was held that Arif, who was a partner of a firm that ran a hotel business and the holder of the insurance policy covering the hotel, did not have an insurable interest in the hotel. This was because the legal owner of the hotel was a separate individual, albeit another of the partners of the firm. To avoid this result, the property would require to be insured in the name of the partnership.

MARINE INSURANCE

An insurable interest is also required in the context of marine insurance. The Marine Insurance Act **6.4.3** 1906 s.4 provides that contracts of insurance by way of gaming or wagering are void, and that a contract of marine insurance is deemed to be one of gaming or wagering where the insured has no insurable interest.[44] The Act also makes clear that the insurable interest need exist only at the time of the loss and not at the time when the insurance contract is entered into.[45]

GOOD FAITH, THE DUTY OF DISCLOSURE AND MISREPRESENTATION

6.5

THE GENERAL DUTY OF UTMOST GOOD FAITH

6.5.1

The contract of insurance is described as a contract uberrimae fidei, or involving the utmost good **6.5.1.1** faith.[46] Lord Mansfield's judgment in *Carter v Boehm*[47] is usually identified as the source of this principle.[48] Although he confirmed that the duty is a reciprocal one,[49] his explanation of the rationale of the rule focused mainly on the insured:

> "Insurance is a contract upon speculation. The special facts, upon which the contingent chance is to be computed, lie most commonly in the knowledge of the insured only: the underwriter trusts to his representation, and proceeds upon confidence that he does not keep back any circumstance in his knowledge to mislead the underwriter into a belief that the circumstance does not exist, and to induce him to estimate the risque, as if it did not exist."[50]

Certain facts material to the insurer's assessment of the risk are known only to the insured, and must therefore be disclosed by him. Such a duty to disclose is the most important aspect of the wider duty of good faith and is considered below.

---

[42] See *Lucena v Craufurd* (1806) 2 Bos. & Pul. (N.R.) 269, in which Lawrence J (at 300–303) set out a wide test for insurable interest. His view on this point was not shared by his colleagues on the bench, and the wider test was not applied in *Macaura v Northern Assurance Co Ltd* [1925] A.C. 619.

[43] *Arif v Excess Insurance Group Ltd*, 1986 S.C. 317.

[44] Insurable interest is defined in s.5(1), (2).

[45] Marine Insurance Act 1906 s.6(1).

[46] W.M. Gloag, *Law of Contract*, 2nd edn (Edinburgh: W. Green, 1929), pp.496–507. Examples of other contracts uberrima fidei identified by Gloag include cautionary obligations and proposals to enter into partnerships; *Life Association of Scotland v Foster* (1873) 11 M. 351, per Lord President Inglis at 359.

[47] *Carter v Boehm* (1766) 3 Burr. 1905.

[48] See also Marine Insurance Act 1906 s.17: "A contract of marine insurance is a contract based on the utmost good faith, and, if the utmost good faith is not observed by either party, the contract may be avoided by the other party."

[49] *Carter v Boehm* (1766) 3 Burr. 1905, per Lord Mansfield at 1909. This point is confirmed in modern case law: see *Life Association of Scotland v Foster* (1873) 11 M. 351, per Lord President Inglis at 359; *Banque Financière de la Cité v Westgate Insurance* [1991] 2 A.C. 249.

[50] *Carter v Boehm* (1766) 3 Burr. 1905, per Lord Mansfield at 1909.

6.5.1.2   The Consumer Insurance (Disclosure and Representations) Act 2012 qualifies the duty to act with the utmost good faith in relation to consumer insurance contracts. There is no general disapplication or removal of the duty, but s.2(5)(a) of the Act modifies the duty to the extent required by the other provisions of the Act regarding disclosure and representations.

6.5.2 THE DUTY OF DISCLOSURE

Consumer insurance contracts

6.5.2.1   In terms of s.2(2) of the Consumer Insurance (Disclosure and Representations) Act 2012, the consumer is under a duty to take reasonable care not to make a misrepresentation to the insurer. This duty replaces any duty relating to disclosure or representations to an insurer which existed in the same circumstances before the Act applied.[51] Section 3(1) of the Act provides that whether or not a consumer has taken reasonable care not to make a misrepresentation is to be determined in light of all the relevant circumstances, and s.3(2) provides examples of things to be taken into account in making such a determination. The standard of care required is that of a "reasonable consumer",[52] subject to two specific provisions, namely, (1) if the insurer was, or ought to have been, aware of any particular characteristics or circumstances of the actual consumer, those are to be taken into account,[53] and (2) a misrepresentation made dishonestly is always to be taken as showing a lack of reasonable care.[54]

In the context of life assurance, s.8 of the 2012 Act provides particular assumptions where an insurance policy is taken out over the life of another person (not being a party to the insurance contract). In this scenario,

     (a)   any information provided to the insurer by the non-contracting party is to be treated as if it were provided by the person who is the party to the contract, but

     (b)   in relation to such information, if anything turns on the state of mind, knowledge, circumstances or characteristics of the party providing the information, it is to be determined by reference to the non-contracting party, and not the party to the contract.[55]

An insurer has a remedy against a consumer for a misrepresentation made by the consumer before the contract of insurance was entered into or varied only if

     (a)   the consumer made the misrepresentation in breach of the duty set out in s.2(2) of the Act (as set out above), and

     (b)   the insurer shows that, without the misrepresentation, the insurer would not have entered into the contract (or agreed to the variation) at all, or would have done so on different terms.[56]

A misrepresentation in respect of which the insurer has a remedy is known as a "qualifying misrepresentation".[57] A qualifying misrepresentation will be classified in terms of the 2012 Act as either (a) deliberate or reckless, or (b) careless.[58] A qualifying misrepresentation will be classified as deliberate or reckless if the consumer

     (a)   knew that it was untrue or misleading, or did not care whether or not it was untrue or misleading, and

---

[51] Consumer Insurance (Disclosure and Representations) Act 2012 s.2(4).
[52] Consumer Insurance (Disclosure and Representations) Act 2012 s.3(3).
[53] Consumer Insurance (Disclosure and Representations) Act 2012 s.3(4).
[54] Consumer Insurance (Disclosure and Representations) Act 2012 s.3(5).
[55] Consumer Insurance (Disclosure and Representations) Act 2012 s.8(2).
[56] Consumer Insurance (Disclosure and Representations) Act 2012 s.4(1).
[57] Consumer Insurance (Disclosure and Representations) Act 2012 s.4(2).
[58] Consumer Insurance (Disclosure and Representations) Act 2012 s.5(1).

(b) knew that the matter to which the misrepresentation related was relevant to the insurer, or did not care whether or not it was relevant to the insurer.[59]

It is for the insurer to show that a qualifying misrepresentation was deliberate or reckless,[60] and a qualifying misrepresentation is deemed to be careless if it is not found to be deliberate or reckless.[61] However, it is to be presumed, unless the contrary is shown, that (a) the consumer had the knowledge of a reasonable consumer, and (b) the consumer knew that a matter about which the insurer asked a clear and specific question was relevant to the insurer.[62]

The remedies open to the insurer for any qualifying misrepresentation depend on the category of the misrepresentation.[63] If the qualifying misrepresentation was deliberate or reckless, the insurer

(a) may avoid the contract and refuse all claims, and
(b) need not return any of the premiums paid, except to the extent (if any) that it would be unfair on the consumer to retain them.[64]

If the qualifying misrepresentation was careless, the insurer's remedies are based on what it would have done if the consumer had complied with its duties in terms of s.2(2) of the Act,[65] and this will vary according to circumstances. Notwithstanding the fact that a misrepresentation was careless in terms of the Act (i.e. not deliberate or reckless), the insurer may still be entitled to avoid the contract and refuse all claims, if it would not have entered into the insurance contract on any terms (in which event it must return the premiums paid).[66] The remedies available to the insurer will also vary if the qualifying misrepresentation was careless and does not relate to any outstanding claim under the policy.[67]

Business insurance contracts

Like the duty of good faith, the duty of disclosure is mutual, although few cases exist that explore the duty as it applies to the insurer.[68] Clearly the duty of good faith is wider in ambit than the duty of disclosure. The duty of good faith applies at all times during the insurance contract: during negotiations; the currency of the insurance contract; and the date when a claim is made.[69] By contrast, the duty of disclosure applies during negotiations, but only up until a binding insurance contract is formed.[70] It revives when the insured renews the contract, such as where the contract is renewed annually.[71] There is, however, no obligation on the insured to disclose factors increasing the risk during the course of the insurance contract.[72] If the

6.5.2.2

---

[59] Consumer Insurance (Disclosure and Representations) Act 2012 s.5(2).
[60] Consumer Insurance (Disclosure and Representations) Act 2012 s.5(4).
[61] Consumer Insurance (Disclosure and Representations) Act 2012 s.5(3).
[62] Consumer Insurance (Disclosure and Representations) Act 2012 s.5(5).
[63] Consumer Insurance (Disclosure and Representations) Act 2012 Sch.1 Pt 1 paras 2–9.
[64] Consumer Insurance (Disclosure and Representations) Act 2012 Sch.1 Pt 1 para.2.
[65] Consumer Insurance (Disclosure and Representations) Act 2012 Sch.1 Pt 1 paras 3 and 4.
[66] Consumer Insurance (Disclosure and Representations) Act 2012 Sch.1 Pt 1 para.5.
[67] Consumer Insurance (Disclosure and Representations) Act 2012 Sch.1 Pt 1 para.9.
[68] Although see *Banque Keyser Ullman SA v Skandia (UK) Insurance Co Ltd* [1990] 1 Q.B. 665, per Steyn J at 772.
[69] The existence of the duty of good faith at the time when a claim is made was confirmed by Lord Penrose in *Fargnoli v G A Bonus Plc*, 1997 S.C.L.R. 12 at 23. The extent of the duty which applies at the time of making a claim may be less than that which applies at the commencement of the contract, see *Manifest Shipping v Uni-Polaris Insurance Co (The Star Sea)* [2001] 1 All E.R. 743.
[70] *Ionides v Pacific Ins Co* (1871) L.R. 6 Q.B. 674. It is common for insurance policies to extend the duration of the duty by stating that the insurer will not be bound until the first premium is received by the insurer, see *MacGillivray on Insurance Law*, 12th edn (2012), para.17–24.
[71] *Law Accident Insurance Society v Boyd*, 1942 S.C. 384; *Lambert v Co-operative Insurance Society Ltd* [1975] 2 Lloyd's Rep. 485; *Kausar v Eagle Star Insurance Co Ltd* [1997] C.L.C. 129; *MacGillivray on Insurance Law*, 12th edn (2012), para.17–25.
[72] Although exceptionally, failure to disclose facts which dramatically increase the risk may be regarded as a breach of the continuing duty of utmost good faith: see *Black King Shipping Corp v Massie (The Litsion Pride)* [1985] 1 Lloyd's Rep. 437. The same is true of the insurer: see *Bank of Nova Scotia v Hellenic Mutual War Risk Association (Bermuda) Ltd (The Good Luck)* [1990] 1 Q.B. 818 CA, reversed on different grounds by the House of Lords in [1992] 1 A.C. 233. Moreover, the insurer may seek to impose such an obligation through the use of an "increase of risk" clause.

parties enter into litigation related to the insurance contract, then both the duty of good faith and the duty of disclosure terminate with the raising of proceedings.[73]

It seems clear that the modern formulation of the duty to disclose goes well beyond the extent that was originally envisaged by Lord Mansfield.[74] There is also an argument that, in a modern context, the insurer relies less on information disclosed by the insured and more on information available from actuaries and experts in order to decide whether to accept the risk and, if so, the level of premium to charge. The duty is of central importance in insurance law, and for this reason is explored in detail below.

The effect on the insured of a breach of the pre-contractual duty of disclosure is significant. Faced with a breach, an insurer can opt to avoid the contract ab initio.[75] Avoidance means that any sums already paid out by the insurer to the insured under the policy must be repaid in full by the insured. All premiums must be refunded by the insurer to the insured under the principles of unjustified enrichment. This will provide only cold comfort to the insured. Breach of the duty of disclosure is almost invariably discovered when the insured makes a claim on the insurance policy in respect of the occurrence of an insured risk. He will not obtain what he expected to, namely, a payment of insurance proceeds triggered by the occurrence of the risk. Attempts to develop the availability of damages as a remedy for breach of the duty of disclosure failed in *Banque Financiére de la Cité v Westgate Insurance*.[76] In this case, due to fraud on an extensive scale, the proceeds under an insurance policy fell far short of meeting the losses arising from the occurrence of the insured risk. This fraud was known to the insurer, but not disclosed to the insured. The insured could have rescinded in response to that breach of duty, but that would have left it considerably worse off, as the proceeds of the policy at least covered some of its loss. The remedy of damages would have been a much more appropriate remedy, operating to cover the remainder of its loss. Nevertheless, it was held that the remedy of damages was not available, leaving the insured with no effective remedy.

Turning to consider the same issue from the insurer's perspective, the insurer will almost never have an interest in seeking damages from an insured. The most disadvantageous aspect of the contract for an insurer is the duty to meet the insured's loss under the policy. It does not stand to suffer a loss from the contract in the classic manner required by the law of contractual damages. By contrast, the remedy of avoidance is an ideal one for the insurer, allowing it to refuse to meet the claim with no penalty (save repayment of the premiums). Although seeming to treat both parties equally by applying the same remedy, the law gives to the insurer the remedy which benefits it most, and to the insured no effective remedy at all.[77]

Actual knowledge of the insured

6.5.2.3 Where the insured is an individual, the duty to disclose will only encompass matters that are within the actual knowledge of the insured.[78] He cannot be expected to disclose matters of which he is unaware.[79] This point was established in *Economides v Commercial Union Assurance Plc*.[80] In this case the insured had indicated that the value of the contents of his home was £16,000, when it was far higher. In the Court of Appeal, the judgments highlighted the fact that the insured was operating on the basis of information provided to him by his father, genuinely thought he was telling the truth, and was under no obligation to establish the true position. It was held that the insurance company was not entitled to avoid liability. Matters are more complex where the insured is a corporate actor, where it is thought that

---

[73] *Manifest Shipping Co Ltd v Uni-Polaris Shipping Co Ltd (The Star Sea)* [2001] 2 W.L.R. 170 HL.
[74] See R. Hasson, "The doctrine of uberrima fides in insurance law—a critical evaluation" (1969) 32 M.L.R. 615.
[75] *Joel v Law Union & Crown Insurance Co* [1908] 2 K.B. 863; Marine Insurance Act 1906 s.17. Avoidance is retroactive, and the contract is therefore treated as though it had never existed.
[76] *Banque Financiére de la Cité v Westgate Insurance* [1991] 2 A.C. 249, per Lord Templeman at 280.
[77] See F. Davidson, "Insurers—Duty of Disclosure and Duty of Care", 1988 S.L.T. (News) 73.
[78] For an interesting example of the impact of knowledge of the insured (in this case an individual with experience of the insurance industry) see *Bate v Aviva Insurance UK Ltd* [2014] EWCA Civ 334.
[79] *Joel v Law Union & Crown Insurance Co* [1908] 2 K.B. 863, per Fletcher Moulton LJ at 884; *Hearts of Oak Building Society v Law Union Insurance* [1936] 2 All E.R. 619, per Lord Goddard at 625.
[80] *Economides v Commercial Union Assurance Plc* [1998] Q.B. 587.

the company's knowledge is the knowledge of those who "represent the directing mind and will of the company, and who control what it does".[81] The Marine Insurance Act 1906 s.18(1) also provides that the insured is deemed to know every circumstance which, in the ordinary course of business, ought to be known by him. This section has, however, been interpreted restrictively by the courts.[82]

"Materiality" and inducement

Section 18 of the Marine Insurance Act 1906 provides that   6.5.2.4

> "the assured must disclose to the insurer, before the contract is concluded, every material circumstance which is known to the assured . . . Every circumstance is material which would influence the judgment of a prudent insurer in fixing the premium or determining whether he will take the risk."[83]

Materiality is judged at the time of formation of the contract, i.e. when the insurer accepts the risk.[84] It is not possible to provide a full picture in this book of the types of facts which tend to be considered material.[85] A particularly difficult issue is the effect of the criminal history or dishonesty of the insured. Criminal convictions for offences of dishonesty are normally treated as material,[86] although the insured is not obliged to disclose convictions which have become "spent" in terms of s.4(3)(a) of the Rehabilitation of Offenders Act 1974.[87] In *North Star Shipping Ltd v Sphere Drake Insurance Plc* it was stated that the insured is required to disclose allegations of serious criminal behaviour which have not yet led to arrest or charge, although the judge criticised this rule.[88] Although it does seem to operate unfairly against an insured, such information will undoubtedly be of the type that would influence the judgment of a prudent insurer in assessing the risk.

Section 18 is silent on the extent of influence that the non-disclosure must have on the hypothetical prudent insurer. This question was considered by the Court of Appeal in *Container Transport International Inc and Reliance Group Inc v Oceanus Mutual Underwriting Association (Bermuda) Ltd*,[89] in which Kerr LJ (referring to the prudent insurer) stated:

> "The word 'influence' means that the disclosure is one which would have had an impact on the formation of his opinion and on his decision-making process in relation to the matters covered by s.18(2)."[90]

The issue was then considered in the important House of Lords case, *Pan Atlantic Insurance Co v Pine Top Insurance Co Ltd*.[91] The decisive influence test was rejected by a narrow majority,[92] despite a forceful dissenting opinion from Lord Lloyd. The insurer need only prove that the issue that was not

---

[81] *MacGillivray on Insurance Law*, 12th edn (2012), paras 17–11, 17–12.

[82] *MacGillivray on Insurance Law*, 12th edn (2012), para.17–12.

[83] Marine Insurance Act 1906 s.18(2).

[84] *Brotherton v Aseguradora Colseguros SA (No.2)* [2003] EWCA Civ 705; [2003] Lloyd's Rep. I.R. 746, per Mance LJ at [39].

[85] See the useful analysis in Birds, *Birds' Modern Insurance Law*, 9th edn (2013), pp.128–140; also see *Bate v Aviva Insurance UK Ltd* [2014] EWCA Civ 334 for discussion regarding materiality and knowledge of the insured.

[86] Even those which have been committed some time ago, see *Schoolman v Hall* [1951] 1 Lloyd's Rep. 139, in which offences committed at least 15 years previously were held to be material.

[87] On "spent" convictions and the operation of the s.4(3)(a) of the Rehabilitation of Offenders Act 1974, see para.6.5.2.6 below.

[88] *North Star Shipping Ltd v Sphere Drake Insurance Plc* [2006] EWCA Civ 378; [2006] Lloyd's Rep. I.R. 519, per Waller LJ at [17]–[20]. This case was distinguished in *Norwich Union Insurance Ltd v Meisels* [2006] EWHC 2811; [2007] Lloyd's Rep. I.R. 69, where Tugendhat J suggested that an allegation which is clearly groundless would not require to be disclosed, preferring the approach of Mance LJ in *Brotherton v Aseguradora Colseguros SA (No.2)* [2003] EWCA Civ 705; [2003] Lloyd's Rep. I.R. 746.

[89] *Container Transport International Inc and Reliance Group Inc v Oceanus Mutual Underwriting Association (Bermuda) Ltd (No.1)* [1984] 1 Lloyd's Rep. 476.

[90] *Container Transport International Inc and Reliance Group Inc v Oceanus Mutual Underwriting Association (Bermuda) Ltd (No.1)* [1984] 1 Lloyd's Rep. 476 at 492.

[91] *Pan Atlantic Insurance Co v Pine Top Insurance Co Ltd* [1995] 1 A.C. 501.

[92] 3:2.

disclosed was one of several factors that a prudent insurer would have taken into account in making his decision to accept the risk and set the premium accordingly.

In *Pan Atlantic*, the House of Lords added a requirement that, to some extent, tempers the harsh effect of the materiality test on the insured. The insurer must prove that the failure to disclose the relevant fact actually induced him to accept the risk and enter into the insurance contract at a specific premium. The source of this extra requirement was, according to their Lordships, the law of misrepresentation.[93] The inducement test is conceptually difficult, involving as it does an analysis of inducement by an omission, in other words the insurer must prove that the omission to disclose induced him to enter into the contract. Since the *Pan Atlantic* decision, the case law on inducement has been conflicting. *St Paul Fire & Marine Insurance Co v McConnell Dowell Construction Ltd* appeared to swing the balance towards protection of the insurer once more.[94] The Court of Appeal indicated that a presumption in favour of inducement existed, and that non-disclosure need only be one of the inducing factors, not the sole inducing factor.[95] Thus the insured is burdened with the onus of proving that the failure to disclose did not induce the insurer to contract.[96] Inducement has been established, where it was held that, had the particular issue been disclosed, it would have provoked the insurer to ask further questions which would in turn have led to the application of a higher premium.[97]

In *Drake Insurance Plc v Provident Insurance Plc* there was an attempt to swing the balance once more in favour of the insured.[98] The case concerned a motor insurance policy taken out by Dr Singh. Two specific events or facts had not been disclosed by the insured to the insurer, Provident. The first was an accident in which Dr Singh's wife had been involved. Whilst the fact of this accident was disclosed, Dr Singh failed to disclose to Provident that, following investigation, his wife was found not to be at fault. The second event was a failure to disclose a speeding conviction. In fact, there was no duty to disclose the first event given that it was an event that did not affect Provident's risk.[99] A duty to disclose did exist in respect of the second event, and Singh failed to discharge that duty. Provident argued that the failure to disclose the speeding conviction was material, and that it had induced them to enter into the contract. A further significant fact in *Drake* was Provident's lack of discretion in setting the premium. Provident operated a "points system". Particular facts, such as speeding convictions or accidents, led to the imposition of a specific number of points. Those points were tallied up, and, if the insured achieved a total of 16 or less, a normal premium would be charged. The "no fault" decision on the accident, if disclosed, would have decreased the points tally. The speeding conviction would have increased the points tally. Thus, had both facts been disclosed, there would have been no overall effect on the premium—the points tally would still have been less than 16. In summary, therefore, although there was an undoubted failure to disclose the conviction, looked at in the whole circumstances of the case, the failure made no difference to the premium charged by Provident.[100]

The Court of Appeal in *Drake* found that Provident did not have the right to avoid for non-disclosure. It had not been induced to enter the contract by reason of the non-disclosure. The decision is, however, a difficult one. It will be recalled that the inducement test looks to the actual, not the hypothetical insurer. It is, of course, impossible to say with confidence what the actual course of events would have been. The Court of Appeal took the view that, if the conviction had been disclosed, Provident would have charged a higher premium. They then reasoned that the imposition of a higher premium would have provoked the insured into disclosing the "no fault" outcome of the accident. One cannot, of course, be certain that this would be the turn of events. At the very least, what the case does suggest is

[93] See also *Gaelic Assignments Ltd v Sharpe*, 2001 S.L.T. 914.
[94] *St Paul Fire & Marine Insurance Co v McConnell Dowell Construction Ltd* [1995] 2 Lloyd's Rep. 116. See also *International Management Group (UK) Ltd v Simmonds* [2003] EWHC 177 (Comm) at [149].
[95] See recent confirmation of this latter point in *Assicurazioni Generali SpA v Arab Insurance Group (BSC)* [2002] EWCA Civ 1642; [2003] 1 W.L.R. 577 CA, per Clarke LJ at [59].
[96] See *Marc Rich v Portman* [1997] 1 Lloyd's Rep. 225 where the past failure of the insurer to take material facts into account did not overcome the presumption in favour of inducement.
[97] *International Management Group (UK) Ltd v Simmonds* [2003] EWHC 177 (Comm) at [145].
[98] *Drake Insurance Plc v Provident Insurance Plc* [2004] Q.B. 601.
[99] Marine Insurance Act 1906 s.18(1); and see para.6.5.2.6 below.
[100] See also *Assicurazioni Generali SpA v Arab Insurance Group (BSC)* [2002] EWCA Civ 1642; [2003] 1 W.L.R. 577 CA.

that inducement must be proved by the insurer. In *Drake*, the onus lay on Provident to prove that Dr Singh would *not* have disclosed the "no fault" outcome. Provident failed to discharge this onus.

There is probably no conflict between the presumption of inducement articulated in the *St Paul* case and the reassertion of the insurer's onus of proving inducement in *Drake*. A presumption of inducement may still operate where the facts that were not disclosed are obviously material.[101]

Finally, it is important to note that the definition of "materiality" in the context of life assurance differs in Scotland compared to England. This is as a result of the decision in the case of *Life Association of Scotland v Foster*.[102] The insured had been asked by the insurer whether she had a rupture and had answered in the negative. She later died as the result of a rupture. It was discovered that, at the time at which she was asked this question, she had a small swelling on her groin which was a symptom of rupture. She was, however, completely unaware that this constituted such a symptom. The First Division of the Inner House held that the insurer could not avoid the insurance contract for non-disclosure given that Mrs Foster, not having any medical knowledge, could not have known that the swelling was material. Lord President Inglis expressed the duty of disclosure in life assurance contracts as follows:

> "His duty is carefully and diligently to review all the facts known to himself bearing on the risk proposed to the insurers, and to state every circumstance which any reasonable man might suppose could in any way influence the insurers in considering and deciding whether they will enter into the contract."[103]

The duty in Scots law in the context of life assurance is framed by reference to what the reasonable man in the position of the insured would consider to be material, not what the prudent insurer would consider to be material.[104] Although Lord President Inglis appeared to suggest that the "reasonable insured" test applied in all types of insurance, in *Hooper v Royal London General Insurance Co Ltd*[105] it was held that the "reasonable insured" test applied only to cases of life assurance. Lord Justice Clerk Ross explained his reasoning by reference to the difference between life assurance and all other types of insurance. In life assurance, the questions asked relate to "personal matters" which are often "peculiarly within the knowledge of the assured" and "are not capable of assessment on any objective basis".[106] He contrasted this position with indemnity insurance where the answers to the questions asked can be objectively ascertained.[107]

Possible constraints on the insurer's right to avoid?

The insurer's remedy for failure to disclose was noted above: he may avoid the contract, but cannot **6.5.2.5** claim damages.[108] There has been an attempt in some English cases to state that the duty of good faith might curtail the insurer's right to avoid. Thus Rix LJ in *Drake* suggested, albeit obiter, that the doctrine of good faith "should be capable of limiting the insurer's right to avoid in circumstances where that remedy, which has been described in recent years as draconian, would operate unfairly."[109] The case law on this point is, however, conflicting.[110] Even in those cases that support this view, there is no indi-

---

[101] Birds, *Birds' Modern Insurance Law*, 9th edn (2013), para.7.10.

[102] *Life Association of Scotland v Foster* (1873) 11 M. 351.

[103] *Life Association of Scotland v Foster* (1873) 11 M. 351 at 359.

[104] An attempt to argue that the prudent insurer test applied to cases of life assurance in Scotland failed in the Outer House, see *Cuthbertson v Friends Provident Life Office* [2006] CSOH 74; 2006 S.L.T. 567.

[105] *Hooper v Royal London General Insurance Co Ltd*, 1993 S.L.T. 679.

[106] *Hooper v Royal London General Insurance Co Ltd*, 1993 S.L.T. 679 at 683.

[107] *Hooper v Royal London General Insurance Co Ltd*, 1993 S.L.T. 679 at 683.

[108] See paras 6.5.2.1 and 6.5.2.2.

[109] *Drake Insurance Plc v Provident Insurance Plc* [2004] Q.B. 601, at [87], citing Lord Lloyd's interpretation of Lord Mansfield's decision in *Carter v Boehm* (1766) 3 Burr. 1905 at 1918 and [89].

[110] Justice Colman in *Strive Shipping Corp v Hellenic Mutual War Risks Association* [2002] EWHC 203 (Comm); [2002] Lloyd's Rep. I.R. 669 had suggested that the insurer would not have the right to avoid where it would be "unconscionable". This case is now inconsistent with the later Court of Appeal decision of *Brotherton v Aseguradora Colseguros SA (No.2)* [2003] EWCA Civ 705; [2003] Lloyd's Rep. I.R. 746.

cation of the steps that an insurer would require to take in order to ensure compliance with the duty of good faith. The parameters of this limitation are, as yet, unclear.

Matters excluded from the duty of disclosure

6.5.2.6 Certain classes of information are excluded from the duty of disclosure both under the common law and in terms of the Marine Insurance Act 1906. Firstly, the insured need not disclose any circumstance that diminishes the risk.[111] Thus, in *The Dora*,[112] the insured was not required to disclose the fact that a yacht would spend a large proportion of its time in the builders' yard, because it was at less risk there than it was at sea.[113]

Secondly, the insured need not disclose any circumstance known or presumed known to the insurer. These include matters of common notoriety or knowledge, and matters that the insurer, in the ordinary course of business, ought to know.[114] An example of this exclusion can be found in *Cohen, Sons & Co v Standard Marine Insurance Co Ltd*.[115] In this case the insurers were held unable to avoid a policy on the grounds that the insured had failed to disclose that an obsolete battleship under tow had no steam power to assist steering, because it was regarded as well known that such vessels often went to sea in this condition.

Thirdly, the insured need not disclose any circumstance that is waived by the insurer.[116] The case law suggests this might occur where the answer given by the insured ought to have put the insurer on inquiry. As Lord Esher MR explained in *Asfar & Co v Blundell*[117]:

> "But it is not necessary to disclose minutely every material fact . . . [T]he rule is satisfied if he discloses sufficient to call to the attention of the underwriters in such a manner that they can see that if they require further information they ought to ask for it."

In *Mann MacNeil & Steeves Ltd v Capital and Counties Insurance Co Ltd*[118] the insured disclosed that the ship was wooden with motor engines. As such, it was dangerously liable to fire damage, and the insurers ought to have been put on their inquiry to ask what cargo it was carrying. They failed to do so, thus failing to ascertain that the cargo carried was petrol. They were held to have waived their right to knowledge of that fact and were unable to avoid the policy.[119]

Waiver may also arise due to the nature of the proposal form. The insurer does not, by asking particular questions, waive his right to disclosure of any material outside the ambit of those questions. By contrast, the insured's duty of disclosure is an onerous one and is not so easily displaced. However, an insurer's question may require to be answered in some detail. Under normal principles of interpretation of contracts, requesting detailed information may indicate a waiver of the right to information not covered by the question. As an example, a particular question may request details of losses suffered in the previous five years. This would tend to suggest that the insurer has waived his right to disclosure of any losses outwith this period, even if those losses would otherwise be considered to be material.[120] An answer provided by the insured may be either incomplete or of such a nature as to put a reasonable insurer on his inquiry. Waiver may be established if the insurer, once put on notice, fails to pursue the particular matter with the insured.[121]

---

[111] Marine Insurance Act 1906 s.18(1).

[112] *Inversiones Manria SA v Sphere Drake Insurance Co, Malvern Insurance Co and Niagara Fire Insurance Co (The Dora)* [1989] 1 Lloyd's Rep. 69.

[113] *Inversiones Manria SA v Sphere Drake Insurance Co, Malvern Insurance Co and Niagara Fire Insurance Co (The Dora)* [1989] 1 Lloyd's Rep. 69, per Phillips J. at 89–90.

[114] Marine Insurance Act 1906 s.18(2).

[115] *George Cohen, Sons & Co v Standard Marine Insurance Co Ltd* (1925) 21 Ll. L. Rep. 30.

[116] Marine Insurance Act 1906 s.18(3).

[117] *Asfar & Co v Blundell* [1896] 1 Q.B. 123 at 129.

[118] *Mann MacNeil & Steeves Ltd v Capital and Counties Insurance Co Ltd* (1920) 124 L.T. 778.

[119] See, in particular, *Mann MacNeil & Steeves Ltd v Capital and Counties Insurance Co Ltd* (1920) 124 L.T. 778, per Atkin LJ at 781.

[120] See Birds, *Birds' Modern Insurance Law*, 9th edn (2013), p.126.

[121] *Container Transport International Inc v Oceanus Mutual Underwriting Assoc (Bermuda) Ltd* [1984] 1 Lloyd's Rep. 476, per Parker LJ at 511–512; *George Cohen, Sons & Co v Standard Marine Insurance Co Ltd* [1925] 21 Ll. L. Rep. 30.

Fourthly, certain circumstances may be treated as not requiring to be disclosed because of express or implied warranties.[122] Warranties, considered in more detail below, are fundamental terms of the insurance contract. Where the insurer can rely on a warranty granted by the insured which will, in effect, guarantee the veracity of a particular fact or facts, there will be no need to rely on the duty of disclosure.[123]

Ordinarily, convictions that are relevant to the risk insured against should be disclosed. However, the insured is not under an obligation to disclose convictions which are "spent" under s.4(3)(a) of the Rehabilitation of Offenders Act 1974. Convictions resulting in a prison sentence of more than two and one-half years can never become spent under the Act. It may be the case, however, that after the passage of a significant period of time, a particular conviction will not be considered to be material.[124]

The impact of the law of agency on the principles of disclosure

Under agency principles, a principal is deemed to be aware of facts which are known to his agent, **6.5.2.7** provided that the agent acquired the knowledge in the course the principal's business.[125] An example of the operation of this principle in an insurance context can be found in *Cruikshank v The Northern Accident Insurance Co Ltd*[126] where the proposal form contained the question: "Are there any circumstances which render you particularly liable to accident?" The insured dictated the response to the insurer's agent: "Slight lameness from birth". The insurers sought to avoid payment of a claim on the basis that the insured had failed to disclose the fact that he was extremely lame. The insurers were held unable to avoid payment because the extent of the lameness must have been visible to the insurer's agent when he met with the insured.

However, it is not always clear whether the principal of an insurance intermediary is the insurer or the insured. It has been held that the agent is acting on behalf of the insured, not the insurer, in the completion of the proposal form.[127] This is because it is the insured's duty to complete the proposal form, and, if he asks the agent to complete it, then that agent does so on the insured's behalf.[128] The agent may also act for the insurer and the insured at the same time. He may act as the insurer's agent, for example, in the acceptance of the risk under a cover note[129] and be treated as the insured's agent for the purposes of disclosure.[130] A clause that purports to have this effect may be challengeable by an insured under the Unfair Terms in Consumer Contracts Regulations 1999.[131]

The 2012 Act sets out certain rules for determining (for the purposes of the Act only) whether an **6.5.2.8** agent through whom a consumer insurance contract is effected is acting as the agent of the consumer or of the insurer.[132] The agent is to be taken as the insurer's agent in each of the following cases,

(a) when the agent does something in the agent's capacity as the appointed representative of the insurer for the purposes of the Financial Services and Markets Act 2000,

(b) when the agent collects information from the consumer, if the insurer has given the agent express authority to do so as the insurer's agent,

(c) when the agent enters into the contract as the insurer's agent, if the insurer had given the agent express authority to do so.[133]

---

[122] Marine Insurance Act 1906 s.18(3)(d).

[123] *The Gunford Ship Co Ltd v Thames and Mersey Marine Insurance Co Ltd*, 1910 S.C. 1072, per Lord President Dunedin at 1084.

[124] *Zurich General Accident and Liability Insurance Co Ltd v Livingston (No.2)*, 1940 S.C. 406, per Lord President Normand at 416.

[125] See the expression of this general rule in the context of Marine insurance in the Marine Insurance Act 1906 s.19.

[126] *Cruikshank v The Northern Accident Insurance Co Ltd* (1895) 23 R. 147.

[127] *McMillan v Accident Insurance Co*, 1907 S.C. 484; *Arif v Excess Insurance Group Ltd*, 1986 S.C. 317 at 319.

[128] *McMillan v Accident Insurance Co*, 1907 S.C. 484, per Lord Justice Clerk Macdonald at 490–491.

[129] *Stockton v Mason* [1978] 2 Lloyd's Rep. 430.

[130] *Arif v Excess Insurance Group Ltd*, 1986 S.C. 317.

[131] Unfair Terms in Consumer Contracts Regulations 1999 (SI 1999/2083); see Sch.2 para.1(n); and see para.6.12 below.

[132] Consumer Insurance (Disclosure and Representations) Act 2012 s.9 and Sch.2 paras 1–3.

[133] Consumer Insurance (Disclosure and Representations) Act 2012 Sch.2 para.2.

In all other cases, it is to be presumed that the agent is acting as the consumer's agent unless, in light of all the relevant circumstances, it appears that the agent is acting as the insurer's agent.[134] The Act provides examples of factors that tend to confirm or show which party the agent is acting for, such as an undertaking by the agent to the consumer to give impartial advice, as opposed to the scenario where the insurer asks the agent to solicit the consumer's custom.[135]

ICOBS—Disclosure[136]

6.5.2.9 ICOBS 8.1.1(3) provides that an insurer must not "unreasonably reject a claim (including by terminating or avoiding a *policy*)".

ICOBS 8.1.2(1)(a) provides that a rejection of a *consumer policyholder's* claim is unreasonable, except where there is evidence of fraud, if it is (in relation to contracts entered into or variations agreed on or before April 5, 2013) for non-disclosure of a fact material to the risk which the *policyholder* could not reasonably be expected to have disclosed.

ICOBS 5.1.4 makes reference to the general rule in ICOBS 8.1.1(3), and then goes on to provide that "Ways of ensuring that a *customer* knows what he must disclose include:

(1) explaining to a *commercial customer* the duty to disclose all circumstances material to a *policy*, what needs to be disclosed, and the consequences of any failure to make such a disclosure;

(2) ensuring that the *commercial customer* is asked clear questions about any matter material to the *insurance undertaking*;

(3) explaining to the *customer* the responsibility of *consumers* to take reasonable care not to make a misrepresentation and the possible consequences if a *consumer* is careless in answering the *insurer's* questions, or if a *consumer* recklessly or deliberately makes a misrepresentation; and

(4) asking the *customer* clear and specific questions about the information relevant to the *policy* being arranged or varied."

MISREPRESENTATION

6.5.3 An insurance contract, like any other contract, can be reduced if one of the parties has been induced to enter into it as a result of an operative misrepresentation. The doctrine of misrepresentation is not particularly important in an insurance context.[137] This is because the insurer is more likely to rely on the wider duty of disclosure. Additionally, the contract can only be reduced where the insured has made a representation prior to conclusion of the contract. Due to the use of "basis of the contract" clauses (discussed below) statements made by the insured are elevated to the level of contractual terms rather than representations.[138] It is easier to rely on actual breach of a term, rather than the more difficult route of misrepresentation, where the onus of proof lies on the insurer.[139]

---

[134] Consumer Insurance (Disclosure and Representations) Act 2012 Sch.2 para.3(1).

[135] Consumer Insurance (Disclosure and Representations) Act 2012 Sch.2 paras 3(3) and 3(4).

[136] Terms in italic below are defined in ICOBS, but should be sufficiently self-explanatory for the purposes of this chapter.

[137] Although the term is now used in consumer insurance contracts to include the duty to disclose information to the insurer.

[138] For the distinction between terms and representations, see W.W. McBryde, *Contract*, 3rd edn (Edinburgh: W. Green, 2007), paras 5–45 to 5–47.

[139] The misrepresentation route is even less attractive to insurers in England in the wake of *Economides v Commercial Union Assurance Co Plc* [1997] 3 All E.R. 636, in which it was held that it was sufficient if the insured honestly believed that what he had said was true and that there was no further requirement that he have reasonable grounds upon which to base his honest belief. As a result of this case, misrepresentation in insurance law differs from other types of misrepresentation in English law. In Scots law, a misrepresentation which induces a contract renders it voidable, even if the misrepresentor has an entirely reasonable belief in the truth of the statement made by him.

FRAUDULENT CLAIMS

An insurer is under no liability to meet a fraudulent claim.[140] The making of a fraudulent claim also **6.5.4**
rules out any valid claim that the insured might have had in relation to the same incident. As explained
by Sir Rodger Parker:

> "On what basis can an assured who asserts, for example, that he has been robbed of five fur coats
> and some valuable silver, when he has only been robbed of one fur coat and no silver, be allowed,
> when found out, to say, 'You must still pay me for the one of which I was truly robbed'?; I can
> see none and every reason why he should not recover at all."[141]

A similar approach was adopted by Lord Penrose in the Scottish case of *Fargnoli v GA Bonus Plc*.[142]
He also considered the more complex issue of the effect of a fraudulent claim on an earlier honest claim
under the same policy. The insurers sought to avoid liability for damage caused to a restaurant by fire
on the basis that a second fire had been wilfully caused by the insured. The insurance policy provided
that, where a fraudulent claim had been made by the insured, "all benefit" of the insurance policy was
to be forfeited by the insured. The insurers argued that the insured's fraud rendered the policy retrospectively void. Lord Penrose applied familiar principles of Scots contract law to find against the
insurers. Relying on *Lloyds Bank v Bamberger*[143] he explained that a material breach of contract permits
the innocent party to rescind, but does not "absolve parties from primary obligations already due for
performance at the time of the rescission".[144] The subsequent fraud by an insured would not, therefore,
permit an insurer to avoid liability in relation to an earlier honest claim.[145] The clause in this particular
case was not a model of good drafting, and it was construed *contra proferentem*, against the insurer.[146]
There might therefore be some doubt as to whether a more carefully drafted clause could render the
policy retrospectively null, although one would imagine that the courts would avoid such a conclusion.
Where the insured is a consumer, the Unfair Terms in Consumer Contract Regulations 1999 might also
strike at such a clause.[147] Because a fraudulent claim does not render the policy retrospectively null, the
insured is not bound to pay back any insurance proceeds received from previous claims made under the
policy.[148]

There may be no bar to recovery where the party guilty of fraud and the party making the claim under
the policy are different legal persons. Thus, in *Bank of Scotland v Guardian Royal Exchange*,[149] where
the benefit of an insurance policy was extended to a bank which was the security-holder over the
subjects, the fact that the owner of the subjects had burned down the subjects did not disentitle the bank
from claiming under the policy. The nature of the bank's interest was determined as a matter of construction of the policy, and was held to be an independent one, not one which derived from the owner.

---

[140] For a discussion of the difference between a fraudulent claim, and "evidence of fraud" in the making of a claim, see *Bate v Aviva Insurance UK Ltd* [2014] EWCA Civ 334.

[141] *Orakpo v Barclays Insurance Services* [1995] L.R.L.R. 443.

[142] *Fargnoli v GA Bonus Plc*, 1997 S.C.L.R. 12.

[143] *Lloyds Bank v Bamberger*, 1993 S.C. 570.

[144] *Fargnoli v GA Bonus Plc*, 1997 S.C.L.R. 12, per Lord Penrose at 22.

[145] See also *Direct Line Insurance v Fox* [2009] EWHC 386 (QB).

[146] *Fargnoli v GA Bonus Plc*, 1997 S.C.L.R. 12, per Lord Penrose at 21; see also *Bass Brewers Ltd v Independent Insurance Co Ltd*, 2002 S.C. 67 for the meaning of "*contra proferentem*".

[147] Unfair Terms in Consumer Contract Regulations 1999 (SI 1999/2083); see Sch.2 para.1(b). See also para.6.12. below.

[148] See also the House of Lords case *H.I.H. Casualty and General Insurance Ltd v Chase Manhattan Bank* [2003] 1 All E.R. 349 where it was held that it is not possible to excuse liability for fraud.

[149] *Bank of Scotland v Guardian Royal Exchange*, 1995 S.L.T. 763.

6.6   THE PROPOSAL FORM

6.6.1 WARRANTIES

Definition

6.6.1.1 The term "warranty" is a slippery one, which may have different meanings in different contexts. In an insurance context it is often defined, using English contractual terminology, as a "fundamental" term. The impact of this description is to identify it as an important term, breach of which would usually entitle the innocent party to avoid the contract.[150] "Warranty" is defined in the Marine Insurance Act 1906 as follows:

> "A warranty . . . means a promissory warranty, that is to say, a warranty by which the assured undertakes that some particular thing shall or shall not be done, or that some condition shall be fulfilled, or whereby he affirms or negatives the existence of a particular state of facts."[151]

The Act also details the consequences of breach of a warranty by the insured:

> "A warranty . . . is a condition which must be exactly complied with, whether it be material to the risk or not. If it be not so complied with, then, subject to any express provision in the policy, the insurer is discharged from liability as from the date of the breach of warranty, but without prejudice to any liability incurred by him before that date."[152]

No special form of words is required in order to create a warranty: "[A]ny form of words expressing the existence of a particular state of facts as a condition of the contract" is sufficient.[153] Nevertheless, the language used must quite clearly indicate that a warranty was intended.[154] Normal rules of contractual interpretation apply to the construction of insurance warranties.[155] In the context of consumer insurance contracts, it is not possible to convert a representation made by a consumer in connection with a proposed insurance contract (or variation of it) into a warranty.[156]

Past/present facts, or as to future facts

6.6.1.2 In certain cases, the insured will only warrant past or present facts. It is, however, possible to warrant that a state of affairs will prevail throughout the duration of the insurance contract. The latter type of warranty is known as a promissory or continuing warranty. In *Woolfall & Rimmer v Moyle*[157] one of the questions in the proposal form asked, "Are your machinery, plant and ways properly fenced and guarded and otherwise in good order and condition?", to which the insured answered, "Yes". It was held that the insured had not made a continuing warranty; in other words, he had not bound himself to ensure that the obligations contained in the question were fulfilled throughout the period of the insurance. The question was interpreted rather as being designed to provide the insurers with a picture of both the existing condition of the machinery and the type of person with whom they were dealing at the time of completion of the proposal form.[158] A similar result was reached in *Kennedy v Smith & Ansvar Insurance Co Ltd*,[159] in which the insured had completed the proposal form together with an "Abstinence and Membership Declaration", indicating that he was a total abstainer from alcohol and had been so

---

[150] Although see the effect in the insurance context described at para.6.6.1.4 below.

[151] See s.33(1).

[152] See s.33(3). The consequences of breach of a warranty are considered in more detail at para.6.6.1.4 below.

[153] *Dawsons Ltd v Bonnin*, 1922 S.C. (HL) 156, per Viscount Findlay at 166.

[154] *Dawsons Ltd v Bonnin*, 1922 S.C. (HL) 156, per Viscount Findlay at 165–167.

[155] See *Hussain v Brown* [1996] 1 Lloyds Rep. 627, per Saville LJ in the context of his discussion of promissory warranties, for which see below.

[156] Consumer Insurance (Disclosure and Representations) Act 2012 s.6. See also "Basis of the Contract" clauses below.

[157] *Woolfall & Rimmer v Moyle* [1942] 1 K.B. 66.

[158] *Woolfall & Rimmer v Moyle* [1942] 1 K.B. 66, per Lord Greene MR at 71.

[159] *Kennedy v Smith & Ansvar Insurance Co Ltd*, 1976 S.L.T. 110. See also *Hussain v Brown* [1996] 1 Lloyd's Rep. 627.

since birth. The defenders provided insurance cover to abstainers at reduced premiums. While driving his car home from a bowls competition with two of his friends, the party had stopped at a local pub and the insured had had one (or perhaps one and a half) pints of lager. When they continued the journey home, the insured's car had careered on to the wrong side of the dual carriageway, and both the passengers were killed. The defenders refused to pay out under the claim, arguing that, at the time of the accident, the abstinence declaration was false because the insured was under the influence of alcohol. The First Division held that the declaration of abstinence did not cover the insured's future behaviour, Lord President Emslie commenting that

> "if insurers seek to limit their liability under a policy by relying upon an alleged undertaking as to the future prepared by them and accepted by the insured, the language they use must be such that the terms of the alleged undertaking and its scope are clearly and unambiguously expressed or plainly implied and that any such alleged undertaking will be construed, *in dubio, contra proferentem*."[160]

As he indicates, because a continuing warranty may place an onerous obligation on the insured, such warranties must be very clearly expressed. An ambiguity will lead to the term being interpreted *contra proferentem*, against the interests of the party who is proposing it.[161] As Lord President Inglis explained in *Life Association of Scotland v Foster*:

> "This rule, founded on plain justice, is quite settled in practice. Insurance companies have the framing of their contracts in their own hands. They may make such conditions as they please, but they are bound so to express them as to leave no room for ambiguity. They must be construed . . . in the sense in which the agreement would be understood by a layman who was about to enter upon an insurance transaction."[162]

Where the warranty is drafted using the present tense, it is unlikely that it will be interpreted as a continuing one.[163]

The effect of a breach of a warranty will differ, depending upon whether it is classed as relating to past/present facts or future ones. If the former, then breach is considered to have occurred when the insurance contract was entered into, and the insurance contract will be avoided ab initio. If the latter, then breach discharges the insurer from liability from the date of the breach, but he will remain liable for claims arising prior to the breach.[164]

Warranties of opinion

The insured may grant a warranty of opinion, effectively meaning that he warrants that facts are true to **6.6.1.3** the best of his knowledge or belief. Should this be the case, he will only be in breach where he has been either dishonest or reckless in his answer. Thus, in *McPhee v Royal Insurance Co Ltd*[165] the insured completed a proposal form by adding the dimensions of the cabin cruiser which he was seeking to insure. The form contained a declaration that the information was provided to the best of his knowledge and belief. Rather than measuring the vessel himself, he telephoned the previous owner of the vessel and, having obtained the dimensions from him, inserted them into the proposal form. It transpired that these dimensions were incorrect and the insurers sought to avoid liability when the vessel was destroyed on the basis that the answers were not true to the best of the proposer's knowledge and belief. In holding that a material misstatement had been made, Lord Robertson explained:

---

[160] *Kennedy v Smith & Ansvar Insurance Co Ltd*, 1976 S.L.T. 110, per Lord President Emslie at 116–117.

[161] For an example of a warranty being construed *contra proferentem*, see *Provincial Insurance Co v Morgan* [1933] A.C. 240. Views differ on the exact meaning of the proferens, see Gloag, at 400–401; McBryde, Contract, 3rd edn (2007), paras 8–38 to 8–43.

[162] *Life Association of Scotland v Foster* (1873) 11 M. 351, per Lord President Inglis at 358. In the second sentence in this quote, the Lord President quotes Cockburn CJ in *Fowkes v The Manchester, etc. Assurance Association* (1863) 32 L.J.Q.B. 153.

[163] *Woolfall & Rimmer v Moyle* [1942] 1 K.B. 66.

[164] This is clear from the wording of s.33(3) of the Marine Insurance Act 1906 quoted above.

[165] *McPhee v Royal Insurance Co Ltd*, 1979 S.C. 304.

"To give true answers to the best of a person's knowledge and belief . . . means that he who gives the answers must have a reasonable basis for his knowledge and belief, and must not act recklessly in giving them."[166]

Effect of a breach of warranty

6.6.1.4 Section 33(3) of the Marine Insurance Act 1906 (quoted above in para.6.6.1.1) provides that the effect of a breach of warranty is to discharge the insurer from liability from the date of the breach, but without prejudice to any liability incurred by the insurer before that date. Despite this discharge of liability under the contract (effectively bringing its purpose to an end), the insurance contract remains in existence.

The House of Lords in *The Good Luck* considered the effect of a breach, with particular reference to the provisions of s.33(3).[167] The facts of the case were complicated. The owner of the ship "The Good Luck" insured it with the defendant insurers. The owners then mortgaged the ship to the plaintiff bank and assigned the benefit of the insurance to that bank. The insurers undertook to notify the bank promptly if the insurers ceased to insure the ship. The ship sailed into the Arabian Gulf, which constituted a breach of warranty. It was hit by Iraqi missiles and became a constructive total loss. The insurers discovered the breach of warranty, but failed to inform the bank. The bank, believing that the ship was covered by insurance, made further advances to the owners that would not have been made had the bank been aware that the ship was no longer insured. The bank sued the insurers for damages for breach of their undertaking. In the House of Lords, Lord Goff interpreted s.33(3) of the Marine Insurance Act 1906 as providing that, where the insured was in breach of a promissory or continuing warranty, the insurer was automatically discharged from liability under the insurance contract upon that breach occurring. The insurer did not need to take any additional steps as regards the contract to achieve that position. In the case of *The Good Luck*, discharge of liability had not been intimated to the bank, and therefore the insurers were in breach of their undertaking to the bank to notify them of that occurrence.

Subsequent to *The Good Luck*, it has been held that it is not open to an insurer to elect to waive a breach of warranty, and that only through estoppel (personal bar) can the insurer be found to have waived the breach.[168] It has also been held that the parties can agree in the contract to a suspension of cover, instead of discharge as a result of breach of warranty.[169]

BASIS OF THE CONTRACT CLAUSES

6.6.2.1 As stated above, no special form of words is required in order to create a warranty. It was previously very common to elevate each statement provided by the proposer on the proposal form to the level of a warranty by using a "basis of the contract" clause. Such a clause, normally located at the bottom of the proposal form, indicates that each of the questions and answers provided forms the basis of the contract between insurer and proposer. The effect on the insured is draconian. Because warranties must be strictly complied with, any inaccuracy in the information could discharge the insurer from liability.[170] Although such practices have been described as "mean and contemptible"[171] in a Scottish case, the validity of such clauses was recognised as part of the operation of the principle of freedom of contract.[172] That case, however, involved a contract between two businesses.

---

[166] *McPhee v Royal Insurance Co Ltd*, 1979 S.C. 304 at 339.

[167] *Bank of Nova Scotia v Hellenic Mutual War Risks Association (Bermuda) Ltd (The Good Luck)* [1992] 1 A.C. 233.

[168] *HIH Casualty & General Insurance v AXA Corporate Solutions* [2002] EWCA Civ 1253. This does not sit easily with s.34(3) of the 1906 Act, which provides that the insurer can waive a breach of warranty.

[169] *'The Lydia Flag'* [1998] 2 Lloyd's Rep 652. Also see para.6.6.3.

[170] See also *Standard Life Assurance Co v Weems* (1884) 11 R. (HL) 48, per Lord Blackburn at 50.

[171] *Glicksman v Lancashire & General Insurance Co Ltd* [1927] A.C. 139, per Lord Wrenbury at 144.

[172] *Unipac (Scotland) Ltd v Aegon Insurance Co Plc*, 1996 S.L.T. 1197 at 1202 (opinion of the court).

In relation to consumer insurance contracts, s.6 of the Consumer Insurance (Disclosure and Representations) Act 2012 specifically prohibits representations made by a consumer in connection with a proposed consumer insurance contract (or variation thereof) being converted into a warranty, whether through a "basis of the contract" clause or otherwise. **6.6.2.2**

CLAUSES DESCRIPTIVE OF THE RISK

In certain cases, what appears to be a warranty has been interpreted as a clause descriptive of, or delineating the risk, perhaps in an attempt to temper the consequences for the insured. Thus, where a particular term has not been complied with, if it is treated as a warranty, the insurer is discharged from liability. If it is treated as descriptive of the risk, the insurer will not be "on risk" during the period when the clause is not being complied with. Once the insured complies with the clause again, the insurer will revert to being "on risk". The consequences for the insured are therefore far less serious where the clause is treated as being descriptive of the risk rather than as a warranty. A clause which is descriptive of the risk may also be referred to as an exception from cover.[173] **6.6.3**

ICOBS—REPRESENTATIONS, CONDITIONS AND WARRANTIES[174]

ICOBS 8.1.1(3) provides that an insurer must not "unreasonably reject a claim (including by terminating or avoiding a *policy*)". **6.6.4**

ICOBS 8.1.2 provides that "A rejection of a *consumer policyholder's* claim is unreasonable, except where there is evidence of fraud, if it is:

(1) in relation to contracts entered into or variations agreed on or before 5 April 2013, for . . . (b) non-negligent misrepresentation of a fact material to the risk; or
(2) in relation to contracts entered into or variations agreed on or after 6 April 2013, for misrepresentation by a *customer* and the misrepresentation is not a *qualifying misrepresentation*; or
(3) for breach of warranty or condition unless the circumstances of the claim are connected to the breach [with additional qualifications for any *pure protection policy*]".

NOTICE

The policy may impose a time limit within which the insured must notify the loss. This can be important as, in certain circumstances, the requirement for timeous notification can amount to a condition precedent for liability under the policy.[175] The question of whether he has complied with the requirements of notice provisions is essentially one of interpretation of the policy itself. In one case, the policy required the insured or his personal representatives to provide notice of an accident "as soon as reasonably possible after it has come to the knowledge of the insured or of the insured's representative".[176] The insured died in an accident in India, and, although her personal representatives were informed of **6.6.5**

---

[173] See *Provincial Insurance v Morgan* [1933] A.C. 240, in which the insured had stated on a proposal form that the lorry to be insured would carry coal. He also signed a declaration stating that his answers were the basis of the contract. On the day on which it was damaged, the lorry had been carrying both coal and timber, although all of the timber had been delivered at the time of the accident. The insurers sought to avoid liability because the insured had failed to comply with the conditions as to goods carried. Lord Rutherford and Lord Wright in the House of Lords considered that the statements were not warranties but merely descriptive of the risk, an approach which had been taken in the Court of Appeal. The result of this approach was that the insurer was not on risk when the lorry was carrying timber, but was on risk once all of the timber had been delivered. The remaining judges in the House of Lords decided the case as a matter of interpretation of a promissory warranty.

[174] Terms in italic below are defined in ICOBS, but should be sufficiently self-explanatory for the purposes of this chapter.

[175] For example, see *Aspen Insurance Ltd v Pectel Ltd* [2008] EWHC 2804.

[176] *Verelst's Administratrix v Motor Union Insurance Co Ltd* [1925] 2 K.B. 137.

her death within one month of the accident, a year had passed before they discovered the existence of the insurance policy and intimated the loss to the insurance company. They were found to have notified the insurers timeously, Roche J explaining that "all existing circumstances must be taken into account",[177] including the means of the administratrix' knowledge of the policy. A similar approach has been taken by Lord Denning, who approved the interpretation of "immediate" as "with all reasonable speed considering the circumstances of the case".[178]

This more lenient approach may, however, be excluded where the clause imposes a specific time limit for notification. In a further case in which there had been a failure to comply with the notification period of 14 days, the insured was held not entitled to recover, even though the injury forming the basis of the insured's claim did not develop for a further eight months.[179] It is possible that an unduly restrictive notice period could be considered "unfair" and thus not binding in terms of the Unfair Terms in Consumer Contracts Regulations 1999.[180]

Where separate parties have insured their individual interests in property and that property is destroyed, both parties may need to notify. It has been held that the holders of a standard security over property were required to notify the insurer of the destruction of property in addition to the owner, even though both parties had insured with the same company.[181]

REPAYMENT OF THE PREMIUM

6.7 Where the risk under the policy is not run, and the insurer was therefore never going to be liable to pay, he is usually bound to return the premium to the insured. Otherwise the insured has paid the premium for nothing. As Lord Mansfield explained:

> "Equity implies a condition that the insurer shall not receive the price of running a risque, if he runs none … If the risque is not run, though it is by the neglect or even the fault of the party insuring, yet the insurer shall not retain the premium."[182]

So, if the contract of insurance is avoided by the insurer, then the premium should be repaid, unless perhaps the insured's conduct that results in the contract being avoided is considered to be fraudulent.[183] The premium may also be recoverable because the insured lacks an insurable interest, or because of breach of warranty on the part of the insured. If the insured has breached a promissory warranty, it may be the case that premiums paid up to the time of breach cannot be recovered, whereas premiums paid after the date of breach are recoverable, on the basis that the risk was run up to the point where the warranty was breached. It is, however, very common in practice for insurance policies to provide that all premiums will be forfeited by the insured in situations of breach of warranty, whether promissory or otherwise. Although there is an argument that such forfeiture clauses may operate as penalty clauses,[184] established authority suggests that they are enforceable.[185] Still, it is likely that such clauses are challengeable (where the insured is a private individual) under the Unfair Terms in Consumer Contracts Regulations 1999.[186]

---

[177] *Verelst's Administratrix v Motor Union Insurance Co Ltd* [1925] 2 K.B. 137 at 142.

[178] *Farrell v Federated Employers Insurance Association Ltd* [1970] 3 All E.R. 632 at 635, where he approved the approach of Fletcher Moulton LJ in *Re Coleman's Depositories Ltd and Life and Health Insurance Association* [1907] 2 K.B. 798. See also *Jacobs v Coster* [2000] Lloyd's Rep. I.R. 506 CA.

[179] *Cassel v Lancashire & Yorkshire Accident Insurance Co Ltd* (1885) T.L.R. 495.

[180] Unfair Terms in Consumer Contracts Regulations 1999 (SI 1999/2083); see Sch.2 para.1(b). See also para.6.12 below.

[181] *Bass Brewers Ltd v Independent Insurance Co Ltd*, 2002 S.C. 67.

[182] *Stevenson v Snow* (1761) Burr. 1237, per Lord Mansfield at 1240.

[183] Anderson v Fitzgerald (1853) 4 H.L. Cas 484.

[184] *Kumar v Life Insurance Corp of India* [1974] Lloyd's Rep. 147, per Kerr LJ at 154. On penalty clauses see McBryde, *Contract*, 3rd edn (2007), paras 22–146 et seq.

[185] *Standard Life Assurance Co v Weems* (1884) 11 R. (HL) 156; *Sparenborg v Edinburgh Life Assurance Co* [1912] 1 K.B. 195.

[186] Unfair Terms in Consumer Contracts Regulations 1999 (SI 1999/2083); see Sch.2 para.1(d). See also para.6.12 below.

If the insured has been at fault in entering into an insurance contract that is considered to be illegal, then he will be barred from recovering the premiums. Taking out an insurance policy on the life of another where the insured has no insurable interest is considered to be illegal under the Life Assurance Act 1774, and so the premiums would not be repayable.[187] Where the insured is innocent of any illegal conduct, for example because she was fraudulently induced by the insurer to enter into an illegal insurance policy, the premiums are repayable.[188]

INDEMNITY   6.8

GENERAL PRINCIPLE

The importance of the indemnity principle was commented on by Brett LJ in *Castellain v Preston*[189]:   **6.8.1**

> "The very foundation . . . of every rule which has been applied to insurance law is this, namely, that the contract of insurance contained in a marine or fire policy is a contract of indemnity, and of indemnity only, and that this contract means that the assured, in case of a loss against which the policy has been made, shall be fully indemnified, but shall never be more than fully indemnified. That is the fundamental principle of insurance, and if ever a proposition is brought forward which is at variance with it, that is to say, which either will prevent the assured from obtaining a full indemnity, or which will give to the assured more than a full indemnity, that proposition must certainly be wrong."[190]

In that case, the indemnity principle was applied in a situation where the insured had signed a contract to sell his house shortly before it was destroyed. Upon signing the contract, risk of damage/destruction had passed to the purchaser,[191] and accordingly he was entitled to recover the full value of the house from the purchaser, even though the house had been destroyed. It was held that he could not also recover the value of the house from the insurer because this would have the effect of over-compensating him.

The insured's loss is calculated at the time of the loss. Prima facie value will be determined by the cost of reinstatement or restoration where the subjects have not been fully destroyed. However, the rule may be displaced if it can be proved that the subjects actually had a different value at the time of the loss. Thus, in *Leppard v Excess Insurance Co*,[192] a cottage was insured for "full value" which was defined as "the amount which it would cost to replace the property in its existing form should it be totally destroyed". The owner had, shortly before the cottage was destroyed by fire, been seeking to sell it at a price of £3,000. It was held that this price represented the market value and was therefore the amount recoverable. Full reinstatement value was not recoverable given that this would have permitted the plaintiff to recover more than his actual loss. It should be borne in mind that the insurance policy may also contain an excess clause which will have an effect on what the insured can recover. Such clauses bind the insured to bear a specific amount or percentage of the loss personally.

The terms of the policy may lead to a departure from the indemnity principle. In particular, the value of the subjects may be specifically stated in the policy. Such a value will conclusively determine the amount recovered by the insured, regardless of whether it exceeds the actual value of the subjects at the time of the loss. As an example, in *Elcock v Thomson*[193] the subjects had been partially damaged. The insured was able to recover a percentage of the agreed value, notwithstanding the fact that this was several times the actual value of the subjects.

---

[187] See s.1; and see para.6.4 above.
[188] *Hughes v Liverpool Victoria Legal Friendly Society* [1916] 2 K.B. 482.
[189] *Castellain v Preston* (1883) 11 Q.B.D. 380.
[190] *Castellain v Preston* (1883) 11 Q.B.D. 380 at 386.
[191] This is an English case. In Scotland, the parties would normally contract out of the common law rule that provides that risk passes on conclusion of missives, and specify that it will pass on completion of the sale.
[192] *Leppard v Excess Insurance Co* [1979] 2 All E.R. 668.
[193] *Elcock v Thomson* [1949] 2 K.B. 755.

A further departure from the indemnity principle occurs in policies which supply "new for old", in other words where the insurer replaces the item rather than paying to the insured its market value, or bears the cost of repair or reinstatement. The insurer may seek to deduct a proportion of the cost of repair on the basis that repairing an item may actually increase its value.

The concept of underinsurance may also have an impact on the amount recoverable by the insured. This issue is covered by the Marine Insurance Act 1906:

> "Where the assured is insured for an amount less than the insurable value or, in the case of a valued policy, for an amount less than the policy valuation, he is deemed to be his own insurer in respect of any uninsured balance."[194]

As a result, where the insured is underinsured, he can recover only the proportion of the sum insured which the damage bears to the value of the subjects. Thus, if subjects worth £2,000 are insured for only £1,000, and suffer £600 damage, then the insured can recover only £300 (50 per cent of the loss). However, this principle only applies in marine insurance. In non-marine cases the insured is entitled to recover the full extent of his loss, notwithstanding the fact that he was underinsured. An insurer can avoid this result by inserting an "average" clause which would, in effect, apply the same principle to non-marine situations. Average clauses, although common in commercial insurance, are rare in policies over domestic heritable property.

6.8.2 SUBROGATION

General principle

6.8.2.1 The principle of subrogation is a consequence of the principle of indemnity and cannot, therefore, arise in cases of life insurance. It is often stated to involve two separate rules. Firstly, as stated in *Castellain v Preston*, the insured must never be more than fully indemnified.[195] He cannot profit from his loss, and any profit which he does make is payable to the insurer. Secondly, where the insurer has indemnified the insured, the insurer is entitled to all the insured's rights against third parties in respect of the loss itself, and any sums that the insured may receive which diminish the loss. The insurer takes the place of, or "stands in the shoes of", the insured in relation to the insured's rights against third parties. As Brett LJ observed in *Castellain v Preston*:

> "[A]s between the underwriter and the assured the underwriter is entitled to the advantage of every right of the assured, whether such right consists in contract, fulfilled or unfulfilled, or in remedy for tort . . . or in any other right . . . legal or equitable."[196]

The sections which follow analyse both aspects of subrogation as they operate in practice.

Insurer must sue in the name of the insured

6.8.2.2 The insurer, once subrogated to the rights of the insured, must sue in the name of the insured. He cannot sue in his own name, as would be the case where the insured had assigned its rights to the insurer. Lord President Rodger confirmed this:

> "[W]here the insured is subrogated to the rights of the assured, it must raise any action in the name of the assured. As Lord Goff explained in his speech in *Esso Petroleum* at p.878F-H (p.663E-F), the payment by the insurer indemnifying the assured does not have the effect of transferring the assured's rights to the insurer and so the insurer cannot simply go ahead and itself

---

[194] Marine Insurance Act 1906 s.81.

[195] Castellain v Preston (1883) 11 Q.B.D. 380, per Brett LJ at 386, quoted above; *Yorkshire Insurance Co Ltd v Nisbet Shipping Co Ltd* [1962] 2 Q.B. 330, per Diplock J at 339–340.

[196] *Castellain v Preston* (1883) 11 Q.B.D. 380, per Brett LJ at 388, cited with approval by Lord Jauncey in *Esso Petroleum Co Ltd v Hall Russell & Co Ltd*, 1988 S.L.T. 874 HL at 1140L.

raise actions based on those rights. Nonetheless, because the insurer has indemnified the assured, the law gives it the right to insist that the assured should authorise it to use the assured's name in proceedings against third parties. If need be, the insurer can take proceedings to compel the assured to grant the necessary authority."[197]

Insurer's right arises only when the insurer has compensated the insured

The insurer must have actually paid the insured before he can be subrogated to the rights of the insured. **6.8.2.3** An example of this principle can be found in the case of *Scottish Union and National Insurance Co v Davis*[198] in which Davis' car had been damaged when a coping stone fell from a building, striking the car. He took the car to a garage to be repaired, and the garage made three, ultimately unsuccessful, attempts at repair, before Davis eventually took the car away. In the meantime, the garage sent their bill direct to the insurers who paid the bill without first checking that the insured's car had been repaired satisfactorily. Davis managed to recover compensation in tort from the owners of the building in settlement of his claim against them. When the insurers claimed to be entitled through subrogation to this sum their claim failed. This was because the insurers had not indemnified Davis in respect of his loss.

Any defect in the insured's title to sue will similarly affect the insurer

Given that subrogation is, in truth, a mechanism which allows the insurer to enforce the rights of the **6.8.2.4** insured, where the insured's title to sue a third party is defective in some respect, this defect will also affect the insurer. In *Simpson & Co v Thomson*[199] two vessels belonging to the same owner collided and one sank. The owner paid a sum into court to compensate the various parties who had suffered a loss as a result of the collision and who therefore had a claim against him under the Merchant Shipping Acts. The owner's insurers paid the owner and then tried to claim a proportion of the fund paid into court. They were unsuccessful because the only action that the insured had, as the owner of a damaged ship, was an action against himself, as the negligent party. It is not possible for the insured to sue himself, and so there was no action for the insurers to be subrogated to.

It has been argued that an insurer was not entitled to be subrogated to the insured's right on the basis that, where the loss was met by the insurer, there was no loss and therefore no right to which to be subrogated to.[200] That argument was rejected, Lord Rodger pointing out that the same argument could be used by any party who was potentially liable to an insured, leaving no room whatsoever for the operation of the principle of subrogation.

Where more than one person has an interest in the same property

Particular problems arise in commercial leases where the landlord generally controls the insurance of **6.8.2.5** the subjects, recovering the cost of the premiums from the tenant either by direct reimbursement or through a service charge. The policy may, for example, cover the subjects against damage by fire. The subjects may, however, be destroyed by a fire which is caused by the negligence of the tenants. The insurers will compensate the landlords as owners of the subjects in terms of the insurance policy. The insurers may then seek to be subrogated to the landlord's rights against the negligent party, namely the tenant. If this principle were permitted to operate, then the tenant would be in the position of having paid for the insurance and yet being liable for the cost of repairing the damage caused to the subjects. Insuring in joint names of the landlord and the tenant, or obtaining for the tenant a waiver by the insurers of their subrogation rights can avoid this result. Neither of these options is attractive to the landlord, and the tenant is most likely to have his "interest" simply noted on the insurance policy, even

---

[197] *Caledonia North Sea Ltd v London Bridge Engineering Ltd*, 2000 S.L.T. 1123, per Lord President Rodger at 1140, referring to the speech of Lord Goff in *Esso Petroleum Co Ltd v Hall Russell & Co Ltd*, 1988 S.L.T. 874.

[198] *Scottish Union and National Insurance Co v Davis* [1970] 1 Lloyd's Rep. 1.

[199] *Simpson & Co v Thomson* (1877) 5 R. (H.L.) 40.

[200] *Caledonia North Sea Ltd v London Bridge Engineering Ltd*, 2000 S.L.T. 1123, per Lord President Rodger at 1134A–1136A, affirmed by 2002 S.L.T. 278 HL.

though the legal effect of noting has not been tested. Even if such mechanisms were not employed, the courts can construe the lease as disclosing no intention to impose ultimate liability on the tenant through the exercise of subrogation rights.[201] This was the outcome in *Mark Rowlands Ltd v Berni Inns Ltd*,[202] where the court was clearly influenced by the particular terms of the lease, specifically that the landlord was obliged to use the insurance proceeds to rebuild the subjects, that the tenant was not liable to repair damage caused by any of the insured risks, and that the insurance was for the benefit of both the landlord and the tenant.

Co-insurance cases

6.8.2.6   Where several parties are insured under the same insurance policy, and damage is caused by the negligence of one of those parties, the insurer may not be able to be subrogated to the rights of one insured against the negligent party. Thus in *Petrofina (UK) Ltd v Magnaload*[203] an insurance policy had been taken out to cover the construction and extension of an oil refinery. The insured was defined as the main contractor, subcontractors and various other parties involved in the construction. Damage was caused by the negligence of one of the subcontractors. The insurers settled a claim by one of the insured parties, and then brought a claim against the negligent subcontractors, claiming to be subrogated to the insured party's right. It was held that the insurers could have no right of subrogation against a negligent party who was also an insured under the same insurance policy.

Over the course of several years, views have changed as to the legal basis of this rule. In *Petrofina* the denial of subrogation rights seems to be based on the necessity to avoid circuity of action. In other words, if the insurers used subrogation rights against the negligent insured, the latter could then claim indemnity against the insurers. Subsequently, however, other case law suggested that the legal basis was that an implied term must be inserted into the contract excluding the exercise of subrogation rights, on the grounds that it would be inconsistent with the insurer's duty to the co-insured.[204] This view seemed to find favour in the House of Lords case *Co-operative Retail Services Ltd v Taylor Young Partnership Ltd*.[205] However, in an English Court of Appeal case, *Tyco Fire & Integrated Solutions (UK) Ltd v Rolls-Royce Motor Cars Ltd*,[206] Rix LJ approved the approach of Lord Hope in *Co-operative* (although Rix LJ's statements were obiter). Referring to the judgment of Brook LJ in the Court of Appeal stage of *Co-operative* and the speech of Lord Hope in the House of Lords in that same case, Rix LJ stated:

> "It . . . appears that the doctrine of circuity of action is no longer favoured (see Brooke LJ at para 69 and Lord Hope at para 64), and that the doctrine of an implied term in the insurance contract has now been replaced by a doctrine of the true construction of the underlying contract for the provision of joint names insurance (Brook LJ at para 73 and Lord Hope at para 65): and that this last doctrine may operate with the assistance of an implied term to the effect that co-insureds cannot sue one another in respect of damage in respect of which they are jointly insured (Lord Hope at para 65).
>
> I too would respectfully wish to adopt Lord Hope's preference to say that 'the true basis of the rule is to be found in the contract between the parties'."[207]

---

[201] See *Barras v Hamilton*, 1994 S.L.T. 949.

[202] *Mark Rowlands Ltd v Berni Inns Ltd* [1986] Q.B. 211.

[203] *Petrofina (UK) Ltd v Magnaload* [1984] Q.B. 127. See also *Hopewell Project Management Ltd v Ewbank Preece Ltd* [1998] 1 Lloyd's Rep. 448; *Fraser Pile & Dredge Ltd v Can-Dive Services Ltd* [2000] 1 Lloyd's Rep. 199.

[204] *Stone Vickers Ltd v Appledore Ferguson Shipbuilders Ltd* [1991] 2 Lloyd's Rep. 288; *National Oilwell Ltd v Davy Offshore Ltd* [1993] 1 Lloyd's Rep. 582.

[205] *Co-operative Retail Services Ltd v Taylor Young Partnership Ltd* [2000] 2 All E.R. 865. See also *Tyco Fire & Integrated Solutions (UK) Ltd v Rolls-Royce Motor Cars Ltd* [2008] EWCA Civ 286, per Rix LJ at [76]. See also Davidson, "Limited Interests in Property, Covenants to Insure and Subrogation", 1994 S.L.T. (News) 1.

[206] *Tyco Fire & Integrated Solutions (UK) Ltd v Rolls-Royce Motor Cars Ltd* [2008] EWCA Civ 286, overturning the decision at first instance [2007] EWHC 3159 (TCC).

[207] *Tyco Fire & Integrated Solutions (UK) Ltd v Rolls-Royce Motor Cars L*td [2008] EWCA Civ 286, per Rix LJ at [75]–[76].

What is clear from *Tyco Fire & Integrated Solutions (UK) Ltd v Rolls-Royce Motor Cars Ltd*[208] is the need to pay particular attention to the manner in which the contracts are drafted. Those contracts may indeed set up a regime that is intended to cover the question of whether the co-insureds are to have a right to sue one another, and therefore whether the insurer can be subrogated to the co-insured's right. According to Rix LJ, the drafting may indicate an intention that the co-insured is *not* to be protected from a claim by the injured co-insured. If that is the case, there is no reason why the insurer cannot exercise subrogation rights.[209] The "rule" in *Co-operative Retail Services Ltd* is not, in fact, a "rule" but rather an implied term that can be defeated by express drafting to the contrary.[210]

Extent of subrogation rights

If the subjects are underinsured, then the insured may seek to recover any shortfall from the negligent party. This could operate in different ways: either the insurer could be entitled to exercise subrogation rights once he has paid out the insurance proceeds (albeit that these are less than the insured's loss), or the insurer could only be entitled to do so once the insured had been fully compensated, including retaining any shortfall the insured has recovered from the negligent party. It appears that the former is the correct analysis: the insurer can exercise his subrogation rights once he has indemnified the insured regardless of whether the insured's actual loss exceeds the amount of the insurance proceeds.[211] **6.8.2.7**

This question was analysed in *Lord Napier and Ettrick v Hunter*,[212] where Lord Templeman in the House of Lords used the following figures to illustrate the issue. He assumed that the loss suffered by the insured was £160,000. The insurers were only liable to meet £125,000 of this amount, and the policy contained an excess of £25,000. The insurers paid the insured £100,000 of insurance proceeds. The insured recovered £130,000 from the third party liable for the loss. Their Lordships considered whether the insured was entitled to retain £60,000 of the amount recovered from the third party, which, when added to the £100,000 insurance proceeds would fully compensate him for his total loss of £160,000, or whether the insurer was entitled to a greater proportion of the amount recovered from the third party, leaving the insured under-compensated. They indicated that the latter alternative was correct. Because there was an excess of £25,000, the insured was considered to be his own insurer for this amount. The insured would be entitled to retain a proportion of the £130,000 recovered from the third party. This would be his uninsured loss (£60,000) minus the excess (£25,000), namely £35,000. The insurers were entitled to the balance of £95,000 (£130,000 minus £35,000). Thus the insured would not be fully compensated for his loss. In the aftermath of this case, it is clear that where a policy contains an excess clause, the insurer is entitled to recover everything that he can through subrogation, before the insured can recover any of the excess from the third party.

The *Napier* case considered the effect of an excess clause rather than the problem of underinsurance. However, Lord Templeman also considered the problem of underinsurance and indicated that the insured is considered to be his own insurer for any loss above the sum insured against.[213]

In rare cases there may be a profit left over after subrogation rights have been exercised by the insurer. If that is the case, the insured is entitled to retain such a profit. The insurer's subrogation rights extend only to the amount which they have paid to the insured, and not to any profit over and above that indemnification. In *Yorkshire Insurance Co Ltd v Nisbet Shipping Co Ltd*[214] a vessel insured for £72,000 was sunk as a result of the negligence of the Canadian Government. The insurer paid to the insured £72,000 in terms of the insurance policy. The insured thereafter successfully sued the Canadian Government. However, between payment of the insurance proceeds and the court action, the pound sterling had been devalued. When the payment made by the Canadian Government following the court

---

[208] *Tyco Fire & Integrated Solutions (UK) Ltd v Rolls-Royce Motor Cars Ltd* [2008] EWCA Civ 286, overturning the decision at first instance [2007] EWHC 3159 (TCC).

[209] *Tyco Fire & Integrated Solutions (UK) Ltd v Rolls-Royce Motor Cars Ltd* [2008] EWCA Civ 286, per Rix LJ at [77].

[210] *Tyco Fire & Integrated Solutions (UK) Ltd v Rolls-Royce Motor Cars Ltd* [2008] EWCA Civ 286, per Rix LJ at [77].

[211] *Lord Napier and Ettrick v Hunter (No.1)* [1993] A.C. 713.

[212] *Lord Napier and Ettrick v Hunter (No.1)* [1993] A.C. 713.

[213] *Lord Napier and Ettrick v Hunter (No.1)* [1993] A.C. 713, per Lord Templeman at 730.

[214] *Yorkshire Insurance Co Ltd v Nisbet Shipping Co Ltd* [1962] 2 Q.B. 330.

action was transmitted to London, it amounted to almost £127,000. The insured accounted to the insurer the sum of £72,000 only. In an action by the insurer in which it sought payment of the remaining £55,000, it was held that the insurer's right was limited to recovery from the insured of the sum paid by the insurer to the insured. Although this case was decided through the application of the Marine Insurance Act 1906,[215] there is no reason to suppose that it does not represent a general rule.

6.8.3 DOUBLE INSURANCE AND CONTRIBUTION

General principles

6.8.3.1 The insured may insure his property with as many insurers as he wishes. Nevertheless, the principle of indemnity will ensure that the insured is not over-indemnified for his loss. The insured, in the event of a loss, may choose which insurer to claim against. Although that insurer cannot, at that stage, object that other insurers are similarly liable, once he has paid the claim, he can demand that the other insurers contribute their share of the loss.[216] Contribution is stated to be subject to further conditions, namely: the insurances must cover the same subjects; the policies must cover the same risks; the same interests must be covered; and the policies must be enforceable.[217]

The legal basis of the right to contribution is not clear. It cannot arise from contract given that the insurers do not have a contractual relationship with one another. In older cases it is identified as an equitable principle,[218] whereas, in a modern context, it has been suggested that its purpose is the avoidance of unjust enrichment.[219]

Contractual clauses play an important role in this area, and their impact on the general rules of contribution is considered below.

Calculating ratios of contribution

6.8.3.2 The rules for determining the amounts of contribution to be paid by each insurer are complex, and may often depend upon insurance practice rather than legal rules. There are two possible approaches. The simpler approach, known as the "maximum liability" approach, dictates that each insurer will pay the proportion of the loss which the sum he has insured bears to the total of all sums insured. This approach can be seen in property insurance where the sum insured by different insurers is likely to be the same. The alternative approach is known as the "independent liability" approach. This approach assumes that there has been no double insurance before calculating the individual insurer's liability as normal. That amount is then assessed as a proportion of all of the insurance taken out by the insured, in order to calculate the contribution payable by that particular insurer.

The right to claim contribution is not confined to cases of co-insurance. In one case,[220] an insurer was found entitled to a 100 per cent contribution from a party who had agreed to indemnify the insured against loss arising from a contract between the insured and that party. On the effect of contribution, Lord Rodger commented:

> "If the insurers and defenders were properly to be regarded as co-obligants on an equal footing in a joint and several obligation to indemnify the pursuers, the insurers would indeed have a right to relief to the extent of a contribution of their pro rata share from the defenders. That is the position which the law has adopted in respect of double insurance where two insurers are liable to indemnify the assured in the events which have happened. Reflecting the commercial reality and the practical understanding of insurers, the law treats the matter as if there were really only one

---

[215] In particular s.79(1).

[216] *Sickness and Accident Assurance Association Ltd v General Accident Assurance Corporation Ltd* (1892) 19 R. 977.

[217] *Legal and General Assurance Society Ltd v Drake Insurance Co Ltd* [1991] 2 Lloyd's Rep. 36, per Lloyd LJ at 38; per Ralph Gibson LJ at 44.

[218] *Legal and General Assurance Society Ltd v Drake Insurance Co Ltd* [1991] Lloyd's Rep. 36, per Nourse LJ at 42.

[219] Birds, *Birds' Modern Insurance Law*, 9th edn (2013), Ch 18.

[220] *Caledonia North Sea Ltd v London Bridge Engineering Ltd*, 2000 S.L.T. 1123; affirmed by 2002 S.L.T. 278 HL.

insurance and the insurers are seen as co-obligants, each liable to bear a one-half share of the liability."[221]

Applying those principles to the facts of the particular case he commented:

> "[I]f, as I have held, both the insurers and the defenders in the present cases are under an obligation to indemnify the pursuers but, as between the defenders and the insurers, the defenders should bear the ultimate liability, then the insurers have a right to total relief from the defenders. It follows that the defenders have no corresponding right of relief against the insurers. In other words, the insurers are like the cautioner who can bring an action of relief to recover the whole of his expenditure from the principal debtor but is not subject to any obligation of relief towards the principal debtor."[222]

This case serves to emphasise the distinction between the right to contribution, which is the insurer's own independent right of relief, and his right to subrogation, where he stands in the place of the insured to enforce the latter's right, in this case a right of indemnity.

"Rateable proportion" clauses

As stated above, where the insured chooses to claim against a particular insurer, it is not open to that insurer to avoid full payment of the claim on the grounds that other insurance policies have been taken out over the same risk. He must meet the claim and only then proceed to claim a contribution from the other insurer. Contractual clauses, known as "rateable proportion" clauses, are used by insurers to avoid this result. Such a clause states that the insurer will only be liable for a rateable proportion of the insured's loss and no more. Assuming that each of the insurers insuring a specific risk has used such a clause, the burden then falls on the insured to claim the relevant proportion from each insurer. Despite having used a rateable proportion clause, the insurer may nevertheless pay the insured's claim in full, perhaps because the existence of further insurance was unknown to the insurer. If the insurer later becomes aware of other insurance, he may seek to recover a contribution from that insurer. **6.8.3.3**

Contribution where the second insurer is not liable to the insured

Difficulties may arise where the second insurer would have had a defence against paying out a claim to the insured. Does the existence of this defence mean that the first insurer will be unable to recover a contribution from the second insurer, or will a contribution be payable nevertheless? This specific question was considered in the case of *Legal and General Assurance Society Ltd v Drake Insurance Co Ltd*,[223] in which a motorist had taken out two policies, both of which included clauses making it a condition precedent to liability that the insured notify the insurer of an incident which might give rise to a claim. When an accident did occur, the insured only notified and claimed against one insurer who paid out in full. There was thus a breach of the second insurance contract, namely the failure to provide that insurer with notice of the accident. It was held that, although the second insurer was not liable to the insured, the first insurer did have an enforceable right of contribution against the second insurer. The Court of Appeal appeared to base its decision on equitable considerations. Their Lordships indicated that questions of contribution should be considered at the time of the loss. In their opinion, in this case, both insurers were potentially liable at the time of the loss.[224] The cover lapsed due to the failure of the insured to notify the second insurers of the accident. The cover therefore could not lapse until after the loss had occurred. However, the second insurer was ultimately found not liable to make payment of any contribution. This was because the first insurer's policy contained a rateable proportion clause. Given that there were two insurance policies in force, the first insurer's liability was limited to one-half of the loss. It is part of the principle of contribution that the first insurer who pays a claim must **6.8.3.4**

---

[221] *Caledonia North Sea Ltd v London Bridge Engineering Ltd*, 2000 S.L.T. 1123, per Lord President Rodger at 1141–1142.
[222] *Caledonia North Sea Ltd v London Bridge Engineering Ltd*, 2000 S.L.T. 1123, per Lord President Rodger at 1142.
[223] *Legal and General Assurance Society Ltd v Drake Insurance Co Ltd* [1991] 2 Lloyd's Rep. 36.
[224] *Legal and General Assurance Society Ltd v Drake Insurance Co Ltd* [1991] 2 Lloyd's Rep. 36, per Lloyd LJ at 38.

pay under a legal liability and not "voluntarily". Because the first insurer was considered to have paid the full amount "voluntarily", no contribution was payable by the second insurer.

The *Drake* decision was questioned in the later case of *Eagle Star Insurance Co v Provincial Insurance Plc*.[225] In particular, doubt was cast on the suggestion that the relevant time for assessing questions of contribution was the time of the loss. The Privy Council suggested that the correct time for this assessment was the date of any judgment against the insurer who pays a claim to the insured. It does not, however, call into question the principle that the insurer claiming contribution must not pay a claim "voluntarily".

Clauses disclaiming liability where double insurance occurs

6.8.3.5 Insurance companies seek to avoid the problems of double insurance by using contractual terms which provide that, if the insured has taken out a second policy to cover the same risk, the original insurer is not liable under the first policy. However, both insurance policies may contain such a clause, which has the effect of leaving the insured with no cover whatsoever. This situation has been considered in several cases, most notably in *Weddell v Road Transport and General Insurance*.[226] In the course of explaining why such clauses could not operate to deny the insured any cover, Rowlatt J commented:

> "In my judgment it is unreasonable to suppose that it was intended that clauses such as these should cancel each other . . . with the result that, on the ground in each case that the loss is covered elsewhere, it is covered nowhere. On the contrary the reasonable construction is to exclude from the category of co-existing cover any cover which is expressed to be itself cancelled by such co-existence, and to hold in such cases that both companies are liable, subject of course in both cases to any rateable proportion clause which there may be."[227]

Although the motivation behind this decision is clear, the reasoning is not. Where Rowlatt J refers to "intention" he is not referring to contractual intention, given that there is no contractual relationship between the two insurers. It may simply be that, as a matter of policy, the courts are not willing to allow the insured to be left without cover.

As might be expected, insurers developed amended exclusion clauses to avoid the result in *Weddell*. In *Steelclad Ltd v Iron Trades Mutual Insurance Co Ltd*[228] each of the policies contained the following clause: "The Company shall not be liable for any loss or damage which is insured or would *but for the existence of this policy* be insured by any other policy."[229]

Referring to the "critical words" of this clause Lord Stott commented:

> "They would appear to have been expressly designed to meet this situation and to close the door to the escape route open to the court in *Weddell*."[230]

An Extra Division of the Inner House decided that the policies would not have cancelled one another out in any event because the wording of the relevant clause in one policy was not sufficiently wide to refer to the other policy. Although the court could therefore have avoided analysing the legal position where both policies use similar exclusion clauses, it did not do so. Following *Weddell*,[231] the court indicated that such clauses would not cancel one another out. Lord Hunter explained:

> "Each of these conditions, regarded separately, would appear to have a sensible and reasonable content. But when they co-exist they would, if applied absolutely literally, produce the absurd and inequitable result that the pursuers are not, and never at any time were, entitled to

---

[225] *Eagle Star Insurance Co v Provincial Insurance Plc* [1993] 3 All E.R. 1.

[226] *Weddell v Road Transport and General Insurance* [1932] 2 K.B. 563.

[227] *Weddell v Road Transport and General Insurance* [1932] 2 K.B. 563, per Rowlatt J at 567.

[228] *Steelclad Ltd v Iron Trades Mutual Insurance Co Ltd*, 1984 S.L.T. 304.

[229] Author's emphasis.

[230] *Steelclad Ltd v Iron Trades Mutual Insurance Co Ltd*, 1983 S.L.T. 347, per Lord Stott at 348.

[231] *Steelclad Ltd v Iron Trades Mutual Insurance Co Ltd*, 1984 S.L.T. 304, per Lord Hunter at 307; per Lord Robertson at 310. See also Davidson, "Double Insurance Exclusion of Liability and Justice" (1986) 54 S.L.G. 3.

be indemnified under either policy . . . In that situation, I do not feel compelled to apply the absolutely literal construction . . .".[232]

PROXIMATE CAUSE

The insurer will not be liable for the insured's losses unless those losses were caused by the risks **6.9** insured against. However, as in other areas of law, identifying the cause of a loss can be a difficult exercise. In marine insurance in terms of the Marine Insurance Act 1906,[233] and in other types of insurance by virtue of the common law,[234] the court must identify the "proximate cause". Lord Shaw summed up the difficulties of the assessment of causation in *Leyland Shipping Co Ltd v Norwich Union Fire Insurance Society Ltd* as follows:

> "The chain of causation is a handy expression, but the figure is inadequate. Causation is not a chain, but a net. At each point influences, forces, events, precedent and simultaneous, meet; and the radiation from each point extends infinitely. At the point where these various influences meet it is for the judgment as upon a matter of fact to declare which of the causes thus joined at the point of effect was the proximate and which was the remote cause. What does 'proximate' here mean? To treat proximate cause as if it was the cause which is proximate in time is, as I have said, out of the question. The cause which is truly proximate is that which is proximate in efficiency."[235]

Thus, the proximate cause is not necessarily the last cause or event. At this stage, as is apparent from the above quote, the practice was to select one cause as "the" proximate cause from a number of competing causes. In more recent times, it has been recognised that there may be several concurrent proximate causes rather than one important proximate cause. Thus in *JJ Lloyd Instruments Ltd v Northern Star Insurance Co Ltd*[236] the concurrent causes of the damage to a ship were found to be its unseaworthiness and adverse sea conditions, only the latter of which was a risk covered by the policy. The Court of Appeal took the view that, where there is no express exclusion of liability, the insured is entitled to recover where there are concurrent causes, at least one of which is an insured risk.[237] It follows from this approach, however, that where liability for one of the concurrent causes is excluded, the insurer will not be liable.[238]

Where human action is involved, it is assumed that such action and not the insured risk is the proximate cause of the loss. An exception to this principle occurs where human action has been taken to avoid the risk. An example of this exception is found in *Johnstone v West of Scotland Insurance Co*,[239] where the house next door to the insured subjects was damaged by fire. A dangerously unstable gable which had been left standing was removed on the instructions of the Dean of Guild. During removal the gable fell on to the insured subjects and destroyed them. Even though the actual damage had been caused as a result of intentional human action, it was held that the proximate cause remained damage by fire. As this was insured under the policy, the insurers were held liable.

The wording of the actual policy may limit the insured's rights in this area. It is common for the policy either to stipulate that the damage must be caused "directly or indirectly" by the insured risk or

---

[232] *Steelclad Ltd v Iron Trades Mutual Insurance Co Ltd*, 1984 S.L.T. 304, per Lord Hunter at 308.

[233] Marine Insurance Act 1906 s.55(1).

[234] *Gray v Barr* [1971] 2 Q.B. 554, per Lord Denning MR at 567; per Salmon LJ at 579; *Wayne Tank and Pump Co Ltd v Employers Liability Assurance Corp Ltd* [1974] Q.B. 57, per Lord Denning MR at 66.

[235] *Leyland Shipping Co Ltd v Norwich Union Fire Insurance Society Ltd* [1918] A.C. 350, per Lord Shaw at 369. See also *Yorkshire Dale SS Co Ltd v Minister of War Transport* [1942] A.C. 691, per Lord Wright at 706.

[236] *JJ Lloyd Instruments Ltd v Northern Star Insurance Co Ltd* [1987] 1 Lloyd's Rep. 32.

[237] Lord Justice Lawton describes this as "settled law"; see *JJ Lloyd Instruments Ltd v Northern Star Insurance Co Ltd* [1987] 1 Lloyd's Rep. 32 at 36; see also the Supreme Court discussion in *Global Process Systems Inc v Syarikat Takaful Malaysia Bhd (The Cendor MOPU)* [2011] UKSC 5.

[238] *Wayne Tank and Pump Co Ltd v Employers Liability Assurance Corp Ltd* [1974] Q.B. 57.

[239] *Johnstone v West of Scotland Insurance Co* (1828) 7 S. 52.

exclude a proximate cause using this expression.[240] In *Coxe v Employers Liability Assurance Corp Ltd*[241] liability was excluded where death was directly or indirectly caused by war. The insured was hit by a train whilst walking along an unlit railway line on his way to inspect sentries guarding the line. It was held that, because he had been acting in pursuance of his military duties, his death had been indirectly caused by war, and that the insurers were not, therefore, liable.

PUBLIC POLICY

6.10 It is of the essence of insurance contracts that the insured cannot deliberately cause the loss insured against. As Lord Atkin explained:

> "The fire assured cannot recover if he intentionally burns down his house, nor the marine assured if he scuttles his ship, nor the life assured if he deliberately ends his own life. This is not the result of public policy, but of the correct construction of the contract."[242]

In spite of Lord Atkin's view, public policy has a role in this area. The insured may be prevented from recovering the insurance proceeds where the insured's act in seeking to cause the loss is criminal, immoral or contrary to public policy. The principles governing this area are those which normally apply to illegal contracts.[243] The insured is not entitled to profit from his own wrong.[244] In one of the most famous cases in this area, *Beresford v Royal Insurance Co*,[245] the insured committed suicide with the express purpose of obtaining for his personal representatives the benefit of five insurance policies. A clause of the policy provided that the policy would be void if the insured committed suicide within the period of one year from its commencement. The insured committed suicide after this period had elapsed. Lord Atkin indicated that there were two issues to be determined in such cases: firstly, the contract must be interpreted using normal principles of interpretation; and, secondly, the court should determine whether the contract was one which could be enforced in a court of law.[246] Although as a matter of construction of the insurance contract the insurers were bound to meet the claim,[247] the contract was not enforceable for reasons of public policy. He explained: "[T]he absolute rule is that the Courts will not recognize a benefit accruing to a criminal from his crime."[248]

In accordance with established principles relating to illegal contracts, illegal acts committed in the course of performance of an otherwise legal contract may not have the effect of denying the insured his claim.[249]

If the insured has contravened a statute, the court will identify what it considers to be the purpose of that statute and determine whether enforcing the contract would be contrary to that purpose.[250]

---

[240] For the impact of exclusions where there is more than one proximate cause, see *Midland Mainline v Eagle Star* [2004] 2 Lloyds Rep 604 CA.

[241] *Coxe v Employers Liability Assurance Corp Ltd* [1916] 2 K.B. 629.

[242] *Beresford v Royal Insurance Co* [1938] A.C. 586, per Lord Atkin at 595. For a more recent example, see *Potter v Zurich Insurance Company* [2009] EWHC 376.

[243] On which see L.J. Macgregor, "Pacta Illicita" in Reid and Zimmermann (eds), *A History of Private Law in Scotland*, (2000) at p.129.

[244] This principle is often expressed using the maxim *ex turpi causa non oritur actio*. If the act committed by the insured is actually criminal, the commission of that act need only be proved on the balance of probabilities and not beyond reasonable doubt: see *Sodden v Prudential Assurance Co Ltd*, 1999 S.C.L.R. 367.

[245] *Beresford v Royal Insurance Co* [1938] A.C. 586.

[246] This approach is also adopted in *Gray v Barr* [1971] 2 Q.B. 554.

[247] *Beresford v Royal Insurance Co* [1938] A.C. 586, per Lord Atkin at 596; per Lord MacMillan at 602.

[248] *Beresford v Royal Insurance Co* [1938] A.C. 586, per Lord Atkin at 599. It should be noted, however, that suicide is no longer a crime, and so the decision, in that respect, is now open to challenge.

[249] See *Euro-Diam Ltd v Bathurst* [1990] 1 Q.B. 517, applying *St Johns Shipping Corp v Joseph Rank Ltd* [1957] 1 Q.B. 267.

[250] *Dalby v India & London Life Assurance Co* (1854) 15 C.B. 365.

ASSIGNATION AND THIRD PARTY RIGHTS

The insurance policy forms a contract between the insured and the insurer and, therefore, normal rules **6.11** of privity of contract exclude the possibility of a relevant claim on the policy by third parties who have suffered a loss caused by the conduct of the insured. Not being parties to that contract, such third parties have no right to sue under the policy, even if the policy is taken out by the insured with the express purpose of covering such a liability. The Third Parties (Rights Against Insurers) Act 1930 operates to temper the strict operation of the rules of privity of contract in this respect. Before the passing of the Act, if the insured became bankrupt, the proceeds of any insurance policy would be paid to the insured's trustee in bankruptcy. It therefore formed part of the general assets to be distributed to the insured's creditors. The 1930 Act prevents the insurance proceeds from being dissipated in this way. In effect, it allows a third party who has a valid claim against an insured who has become bankrupt to proceed directly against the insurer.[251] It thus operates as a statutory assignation of the insured's rights under the insurance policy to the injured third party, giving that third party a preferred status in comparison with the insured's other general creditors.

Because the Act operates as a statutory form of assignation, the third party can obtain no better right against the insurer than that of the original insured. The third party "stands in the shoes of" the insured in any action against the insurer. This principle leads to certain practical restrictions in the operation of the Act. The insured's liability to the third party must be established before the third party has any right under the Act.[252] Additionally, any defence that the insurer could have raised against the insured can similarly be raised against the third party.[253] However, the insurer is not barred from challenging the insured's liability to the third party simply because the insurer decided not to defend the third party's action against the insured.[254] The Act has been interpreted as protecting the third party's rights only where he has suffered a loss through either the negligence of, or a breach of contract by, the insured.[255] It does not assist a third party who is seeking to claim professional fees, such as legal fees, under an insurance policy taken out by the insured.[256] These limitations were recognised in a joint consultation paper by the English and Scottish Law Commissions.[257]

Provided that the policy itself contains no prohibition on assignation, it is open to the insured to assign his interest in the insurance policy. Where the policy insures the life of the insured, it does not matter that the assignee has no insurable interest in the life of the insured.[258] This is because the insurable interest need only exist at the time when the insurance policy is taken out.[259] In indemnity insurance, however, the insured must have an insurable interest at the date of the loss. As a result, the subjects insured must also be assigned or transferred to the assignee so that the assignee can meet this requirement.

The assignee can obtain no better right under the insurance policy than the insured.[260] An example of the operation of this principle can be seen in *Scottish Equitable Life Assurance Society v Buist*,[261] in which the insured's actual state of health and his addiction to alcohol had not been disclosed to the insurers. The policy was then assigned before the insured died at the age of 30. Because the assignee could obtain no better right under the policy than the insured, the insurers were found entitled to avoid

---

[251] Third Parties (Rights Against Insurers) Act 1930 s.1(1).

[252] *Saunders v Royal Insurance Plc*, 1998 S.C.L.R. 1118.

[253] *Saunders v Royal Insurance Plc*, 1998 S.C.L.R. 1118.

[254] *Cheltenham & Gloucester Plc v Sun Alliance and London Insurance Plc*, 2001 S.C.L.R. 670.

[255] *Tarbuck v Avon Insurance Plc* [2001] 2 All E.R. 503.

[256] *Tarbuck v Avon Insurance Plc* [2001] 2 All E.R. 503.

[257] Law Commission and Scottish Law Commission, *Third Parties—Rights Against Insurers*. The Stationery Office, 2001. Law Com. Consultation Paper No.272; Scot. Law Com. Consultation Paper No.184. Cm.5217. At the time of writing, the Third Parties (Rights Against Insurers) Act 2010, which will replace the 1930 Act, is yet to come into force.

[258] *Brownlee v Robb*, 1907 S.C. 1302.

[259] *Dalby v India & London Life Assurance Co* (1854) C.B. 365

[260] This is due to the operation of the principle *assignatus utitur jure auctoris*, or the assignee exercises the right of his cedent.

[261] *Scottish Equitable Life Assurance Society v Buist* (1877) 4 R. 1076.

the assignee's claim. As is the case with the transfer of other incorporeal rights, the insured, in addition to assigning his right to the policy, must intimate the assignation to the insurer.[262]

THE UNFAIR TERMS IN CONSUMER CONTRACTS REGULATIONS 1999

6.12 Insurance contracts do not fall within the ambit of the Unfair Contract Terms Act 1977.[263] They are, however, regulated by the Unfair Terms in Consumer Contracts Regulations 1999.[264] Although it is not possible to provide a full analysis of the regulations here, certain points can be made about their effect within an insurance context. It is important to note that they only protect "consumers", this term being defined as natural persons not acting for the purposes of a trade, business or profession.[265] They are also aimed at standard form contracts, and so would embrace any term of an insurance contract that has not been individually negotiated.[266]

Two particular protections within the regulations are relevant in an insurance context. Firstly, reg.7 requires that any written term of the contract should be in plain and intelligible language, with any doubt as to interpretation being resolved in favour of the consumer.[267] This suggests that such contracts should be intelligible to the normal layperson.[268] Insurance contracts often fall short of this standard.[269] Secondly, certain terms of the insurance contract could be considered "unfair" in terms of reg.5, and thus not binding on the consumer.[270] A term is unfair if,

> "contrary to the requirements of good faith, it causes a significant imbalance in the parties' rights and obligations arising under the contract, to the detriment of the consumer".[271]

There are, however, two important exceptions to the fairness test, contained in reg.5.[272] Firstly, the test cannot be applied to a term which concerns the adequacy of the price as against the goods or services supplied.[273] It could not, therefore, be used to challenge the level of the premium in an insurance contract. Secondly, the test cannot be applied to a term which defines the main subject matter of the contract.[274] Some guidance on this point can be drawn from recital 19 of the preamble to the Directive, which suggests that "terms which define or circumscribe the insured risk and the insurer's liability" fall within the scope of that phrase. In all cases, however, the term must be in plain and intelligible language, and a term that falls short of this standard will remain challengeable notwithstanding the terms of these exceptions.[275] When the impact of the exceptions is considered, it seems clear that many of the most

---

[262] See *Strachan v McDougle* (1835) 13 S. 954, where an unintimated assignation was defeated by an arrestment.

[263] Unfair Contract Terms Act 1977 s.15(3)(a)(i).

[264] Unfair Terms in Consumer Contracts Regulations 1999 (SI 1999/2083), as amended by the Unfair Terms in Consumer Contracts (Amendment) Regulations 2001 (SI 2001/1186) (hereinafter "1999 Regulations"), implementing Directive 93/13 on unfair terms in consumer contracts [1993] OJ L95/29. See also the earlier implementation of the Directive in the Unfair Terms in Consumer Contracts Regulations 1994 (SI 1994/3159).

[265] 1999 Regulations reg.3(1).

[266] 1999 Regulations reg.5(1).

[267] See *Re Drake Insurance Plc* [2001] Lloyd's Rep. I.R. 643.

[268] Although see *Bankers Insurance Co Ltd v South* [2004] Lloyd's Rep. I.R. 1, where this argument failed, even though it was not clear to the consumer from the definitions in the policy whether the activity he was pursuing was covered by its terms.

[269] Indeed, early OFT guidance indicated that a term which is obscure could be unfair for that reason alone, see OFT, *Unfair Contract Terms Bulletin No.4*, p.22; and see *Kindlance Ltd v Murphy* Unreported 1997 High Court of Northern Ireland.

[270] 1999 Regulations reg.8(1).

[271] 1999 Regulations reg.5(1). Terms are likely to be considered unfair if they give to the insurer an unfair advantage; see reg.6(1) and Sch.2.

[272] 1999 Regulations reg.6(2).

[273] 1999 Regulations reg.6(2)(b).

[274] 1999 Regulations reg.6(2)(a).

[275] See *Pearl Assurance Plc v Kavanagh* [2001] C.L.Y. 3382.

important terms of an insurance contract are not challengeable as "unfair". A "basis of the contract" clause does not fall within either exception and may therefore be challengeable, on the basis that it would allow the insurer to escape liability in the event of a non-material misstatement by the insured in the proposal form.[276] The same would be true of a term which deems every term of the contract to be material.[277]

---

[276] As in *Dawsons Ltd v Bonnin*, 1922 S.C. (HL) 156.

[277] See the views of Lord Greene MR in *Zurich General Accident and Liability Insurance Co Ltd v Morrison* [1942] K.B. 53 at 58.

Chapter 7

PERSONAL INSOLVENCY

INTRODUCTION

7.1 This area of the law concerns itself with the sequestration of an insolvent debtor's estate—its removal and deposit in the hands of a neutral third person, its realisation and ultimate distribution amongst the creditors of the estate. This may occur, either through the granting of a voluntary trust deed for creditors, or through formal sequestration—the process whereby an individual is made bankrupt, following an application to the Accountant in Bankruptcy or a petition to the sheriff.[1] The law in this area is mainly statutory, being governed by the Bankruptcy (Scotland) Act 1985, as amended.

The Act, which largely gave effect to the Scottish Law Commission Report on Bankruptcy and Related Aspects of Insolvency and Liquidation,[2] represented a major revision and restatement of the Scots law of bankruptcy, repealing the Bankruptcy Acts of 1621 and 1696 and the Bankruptcy (Scotland) Act 1913. Among the reforms introduced by the Act were:

(1) the introduction of the office of interim trustee, with an interim trustee requiring to be appointed in every judicial sequestration;

(2) the requirement that a permanent trustee be appointed or elected in every judicial sequestration;

(3) the requirement that trustees be qualified insolvency practitioners;

(4) the making available of funds from the public purse to meet the expenses of judicial sequestration, where the estate was insufficient to meet these;

(5) the removal of the requirement for public examination of the debtor;

(6) the imposition of certain restraints on the permanent trustee's power to sell the family home;

(7) the introduction of new rules regarding gratuitous alienations and unfair preferences;

(8) the automatic discharge of the debtor three years after the date of sequestration (unless a deferment were granted); and

(9) the introduction of the concept of the protected trust deed.

The Act itself, however, was subject to significant reform within 10 years of coming into effect, through the agency of the Bankruptcy (Scotland) Act 1993. The main reason for this second measure was the unforeseen consequences of reforms designed to remove much of the stigma from bankruptcy, together with the provision of public funding to meet trustees' fees and outlays where the assets of the estate were insufficient for that task. This meant that, whereas before there was little point in seeking to sequestrate a debtor who had very few assets, it suddenly became a very attractive option—at least for insolvency practitioners. The availability of the trust deed route to sequestration also made it a very straightforward option, in that a debtor could sign a trust deed and the trustee could immediately petition for sequestration without involving a creditor. Thus a totally unexpected explosion in the number of sequestrations resulted, with a staggering increase in the cost to the public purse. The 1993 Act then addressed these problems by:

(1) making it possible for the Accountant in Bankruptcy to act as interim and/or permanent trustee and effectively ensuring that she would be so appointed in most cases where the

---

[1] In the English case of *Holtham v Kelmanson* [2006] B.P.I.R. 1422 it was held that the administration of a bankrupt's estate was not a process that resulted in the determination of the civil rights and obligations of the bankrupt within the terms of art.6 of the European Convention on Human Rights: see Evans-Lombe J at [17].

[2] Scottish Law Commission, *Report on Bankruptcy and Related Aspects of Insolvency and Liquidation* (HMSO, 1982), Scot. Law Com. No.68.

estate was insufficient to meet the expenses of sequestration (in this way, greater public control was exercised over the cost of sequestration process);

(2) the creation of a new scheme for summary administration of small estates, whereby a streamlined and thus less costly procedure may be followed (this has now been abolished);

(3) the imposition of greater restrictions on the right of a trustee under a trust deed to petition for sequestration;

(4) making it more difficult for debtors to seek sequestration without the concurrence of creditors; and

(5) making it easier for debtors to seek sequestration via the device of the protected trust deed, in the hope that there would be more resort to this route, avoiding the costs and procedural complexities of judicial sequestration.

The Act was subject to further major amendment via the Bankruptcy and Diligence etc. (Scotland) Act 2007. As far as bankruptcy is concerned, the Act sought to support entrepreneurial attitudes by allowing debtors to escape earlier from the consequences of bankruptcy, while protecting the public against culpable behaviour.[3] This took the form of reducing the period after which the debtor is automatically discharged from sequestration from three years to one year,[4] but balancing that by introducing the device of a bankruptcy restrictions order which may be sought by the Accountant in Bankruptcy where the behaviour of the debtor argues for the imposition of continuing controls in the public interest. Among the other reforms introduced by the 2007 Act were:

- the introduction of the concept of a bankruptcy restrictions undertaking to provide a negotiated alternative to a bankruptcy restrictions order;
- the effective amalgamation of the offices of interim trustee and permanent trustee. Although the interim trustee will continue to have a minor role in the brief period between the application for and grant of sequestration, from the latter date all the duties formerly undertaken by the interim trustee and permanent trustee will be undertaken by an officer known as the trustee in sequestration;
- the removal of any need for the trustee in sequestration to call a statutory meeting of creditors;
- entrusting the task of considering applications by debtors to be sequestrated to the Accountant in Bankruptcy rather than the sheriff[5];
- confining the task of considering petitions by creditors for a debtor to be sequestrated to the sheriff court[6];
- no longer giving the trustee in sequestration the right to the debtor's non-vested contingent interests[7];
- limiting the time during which the trustee in sequestration can assert the right to the family home, in that if the trustee has not taken an appropriate step to assert that claim within three years of the date of sequestration, the home re-vests in the debtor;
- lowering the threshold of creditor approval for a debtor to be discharged under a composition contract, and having such arrangements approved by the Accountant in Bankruptcy rather than the sheriff; and

---

[3] See the policy memorandum which accompanied the Bill, paras 154–155.

[4] Thus aligning the law with the position in England.

[5] The Executive considered this was "largely an administrative process", and that valuable court time should not be taken up by it. See the policy memorandum, para.201.

[6] The Executive considered that as the grant of sequestration had very serious consequences and as the debtor might object to being sequestrated, it was proper that such petitions be considered by the court. However, it saw no need why the time of the Court of Session should be taken up by considering such petitions. See the policy memorandum, paras 204–205.

[7] Typically, this might be a future inheritance. The Executive considered that in practice these rights had little value for creditors while it was not cost effective for a trustee to hang on in office on the chance that such an asset might vest. At the same time the debtor could be left in limbo, uncertain as to whether the creditors had abandoned their claim. See the policy memorandum, paras 231–233.

- the abolition of the certificate of summary administration,[8] and the streamlined procedure used under Sch.2 in small assets cases.

Since then the 1985 Act has been further amended by Pt 2 of the Home Owner and Debtor Protection (Scotland) Act 2010. These amendments include:

- the removal of the possibility of a debtor applying for his own sequestration with the consent of a concurring creditor or creditors and its replacement with the possibility of a debtor application on the basis of a certificate of sequestration granted by an authorised person;
- the extension of the protections regarding to sale of the debtor's family home to sales by trustees under trust deeds.

Most recently, the Bankruptcy and Debt Advice (Scotland) Act 2014 looks to make a number of further amendments. The intention is to follow this measure with consolidating legislation, with that legislation and the changes effected by the 2014 Act coming into force in Spring 2015. The authors might therefore have waited for a further year before bringing out this edition, so that the new regime could be accurately described. However, since the appearance of this edition has already been delayed by the imminence of this legislation, it has been decided to make reference to the changes effected by the 2014 Act, even though they will not yet be in force when the book first appears. The key reforms introduced by the 2014 Act are therefore:

- A significant increase in consumer debt led the Accountant in Bankruptcy Service to the view that there should be a "Financial Health Service", providing access to "fair and just processes of debt advice, debt relief and debt management", and thus "rehabilitation to individuals and organisations in relation to their financial pressures".[9] Thus the Act deals with the provision of advice and financial education for debtors.
- A key principle of the Act is that "those who can pay should pay".[10] Thus the Scottish Government is developing a common financial tool across all debt relief and debt management solutions which will calculate the contribution which an individual should make from any surplus income he may have. For bankrupt individuals this will operate within debtor contribution orders, but separate regulations will be made in respect of debt arrangement schemes and protected trust deeds. The tool which will be adopted is the Money Advice Trust's Common Financial Statement, which is a detailed budgeting format enabling an accurate overview of the debtor's income and expenditure to be produced. It contains "trigger figures" to identify levels of monthly expenditure deemed reasonable across a number of areas of expenditure.
- The low income, low asset route into bankruptcy is replaced with a new minimal asset process, designed for debtors whose only income is derived from social security benefits or whom the common financial tool has identified as unable to make a contribution to what is owed. The Accountant in Bankruptcy will act as trustee in such cases, and since nothing will be paid to creditors, the administration will be minimal, and the debtor will be discharged six months after the date of sequestration.
- Currently, in relation to debt arrangement schemes, reg.30 of the Debt Arrangement Scheme (Scotland) Regulations 2011[11] imposes a six-week moratorium on diligence, preventing any creditor doing any form of diligence on the debtor's estate for a six-week period following intimation of the intention to apply for approval of a debt payment programme. A similar moratorium applies where a debtor intimates an intention to apply for bankruptcy or for protection of a trust deed for creditors.

---

[8] The Executive noted that the procedure was not used in practice and served no useful purpose. See the policy memorandum, para.303.
[9] Policy Memorandum, para.3.
[10] Policy Memorandum, para.34.
[11] (SSI 2011/141).

- At the moment acquirenda only vest up to the date of discharge, after which they vest in the debtor. Similarly, if a contingent interest has not been realised by the date of discharge, it reinvests in the debtor. In both cases the Act extends the period for which such rights vest in the trustee for four years after the date of sequestration.
- The Act also alters the position whereby a debtor is automatically discharged from bankruptcy after a year from the date of sequestration unless the trustee has applied to the sheriff for deferral of discharge. Debtors subject to the minimal asset process will be discharged six months after the date of sequestration. Any other debtor will only be discharged when the trustee applies to the Accountant in Bankruptcy for such discharge on the basis that the debtor has fully co-operated and all necessary steps have been completed. The earliest this can happen is 10 months after the award. The possibility of discharge on composition is removed.
- A large number of functions which the framers of the legislation consider to be administrative are transferred from the sheriff to the Accountant in Bankruptcy. A number of types of decision made by the Accountant in Bankruptcy may be appealed to the sheriff. The Act will now require such appellants to ask the Accountant in Bankruptcy to review certain such types of decision prior to making an appeal.

The reforms which will be effected by the 2014 Act are considered in detail below. Such passages are italicised for ease of identification.

THE ACCOUNTANT IN BANKRUPTCY

Before examining the rules governing sequestration, it is worth noting the role of an official who guar- **7.1.1** antees some degree of public oversight of the process. The office of Accountant in Bankruptcy (hereafter the AIB) was created in 1856 and from 1889–1993 was coincident with that of Accountant of Court. The two offices are now separate, testifying to the increased significance of the office following the 1993 Act while, following the 2007 Act, the AIB is now an officer of the court.[12] A major innovation introduced by the 2007 Act is that the AIB may now determine applications by debtors to be sequestrated. Otherwise, the functions of this official are as follows[13] (all references are to the 1985 Act, as amended):

- the supervision of the performance of those involved in the sequestration process, as well as trustees under protected trust deeds;
- the maintenance of a register of insolvencies;
- the preparation of an annual report; and
- the reporting of suspected offences to the Lord Advocate.

Supervisory role of the Accountant

The AIB supervises the performance of interim trustees, trustees in sequestration and commissioners. **7.1.1.1** This is not generally a directive role.[14] She issues *Notes for Guidance for Interim and Permanent Trustees*, which notes provide checklists of documents to be sent to her by interim trustees and trustees in sequestration. The AIB investigates complaints against interim trustees, trustees in sequestration and commissioners. Where she takes the view that anyone subject to her supervision has failed without reasonable excuse to perform any duty, she shall report the matter to the sheriff, who may remove the individual from office or impose another appropriate sanction.[15] If she has reasonable grounds to suspect that anyone subject to her supervision has committed an offence, she must report the matter to the Lord Advocate.[16]

---

[12] See s.1(1A).
[13] See s.1A.
[14] See Sch.2A para.3.
[15] See s.1A(2).
[16] See s.1A(3).

The Accountant as interim trustee/trustee in sequestration

7.1.1.2 It will be seen below that the AIB may be appointed to act as interim trustee or trustee in sequestration. Needless to say, the AIB may delegate any of her functions to her staff, and in relation to her functions, "in respect of the sequestration of the estate of any debtor" may appoint agents.[17] Thus she may subcontract the conduct of certain sequestrations to qualified insolvency practitioners for a fixed fee.

WHO CAN BE SEQUESTRATED?

7.1.2 The following categories of entity may be sequestrated in terms of ss.5 and 6 of the Act:

- living debtors[18];
- deceased debtors;
- trusts;
- partnerships and limited partnerships, including in both cases dissolved partnerships;
- bodies corporate, but not companies under the Companies Acts; and
- unincorporated bodies, e.g. clubs and trade unions.[19]

7.1.3 WHO CAN SEEK SEQUESTRATION?

Debtor applications

7.1.3.1 Whereas hitherto sequestration could only be sought by petitioning the court, the 2007 Act introduced the possibility of sequestration being granted by the AIB where a debtor applies for his own sequestration.[20] A debtor[21] can so apply if[22]:

(1) he owes at least £3,000 at the date of presentation of the petition; and

(2) sequestration has not been awarded against him during the previous five years (to guard against the, possibly mythical, individual who employs serial, self-arranged sequestration as a means of escaping from his debts); and

(3) *he has obtained the requisite advice from a money adviser[23] (see para.7.1.3.3),*

(4) *he has given a statement of undertakings (see para.7.1.5) including an undertaking to pay to the trustee an amount determined by the common financial tool[24],*

(5) one of the following situations pertains:

    (a) he has handed over his estate to a trustee under a voluntary trust deed for the benefit of his creditors, and the trustee has tried unsuccessfully to make the trust deed protected—see para.7.4.7.2 below;

    (b) he is apparently insolvent—see para.7.1.4 below;

---

[17] See s.1B.

[18] Debtors must be sequestrated individually, unless one is sequestrating a firm or association. It is therefore not competent to bring a single petition to sequestrate spouses who are not in partnership): *Campbell v Dunbar*, 1989 S.L.T. (Sh Ct) 29.

[19] But where an individual operated under a trading name, it was held incompetent to seek to sequestrate him under that name, since it is not possible to sequestrate a body which has no real legal existence: *Accountant in Bankruptcy v Butler*, 2007 S.L.T. (Sh Ct) 200.

[20] For the detailed procedure to be followed in such cases see Bankruptcy (Scotland) Regulations 2008 (SSI 2008/82) reg.14 and Forms 9–16.

[21] It has been held that it is incompetent for someone with power of attorney to sign for the debtor, and it was doubted whether any mandatory could be authorised to apply for sequestration: *Toni, Petitioner*, 2002 S.L.T. (Sh Ct) 159.

[22] Bankruptcy (Scotland) Act 1985 s.5(2B).

[23] *This would be as a result of s.5(2B)(ba), added by the 2014 Act. That Act also adds s.5(4BA), which indicates that the application must include a declaration by the adviser that the required advice has been given, and must specify the adviser's name and address.*

[24] This would be as a result of s.5(2B)(bb), added by the 2014 Act.

(c) he is unable to pay his debts and all of the conditions prescribed by s.5A apply. That section deals with applications by low income low asset debtors and the conditions are that the debtor's gross[25] weekly income on the date of application does not exceed 40 times the hourly rate of the national minimum wage (currently £6.50 thus giving a weekly income ceiling of £260[26]); the total value of his assets on that date does not exceed £10,000 (and no single asset exceeds £1,000 in value[27]); and he does not own any land. A person in receipt of an income related benefit as defined in s.191 of the Social Security Administration Act 1992, or an income-based jobseeker's allowance as defined by s.1(4) of the Jobseekers Act 1995 or a working tax credit as defined by s.1(1)(b) of the Tax Credits Act 2002, shall be treated as having no income.[28] This is because these benefits are already income based and means tested. All other social security benefits and tax credits are not taken into account in calculating income.[29] Only the debtor's personal income is taken into account[30]—i.e. the debtor is not to be pushed over the threshold because of income received by another member of the family. A debtor applying under this scheme must complete and return to the AIB a statutory declaration that he meets the necessary criteria,[31] and if he fails to do so the AIB shall refuse to grant the application unless she is satisfied that he is apparently insolvent.[32] In such a case the notice published by the trustee in the *Edinburgh Gazette* (see para.7.2.14.) must state that the debtor has met the conditions for a low income/low asset sequestration, and that since no dividend is expected creditors are not invited to make a claim in such a sequestration.[33]

The 2014 Act looks to replace the low income, low asset route into bankruptcy with a new minimal assets process whereby debtors can arrange their own sequestration. As in low income, low asset cases, in the new minimal assets process the AIB will not appoint a trustee, but instead will be automatically deemed to be the trustee.[34] The criteria for access to this new procedure are more restrictive. It is designed for debtors whose only income during the six months prior to application is derived from social security benefits—which of course do not vest in the trustee in bankruptcy—or who has been assessed by the common financial tool as being unable to make a contribution.[35] Further conditions are that:

- *on the date of application the debtor's debts are not less than £1,500 and not more than £17,000[36];*
- *the total value of his assets on the above date, leaving liabilities out of the account, does not exceed £2,000, with the value of no single asset exceeding £1,000.[37] In making this calculation, assets which do not vest in the AIB as trustee will not be taken into account.[38] Nor will any vehicle owned by the debtor which is worth £3,000 or less and which is reasonably required by him[39];*
- *the debtor does not own land[40];*

---

[25] Bankruptcy (Scotland) Act 1985 (Low Income, Low Asset Debtors etc.) Regulations 2008 (SSI 2008/81) reg.2(7).

[26] Bankruptcy (Scotland) Act 1985 (Low Income, Low Asset Debtors etc.) Regulations 2008 (SSI 2008/81) reg.2(1). For how the calculation is made when a person is paid monthly, or paid otherwise than weekly or monthly, see reg.2(2)–(3). And for the position where a person's weekly income varies see reg.2(8).

[27] Bankruptcy (Scotland) Act 1985 (Low Income, Low Asset Debtors etc.) Regulations 2008 (SSI 2008/81) reg.3(1)–(2). In making this calculation assets which do not vest in the trustee are not taken into account: reg.3(3). See para.8.2.12.

[28] Bankruptcy (Scotland) Act 1985 (Low Income, Low Asset Debtors etc.) Regulations 2008 (SSI 2008/81) reg.2(2).

[29] Bankruptcy (Scotland) Act 1985 (Low Income, Low Asset Debtors etc.) Regulations 2008 (SSI 2008/81) reg.2(5).

[30] Bankruptcy (Scotland) Act 1985 (Low Income, Low Asset Debtors etc.) Regulations 2008 (SSI 2008/81) reg.2(6).

[31] Bankruptcy (Scotland) Regulations 2008 (SSI 2008/82) reg.15(1) and Form 17.

[32] Bankruptcy (Scotland) Regulations 2008 (SSI 2008/82) reg.15(2).

[33] Bankruptcy (Scotland) Regulations 2008 (SSI 2008/82) reg.15(3).

[34] *See s.2(1D).*

[35] *See s.5(2ZA)(a).*

[36] *See s.5(2ZA)(b).*

[37] *See s.5(2ZA)(c)–(d).*

[38] *See s.5(2ZB)(a).*

[39] *See s.5(2ZB)(b).*

[40] *See s.5(2ZA)(e).*

- *he has applied for and been granted a certificate for sequestration by an authorised person in terms of s.5B (see below)[41];*
- *he has not been made bankrupt during the 5 years leading up to the date of application, nor been made bankrupt through the minimal assets process during the 10 years leading up to the date of application.[42]*

Regulations may be made regarding how assets may be valued and otherwise to vary the limits set out above.[43]

The consequences of the application of the minimal assets process are set out at various points below. Broadly speaking, they are that the debtor will be discharged automatically six months after the date on which sequestration is awarded, while no claims may be submitted by creditors, so that no statutory meeting of creditors will be held. However, in certain circumstances the AIB is under a duty to consider whether these consequences should cease to apply.[44] Those circumstances are that:

- *the AIB becomes aware that the application contains an error or deliberately misrepresents or fails to state a fact, with the result that debtor was not at that time a debtor who met the criteria for access to this new process[45];*
- *at any time after the date of the application, the total value of the debtor's assets (leaving out of the account liabilities and assets which do not vest in the trustee) exceeds £5,000, or the AIB assesses the debtor under the common financial tool as being able to make a contribution[46];*
- *at any time after the date of sequestration the AIB is not satisfied that the debtor has co-operated with the trustee and considers that it would be of financial benefit to the estate and in the interests of the creditors if the consequences were to cease to apply.[47]*

If the AIB does consider that the consequences should cease to apply, she should notify the debtor of that fact, indicating which of the above circumstances she believes to apply to the debtor, and that the debtor has 14 days from the date of notification to make representations to her.[48] On the expiry of that 14 day period, having taken into account any representations made by the debtor, the AIB must decide whether the consequences should indeed cease to apply,[49] and if that is the decision reached, must as soon as practicable give the debtor written notice of the decision and its effect.[50] If such notice is given, the debtor has 14 days from the date when the notice is given to appeal to the sheriff.[51] If such an appeal is granted, the consequences will continue to apply.[52] If no such appeal is made, or if it is refused, abandoned or withdrawn, the consequences will cease to apply.[53]

(d) he has, within the 30 days leading up to the making of the application,[54] been granted a certificate of sequestration by an authorised person, to that person that he is unable to pay his debts as they become due. This route to sequestration was introduced by the Home Owner and Debtor Protection (Scotland) Act 2010 to replace the route whereby a debtor could apply with the concurrence of a qualified creditor. An authorised person

---

[41] *See s.5(2ZA)(f).*
[42] *See s.5(2ZA)(g)–(h).*
[43] *See s.5(2ZC)–(2ZD).*
[44] *See Sch.A1, para.2(1)–(2).*
[45] *See Sch.A1, para.2(3)–(4).*
[46] *See Sch.A1, para.2(5).*
[47] *See Sch.A1, para.2(6).*
[48] *See Sch.A1, para.3(1)–(2).*
[49] *See Sch.A1, para.3(3).*
[50] *See Sch.A1, para.3(4).*
[51] *See Sch.A1, para.4(1)–(3).*
[52] *See Sch.A1, para.4(4).*
[53] *See Sch.A1, para.4(5).*
[54] Bankruptcy (Certificate for Sequestration) (Scotland) Regulations 2010 (SSI 2010/397) reg.7.

might be a qualified insolvency practitioner or someone who works for such a practitioner and has been given authority by the practitioner to grant certificates.[55] It might also be a person who works as a money adviser for a local authority, or an accredited organisation or a citizens advice bureau which is a full member of the Scottish Association of Citizens Advice Bureaux—Citizens Advice Scotland.[56] It might equally be a person who is approved for the purposes of the Debt Arrangement Scheme.[57] However, an authorised person may not be an associate of the debtor[58] (see para.7.2.16.1). No fee may be charged for issuing such a certificate.[59] The certificate can only be granted on application by the debtor[60] and only if he can demonstrate that he is unable to pay his debts as they become due.[61] It would simply indicate that fact.[62] Prior to granting a certificate for sequestration the authorised person must provide the debtor with a copy of a Debt Advice and Information Package; advise him of the options of a voluntary repayment plan, a debt payment programme under the Debt Arrangement Scheme or a trust deed; and advise him of the consequences of sequestration.[63] (*The 2014 Act would replace the concept of an authorised person in s.5B with that of a money adviser.*)

The culmination of these conditions aims to protect against debtors applying for sequestration against the interests of their creditors. *Where the AIB considers that a debtor application is incomplete or lacks key information or evidence, or any relevant fee or charge is outstanding, she must give the debtor written notice of this and require that the information, evidence, fee or charge be provided or paid within 21 days or such longer period as she may specify.[64] She may refuse to award sequestration if, after the expiry of such period, she considers that the application remains incomplete or the information or evidence remains insufficient, or the fee or charge remains outstanding.[65] Where the AIB considers that an award of sequestration on a debtor application may not be appropriate, she must give written notice specifying why and indicating any further information to be provided within 21 days or such longer period as she may specify.[66] She may refuse to award sequestration if after the expiry of such period she remains of the view that an award of sequestration is not appropriate.[67]*

Although the device of a debtor application is primarily designed with individual debtors in mind, it is also possible for debtor applications to be made in respect of:

- trusts, by a majority of trustees;
- partnerships, by the firm; and
- bodies corporate and unincorporated bodies, by a person authorised to act on behalf of the body.

---

[55] Bankruptcy (Certificate for Sequestration) (Scotland) Regulations 2010 (SSI 2010/397) reg.3(1)(a).

[56] Bankruptcy (Certificate for Sequestration) (Scotland) Regulations 2010 (SSI 2010/397) reg.3(1)(b).

[57] Bankruptcy (Certificate for Sequestration) (Scotland) Regulations 2010 (SSI 2010/397) reg.3(1)(b)(ii).

[58] Bankruptcy (Certificate for Sequestration) (Scotland) Regulations 2010 (SSI 2010/397) reg.3(2).

[59] Bankruptcy (Certificate for Sequestration) (Scotland) Regulations 2010 (SSI 2010/397) reg.6.

[60] Bankruptcy (Scotland) Act 1985 s.5B(2).

[61] See s.5B(3). But if the debtor suggests that this is so, it would appear that the authorised person should take his word for it. The Explanatory Notes to the Bankruptcy (Certificate for Sequestration) (Scotland) Regulations 2010 state that the person "will be entitled to rely on statements and paperwork provided by the debtor in granting a certificate for sequestration. In particular, an authorised person is entitled to rely on the information provided by a debtor as to their financial circumstances".

[62] See s.5B(1). For the form of certificate see Bankruptcy (Certificate for Sequestration) (Scotland) Regulations 2010 (SSI 2010/397) reg.5 and Sch.

[63] Bankruptcy (Certificate for Sequestration) (Scotland) Regulations 2010 (SSI 2010/397) reg.4: in particular that an award of sequestration, if granted, is recorded in a public register and may result in one or more of the debtor: being refused credit, or being offered credit at a higher rate, whether before or after the date of discharge; not being able to remain in his current place of residence; being required to relinquish his property; requiring to make contributions from income for the benefit of creditors; still being liable for some debts; as well as his past financial transactions being investigated, damage to his business interests and employment prospects, plus other restrictions or requirements being imposed on him.

[64] *See s.11A(1)–(3). Sections 11A and 11B are not really new provisions, since they effectively restate reg.14 of the Bankruptcy (Scotland) Regulations 2008 (SSI 2008/88). The opportunity is being taken to put these requirements within primary legislation: see Explanatory Notes para.24.*

[65] *See s.11A(4).*

[66] *See s.11B(1)–(2).*

[67] *See s.11B(3).*

In all the above cases the concurrence of a qualified creditor or qualified creditors (see next paragraph) is required.[68]

Sequestration of living debtors—petitions

7.1.3.2 Who can petition for the sequestration of a debtor? A qualified creditor (or creditors) may do so if the debtor is apparently insolvent (see para.7.1.4) but only if the creditor has presented the debtor with a debt advice and information package under the Debt Arrangement and Attachment (Scotland) Act 2002, not less than 14 days and not more than 12 weeks before the presentation of the petition.[69] A qualified creditor is someone who, at the date of presentation of the petition, is owed at least £3,000, while qualified creditors are at that date in aggregate owed at least £3,000.[70] Contingent or future debts or amounts payable under confiscation orders do not count.[71] Moreover, the Debt Arrangement and Attachment (Scotland) Act 2002 creates a national debt arrangement scheme to enable multiple debts to be paid in accordance with a debt arrangement programme over a period of time. This witnesses a debtor, having obtained the advice of a money adviser, applying to the Scottish Ministers for approval of a debt arrangement programme.[72] No creditor may found on any debt owed by a debtor whose debts are being paid under an approved debt arrangement programme in presenting or concurring in the presentation of a petition for sequestration.[73] This relates not only to debts covered by the programme, but to any other debt, provided the creditor has received proper notice of the approval of the debt arrangement programme.[74]

A trustee under a trust deed may also petition.[75] As an alternative to sequestration, a debtor can seek to place his estate in trust for the benefit of his creditors. However, such an arrangement may not work as well as hoped. So the trustee can petition if either the debtor has failed to comply with an obligation under the trust deed with which he could reasonably have complied, or with any instruction or requirement reasonably given to or made of him by the trustee for the purposes of the trust deed.[76] Alternatively, the trustee can petition simply on the basis that it would be in the best interest of the creditors that sequestration be awarded.[77]

Money advice

7.1.3.3 *The 2014 Act would amend the 1985 Act so as to provide that an application for the sequestration of a living debtor's estate may not validly be made until the debtor has obtained from a money adviser advice on the debtor's financial circumstances, the effect of the proposed sequestration on his estate, the preparation of the application, and such other matters as may be prescribed by regulations.[78] This is because it is government policy to make money advice compulsory for all debtors prior to obtaining access to any form of statutory debt relief. A money adviser may not be an associate of the debtor (see para.7.2.16.1), and must be of a description or fall into a class prescribed by regulations.[79] The regulations in question[80] indicate that those who can be money advisers in this context are a qualified insolvency practitioner, a person who works for a qualified insolvency practitioner and has been authorised by that practitioner to act as a money adviser on their behalf, a person who works as a money adviser for an accredited organisation, a person who works as a money adviser for a citizens*

---

[68] See ss.6(3)(a), 6(4)(a), 6(6)(a).

[69] See s.5(2D) and Bankruptcy (Scotland) Regulations 2008 (SSI 2008/82) reg.12.

[70] See s.5(4). In determining whether the £3,000 threshold is reached, interest and the expenses of doing diligence are both taken into account: *Arthur v SMT Sales and Service Co Ltd (No.2)*, 1999 S.C. 109.

[71] See s.5(4).

[72] See Debt Arrangement and Attachment (Scotland) Act 2002 ss.2–3.

[73] Debt Arrangement and Attachment (Scotland) Act 2002 s.4(3).

[74] Debt Arrangement and Attachment (Scotland) Act 2002 s.4(5).

[75] See s.5(2).

[76] See s.5(2C)(a). See *Young, Petitioner* [2007] CSOH 194.

[77] See s.5(2C)(b).

[78] *See s.5C(1).*

[79] *See s.5C(2).*

[80] *Debt Arrangement Scheme (Scotland) Regulations 2011 (SSI 2011/141) reg.8.*

advice bureau, which is a full member of the Scottish Association of Citizens Advice Bureaux—Citizens Advice Scotland, and a person who works as a money adviser for a local authority.

Deceased debtors

If it is sought to sequestrate the estate of a deceased debtor, the petition may be made by[81]:
7.1.3.4

- the executor or a person entitled to be appointed as such; or
- a qualified creditor or qualified creditors; or
- the trustee under a voluntary trust deed.

As sequestration in these circumstances may simply be a means of paying off creditors on the estate, if an executor or trustee petitions, it is not necessary that the debtor is insolvent, and the petition may be presented at any time.[82] Nor is there any need to show insolvency when a qualified creditor or qualified creditors petition at least six months after the debtor's death.[83] However, if a qualified creditor or qualified creditors petition before that date, the debtor must have been apparently insolvent within the four months prior to his death.[84]

Trusts

A majority of the trustees may make a debtor application with the concurrence of a qualified creditor or qualified creditors. Otherwise if it is sought to sequestrate a trust, the petition may be made by:
7.1.3.5

- a temporary administrator; or
- a Member State liquidator appointed in the main proceedings; or
- a qualified creditor or qualified creditors if the trustees are apparently insolvent.[85]

Partnerships

A partnership itself may make a debtor application with the concurrence of a qualified creditor or qualified creditors (the Partnership Act 1890 s.24(8) narrates that, while ordinary matters connected with the partnership business can be decided by a majority of the partners, no change in the nature of that business can be made without the consent of all existing partners; thus, in the absence of special agreement in the partnership deed, such a step would require the assent of all partners).
7.1.3.6

Otherwise if it is sought to sequestrate a partnership or limited partnership, the petition may be made by[86]:

- a temporary administrator; or
- a Member State liquidator appointed in the main proceedings;
- a trustee under a trust deed;
- a qualified creditor or qualified creditors, if the firm has been apparently insolvent within the four months prior to the petition.

Bodies corporate or unincorporated

A person authorised to act on its behalf may make a debtor application on behalf of a body corporate or unincorporated body. Otherwise if it is sought to sequestrate such a body, the petition may be made by:
7.1.3.7

---

[81] See s.5(3). *The Policy Memorandum to the 2014 Act (para.108) comments that currently a petition for sequestration by an executor is presented before the sheriff so that the debtor has the opportunity to indicate why sequestration should not be granted. This obviously makes no sense, so s.5(3) and related provisions are to be amended so that the executor of an insolvent debtor will simply make a debtor application to the AIB.*

[82] See s.8(3)(a).

[83] See s.8(3)(b)(ii).

[84] See s.8(3)(b)(i).

[85] See s.6(3).

[86] See ss.6(4), 8(2).

- a temporary administrator; or
- a Member State liquidator appointed in the main proceedings; or
- a qualified creditor if the body has been apparently insolvent within the four months prior to the petition.[87]

APPARENT INSOLVENCY

7.1.4 It will have been seen above that in a number of circumstances an application or petition is only competent if the debtor has been "apparently insolvent". The term insolvency has a number of meanings. So-called absolute insolvency arises where the debtor's total liabilities exceed his total assets. It is entirely possible for someone to be in this condition for a considerable period of time without evident financial difficulty, as an individual may be able to pay his debts as they fall due, while suffering from significant underlying insolvency. Absolute insolvency does not lead directly to sequestration, although it is not without legal significance in this context, as it is a precondition for common law challenges to gratuitous alienations and fraudulent preferences (see para.7.2.16.3). Simple or practical insolvency occurs when a debtor is unable to pay his debts as they fall due. It may arise merely because the debtor is facing liquidity problems, and so is not necessarily indicative of absolute insolvency, although the two can obviously co-exist. Simple insolvency is not the same thing as apparent insolvency, although it often quickly leads to apparent insolvency. Simple insolvency is what is required for the exercise of the possessory remedies of unpaid sellers under the Sale of Goods Act 1979 (see para.1.14.1).

By contrast, apparent insolvency is a term of art created by the 1985 Act to describe a number of situations which are broadly indicative of serious financial problems on the part of the debtor, and which thus may be regarded as establishing a prima facie case for sequestration. Thus for the debtor apparent insolvency can be constituted by any of the following circumstances[88]:

(1) actually being sequestrated—where a petition is presented by a debtor with the concurrence of a qualified creditor, it is possible that he may not have been apparently insolvent before that point;
(2) being adjudged bankrupt in England, Wales or Northern Ireland;
(3) not being a person whose property is for the time being affected by a restraint order or subject to a confiscation or charging order,[89] he gives notice to his creditors that he has ceased to pay his debts in the ordinary course of business;
(4) becoming subject to main insolvency proceedings in an EC Member State other than the UK;
(5) granting a voluntary trust deed for his creditors;
(6) the revocation of a debt payment programme under the Debt Arrangement and Attachment (Scotland) Act 2002.

But where the debtor applies for his own sequestration without the concurrence of a qualified creditor or qualified creditors, neither (3) nor (5) is indicative of apparent insolvency.[90] This provision is clearly designed to prevent a debtor arranging his own sequestration via a self-created act of apparent insolvency.

(7) being served with a charge for payment and the expiry of the days of charge (14) without payment. A charge is a formal requisition of payment served by a judicial officer;
(8) a decree of adjudication over any part of his estate is granted;
(9) where any debt is being paid under a debt payment programme and the programme is revoked;

---

[87] See s.6(6).

[88] See s.7(1).

[89] Restraint orders and confiscation orders are made under the Proceeds of Crime Act 2002, while charging orders can be made under s.78(2) of the Criminal Justice Act 1988 or s.27(2) of the Drug Trafficking Act 1994.

[90] See s.5(2B)(c).

The fact that a debtor has failed to pay after being served with a charge for payment is usually a good indicator of insolvency, but not invariably so, such as where it results from a stubborn refusal to pay a particular debt. Similarly, although a solvent debtor would not normally grant a voluntary trust deed for his creditors, this may occasionally happen, e.g. as a safeguard against a debtor's improvidence. Therefore, the circumstances outlined in (5), (7), (8) or (9) do not create apparent insolvency if it can be shown that the debtor was able and willing to pay his debts as they fell due, or would have been so willing but for being subject to a restraint, confiscation or charging order.

> (10) a creditor in respect of a liquid debt of at least £750 (or an aggregate of liquid debts amounting to at least that sum) having served on the debtor by personal service via an officer of the court, a notice in prescribed form[91] requiring him either to pay the debt or find security for its payment, and three weeks having expired from that service without payment being made, or the debtor intimating to the creditor by recorded delivery that he denies that there is a debt or that the sum claimed is immediately payable.

A debt is liquid when the amount is settled and it is immediately payable. The three-week time period is strictly enforced, even though it may bear harshly on ordinary individuals, and a debtor who fails to record his objection as required may find that he is precluded from challenging the liquidity of the debt.[92] The prescribed form of notice demands that clear evidence of the existence of the debt be attached thereto. If this is not done, the debtor's apparent insolvency is not properly constituted, and sequestration as a result may not be competent.[93] It has also been held that the effect of serving a notice under this provision prevents that creditor seeking sequestration on the basis that the debtor is apparently insolvent by virtue of the fact that he has not paid the debt after having been served with a charge for payment.[94]

Under (1) and (2) the debtor's apparent insolvency continues until his discharge, and under (4) until the main proceedings have ended, while otherwise it continues until he becomes able to pay his debts and pays them as they become due.[95]

A partnership may be apparently insolvent either through its own apparent insolvency, or through the apparent insolvency of a partner for a debt of the firm.[96] An unincorporated body may be apparently insolvent if, in respect of a debt of the body, someone representing the body or someone holding its property as a fiduciary is apparently insolvent.[97]

THE MECHANICS OF APPLICATIONS AND PETITIONS

7.1.5 The first thing to be asked is whether the AIB has jurisdiction to award sequestration. She will have jurisdiction if the debtor habitually resided or had an established place of business in Scotland during the year prior to the application.[98] As regards a firm, body corporate, or unincorporated body, it must either have had an established place of business in Scotland during the year prior to the application, or have been constituted or formed under Scots law and at any time carried on business in Scotland.[99] The latter criterion allows the sequestration in Scotland of an entity which no longer operates in Scotland, or which has long ceased to operate at all. A debtor must state in his application whether his centre of main interests is situated in the UK or another Member State and whether he possesses an establishment in the UK or another Member State.[100] If, to his knowledge, there is a Member State liquidator

---

[91] Bankruptcy (Scotland) Regulations 2008 (SSI 2008/82) Form 1.
[92] *Guthrie Newspaper Group v Gordon*, 1992 G.W.D. 22–1244.
[93] *Lord Advocate v Thomson*, 1994 S.C.L.R. 96.
[94] *Unity Trust Bank v Ahmed*, 1993 S.C.L.R. 53.
[95] See s.7(2).
[96] See s.7(3)(a).
[97] See s.7(3)(b).
[98] See s.9(1A).
[99] See s.9(2A).
[100] See s.6B(1).

appointed in main proceedings in relation to him, he must send a copy of the application to that liquidator as soon as is reasonably practicable.[101] *When the executor of a deceased debtor makes a debtor application, it is the executor who must provide this information.*[102]

There are detailed regulations concerning the procedure to be followed in the making of debtor applications.[103] However, the Act provides that an application may be made at any time,[104] and the debtor must send a statement of his assets and liabilities along with the application.[105] It is a criminal offence for a debtor, without reasonable excuse, to fail to send this statement, to fail to disclose any material fact therein, or to make a material misstatement therein.[106] *The 2014 Act would no longer regard failure to send the statement as a criminal offence, but it would also require the debtor to send a statement of undertakings along with the application.*[107] The making of or the concurring in an application prevents the running of periods of prescription and limitation in relation to the debtor's debts.[108] If, before sequestration is awarded, it becomes apparent that a creditor concurring in a debtor application was ineligible to concur in the application, i.e. was not a qualified creditor, the AIB must withdraw him from the application. Another creditor may then concur in his place but must notify the AIB of that fact.[109]

As regards petitions, a sheriff has jurisdiction to award sequestration if the debtor habitually resided or had an established place of business in the sheriffdom during the year prior to the presentation of the petition or the death of the debtor.[110] As regards a firm, body corporate, or unincorporated body, it must either have had an established place of business in the sheriffdom during the year prior to the presentation of the petition, or have been constituted or formed under Scots law and at any time carried on business in the sheriffdom.[111] Where the sheriff has jurisdiction to sequestrate a firm, then he also has jurisdiction to sequestrate any partner thereof, even though he might not otherwise have jurisdiction over him.[112] In the case of a limited partnership, an extra requirement is that it must be registered in Scotland.[113] A petition must state, so far as this is within the petitioner's knowledge, whether the debtor has his main place of business in another state, and if the petitioner is aware that a liquidator has been appointed in relation to the debtor in another Member State, he must send a copy of the petition to that liquidator.[114] Business means the carrying on of any activity, whether for profit or not,[115] so that "place of business" will have a much wider meaning than might be anticipated. A petition may be presented to the sheriff court in any sheriffdom where the residence or place of business is situated.[116]

The Act also recognises the possibility that other insolvency proceedings[117] or proceedings seeking an analogous remedy[118] are already in train in relation to the debtor or his estate. If the debtor or anyone

[101] See s.6B(2).

[102] *See s.6B(2A).*

[103] See Bankruptcy (Scotland) Regulations 2008 (SSI 2008/82) reg.14 and Forms 9–16.

[104] See s.8A(1). But regulations may be made prescribing a period within which it will be possible to apply for the sequestration of a limited partnership; s.8A(2).

[105] See s.5(6A).

[106] See s.5(9), (10).

[107] *See s.5(6B). While debtors already sign a Statement of Undertakings at the beginning of the bankruptcy process, this has not previously had a statutory basis. The statement of undertakings requires the debtor to confirm that he has made a full disclosure of all assets which he owned or in which he had an interest at the date of sequestration. He further undertakes to inform the trustee if he inherits, wins or otherwise acquires further assets during the period of sequestration. He must also confirm that he shall immediately inform the trustee of any change of address or change in his financial circumstances during the period of the sequestration. Finally he must confirm that he understands his legal obligations arising out of sequestration and its other implications.*

[108] See s.8A(3).

[109] See s.8A(4).

[110] See s.9(1).

[111] See s.9(2),

[112] See s.9(3).

[113] Bankruptcy (Scotland) Regulations 2008 (SSI 2008/82) reg.12.

[114] See s.6A.

[115] See s.73.

[116] See s.9(1), (4).

[117] i.e. debtor applications, petitions for sequestration, petitions for the appointment of a judicial factor on the debtor's estate or the actual appointment of a judicial factor and petitions for the winding up of companies: see s.10(2).

[118] i.e. a bankruptcy order, individual voluntary arrangement or an administration order in England and Wales, corresponding remedies in Northern Ireland, or analogous remedies in any other country; see s.10(7).

petitioning for sequestration becomes aware of such proceedings, he must as soon as possible notify the sheriff to whom the petition was presented.[119] Similarly, the debtor or any creditor concurring in a debtor application must notify the AIB as soon as possible.[120] Failure to do so on the part of the debtor might lead to a criminal conviction,[121] while a petitioner might be made liable for the expenses of the petition, and a concurring creditor might be made liable for the expenses of the debtor application. On being notified of the other proceedings, the AIB may determine or dismiss the debtor application.[122] In the case of a petition, the sheriff may, on his own motion, or at the instance of an interested party, allow the petition to proceed, or may sist or dismiss it.[123] A sheriff may also on his own motion, or at the instance of an interested party, direct the AIB to dismiss a debtor application.[124] *If the AIB has already awarded sequestration when directed to dismiss an application, she must recall the award.*[125] *The effect of that recall is, so far as is practicable, to restore the debtor and any other person affected by the sequestration to the position they would have been in if the sequestration had not been awarded.*[126] *However, the recall does not affect the interruption of prescription caused by the presentation of the petition, the making of the debtor application, nor the submission of a claim by a creditor.*[127] *Nor does it invalidate any transaction entered into before recall by the interim trustee or trustee with a person acting in good faith, nor affect a bankruptcy restrictions order which has not been annulled by the sheriff.*[128] Additionally, the Court of Session has the power, of its own motion, or at the instance of an interested party, to order that petitions be heard together, or to direct a sheriff to sist or dismiss a petition.[129]

THE AWARD OF SEQUESTRATION

Where a debtor application is made, the AIB must award sequestration forthwith if satisfied that: **7.1.6**

- the application is made in accordance with the Act and any provisions made under the Act;
- the statement of assets and liabilities (see para.7.2.7) has been sent with the application; and
- the conditions for a debtor application (see para.7.1.3.1) are met.[130]

Where a petition is presented by the creditor or a trustee under a trust deed, the sheriff will grant warrant to cite the debtor to appear before him to show cause why sequestration should not be granted.[131] Sequestration will not be awarded if either[132]:

(1) cause is shown why it is not competent; or
(2) the debtor forthwith pays or satisfies the debt in respect of which he became apparently insolvent and any other debt he owes to the petitioner and any concurring creditor (or produces written evidence of payment/satisfaction, or gives or shows sufficient security for such debt(s)).

---

[119] See s.10(3)(a).
[120] See s.10(3)(b).
[121] See s.10(6).
[122] See s.10A(4), (6).
[123] See s.10A(1), (5).
[124] See s.10A(3).
[125] *See s.10A(3A). After granting such a recall, the AIB must send a certified copy of her decision to the Keeper of the Register of Inhibitions for recording in that register: see s.10A(3D).*
[126] *See s.10A(3B).*
[127] *See s.10A(3C)(a).*
[128] *See s.10A(3C)(b)–(c).*
[129] See s.10A(2).
[130] See s.12(1). *After the amendments made by the 2014 Act, this would include a debtor application made by the executor of a deceased debtor: see s.12(1B).*
[131] See s.12(2).
[132] See s.12(3A).

As regards showing sufficient security for a debt, in *Clydesdale Bank Plc v Grantly Developments*[133] the firm sought to resist the petition presented by the bank on the basis that the bank already held standard securities over the property of the firm. Lord Nimmo Smith reacted as follows[134]:

> "I have found some difficulty in following this argument . . . [T]he Act makes it clear that the debtor can only escape an award of sequestration if he *forthwith* . . . pays the debt or gives or shows that there is sufficient security for the *payment* of the debt. . . . [A] standard security is only sufficient security if it is capable of realisation forthwith and will accordingly result in payment of the whole debt without undue delay."

Again in *Commissioners of Customs and Excise v Zaoui*[135] Lord Prosser stated:

> "The sufficiency of any security must be demonstrated to the satisfaction of the court *forthwith*. I think the word can be read as having somewhat more scope than the word 'immediately', but I cannot envisage it as covering more than a matter of days . . . Once a debtor appears before the court to show cause why sequestration should not be awarded, the statute requires him to do so at that hearing, although perhaps with some brief deferment or continuation. More fundamentally . . . I am satisfied that the offering of security is not the giving of security."

Following the 2007 amendments, it is now also possible for a sheriff to continue a petition for up to 42 days if the debtor can satisfy him that within 42 days of appearing before him, he (the debtor) will pay or satisfy the debt in respect of which he became apparently insolvent and any other debt due to the petitioner.[136] Moreover, a sheriff may continue a petition for as long as he thinks fit if satisfied[137]:

- that a debt payment programme under the Debt Arrangement and Attachment (Scotland) Act 2002 relating to the debt in respect of which the debtor became apparently insolvent and any other debt due to the petitioner has been applied for and not yet been approved or rejected; or
- that a debt payment programme will be applied for.

One of the effects of a debt payment programme being approved in respect of a particular debt is that the creditor cannot seek the debtor's sequestration in relation to that debt.[138] Consequently, if a decision on the approval of such a programme is pending, it makes sense to keep the sequestration proceedings open in the meantime.

Apart from such specialities, the sheriff shall forthwith make the award if satisfied[139]:

(1) that if the debtor has not appeared, proper citation has been made;
(2) that the petition has been presented in accordance with the provisions of the Act;
(3) that the requirements relating to copies of the petition are satisfied;
(4) in the case of a creditor, the requirements as to apparent insolvency have been fulfilled; and
(5) in the case of a trustee, that the matters averred in his petition are true (see para.7.1.5).

When these preconditions are met, sequestration must be awarded, the sheriff having no discretion in the matter.[140] Obviously, if there is doubt as to whether those preconditions are indeed met, or whether a defence to the petition has been established, and some enquiry has to be made into the facts, the proceedings may be continued or even sisted, despite the requirement that the award be made "forthwith".[141] And in *Chris Hart Business Sales Ltd v Campbell*[142] the petition was not granted in light of an interim interdict preventing the petitioner seeking the debtor's sequestration.

---

[133] *Clydesdale Bank Plc v Grantly Developments*, 2000 S.C.L.R 771.
[134] *Clydesdale Bank Plc v Grantly Developments*, 2000 S.C.L.R 771 at 777F–778A.
[135] *Commissioners of Customs and Excise v Zaoui*, 2001 S.L.T. 201 at 206C–D.
[136] See s.12(3B).
[137] See s.12(3C).
[138] Under s.4(3) of the 2002 Act.
[139] See s.12(3).
[140] See, e.g. *Sales Lease Ltd v Minty*, 1993 S.L.T. (Sh Ct) 52 at 54.
[141] See, e.g. *Royal Bank of Scotland Plc v Forbes*, 1988 S.L.T. 73.
[142] *Chris Hart Business Sales Ltd v Campbell*, 1993 S.C.L.R 383.

Date of sequestration

In the case of a debtor application, the date of sequestration will be the date of the award.[143] In the case **7.1.6.1** of a petition, the date will be the date on which the sheriff grants warrant to cite the debtor.[144] Where more than one warrant is granted, the date of the first will be the date.[145] It is vitally important to know the date of sequestration, as many of the consequences of sequestration operate from, or by reference to, that date.

RECALL OF SEQUESTRATION

While a petitioner or a concurring creditor may appeal against a sheriff's refusal to award sequestration,[146] **7.1.7** and a debtor or a concurring creditor may appeal to the sheriff against the AIB's refusal to award sequestration on a debtor application,[147] a decision to award sequestration is not subject to appeal.[148] However, in certain circumstances the award may be recalled. A petition for recall must be presented to the sheriff, and may be presented by the debtor, any creditor or other person having an interest, the trustee in sequestration, or the AIB.[149] The sheriff may recall the award if he is satisfied that in all the circumstances, including those arising after sequestration, it is appropriate to do so.[150] This clearly gives the sheriff considerable discretion, and Lord Prosser has suggested that recall should be granted if it can be done "without apparent prejudice to creditors".[151] However, given that there are generally good reasons why sequestration was granted in the first place, this may be difficult to establish.[152] The Act lists three specific grounds on which sequestration may be recalled, without prejudice to the sheriff's general power to recall. These are[153]:

- the debtor has paid his debts in full or provided sufficient security for their payment. It would not be sufficient for the debtor to aver that such payment could be made or security be provided[154] *(The reference to providing sufficient security for their payment would be removed by the 2014 Act, since the Policy Memorandum (para.249) indicates that the phrase has caused confusion, as it is not clear what it means. The 2014 Act will also add s.17(2A), which indicates that where the sheriff intends to recall the award on this ground, the order may not be made before the payment in full of the outlays and remuneration of the interim trustee and trustee, and may be subject to conditions which are to be fulfilled before the order takes effect.)*;
- the majority in value of the creditors reside in a country other than Scotland, and it is more appropriate that the debtor's estate be administered there; and
- one or more other awards of sequestration of the estate or analogous awards have been granted. Where a petition is presented in such a case, the court may decide to recall the other award(s).

---

[143] See s.12(4)(a).

[144] See s.12(4)(b).

[145] See s.12(4)(b).

[146] See s.15(3).

[147] See s.15(3A). *The 2014 Act intends that instead of such an appeal an application may be made for a review of the refusal within 14 days of the refusal: see s.15(3A)–(3B). The AIB must then take into account any representation made by an interested person made within 21 days of the application, and must confirm the refusal or award sequestration within 28 days of the application: see s.15(3C). If refusal is confirmed, the debtor or a concurring creditor may then appeal against the decision within 14 days of it being made: see s.15(3D).*

[148] See s.15(4).

[149] See s.16(1).

[150] See s.17(1). One such situation might be where a debtor has been sequestrated in respect of the debts of a firm with which she has no connection: *Barlow v City Plumbing Supplies Holdings Ltd*, 2009 S.C.L.R. 350.

[151] *Button v Royal Bank of Scotland Plc*, 1987 G.W.D. 27–1019.

[152] See, e.g. *Grantly Developments v Clydesdale Bank Plc*, 2002 G.W.D. 11–339; where an Extra Division held that it was not a good ground for recall that the debtor insisted that he had no assets, this being a matter which the process of sequestration was designed to ascertain.

[153] See s.17(1)–(2).

[154] *Martin v Martin's Trustee*, 1994 S.L.T. 261.

Where recall is sought under any of these three specific grounds, no time limit applies to the presentation of the petition, although the deeper into the process presentation is made, the less likely the petition is to be granted.[155] Otherwise, the petition must be presented within 10 weeks of the award of sequestration.[156]

The sheriff may refuse to recall the award, or order that the sequestration continue subject to such conditions as he thinks fit.[157] Recall restores the debtor and any other person affected by the sequestration so far as possible to the same position he would have been in had sequestration not been awarded,[158] and the sheriff has the power to make any order necessary to achieve this.[159] Nonetheless, if a period of prescription was interrupted by the presentation of the petition for sequestration, the recall of an award does not affect that interruption.[160] Nor does the recall invalidate any transaction entered into prior to the recall by the trustee in sequestration with a person acting in good faith.[161] The sheriff on recall must make provision for payment of the outlays and remuneration of the interim trustee and (where relevant) the trustee in sequestration. He may either direct that the payment be made out of the debtor's estate or require the petitioner for sequestration to pay.[162] He may also direct that payment of the expenses of a petitioning or concurring creditor be made out of the debtor's estate.[163] The question of whether the sheriff could impose a personal liability on the debtor to pay the outlays and remuneration of the trustee, should his estate be inadequate for that purpose, was considered in *Hall v Crawford*.[164] The majority of the court took the view that it was not open to the sheriff to impose personal liability in terms of s.17(3)(a), although it was also thought[165] that his power under s.17(3)(c) to make such further order as it considers necessary and reasonable would entitle him to impose such liability. Lord Marnoch opined[166]:

> "the real 'moral' to be derived from the case is that a trustee should oppose a motion for recall of sequestration unless and until he is satisfied that . . . he will be in a position to pay for his outlays and remuneration 'out of' the funds in his hands, or alternatively that he has made some other secure arrangement for their payment."

In addition to the provisions outlined above, a non-entitled spouse who has occupancy rights in the matrimonial home under the Matrimonial Homes (Family Protection) (Scotland) Act 1981 may apply for a recall on the basis that the purpose of the sequestration was wholly or mainly to defeat those occupancy rights.[167] The 1981 Act confers occupancy rights upon a spouse who is not permitted or entitled to occupy the matrimonial home, and s.41 gives the right of recall to such a spouse in order to deal with the possibility that the other spouse might seek to thwart those rights by arranging for his own sequestration. The trustee in sequestration must intimate the sequestration to any such non-entitled spouse within 14 days of being appointed.[168] The non-entitled spouse may then petition for recall within 40 days of the date of the trustee's appointment or 10 weeks of the award of sequestration. The sheriff may instead of granting recall make any other order as he thinks fit to protect the occupancy rights.[169] Section 41A contains more or less identical provisions governing the position of a non-entitled partner under the Civil Partnership Act 2004.

---

[155] *Van Overwaele v Hacking and Paterson (No.1)*, 2002 S.C. 62.

[156] See s.16(4). The court will not entertain a petition which is not presented timeously: *Sutherland v Advocate General for Scotland*, 2006 S.C. 682. But in *Barlow v City Plumbing Supplies Holdings Ltd*, 2009 S.C.L.R. 350; Lord Hardie suggested that if the debtor had not applied within the time period because she was unaware of the sequestration, the award might be reduced. *The 2014 Act would remove the time limit.*

[157] See s.17(6).

[158] See s.17(4).

[159] See s.17(3)(c).

[160] See s.17(5)(a).

[161] See s.17(5)(b).

[162] See s.17(3)(a).

[163] See s.17(3)(b).

[164] *Hall v Crawford*, 2002 S.C.L.R. 464.

[165] See Lord Marnoch at *Hall v Crawford*, 2002 S.C.L.R. 464 at 472B.

[166] *Hall v Crawford*, 2002 S.C.L.R. 464 at 472B–C.

[167] See s.41(1).

[168] See s.41(1).

[169] See s.41(1)(b)(ii).

The 2014 Act contemplates that where the only ground for recall is that the debtor can pay his debts in full (except where he is claiming that he was not apparently insolvent at the date of sequestration) an application for recall must be made to the AIB rather than the sheriff.[170] The basic procedure for making such an application (under s.17A) is fairly similar to the presentation of a petition for recall under s.16. However, several other new provisions are introduced. Thus s.17B elaborates on the procedure to be followed. It insists that the trustee must prepare a statement on the debtor's affairs, so far as these matters are within the trustee's knowledge.[171] The statement must be submitted at the same time as the application, or if someone other than the trustee makes the application, within 21 days of notice of the application being given.[172] The trustee must also notify every known creditor that an application had been made. This must be done within seven days of the application being made, or if someone other than the trustee had made the application, within seven days of notice of the application being given.[173] The statement must indicate whether the debtor has agreed to the claims of the trustee and interim trustee for outlays reasonably incurred and for remuneration for work reasonably undertaken, including in both cases any outlays and remuneration yet to be incurred.[174] It must also state whether or not the debtor's debts (including the outlays and remuneration of the interim trustee and trustee) have been paid in full.[175] Where they have not been so paid, the statement must provide details of any unpaid debt and indicate whether, in the trustee's opinion, the debtor's assets are likely to be sufficient to pay the debts (including the outlays and remuneration of the interim trustee and trustee) in full within eight weeks of the submission of the statement.[176] Finally, the statement must provide details of any distribution of the debtor's estate. If a creditor has not previously submitted a claim, in order to be included in the statement he must do so within 14 days of such notice being given.[177] (See para.7.3.3 for how a claim should be submitted.) Should any such claim be submitted, the trustee must update and resubmit the statement within seven days of the expiry of that 14 day period.[178] The trustee must also update and resubmit the statement if it did not state that the debtor's debts had been paid in full, and the trustee is able to make that statement before the application is determined by the AIB.

The 2014 Act contemplates that the AIB may grant recall of an award of sequestration. If the AIB does not grant a recall or interim recall, the sequestration will continue, but subject to such conditions as she thinks fit.[179] The AIB may grant a recall of an award of sequestration where the trustee has notified her in the statement submitted under s.17B that the debtor's debts have paid in full (including the outlays and remuneration of the interim trustee and trustee), and if she is satisfied that it is appropriate to do so.[180] The effect of that recall is, so far as is practicable, to restore the debtor and any other person affected by the sequestration to the position they would have been in if the sequestration had not been awarded.[181] However, the recall does not affect the interruption of prescription caused by the presentation of the petition, the making of the debtor application, nor the submission of a claim by a creditor.[182] Nor does it invalidate any transaction entered into before recall by the interim trustee or

---

[170] *See s.16(1A), (1B).*

[171] *See s.17B(2).*

[172] *See s.17B(3).*

[173] *See s.17B(6).*

[174] *See s.17B(4)(a). If the statement indicates that this is not agreed, the trustee must at the same time as submitting the statement provide the AIB with his accounts of his intromissions with the debtor's estate for audit, plus details of his claim for outlays and remuneration, as well as such other information as the AIB reasonably requests: see s.17C(1)–(2). The AIB must then within 28 days of the expiry of the period mentioned in s.17B(9) (discussed below) issue a determination fixing the amount of outlays and remuneration payable to the trustee: see s.17C(3). Within the same period the AIB may also determine the expenses reasonably incurred by a creditor who petitioned for sequestration or concurred in a debtor application: see s.17C(3A)). If a debtor satisfies the sheriff that he has a pecuniary interest in the outcome of an appeal, he may appeal to the sheriff against a determination under s.17C(3) within 8 weeks after the end of an accounting period, and the decision of the sheriff will be final: see s.17C(4).*

[175] *See s.17B(4)(b).*

[176] *See s.17B(4)(c).*

[177] *See s.17B(7)–(8).*

[178] *See s.17B(9).*

[179] *See s.17E(4).*

[180] *See s.17E(1).*

[181] *See s.17E(2).*

[182] *See s.17E(3)(a).*

trustee with a person acting in good faith, nor affect a bankruptcy restrictions order which has not been annulled by the sheriff.[183] *After granting such a recall, the AIB must without delay send a certified copy of her decision to the Keeper of the Register of Inhibitions for recording in that register.*[184]

Provision is also made for the AIB to grant recall of an award of sequestration where she is herself the trustee and considers that recall should be granted on the ground that the debtor has paid or is able to pay his debts in full, including the outlays and remuneration of the interim trustee and trustee.[185] *In that case she must notify the debtor and every known creditor that such is the position.*[186] *If a creditor has not previously submitted a claim, in order that his claim to a dividend from the debtor's estate should be considered he must do so within 14 days of such notice being given.*[187] *Before granting interim recall the AIB must take into account any representations made by an interested person made within 21 days of such notice being given, and determine her fees and outlays.*[188] *The AIB may grant recall if she is satisfied that the debtor's debts have paid in full (including the outlays and remuneration of the interim trustee and trustee) within eight weeks of the expiry of the above mentioned 21 day period, and that it is appropriate to do so.*[189] *The effect of recall is the same as if the AIB had not been the trustee.*[190] *After granting such a recall, the AIB must without delay send a certified copy of her decision to the Keeper of the Register of Inhibitions for recording in that register.*[191]

Whether or not the AIB is the trustee, she may always refer an application for recall to the sheriff to be dealt with as if it were a petition for recall.[192]

The debtor, a creditor, the trustee or any other interested person may apply to the AIB for a review of her decision to grant or refuse to grant recall or interim recall, or her determination of the expenses reasonably incurred by a petitioning or concurring creditor, within 14 days of the date of the relevant decision or determination.[193] *The AIB must confirm, amend or revoke the decision or determination within 28 days of the application, but must take into account any representations made by an interested person within 21 days of the application.*[194] *The debtor, a creditor, the trustee or any other interested person may then appeal to the sheriff against the AIB's review decision within 14 days of that decision.*[195] *Equally, such a person may appeal to the sheriff against the AIB's determination of the amount of the outlays and remuneration payable to the trustee or the amount of her own outlays and fees when acting as trustee,*[196] *the sheriff's decision in this case being final.*[197] *In upholding an appeal against the AIB's decision to grant or refuse to grant interim recall, the sheriff may quash the decision and remit the case to the AIB.*[198]

7.2   THE SEQUESTRATION PROCESS

APPOINTMENT OF AN INTERIM TRUSTEE

7.2.1 It used to be the case that the first step in any sequestration would be the appointment of an interim trustee to take over the administration of the debtor's estate prior to the election or appointment of a

---

[183] *See s.17E(3)(b)–(c).*
[184] *See s.17E(5).*
[185] *See s.17F(1).*
[186] *See s.17F(2).*
[187] *See s.17F(3)–(4).*
[188] *See s.17F(5).*
[189] *See s.17F(9).*
[190] *See s.17F(10).*
[191] *See s.17F(11).*
[192] *See s.17G.*
[193] *See s.17H(1)–(3).*
[194] *See s.17H(4)–(5).*
[195] *See s.17H(5)(a).*
[196] *See s.17H(5)(b).*
[197] *See s.17H(6).*
[198] *See s.17H(7).*

permanent trustee. However, following the 2007 Act those offices are amalgamated into that of the trustee in sequestration. Thus an interim trustee now may only be appointed for the limited period between a petition for sequestration being presented and sequestration being awarded, while his sole function is to safeguard the estate until the decision whether or not to award sequestration is taken.[199] There need not be an interim trustee, but one may be appointed where the petition is presented by a creditor or a trustee under a trust deed, and either the debtor consents or cause is shown for the appointment,[200] e.g. a risk to the estate. Where the petition nominates a qualified insolvency practitioner who has given a written undertaking to act as interim trustee, the sheriff may appoint that person,[201] but where such a person is not appointed then the sheriff must appoint the AIB to act as interim trustee.[202] In cases where it is obvious that the available assets will be insufficient even to meet the outlays and remuneration of the interim trustee, it is most unlikely that a private insolvency practitioner would be willing to accept nomination. In such cases the AIB will inevitably be appointed. An interim trustee must inform the debtor of his appointment as soon as is practicable.[203]

Where the interim trustee dies in office, the sheriff will appoint a new interim trustee, on the application of the debtor, a creditor or the AIB.[204] An interim trustee (not the AIB) who wishes to resign may apply to the sheriff for authority to do so, and the sheriff shall grant such an application if satisfied[205]:

(a) that the interim trustee is unable to act by virtue of a provision of the Act, or because he is incapable within the meaning of s.1(4) of the Adults with Incapacity (Scotland) Act 2000 or is subject to some other incapacity which prevents him from acting; or
(b) that he has so conducted himself that he should no longer continue to act.

The interim trustee may also be removed by the sheriff on either of the above grounds on the application of the debtor, a creditor or the AIB,[206] or following upon a report to the court by the AIB that he has failed to perform any of his duties without reasonable excuse.[207] In the last case, the sheriff shall appoint a replacement on the application of the AIB.[208] Otherwise, he will automatically appoint a replacement.[209]

THE POWERS OF THE INTERIM TRUSTEE

The interim trustee is granted extensive powers to ensure the interim preservation of the debtor's estate. **7.2.2** Firstly, a general power to direct the debtor as to the management of the estate is conferred.[210] If the debtor thinks any such direction is unreasonable, he may apply to the sheriff, who may set aside the direction or substitute his own, although the debtor must comply with the original direction until the appeal is finally determined.[211] *(Under the 2014 Act reforms, while this would continue to be the case where the AIB is not the interim trustee, where she is the interim trustee, instead of applying to the sheriff the debtor would apply to the AIB for a review of that direction.[212] The AIB must confirm, amend or revoke the direction within 28 days of the application, but must take into account any*

---

[199] See s.2(6A). The interim trustee must also supply such information to the AIB as the latter considers necessary to enable her to discharge her functions under the Act: s.2(6B). This duty continues even after he has left office.
[200] See s.2(5).
[201] See s.2(6)(a).
[202] See s.2(6)(b).
[203] See s.2(7)(b).
[204] See s.13(5).
[205] See s.13(2)–(3).
[206] See s.13(2)–(3).
[207] See s.1A(2).
[208] See s.13(1).
[209] See s.13(2), (4).
[210] See s.18(1).
[211] See s.18(4).
[212] *See s.18(3A).*

representations made by an interested person within 21 days of the application.[213] *The debtor may then apply to the sheriff within 14 days of the AIB's review decision.*[214]*)* The aforementioned general power is supplemented by a number of specific powers. These include the power to[215]:

(1) require the debtor to deliver up money, valuables, business or financial documents;

(2) place anything mentioned in (1) in safe custody;

(3) require the debtor to deliver up perishable goods, and arrange their sale or disposal (while generally the sale of any property is a function restricted to the trustee in sequestration, the need for this exception is obvious);

(4) make an inventory or valuation of the debtor's property;

(5) require the debtor to implement any transaction the debtor has undertaken, e.g. a beneficial contract;

(6) effect or maintain insurance policies in respect of the debtor's business or property;

(7) carry on the debtor's business and borrow money insofar as such borrowing is necessary to safeguard the estate; and

(8) request the supply of gas, electricity, water or telecommunications services for the purposes of the debtor's business.[216]

Moreover, he can ask the sheriff for a warrant to enter and search the debtor's home or business premises (but not elsewhere) to search for and take possession of money, etc.; which warrant the sheriff may grant on cause shown.[217] More generally, the sheriff, on the interim trustee's application, may grant such other order to safeguard the estate as it thinks appropriate.[218] Thus in *Scottish & Newcastle Plc, Petitioner*[219] the court authorised the sale of licensed premises—a power which only the trustee in sequestration would normally have. Of course this case relates to a period when the interim trustee would continue in office for a significant period after sequestration was awarded. Since he is now only appointed for a limited period, it is unlikely that a sheriff will have occasion to make such an order again. The debtor is guilty of an offence if he fails without reasonable excuse to comply with any direction or requirement or obstructs the interim trustee in any search.[220]

INTERIM TRUSTEE—TERMINATION OF FUNCTIONS AND DISCHARGE

7.2.3 In relation to an interim trustee who is not the AIB, if he is not appointed the trustee in sequestration, he must on sequestration being awarded hand over everything relating to the sequestration, and thereupon shall cease to act.[221] Within three months of the sheriff awarding (or refusing to award) sequestration, the interim trustee shall[222]:

(1) submit to the AIB his accounts of his intromissions (if any) with the estate and a claim for his outlays reasonably incurred and for remuneration for work reasonably undertaken; and

(2) send a copy of the above submission to the debtor, the person who petitioned for sequestration and (where sequestration was awarded) to the trustee in sequestration and to all creditors known to the interim trustee.

His accounts are audited by, and the actual amount of outlays and remuneration payable determined by, the AIB, who must send a copy of the determination to the interim trustee and everyone entitled to a

---

[213] See s.18(3B).

[214] See s.18(3C)–(3D).

[215] See s.18(2).

[216] See s.70. The supplier may not make it a condition of the continuation of the supply that outstanding charges are paid, but is entitled to insist that the interim trustee personally guarantees the payment of any charges: s.70(2).

[217] See s.18(3)(b).

[218] See s.18(3)(c).

[219] *Scottish & Newcastle Plc, Petitioner*, 1992 S.C.L.R. 540.

[220] See s.18(5).

[221] See s.13A(2).

[222] See s.13A(4).

copy of the submission.[223] Where sequestration has been awarded, the AIB shall also send a copy of the audited accounts and determination to the trustee in sequestration, who shall insert them in the sederunt book.[224] Within 14 days of the AIB's determination being issued, it may be appealed to the sheriff by the interim trustee, the trustee in sequestration, the debtor or any creditor.[225] When the interim trustee receives a copy of the AIB's determination he may apply to the AIB for a discharge, sending a notice of that application to any person entitled to a copy of his submission and informing them of the effect of a discharge and their right to make written representations regarding the application to the AIB within 14 days of notification.[226] Once that 14-day period has expired, the AIB, having considered any such representations, shall grant or refuse a certificate of discharge, notifying all persons who were entitled to make representations.[227] All such persons and the interim trustee may appeal that decision to the sheriff, who may confirm the AIB's decision, or revoke any certificate granted, or order that one be granted if it has been refused.[228] The sheriff's decision is final.[229] *The 2014 Act contemplates that, instead of an appeal, such individuals may apply to the AIB for a review of her decision within 14 days of it being made.[230] The AIB must confirm, amend or revoke the decision within 28 days of the application, but must take into account any representations made by an interested person within 21 days of the application.[231] An appeal may then be made to the sheriff against the AIB's review decision within 14 days of that decision.[232]* The grant of a discharge discharges the interim trustee from all liability (other than liability for fraud) in the exercise of his functions.[233] The sheriff may make such order in relation to liability for the outlays and remuneration of the interim trustee as may be appropriate.[234] A similar set of provisions, suitably adapted, deals with the situation where the AIB is the interim trustee.[235]

THE APPOINTMENT OF THE TRUSTEE IN SEQUESTRATION

Prior to the 2007 amendments, the interim trustee remained in office after the award of sequestration **7.2.4** until the statutory meeting of creditors elected the permanent trustee or the permanent trustee was appointed by the court when nobody was elected to that office. Now the interim trustee (if any) ceases to hold office on the award of sequestration, and the trustee in sequestration is thereupon appointed. Where sequestration is awarded by the AIB on a debtor application, and that application nominates a person to be trustee, states that person is a qualified insolvency practitioner who has given an undertaking to act, and has a copy of that undertaking attached, then if it appears to the AIB that the person satisfies those conditions, she may appoint that individual.[236] If no person is nominated, or the AIB decides not to appoint that person, the AIB herself will be automatically appointed as the trustee in sequestration.[237] Moreover, the AIB will be automatically appointed as the trustee in all instances of applications by low income, low asset debtors.[238]

Where sequestration is awarded by the sheriff and an interim trustee has been appointed, the sheriff may appoint the interim trustee as the trustee in sequestration.[239] Alternatively, he may appoint

---

[223] See s.13A(5)(a)–(c).
[224] See s.13A(5)(d). Of course, where the AIB herself becomes the trustee there is no need for such material to be sent before it is inserted: s.13A(6).
[225] See s.13A(7).
[226] See s.13A(8)–(9).
[227] See s.13A(10).
[228] See s.13A(11)–(13).
[229] See s.13A(15).
[230] *See s.13A(10A)–(10B).*
[231] *See s.13A(10C).*
[232] *See s.13A(11).*
[233] See s.13A(16).
[234] See s.13A(3).
[235] See s.13B.
[236] See s.2(1A).
[237] See s.2(1B).
[238] See s.2(1C).
[239] See s.2(2A)(a).

an individual nominated in the petition[240] provided it appears to the sheriff that that person is a qualified insolvency practitioner who has given an undertaking to act, and a copy of that undertaking has been lodged with the sheriff.[241] If the sheriff appoints neither such individual, he must appoint the AIB.[242] Where there is no interim trustee, the sheriff's options are practically identical, save that obviously he cannot appoint the interim trustee.[243]

Where sequestration follows on a petition the trustee must inform the debtor of his appointment as soon as practicable,[244] *at the same time sending the debtor for signing a statement of undertakings in prescribed form.[245]*

RESIGNATION/REMOVAL/DEATH OF THE TRUSTEE

7.2.5　A trustee must apply to the AIB if he wishes to resign office,[246] and authority to do so can only be given on two grounds—inability to act, or misconduct.[247] The AIB may make such authority subject to the election of a new trustee, and to such conditions as she thinks appropriate.[248] If a trustee (other than the AIB) dies, it is the duty of the commissioners (see para.7.3.2 below), or the AIB if there are none, to call a meeting of creditors to elect a new trustee.[249] The same is true if the trustee is permitted to resign, except where the application has been granted subject to the election of a new trustee, in which case the resigning trustee must himself call a meeting of creditors to elect a new trustee.[250] Where the trustee was appointed rather than elected to begin with,[251] or where no replacement trustee is elected, the AIB or her nominee may apply to the sheriff for appointment in place of a deceased or resigning trustee.[252] *The 2014 Act intends that where no replacement trustee is elected, the AIB shall appoint as trustee any person who applies for appointment within 14 days of the meeting.[253] If no such person applies, the AIB may appoint anyone who consents to the appointment.[254] In the absence of such appointment, the AIB is deemed to be the trustee.[255] Any person appointed must of course be eligible to act as replacement trustee[256] (see para.7.2.10).*

It is also possible for a trustee (other than the AIB)[257] to be removed. The trustee may be removed by a majority of those creditors entitled to vote on the issue, provided they elect a new trustee forthwith.[258] A trustee may also be removed by the sheriff. One situation where that might occur is where the AIB has reported the trustee to the sheriff under s.1A(2) for failure to perform his duties, and the sheriff decides to remove him from office (see para.7.1.1.1). Otherwise the sheriff may remove a trustee under s.29 if cause is shown. If the cause is that he is unable to act (for a reason other than death) or has so conducted himself that he should no longer continue to act, then the debtor, the AIB, or any commissioner or creditor may apply for his removal.[259] If any other cause is advanced, the AIB, the commissioners, or a

---

[240] See s.2(2A)(b).
[241] See s.2(2B).
[242] See s.2(2C).
[243] See s.2(2).
[244] See s.2(7).
[245] *See s.2(8).*
[246] For the form of application see Bankruptcy (Scotland) Regulations 2008 (SSI 2008/82) Form 19.
[247] See s.28(1).
[248] See s.28(1A).
[249] See s.28(3).
[250] See s.28(2).
[251] See Sch.2 para.3(2).
[252] See s.28(5).
[253] *See s.28(5)(a).*
[254] *See s.28(5)(b).*
[255] *See s.28(5B).*
[256] *See s.28(5A).*
[257] See s.29(10).
[258] See s.29(1)(a).
[259] See s.29(6), (9).

person representing not less than a quarter in value of the creditors may apply.[260] In either case, if the sheriff is satisfied that cause has been shown he may remove the trustee. In the latter case the trustee is entitled to have an opportunity to be heard before the sheriff makes a decision.[261] The trustee, the AIB, the commissioners, or any creditor may appeal against the sheriff's decision within 14 days of it being made.[262] In the former case the sheriff may declare the office of trustee to be vacant.[263] If in either case the sheriff removes the trustee, the commissioners (or the AIB if there are none) must call a meeting of creditors no more than 28 days after removal to elect a new trustee.[264] *The 2014 Act would transfer the sheriff's functions in this context to the AIB. Thus in both cases application would be made to the AIB rather than the sheriff, while the AIB would require to be satisfied that a relevant reason for removal applies, either on the application of an appropriate person[265] or on her own initiative. The AIB must order that an application under s.29(1A) be served on the trustee, giving him an opportunity to make representations before reaching a decision, and must enter particulars of the application in the register of insolvencies.[266] The trustee, the debtor, the commissioners, or any creditor may apply to the AIB for a review of her decision or declaration within 14 days of it being made.[267] The AIB must confirm, amend or revoke the decision or declaration within 28 days of the application, but must take into account any representations made by an interested person within 21 days of the application.[268] The same individuals may then appeal to the sheriff against the AIB's review decision within 14 days of that decision.[269]*

THE FUNCTIONS OF THE TRUSTEE IN SEQUESTRATION

The trustee's functions include[270]:   **7.2.6**

- recovering, managing and realising the debtor's estate, wherever situated;
- distributing the estate among the creditors according to their respective entitlements;
- ascertaining the reasons for the debtor's insolvency and the circumstances surrounding it; and
- ascertaining the state of the debtor's liabilities and assets.

However the trustee should discharge the above functions only insofar as he believes that it would be of financial benefit to the estate and in the interests of the creditors to do so[271]:

- providing an accurate record of the sequestration process through maintaining a sederunt book into which all key documents are inserted (he must also give the debtor and all creditors known to him written notice that the book is available for inspection at an address specified by him)[272];

---

[260] See s.29(1)(b).

[261] See s.29(2).

[262] See s.29(4).

[263] See s.29(6).

[264] See s.29(5)–(6).

[265] *Obviously, the AIB herself would no longer make an application. Otherwise the individuals who may make an application under the situation contemplated by s.29(1)(b) are as before: see s.29(1A). In the other situation, only the debtor, the commissioners or a creditor may apply, i.e. an individual commissioner may no longer apply: see s.29(6A). The AIB may also ask a sheriff for a direction before making any order or declaration or undertaking any review under this section: see s.29(6I). No party may ask for a review of the AIB's decision in relation to a matter on which she has applied to the sheriff for a direction: see s.29(6J).*

[266] *See s.29(2).*

[267] *See s.29(3A)–(3B), (6E)–(6F).*

[268] *See s.29(3C), (6G).*

[269] *See s.29(4), (6H).*

[270] See s.3.

[271] See s.3(8).

[272] See s.3(1)(e). *The 2014 Act contemplates that the sederunt book should henceforward be kept in electronic form and certainly sent to the AIB in this form: see s.57(1A). It is also intended that the AIB shall record the information contained in the book in the Register of Insolvencies: see s.58A(4)(b)(ii). Moreover, the 2014 Act adds a new Sch.3A to the 1985 Act, listing in one place (as opposed to being spread across the Act) the documents which have to be placed in the sederunt book.*

- keeping regular accounts available for inspection by all interested parties[273];
- supplying the AIB with such information as she considers necessary to enable her to discharge her functions under the Act. (This last function persists even after he has ceased to act in the sequestration.)

Moreover, if the trustee has reasonable grounds to suspect that an offence has been committed in relation to a sequestration, whether by the debtor or any other person, or that the debtor's behaviour might result in the grant of a bankruptcy restrictions order, he must report such matters to the AIB.[274] Such a report attracts absolute privilege.[275]

STATEMENT OF ASSETS AND LIABILITIES

7.2.7 In order that the trustee may discharge his function of ascertaining the reasons for the debtor's insolvency the debtor must supply the trustee with a statement of his assets and liabilities, containing, inter alia, a list of his assets and liabilities and a list of his income and expenditure. In the case of a debtor application, the debtor must send the statement to the AIB along with the application[276] and, should the AIB then be appointed trustee, the debtor need take no further steps. Should the AIB not be appointed trustee, the debtor must send the statement which accompanied the application to the trustee not more than seven days after the appointment.[277] Where the award follows on a petition, the debtor must prepare a statement from scratch and send it to the trustee not more than seven days after the latter has informed him of his appointment.[278] It is a criminal offence for the debtor, without reasonable excuse, to fail to send this statement, to fail to disclose any material fact therein, or to make a material misstatement therein.[279] *The 2014 Act would no longer regard failure to send the statement as a criminal offence.*

Once the trustee receives the statement of assets and liabilities referred to in the previous paragraph, he shall prepare a statement of the debtor's affairs, indicating whether the assets are likely to be able to pay any dividend whatever in respect of preferred, ordinary and postponed debts[280] (see para.7.3.8). This requires him to estimate the value of the debtor's assets, and the value of the probable expenses of the sequestration. Not less than four days before the statutory meeting (see para.7.2.9), or where he does not intend to hold a meeting not more than 60 days after sequestration is awarded, the trustee (unless she is the AIB) must send the AIB a copy of both the aforesaid statements, together with written comments as to the causes of the insolvency and the extent to which the conduct of the debtor may have contributed thereto.[281] Such comments attract absolute privilege.[282]

CALLING THE STATUTORY MEETING

7.2.8 The interim trustee used to have to call a statutory meeting of creditors, the main purpose of which was to elect the permanent trustee. However, in many cases the meeting was fairly pointless, serving only to prolong the process and increase its expense. Thus where the interim trustee was the AIB, she was

---

[273] *But this requirement and the requirement to maintain a sederunt book do not apply where the minimal assets process operates: Sch.A1 para.1(2).*
[274] See s.3(3)–(3A).
[275] See s.3(4).
[276] See s.5(6A).
[277] See s.19(1).
[278] See s.19(2).
[279] See s.19(3), (4).
[280] See s.20(1). *Where the minimal assets process applies, the AIB must prepare a statement of the debtor's affairs, indicating that because s.5(2ZA) applies to the debtor, the creditors may not submit any claims. The AIB must then send a copy of the statement to every known creditor: s.20(1A)–(1B).*
[281] See s.20(2).
[282] See s.20(3).

allowed to elect not to hold the meeting, subject to the right of a certain proportion of creditors to insist that one be held. Following the 2007 amendments, that discretion is extended to every trustee in sequestration. Currently, therefore, within 60 days of the award of sequestration, or such longer period as the sheriff may allow, the trustee must give notice to every creditor known to him of whether he intends to call the statutory meeting.[283] If he indicates that he does not intend to hold the meeting, within seven days of the giving of that notice any creditor can request that a meeting be held,[284] and if a quarter in value so request, the meeting must be held within 28 days of the giving of the notice or such longer period as the sheriff on cause shown might allow.[285] If he indicates that he does intend to hold the meeting, it must be held within 28 days of the giving of the notice.[286] Not less than seven days before the meeting he shall notify any known creditor and the AIB of the date, time and place of the meeting, inviting the submission of claims not already submitted.[287] The creditors are entitled to continue the meeting to a date not more than seven days after the expiry of the period within which the meeting must normally be held, while the sheriff might allow them to continue the meeting to a later date on cause being shown.[288] Where no meeting is held, the trustee (unless she is the AIB) must report to the AIB on the circumstances of the sequestration.[289]

THE STATUTORY MEETING

Where the statutory meeting is held, it must be chaired, at least to begin with, by the trustee.[290] The **7.2.9** quorum is a single creditor entitled to vote.[291] When the meeting is attended by creditors, the first task of the trustee is to accept or reject in whole or in part the claim (see para.7.3.3) of each creditor (and to convert any claim stated in foreign currency into sterling).[292] Acceptance (partial or otherwise) of a claim determines a creditor's entitlement to vote at the meeting.[293] Having decided which claims he will accept, the trustee shall invite the creditors to elect one of their number as chairman, although failing such election he remains in the chair.[294]

Thereafter, the trustee makes available for inspection the statement of assets and liabilities prepared by the debtor and the statement of the debtor's affairs prepared by himself (see para.7.2.7).[295] He must answer to the best of his ability any questions put by the creditors, and must consider any representations they make,[296] e.g. in regard to possible gratuitous alienations by the debtor. As a result of what he has heard, he may decide that it is necessary to revise the statement of the debtor's affairs,[297] and if he does so, he must as soon as possible send a revised copy to every creditor of whom he is aware.[298] Finally, in light of what he has heard, he must once more express an opinion as to whether the assets are likely to be able to pay any dividend whatever in respect of preferred, ordinary and postponed debts.[299]

---

[283] See s.21A(2). *That notice must be accompanied by his statement of the debtor's affairs, and explain the rights of creditors to call a meeting: s.21A(3). In cases where the minimal asset process applies there will be no statutory meeting, so that none of the provisions of ss.21A–28 will apply: Sch.A1 para.1(5).*
[284] See s.21A(4).
[285] See s.21A(5).
[286] See s.21A(6).
[287] See s.21A(7). He must also notify the creditors of his duties under s.23(3) to provide information about the debtor's affairs.
[288] See s.21A(8).
[289] See s.21B and Bankruptcy (Scotland) Regulations 2008 (SSI 2008/82) Form 18.
[290] See s.23(1).
[291] See Sch.6 para.12.
[292] See s.23(1)(a).
[293] See s.23(2).
[294] See s.23(1)(b).
[295] See s.23(3)(a).
[296] See s.23(3)(b).
[297] See s.23(3)(d).
[298] See s.23(5).
[299] See s.23(3)(c).

At the conclusion of the meeting, the creditors shall proceed to the confirmation of the trustee or the election of a replacement trustee.[300] The result is determined by a majority in value of creditors who vote, or their mandatories.[301] Although otherwise entitled to vote at creditors' meetings, no postponed creditor (see para.7.3.8.2) may vote in the election of the trustee, and nor may any creditor whose debt is acquired (unless by succession) after the date of the sequestration.[302]

The meeting (or any subsequent meeting of creditors) may elect between one and five of their number as commissioners (see para.7.3.2), to supervise and advise the trustee.[303] There do not have to be commissioners.[304]

CONFIRMATION OR REPLACEMENT OF THE TRUSTEE

7.2.10 As noted above, the meeting will either confirm the existing trustee in office or elect a replacement. The debtor cannot be elected.[305] Nor can the AIB,[306] nor anyone whose interests are opposed to the general interests of the creditors.[307] Additionally, in order to be eligible for election, an individual must be a qualified insolvency practitioner,[308] and give a written undertaking to act.[309] There must be a single trustee. The office cannot be held jointly.[310]

On election of a replacement trustee, the original trustee must report the proceedings at the meeting to the sheriff.[311] The debtor, any creditor, the original trustee, the replacement trustee or the AIB may within four days of the meeting object to the sheriff concerning the election.[312] If there is a timeous objection, the sheriff shall forthwith give the parties an opportunity to be heard thereon, and shall give his decision,[313] which shall be final.[314] If he sustains the objection, the sheriff shall order the original trustee to arrange a new trustee vote to elect the replacement trustee.[315] If he does not sustain the objection, or if no timeous objection is made, the sheriff shall forthwith confirm the elected person as replacement trustee.[316] *The 2014 Act contemplates that the original trustee must report the proceedings at the meeting to the sheriff only where that trustee was the AIB.[317] Otherwise the report should be made to the AIB.[318] Equally, unless that trustee was the AIB, any objection should be made to the AIB, and it will be the AIB who declares the elected person to be replacement trustee in the absence of a timeous objection.[319] That Act would also add ss.25A and 25B, concerning the procedure for objecting to the election. Where an objection is made to the AIB, she must without delay give the original and replacement trustees, the objector and any other interested person the opportunity to make written submissions, and thereafter she must make a decision.[320] If she decides to reject the objection, she must without delay declare the elected person to be the trustee.[321] If she decides to sustain the objection, she*

---

[300] See s.24(1).
[301] See Sch.6 paras 11, 13.
[302] See s.24(3).
[303] See s.30(1).
[304] See Sch.2 para.6.
[305] See s.24(2)(a).
[306] See s.24(2)(f).
[307] See s.24(2)(c).
[308] See s.24(2)(b).
[309] See s.24(2)(e).
[310] *Inland Revenue Commissioners v MacDonald*, 1988 S.L.T. (Sh Ct) 7.
[311] See s.25(1)(a).
[312] See s.25(1)(b).
[313] See s.25(3).
[314] See s.25(5).
[315] See s.25(4)(b).
[316] See ss.25(2), 25(4)(a).
[317] *See s.25(2)(b).*
[318] *See s.25(2)(a).*
[319] *See s.25(3), (5).*
[320] *See s.25A(2), and see s.25B(2) for very similar provisions regarding the sheriff.*
[321] *See s.25A(3)(a), and see s.25B(3)(a) for very similar provisions regarding the sheriff.*

must order the original trustee to arrange a new meeting at which a new trustee vote will be held.[322] Any of the same individuals may then apply to her for a review of her decision within 14 days of it being notified.[323] The AIB must confirm, amend or revoke the decision within 28 days of the application, but must take into account any representations made by an interested person within 21 days of the application.[324] The debtor, the objector or any other interested person may then appeal to the sheriff against the AIB's review decision within 14 days of that decision.[325] A very similar regime applies to applications and appeals to the sheriff under s.25B, save that any decision of the sheriff is final and thus not subject to review or appeal.[326]

When the original trustee is not confirmed in office, he shall on confirmation of the replacement trustee hand over everything in his possession relating to the sequestration and cease to act.[327] Within three months of confirmation of the replacement trustee, the original trustee must submit to the AIB an account of any intromissions with the estate and a claim for outlays reasonably incurred and work reasonably undertaken[328] (including, if applicable, outlays incurred and work undertaken as interim trustee).[329] The AIB shall audit the accounts and determine the amount payable,[330] which determination may be appealed to the sheriff within 14 days of issue by the debtor, any creditor, the original trustee or the replacement trustee, and the sheriff's decision is final.[331] These provisions do not apply where the AIB was the original trustee.[332]

If no creditor entitled to vote attends the meeting, or if no replacement trustee is elected, then the original trustee (unless she is the AIB) must forthwith notify the AIB, report to the sheriff, and continue to act as trustee.[333] Where, in such a case, the AIB is the original trustee, she must forthwith report to the sheriff and continue to act as trustee.[334]

VESTING OF THE ESTATE IN THE TRUSTEE

7.2.11 By virtue of the trustee's appointment, the debtor is divested of his entire estate, which vests in the trustee as at the date of sequestration.[335] Vesting includes all powers the debtor might have had in relation to the estate.[336]

Acquirenda

7.2.11.1 Moreover, any estate which the debtor acquires after the date of sequestration and prior to discharge, e.g. as a result of inheritance, similarly automatically vests in the trustee. *The 2014 Act takes the view that the interests of creditors are not properly served if the trustee can only claim acquirenda which vest in the debtor prior to discharge. Instead the trustee will be able to claim acquirenda which vest in the debtor within the four years following the date of sequestration.[337]* The Act provides that any person

---

[322] *See s.25A(3)(b), and see s.25B(3)(b) for very similar provisions regarding the sheriff.*

[323] *See s.25A(5)–(6).*

[324] *See s.25A(7).*

[325] *See s.25A(8).*

[326] *See s.25B(5).*

[327] See s.26(1).

[328] See s.26(2).

[329] See s.26(2A).

[330] See s.26(3). He must also send a copy of the determination to both the original and the replacement trustee, while the latter must insert the determination and audited accounts in the sederunt book.

[331] See s.26(4).

[332] See s.26(5A).

[333] See s.24(4).

[334] See s.24(3A).

[335] See s.31(1). This is not incompatible with art.1 of Protocol 1 of the European Convention on Human Rights; see *Krasner v Dennison* [2001] Ch. 76 CA.

[336] See s.31(8); e.g. exercising voting rights under shares which were part of the debtor's estate: *Cumming's Trustee v Glenrinnes Farms Ltd*, 1993 S.L.T. 904.

[337] *See s.32(10).*

who holds any such estate must convey or deliver the estate to the trustee.[338] However, if such a person has in good faith and without knowledge of the sequestration, conveyed any estate to the debtor, he shall incur no liability to the trustee except to account for any proceeds of the conveyance which are in his hands.[339] *The 2014 Act proposes to add that where the trustee knows or becomes aware of any estate vested in him which comprises funds held by a bank, he must serve a notice on the bank informing it of the sequestration and giving sufficient specification to allow the bank to identify the debtor and the funds held.*[340] *Such a notice must be in writing and may be sent by first class post or registered or recorded delivery or sent in some other manner, including electronically, which he reasonably considers likely to cause it to be delivered to the bank on the same or the following day.*[341] *The notice is then deemed to be delivered on the day after it is sent.*[342] The consequences of a person conveying property to the debtor although aware of his sequestration are described by Lord Macfadyen in *Rankin's Trustee v H C Somerville & Russell*[343]:

> "[I]f the holder [of property] in fact conveys, delivers or pays the property to the debtor, he thereby wrongfully disposes of the property which belongs to the trustee for the benefit of the creditors. In that situation the trustee is entitled to seek the appropriate remedy against the former holder. If the property which has been paid away to the debtor is cash, that remedy will be a money claim."

A debtor must immediately inform the trustee of any *acquirenda*, on pain of committing an offence,[344] and may not validly deal with this property.[345] Naturally, anything acquired with *acquirenda* also vests in the trustee.[346]

Tantum et tale

7.2.11.2 The trustee effectively gains the same rights as the debtor to the estate, and is thus subject to any limitations which affected the debtor.[347] Moreover, the Act specifically states that the right of any secured creditor is preferable to the rights of the trustee, and that the vesting of the estate in the trustee does not defeat a landlord's hypothec.[348]

Specialities of moveable property

7.2.11.3 The trustee acquires the debtor's entire moveable estate, including any rights to payment which the latter may have, e.g. a right to claim rent.[349] However, there is a difference between acquiring rights and undertaking onerous obligations, such as that of a tenant under a lease, and the trustee will not be liable for such obligations unless he adopts the contract[350] (see para.7.2.15). Again, while the Act provides that where delivery or possession or intimation of its assignation would normally be required to complete title to moveables, such delivery, possession or intimation will be deemed,[351] where some

---

[338] See s.32(6).

[339] See s.32(6)(i). And a trustee has no remedy against a bank in respect of any banking transaction entered into before the receipt of the notice under s.32(5A), whether or not the bank was aware of the sequestration: see s.32(6)(ia).

[340] *See s.32(5A).*

[341] *See s.32(5B)(a).*

[342] *See s.32(5B)(b).*

[343] *Rankin's Trustee v H C Somerville & Russell*, 1999 S.L.T. 65 at 71–72.

[344] See s.32(7).

[345] *Alliance and Leicester Building Society v Murray's Trustee*, 1994 S.C.L.R. 19.

[346] *Royal Bank of Scotland Plc v Macgregor*, 1998 S.C.L.R. 923—property acquired by a loan taken out after the date of sequestration vests in the trustee, albeit subject to security granted in relation thereto.

[347] *Heritable Reversionary Co Ltd v Millar* (1892) 19 R. (HL) 43.

[348] See s.33(2), (3). It is now of course the case that the extent of a landlord's hypothec has been significantly restricted by s.208 of the 2007 Act: see para.5.4.2.1 above.

[349] *Mitchell's Trustee v Pearson* (1834) 12 S. 322.

[350] *Myles v City of Glasgow Bank* (1879) 6 R. 718; *MacDonald's Trustees v Cunningham*, 1997 S.C.L.R. 986.

[351] See s.31(4).

further step is necessary to complete title, e.g. registration, the title of the trustee is not perfected until that step occurs,[352] and the rights of the trustee may be defeated if a third party registers title first.[353]

Damages

If damages awarded to the debtor form part of the estate then they will vest in the trustee. More importantly, a trustee can raise an action in respect of patrimonial loss suffered by the debtor.[354] On the other hand, it has always been recognised that a right to sue for *solatium* is a right purely personal to the debtor, so that only the debtor can raise such an action.[355] Yet as soon as an action to recover *solatium* is raised, the right to any damages paid (or indeed to any sum received in settlement of the claim) vests in the trustee, even if damages (or the amount agreed on) are only paid after the debtor is discharged.[356] It is specifically provided that an award under the Criminal Injuries Compensation Scheme does not vest in the trustee.[357] **7.2.11.4**

Obviously, if damages are paid in respect of the wrongful dismissal of the debtor from employment, they will vest in the trustee. Actual remuneration from employment counts as income, and so will not vest (see para.7.2.12.2). A question arises in relation to payment in lieu of notice. If this is regarded as remuneration from employment, it will not vest, but if it were to be treated as liquidated damages, then it might be argued that it should vest. It is suggested that redundancy payments, compensation for unfair dismissal and other compensation in respect of the infringement of employment rights are equivalent to damages and thus should vest. The same argument might be made in respect of contractual compensation on dismissal, e.g. contractually enhanced redundancy payments, or ex gratia payments. It has to be recorded, nonetheless, that the notes by the Accountant in Bankruptcy for the guidance of trustees refer[358] to the case of Patrick McGrail, heard in Glasgow Sheriff Court on August 10, 1990, in which certain of the above matters were discussed. The trustee in that case conceded that payment in lieu of notice did not vest. The sheriff held that the statutory redundancy payment was alimentary in nature, so did not vest, but that a contractually enhanced redundancy payment and an ex gratia payment both did vest.

Pensions

Under occupational pension schemes the fund from which the pension is payable is not owned by the debtor, so that where he receives any sum (including a lump sum) from an occupational pension, it is treated as income and so will not vest in the trustee. A personal pension usually takes the form of an annuity purchased by a fund invested and owned by the debtor, so that although payments take the form of income, that income derives from estate vested in the trustee (the pension fund). Thus traditionally, personal pensions vested in the trustee.[359] Yet personal pensions no longer so vest in sequestrations awarded after May 29, 2000.[360] It may be added that the trustee may, in terms of ss.36A–36C of the 1985 Act, seek a court order to recover excessive contributions to pension schemes (whether personal or occupational) (see para.7.2.16.5). **7.2.11.5**

Contingent interests

The trustee even takes over contingent interests of the debtor. Section 31(5) provides: **7.2.11.6**

---

[352] *Cumming's Trustee v Glenrinnes Farms Ltd*, 1993 S.L.T. 904.
[353] *Morrison v Harrison* (1876) 3 R. 406.
[354] *Muir's Trustee v Braidwood*, 1958 S.C. 169.
[355] *Watson v Thompson*, 1991 S.C. 447.
[356] *Coutts Trustees v Coutts*, 1998 S.C.L.R. 729.
[357] Criminal Injuries Compensation Act 1995 s.7(2).
[358] Accountant in Bankruptcy, Notes for Guidance of Trustees, para.6.23.1.
[359] See *Rowe v Sanders* [2002] 2 All E.R. 800.
[360] See ss.11–13 of the Welfare Reform and Pensions Act 1999.

"Any non-vested contingent interest which the debtor has shall vest in the trustee as if an assignation of that interest had been executed by the debtor and intimation thereof made at the date of sequestration."

The most obvious type of non-vested contingent interest arises where the debtor has been left a legacy in a will, but the testator is still alive at the date of sequestration. The trustee used to be able to claim such an interest even though it did not vest until some time after the debtor had been discharged.[361] However, s.31(5A) now provides that if the interest has not actually vested at the time of the debtor's discharge, it is reinvested in the debtor. In other words, whereas under the old law in the scenario above the trustee could claim the legacy whether the testator died before or after the debtor was discharged, under the law as it presently stands the trustee may only claim the legacy if the testator dies before the debtor is discharged. Should the testator die after the debtor is discharged, the debtor retains the legacy. *The 2014 Act takes the view that the interests of creditors are not properly served if the trustee can only claim a contingent interest if it vests in the debtor prior to discharge. Instead s.31(5A) will be amended so that the trustee will be able to claim a contingent interest if it vests in the debtor within the four years following the date of sequestration.*

Specialities of heritable property

7.2.11.7   Although the award of sequestration vests heritable property in the trustee, he does not acquire a real right in the property until his title is properly registered. Thus in *Fleming's Trustee v Fleming*[362] Lord Sutherland noted:

"It is clear . . . that the effect of vesting of the bankrupt's estate in the trustee is that he gets a personal right only, and if there is a prior disponee of heritable property, a race to the register will result."

Thus if heritage had been sold by the bankrupt prior to sequestration, but the purchaser did not register his title before the trustee registered his, that heritage vested in the trustee rather than the purchaser.[363] However, the amendments effected by the 2007 Act make it less likely that such an unfortunate situation will arise, as the trustee is placed under a handicap in the "race to the register", in that the trustee is precluded from registering title to heritage for 28 days after the registration of the award of sequestration in the register of inhibitions.[364]

Debtor dealing with the estate

7.2.11.8   Any dealing with the estate by the debtor after sequestration, e.g. purported sales, is ineffective in a question with the trustee,[365] unless the person seeking to uphold the dealing can establish that the person dealing with the debtor was at the time of the dealing unaware of the sequestration, had then no reason to believe that the estate was the subject of sequestration proceedings, and can establish that the trustee[366]:

---

[361] See, e.g. *Stuart's Trustee v H.J. Banks & Co Ltd*, 1998 S.C.L.R. 1109; discussed in Davidson and Macgregor, *Commercial Law in Scotland* (Edinburgh: W. Green, 2003).

[362] *Fleming's Trustee v Fleming*, 2000 S.C. 206 at 209C. That case shows the other side of coin where the trustee is slow to take title. The debtor lived in the matrimonial home to which title had been taken in the name of himself and his wife and to the survivor of them. When he died, it was held that as the trustee had not registered his title, he did not have a real right to the debtor's share of the house, which passed to the debtor's wife under the special destination. However, this was ultimately of little benefit to the widow, since as Lord Sutherland pointed out (at 212B–C): "The share passing under the special destination can only be taken with such qualifications as could be pleaded against the institute. The substitute takes no greater right than that possessed by the institute. The institute's share was vested in the trustee and was liable for the debtor's debts. . . . On the death of the debtor his share passed under the special destination with the same qualifications." In other words, the widow obtained her husband's share of the property, but could be sued for its value. See also *Halifax Plc v Gorman's Trustee*, 2000 S.L.T. 1409.

[363] *Burnett's Trustee v Grainger*, 2004 S.C. (HL) 19.

[364] See s.31(1A)–(1B).

[365] See s.32(8). *The 2014 Act would add that this does not apply to a banking transaction entered into before the receipt of the notice under s.32(5A), whether or not the bank was aware of the sequestration: see s.32(9C).*

[366] See s.32(9).

- had abandoned the property concerned to the debtor, e.g. as not being worth the expense of recover;
- had expressly or impliedly authorised the dealing;
- is otherwise personally barred from challenging the dealing; or
- can establish that the dealing:

  - features performance of an obligation undertaken before the sequestration by the person obliged to the debtor, e.g. payment of a debt;
  - is the purchase of goods from the debtor for which the buyer has paid the debtor or is willing to pay the trustee;
  - is a banking transaction in the ordinary course of business, e.g. honouring a cheque; or
  - constitutes the transfer of incorporeal moveable property, or the creation, transfer, variation or extinction of a real right in heritable property, for which the person dealing with the debtor has given adequate consideration to the debtor, or is willing to give adequate consideration to the trustee, and the dealing requires the delivery of a deed which delivery occurs during the period between the date of sequestration and seven days after the date when the award of sequestration is recorded in the register of inhibitions.[367]

This last category of protected dealing is added by the 2007 Act and seeks to protect persons dealing with the debtor who fall foul of the "registration gap", i.e. who are dealing with a form of property of a kind which requires interests therein to be registered, but who could not be expected to know about the sequestration even if they had searched the appropriate registers, due to the gap which normally occurs between the award of sequestration and its registration. In *Brown's Trustee, Applicant*[368] the debtor had continued to trade after the date of sequestration. The trustee proposed to write to relevant parties to request payment of sums received from the debtor on or after the date of sequestration and to invite them to submit a claim in the sequestration for such sums. In order to safeguard his position he applied under s.3(6), which provides that a "trustee may apply to the sheriff for directions in relation to any particular matter arising in the sequestration".[369] Sheriff Holligan[370] observed that "what the trustee proposes is an appropriate act of administration for the trustee to take", and made a direction accordingly. The sheriff[371] was also of the view that liabilities incurred by the debtor after the date of sequestration could not be liabilities in the sequestration unless they fell within one of the categories set out above.

ESTATE EXCLUDED FROM VESTING

Certain estate is exempted from vesting.   **7.2.12**

Property held in trust

Property which the debtor holds in trust for another is specifically excluded from vesting.[372] Thus in **7.2.12.1** *Council of the Law Society v McKinnie*[373] the First Division held that funds held in a solicitor's client

---

[367] See s.32(9ZA).

[368] *Brown's Trustee, Applicant*, 2010 S.L.T. (Sh Ct) 45.

[369] *It may be noted that the 2014 Act would amend s.3(6) so that only the AIB when acting as a trustee would apply directly to the sheriff for directions. Where the AIB is not the trustee a new s.3A would indicate that the trustee would apply to the AIB for directions, although the AIB could in turn apply to the sheriff for a direction, e.g. if the matter was very complicated. Additionally, the trustee may apply to the AIB for a review of a direction made by the latter within 14 days of it being made. The AIB must then take into account any representation made by the trustee, the debtor, a creditor or any other interested person made within 21 days of the application, and must confirm amend or revoke the direction within 28 days of the application. The trustee may then appeal against this decision within 14 days of it being made.*

[370] *Brown's Trustee, Applicant*, 2010 S.L.T. (Sh Ct) 45 at [16].

[371] *Brown's Trustee, Applicant*, 2010 S.L.T. (Sh Ct) 45 at [11].

[372] See s.33(1)(b). Thus a court would not reduce a gratuitous alienation of heritable property made by a bankrupt debtor in favour of his wife, if the wife could show that although the title had been in her husband's name, he had actually held the property in trust for her: *Accountant in Bankruptcy v Mackay*, 2004 S.L.T. 777.

[373] *Council of the Law Society v McKinnie*, 1993 S.L.T. 238.

account were held in a fiduciary capacity, and thus were immune from vesting. This rule will apply as long as property or funds held in trust (or at least the assets into which they have been converted) can be identified.[374] If trust property cannot be identified, the rule cannot be applied,[375] although the court will allow funds held in trust to be recovered, if they have been paid, along with other monies, into an account which is in credit.[376]

Income

7.2.12.2 Income received by the debtor vests in the debtor unless it is income derived from estate vested in the trustee.[377] Thus if the debtor's mother provides for the rents from properties she owns to be paid to the debtor, he may retain that money. But rents from properties the debtor owns count as income derived from estate vested in the trustee, and thus also vest in the trustee.

Creditors cannot use diligence to attach the debtor's income in respect of pre-sequestration debts.[378] It would seem to follow that income can be attached in respect of post sequestration debts. In this context, diligence includes the making of a deduction from earnings under the Child Support Act 1991. Other deductions from money which would otherwise be payable to the debtor do not amount to diligence.[379]

In *Accountant in Bankruptcy v Halifax Plc*[380] the defenders had issued free shares to a bankrupt, despite a claim by the AIB (acting as trustee) that they were his. Lord Penrose rejected their contention that the shares were income and not *acquirenda*, noting:

> "In my opinion, the expression 'income' is not apt to include a price paid, in whatever form, to a debtor effectively to accept the substitution of a different creditor on a subsisting loan. It is clear that the property would be acquirenda . . . If the vesting day under the transfer agreement was earlier than the date of sequestration . . . the right to shares would be part of his estate on sequestration. If there remained some unfulfilled requirement . . . the right would be properly described as contingent, and s.31(5) would apply. If any requirement had to be performed by the bankrupt personally, s.64 would oblige him to do that act and there would be power in the sheriff to order performance if need be."

It may be assumed that assets the debtor acquires from income do not vest in the trustee.

Income payment orders and agreements/*Debtor contribution orders*

7.2.12.3 Despite the reference above to a debtor retaining his income, if the trustee considers the debtor's income to be excessive, he may, at any time prior to the debtor's discharge,[381] apply to the sheriff for an order that the excess be paid over to him.[382] The sheriff will allow the debtor a suitable amount to provide for his aliment and "relevant" obligations. Those obligations are his alimentary obligations, any obligation to make a periodical allowance to a former spouse or civil partner, and any obligation to pay child support maintenance under the Child Support Act 1991.[383] The sheriff need not allow the debtor sufficient income to allow him to comply with a previous court order relating to aliment or periodical allowance.[384] In other words, if having worked out the amount the debtor requires to aliment himself, the sheriff is then faced with the plea that the debtor is also bound to pay his ex-wife £1,000 per month by way of periodical allowance, he may decide to allow all of that sum or only part of it. The

---

[374] *Newton's Executrix v Meiklejohn's Judicial Factor*, 1959 S.L.T. 71; *Smith v Liquidator of James Birrell Ltd (No.2)*, 1968 S.L.T. 174.
[375] *Hofford v Gowans*, 1909 1 S.L.T. 153.
[376] *Magistrates of Edinburgh v McLaren* (1881) 8 R. (HL) 140.
[377] See s.32(1).
[378] See s.32(5).
[379] *Mulvey v Secretary of State for Social Security*, 1997 S.L.T. 753.
[380] *Accountant in Bankruptcy v Halifax Plc*, 1999 S.C.L.R. 1135 at 1143F–1144B.
[381] See s.32(2WA).
[382] See s.32(2).
[383] See s.32(3).
[384] See s.32(3).

sheriff has complete discretion here, and is not bound by any formula, but should determine a suitable amount balancing the interests of the debtor and the creditors.[385] Should the debtor's circumstances change, he, the trustee, or any other interested person, e.g. a creditor, may apply to the sheriff for the variation or recall of the payment order.[386]

Previously, such orders would have only operated until the date of the debtor's discharge. However, with the new statutory regime contemplating that the debtor will normally be automatically discharged within one year, creditors would obviously have been in the position of benefiting from the debtor's income for a very restricted period of time. Accordingly the 2007 amendments seek to achieve some sort of balance by allowing the sheriff to specify the period for which an order is to have effect, which period may extend for up to three years and thus might indeed end after the debtor has been discharged.[387] Another innovation is that such an order may provide that a third person is to pay to the trustee a specified proportion of money due to the debtor by way of income.[388] In other words, instead of the order directing the debtor to pay 25 per cent of his salary to the trustee, it might direct the debt-or's employer to do so. A debtor who fails to comply with such an order now commits a criminal offence.[389]

As an alternative to being subject to an order, the debtor might enter into a written agreement with the trustee whereby he pays a specified proportion of his income to the trustee, or a third party pays to the trustee a specified proportion of money due to the debtor by way of income.[390] A third person who pays a sum of money to the trustee under an agreement or an order is discharged of liability to the debtor to that extent.[391] Such an agreement may also operate for up to three years.[392] The trustee, unless she is the AIB, must send a copy of the agreement (and any variation thereof) to the AIB, and if this is done it may be enforced like an order.[393] Such agreement may be varied by written agreement or by the sheriff on application by the debtor, the trustee, or any other interested person.[394] The sheriff may not vary an agreement so that it includes anything which could not appear in an order, and must vary an agreement if this is necessary to provide for the debtor's aliment and "relevant" obligations.[395] If the debtor fails to honour the agreement, the trustee may apply to the sheriff for an order on the same terms as and for the same period as that agreement.[396] Such an application may be made even after the date of the debtor's discharge.

However, the 2014 Act will repeal ss.32(2) to 32(4L) and abolish the above scheme. Instead it creates seven new sections to deal with payments of the debtor's contribution. Rather than the trustee applying to the sheriff for an income payment order, the AIB must make an order fixing the debtor's contribution,[397] even if it is fixed at zero.[398] The AIB must use the common financial tool to assess the debtor's contribution.[399] It is noted above (para.7.2.11.5) that personal pensions no longer vest in the trustee, but a debtor's personal pension can be taken into account in deciding whether to a make a debtor contribution order.[400] Where the debtor applies for his own sequestration, the order must be made at the same time as the award of sequestration.[401] Where sequestration has been awarded following a petition, e.g. by a qualified

---

[385] *Brown's Trustee v Brown*, 1995 S.L.T (Sh Ct) 2.

[386] See s.32(4).

[387] See s.32(2XA).

[388] See s.32(2YA).

[389] See s.32(2ZA).

[390] See s.32(4B). Such agreement must be entered into prior to discharge; s.32(4C). For the form of such an agreement see Bankruptcy (Scotland) Regulations 2008 (SSI 2008/82) reg.18.

[391] See s.32(4J).

[392] See s.32(4D).

[393] See s.32(4E), (4K).

[394] See s.32(4G).

[395] See s.32(4H).

[396] See s.32(4L).

[397] *See s.32A(1).*

[398] *See s.32A(2A).*

[399] *See s.32A(2).*

[400] *See s.32A(3).*

[401] *See s.32A(1)(a).*

creditor, the order must be made after considering proposals from the trustee.[402] The trustee must send initial proposals within six weeks of the date of sequestration.[403] Instead of or perhaps as well as payments having to be made directly by the debtor, for the first time the legislation allows an order to direct that a third party must pay to the trustee a specified proportion of money which the third party owes the debtor by way of income.[404] Typically, the order will direct that the debtor's employer pays over a particular proportion of the former's wages to the trustee. In such a case the debtor must instruct the employer to deduct specified amounts from his earnings and pay these over to the trustee.[405] Should the debtor fail to give such an instruction and misses two payments, the trustee may give the instruction.[406] Whether the instruction is given by the debtor or the trustee, the employer must comply with it.[407] Where the employer (or any other third person) pays a sum of money to the trustee, he is discharged from liability to the debtor to the extent of that sum.[408] Regulations may provide for the form in which an instruction should be given, and more importantly, how it affects an employer and the consequences of an employer's failure to comply with it.[409] It is expected that the form will mirror that of a payment instruction given to an employer under the Debt Arrangement Scheme (Scotland) Regulations 2011 (Form 3).[410] Equally, it is expected that the regulations will otherwise mirror reg.32 of the 2011 Regulations. If so, they will provide that once the employer receives an instruction, he must while it remains in effect deduct the sum specified on every pay day and pay the sum deducted to the trustee as soon as reasonably practicable. He must continue to do so until the instruction is recalled by the debtor or the trustee. An employer who makes such a deduction is entitled to charge a fee equivalent to the fee for operating diligence under s.71 of the Debt Arrangement and Attachment (Scotland) Act 2002 and deduct this from the balance of the employee's earnings. An employer who fails without good cause to make an instructed payment is liable to pay on demand the relevant amount to the trustee, and will not be entitled to recover that amount from the debtor. An employer's obligation to make a payment shall be extinguished one year from the date on which liability arose unless court proceedings to recover the amount are commenced within the period. Payment of such sums as directed by the order relieves the third party of any further liability to the debtor in respect of those sums.[411] In other words, if an employer pays £100 of the debtor's £300 wage to the trustee as ordered, the debtor cannot claim to be owed that £100. As soon as an order is made, the AIB must notify in writing the debtor, the trustee and any third party mentioned in the order,[412] but the order must not take effect until more than 14 days after such notification.[413]

An order (assuming the contribution is not zero) must indicate the date of first payment,[414] the intervals at which payment must be made and the payment period.[415] That period will usually be 48 months from the date when the order directs the first payment should be made[416] and hence (as was previously the case) continue well beyond the date on which the debtor is discharged.[417] However, a longer period may be determined by the trustee if the debtor fails to make contributions.[418] For example, if over the 48-month period the debtor has missed five monthly payments, the period might be increased by five

---

[402] *See s.32A(1)(b).*

[403] *See s.32A(1A).*

[404] *See s.32A(4).*

[405] *See s.32D(2). Although the discussion here is couched in terms of an instruction being given to an employer, s.32D can also operate in relation to any third party who pays the debtor earnings or other income: see s.32D(3).*

[406] *See s.32D(4).*

[407] *See s.32D(5).*

[408] *See s.32D(6).*

[409] *See s.32D(7).*

[410] *(SSI 2011/141).*

[411] *See s.32A(5).*

[412] *See s.32A(6).*

[413] *See s.32A(7).*

[414] *See s.32B(4A).*

[415] *See s.32B(1).*

[416] *See s.32B(2)(a).*

[417] *The majority of respondents to the consultation on reform were in favour of a standardised payment period rather than an indefinite period: see policy memoradum, para.49, and it was thought that four years struck the appropriate balance between the interests of debtors and creditors; see policy memoradum para.51.*

[418] *See s.32B(2)(c)(i).*

months. Alternatively, the trustee and debtor may agree on a longer period,[419] e.g. where it suits the debtor to make a smaller contribution for a certain period of time, and this is made up for by the payment period being extended. A shorter period is also possible, but only in the unusual event that the payments made over the periods, together with the distribution of the estate, are sufficient to pay off all the debts and expenses of the sequestration in full.[420] Payments will usually be monthly, but might be weekly, depending on the debtor's circumstances. The debtor, the trustee or any other interested person may apply to the AIB for a review of an order within 14 days of it being made.[421] The order is then suspended until the determination of that review.[422] The AIB must confirm, amend or revoke the order within 28 days of the application, but must take into account any representations made by an interested person within 21 days of the application.[423] The debtor or the trustee may then appeal to the sheriff against the AIB's review decision within 14 days of that decision.[424]

The effect of the order is that the debtor is liable to pay the amount of the order which is set by the AIB or varied by the trustee (see below),[425] and that liability will continue after discharge.[426] The only qualification to this is that the order ceases to have effect in the unlikely event that the trustee finds that the debtor's estate and income is enough to pay off in full all debts owed by the debtor and the expenses of the sequestration.[427]

The trustee may vary or quash a debtor contribution order in a variety of circumstances. One situation may be where he sends a report to the AIB concerning the debtor's conduct in the sequestration as a precursor to the debtor's discharge, or, where the trustee is the AIB, actually grants that discharge.[428] The other situation is where he does so, either on his own initiative, or on the application by the debtor, following a change in the debtor's circumstances.[429] In all cases he must consider the action to be appropriate, and he will largely be guided by the common financial tool.[430] This may indicate that, at least for the time being, the debtor cannot make any contribution, or can be expected to make a reduced (or indeed increased) contribution. It should be remembered that the effect of a debtor contribution order may extend beyond discharge, so it will not always be appropriate to quash the order upon discharge. The legislation gives the trustee the necessary flexibility to deal with changes in the debtor's circumstances. If the trustee varies or quashes a debtor contribution order on his own initiative, that decision cannot take effect until at least 14 days have elapsed from the date of the decision.[431] Where the trustee varies or quashes a debtor contribution order, or refuses an application by the debtor, he must immediately give written notification to certain key individuals—the debtor, the AIB (unless the AIB and the trustee are one and the same), any third person, such as an employer, who is required to make a payment under a debtor contribution order, and any other interested person.[432]

The legislation also embraces the concept of a payment break, which was first introduced as regards debt payment programmes by reg.37(1)(h) and (3) of the Debt Arrangement Scheme (Scotland) Regulations 2011. It is designed to reflect the fact that circumstances may arise whereby the debtor is temporarily unable to continue to make payments.[433] It is for the debtor to apply to the trustee for a payment break,[434] and the application must specify the period sought,[435] although this cannot exceed

---

[419] *See s.32B(2)(c)(ii).*

[420] *See s.32B(2)(b) and s.32B(3).*

[421] *See s.32BA(1)–(2).*

[422] *See s.32BA(3).*

[423] *See s.32BA(4).*

[424] *See s.32BA(5).*

[425] *See s.32C(1).*

[426] *See s.32C(2).*

[427] *See s.32C(3).*

[428] *See s.32E(1)(c).*

[429] *See s.32C(1)(a)–(b)).*

[430] *See s.32E(2).*

[431] *See s.32E(3).*

[432] *See s.32E(4)–(5).*

[433] *The policy memorandum notes (at para.69) that such breaks happen in practice on an informal basis, and it was thought that this should be placed on a statutory footing.*

[434] *See s.32F(1).*

[435] *See s.32F(5).*

six months.[436] The debtor may not apply more than once.[437] The ground on which the application may be made is that there has been a reduction of at least 50 per cent of the debtor's disposable income (as determined by the common financial tool)[438] as a result of any of these circumstances[439]:

- *a period of unemployment or change in employment;*
- *a period of leave from employment because of the birth or adoption of a child or the need to care for a dependant;*
- *a period of illness of the debtor;*
- *a divorce or dissolution or civil partnership;*
- *a separation from the debtor's spouse or civil partner;*
- *the death of someone who, along with the debtor cared for a dependant of the debtor.*

If the trustee thinks a break is fair and reasonable, he may grant a break on such conditions and for such period as he thinks fit.[440] This period may thus be shorter than that sought by the debtor. If the trustee decides not to grant a break, he must notify the debtor of this, laying out his reasons.[441] If he decides to grant a break, he must provide written notification to the debtor, the AIB (unless the AIB and the trustee are one and the same), and any third person, such as an employer, who is required to make a payment under a debtor contribution order.[442] It is important to appreciate that the grant of a break does not relieve the debtor of the obligation to make the relevant payments, but simply defers that obligation, with the result that the period of a debtor contribution order is extended by the period of the break.[443] Thus if a break of four months is granted, the period for which a debtor must make contributions under the order will be extended by four months.

Should the debtor or any other interested person disagree with the trustee's decision to vary or quash a debtor contribution order or to allow a payment break, he has 14 days from the date of the relevant decision to apply to the AIB for a review of that decision.[444] Any decision to vary or quash a debtor contribution order on the trustee's own initiative following a change in the debtor's circumstances is then suspended until the AIB has decided upon the review, but decisions are not otherwise affected by the fact of the review.[445] The AIB must confirm, amend or revoke the decision within 28 days of the application, but must take into account any representations made by an interested person (including the debtor) within 21 days of the application.[446] This would seem to mean that the AIB will wait at least 21 days in order to see if any representations are made. A representation made after that 21-day period need not be taken into account. Either the trustee or the debtor may appeal to the sheriff against the AIB's decision within 14 days of that decision.[447]

Social security payments

7.2.12.4 Legislation indicates that most such payments are inalienable and do not vest in the trustee.[448] Nor do deductions from awards of compensation to reflect social security payments, nor overpayments of

---

[436] *See s.32F(2).*
[437] *See s.32F(3)(b).*
[438] *See s.32F(3)(a).*
[439] *See s.32F(4).*
[440] *See s.32F(6).*
[441] *See s.32F(8).*
[442] *See s.32F(7).*
[443] *See s.32F(9).*
[444] *See s.32G(1)–(2).*
[445] *See s.32G(3).*
[446] *See s.32G(4).*
[447] *See s.32G(5).*
[448] See the Social Security Contributions and Benefits Act 1992 s.122; and the Social Security Administration Act 1992 ss.187, 191. The benefits concerned include attendance allowance, benefits for widows and widowers, child benefit, disability living allowance, disability working allowance, family credit, guardian's allowance, housing benefit, income support, industrial injury benefit, invalid care allowance, invalidity benefit, jobseeker's allowance, sickness benefit, severe disablement allowance, state maternity allowance, state retirement pensions and unemployment benefit.

benefit recovered by the authorities, nor repayments from the social fund which the debtor was obliged to make.[449]

Criminal injuries compensation

An award made under the statutory scheme does not vest in the trustee.[450]   **7.2.12.5**

Property exempted from attachment

Property kept outwith a dwellinghouse in respect of which attachment is incompetent by virtue of s.11 of **7.2.12.6** the Debt Arrangement and Attachment (Scotland) Act 2002, does not vest in the trustee.[451] This covers:

(1) any implements, tools of trade, books or other equipment reasonably required by the debtor in the practice of his profession, trade or business (not exceeding in aggregate value £1,000);

(2) any vehicle, the use of which is reasonably required by the debtor as above (not exceeding £3,000 in value);

(3) a mobile home which is the debtor's only or principal residence;

(4) any tools or other equipment reasonably required for keeping in good order and condition any garden or yard adjacent to or associated with a dwellinghouse in which the debtor resides; and

(5) money in the sense of cash, negotiable instruments, postal orders and government payment instruments.

Essential assets

Similarly, property kept in a dwellinghouse which is not a non-essential asset for the purposes of Pt 3 **7.2.12.7** of the Debt Arrangement and Attachment (Scotland) Act 2002, does not vest in the trustee.[452] (In other words, assets regarded as essential do not vest.)

None of the following will therefore vest:

(1) clothing reasonably required by the debtor or any member of the debtor's household;

(2) any implements, tools of trade, books or other equipment reasonably required by any member of the debtor's household in the practice of their profession, trade or business (not exceeding in aggregate value £1,000);

(3) medical aids or equipment reasonably required by the debtor or any member of the debtor's household;

(4) books or other articles reasonably required for the education or training of the debtor or any member of the debtor's household (not exceeding in aggregate value £1,000);

(5) toys of a child who is a household member;

(6) articles reasonably required for the care or upbringing of such a child;

(7) the following articles in the dwelling reasonably required for the use of the debtor or a member of his household, viz beds; bedding; household linen; chairs; settees; tables; food; lights and fittings; heating appliances; curtains; floor coverings; anything used for cooking, storing or eating food; refrigerators; anything used to clean the house or clean, mend, dry or press clothes; refrigerators; items of domestic safety; tools used to repair or maintain the house or household articles; furniture used to store clothing, bedding, household linen, articles used to clean the house, or utensils used to cook and eat food; computers and accessory equipment; microwave ovens; radios; telephones; and televisions.

---

[449] See the Social Security Administration Act 1992 ss.71(10B), 78(3B), 82, 89(2). The House of Lords held in *Mulvey v Secretary of State for Social Security*, 1997 S.C. (HL) 105 that the right of the Secretary of State to deduct sums from the debtor's income support to cover loans made from the social fund prior to sequestration was unaffected by the debtor's sequestration. The view was taken that, as the social security system operated outwith the normal rules of bankruptcy, this could not be equated with a creditor withholding money due to the debtor on the basis of compensation. (Compensation cannot usually be pleaded, as it allows that creditor to benefit unfairly.)

[450] Criminal Justice Act 1988 s.117.

[451] See s.33(1)(a).

[452] See s.33(1)(aa).

It can thus be appreciated that most standard household items do not vest.

Property excluded under the Proceeds of Crime Act 2002

7.2.12.8 The 2002 Act provides for the confiscation of the assets of persons convicted of criminal offences. It is not proposed to go into the detail of this rather arcane area. However, among the devices it employs are confiscation orders, restraint orders which interdict individuals from dealing with any realisable property held by them, and orders appointing enforcement and director's receivers in England and Northern Ireland and enforcement administrators in Scotland to manage affected property. Essentially, property affected by any such order will not be regarded as part of the debtor's estate at the date of sequestration.[453] However, where an order is quashed or discharged, or where a surplus remains after satisfaction of that order, the relevant property or surplus will vest in the trustee.[454] Where sequestration has already been awarded, no property which is part of the estate, nor any of the debtor's income which has been ordered to be paid to the trustee, can be affected by any order under the 2002 Act.[455]

RECOVERY OF ESTATE AND DOCUMENTS

7.2.13 Although the estate automatically vests in the trustee, he must take practical steps to ingather it. Thus, as soon as possible after appointment, the trustee should take possession of the estate and any document in the debtor's possession or control which relates to his assets or his business or financial affairs.[456] The trustee is also entitled to have access to and copy all documents relating to such matters which have been sent by the debtor to a third party, and if access is obstructed, he may apply to the sheriff for an order that the person obstructing should cease to obstruct.[457] Similarly, he may require delivery of any title deed or document of the debtor held by a third party, but this is subject to any right of lien the third party may have over the deed or document.[458] Bell indicates that a lien gives the holder preference over all creditors, whether secured or not, and the deeds or documents may only be recovered by paying the debt or finding security for its payment.[459] Any person who damages, conceals, disposes of or removes from Scotland any part of the estate or any document which relates to the debtor's assets or business or financial affairs may commit an offence.[460]

INFORMATION AND EXAMINATIONS

7.2.14 The trustee may require information to carry out his functions, and is given extensive powers to enable him to secure it. Thus he may request the debtor or any other person to appear before him to give information regarding the debtor's assets, the debtor's dealings with them, or the conduct of the debtor's affairs.[461] Moreover, if he considers it necessary, i.e. where informal meetings have not yielded the information sought, then the trustee can apply to the sheriff for a private examination of any such person.[462] Although the trustee need not indicate what he hopes to discover through the examination,[463] the granting of the application appears to lie at the sheriff's discretion.[464] Alternatively, the trustee can

---

[453] Proceeds of Crime Act 2002 s.420(2); but to obtain a good title to heritage, the restraint order must be recorded in the Land Register or Register of Sasines before the award of sequestration: s.420(3).

[454] Bankruptcy (Scotland) Act 1985 ss.31A–31C.

[455] Proceeds of Crime Act 2002 s.421.

[456] Bankruptcy (Scotland) Act 1985 s.38(1)(a).

[457] See s.38(2), (3).

[458] See s.38(4).

[459] Bell, *Commentaries*, 7th edn, II, 108.

[460] See s.67(2).

[461] See s.44(1).

[462] See s.44(1).

[463] *Park v Robson* (1871) 10 M. 10.

[464] See s.44(2).

apply to the sheriff for a public examination of any such person as mentioned above, and must do so if so requested by the AIB, the commissioners (see para.7.3.2), or one-quarter in value of the creditors.[465] Although such an application should normally be made not less than eight weeks before the end of the first accounting period (see para.7.3.3), it can be made at any time on cause shown.[466] If the application is properly made, it must be granted by the sheriff.[467]

An individual will be ordered to appear for private or public examination not earlier than eight days nor later than 16 days after the order, at a time specified in the order,[468] although if that individual is prevented from attending for any good reason, the sheriff may appoint a commissioner to conduct the examination.[469] (This is a commissioner in the sense of a person who takes evidence on commission, rather than one of the creditor commissioners who supervise the trustee.) Outside of this speciality, an individual who fails, without reasonable excuse, to appear commits an offence.[470] On the application of the trustee, the sheriff, if satisfied that this is necessary to secure the attendance of the relevant individual at the examination, may grant a warrant for his arrest and delivery to the place of examination.[471] Either the sheriff or the commissioner may order any individual to produce any document in his custody or control relating to the debtor's assets, his dealings with them, or his conduct in relation to his business or financial affairs, and to deliver a copy to the trustee.[472]

The main differences between a private and public examination, apart from the latter being held in open court,[473] are that:

- when the sheriff makes an order for a public examination, the trustee must publish notice thereof in the *Edinburgh Gazette*, sending a copy to every known creditor (and to the debtor if he is not the person being examined), and informing them of their right to participate in the examination[474]; and
- whereas at a private examination only the trustee (or a solicitor or counsel acting for him), or the debtor if he is not the person being examined, may question the relevant individual, in a public examination any creditor may ask questions.[475]

Questions are confined to matters relating to the debtor's assets, his dealings with them, or his conduct in relation to his business or financial affairs.[476] The legal adviser of the witness may not ask questions in order to clarify his client's evidence, but may object to questions which stray beyond the permissible issues.[477] The sheriff (and presumably the commissioner) may also ask questions, although this is not explicitly stated in the Act.[478] Examinations before a sheriff are on oath,[479] so that perjury becomes possible, while refusal to answer invites a finding of contempt, although in *Paxton v HM Advocate*[480] it was held that such a finding was not open where the refusal to answer occurred when the examination had continued after the sheriff had left the bench. The witness is not excused from answering a question merely because the answer may incriminate him, or on grounds of confidentiality.[481] Nonetheless, his evidence is not admissible against him in any subsequent criminal proceedings, other than proceedings

---

[465] See s.45(1)(a), (b).

[466] See s.45(1).

[467] See s.45(2).

[468] See ss.44(2), 45(2).

[469] See s.46(2).

[470] See ss.44(3), 45(4).

[471] See s.46(1).

[472] See s.46(4).

[473] See s.45(2).

[474] See s.45(3) and Bankruptcy (Scotland) Regulations 2008 (SSI 2008/82) Form 6. *The 2014 Act intends that instead of publishing the notice in the Gazette, the trustee should send it to the AIB, who will enter particulars thereof in the Register of Insolvencies.*

[475] See s.47(2).

[476] See s.47(2).

[477] *Holmes, Petitioner*, 1988 S.L.T. (Sh Ct) 47.

[478] *Holmes, Petitioner*, 1988 S.L.T. (Sh Ct) 47.

[479] See s.47(1).

[480] *Paxton v HM Advocate*, 1984 S.L.T. 367.

[481] See s.47(3).

in respect of perjury.[482] This implies that the evidence may be admissible against him in subsequent civil proceedings. A public examination may be sought in order to impress upon the witness how serious the issue may be, but might be a double edged sword in that it may also serve to alert all and sundry that the sequestration may not be proceeding entirely smoothly.

In this context it may also be noted that the trustee can also seek a private examination of a creditor or other person regarding the amount or validity of the creditor's claim.[483]

MANAGEMENT OF THE ESTATE

7.2.15 Although the main function of the trustee is to realise the estate and distribute the proceeds amongst the creditors, in order to protect the estate he may have to manage it, sometimes over an extended period of time. To begin with, however, as soon as possible after being appointed he must consult with the AIB regarding the exercise of his functions,[484] unless of course she is the AIB. Moreover, he must comply with general or specific directions given by[485]:

- the creditors, i.e. a majority in value of those voting at a creditors' meeting. A trustee might seek such a meeting specifically in order to receive directions in relation to issues where he is reluctant to proceed on his own initiative; or
- the court at the behest of the commissioners; or
- the AIB.

The only exception to the above is that directions given by the creditors or the AIB may be ignored if the trustee has to sell perishable goods, and he believes that compliance would adversely affect the sale.[486] The above duties do not apply where the trustee is the AIB.[487]

Certain specific powers are conferred on the trustee, but he should only exercise them insofar as he believes that it would be of financial benefit to the estate and in the interests of creditors to do so.[488] These powers are[489]:

- to carry on the debtor's business. The business may have certain contracts which, if performed, may significantly benefit the estate, or which if not performed may increase its liabilities. The continuation of the business may also make it easier to sell with its goodwill intact;
- to close down the business;
- to bring, defend or continue any legal proceedings relating to the estate; to create a security over any part of the estate. It may be that he needs to borrow money in order to run the business;
- to make payments or incur liabilities in order to acquire property which is the subject of a right or option, e.g. exercising the right to buy shares at specially discounted rates, which he knows he will be able to resell at a profit;
- to borrow money insofar as necessary to safeguard the estate; and
- to insure the debtor's business or property.

The trustee may also adopt any contract entered into by the debtor prior to sequestration if he considers that adoption would be beneficial, unless such adoption is excluded by the express or implied terms of the contract.[490] Many contracts expressly prohibit adoption in this context, or give a party a right not to

---

[482] See s.47(3)(a); although a witness may not be forced to disclose any information received from a person who is not being examined, where it is confidential between them: s.47(3)(b).
[483] See s.48(5), (6).
[484] See s.39(1).
[485] See s.39(1).
[486] See s.39(6).
[487] See s.39(1A).
[488] See s.39(9).
[489] See s.39(2).
[490] See s.42(1).

allow adoption, or more generally exclude assignation. Where a contract involves an element of *delectus personae* in relation to the debtor, then adoption is impliedly excluded.[491] The trustee may equally decline to adopt any contract.[492] While this is quite likely to amount to a breach of contract, giving the other party a claim for damages which may be considered in the sequestration,[493] a court will not order the trustee to implement the contract.[494] A party who invokes a right to elect to terminate the contract on the debtor's sequestration has no claim against the estate.[495] If the trustee does adopt, he will generally become personally liable for performance, including obligations which had arisen prior to vesting.[496] The trustee may equally enter into new contracts, if he considers that to do so would be beneficial.[497] Such a step is very likely where he is carrying on the debtor's business. The trustee will certainly become personally liable for performance of such new contracts.[498]

There may be other pitfalls for an unwary trustee. The case of *Vale Sewing Machines v Robb*[499] involved a liquidator, but would seem equally applicable to a case of personal insolvency. The company in liquidation had among its assets certain goods which were subject to a retention of title clause (see para.1.8.3). The seller of these goods left the liquidator in no doubt that, as the company still owed money on these goods, property therein had not passed to it. Nonetheless, the liquidator proceeded to resell the goods. He was held personally liable to the owner. The sheriff added[500]:

> "The defender indicated to me that the proceeds of sale have been placed in a suspense account pending resolution of this action. The action is raised against him personally and the decree is one on which he alone is personally liable. He is not entitled to apply any part of the liquidation funds to satisfy that decree as they would amount to a misappropriation of funds held for the general body of creditors."

Just because a contract is allowed to continue for some time before being terminated does not mean it is adopted. So in *Lindop v Stewart Noble & Sons Ltd*[501] the fact that an employee had continued in employment for almost four weeks before being dismissed did not mean that his contract was adopted. Generally, enforcing rights under a contract which involve no element of performance does not infer adoption, e.g. the collection of money due under the contract,[502] or even suing upon the contract.[503] Adoption will not be inferred even if the trustee takes limited steps to protect the position of the estate, so that the lease of a farm was not adopted, simply by the trustee involving himself in its running prior to sale.[504] But where a trustee invoked a term in a lease obliging the landlord to purchase sheep, that was held to be an adoption allowing the landlord to invoke reciprocal obligations in the lease.[505] If the trustee fails to indicate an intention to adopt within a reasonable time, then he will be held to have abandoned the contract.[506] If the other party wishes a clear decision on adoption, he may write to the trustee requesting a decision.[507] The trustee then has 28 days from the receipt of the request (or such longer period as the court may allow) to adopt or refuse to adopt the contract.[508] If the trustee does not reply in writing to the request within the period allowed, he is deemed to have refused to adopt the

---

[491] *Anderson v Hamilton & Co* (1875) 2 R. 355.
[492] See s.42(1).
[493] *Crown Estate Commissioners v Liquidators of Highland Engineering Ltd*, 1975 S.L.T. 58.
[494] *Crown Estate Commissioners v Liquidators of Highland Engineering Ltd*, 1975 S.L.T. 58.
[495] *Buttercase v Geddie* (1897) 24 R. 1128.
[496] *Dundas v Morison* (1857) 20 D. 225.
[497] See s.42(4).
[498] *Mackessack & Son v Molleson* (1886) 13 R. 445.
[499] *Vale Sewing Machines v Robb*, 1997 S.C.L.R. 797.
[500] *Vale Sewing Machines v Robb*, 1997 S.C.L.R. 797 at 800B.
[501] *Lindop v Stewart Noble & Sons Ltd*, 1999 S.C.L.R. 889.
[502] *Mitchell's Trustees v Pearson* (1834) 12 S. 322.
[503] *Sturrock v Robertson's Trustee*, 1913 S.C. 582.
[504] *McGavin v Sturrock's Trustee* (1891) 18 R. 576.
[505] *Craig's Trustee v Lord Malcolm* (1900) 2 F. 541.
[506] *Crown Estate Commissioners v Liquidators of Highland Engineering Ltd*, 1975 S.L.T. 58.
[507] See s.42(2).
[508] See s.42(2).

contract.[509] *The 2014 Act makes provision for that 28 day period to be extended. Where the AIB is the trustee, an application for extension is made by the AIB to the sheriff, otherwise the trustee applies to the AIB.[510] The trustee may apply to the AIB for a review of her decision within 14 days of it being made.[511] The AIB must confirm, amend or revoke the decision within 28 days of the application, but must take into account any representations made by an interested person within 21 days of the application.[512] The trustee may then appeal to the sheriff against the AIB's review decision within 14 days of that decision.[513] It is also possible for the AIB to ask a sheriff for a direction before making any decision or undertaking any review.[514] No party may ask for a review of the AIB's decision in relation to a matter on which she has applied to the sheriff for a direction.[515]*

CHALLENGEABLE TRANSACTIONS

7.2.16   In seeking to deal with the debtor's estate, the trustee may discover that the debtor had disposed of parts of it prior to sequestration. The law of bankruptcy could not operate effectively if there was no means of challenging disposals which had the effect of unfairly prejudicing the body of creditors. Accordingly, procedures for challenge are laid down. It should be noted, however, that no decree to reduce a gratuitous alienation or unfair preference can be granted under the Act in respect of property which is the subject of the "tainted gift" provisions of the Proceeds of Crime Act 2002.[516]

Gratuitous alienations

7.2.16.1   Under s.34(1) such transactions may be challenged in the Court of Session by a creditor, the trustee in sequestration, the trustee under a protected trust deed, or the judicial factor on a deceased's estate.[517] The essence of a gratuitous alienation is that the debtor has simply given up some part of his estate. It must be shown that there has been a transfer of the debtor's property (including a cash payment), or a renunciation of a right,[518] as where a debtor gave up his right to the assignation of a lease.[519] In the context of corporate insolvency, it has been held that the giving of a guarantee amounts to an alienation.[520] An alienation will be challengeable if made to an associate of the debtor within five years of the date of the debtor's sequestration (or of his death, or the granting of a protected trust deed).[521] If made to any other person, the relevant period is two years.[522] The term associate is defined[523] so as to embrace a wide variety of individuals who are seen as having close ties, emotional or financial, with the debtor. So an associate may be:

(1)   a spouse or civil partner, including any former or reputed spouse or civil partner;

(2)   certain relatives of the debtor or his spouse or civil partner (including any former or reputed spouse or civil partner), i.e. any direct ancestor or descendant, any sibling, uncle, aunt, niece or nephew, in all cases, treating an illegitimate child as legitimate, treating any adopted child as a natural child, and treating any half blood relationship as of the whole blood;

---

[509] See s.42(3).
[510] *See s.42(2A).*
[511] *See s.42(2B).*
[512] *See s.42(2C).*
[513] *See s.42(2D).*
[514] *See s.42(2E).*
[515] *See s.42(2F).*
[516] Proceeds of Crime Act 2002 s.422.
[517] A creditor may seek to reduce a gratuitous alienation even if the trustee in sequestration has taken steps to do so: *Accountant in Bankruptcy v Brown*, 2009 S.L.T. 1115.
[518] Bankruptcy (Scotland) Act 1985 s.34(2)(a).
[519] *Ahmed's Trustee v Ahmed (No.2)*, 1993 S.L.T. 651.
[520] *Jackson v Royal Bank of Scotland Plc*, 2002 S.L.T. 1123.
[521] See s.34(3)(a).
[522] See s.34(3)(b).
[523] See s.74.

(3) the spouse or civil partner (including any former or reputed spouse or civil partner) of any such relative;

(4) business partners and their associates, a firm itself being an associate of any of its members;

(5) the debtor's employer or employee (and for this purpose any director or other officer of a company is treated as its employee); or

(6) a company if the debtor alone, or the debtor and his associates control it. A company is an associate of another company if the same person controls both, or a person controls one and his associates (or he and his associates) control the other. Equally, a company may be an associate of another company if a group of two or more persons controls each company, and the groups either consist of the same persons or their associates. Control occurs where the directors of a company (or of another company which controls the first) are accustomed to act in accordance with the instructions of a person or group, or where a person or group is entitled to exercise or control the exercise of one-third of the voting power at any general meeting of the company (or of another company which controls the first).

A mere friend of the debtor, no matter how close, or even a fiancée is not an associate.

In order to determine when an alienation took place, the Act[524] directs that this shall be when the alienation became completely effectual. In relation to moveables this is taken to be the date of delivery,[525] while in relation to heritage, it is taken to be the date of recording of the disposition.[526] The same argument must also apply to any transaction where some form of registration is necessary to complete title.

There are three absolute defences to a challenge:

- that at any time after the alienation, the debtor's assets exceeded his liabilities[527];

The Act attempts to open to challenge alienations by individuals who are plainly insolvent. Thus alienations during periods of temporary insolvency are not challengeable. It has been held that assets which are beyond the reach of creditors, e.g. pension rights, should not be taken into account in this context.[528]

- that the alienation was for adequate consideration[529];

In other words, that the alienation was not gratuitous at all. In *McFadyen's Trustee v McFadyen*[530] it was held that the term "consideration" should be accorded its ordinary meaning as something of value given in return for something else. In that case, a mother purchased a house for her son and paid all the running costs. He then transferred title to her gratuitously, and it was held that this amounted to a gratuitous alienation, as her contribution of the price and payment of the costs could not be treated as consideration. In similar fashion in *Matheson's Trustee v Matheson*[531] Lord Marnoch held consideration could not be provided in respect of a disposition of a house by a husband to his wife by a number of past gifts she had made to him. A payment cannot be treated as amounting to consideration if it was not so intended at the time. On the other hand, the fact that a disposition of heritage narrates that it is for, "love, favour and affection" does not prevent the debtor seeking to prove that in reality adequate consideration was given.[532]

In *Cay's Trustee v Cay*[533] a husband who had given a large sum of money to his wife sought to argue that adequate consideration had been provided by her undertaking to aliment him. Predictably, this argument received short shrift from Lord McCluskey, who opined[534]:

---

[524] See s.34(3).

[525] *Craiglaw Developments Ltd v Wilson*, 1997 S.C.L.R. 1157.

[526] *Grant's Trustee v Grant*, 1986 S.L.T 220; *Accountant in Bankruptcy v Orr*, 2005 S.L.T. 1019.

[527] See s.34(4)(a); if this defence is pleaded, clear evidence of this fact must be provided: *Lombardi's Trustee v Lombardi*, 1982 S.L.T. 81. In determining the issue a "balance sheet" approach must be adopted, taking into account the debtor's claims against third parties and their counterclaims against him, even though these are not liquid: see Lord McEwan in *Accountant in Bankruptcy v Sneddon* [2008] CSOH 11 at [26].

[528] *McGruther v Walton*, 2004 S.C.L.R. 319.

[529] See s.34(4)(b).

[530] *MacFadyen's Trustee v MacFadyen*, 1994 S.L.T. 1245.

[531] *Matheson's Trustee v Matheson*, 1992 S.L.T. 685.

[532] *Nottay's Trustee v Nottay*, 2001 S.L.T. 769.

[533] *Cay's Trustee v Cay*, 1998 S.C.L.R 456.

[534] *Cay's Trustee v Cay*, 1998 S.C.L.R 456 at 461B–C.

"It cannot be maintained that this transfer of funds effected any alteration in the defender's obligation to aliment the debtor or in the debtor's corresponding legal right to demand such aliment. The legal rights of the defender and debtor *inter se* in relation to aliment remained after the transfer of funds exactly as they had been before. Accordingly, it cannot be said that the transfer of funds constituted a consideration in the form of a newly created legal right to be enjoyed by the debtor against the defender."

In regard to determining whether the consideration is adequate when genuine consideration is supplied, Lord Cullen observes in *Lafferty Construction v McCombe*[535]:

"I do not take the view that it is for the defender to establish that the consideration was the best which could have been obtained in the circumstances. On the other hand, the expression 'adequate' implies the application of an objective standpoint. The consideration should be not less than would reasonably be expected in the circumstances, assuming that persons in the position of the parties were acting in good faith and at arms length."

In this context, the Second Division in the *Cay* case was prepared to concede that consideration could be found in an undertaking by Mrs Cay to assume liability for certain of her husband's debts, but held that the alienation was inadequate since that liability could not exceed £20,000, while the alienation was in the region of £35,000. Again, in *Kerr v Aitken*[536] a husband and wife jointly owned a house and a further parcel of land, the latter being subject to a standard security in favour of a bank. He sought to argue that consideration for his otherwise gratuitous alienation of his half of the house in favour of her was supplied by her waiving her right of relief against him should the bank enforce the standard security to recover the amount of his overdraft. The argument was rejected because there was no suggestion that a right of relief against him was worth anything.

- That the alienation was a permitted gift, i.e. a birthday, Christmas or other conventional gift, or charitable donation (but in this last case not to an associate).[537]

Any such gift or donation will still be open to challenge if not "reasonable", obviously a significant qualification in this context. A donation is charitable if made for any charitable, benevolent or philanthropic purpose, whether or not this is regarded as charitable within the meaning of any rule of law.[538]

If an alienation is successfully challenged, then the court shall grant decree of reduction or order restoration of property to the estate or such other redress as may be appropriate.[539] Nevertheless, a third party who has acquired any property in good faith and for value shall not be prejudiced.[540] Thus where a third party is involved, it may be most appropriate to order the original recipient of the alienation to pay over to the estate the proceeds of the sale to the third party. But where a third party is not involved, restoration would seem to be the main remedy, if possible. In *Short's Trustee v Chung*[541] S sold to C two flats in Glasgow in October 1986 for £2,500 each. C gifted them to his wife in May 1987 and S was sequestrated in June 1987. A valuer acting for the trustee valued the flats as at October 1986 at £6,500 and £7,000. The Lord Ordinary decided that the alienations were not for adequate consideration and granted reduction of the transactions. Mrs C was not protected as she had not given value for the property. Mrs C then appealed on the basis that the remedy of reduction was inequitable as, due to the rise in property prices, it allowed the debtor's estate to benefit by more than the difference between the sum paid and the actual market value of the property at the time of sale. She contended that the appropriate remedy would have been to order her to pay £8,500 (the difference between the sum paid and the actual market value of the property at the time of sale). The Second Division responded as follows[542]:

---

[535] *Lafferty Construction v McCombe*, 1994 S.L.T. 858 at 861D.

[536] *Kerr v Aitken* [2000] B.P.I.R. 278.

[537] See s.34(4)(c).

[538] See s.34(5).

[539] See s.34(4).

[540] See s.34(4).

[541] *Short's Trustee v Chung (No.1)*, 1991 S.L.T. 472.

[542] *Short's Trustee v Chung (No.1)*, 1991 S.L.T. 472 at 476K. For a final twist in the tale of this saga see *Short's Trustee v Keeper of the Registers of Scotland*, 1996 S.C. (HL) 14; and *Short's Trustee v Chung (No.2)*, 1997 S.C.L.R. 1181.

"It is clear that the general purpose [of s.34] is to provide that as far as possible any property which has been improperly alienated should be restored to the debtor's estate. In the case of a disposition of heritable property this can easily be done by reduction of that disposition. We consider that the reference to 'such other redress as may be appropriate' is not intended to give the court a general discretion to decide a case on equitable principles, but is designed to enable the court to make an appropriate order in a case where reduction or restoration of the property is not a remedy which is available."

Equally, in the *Cay* case it was argued on behalf of Mrs Cay that she should not be obliged to repay the whole £35,000, as she had used the money partly to pay off £20,000 of her husband's debts. The Second Division followed its previous line that s.34(4) does not, "create any general discretion to decide on equitable principles to order something less than a full return of the alienated property".[543] Nor was there any room for the doctrine of set off to apply, as "there was no *concursus debiti* and *crediti*".[544]

By contrast, in *Nottay's Trustee v Nottay*[545] the debtor's spouse, having been given certain equipment by the debtor, was asked to pay for it by the trustee. She argued that, as she had sold it on, but had been compelled to sue the buyer for payment, the trustee should really be seeking the return of the property from the buyer. Lord Clarke said[546] that the case

"is distinguishable from *Short* and *Cay*, where the relevant property could be reconveyed by reduction of the relevant disposition. In the present case, the property is moveable, has been sold to a third party, and the whereabouts of the goods are unknown. It is also nothing to the point that the second defender may not herself have received consideration for the goods, if there was a gratuitous alienation in terms of s.34. The pursuer is entitled to seek appropriate redress from her which, in this case, would appear to be the value of the goods in question."

Unfair preferences

Such a transaction may be challenged in the same court and by the same categories of person as in regard to gratuitous alienations above.[547] To be challengeable, the preference must have occurred no more than six months before the date of sequestration (or the date of granting of a protected trust deed, or the date of death if sequestration of the appointment of a judicial factor follows within 12 months of death).[548] A preference is unfair if a creditor is preferred to the prejudice of the general body of creditors.[549] An example might be the granting of a security to a hitherto unsecured creditor, but a simple payment of a debt might in certain circumstances suffice. An interesting example from the corporate sphere is found in the case of *Baillie Marshall Ltd (in liquidation) v Avian Communications Ltd*,[550] where A Ltd acquired the business of B Ltd for a consideration which included the payment of B Ltd's trade creditors, but not their other creditors, with the aim of preserving the goodwill attached to B Ltd's business.

7.2.16.2

Certain transactions cannot be challenged:

(1) any transaction in the ordinary course of trade or business[551];

In *Nordic Travel Ltd v Scotprint Ltd*,[552] Lord Cameron adopts the following definition thereof:

---

[543] *Cay's Trustee v Cay*, 1998 S.C.L.R 456 at 464B.
[544] *Cay's Trustee v Cay*, 1998 S.C.L.R 456 at 463C.
[545] *Nottay's Trustee v Nottay*, 2001 S.L.T. 769.
[546] *Nottay's Trustee v Nottay*, 2001 S.L.T. 769 at 774C–D.
[547] See s.36.
[548] See s.36(1).
[549] See s.36(1).
[550] *Baillie Marshall Ltd (in liquidation) v Avian Communications Ltd*, 2002 S.L.T. 189.
[551] See s.36(2)(a).
[552] *Nordic Travel Ltd v Scotprint Ltd*, 1980 S.C. 1 at 29.

"[A] transaction which it would be usual for a creditor or debtor to enter as a matter of business in the circumstances . . . uninfluenced by any belief on the part of the creditor that the debtor might be insolvent."

So the payment of debts as they fall due would be in this category, as would the delivery of orders to customers. But returning goods to a supplier because of fears that the account would not be paid would not be, and would therefore amount to an unfair preference.[553] In *Balcraig House's Trustee v Roosevelt Property Services Ltd*[554] some four months before the date of sequestration a firm which ran a hotel "sold" its contents to a company, although the firm continued in possession of these goods. The consideration for this transaction was said to be a sum of money which the company had loaned the firm four years earlier, but which had never been repaid. Lord Maclean took the view that this transaction was an unfair preference as the debtor was in effect voluntarily transferring assets to one creditor in respect of a debt already incurred. Even if it were a true sale, it could not be seen as within the ordinary course of the firm's business as a hotel.

(2)   any payment in cash in respect of a debt then payable—unless there is collusion[555];

It follows that cash payment of a debt not yet due would amount to a preference.[556] Payment by banker's drafts, cheques or other bills of exchange amounts to cash payment.[557] But it would normally be an unfair preference for a debtor to indorse to a creditor a bill drawn up in his favour.[558] As far as collusion is concerned, Lord President Emslie defines it thus in the *Nordic* case[559]:

"The creditor who has been preferred has been apprised of the debtor's situation and duties, and enters into a transaction with him for the purpose of deceiving and defeating the rest of his creditors" and

"There is no authority for the view that the word 'collusion' is apt to include a creditor's knowledge of the insolvency of the debtor at the time of payment. The word . . . is intended to refer to participation by the creditor whose co-operation is necessary to achieve the result, in some device or transaction designed particularly to confer upon him a preference which would itself be [unfair]."

(3)   a transaction where the debtor and the other party undertake reciprocal obligations—*nova debita*[560];

An example would be where a party demands security in return for advancing money to the debtor— but not where the debtor grants a security in relation to a loan that has already been made. In *Thomas Montgomery & Sons v Gallacher*[561] the suppliers of G became concerned by his tardiness in failing to pay his account on the proper date. Accordingly, in return for agreeing to continue to supply him, they persuaded him to grant a heritable security over his trade premises. That security was stated to be "in respect of credit facilities presently granted to me and for future credit facilities". Lord Stewart took the view that transactions entered into after this agreement were *nova debita* and thus validly covered by the security. The granting of the security in respect of existing transactions would, however, have been an unfair preference. Yet the issue did not arise since G had continued to make payments in respect of goods supplied, and on the basis of the rule in *Clayton*'s case (see para.5.6.1.4) it was assumed that such payments should be ascribed to the earlier transactions, with the result that these earlier debts had been settled.

---

[553] *Morton's Trustee v The Fifeshire Auction Co Ltd*, 1911 1 S.L.T. 405.
[554] *Balcraig House's Trustee v Roosevelt Property Services Ltd*, 1994 S.L.T. 1133.
[555] See s.36(2)(b).
[556] *Whatmough's Trustee v British Linen Bank*, 1932 S.C. 525 per Lord President Clyde at 543.
[557] *Whatmough's Trustee v British Linen Bank*, 1934 S.C. (HL) 51.
[558] *Horburgh v Ramsay* (1885) 12 R. 1171; but see *Watson v Young* (1826) 4 S. 507.
[559] *Nordic Travel Ltd v Scotprint Ltd*, 1980 S.C. 1 at 11 and 19.
[560] See s.36(2)(c).
[561] *Thomas Montgomery & Sons v Gallacher*, 1982 S.L.T. 138.

In *Nicoll v Steelpress (Supplies) Ltd*[562] (a case decided under the equivalent provisions of the Insolvency Act 1986) S Ltd became worried when one of the companies it supplied fell further and further behind in the payment of its account. Accordingly, it arranged that it would only continue to supply the company if each order was met by a payment which would go some way towards clearing off the existing debt, e.g. on one occasion goods invoiced at under £350 were released in exchange for a cheque for £10,500. It was held that this amounted to an unfair preference. An Extra Division of the Inner House opined[563]:

> "The principle is that the consideration given to the debtor in the transaction cannot be less than full value to qualify for the exception. Strict equivalence is necessary in that the debtor's estate must not be diminished as a result of the transaction."

Once again, this exception does not apply where there is collusion.[564]

    (4)   the grant of a mandate to pay over arrested funds, as long as there has been a decree for payment or a warrant for summary diligence, and that decree/warrant has been proceeded by an arrestment on the dependence or followed by an arrestment in execution.[565]

The result of a successful challenge is identical to a successful challenge of a gratuitous alienation. The facts of *Baillie Marshall Ltd (in liquidation) v Avian Communications Ltd*[566] (a case decided under the equivalent provisions of the Insolvency Act 1986), are rehearsed above. The liquidator sought damages from the company which had bought the liquidated company's business in return for, inter alia, the payment of the latter's trade creditors. The measure of damages sought represented the amount which the other creditors would have received by way of dividend, but for the transaction. It was held that such an action was not competent. Relying on cases decided in relation to gratuitous alienations under the bankruptcy legislation, Lord Kingarth took the view that restoration of property is the primary remedy envisaged by the statute, and the words, "or such other redress as may be appropriate", should be construed as relating to redress of the same general character, and not as giving the court a general equitable jurisdiction.

Challenging gratuitous alienations/fraudulent preferences at common law

Any creditor has the right to challenge a gratuitous alienation at common law and by virtue of s.34(8) **7.2.16.3** this right of challenge is extended to the trustee in sequestration (as well as a trustee under a protected trust deed or any judicial factor). For a challenge to succeed at common law, it must be shown not only that the alienation was gratuitous, but that it prejudiced lawful creditors, and most importantly, that at the time of the alienation the debtor was absolutely insolvent or was made so by the alienation and is still absolutely insolvent at the time of challenge. Absolute insolvency (as opposed to apparent insolvency: see para.7.1.4) occurs when the debtor's liabilities exceed his assets.[567]

    In much the same way, s.36(6) gives a trustee in sequestration (as well as a trustee under a protected trust deed or any judicial factor) the same right to challenge a fraudulent preference at common law. Despite the use of the term fraudulent, there is no need for an actual dishonest intention to be shown. The criteria are that the transaction was a voluntary act of the debtor,[568] undertaken when he was absolutely insolvent and knew himself to be so,[569] which transaction preferred one creditor to the prejudice of others.[570] Although the debtor must be aware of his insolvent state, the state of knowledge of the preferred creditor is irrelevant. As Lord Justice Clerk Hope puts it in *McCowan v Wright*[571]:

---

[562] *Nicoll v Steelpress (Supplies) Ltd*, 1992 S.C.L.R. 332.
[563] *Nicoll v Steelpress (Supplies) Ltd*, 1992 S.C.L.R. 332 at 338B.
[564] See s.36(2)(c).
[565] See s.36(2)(d).
[566] *Baillie Marshall Ltd (in liquidation) v Avian Communications Ltd*, 2002 S.L.T. 189.
[567] See s.73(2).
[568] See Lord President Emslie in *Nordic Travel Ltd v Scotprint Ltd*, 1980 S.C. 1 at 10.
[569] *McCowan v Wright* (1853) 15 D. 494.
[570] *McCowan v Wright* (1853) 15 D. 494
[571] *McCowan v Wright* (1853) 15 D. 494 at 498.

"The creditors are equally injured—the prejudice to them is the same, whether the receiver at the time knew that the security was a fraud against them or not; and if it was a fraud . . . it does not become less so that he did not at the time know it was a fraud."

Lord President Emslie notes in *Nordic Travel Ltd v Scotprint Ltd*[572]:

"The creditor's knowledge of his debtor's absolute insolvency at the time when the debtor performs an act in his favour is quite irrelevant in deciding whether or not the act is a fraudulent preference. If a particular act by an insolvent debtor to his creditor is *per se* unobjectionable and lawful, I am unable to see how his creditor's mere knowledge of his insolvency can make it objectionable and unlawful."

Defences (1)–(3) considered in the previous subparagraph in relation to unfair preferences apply in this context also.

If the appropriate conditions are met, then a transaction might be challenged as a gratuitous aliena-tion or fraudulent preference whenever it occurred, i.e. the time limits laid down by the Act do not apply. A transaction can indeed be challenged prior to the commencement of the sequestration process, although obviously it would be a creditor rather than the trustee who would make such a challenge.

Finally, it should be remembered that whether a transaction is being challenged at common law or under statute, the court cannot recover money or property from a defender who is outside Scotland.[573]

Capital sum payable on divorce

7.2.16.4 While a decree ordering the transfer of property and/or the payment of a certain sum on the debtor's divorce could hardly be described as either a gratuitous alienation or unfair preference, it may appear unduly generous with the benefit of hindsight. Thus if, within five years of the order, the debtor's estate has been sequestrated, or he has granted a trust deed which has become protected, or he has died and within 12 months after his death he has either been sequestrated or a judicial factor has been appointed to admin-ister his estate, the appropriate person (the trustee in sequestration, the trustee under the trust deed or the judicial factor) may request the court to recall an order.[574] It must be shown that the debtor was absolutely insolvent at the date of the order, or was so rendered by the order.[575] The court, having regard to all the circumstances, including the financial and other circumstances of the person against whom the order would be made, may order repayment of the whole or part of the sum paid, the retransfer of the whole or part of any property transferred, or payment of the whole or part of the proceeds from the sale of property.[576]

Excessive pension contributions

7.2.16.5 While any sums paid to the debtor from an occupational or personal pension scheme do not vest in the trustee, such amounts obviously derive to some extent from contributions made to such schemes by or on behalf of the debtor. It is therefore possible that during the period leading up to the sequestration, the debtor may have been investing considerable sums in such a scheme to safeguard his ultimate pension position, to the detriment of his creditors. For that reason the trustee may apply to the court in such circumstances.[577] If the court is satisfied that the debtor's rights under the scheme are to any extent derived from excessive contributions, it may make such order as it thinks fit for restoring the position to what it would have been had the excessive contributions not been made.[578] Such an order may in particular require those responsible for the scheme to pay over an amount to the trustee, and/or to reduce the benefits paid by the scheme to the debtor or to any other person, e.g. a dependant of the debtor, where these

---

[572] *Nordic Travel Ltd v Scotprint Ltd*, 1980 S.C. 1 at 14.
[573] *Reid v Ramlort Ltd*, 1998 S.C. 887, IH.
[574] See s.35(1), (2).
[575] See s.35(2).
[576] See s.35(2).
[577] See s.36A(1).
[578] See s.36A(2).

benefits derive from the rights of the debtor.[579] The maximum amount that may be ordered to be paid is the amount of the excessive contributions, or the value of the debtor's rights under the scheme, whichever is the lesser.[580] Before it can make an order, the court must be satisfied that the making of the excessive contributions has unfairly prejudiced the creditors,[581] and in so deciding shall consider whether any contributions were made for the purpose of putting assets beyond the reach of creditors, and whether contributions appear excessive in view of the debtor's circumstances when they were made.[582] In deciding whether contributions are excessive, no account is to be taken of any debit on the debtor's benefits on account of pension sharing.[583] In other words, the court is not allowed to take into account that a debtor has to share a pension with an ex-spouse in working out whether contributions were excessive.

Extortionate credit transactions

It is not unknown for debtors who are sinking deeper into financial difficulties to enter into very unwise **7.2.16.6** credit transactions. The trustee can challenge any credit transaction entered into within three years prior to the date of sequestration on the basis that it is extortionate.[584] A credit transaction is extortionate if, having regard to the risk accepted by the credit supplier, its terms required grossly exorbitant payments to be made, or it otherwise grossly contravened the ordinary principles of fair dealing.[585] It will be presumed that a transaction is extortionate, and so it will fall to the credit supplier to prove the contrary.[586] These criteria are essentially the same as those applied in order to determine whether a credit bargain is extortionate in terms of the now repealed s.138 of the Consumer Credit Act 1974 (see para.3.9 of the first edition of this work), so case law thereunder may be instructive. Where the court finds a credit transaction to be extortionate, it may do any one or more of the following things[587]:

- set aside the obligation in whole or in part;
- vary the terms of the obligation or any associated security;
- require repayment to the trustee of any sums paid by the debtor;
- require the surrender to the trustee of any property held as security for the purposes of the transaction;
- direct accounts to be taken between any persons.

Obviously any money or property returned under this provision vests in the trustee.[588]

REALISATION OF THE ESTATE

While the trustee may have to manage the estate, his main concern will be to sell it off, including any **7.2.17** debts owing to the estate.[589] Any part of the estate may be sold either by public sale or private bargain.[590] However, it is incompetent for the trustee, or any associate of his, or a commissioner to purchase any part of the estate.[591] The meaning of the term "incompetent" in this context is not clear. It may be that s.39(8) is intended as a qualification of s.39(7), which recites that the validity of the title of any purchaser shall not be challengeable on the ground that there has been a failure to comply with s.39. If so, then it is possible that s.39(8) intends to suggest that such sales are void, with the result that any

---

[579] See s.36A(2), (3).
[580] See s.36B(4).
[581] See s.36A(2)(b).
[582] See s.36A(6).
[583] See s.36A(3), (4).
[584] See s.61(2).
[585] See s.61(3).
[586] See s.61(3).
[587] See s.61(4).
[588] See s.61(5).
[589] See s.39(5).
[590] See s.39(3).
[591] See s.39(8).

purchaser from the trustee, etc. cannot obtain a good title. It must also be remembered that a trustee in sequestration is a fiduciary.[592] Thus if, for example, a trustee were to sell part of the property of the estate to another on the understanding that the property would then be resold to the trustee, such a transaction would be voidable at common law, and the trustee liable in damages to the estate.[593]

The trustee may sell heritage despite it being subject to an inhibition.[594] Where heritage is subject to a security then either the trustee or the secured creditor may sell. Generally, once the trustee has intimated his intention to sell, the secured creditor may not take steps to sell the property, and vice versa.[595] Nonetheless, if either party has intimated his intention to sell, then delays unduly in doing so, the other may seek the authority of the sheriff to proceed with the sale himself.[596] Moreover, the trustee may not sell heritage without the concurrence of any secured creditor, unless he obtains a sufficiently high price to discharge the securities.[597]

There may also be difficulties if the trustee (or a trustee under under a trust deed[598]) wishes to sell the family home. This is the place where immediately before the date of sequestration (or the day immediately before the date the trust deed was granted)[599] the debtor's spouse or civil partner (with or without the debtor) or former spouse or civil partner resided, or the debtor resided with a child of the family.[600] The width of the definition means that more than one residence could qualify as the family home. A child of the family includes any child or grandchild of the debtor, his spouse or civil partner, or former spouse or civil partner, as well as any person who has been brought up and accepted as if they were the child of any of those individuals.[601] The actual age of the child is irrelevant.[602] The inspiration of the provisions in this area is the recognition that, while it is obviously not acceptable that debtor's family should continue indefinitely to occupy accommodation of a high standard while his creditors await payment, nonetheless, the family could experience genuine hardship through the immediate sale of their home.[603] Accordingly, the trustee requires to obtain the consent of the spouse or debtor, and if that cannot be obtained, the authority of the sheriff, if he wishes to sell.[604] (The debtor's consent need only be sought if living with a child of the family, but not if he is living with a spouse or civil partner, or former spouse or civil partner.) It will be seen that the Act protects the interests of the family. There is no need to seek any consent or authority if the debtor occupies a house alone or with someone, e.g. a lover or parent, who is not part of the family as defined above. Nor indeed is consent required when a child occupies a house alone.

Where the trustee is unable to obtain the necessary consent, he will be obliged to apply to the sheriff for authority to sell. Before commencing proceedings to obtain such authority, the trustee (or a trustee acting under a trust deed) must give notice of the proceedings to the local authority[605] in whose area the home is situated.[606] The sheriff will take into account all the circumstances of the case, including[607]:

---

[592] *York Buildings Co v Mackenzie* (1795) 3 Pat. 378.

[593] *Fraser v Hankey & Co* (1847) 9 D. 415; *Whyte's Trustee v Burt* (1851) 13 D. 679.

[594] See s.31(2).

[595] See s.39(4)(b).

[596] See s.39(4)(c).

[597] See s.39(4)(a).

[598] While the discussion in the text refers to the trustee in sequestration, as a result of amendments to s.40(1)–(3) introduced by s.11(a) of the Home Owner and Debtor Protection (Scotland) Act 2010, a trustee under a trust deed must similarly seek the consent of the relevant person or the permission of the sheriff before he is able to sell the family home.

[599] See s.40(4)(d).

[600] See s.40(4)(a).

[601] See s.40(4)(b).

[602] See s.40(4)(b).

[603] See para.1118, Review Committee on Insolvency Law and Practice, *Report of the Review Committee on Insolvency Law and Practice* (HMSO, 1982), Cmnd.8858.

[604] See s.40(1).

[605] Meaning a council constituted under s.2 of the Local Government Act 1994: s.40(4)(ba).

[606] See s.40(3A). For the form of notice see the Bankruptcy (Scotland) Regulations 2008 (SSI 2008/82) reg.19A and Form 24.

[607] See s.40(2). In *Burns's Trustee v Burns*, 2001 S.L.T. 1383; a debtor was sequestrated in respect of a debt under £1,000. He refused to co-operate with the sequestration, so that the expenses of its administration amounted to £30,000. Even though sale of the family home would realise no more than £20,000, Lord Philip consented to its sale, observing (at [16]) that s.40(2) "enjoins me to have regard to all the circumstances of the case. I consider that these include both the public interest and the first defender's behaviour ... It is in the public interest that expenses of administration paid for by the public purse should be recouped ... [while] it would not be in the public interest if the first defender were to be seen to benefit from his recalcitrance".

- the needs and financial resources of the spouse/former spouse, civil partner/former civil partner or any child of the family;
- the length of time the home has been used as a residence by any of the above individuals;
- the interests of creditors.

The sheriff may decide to refuse the application. He might do so, for example, when the amount which might be secured from the sale would be modest in comparison with the dislocative effect of the sale on the family, but in extreme cases applications have been refused even where the family home was the debtor's major asset, in light of the trauma which sale might cause.[608] Even if the sheriff authorises the sale of the home, he may postpone the granting of the application for up to three years, or grant it subject to conditions.[609] In *McMahon's Trustees v McMahon*[610] it was held that such conditions could validly include the payment of part of the proceeds of sale to certain of the debtor's dependants. It may be noted that the Act directs that the sheriff must take into account the same factors, and has the same powers where the trustee raises an action for the division and sale of the family home[611] (which would be required if the house were not owned solely by the debtor), or an action to obtain vacant possession.[612] In this latter respect the legislation is ambiguous since it seems to suggest that even where the sheriff has granted an application to sell a family home in terms of s.40(2), the same factors require to be considered anew if it proves necessary to raise an action to obtain vacant possession, as would be the case if the occupant of the home refuses to leave. However, in *Blackburn v Cowie*[613] the Inner House rejected such an interpretation as absurd, since it could lead to the situation where, authority to sell a family home having been granted under s.40(2), should it then prove necessary to raise an action to evict the family, a different sheriff taking into account the same considerations might refuse that application under s.40(3)(b). Accordingly, it was held that the proper interpretation of the legislation was that, if an application for sale has been granted, there is no need to consider the same factors again should it be necessary to raise an action to recover possession. *This would be clarified by the 2014 Act.* In the view of the court, s.40(3)(b) would apply to the situation where the trustee did not intend to sell the family home, but wished rather to obtain vacant possession, so that he might lease it for the benefit of the bankrupt estate.

It might be added that the above safeguards only apply where the trustee wishes to sell the family home. There are no such safeguards where a secured creditor exercises the right to sell the property over which it has security, even if that property is a family home.

Following the 2007 amendments, the Act now provides a time limit within which the trustee must take steps to sell the family home otherwise it will be reinvested in the debtor. It was felt that the Act previously allowed the debtor's family to be left "in limbo", making it more difficult for debtors to move on and restart.[614] Thus three years after the date of sequestration any right or interest in the debtor's family home which vested in the trustee will cease to form part of the sequestrated estate and be reinvested in the debtor, unless the trustee takes certain types of action.[615] The sorts of action which will prevent the family home being reinvested in the debtor are where the trustee[616]:

---

[608] See, e.g. *Gourlay's Trustee, Petitioner*, 1995 S.L.T. (Sh Ct) 7; but compare *Salmon's Trustee v Salmon*, 1989 S.L.T. (Sh Ct) 49.

[609] See s.40(2).

[610] *McMahon's Trustees v McMahon*, 1997 S.C.L.R. 439.

[611] See s.40(3)(a). If a house is not owned solely by the debtor, the trustee's options are limited prior to sale. In *Stewart's Trustee v Stewart*, 2012 S.L.T. (Sh Ct) 231; Sheriff Mann held that a trustee in bankruptcy was in no better a position than any other *pro indiviso* proprietor, and one proprietor could not eject the other. Therefore he refused to grant an order for ejection of the co-proprietor. Similarly he refused to grant an order for possession, since the trustee in bankruptcy would not wish to move in with the co-owner and could not install a tenant without the latter's consent. Practically, even the debtor could not be ejected, since she would retain the right to occupy through the tolerance of her co-owner: see paras 7–10. See also *Reith v Paterson*, 1993 S.C.L.R. 921; and *Langstane (S.P.) Housing Association v Davie*, 1993 S.C.L.R. 158.

[612] See s.40(3)(b).

[613] *Blackburn v Cowie*, 2008 S.L.T. 437; see especially paras 28–32.

[614] See the policy memorandum which accompanied the Bill, para.231.

[615] See s.39A(2).

[616] See s.39A(3).

- disposes of or otherwise realises the right or interest, e.g. sells the home;
- concludes missives for its sale;
- sends a memorandum to the Keeper of the Register of Inhibitions in order to continue the inhibiting effect of registering the original award for a further period;
- registers a notice of title to the right or interest in the Land Register or Register of Sasines;
- commences proceedings to obtain the authority of the sheriff to sell the right or interest, or commences an action for division or sale of the family home or to obtain vacant possession of the family home;
- challenges the earlier disposal of the home as a gratuitous alienation;
- agrees with the debtor that the right or interest shall be reinvested in the debtor in return for the debtor incurring a specified liability, in other words the debtor agrees to pay in order to be allowed to hang on to the home.[617]

Where the debtor fails to inform the trustee or AIB of his right or interest in the family home within three months of the date of sequestration, the three-year period shall run from the date when the trustee or AIB becomes aware of that interest.[618] Moreover, the sheriff on application by the trustee may extend the period if he thinks appropriate.[619] Regulations may be made for a shorter period to operate in certain circumstances, or for the section not to apply in certain circumstances, or to be disapplied by the sheriff in certain circumstances, or for compensation to be paid.[620]

Following upon the realisation of the estate, the trustee would proceed to distribute it as directed by the Act. The order of distribution is considered at para.7.3.8, in the section dealing with creditors, which now follows.

THE CREDITORS

7.3 This treatment, having so far considered the subject from the standpoint of the debtor or trustee, now turns to look at sequestration from the perspective of the creditors. Before considering the relationship of creditors to the sequestration process, it is useful to consider the impact that pre-sequestration activities may have on that process, i.e. the relationship between sequestration and diligence.

SEQUESTRATION AND DILIGENCE

7.3.1 Obviously, when an individual is in financial difficulties and his creditors are not receiving payment, one or more creditors may be tempted to do diligence on the debtor's estate in order to obtain payment. Diligence is of course the process whereby the debtor's property is attached in order to facilitate recovery of his debts. The main forms of diligence are attachment of money, arrestment and attachment of moveables, and inhibition and attachment of land in relation to heritage (the 2007 Act having abolished adjudication). The point of doing diligence is of course to give a creditor a preferential right to the asset(s) upon which diligence is done. If a number of creditors seek to do diligence upon a certain asset, priority tends to be determined in terms of the date on which diligence was done—the earlier a creditor did diligence the more advantageous his position. Yet the law of personal insolvency is premised on the basis that creditors are treated fairly, and for the most part equally. That aim would hardly be served if a creditor could ensure full payment simply by being the first to rush to diligence. Accordingly, there are special rules regarding diligence.

---

[617] See s.39A(5).
[618] See s.39A(6).
[619] See s.39A(7).
[620] See s.39A(8).

Equalisation of diligence and apparent insolvency

Certain rules apply to diligence even though outwith the context of the sequestration process. Thus all **7.3.1.1** arrestments and attachments executed within the period 60 days before the constitution of apparent insolvency (see para.7.1.4) and four months thereafter are treated as if they had been executed on the same date.[621] So, if an act of apparent insolvency is committed on July 31, any diligences done during the period between June 1 and November 30 are treated as if they had been done on the same day. The result of course is that they are all ranked equally. This is known as equalisation of diligence, and ensures equal treatment of creditors. The Act also states that, if there is any judicial process relating to the arrestments or attachments, any creditor who can produce liquid grounds of debt or a decree for payment within the aforesaid period is entitled to share equally in the assets affected by the diligence.[622] The above example is very straightforward. Yet, if an individual is experiencing financial difficulties, more than one instance of apparent insolvency may arise, so that there may be overlapping equalisation periods. This can give rise to issues of great complexity to which the current law provides no obvious solution.[623] Subject to this point, a creditor who has effected diligence before the equalisation period begins retains the benefit of that diligence.

It may be noted that none of the above provisions apply to an earnings arrestment, a current maintenance arrestment, or a conjoined arrestment order.[624] This is because there can only be one earnings arrestment and current maintenance arrestment effective against a debtor at any one time. If any other creditor wishes to share in the earnings of a debtor, a conjoined arrestment order must be sought.

Equalisation of diligence does not apply to inhibitions, which by their nature do not attach to a specific asset.

Diligence and sequestration

As might be expected, actual sequestration has an effect on diligence. Thus, broadly speaking, any dili- **7.3.1.2** gence done within 60 days prior to the date of sequestration or any time thereafter is effectively cut down.[625] So no arrestment or attachment (including interim attachment or money attachment) within the aforesaid period is effectual, and any estate so arrested or attached, or the proceeds of sale thereof must be handed over to the trustee.[626] There is no need for arrestment or attachment to be subsisting at the date of sequestration.[627] If estate has been arrested or attached during the crucial period, it or the proceeds of its sale must be handed over, even if the arrestment or attachment has been withdrawn or otherwise fallen.[628] There is no suggestion in the terms of the Act that a third party who has acquired estate in good faith from the arresting/attaching creditor may retain it. Therefore, the trustee should be able to demand that such a third party hands over the estate. The arresting/attaching creditor is nonetheless entitled to certain expenses to be paid from the estate or the proceeds of its sale, i.e. expenses incurred[629]:

- in obtaining warrant for interim attachment or the extract of the decree or other document on which the arrestment or attachment proceeded;
- in executing the arrestment or attachment;
- in taking any further action in respect of the diligence.

None of the above provisions applies to an earnings arrestment, a current maintenance arrestment, a conjoined arrestment order, or deductions from earnings orders under the Child Support Act 1991.[630]

---

[621] See s.75(1)(b) and Sch.7 para.24(1).
[622] See Sch.7 para.24(3).
[623] See paras 5.42–5.53, Scottish Law Commission, *Equalisation of Diligences* (HMSO, 1987) Scot. Law Com. Discussion Paper No.79.
[624] See Sch.7 para.24(8).
[625] See s.37.
[626] See s.37(4).
[627] See s.37(4).
[628] As to the previous law see *Johnston v Cluny Estate's Trustee*, 1957 S.L.T 293.
[629] See s.37(5).
[630] See s.37(5A).

Yet sequestration terminates such arrestments and orders, although the trustee must apply for the recall of a conjoined arrestment order.[631]

Similarly, no land attachment created within six months prior to the date of sequestration creates a preference for the creditor who creates it,[632] although he is nonetheless entitled to certain expenses to be paid from the land or the proceeds of its sale,[633] while land attachment created after the date of sequestration is completely ineffective.[634] But where a contract to sell the land has been concluded, the trustee must concur in and ratify the deed implementing the contract, and will receive that portion of the proceeds of sale which would otherwise be due to the debtor.[635] Yet s.37(8C) does not apply where the deed is not registered within 28 days after the recording in the Register of Inhibitions of the certified copy of the order of the sheriff granting warrant to cite the debtor to appear before him to show cause why sequestration should not be granted, or of the certified copy of the determination of the AIB awarding sequestration.[636] Again, where a decree of foreclosure has been granted, but the extract not registered, the creditor may complete title by registering that extract, provided this is done within the period just described.[637]

As inhibition does not attach to specific assets, no provision is made for the handing over of any estate to the trustee, nor for the creditor to recover any expenses in connection with the inhibition. Yet where an inhibition has been effected within 60 days prior to the date of sequestration, the trustee acquires any right of challenge competent to the inhibitor and any right the inhibitor would have to receive payment for discharging the inhibition.[638] Again, no poinding of the ground (required to give a heritable creditor security over moveables on the subjects) is effectual if executed within that period, save in respect of the rights of a secured creditor to certain types of interest in his debt.[639]

While sequestration does not itself amount to diligence,[640] the Act treats it as having the effect of the appropriate form of diligence. Thus s.37(1) recites that, as from the date of sequestration, the award of sequestration has the effect in relation to any diligence done of an arrestment in execution and decree of furthcoming, an arrestment in execution and warrant of sale, and an attachment, in favour of the creditors according to their respective entitlements. In other words, it is as if each creditor did the appropriate form(s) at the date of sequestration. This has significant consequences where the date of sequestration occurs within four months of the constitution of apparent insolvency. Since, as described above, all arrestments and attachments executed within the period 60 days before the constitution of apparent insolvency and four months thereafter are treated as if they had been executed on the same date, all arrestments and attachments within that period will be equalised with the sequestration itself, and so will effectively be cut down. This is illustrated by *Stewart v Jarvie*.[641] Diligence was done on October 16, 1936, and apparent insolvency constituted on November 27, 1936. Sequestration was awarded on January 4, 1937. It can be appreciated then that diligence was done more than 60 days prior to the date of sequestration, so that it was not automatically cut down. Nonetheless, the sequestration did occur within four months of the constitution of apparent insolvency, and the diligence was executed less than 60 days prior to that latter date, so that the diligence was equalised with the sequestration and the creditor concerned gained no priority over the other creditors in the sequestration. Lord Fleming explained the matter thus[642]:

> "It is important to note that, on the one hand, the appellant's arrestment was used within 60 days prior to the constitution of [apparent insolvency], and that, on the other hand, sequestration took

---

[631] Debtors (Scotland) Act 1987 ss.72, 66.
[632] See s.37(5B).
[633] See s.37(5C) for details.
[634] See s.37(8A).
[635] See s.37(8C).
[636] See s.37(8D).
[637] See s.37(8E).
[638] See s.37(2), (3).
[639] See s.37(6).
[640] *G & A Barnie v Stevenson*, 1993 S.C.L.R. 318.
[641] *Stewart v Jarvie*, 1938 S.C. 309.
[642] *Stewart v Jarvie*, 1938 S.C. 309 at 312.

place within 4 months thereafter . . . Applying [the legislation] to the case in hand, the result is that on January 4 the sequestration is to be regarded as equivalent to an arrestment used for behoof of all the creditors equally. And accordingly the appellant's claim for a preference over the other creditors must be dealt with on the footing that, in addition to the arrestment he used on October 16, there was also used for the behoof of the general body of the creditors, an arrestment on January 4. . . . The appellant is not entitled to any preference over the other creditors, for his arrestment and their arrestment are equalised. The appellant is entitled to be ranked on the arrested fund for the amount of his claim, but equally all the other creditors are entitled to be ranked thereon *pari passu* with him for the amount of their respective claims."

Of course, if diligence has been effected too early to be struck down by the sequestration, it remains effective. It may well be that the effect of the diligence is to transfer ownership of the asset concerned to the creditor. If, however, ownership is retained by the debtor, the asset will vest in the trustee and the diligence is treated as a security over the asset.

Moratorium on diligence   7.3.1.3

While an award of sequestration effectively cut down any diligence done at least 60 days prior to the date of sequestration, the law did not prevent diligence being granted during the period leading up to sequestration. The granting of a protected trust deed did not even cut down prior diligences. By contrast, in relation to debt arrangement schemes regulation 30 of the Debt Arrangement Scheme (Scotland) Regulations 2011 imposes a six-week moratorium on diligence, preventing any creditor doing any form of diligence on the debtor's estate for a six-week period following intimation of the intention to apply for approval of a debt payment programme. The 2014 Act aims to apply such a scheme to any intimation by a debtor of the intention to apply for approval of a debt payment programme, or sequestration, or the granting of a protected trust deed, thus achieving uniformity of treatment across all debt relief and debt management solutions. Thus it is now provided that a person may give written notice to the AIB of his intention:

- *to make a debtor application for sequestration[643]; or*
- *to seek to have a trust deed protected[644]; or*
- *to apply for approval of a debt payment programme.[645]*

As under the Debt Arrangement Scheme (Scotland) Regulations, such a person may not give notice if he has done so in the previous 12 months.[646] The AIB on receiving a notice must without delay register the name of the person giving the notice and such other details as she considers appropriate in the register of insolvencies and the register of debt payment programmes.[647] A moratorium on diligence will then apply to that person,[648] meaning that it is not competent for the relevant period to serve a charge for payment in respect of any debt owed by the person, or commence or execute any diligence to enforce payment of such a debt, or to found on such a debt as a basis for seeking sequestration.[649] Nor where a creditor has arrested funds which are due to the debtor may those funds be released to the debtor.[650] Normally an arrestee must release the arrested funds to the creditor within 14 weeks of

---

[643] *See s.4A(1)(a), s.4B(1).*

[644] *See s.4A(1)(b).*

[645] *See s.4A(1)(c).*

[646] *See s.4A(2), s.4B(3). The Policy Memorandum (para.93) indicates that this "ensures that the restriction on creditors taking further action is not extended and repeated without limit".*

[647] *See s.4A(3)–(4), s.4B(3).The aim is to ensure that the moratorium is "registered on a public register that can be accessed by interested parties", Policy Memorandum (para.94).*

[648] *See s.4C(2).*

[649] *See s.4C(3)(a)–(c). However, it is still competent to (a) auction an article which has been attached in accordance with the Debt Arrangement and Attachment (Scotland) Act 2002 where either notice has been given to the debtor under s.27(4) of that Act, or the article has been removed or notice of removal given under s.53 of that Act; (b) implement a decree of furthcoming; (c) implement a decree or order for sale of a ship (or share of it) or cargo; (d) execute an earnings arrestment, a current maintenance arrestment or a conjoined arrestment order which came into effect before the moratorium begins: see s.4C(5).*

[650] *See s.4C(3)(d).*

the date of service of a final decree on the debtor or the date of service of a schedule of arrestment on the debtor. However, the running of this 14-week period is suspended for the duration of the moratorium.[651]

The primary assumption is that the period of the moratorium begins on the day when the AIB makes the relevant entry in the register of insolvencies, and ends six weeks after that day.[652] *However, the moratorium may end prior to that date if an entry is made in the register of insolvencies recording the award of sequestration or the granting or refusal of protected status to a trust deed.*[653] *The position is similar if an entry is made in the DAS register recording the approval of a debt payment programme, or if written notice is given to the AIB of the withdrawal of the notice.*[654] *It is also possible for the moratorium to end later than the normal date. Thus, where the AIB has not awarded sequestration, it is possible under s.15(3A) for the debtor or a creditor concurring in a debtor application to request a review of that decision (see para.7.1.7). Under s.15(3C) the AIB must ultimately confirm that decision or award sequestration. Where the AIB has not made the decision under s.15(3C) at the end of the standard moratorium period, the moratorium period continues until written notice is given to the AIB of the withdrawal of the notice, or the day when an entry is made in the register of insolvencies recording the award of sequestration.*[655] *Should the AIB, under s.15(3C), confirm the decision not to award sequestration, the period ends on the date when that confirmation decision is made.*[656] *Alternatively, no request to review the decision under s.15(3A) may be made within the period allowed by s.15(3B)—14 days from the date of refusal. If the expiry of that period runs beyond the standard moratorium period, the moratorium period will continue until the former period expires.*[657] *Similarly, where an entry has been made in the register of insolvencies recording an application for a trust deed to receive protected status and the decision whether or not to grant that status has not been made at the end of the standard moratorium period, the moratorium period continues until written notice is given to the AIB of the withdrawal of the notice of intention to apply, or the day when an entry is made in the register of insolvencies recording the grant of protected status.*[658] *If no such entry is made, i.e. if protected status is not granted, the moratorium period will be of 13 weeks duration.*[659] *Where an individual has sought approval of a debt payment programme, and that application has not been determined at the end of the standard moratorium period, the moratorium period continues until written notice is given to the AIB of the withdrawal of the notice of intention to apply, or the day when an entry is made in the DAS register recording the approval or rejection of the programme.*[660]

THE CREDITORS' SUPERVISION OF THE INSOLVENCY PROCESS—COMMISSIONERS

7.3.2 It is possible for the creditors to elect from among their fellows commissioners to advise and supervise the trustee.[661] When sequestration was a process controlled by the creditors, election of commissioners was mandatory. Now, however, there need not be commissioners (and often none will be elected), while it is not permitted to have commissioners in any sequestration where the trustee is appointed rather than elected.[662] They may be elected at the statutory meeting of creditors or at any subsequent meeting of creditors, and there may be any number of commissioners from one to five at any one

---

[651] *See s.4C(4).*
[652] *See s.4D(1)(a), s.4D(1)(b)(i).*
[653] *See s.4D(2)(a)–(b).*
[654] *See s.4D(2)(c)–(d).*
[655] *See s.4D(3), s.4D(4)(a) and (c).*
[656] *See s.4D(3), s.4D(4)(b)(ii).*
[657] *See s.4D(3), s.4D(4)(b)(i).*
[658] *See s.4D(5), s.4D(6)(a) and (c).*
[659] *See s.4D(5), s.4D(6)(b).*
[660] *See s.4D(7)–(8).*
[661] See s.4.
[662] See Sch.2 para.6.

time.[663] They will be elected by those creditors who are qualified to elect the trustee[664] (see para.7.2.9). To qualify for election individuals must be creditors or mandatories of creditors. A mandatory is someone a creditor has authorised in writing to represent him at a meeting.[665] (The creditor must lodge that authorisation with the trustee prior to the meeting.)[666] Certain individuals are disqualified—the debtor, an associate (see para.7.2.16.1) of the debtor or of the trustee, a person who holds an interest opposed to the general interests of creditors—and should a commissioner become such a person, he is no longer entitled to continue in that role.[667]

A commissioner may resign at any time,[668] and may be removed from office:

- by the creditors at a meeting called for that purpose[669];
- if an elected trustee is replaced by an appointed trustee[670];
- where he is a mandatory, by the creditor recalling the mandate, and intimating that recall in writing to the trustee[671];
- by the sheriff, following on a report by the AIB that he has failed without reasonable excuse to perform his legal duties[672];
- *by the order of the sheriff if he is satisfied that the commissioner is no longer acting in the interests of the efficient conduct of the sequestration.[673] Such an order may be made on the application of the AIB, the trustee, or a person representing not less that one quarter of the value of the creditors.[674] The sheriff must order that the application be served on the commissioner and intimated to any creditor who has given the commissioner a mandate, and must before deciding to make an order give the commissioner an opportunity to make representations.[675] Whether or not he decides to remove the commissioner from office, he may make such other order as he thinks fit.[676] The AIB, the trustee, any commissioner or any creditor may appeal against the sheriff's decision within 14 days of it being made.[677]*

The general functions of a commissioner are to supervise the intromissions of the trustee with the estate, and to advise him.[678] They are subject to certain mandatory duties. Thus, when they become aware that the trustee has resigned, died, or been removed from office by the sheriff, they must call a meeting of creditors to elect a replacement.[679] Within six weeks of the end of an accounting period (see next paragraph), they must determine the amount of outlays and remuneration payable to the trustee, and may audit his accounts.[680] They must consider any offer of composition reported by the trustee and decide whether it should be placed before the creditors.[681] In addition, their consent is required if the trustee is[682]:

- to vary the length of an accounting period, other than the first;
- to accept a claim in other than prescribed form;
- to pay preferred debts earlier than would otherwise be the case;
- to postpone payment of a dividend to the ordinary creditors;

---

[663] See s.30(1).
[664] See ss.24(3), 30(1).
[665] See Sch.6 para.11(1).
[666] See Sch.6 para.11(2).
[667] See s.30(2).
[668] See s.30(3).
[669] See s.30(4)(b).
[670] See Sch.2 para.6.
[671] See s.30(4)(a).
[672] See s.1A(2).
[673] *See s.30(4)(c).*
[674] *See s.30(5).*
[675] *See s.30(6).*
[676] *See s.30(7).*
[677] *See s.30(8).*
[678] See s.4.
[679] See ss.28(2), (3) and 29(5), (6).
[680] See s.53(5).
[681] See Sch.4 paras 4, 5.
[682] See ss.52, 65(1).

- to refer any claim or question to arbitration;
- to compromise any claim.

There are also powers which they may exercise at their discretion:

- to inspect the trustee's accounts at all reasonable times[683];
- to require the trustee to apply to the sheriff for an order for the public examination of the debtor or other relevant person[684];
- to dispense with the taxation of an account in respect of legal services incurred by the trustee[685];
- to require the trustee to call a meeting of commissioners, or to call a meeting of commissioners themselves if the trustee fails timeously to respond to such a request.[686]

Although the trustee must "have regard" to advice offered by the commissioners,[687] he need not take that advice. Nonetheless, the commissioners may apply to the sheriff for the trustee to be given directions regarding the recovery, management and realisation of the estate with which directions he must comply.[688] The Act also provides that where a "person having an interest" is dissatisfied with any act, omission or decision of the trustee, he may apply to the sheriff who can confirm, annul or modify any such act or decision, or give the trustee such directions as he thinks fit.[689] It is submitted that a commissioner is a "person having an interest". As a last resort commissioners may apply to the sheriff (*the AIB following the 2014 Act*) for the trustee's removal from office.[690] The performance of commissioners is itself subject to the supervision of the AIB, who must report any suspected offences committed by a commissioner to the Lord Advocate.[691] If the AIB considers that a commissioner has failed without reasonable excuse to perform a legal duty, she must report this to the sheriff, who may remove the commissioner from office, or censure him, or make such other order as seems appropriate.[692]

Commissioners owe fiduciary duties to the debtor and creditors.[693] While a commissioner is specifically precluded from buying any part of the estate,[694] he might also be liable in respect of any transaction related to the estate from which he might benefit, or which might be inimical to interests of the debtor and/or creditors. Moreover, a commissioner must act gratuitously and is not even entitled to expenses. Indeed, if a commissioner also acts as solicitor for the trustee, he may recover his outlays only, and cannot charge for his legal services.[695] If the trustee pays fees to such a commissioner, the AIB will hold him personally liable to the estate for such a sum.[696]

SUBMISSION OF CLAIMS

7.3.3 Although a few creditors may become commissioners, and the law of diligence will impact on many creditors, all creditors will be interested in submitting claims on the estate and receiving some sort of payment. (*No claims may be submitted where the minimal assets process applies.*[697]) Claims must be submitted in the prescribed form,[698] which requires details of each debt, and any security for a debt, and

---

[683] See s.3(1)(f).
[684] See s.45(1).
[685] See s.53(2A).
[686] See Sch.6 paras 17, 18.
[687] See s.3(2).
[688] See s.39(2).
[689] See s.3(7).
[690] See s.29(1).
[691] See s.1A(1), (3).
[692] See s.1A(2).
[693] *Campbell v Cullen*, 1911 1 S.L.T. 258.
[694] See s.39(8).
[695] *Geddes' Trustee, Petitioner* Unreported April 6, 1985 (CSOH).
[696] Accountant in Bankruptcy, *Notes for Guidance of Interim and Permanent Trustees*, para.7.7.
[697] *See Sch.A1 para.1(5).*
[698] See s.22(2)(a) and Form 4.

must be signed by the creditor or his agent. A claim must be accompanied by an account or voucher which constitutes prima facie evidence of the debt.[699] However, any failure to meet such requirements can be sanctioned by the trustee, but if there are any commissioners, such a step requires their consent.[700] Moreover, the Act states that a creditor who neither resides nor has a place of business in the UK may be permitted to submit an informal claim in writing.[701] Indeed, where the trustee knows where such a creditor resides or has a place of business, then he must write to him to inform him of his right to make a claim—unless he has already done so in notifying him of the statutory meeting.[702] A claim may be stated in foreign currency, where a court order, contract or bill of exchange requires payment to be made in that currency.[703] The claim will be converted into sterling at the rate of exchange for that currency at the mean of the buying and selling spot rates prevailing in the London market at the close of business on the date of sequestration.[704] It is an offence for a creditor to submit a false claim, account or voucher (subject to a defence that he neither knew nor had reason to believe that it was false), and for the debtor who knows of such an offence to fail as soon as is practicable to report it to the trustee.[705] The submission of a claim interrupts the running of prescription,[706] and bars any enactment relating to the limitation of actions.[707]

A creditor may submit a claim at or before the statutory meeting in order to be entitled to vote at that meeting,[708] and if this claim is accepted by the trustee, it does not require to be resubmitted in order to be entitled to vote in subsequent meetings, nor to be entitled to share in dividends.[709] So it is very common for a creditor to submit a claim before the statutory meeting, not because he intends to vote at or even be present at that or any other meeting, but simply to secure his right to share in dividends. A claim under a confiscation order under the Proceeds of Crime Act 2002 may not be submitted to the trustee.[710]

If a creditor does not submit a claim at or before the statutory meeting, then in order to be entitled to vote at any meeting, he must submit a claim at or before that meeting, and to be entitled to participate in a dividend, a claim must be submitted not later than eight weeks before the end of an accounting period.[711] Again, once a claim is made, it does not require to be resubmitted.[712] *The 2014 Act would further demand that a claim must be submitted no more than 120 days after the trustee has given notice to creditors inviting them to submit claims.[713] However, a late claim may be entertained if there were exceptional circumstances which prevented it being submitted within the time limit, and the claim is submitted not later than eight weeks before the end of the then current accounting period.[714]* Accounting periods are usually successive periods of 12 months running from the date of sequestration, although the length of any period after the first may be varied by the trustee in conjunction with the commissioners, or with the AIB if there are no commissioners.[715] Obviously, where the AIB is the trustee, the length of such subsequent accounting periods lies within her discretion. *The 2014 Act intends to allow the trustee to shorten the first accounting period to a period of not less than six months should he consider that sufficient funds are ingathered to pay a dividend.[716] That decision will be taken by the*

---

[699] See s.22(2)(b).

[700] See ss.22(2), 48(3).

[701] See s.22(3)(b).

[702] See s.22(3)(a).

[703] See ss.22(6), 48(7); Bankruptcy (Scotland) Regulations 2008 (SSI 2008/82) reg.4

[704] See ss.23(1)(a), 49(3); Bankruptcy (Scotland) Regulations 2008 (SSI 2008/82) reg.5.

[705] See ss.22(5), 48(7).

[706] Prescription and Limitation (Scotland) Act 1973 s.9(1).

[707] See s.22(8).

[708] See s.22(1).

[709] See s.48(2).

[710] Proceeds of Crime Act 2002 s.420(4).

[711] See s.48(1).

[712] See s.48(2).

[713] *See s.48(1A)–(1B).*

[714] *See s.48(1C). The aim of the introduction of a timeframe is to establish as soon as possible the exact amount owed, so that dividend payments can be calculated: see Policy Memorandum, para.117.*

[715] See ss.52(2), 52(2ZA).

[716] *See s.52(2ZB).*

trustee alone if she is the AIB. Otherwise the period will be agreed between the trustee and the commissioners, or between the trustee and the AIB if there are no commissioners. A creditor who has submitted a claim may always subsequently submit a further claim specifying a different amount,[717] save that a secured creditor may not in such a claim specify a different value for his security if the trustee has required him to discharge, convey or assign it in accordance with the Act.[718]

WHAT MAY BE CLAIMED

7.3.4 Generally, a creditor may claim the amount owed plus interest due at the date of sequestration.[719] As to interest after the date of sequestration see para.7.3.8.

Debts due after the date of sequestration

7.3.4.1 If a debt is due after the date of sequestration, then it is simply treated as due at that date, but subject to deduction of interest at the higher of the prescribed rate at the date of sequestration and the rate which would otherwise apply to that debt.[720] Where the debt is due significantly after the date of sequestration, this approach can severely reduce its amount.

Secured creditors

7.3.4.2 A creditor who holds a security over any part of the debtor's estate should deduct the value of the security (as estimated by him) from the claim, unless he surrenders it for the benefit of the estate (or undertakes to do so in writing).[721] Although the creditor estimates the value of the security, the trustee may, at any time after the expiry of 12 weeks from the date of sequestration, require the creditor to discharge the security, or convey or assign it to the trustee, on payment of the value so specified.[722] The amount of that payment is then deducted from the debt. The fact that the trustee can discharge the security by paying the creditor what the latter says it is worth obviously discourages the creditor from undervaluing a security in order to maximise the amount of his claim. Unless the trustee has already exercised this power, it is always open for a creditor to resubmit a claim, based on a different estimate of the value of the security.[723] Since the Act focuses on securities over the debtor's estate,[724] it follows that any security held by the creditor over another's estate, e.g. a parent of the debtor, or security in the form of a cautionary obligation, is not deducted from the claim.

Aliment or periodical allowance

7.3.4.3 Claims for arrears of aliment or periodical allowance in respect of the period prior the date of sequestration can only be made if due by virtue of a court decree or written agreement, and if in the case of a spouse or civil partner (or an ex-spouse or civil partner claiming for a child) the parties were living apart during the period to which the claim relates.[725] Such claims arising after the date of sequestration cannot be allowed at all,[726] and would have to be made against the debtor himself.

---

[717] See ss.22(4), 48(4).
[718] See s.48(4) and Sch.1 para.5(2).
[719] See Sch.1 para.1(1).
[720] See Sch.1 para.1(2).
[721] See Sch.1 para.5(1).
[722] See Sch.1 para.5(2).
[723] See s.48(4).
[724] See s.73(1).
[725] See Sch.1 para.2.
[726] See Sch.1 para.2(1)(b).

Contingent debts

A contingent debt "is a debt which has no existence now but will only emerge and become due upon **7.3.4.4** the occurrence of some future event".[727] That event may never occur, but even if it is bound to occur, its exact date cannot be determined. Where the existence or amount of a debt depends upon a contingency, the creditor may choose either to wait until that contingency has arisen, or have the debt valued by the trustee, or by the sheriff (*the AIB following the 2014 Act*) if there is no trustee.[728] Where the debt is valued by the trustee, any interested party may appeal to the sheriff, who may affirm or vary that valuation.[729] *(Following the 2014 Act, any interested person may instead apply to the AIB for a review of the valuation within 14 days of it being made.[730] The AIB must confirm or vary the valuation within 28 days of the application, but must take into account any representations made by an interested person within 21 days of the application.[731] Any interested person may then appeal to the sheriff against the AIB's review decision within 14 days of that decision.[732] It is also possible for the AIB to ask a sheriff for a direction before making any decision on a review.[733] An appeal to the sheriff may not be made in relation to a matter on which the AIB has asked the sheriff for a direction.[734])* The amount of the valuation determines the amount of the creditor's claim. The risk that the creditor runs in submitting to valuation is that the debt may be undervalued, while the risk of waiting for the contingency to arise is that it may not arise. In relation to contingent creditors Lord President Inglis observes in *Mitchell v Scott*[735]:

> "If . . . contingent creditors, i.e. those whose debts are not yet payable and may never become payable, were not entitled to claim in the sequestration, their debts would be gone forever, because the bankrupt's discharge would finally put an end to them."

In *Crighton v Crighton's Trustee*[736] the husband of the debtor, having raised an action of divorce (in which he claimed a capital sum) some time before the debtor was sequestrated, was granted a divorce and awarded a capital sum of £157,000 after the date of sequestration. The trustee rejected his claim on the basis that it only emerged after sequestration. However, both the sheriff and sheriff-principal held that the trustee had to accept the claim as being a contingent debt due by the debtor at the date of sequestration. Sheriff Principal Hay opined[737]:

> "The debtor's obligation to the claimant to share the matrimonial property fairly with him . . . arose at the latest when he raised the action of divorce and craved payment of a capital sum. . . . From that point on . . . the debtor was under a contingent liability to pay the claimant whatever capital sum might be awarded."

Debts due under composition contracts

Although a sequestration may be ended by a composition contract (see para.7.4.5), the sequestration **7.3.4.5** may revive if that contract fails. In such a case, each creditor may resurrect his original claim, less any amount actually paid under the composition contract.[738]

---

[727] *Fleming v Yeaman* (1884) 9 App. Cas. 966, per Lord Watson at 976.
[728] See Sch.1 para.3.
[729] See Sch.1 para.3(3).
[730] *See Sch.1 para.3(3)–(4).*
[731] *See Sch.1 para.3(5).*
[732] *See Sch.1 para.3(6).*
[733] *See Sch.1 para.3(7).*
[734] *See Sch.1 para.3(8).*
[735] *Mitchell v Scott* (1881) 8 R. 875 at 879.
[736] *Crighton v Crighton's Trustee*, 1999 S.C.L.R. 16.
[737] *Crighton v Crighton's Trustee*, 1999 S.C.L.R. 16 at 22C.
[738] See Sch.1 para.4.

Claims against partners for partnership debts

7.3.4.6 Partnerships may be sequestrated without the sequestration of individual partners, and vice versa. However, while a firm is not liable for the debts of individual partners incurred as individuals, individual partners do have a residual liability for the debts of the firm, i.e. if the firm proves unable to pay its own debts, creditors may proceed against individual partners.[739] Thus a partner may ultimately be sequestrated in respect of the firm's debts. Since a creditor must first seek to obtain whatever he can from the firm before turning to its partners, the Act provides that a creditor proceeding against the estate of an individual partner in respect of the debt of the firm must deduct the value of his claim against the firm from his claim against the partner.[740] That value is estimated by the creditor himself, but that estimate need not be accepted by the trustee. Firms may have a great number of partners, and a creditor may be simultaneously pursuing claims against a good many partners. Yet the value of such claims does not have to be deducted.

CO-OBLIGANTS

7.3.5 It may be the case that a creditor can require someone other than the debtor to pay a debt, as where the debtor is jointly and severally liable with one or more persons, or where someone is a cautioner for the debt. Usually such a co-obligant will have a right of relief against the debtor. However, special rules apply in the context of sequestration. Thus the common law prohibition against double ranking will apply. So, for example, a cautioner who has been required to pay all or any part of the principal debt normally has a right of relief against the debtor.[741] That would mean that, if the cautioner pays the whole of the principal debt, he may make a claim in the sequestration. (Indeed the Act itself indicates that a co-obligant who has paid the debt may obtain, at his own expense, an assignation of the debt, and thereafter, claim, vote and obtain a dividend.[742]) But if the creditor makes a claim in the sequestration, and then pursues the cautioner for the remainder of the principal debt, the latter may not make a claim in the sequestration in respect of the sum he had to pay, as it is unfair to the creditors that what is essentially the same debt should be allowed to rank twice on the estate.[743]

The Act also regulates the rights of co-obligants. Thus while the common law envisaged various ways in which a co-obligant could be released by the actions of the creditor, it is now provided that a co-obligant is not freed from liability by the discharge of the debt, or by the creditor voting, or drawing a dividend, or assenting to (or at least not opposing) a composition or the debtor's discharge.[744] Where a co-obligant holds a security over the debtor's estate, he must account for it to the trustee so as to put the estate in the same position as if he had paid the debt and then had his claim accepted after deducting the value of the security.[745] This provision deals with the situation where, for example, a cautioner holds a security over the debtor's estate. If the creditor makes a claim against the debtor's estate and receives a dividend, he will pursue the cautioner for the remainder of the debt. As noted above, the cautioner in such a scenario may not make a claim in the sequestration in respect of the sum he has had to pay, because of the rule against double ranking. But if he is allowed to enforce his security against the estate, the rule against double ranking is to some extent avoided. The provision prevents this by effectively depriving him of the benefit of the security.

---

[739] Partnership Act 1890 s.9. A creditor has no claim against an individual partner unless the firm is unable to pay; see *Brickmann's Trustee v Commercial Bank* (1901) 38 S.L.R. 766.

[740] See Sch.1 para.6.

[741] *Smithy's Place Ltd v Blackadder*, 1991 S.L.T. 790.

[742] See s.60(3).

[743] *Mackinnon v Monkhouse* (1881) 9 R. 393.

[744] See s.60(1).

[745] See s.60(2).

BALANCING OF ACCOUNTS

Sometimes a creditor will also owe money to the debtor. Clearly, the creditor would prefer not to pay the **7.3.6** debtor in full and then make a claim for the full amount he is owed by the debtor, as he is likely to be able to recover only a fraction of the latter sum. Rather he would wish to set off the sum he owes against the sum owed by him, so that he either is treated as owing the balance due to the debtor, or else he can make a claim for the balance owing to him. This is permitted in the context of insolvency,[746] and indeed an illiquid debt may be set off against a liquid debt,[747] so that the creditor may set off a future or contingent debt owed by the debtor against a liquid debt owed by him.[748] Moreover, it is open to a creditor who has a claim which is partly preferential or partly secured to choose to set off the debt owed by him against any part of his claim which is neither preferential or secured.[749] One major qualification is that a debt arising before insolvency may only be set off against a debt similarly arising,[750] and equally a debt arising after insolvency may only be set off against a debt also arising after insolvency.[751] It has been said that[752]

> "bankruptcy law presupposes reciprocal obligations which are both existing at the time of the declaration of insolvency, although only one of them is, it may be, immediately exigible. It has no application to the case of a new obligation arising after bankruptcy or declaration of insolvency."

In this context the meaning of insolvency is rather vague. It would appear that sequestration proceedings need not actually have commenced, and that indeed a party is insolvent if his "pecuniary responsibility and circumstances had materially altered to the worse",[753] although the mere fact that a party is experiencing losses is insufficient, if there is no suggestion that his liabilities exceed his assets, or that he is experiencing difficulty in meeting his liabilities when they fall due.[754]

It may be noted that if a creditor has claimed in the debtor's sequestration, a co-obligant of the debtor cannot attempt to set off any right of relief he may claim against the debtor against any debt which he may owe the debtor.[755] Consider the example of a debt which is reinforced by a cautionary obligation. If the creditor makes a claim against the debtor's estate and receives a dividend, he will pursue the cautioner for the remainder of the debt. The cautioner in such a scenario may not make a claim in the sequestration in respect of the sum he has had to pay, because of the rule against double ranking. But if he is allowed to set off his right of relief against a debt which he would otherwise have to pay to the debtor's estate, that estate is diminished and the rule against double ranking is to some extent avoided. Thus the rule against double ranking precludes such set-off. If the Crown is a creditor, set-off cannot be allowed in respect of any claim for taxes, duties or penalties, nor can any claim for the repayment of taxes, duties or penalties be set off against any other claim by the Crown.[756] Otherwise set-off is generally available when the debts in question relate to the same government department, although the leave of the court is required if the Crown is to be allowed to plead set-off when different government departments are involved.[757] Leave is usually given.[758] It has been suggested (obiter) that if the Crown is due to return any sum as a gratuitous alienation or unfair preference, it would be unfair to the creditors as a whole to allow this to be set off against debts due to the Crown.[759]

---

[746] See *Ross v Ross* (1895) 22 R. 461, per Lord McLaren at 465.
[747] See *Scott's Trustees v Scott* (1887) 14 R. 1043, per Lord President Inglis at 1051.
[748] *Hannay & Sons Trustee v Armstrong & Co* (1877) 4 R. (HL) 43.
[749] *Turner v Inland Revenue Commissioners*, 1994 S.L.T. 811.
[750] *Taylor's Trustee v Paul* (1888) 15 R. 313.
[751] *Liquidators of Highland Engineering v Thomson*, 1972 S.C. 87.
[752] *Asphaltic Limestone Concrete Co v Corp of Glasgow*, 1907 S.C. 463, per Lord McLaren at 474.
[753] *Paul & Thain v Royal Bank of Scotland* (1869) 7 M. 361, per Lord Ormidale at 364.
[754] *Busby Spinning Co Ltd v BMK Ltd*, 1988 S.C. 70, per Lord Cullen at 72, 73.
[755] *Anderson v Mackinnon* (1876) 3 R. 608.
[756] Crown Proceedings Act 1947 s.35(2)(b).
[757] Crown Proceedings Act 1947 s.35(2)(c), (d).
[758] *Smith v Lord Advocate (No.2)*, 1980 S.C. 227.
[759] *John E Rae (Electrical Services) Linlithgow Ltd v Lord Advocate*, 1994 SLT 788, per Lord Clyde at 791.

ADJUDICATION OF CLAIMS

7.3.7 Turning now to how claims are dealt with, it may be noted that at the commencement of any meeting of creditors the trustee accepts or rejects the various claims. This determines the right of any creditor to vote at the meeting.[760] The trustee will only accept or reject claims for the purpose of paying a dividend if there are funds available, but where he engages in such adjudication, he must do so not later than four weeks before the end of the relevant accounting period.[761] The two types of adjudication have no bearing on each other. As noted above (para.7.3.3), a claim must be submitted not later than eight weeks before the end of that accounting period in order to be considered, but it should be remembered that once a claim is made, it does not require to be resubmitted.[762] Thus a claim may well have been submitted during an earlier accounting period. If the trustee requires to be satisfied as to the amount or validity of a claim, he may ask the creditor or any other person whom he believes to have such evidence to produce further evidence, and if that individual refuses or delays in doing so, the trustee may apply to the sheriff for an order for his private examination before the sheriff.[763] If the trustee rejects a claim in whole or in part, he must forthwith inform the creditor of his reasons.[764] A claim may be referred to arbitration or compromised, but if there are commissioners, they must consent.[765] On accepting or rejecting any claim, the trustee must, as soon as is reasonably practicable, send a list of every such claim and its amount to the debtor and every creditor known to him.[766] Any aggrieved creditor may appeal to the sheriff against the decision to accept or reject a claim, or to give a claim a particular ranking,[767] but the debtor may only appeal if he satisfies the sheriff that he has or is likely to have a pecuniary interest in the outcome of the appeal.[768] Where the acceptance or rejection is for the purpose of determining the right of a creditor to vote at a meeting, an appeal must be made within two weeks of that decision.[769] Where the acceptance or rejection is for the purpose of determining the right of a creditor to share in a dividend, an appeal must be made not later than two weeks before the end of the relevant accounting period.[770] Where a creditor appeals against an adjudication, the debtor may not demand to be sisted as a party to the proceedings in order to argue that the trustee made the correct decision.[771] *The 2014 Act contemplates that instead of an appeal to the sheriff an application may be made to the AIB for a review of the relevant decision.[772] Where the acceptance or rejection is for the purpose of determining the right of a creditor to vote at a meeting, an application must be made within 14 days of the decision.[773] Where the acceptance or rejection is for the purpose of determining the right of a creditor to share in a dividend, an application must be made within 28 days of the decision.[774] The AIB must take into account any representation made by an interested person within 21 days of the making of the application and must confirm, amend or revoke the decision within 28 days of the making of the application.[775] The debtor or any creditor may appeal to the sheriff against the later decision within 14 days of it being made.[776]*

---

[760] See s.49(1).

[761] See s.49(2).

[762] See s.48(1), (2).

[763] See s.48(5), (6).

[764] See s.49(4), (7).

[765] See s.65(1).

[766] See s.49(2A).

[767] See s.49(6).

[768] See s.49(6A).

[769] See s.49(6)(a).

[770] See s.49(6)(b).

[771] *McGuinness v McGuinness' Trustee*, 1993 S.C.L.R. 755.

[772] *See s.49(6). Again the the debtor may only apply if he satisfies the AIB that he has or is likely to have a pecuniary interest in the outcome of the appeal: see s.49(6A).*

[773] *See s.49(6B)(a).*

[774] *See s.49(6B)(b).*

[775] *See s.49(6C).*

[776] *See s.49(6D). But the debtor may only appeal if he satisfies the sheriff that he has or is likely to have a pecuniary interest in the outcome of the appeal: see s.49(6E).*

DISTRIBUTION OF ESTATE

At the end of each accounting period, the trustee will distribute such assets as he has managed to realise **7.3.8**
during that period to cover certain expenses and to pay dividends to those creditors whose claims he
has accepted. Broadly speaking, the Act accords priority to the expenses of the sequestration itself, with
certain debts being seen as more deserving and others as less deserving than the great mass of ordinary
debts. It may also be remembered that the Act does not affect the rights of secured creditors nor of
creditors who may have a lien over title deeds.[777] Effectively, a secured creditor will receive the value
of his security before the estate benefits from the asset realised. Subject to these points, the estate will
be distributed in the following order[778]:

- the outlays and remuneration of the interim trustee;
- the outlays and remuneration of the trustee in sequestration;
- where the debtor was deceased at the date of sequestration, deathbed and funeral expenses
  reasonably incurred, and expenses reasonably incurred in administering the deceased's estate
  (unreasonable expenses are treated as ordinary debts, while any such expenses in relation to a
  debtor who dies after the date of sequestration do not count as debts in the sequestration);
- the expenses of a creditor who has petitioned for sequestration or concurred in the debtor's
  application for sequestration;
- preferred debts (but not interest thereon up to the date of sequestration);
- ordinary debts;
- interest on preferred debts and interest on ordinary debts after the date of sequestration;
- postponed debts.

Where funds are insufficient to pay any of the above classes of debt in full, the creditor will be paid a
rateable proportion,[779] e.g. if the funds available will only pay 20 per cent of the ordinary debts, then
each ordinary creditor will receive 20 per cent of his claim. In the unlikely event of all the above debts
being paid in full, any surplus will be paid to the debtor,[780] although if the sequestration amounts to
secondary proceedings in a cross-border insolvency, any surplus must be transferred to the main proceedings in another EU state.[781] A surplus includes any kind of estate, but not an unclaimed dividend.[782]

Preferred debts

Certain debts must be paid in full before any ordinary creditor receives anything. These used to include **7.3.8.1**
certain debts due to the Inland Revenue and Customs and Excise, and certain social security payments,
but now mainly comprehend certain payments due to employees. More specifically, they are[783]:

- contributions to occupational pension schemes and state scheme premiums;
- European Coal and Steel Community levies and surcharges;
- certain payments ordered under the Reserve Forces (Safeguard of Employment) Act 1985;
- accrued holiday pay up to the date of sequestration, where the employment has been terminated (whether before or after that date); and
- arrears of wages for up to four months prior to the date of sequestration—subject to a maximum
  of £800 per employee. Arrears of wages beyond the limit would be treated as an ordinary debt. It
  is not clear whether the limit refers to gross or net wages. Wages is defined so as to include
  certain payments due under statute when the employee is absent from work for good cause. (If
  anyone advances money to pay arrears of wages or holiday pay, they will have a preferential

---

[777] See s.51(6).
[778] See s.51(1).
[779] See s.51(4).
[780] See s.51(5).
[781] See s.51(5A).
[782] See s.51(5).
[783] See Sch.3.

claim, if the money was in fact used to pay the employee and he would have had a preferential claim.)

In relation to all the above categories, if the debtor was deceased at the date of sequestration, then the crucial date is the date of death rather than the date of sequestration.

Postponed debts

7.3.8.2 Obviously these are debts which can only be paid when every other claim is met in full. As it is not unusual for ordinary creditors to receive nothing, it may be appreciated that it is very rare for postponed creditors to receive anything. Postponed debts are[784]:

- a loan to the debtor in return for a share of the profits of his business, which is postponed to the claims of other creditors under s.3 of the Partnership Act 1890. Such a person has to some degree tied himself to the fortunes of the debtor's business. Thus, since he will benefit more than an ordinary creditor if the business prospers, it is fair that he should have a lower priority than an ordinary creditor if the business struggles;
- a loan made by the debtor's spouse or civil partner; and
- the creditor's right to anything vesting in the trustee as a result of a successful challenge of a gratuitous alienation (or to the proceeds of the sale of such a thing).

7.4
THE DEBTOR

EFFECT OF SEQUESTRATION ON THE DEBTOR

7.4.1 Turning from the creditors to consider the effect of sequestration on the debtor, it can be observed that various effects have already been noted, such as the vesting of his estate and any *acquirenda* in the trustee, and his prohibition from dealing with the estate; the possibility that he might be ordered to contribute excess income to the trustee; his duty to co-operate with the trustee; his liability to examination; and the possibility that he may commit certain offences. However, there remain certain effects of the process which are yet to be discussed, primarily certain general offences which might be committed by the debtor, and his disability from holding certain offices and carrying on certain professions.

Section 67 enumerates the general offences which the debtor may commit. These are:

- during the relevant period, making a false statement to a creditor or someone concerned in the administration of his estate regarding his business or financial affairs, unless he neither knew nor had reason to believe that the statement was false;
- during the relevant period, concealing, destroying, damaging, disposing of or removing from Scotland any part of his estate or document relating to his assets or his business or financial affairs, unless he can show that he did not do so with intent to prejudice the creditors;
- failing to return to Scotland in compliance with a court order after the date of sequestration;
- during the relevant period, falsifying a document relating to his assets or his business or financial affairs, unless he can show that he had no intention to mislead the trustee, a commissioner or any creditor;
- failing to report to the trustee such a falsification by a third party within a month of becoming aware thereof;
- during the relevant period, making a gratuitous alienation or unfair preference, unless he can show that he did not do so with intent to prejudice the creditors;
- during the year leading up to the date of sequestration, otherwise than in the ordinary course of business, pledging or disposing of property obtained on credit, unless he can show that he

---

[784] See s.51(3).

did not do so with intent to prejudice the creditors. This offence can only be committed if he is engaged in trade or business;

- obtaining credit to the extent of £500 (*due to rise to £2,000 by virtue of s.47 of the 2014 Act*), or credit of any amount where his debts already amount to £1,000 or more, without advising the other party that he has been sequestrated and is not yet discharged.[785] Under s.67 "the relevant period" is the period commencing one year before the date of sequestration and concluding with the debtor's discharge.

Looking briefly at the disabling effects of sequestration, it may be observed that, for example, certain professions may not be practised by undischarged bankrupts, most notably that of solicitor,[786] and certain public offices, such as acting as a member of either House of Parliament, are closed to them,[787] while it is actually an offence for an undischarged bankrupt to act as a director of a company or be involved in its promotion, formation or management, except with the leave of the court.[788] Again, s.33(1) of the Partnership Act 1890 indicates that, subject to the contrary agreement of the partners, a partnership is dissolved by the bankruptcy of any partner, while a company's articles of association will usually remove a director from office if he becomes bankrupt.[789] The last example serves as a reminder that all manner of contractual disqualifications or terminations may result from insolvency.

Financial education for the debtor

The 2014 Act added a new s.43B to the Act, the Policy Memorandum[790] stating that the policy behind **7.4.2** *the provision was "to introduce a financial education role as part of the Financial Health Service", seeking to prevent individuals encountering repeated financial difficulties by ensuring that they have the skills to avoid ending up in financial difficulty in the future. Not every debtor is required to undertake financial education. Rather the provision is aimed at debtors "whose financial history and circumstances identify them as being particularly vulnerable to problems arising as a result of recurring debts".[791] Thus the trustee[792] must notify a living debtor that he is required to undertake a prescribed course of financial education specified by the trustee if, in the trustee's opinion, undertaking the course would be appropriate for the debtor and any of following circumstances apply[793]:*

(1) In the five years leading up to sequestration:

- *the debtor has been sequestrated;*
- *the debtor has granted a protected trust deed;*
- *the debtor has been subject to an analogous remedy within the meaning of s.10(7): see footnote 118;*
- *the debtor participated in a debt management programme, under which he made regular payments.*

(It can be appreciated that the above criteria indicate that the debtor has experienced serious financial difficulties in the relatively recent past.)

---

[785] In calculating the amount of credit obtained or the amount of the debtor's existing debts, no account is taken of any money owed to providers of utilities or by way of council tax: s.67(9A). A similar offence can be committed by anyone subject to a bankruptcy restrictions order who obtains credit in such circumstances without advising the provider that he is subject to the order.

[786] Solicitors (Scotland) Act 1980 s.18(1).

[787] Insolvency Act 1986 s.427; see also Enterprise Act 2002 s.268.

[788] Company Directors Disqualification Act 1986 s.11(1).

[789] That would be the effect of art.81(b) of Table A of the Companies (Tables A to F) Regulations 1985 (SI 1985/805). Table A is a set of model articles, which may be adopted in whole or in part by a company, but which will apply automatically if a company does not register articles: Companies Act 1985 s.8.

[790] *Policy Memorandum, paras 29–30.*

[791] *Explanatory Notes, para.7.*

[792] *See s.43B(1). The trustee must decide whether to issue such a notification within six months of the date of the award of sequestration, or if the trustee was initially unable to ascertain the whereabouts of the debtor, as soon as reasonably practicable after he ascertains those whereabouts or is contacted by the debtor: see s.43B(2A).*

[793] *See s.43B(2).*

(2) *The debtor is subject to, or under investigation with a view to an application being made for, a bankruptcy restrictions order (see para.7.4.4).*

(3) *The trustee considers that the pattern of the debtor's behaviour, whether before or after the award of sequestration, is such that he would benefit from a financial education course. Thus if the trustee perceives that the debtor does not manage money well or is prone to reckless spending, he may direct the debtor to take an appropriate course.*

(4) *The debtor agrees to undertake a financial education course—in other words he decides that he would benefit from financial education and volunteers to take a course.*

There are, however, a couple of situations where a debtor is not obliged to undertake a financial education course. One is where he has already completed such a course in the five years leading up to the date of sequestration.[794] The other is where his health (including disability or mental illness) in the opinion of the trustee prevents him participating in or completing such a course.[795] Financial education is to be targeted at specific types of vulnerable debtor, and it is intended that its content, format and delivery will be laid out in regulations.[796]

7.4.3 DISCHARGE OF THE DEBTOR

Automatic discharge of the debtor

7.4.3.1 Given the above effects of sequestration, the debtor will obviously be concerned to know when he can obtain a discharge. Under the previous legislation, the debtor had to apply to the court for a discharge. Thus through ignorance, impecuniosity, reluctance to appear before a court, or just sheer inertia, many bankrupts did not make that application and thus remained forever undischarged. Accordingly, the Act originally contemplated that a debtor would be automatically discharged three years after the date of sequestration, unless a creditor or the trustee had applied to the sheriff for a deferment. However, following the 2007 amendments, that period has been reduced to one year.[797] A debtor who has been discharged may apply to the AIB for a certificate, which she must grant if satisfied of the discharge.[798] Such a certificate is not necessary for a discharge, but might provide useful evidence of the fact of discharge.

While currently the legislation operates on the basis that the debtor will be automatically discharged unless the trustee applies to the sheriff for deferment, the Policy Memorandum[799] to the 2014 Act describes the latter as "a costly and time consuming process" which "is not often utilised". That Act then does not believe in automatic discharge (subject to the exception set out below). Instead it looks "to introduce a new process of discharge . . . linking a debtor's co-operation with their discharge".[800] Thus where the AIB is not the trustee, the Act envisages that she will discharge the debtor where she considers it appropriate to do so, by granting a certificate of discharge in due form, as long as at least 12 months have elapsed from the date on which sequestration is awarded.[801] Before deciding whether to discharge the debtor, the AIB must consider the trustee's report and take into account any timeous, relevant representations.[802] The trustee must send the report to the AIB without delay once 10 months have elapsed from the date on which sequestration is awarded, and it must be made before sending the AIB the documentation which the trustee sends when applying for his own discharge[803] (see para.7.4.6). The report must include information about:

---

[794] *See s.43B(3)(b).*
[795] *See s.43B(3)(a).*
[796] *See s.43B(4).*
[797] *See s.54(1), (3).*
[798] See s.54(2); Bankruptcy (Scotland) Regulations 2008 (SSI 2008/82) Form 7.
[799] *para.139.*
[800] *Policy Memorandum, para.138.*
[801] *See s.54(2).*
[802] *See s.54(3).*
[803] *See s.54(4).*

- *the debtor's assets, liabilities, financial and business affairs and his conduct in relation thereto;*
- *the sequestration and his conduct in relation thereto.*[804]

It must also include a statement of whether the trustee has carried out all of his functions,[805] *and a statement of whether, in the opinion of the trustee, the debtor has:*

- *complied with any debtor contribution order;*
- *co-operated with the trustee as required by the Act;*
- *complied with the statement of undertakings (see para.7.1.5),*
- *made a full and fair surrender of his estate;*
- *made a full disclosure of all claims he is entitled to make against others; and*
- *delivered to the trustee every document under his control relating to his estate, financial and business affairs.*[806]

The trustee must, at the same time as sending the report to the AIB, give the debtor and every known creditor a copy and a notice informing them that that they have a right to make representations to the AIB in the 28 days following the giving of this notice.[807] *If the AIB grants a discharge, it cannot take effect until at least 14 days have elapsed from the notification of the decision.*[808]

Where the AIB is the trustee, the Act envisages that she will discharge the debtor of her own initiative, and may do so at any time after 12 months have elapsed from the date on which sequestration is awarded by granting a certificate of discharge in prescribed form.[809] *As soon as practicable after that date she must decide whether to discharge the debtor, notifying the debtor and every known creditor of her decision, and sending them a report on:*

- *the debtor's assets, liabilities, financial and business affairs and his conduct in relation thereto;*
- *the sequestration and his conduct in relation thereto.*[810]

If the AIB decides not to discharge the debtor, she must as soon as practicable after 12 months have elapsed from the date of refusal, decide whether to discharge the debtor, sending such notification and report.[811] *In other words, the AIB must consider the situation anew every 12 months until she eventually decides to discharge the debtor, although that day may never arise. Again such discharge cannot take effect until at least 14 days have elapsed from the notification of the decision.*[812]

The reason why such discharge cannot take effect until at least 14 days have elapsed from the notification of the decision is that any creditor may apply to the AIB for a review of a decision to discharge the debtor,[813] *such discharge being suspended until the AIB has determined the review.*[814] *Equally, the trustee or the debtor may apply to the AIB for a review of a decision not to discharge the debtor.*[815] *All such applications must be made within 14 days of notification of the decision.*[816] *The AIB must take into account any representation made by an interested person within 21 days of the making of the application and must confirm or revoke her original decision within 28 days of the making of the application.*[817] *The trustee, the debtor or any creditor may appeal to the sheriff against the later decision within 14 days of it being made.*[818]

---

[804] *See s.54(5)(a).*
[805] *See s.54(5)(c).*
[806] *See s.54(5)(b).*
[807] *See s.54(6).*
[808] *See s.54(7).*
[809] *See s.54A(1)–(2).*
[810] *See s.54A(3)–(4).*
[811] *See s.54A(5)–(6).*
[812] *See s.54A(7).*
[813] *See s.54B(2).*
[814] *See s.54B(4).*
[815] *See s.54B(1).*
[816] *See s.54B(3).*
[817] *See s.54B(5).*
[818] *See s.54B(6).*

One situation remains where a debtor is discharged automatically. A debtor who is subject to the new minimal assets process will be discharged automatically six months after the date on which sequestration is awarded,[819] and may apply to the AIB for a certificate of discharge.[820] The only exception to this is where a debtor subject to the new process is transferred to an ordinary sequestration under Sch. A1 (see para.7.1.3.1). However, a debtor who is thus automatically discharged is subject to restrictions for the six months following the date of discharge.[821] Thus before the debtor (whether alone or jointly with another person, e.g. a spouse) can obtain credit of £2,000 or more, or credit of any amount where the debtor owes at least £1,000, he must inform the potential creditor that he is subject to this restriction.[822] Moreover, if the debtor ran a business at the time of sequestration, he may not do business with anyone under another business name, unless he also informs any person with whom he is doing business of the name of the previous business.[823] If the debtor breaches either of these conditions, the restriction will continue for a further 12 months,[824] and any further breach during this extra 12 month period will constitute an offence.[825] If found guilty of such an offence in summary proceedings the debtor will be liable to a fine of up to £10,000, or a prison term of up to three months (or up to 6 months if he has previously been convicted of an offence inferring dishonest appropriation or an attempt at such appropriation), or to both such fine and imprisonment.[826] If found guilty of such an offence on indictment, the debtor will be liable to an unlimited fine or a prison term of up to two years, or to both such fine and imprisonment.[827]

The 2014 Act also makes provision for the situation where the trustee, having made reasonable enquiries, is unable to ascertain the debtor's whereabouts, and thus cannot carry out his functions under the Act.[828] In such a case the trustee should send a deferral notice in prescribed form to the debtor's last known address and to every known creditor, as well as applying in prescribed form to the AIB for a deferral (assuming the trustee is not the AIB).[829] Such an application must be made no earlier than eight months but no later than 10 months after the date on which sequestration is awarded.[830] After receiving an application, the AIB must take into account any representations made by an interested person within 14 days of the making of the application, and if satisfied that the trustee is indeed unable to ascertain the debtor's whereabouts and that it would not be reasonably practicable for the trustee to continue to search, must issue a certificate indefinitely deferring the debtor's discharge.[831] Where the AIB is also the trustee, she will issue a certificate on her own initiative if satisfied that it would not be reasonably practicable to continue to search, having taken into account any representations made by an interested person within 14 days of the deferral notice being given.[832] Where a certificate is issued, the AIB must make an appropriate entry in the register of insolvencies.[833]

Where a certificate is issued, a trustee who is not the AIB may wish to resign. The legislation allows him to apply to the AIB for authority to do so, and this authority must be granted as long as this application is made within six months of the certificate being issued and as long as in the interim the trustee has not ascertained the debtor's whereabouts nor been contacted by the debtor.[834] Where authority is granted, the AIB is deemed to be the new trustee and the former trustee must inform every known

---

[819] *See s.54C(1).*
[820] *See s.54C(2).*
[821] *See s.55A(6).*
[822] *See s.55A(1)–(3).*
[823] *See s.55A(4)–(5).*
[824] *See s.55B(1).*
[825] *See s.55B(2).*
[826] *See s.55B(3).*
[827] *See s.55B(4).*
[828] *See s.54D(1).*
[829] *See s.54D(2).*
[830] *See s.54D(3).*
[831] *See s.54D(4)–(5).*
[832] *See s.54D(6).*
[833] *See s.54D(7).*
[834] *See s.54E(2)–(4). An application must contain details of every creditor known to the trustee: see s.54E(2A).*

creditor of this.[835] *However, the former trustee may not recover his outlays and remuneration except in a claim in the final distribution of the estate*[836] *(see para.7.3.8).*

Where a certificate is issued, there remains the possibility that trustee might thereafter ascertain the debtor's whereabouts or be contacted by the debtor. Where the AIB is also the trustee, she may discharge the debtor at any time after 12 months have elapsed from the date when the whereabouts were ascertained or contact was made.[837] *Where the AIB is not the trustee, the trustee must prepare and send to the AIB a report of the kind he would send under s.54 (discussed above).*[838] *This must be done without delay once 10 months have elapsed from the date on which the debtor's whereabouts were ascertained or contact was made with the trustee, whichever is the earlier.*[839] *The process whereby the AIB may thereafter discharge or decide not to discharge the debtor is then as described under s.54.*[840] *Equally, very similar provisions apply under s.54G to the procedure under s.54B (discussed above) for seeking a review by the AIB of a decision to discharge or to refuse to discharge the debtor, with the same possibility of an appeal to the sheriff.*

Deferment

The trustee or any creditor may seek to prevent the debtor's automatic discharge by making an application for its deferment, and prima facie in order to be valid such an application must be made within nine months of the date of sequestration.[841] However, a sheriff is entitled to overlook defective procedure,[842] and in so doing may extend or waive any time limit under the Act.[843] (*The 2014 Act would allow the AIB rather than the sheriff to cure defective procedure consisting of a clerical or incidental error in a required document or a failure to comply with a time limit.*[844]) It has therefore been held that a court may extend the above time limit.[845] Where an application is received timeously, but cannot be disposed of within the one year period, it appears that the discharge is effectively suspended until the determination of the application.[846] If it is not received timeously, there seems to be some dispute as to whether the discharge is effectively suspended until the determination of the application for the court to extend the time limit (and if that application is successful, until the determination of the application proper),[847] or whether an interim discharge might be granted.[848] On receipt of the application, the sheriff shall order a copy to be served on the debtor, and (if the application is made by a creditor) on the trustee.[849] He shall also order the debtor within 14 days to lodge a declaration that he has made[850]:

(1) full and fair surrender of his estate;
(2) full disclosure of claims he is entitled to make against others;
(3) delivery to the trustee of every document relating to the estate or his affairs.

7.4.3.2

---

[835] *See s.54E(5)(a)–(b).*
[836] *See s.54E(5)(c).*
[837] *See s.54F(2).*
[838] *See s.54F(4A).*
[839] *See s.54F(4).*
[840] *See s.54F(8)–(10).*
[841] See s.54(3).
[842] See s.63(1)(a).
[843] See s.63(2)(c).
[844] *See s.63A(1). The AIB could do so either of her own initiative or on the application of an interested person: s.63A(2). The AIB or the applicant must notify all interested persons that they may make representations on the issue within 14 days of that notice, and the AIB must take any such representations into account before making the decision: s.63A(3)–(6). Any interested person may then apply to her for a review of her decision to make or refuse to make an order within 14 days of the decision being made: s.63B(1)–(2).The AIB must confirm, amend or revoke the decision within 28 days of the application, but must take into account any representations made by an interested person within 21 days of the application: s.63B(3). Any interested person may then appeal to the sheriff against the AIB's review decision within 14 days of that decision, the decision of the sheriff being final: s.63B(4)–(5).*
[845] *Pattison v Halliday*, 1991 S.L.T 645.
[846] *Clydesdale Bank Plc v Davidson*, 1994 S.L.T. 225.
[847] *Whittaker's Trustee v Whittaker*, 1993 S.C.L.R. 718.
[848] *Pattison v Halliday*, 1991 S.L.T 645.
[849] See s.54(4)(a).
[850] See s.54(4)(b).

Failing the timeous lodging of such a declaration, the sheriff must automatically grant a deferment for a period not exceeding two years.[851] If the declaration is lodged, then there will be a hearing not earlier than 28 days after that lodging, and the sheriff will order the applicant to notify the debtor and (if appropriate) the trustee (or the AIB if the trustee has been discharged) of the date of the hearing.[852] The trustee (or the AIB if the trustee has been discharged) shall then lodge, not later than seven days before the date of the hearing, a report on the debtor's assets and liabilities, his financial and business affairs, his conduct in relation thereto, and on the sequestration and his conduct in the course of it.[853] The debtor, the applicant and any creditor may make representations at the hearing. The sheriff will then either dismiss the application, or grant a deferment for a period not exceeding two years, subject to the right of the applicant or the debtor to appeal against that decision within 14 days of it being made.[854] Yet although the Act says nothing about the grounds for granting a deferment, the sheriff will not take this course unless good cause is shown,[855] and an applicant must clearly set out in the application the grounds on which deferral is sought.[856] Deferment has been granted on the basis of the debtor's dishonest[857] or obstructive[858] behaviour, and (arguably unnecessarily) where the trustee wished to sist himself to a reparation action by the debtor.[859] If deferment is granted, the debtor can nonetheless petition at any time for a discharge, provided he lodges the declaration.[860] A hearing will then be held in much the same way as described above.[861] The refusal of a petition is no bar to subsequent petitions. Equally, a further deferment may be applied for not later than three months before the end of the period of deferment, so that theoretically if such applications continue to be made, the discharge may be postponed indefinitely.[862]

Effects of discharge

7.4.3.3 There are three main effects:

(1) the debtor ceases to be disqualified from the various offices and professions which are not open to undischarged bankrupts;

(2) any estate acquired by the debtor after discharge vests in him, rather than the trustee, and any contingent interest which has not vested at the date of discharge is reinvested in the debtor;

(3) the debtor is discharged from all debts due at the date of sequestration, with the following exceptions[863]:

(a) any liability to pay a fine or other penalty due to the Crown, including payment under a confiscation order under the Proceeds of Crime Act 2002;

(b) any liability to pay a fine imposed by a district court;

(c) any liability under a order obliging him to pay compensation for any injury loss or damage caused by an offence of which he has been convicted;

(d) any liability to forfeiture of bail money under s.1(3) of the Bail (Scotland) Act 1980;

(e) any liability incurred by reason of fraud or breach of trust;

(f) any liability to pay aliment or a periodical allowance on divorce (where these cannot be included in a claim in the sequestration);

---

[851] See s.54(4).

[852] See s.54(5)(a), (b).

[853] See s.54(5).

[854] See s.54(6).

[855] *Crittal Warmliffe Ltd v Flaherty*, 1988 G.W.D. 22–930.

[856] *Chowdhury's Trustee v Chowdhury*, 1996 S.C.L.R. 948.

[857] See *Accountant in Bankruptcy v Campbell*, 2012 S.L.T. (Sh. Ct.) 35. Sheriff Holligan said (at [16]) that "[t]he structure of s.54 assumes that the court will deal with the matters on the basis of the debtor's declaration and the trustee's report. I consider that it would only be in very exceptional circumstances (and much to be discouraged) that any evidence would be led."

[858] *Nicol's Trustee v Nicol*, 1996 G.W.D. 10–531.

[859] *Watson v Henderson*, 1988 S.C.L.R. 439.

[860] See s.54(8).

[861] See s.54(8).

[862] See s.54(9).

[863] See s.55(1), (2).

(g) any liability to pay child support maintenance;

(h) any liability in respect of a student loan[864]—a student loan is not treated as a debt in a sequestration.

This does not mean that the bankrupt estate ceases to be liable for debts when the debtor is discharged. Rather the debtor as an individual is protected from future personal liability for the debts in question As Sheriff Way puts it in *Young v Accountant in Bankruptcy*,[865] s.55 "provides a mechanism for a bankrupt to move on in life free from the spectre of being pursued for past debts save for those (largely alimentary) continuing obligations that that section preserves". As Sheriff Way continues, "[t]rustees can and do take many years to complete the administration of estates". Thus the sequestration may continue for some time after the debtor is discharged, with the trustee continuing to realise estate and meet the claims of creditors. Accordingly, in the case in question the sheriff had no difficulty in rejecting the remarkable proposition that qualifying claims were extinguished by the bankrupt's discharge. The trustee was entitled and indeed obliged to continue to realise estate and meet qualifying claims. That is in part why s.55(2)(e) states that the debtor's obligation to co-operate with the trustee continues after discharge. Moreover, discharge cannot prejudice the rights of a secured creditor.[866] Nor does discharge reinvest the debtor in his former estate, unless he is discharged through composition[867] (see para.7.4.5). It may also be noted that discharge relates only to debts as at the date of sequestration, not to debts incurred after that date.

CONTINUING RESTRICTIONS ON DEBTORS FOLLOWING DISCHARGE— BANKRUPTCY RESTRICTIONS ORDERS AND UNDERTAKINGS

While the 2007 reforms reduced the period for automatic discharge to one year, thus allowing debtors **7.4.4** to escape the consequences of bankruptcy and make a fresh start much earlier, this is sought to be balanced by the introduction of devices to impose continuing restrictions on the activities of debtors whose conduct has suggested that they may pose a threat to the public interest. These devices are bankruptcy restrictions orders and undertakings.

An application for a bankruptcy restrictions order may only be made by the AIB in respect of a living debtor.[868] The application must be made to the sheriff within the period beginning with the date of sequestration and ending on the date when the debtor's discharge becomes effective, unless the sheriff permits an application to be made after the latter date.[869] The sheriff shall grant the order if he thinks it appropriate in light of the debtor's conduct, whether before or after the date of sequestration.[870] In particular, he shall take into account any of the following kinds of behaviour[871]:

- failing to keep records which account for the loss of a property by him or his business, where that loss occurred in the period beginning two years before the date of the petition/application for sequestration and ending with the date of the application for the order;
- failing to produce such records when they are demanded by the AIB, the interim trustee or the trustee in sequestration;
- making a gratuitous alienation or any other sort of challengeable alienation;
- creating an unfair preference or any other sort of challengeable preference;
- making an excessive contribution to a pension scheme (see para.7.2.16.5);
- failing to supply goods or services which were wholly or partly paid for, leading to a creditor submitting a claim to the trustee in sequestration;

---

[864] Education (Student Loans) Act 1990 Sch.2 para.6.
[865] *Young v Accountant in Bankruptcy*, 2010 S.L.T. (Sh Ct) 37 at [5].
[866] See s.55(3).
[867] *Buchanan v McCulloch* (1865) 4 M. 135.
[868] See s.56A.
[869] See s.56D.
[870] See s.56B(1).
[871] See s.56B(2).

- trading prior to sequestration when he knew or ought to have known that he was unable to meet his debts;
- incurring prior to sequestration a debt which he had no reasonable expectation of being able to pay;
- failing to account satisfactorily to the sheriff, the AIB, the interim trustee or the trustee in sequestration for a loss of property or an insufficiency of property to meet his debts;
- having between the date of the petition/application for sequestration and the date sequestration was awarded engaged in gambling, speculation or extravagance which may have materially contributed to or increased the extent of his debts;
- neglect of business affairs of a kind which may have materially contributed to or increased the extent of his debts.

The sheriff must also consider whether the debtor has previously been sequestrated and remained undischarged from that sequestration at any time within the five years prior to the current sequestration.[872]

It is also the case that, between the time of making the application for an order and the determination of that application, the AIB may apply for an interim bankruptcy restrictions order.[873] The sheriff may grant such an order if he thinks (a) that there that there are prima facie grounds to suggest that the application for the ordinary bankruptcy restrictions order will be successful, and (b) the making of the interim order is in the public interest.[874] An interim order takes effect as soon as it is made and operates until the application for the ordinary order is determined, or a bankruptcy restrictions undertaking is accepted, or it is discharged on the application of the debtor or the AIB.[875]

If the sheriff makes a bankruptcy restrictions order, it comes into force on the date when it is made and operates for a specified period of not less than two and not more than 15 years,[876] although if an interim order has already been made, those periods are calculated by reference to the date when the interim order came into effect.[877] The length of the period chosen by the sheriff will no doubt reflect the culpability of the debtor's behaviour and/or the extent of the risk to the public interest he represents. Once an order has been made, the sheriff on application by the debtor can annul the order or provide for it to last for a shorter period (though not for less than two years).[878] The notes to the Act provided by the Scottish Executive observe that no grounds are provided for the exercise of the sheriff's discretion, it being "left to the sheriff to consider whether such action is appropriate in all the circumstances". The effect of an order is that a person subject to it may not be appointed as a receiver,[879] nor may hold office as a member of a local authority nor be nominated for or elected to such office.[880] Moreover, the sheriff may specify in the order that s.67(9) is to apply to the debtor.[881] This means that for the duration of the order the debtor commits an offence if he obtains credit in excess of £500 in a single transaction or any amount of credit over £1,000, without informing the creditor of the fact that he is subject to a bankruptcy restrictions order.

A bankruptcy restrictions undertaking may be offered to the AIB by any debtor not subject to a bankruptcy restrictions order.[882] It is simply an agreement whereby the debtor is subject to the same restrictions as under an order, obviating the need to seek an order. The criteria to which the AIB must have regard in deciding whether to accept an undertaking are those which the sheriff must take into account in making the order.[883] The undertaking takes effect on being accepted, and the minimum and maximum

---

[872] See s.56B(4).
[873] See s.56F(1).
[874] See s.56F(2).
[875] See s.56F(3), (4).
[876] See s.56E(1), (2).
[877] See s.56F(6).
[878] See s.56E(3).
[879] As a result of Bankruptcy and Diligence etc. (Scotland) Act 2007 s.3, inserting s.51(3)(ba) into the Insolvency Act 1986.
[880] As a result of Bankruptcy and Diligence etc. (Scotland) Act 2007 s.3, inserting s.31(1)(ba) into the Local Government (Scotland) Act 1973.
[881] See s.56C.
[882] See s.56G(2).
[883] See s.56G(2).

periods of duration are the same as for an order.[884] Equally, the debtor in the undertaking may agree that he is subject to s.67(9).[885] The sheriff on application by the debtor can annul the undertaking or vary it, including providing for it to last for a shorter period.[886] (*The 2014 Act would abolish bankruptcy restrictions undertakings, repealing s.56G.*)

The AIB is under a duty to enter any order, interim order or undertaking in the Register of Insolvencies.[887]

If the award of sequestration is recalled, the sheriff has discretion to annul any such order or undertaking, and no new order may be made or undertaking accepted.[888] If he does not, the debtor has 28 days from the date of recall to appeal to the sheriff principal, whose decision is final.[889]

The 2014 Act creates the added possibility that, rather than applying to the sheriff, the AIB may herself make a bankruptcy restrictions order, having first notified the debtor that (a) this is her intention and (b) that he has a right to make representations in relation thereto, and having taken any such representations into account.[890] The grounds for making an order are as before with the addition of an extra ground[891]—failing to supply accurate information to an authorised person for the purpose of granting a certificate of sequestration (see para.7.1.3.1). The period within which an order may be made is also the same, but the AIB may apply for such an order or indeed make such an order after that date only with the permission of the sheriff.[892] The period for which an order may be granted will be between two and five years if it is made by the AIB, but between five and 15 years if it is made by the sheriff,[893] suggesting that the AIB will only apply to the sheriff for an order if she considers that an extensive period of restriction is appropriate. The debtor may apply to the AIB for a review of her decision to grant an order within 14 days of the date of that decision.[894] The AIB must confirm, amend or revoke the decision within 28 days of the application, but must take into account any representations made by an interested person within 21 days of the application.[895] The debtor may then appeal to the sheriff against the AIB's review decision within 14 days of that decision.[896] It also falls to the AIB to make an interim bankruptcy restrictions order as an alternative to applying to the sheriff for such an order. The AIB could make such an order any time after she has notified the debtor of her intention to make a full bankruptcy restrictions order and before such an order is made.[897] If the award of sequestration is recalled, it is the AIB rather than the sheriff who has discretion to annul an order.[898] If the AIB refuses to annul an order, the debtor may apply to her for a review of that decision within 14 days of the date of the refusal.[899] The AIB must confirm, amend or revoke the decision within 28 days of the application, but must take into account any representations made by an interested person within 21 days of the application.[900] The debtor may then appeal to the sheriff against the AIB's review decision within 14 days of that decision, the sheriff's decision being final.[901]

---

[884] See s.56G(3), (4).

[885] See s.56H.

[886] See s.56G(5).

[887] See s.1A(1)(b)(iia). But the 2014 Act would add s.1A(5) allowing for regulations to be made which prescribe circumstances where information need not be included in the Register of Insolvencies if in the opinion of the AIB its inclusion would be likely to jeopardise the safety or welfare of any person.

[888] See s.56J(1).

[889] See s.56J(2), (3).

[890] *See s.56A.*

[891] *See s.56B(2)(ba).*

[892] *See s.56D(2).*

[893] *See s.56E(2).*

[894] *See s.56E(4)–(5).*

[895] *See s.56E(6).*

[896] *See s.56E(7). The sheriff may in determining that appeal or otherwise on an application by the AIB order that the debtor may not make another application for review for such period as the order may specify: see s.56E(8).*

[897] *See s.56F(1).*

[898] *See s.56J(4).*

[899] *See s.56J(5)–(6).*

[900] *See s.56J(7).*

[901] *See s.56J(8)–(9).*

DISCHARGE ON COMPOSITION

7.4.5 A composition contract, whereby a debtor is relieved of liability for his debts in return for part payment, may be used as an alternative to sequestration. But it is possible for a debtor who has been sequestrated to obtain early discharge through composition, this process being known as judicial composition and being governed by the Act.[902] The process cannot begin until the trustee is appointed.[903] An offer would be made to him, which he would then communicate to the commissioners (or if there are none to the AIB),[904] who would decide whether the offer should be placed before the creditors. A positive decision on that issue would be prompted by the view that the offer—which must be at least 25p in the £—will be timeously implemented, and by satisfaction with the caution or other security[905] to be provided for its implementation.[906] If the offer is to be placed before the creditors, the trustee must publish in the *Edinburgh Gazette* a notice stating that an offer has been received and where its terms may be inspected.[907] Not later than a week after the publication of the notice he must send to every creditor known to him a copy of the terms of the offer.[908] Where within five weeks of the publication of the notice the trustee has not received written notification of rejection from a majority in number or at least a third in value of the creditors, he shall approve the offer.[909] Where an offer is approved, any creditor who has not received a copy of its terms or who notified his rejection may appeal to the AIB against the approval within 28 days.[910] The AIB may then approve or reject the offer.[911] Once various formalities are complied with, the AIB shall then grant certificates discharging the debtor and trustee,[912] whereupon the sequestration ends and the debtor is reinvested in his estate.[913] However, if any creditor can satisfy the Court of Session that there has been or is likely to be a default in payment, or that for any reason the composition cannot be proceeded with without undue delay or without injustice to the creditors, or at all, it may recall the approval of the offer and the grant of certificates, with the effect that the sequestration revives.[914] Only two offers of composition may be made during the course of a sequestration.[915] It is now provided that, even if the debtor is discharged on composition, any bankruptcy restrictions order (including interim orders) or bankruptcy restrictions undertaking to which he was subject will continue in force, although no order may be made after discharge.[916] *Section 17 of the 2014 Act would abolish the possibility of discharge on composition, repealing ss.56 and 56K and Sch.4.*

THE END OF THE SEQUESTRATION PROCESS

7.4.6 The approval of a composition offer, as described above, leads to the conclusion of the sequestration. The trustee shall submit to the commissioners (or to the AIB if there are none) his accounts for audit, along with a claim for his outlays and remuneration.[917] Where such documents are sent to the commissioners, a copy must be sent to the AIB.[918] The trustee must also take all reasonable steps to ensure that the interim trustee (if a different person) has also sent such documents.[919] The trustee then sends to the

---

[902] See s.56 and Sch.4.
[903] See Sch.4 para.1(1).
[904] See Sch.4 para.2.
[905] See Sch.4 para.1(2).
[906] See Sch.4 para.3.
[907] See Sch.4 para.4(b).
[908] See Sch.4 para.4(c).
[909] See Sch.4 para.6.
[910] See Sch.4 para.8B(1).
[911] See Sch.4 para.8B(2).
[912] See Sch.4 paras 9–11.
[913] See Sch.4 para.16.
[914] See Sch.4 para.17.
[915] See Sch.4 para.15.
[916] See s.56K.
[917] See Sch.4 para.9(1)(a); and see para.9(1A) where the AIB is the trustee.
[918] See Sch.4 para.9(1)(a); and see para.9(1A) where the AIB is the trustee.
[919] See Sch.4 para.9(1)(b).

AIB a declaration that all necessary charges in connection with the sequestration have been paid or satisfactory provision made in respect of their payment, while a bond of caution or other security must be lodged by or on behalf of the debtor.[920] As explained in the previous paragraph, once these documents have been lodged, the AIB grants certificates discharging the debtor and the trustee.[921]

If a sequestration is not ended by composition, in one sense it never ends. It has already been seen that the discharge of the debtor does not end the sequestration, and nor will the discharge of the trustee. If, following such discharge, significant new assets appear, it is open to appoint a new trustee.[922] Nonetheless, in most cases the discharge of the trustee will mark a practical end to the sequestration.[923] This will usually be sought when the estate has no further assets which are capable of being realised, and any funds available to the trustee are not sufficient to justify a further distribution.

When the trustee has made the final division of the estate, and inserted his final audited accounts in his sederunt book, he must deposit unapplied balances and unclaimed dividends in an appropriate bank or institution, and send the AIB the deposit receipt and a copy of the audited accounts.[924] At the same time as sending these documents he may apply to the AIB for a discharge.[925] It is not necessary to apply for a discharge, but it will mean that he is discharged from all liability to the creditors (other than for fraud) in respect of the exercise of his functions.[926] Such discharge would also cover any period during which he acted as interim trustee.[927] The trustee shall notify the debtor and all creditors known to him of his application, informing them that they are entitled within 14 days to make representations to the AIB regarding the application.[928] In light of the documents submitted and any representations made, the AIB will either grant or refuse the discharge, notifying the trustee, the debtor and any creditors who have made representations.[929] Any of these parties may, within a further 14 days, appeal against the decision to the sheriff, whose decision will be final.[930] *The 2014 Act contemplates that, instead of an appeal to the sheriff, an application to the AIB for a review of her determination should be made within 14 days thereof.[931] Thus a discharge granted cannot have effect until that 14-day period has expired and will not receive effect if an application for a review is made.[932] The AIB must confirm, amend or revoke the determination within 28 days of the application, but must take into account any representations made by an interested person within 21 days of the application.[933] An appeal then lies to the sheriff against that decision as described above.[934]*

Where the AIB acts as trustee the procedure is very similar, except that she obviously will not apply to herself for a discharge.[935] Instead, she must send to the debtor and all creditors known to her, a copy of her determination of her fees and outlays, and a notice informing them that[936]:

(1) she has started the procedure leading to her discharge; and
(2) they may within 14 days appeal to the sheriff against her determination and/or discharge.

---

[920] See Sch.4 para.10.
[921] See Sch.4 para.11.
[922] *Northern Heritable Securities Investment Co v Whyte* (1888) 16 R. 100.
[923] *Buchanan v McCulloch* (1865) 4 M. 135.
[924] See s.57(1)(a), (b). *The 2014 Act s.19 envisages that these provisions will be amended so that the trustee pays to the AIB any unapplied balances and unclaimed dividends. It will then be for the AIB under s.57(1B) to deposit these in an appropriate bank or institution.*
[925] See s.57(1)(c).
[926] See s.57(5).
[927] See s.57(5).
[928] See s.57(2).
[929] See s.57(3).
[930] See s.57(4), (4A).
[931] *See s.57(3B)–(3C).*
[932] *See s.57(3A).*
[933] *See s.57(3D).*
[934] *See s.57(4).*
[935] See s.58A.
[936] See s.58A(4).

Once more, the decision of the sheriff will be final.[937] Where no appeal is made or an appeal is refused, the AIB will be discharged.[938] *The 2014 Act contemplates that instead of an appeal to the sheriff, an application to the AIB for a review of her discharge may be made along the lines mentioned above, with an appeal then lying to the sheriff.*[939]

Paragraphs 188 to 190 of the Policy Memorandum to the 2014 Act note that assets which should have vested in the trustee can come to light after the trustee has been discharged. This may lead to an application to the sheriff asking for the case to be reopened, which is a costly step. Accordingly, s.58B would allow the AIB to intervene when she becomes aware of newly identified estate[940] with a value of at least £1,000 after the trustee has been discharged but within five years of the date of sequestration.[941] In such a case the AIB may reappoint herself if she was formerly the trustee.[942] Where she was not formerly the trustee, she may appoint herself or reappoint the former trustee on the latter's application.[943] However, the AIB can only take such a step if in her opinion the value of the newly identified estate is likely to exceed the costs of both (re)appointment and the recovery, management, realisation and distribution of the estate.[944] Accordingly, a discharged trustee who applies for reappointment must provide the following information to the AIB[945]:

- the estimated value of the newly identified estate;
- the reason why it forms part of the debtor's estate;
- the reason why it was not recovered;
- his estimated outlays and remuneration following reappointment;
- the likely distribution of the estate following reappointment.

Where a discharged trustee does not apply for reappointment, he must provide the AIB of details of newly identified estate of which be becomes aware, if it has a value of at least £1,000.[946] He must then provide the above information to the AIB if she so requests.[947] Where the AIB was formerly the trustee, she must simply record and consider this information.[948] Where such an application has been made, and the AIB proposes to (re)appoint, she must notify the debtor and any other person she considers to have an interest, informing them that they may make representations in relation to the application and proposed (re)appointment within 14 days of the notice being given.[949] Before (re)appointing the AIB must take any such representations into account.[950] If she (re)appoints, she must notify the debtor and soon as practicable, reminding him of his duties to co-operate with the trustee.[951] Any decision to (re)appoint or not to (re)appoint may be appealed to the sheriff by an interested person within 14 days of being made.[952]

PROTECTED TRUST DEEDS

7.4.7 Having considered the formalities of the sequestration process, it may be useful to deal briefly with some alternatives to sequestration. Creditors may enter into all manner of informal arrangements with

---

[937] See s.58A(6).
[938] See s.58A(7).
[939] See s.58A(4A)–(4C), (5), (6).
[940] Any part of the estate which vested in the trustee, but which was not recovered before his discharge: see s.58B(2).
[941] See s.58B(1).
[942] See s.58B(3)(b).
[943] See s.58B(3)(a).
[944] See s.58B(4).
[945] See s.58B(5), (7).
[946] See s.58B(5A)(a).
[947] See s.58B(5A)(b).
[948] See s.58B(6).
[949] See s.58C(1)–(2).
[950] See s.58C(3).
[951] See s.58C(4)–(5).
[952] See s.58D.

debtors rather than press for sequestration. Such arrangements, however, typically do not prevent any creditor deciding to opt for sequestration at any time. Again, it was observed earlier that a composition contract, whereby a debtor is relieved of liability for his debts in return for part payment, may be used as an alternative to sequestration (as opposed to judicial composition which ends the sequestration process). This will of course only bind those creditors who become party to the contract, while their rights are restored should the debtor default.

Simple trust deeds

Traditionally, perhaps the most popular alternative to sequestration is for the parties to arrange that the **7.4.7.1** debtor simply places his estate, or an agreed part thereof, in trust for the benefit of the creditors. This procedure is quicker, cheaper and more straightforward, while from the debtor's point of view none of the disabilities in terms of holding office, etc. ensue. The process is also almost entirely private. Yet the Act does not ignore private trust deeds altogether.

First of all, it is necessary to note that the Act defines a trust deed in s.5(4A). This used to indicate that a trust deed meant a voluntary trust deed granted by or on behalf of the debtor whereby his estate (other than estate which would not vest in the trustee if he were sequestrated) is conveyed to the trustee for the benefit of his creditors generally. This has now been expanded to include a trust deed which does not convey the whole or part of the debtor's dwellinghouse[953] where a secured creditor holds a security over it, and that creditor has, at the debtor's request, agreed before the trust deed is granted not to claim under the deed for any of the debt in respect of which the security is held. However, subject to these exceptions, the definition would exclude any trust deed which only conveyed part of the debtor's estate to the trustee. Such an arrangement would not be entirely inoperative, but would be subject to the common law rather than the Act. It is only trust deeds (including protected trust deeds) meeting the definition under s.5(4A), which are subject to the Act and any reference in this chapter to a trust deed or a trustee under a trust deed should be read accordingly.

As regards how the Act deals with trust deeds, whatever the deed may say, the Act allows the debtor, the trustee or any creditor to require that the trustee's accounts are audited and his remuneration fixed by the AIB.[954] Equally, it permits a trustee to record certain notices in the Register of Inhibitions, extends the provisions of Sch.1 to valuation of claims (unless the deed provides otherwise), and stipulates that the submission of a claim to a trustee shall bar any provisions relating to limitation of actions.[955] Moreover, in terms of the Insolvency Act 1986, any individual who acts as a trustee without being a qualified insolvency practitioner commits a criminal offence.[956] In the main, however, none of the statutory obligations and sanctions apply, and in particular gratuitous alienations and unfair preferences cannot be challenged. Nor is there anything to prevent any dissident creditor undermining the process at any time by seeking to do diligence on the estate or indeed petitioning for sequestration. If sequestration is granted, which of course it should be, given that the granting of a trust deed for creditors is an act of apparent insolvency allowing any creditor to petition,[957] the trustee under the deed must hand over the estate to the trustee in sequestration.[958] (It should indeed be remembered that the trustee under a deed may himself petition for sequestration if the trust deed process does not go according to plan.[959]) It was to deal with some of these disadvantages that the concept of a protected trust deed was introduced.

---

[953] This is a dwellinghouse (including any yard, garden, outbuilding or other pertinents) which, on the day before the date the deed was granted, was the sole or main residence of the debtor, who (either alone or in common with any other person) owned it or leased it under a lease exceeding 20 years: s.5(4AA). A dwellinghouse may be a sole or main residence even though it is used by the debtor for the purposes of a trade, profession or business: s.5(4AB).

[954] See Sch.5 para.1.

[955] See Sch.5 paras 2–4.

[956] See ss.388(2)(b), 389(1).

[957] See ss.5(2)(b), 7(1)(c)(i).

[958] *Salaman v Rosslyn's Trustees* (1900) 3 F. 298.

[959] See s.5(2)(c), (2C).

Protected trust deeds—introduction

7.4.7.2 The main advantage of a protected trust deed is that they bind all creditors, and they have become very popular as an alternative to sequestration, with several thousand being recorded in the Register of Insolvencies each year. Because of concerns as to how well the schemes were managed, the law regulating their operation, which was formerly to be found in Sch.5 to the Act, was tightened by the Protected Trust Deeds (Scotland) Regulations 2008.[960] These were subject to minor amendment by the Protected Trust Deeds (Scotland) Amendment Regulations 2010.[961] However, both the 2008 and 2010 Regulations are revoked and replaced by the Protected Trust Deeds (Scotland) Regulations 2013,[962] which now contain the law in this area. The impetus for the new Regulations was concern over the performance of protected trust deeds, since over a third of protected trust deeds paid no dividend to creditors whatsoever, any funds generated being swallowed up by the costs of administering the deed. Often debtors were recruited by "lead generator" firms, who would sell on the debtors to actual insolvency firms for substantial fees, which fees would become part of the costs of administering the deed. It was also felt that "lead generator" firms, in order to maximise their profits, would recruit debtors for whom the protected trust deed route was not the optimal solution to their debt problems. In order to deal with such abuses, the 2013 Regulations introduce a number of new controls:

- a new minimum debt level of £5,000;
- a deed being ineligible for protection if all the debts can be fully repaid with 48 months;
- pre-trust deed fees no longer to be capable of being part of administration costs;
- trustees no longer to be able to charge an hourly rate, instead having to charge a fixed upfront fee, augmented by a percentage of funds ingathered;
- creditors to be aware of the fees to be charged before they agree to the trust deed;
- no contributions to be paid from the debtor's social security benefits.

The new regulations will almost certainly lead to a significant diminution in the number of protected trust deeds registered. Their detail is considered below.

Requirements for protection

7.4.7.3 Certain requirements must be met if a trust deed is to become protected, and if they are met the deed will have protected status from the date when the deed is registered in the Register of Insolvencies.[963] First of all, the debtor must be a "person" who is capable of being sequestrated[964] (see para.7.1.2), but must not be a person who has been sequestrated and whose trustee remains undischarged.[965] Secondly, the total amounts of the debtor's debts (including interest) at that date the deed is granted must be at least £5,000. Thirdly, the trustee must be a person who would not be disqualified from acting as the replacement trustee were the debtor to be sequestrated.[966] This means that, inter alia, he requires to be a qualified insolvency practitioner. Fourthly, the deed must state that all the debtor's estate, other than that which would not vest in a trustee in a sequestration, has been conveyed to the trustee,[967] and that the debtor has agreed to convey to the trustee any estate which is acquired by the debtor during the four years after the trust deed is granted, which would have been conveyed to the trustee if it had been part of the debtor's estate on the date on which the trust deed was granted.[968] (In other words the deed must state that the debtor has agreed to convey *acquirenda*.) It must also state that a contribution from

[960] Protected Trust Deeds (Scotland) Regulations 2008 (SSI 2008/143).
[961] Protected Trust Deeds (Scotland) Amendment Regulations 2010 (SSI 2010/398).
[962] Protected Trust Deeds (Scotland) Regulations 2013 (SSI 2013/318). However, the 2008 Regulations (as amended by the 2010 Regulations) continue to apply to any trust deed granted before November 28, 2013: see 2013 Regulations reg.31(1).
[963] See reg.3.
[964] See reg.4(1).
[965] See reg.4(2).
[966] See reg.5.
[967] See reg.7(1)(a).
[968] See reg.7(1)(b).

income is payable where this applies.[969] It is expected that when the debtor is identified as having excess income once allowed expenditure is taken into account in terms of the Common Financial Measure (*soon to be replaced by the common financial tool*), all such income should be paid over to the trustee.[970] Thus where this is so, the trust deed must state that the debtor must during the payment period pay the relevant contribution at regular intervals.[971] In determining the amount of any contribution, the trustee may take account of any social security benefit paid to the debtor, but the contribution must not include an amount derived from that benefit.[972] The contribution period must be at least 48 months,[973] but the trustee may determine a shorter period if he believes that the relevant contributions will allow the debtor's debts at the date of granting the deed to be paid in full.[974] A longer period may be agreed with the debtor, but can be determined by the trustee to reflect any period during which the debtor ceased to make a contribution.[975] If the trustee decides to shorten or lengthen the period, he must notify the debtor without delay.[976] It was noted in para. 7.4.7.1 that a trust deed may not convey the whole or part of the debtor's dwellinghouse where a secured creditor holds a security over it, and that creditor has, at the debtor's request, agreed before the trust deed is granted not to claim under the deed for any of the debt in respect of which the security is held. In other words if the debtor's home is subject to a large mortgage, then it might make sense to exclude it from the property held under the trust, and to exclude the creditor from the deed. If that creditor is to be excluded from the deed, prior to the debtor granting the trust deed the trustee must provide the debtor and the secured creditor with a valuation made by a chartered surveyor or other suitably qualified third party of property concerned, and the secured creditor must agree in prescribed form.[977] The trust deed must then state details of the secured creditor and of the relevant debt.[978] Fifthly, before the deed is granted, the trustee must provide the debtor with a copy of a Debt Advice and Information Package and advise him that granting the deed may have certain results.[979] The trustee and debtor must then sign a statement confirming that the trustee has fulfilled these duties.[980] Sixthly, the trust deed having been delivered to him, the trustee must without delay send a notice in prescribed form to the AIB for publication by registration in the Register of Insolvencies.[981] Seventhly, no later than seven days after registration the trustee must send to every creditor[982] known to him, a copy of that notice, a copy of the trust deed, a statement of the debtor's affairs prepared by the trustee, a copy of the form which invites a statement of claim from creditors, and a statement in prescribed form of the anticipated realisations from the deed.[983] The trust

---

[969] See reg.7(1)(c).

[970] See regs 8(5), 10(1)(d)(ii).

[971] See reg.8(1).

[972] See reg.21(4).

[973] See reg.8(2)(a).

[974] See reg.8(2)(b), 8(3). If the debtor is a living individual, contributions must be less than that sum: reg.8(4).

[975] See reg.8(2)(c).

[976] See reg.20(1).

[977] See reg.6.

[978] See reg.7(2).

[979] See reg.7(3)(a)–(b). These results are the sequestration of his estate; being refused credit, whether before or after discharge; not being able to remain in his current place of residence (unless this is excluded from the deed); being required to relinquish property he owns; being required to make contributions from his income for the benefit of creditors; damage to his business interests and employment prospects; and the fact that he has granted a trust deed becoming public information.

[980] See reg.7(3)(c).

[981] See reg.9.

[982] Apart from a creditor who holds a security over the debtor's dwellinghouse which has been excluded from the trust deed.

[983] See reg.10(1). The statement of affairs must contain, inter alia: a list of the debtor's assets and liabilities; a statement of the debtor's income and expenditure in the form of the Common Financial Statement as at the date when the trust deed was granted; a statement as to the extent to which those assets and income will not vest in the trustee; a statement as to any contribution from income which the debtor is expected to make; a statement whether, on the basis of the information then available, the creditors are likely to be paid a dividend; where a creditor holds a security over the debtor's dwellinghouse which has been excluded from the trust deed the effect on the dividend of that exclusion; a valuation made by a third party of the dwellinghouse and the amount of the debt owed to any secured creditor of that dwellinghouse who has been excluded from the trust deed; a statement that the trustee must on request provide a copy of any valuation relating to an asset of the debtor made by a third party which the trustee holds; any statement showing the amount due by a debtor under a security, and any document showing the present income of the debtor; details of any protected trust deed under which, in the preceding six months, the debtor has been discharged or refused a discharge; and a statement explaining the conditions which must be fulfilled before the trust deed becomes protected and the consequences of that happening.

deed will then have to be acceded to by the notified creditors,[984] and that will occur unless, within five weeks of the publication of the notice, the trustee has received written objections from a majority in number or at least one-third in value of the creditors.[985]

As soon as reasonably practicable after the expiry of that five week period (and not later than four weeks after that expiry), the trustee must send the AIB[986] a copy of the trust deed; either a copy of every agreement by a secured creditor excluded from the deed or a statement that no such agreement has been obtained; a statement that he has not received the requisite number of objections; a copy of the signed statement referred to in reg.7(3)(c); a copy of the statement of the debtor's affairs; a copy of any agreement not to realise certain heritable estate and to relinquish the trustee's interest in that estate in return for payment made by the debtor (see next paragraph); a statement that all the necessary conditions have been met and all the necessary documents have been sent; where the debtor is to make a contribution from income, a statement that the trustee assessed the debtor's expenditure against the prevailing trigger figures under the Common Financial Statement, explaining any instance in which those trigger figures are exceeded. The AIB must register the trust deed in the Register of Insolvencies making it protected if she has received the above documents and the prescribed conditions have been met, unless she is not satisfied that a contribution from income is appropriate or believes that the debtor's expenditure is excessive.[987] Once the AIB has notified the trustee of the registration of the trust deed or her refusal to do so, the trustee must notify the debtor and every known creditor within seven days.[988]

Effects

7.4.7.4 The main effects of a trust deed becoming protected are as follows:

- An objecting creditor, or a creditor who did not receive the notice, has no higher right to recover the debt than an acceding creditor.[989] It is, however, provided that an objecting creditor, or a creditor who did not receive the notice, may present a petition for sequestration within five weeks of the registration of the notice of the intention to seek protected status sent by the trustee to the AIB.[990] The sheriff will award sequestration if he considers it to be in the best interests of the creditors.[991] Moreover, such a creditor may present a petition for sequestration at any time on the grounds that distribution of the estate is unduly prejudicial to any creditor or class of creditors.[992] In this case the sheriff will award sequestration if he considers that the ground is established.[993]
- The debtor cannot apply for sequestration.[994]
- Broadly speaking, any diligence against earnings ceases to have effect and no new diligence is effective.[995]
- Where the debtor is required to pay a contribution from earnings and has failed to pay the required amount on two consecutive occasions, at the trustee's request the debtor must give his employer an instruction in prescribed form to make deductions of specified amounts from the debtor's earnings and pay these to the trustee.[996] If the debtor fails to give the employer

---

[984] The creditor who holds a security over the debtor's dwellinghouse which has been excluded from the trust deed is not a notified creditor and thus cannot vote on a trust deed becoming protected.

[985] See reg.10(2).

[986] See reg.11(1).

[987] See reg.11(2). For an appeal against her refusal to do so see para.8.4.7.10.

[988] See reg.11(3).

[989] See reg.12(1)(a). In *Junespear Ltd v Dear*, 2008 S.L.T. (Sh Ct) 69; Sheriff Principal Dunlop notes of the previous regulations (at paras 22–23) that while a debt owed to a non-acceding creditor is not extinguished by the protected trust deed procedure and that the debtor's discharge is not binding on such a creditor, the debtor "is for all practical purposes free from those claims" and thus "*in effect*" is discharged.

[990] See reg.17(1)(a). Provided the apparent insolvency founded on in the petition in constituted with four months of the petition being presented: see reg.17(2).

[991] See reg.17(3)(a).

[992] See reg.17(1)(b).

[993] See reg.17(3)(b).

[994] See reg.12(1)(b).

[995] See reg.13.

[996] See reg.14(1)–(2).

this instruction, the trustee may do so directly.[997] The employer must pay over the sums deducted as soon as it is reasonably practicable to do so.[998] An employer who fails to make a payment without good cause is liable to the trustee for that amount, and may not recover such an amount from the debtor.[999] An employer who makes a payment may also charge a fee equivalent to the fee payable for doing diligence on earnings under s.71 of the Debtors (Scotland) Act 1987 and deduct this from the earnings.[1000] After the discharge of the debtor, the trustee must notify the employer without delay that the instruction has been recalled.[1001]

- It was seen that in certain circumstances the debtor's dwellinghouse may be excluded from the estate conveyed to the trustee (see previous paragraph). It is also possible for a trustee to agree in relation to a specified item of heritage which has been conveyed, not to realise it, to relinquish any interest in it, and to recall any notice of inhibition in relation thereto, provided certain conditions are met.[1002] These conditions are that the debtor must pay an amount determined by the trustee by a date determined by the trustee, continue to make a contribution from income beyond the agreed/determined period for a period determined by the trustee, and co-operate with the administration of the trust.[1003] The idea here is to allow the debtor to keep such property only if its value is recovered by the trustee, so the amount paid must be in accordance with a valuation made by a chartered surveyor or other suitably qualified third party.[1004] If the debtor fails to fulfil any condition the trustee may withdraw from the agreement.[1005] As soon as practicable, the trustee must send a copy of the agreement in prescribed form to the AIB and every known creditor other than a secured creditor who has consented to be excluded from a trust deed.[1006]
- If the funds from the estate are sufficient, the trustee must pay a dividend to creditors no later than six weeks after the end of the first dividend period—24 months from the date the deed was granted.[1007] Subsequent dividend periods then arise every six months thereafter.[1008] Funds will be sufficient if, after deducting the trustee's fees and outlays and making allowance for future contingencies, a dividend of at least 5 pence in the £ can be paid.[1009]
- The trustee or any creditor can challenge an unfair preference[1010] or gratuitous alienation,[1011] while the former can also challenge an order for the payment of a capital sum on divorce.[1012]
- A secured creditor who has consented to be excluded from a trust deed is not entitled to make a claim under the deed in respect of any of the debt in respect of which the security is held; to do diligence against the assets conveyed to the trustee under the protected trust deed; nor to petition for the sequestration of the debtor during the subsistence of the deed.[1013]

Discharge of debtors

It is contemplated that the debtor will be discharged on the application of the trustee, made either at the debtor's request or after four years from the date when the deed was granted.[1014] A debtor will be discharged from all debts and obligations for which he was liable at the date the trust deed was granted if: **7.4.7.5**

---

[997] See reg.14(3).
[998] See reg.14(4)–(5).
[999] See reg.14(6).
[1000] See reg.14(7).
[1001] See reg.14(8).
[1002] See reg.15(2).
[1003] See reg.15(3).
[1004] See reg.15(4).
[1005] See reg.15(5).
[1006] See reg.15(6).
[1007] See reg.16(1)(a).
[1008] See reg.16(1)(b).
[1009] See reg.16(2).
[1010] See s.36(1), (4), (6).
[1011] See s.34(1), (2), (8).
[1012] See s.35(1), (2).
[1013] See reg.12(3).
[1014] See reg.24(8).

(1) the trustee makes a statement that to the best of his knowledge the debtor has met his obliga-
     tions[1015] under the deed and co-operated with the administration of the trust; and
(2) any notice of inhibition under para.2 of Sch.5 to the Act has been recalled or has expired.[1016]

If those conditions are met, the trustee must send the AIB an application in prescribed form containing
such a statement with a copy to the debtor.[1017] The AIB must, on receiving that application, register it
in the Register of Insolvencies, the date of registration being the date of discharge.[1018] She must without
delay notify the trustee of the fact of registration and discharge, and the trustee must notify every known
creditor of these facts within seven days of receipt.[1019] However, the AIB may refuse to register the
application if she is not satisfied that the debtor has met his obligations under the deed and co-operated
with the administration of the trust.[1020] She must provide written notification of the refusal and the
reasons for it to the debtor and the trustee, the latter must then send a copy of the notification to every
known creditor within seven days of receipt.[1021] Similarly, if the trustee decides not to make an application in the first place, whether at the debtor's request or at the end of the relevant period, then he will
inform the debtor in writing of, that fact and the reason for refusal, the fact that the debtor is not
discharged from his debts and obligations, and the fact that the debtor may apply to the sheriff for a
direction under reg.28(1) (see para.7.4.7.10).[1022] The trustee must then send a copy of this notification
to the AIB within 21 days.[1023] Discharge does not affect student loans,[1024] nor any liability arising after
the date the trust deed was granted, nor any debt from which discharge cannot be granted in terms of
s.55(2) of the Act (see para.7.4.3.3), nor does it affect the rights of secured creditors (including a creditor with a security over a dwelling house which was excluded from the deed).[1025]

Supervision of trustees

7.4.7.6 Provision is also made for the supervision of trustees under protected trust deeds by the AIB. Thus she
may give directions to the trustee as to how to conduct the administration of the trust deed.[1026] Such a
direction may be made on the initiative of the AIB or (at the AIB's discretion) at the request of the
trustee, the debtor or any creditor.[1027] The terms of any direction should be intimated to the debtor and
all known creditors.[1028] The trustee must comply with a direction within 30 days unless the trustee
appeals to the sheriff against the direction, in which case he must comply within 30 days of the appeal
being withdrawn or dismissed.[1029] If it appears to the AIB that the trustee has failed without reasonable
excuse to comply with a direction, she may report the matter to the sheriff who, after hearing the
trustee, may censure him or make such other order as may be required.[1030]

Obligations of trustees

7.4.7.7 The trustee has certain information and notification obligations. Thus if he decides to shorten or
lengthen the period for which the debtor must pay contributions, he must notify the debtor without

---

[1015] Neither refusing to consent to the sale of his dwellinghouse where it is excluded from the trust deed, nor refusing to consent
to the sale of his family home (see para.7.2.17) may be treated as a failure to meet his obligations: see reg.24(7).
[1016] See reg.24(1)–(2).
[1017] See reg.24(1)–(2). For an appeal against a refusal to send an application see para.7.4.7.10.
[1018] See reg.24(3).
[1019] See reg.24(4)–(5).
[1020] See reg.24(11). For an appeal against her refusal see para.7.4.7.10.
[1021] See reg.24(12)–(13).
[1022] See reg.24(8)(a).
[1023] See reg.24(8)(b).
[1024] See reg.24(9)–(10).
[1025] See reg.24(6).
[1026] See reg.19(1). For an appeal against such a direction see para.7.4.7.10.
[1027] See reg.19(3).
[1028] See reg.19(2).
[1029] See reg.19(4)–(5).
[1030] See reg.19(6).

delay.[1031] Moreover, whether or not he is still acting as trustee, he must supply the AIB with such information relating to the trust deed as the latter considers necessary to discharge her statutory functions.[1032] If it appears to the AIB that the trustee has failed without reasonable excuse to supply requested information, she may report the matter to the sheriff who, after hearing the trustee, may censure him or make such other order as may be required.[1033] If the trustee is replaced, the new trustee must inform the AIB without delay.[1034] Moreover, at intervals of not more than 12 months beginning with the date the trust deed is granted and by no more than six weeks after the end of each interval, the trustee must send to the AIB, the debtor and each creditor a report in prescribed form on his management of the trust during the previous period,[1035] and a statement of his accounts of his intromissions in administering the trust during the period.[1036] Within 14 days of receiving this statement, the debtor or any and each creditor may require the AIB to exercise her supervisory function under s.1A(1)(a)(iia) of the 1985 Act by carrying out an examination of the administration of the trust deed by the trustee.[1037] The trustee must also retain certain documents (or copies thereof) for at least 12 months after his discharge.[1038]

Remuneration of trustees

The trustee is entitled to remuneration for work done in administering the trust deed. This remuneration **7.4.7.8** may take the form of a fixed fee intimated to creditors before the deed becomes protected, an additional fee based on a percentage of the total assets and contributions he manages to realise, and any outlays he incurs after the deed is granted.[1039] That fixed fee may include an amount for work done in seeking a secured creditor's consent to the exclusion of a dwellinghouse from the deed prior to the deed becoming protected, whether or not that consent is obtained.[1040] The AIB may at any time audit the trustee's accounts and fix his outlays, and any audit fee charged by the AIB may be recovered from the debtor's estate.[1041] However, any debt due to a third party before the granting of the trust deed does not rank higher than any other creditor's claim.[1042] This is to prevent the arrangement fees of debt management companies in respect of setting up protected trust deeds becoming part of the costs of the administration of the deed. Work done by third parties at the trustee's behest will form part of his outlays, but will be subject to proper audit and supervision. In the event of unforeseen circumstances, the fixed fee can be increased if a majority in value of creditors approves.[1043] If such approval is sought but not gained, then the AIB may approve if satisfied that a majority in number of creditors have not refused to approve the increase and that the increase is required for work to be completed by the trustee for the benefit of the creditors that was not foreseen when the fixed fee was intimated.[1044] When the AIB approves the increase, she may also determine its amount.[1045]

[1031] See reg.20(1).

[1032] See reg.20(2).

[1033] See reg.20(3).

[1034] See reg.20(4).

[1035] See reg.21(2). This allows evaluation of the performance of the trust against the expectations given to creditors.

[1036] See reg.21(1).

[1037] See reg.21(3).

[1038] See reg.22. The documents are: the trust deed, the statement signed by the debtor and trustee that the latter has advised the debtor correctly before the deed is signed, the notice that the deed is granted which is registered in the Register of Insolvencies, the statement of the debtor's affairs, the statement of anticipated realisations, the statement of realisations and distribution sent by the trustee on discharge, all statements of objection or accession received from creditors, any agreement not to realise a specified item of heritage, all reports sent under reg.21(2), any adjudication of a creditor's claim, any scheme of division among creditors, any circular sent to creditors with accounts, the debtor's discharge, the application to creditors for the trustee's discharge, any court decree, direction or order relating to the administration of the trust, any other document relating to the administration of the trust which the AIB has prior to the trustee's discharge indicated should be retained.

[1039] See reg.23(1).

[1040] See reg.23(5).

[1041] See reg.23(7)–(8).

[1042] See reg.23(6).

[1043] See reg.23(2)(a).

[1044] See reg.23(2)(b), (3).

[1045] See reg.23(4). For an appeal against that determination see para.7.4.7.10.

Discharge of trustee

7.4.7.9 Within 28 days of making the final distribution of the estate[1046] among the creditors a trustee must seek to obtain a discharge from acceding creditors by making an application to the AIB in prescribed form and including the accounts of his intromissions for the final accounting period (see para.7.4.7.7).[1047] Where a majority of the creditors in value have consented to that discharge within 14 days from the date of the application the trustee is discharged,[1048] and any creditor who does not respond to the application within that period is deemed to have consented.[1049] Such a discharge also discharges any previous trustee of the deed unless an interested party obtains a contrary ruling from the sheriff.[1050] Immediately upon obtaining his discharge the trustee must confirm this fact to the AIB and send her a statement of realisation and distribution of the estate in prescribed form for registration in the Register of Insolvencies.[1051] However, a creditor who objected to the trust deed, or who did not receive a copy of the notice, may within 28 days of such registration apply to the sheriff for an order that the creditor should not be bound by the trustee's discharge.[1052] This option is open where the creditor has not petitioned for the debtor's sequestration under reg.17, or even where such a petition has been refused. The order may be granted if the sheriff is satisfied that the trustee's intromissions with the estate have been so unduly prejudicial to that creditor's claim that the creditor should not be bound by the trustee's discharge.[1053] The sheriff clerk must send a copy of any such order to the trustee and also to the AIB for registration in the Register of Insolvencies.[1054]

Appeals and directions

7.4.7.10 The trustee can appeal to the sheriff regarding certain matters, as can the debtor or any creditor, provided in the latter cases they can satisfy the sheriff that they have or are likely to have a pecuniary interest in the outcome of the appeal.[1055] These matters are[1056]:

- the AIB's refusal to register a trust deed where she is not satisfied that a contribution from income is appropriate or believes that the debtor's expenditure is excessive (see para.7.4.7.3);
- the AIB's determination of the remuneration payable to the trustee(see para.7.4.7.8);
- any direction from the AIB to the trustee as to how to conduct the administration of the trust deed (see para.7.4.7.6);
- the AIB's refusal to register the debtor's application for discharge if she is not satisfied that the has met his obligations under the deed and co-operated with the administration of the trust (see para.7.4.7.5).

Any such appeal would require to be made within 21 days of that determination or direction.[1057] Additionally, the trustee may appeal to the sheriff against the refusal by the creditors to grant him a discharge[1058] (see para.7.4.7.9), while the debtor may appeal to the sheriff against the refusal by

---

[1046] i.e. the date on which all of the estate which is to be distributed amongst the creditors has been placed beyond the control of the trustee see reg.25(4).

[1047] See reg.25(2)–(3). For an appeal against a refusal to grant a discharge see para.7.4.7.10.

[1048] See reg.25(6).

[1049] See reg.25(5).

[1050] See reg.25(9). The sheriff would exercise this power under reg.28: see next paragraph.

[1051] See reg.25(7).

[1052] See reg.18(1), (4).

[1053] See reg.18(2). The sheriff must be satisfied on grounds other than those which would have justified a petition for the debtor's sequestration under reg.17(1)(b) on the basis that the provision for the distribution of the estate under the trust deed was or was likely to be unduly prejudicial to a creditor or class of creditors.

[1054] See reg.18(3).

[1055] See reg.27(2).

[1056] See reg.27(1).

[1057] See reg.27(5).

[1058] See reg.27(3).

the trustee to apply for his discharge[1059] (see para.7.4.7.5). In all the above cases the decision of the sheriff is final.[1060] Moreover any interested person may at any time apply to the sheriff for a direction as regards the administration of a trust deed.[1061] Such a direction may include making any order the sheriff thinks fit to make in the interests of justice including an order to cure any defect in procedure.[1062]

[1059] See reg.27(4).
[1060] See reg.27(7).
[1061] See reg.28(1).
[1062] See reg.28(2).

Chapter 8

PARTNERSHIP

INTRODUCTION   8.1

THE IMPORTANCE OF PARTNERSHIPS

Partnerships are the business entity of choice for many businesses, whether professional or **8.1.1** non-professional. It is a misconception to think of a partnership as a small business entity. Partnerships were, at one stage, limited to 20 partners in number, although exclusions applied to certain professions, solicitors included. These restrictions were removed and all partnerships can be unlimited in size.[1] Moreover, whilst a firm may have few partners, it may have many employees.

---

[1] See Regulatory Reform (Removal of 20 Partner Limit in Partnership etc) Order 2002 (SI 2002/3203). The limit was removed with effect from December 2002.

WHY CHOOSE A PARTNERSHIP?

8.1.2 There are many reasons why a partnership as a business entity may be more attractive than a limited liability company. One of the most important advantages is that of privacy of financial information. Firm accounts can remain private, in contrast to the stringent requirements for preparation and publication of annual accounts for a limited company. The creation of a partnership does not involve the same degree of formality and expense as is involved in the creation of a limited company. Flexibility in management is also possible given that there are few rules governing the creation and running of a firm. Each partner may participate in the management of the firm, and the partners as a whole can include in their partnership agreement more detailed rules on the management of the partnership.[2]

On the other hand, trading as a limited company may be more attractive to a particular business. The most obvious advantage is limited liability itself. As is explored in more detail later in this chapter, partners are jointly and severally liable for the debts of the firm.[3] However, the advantage of limited liability for companies is often more illusory than real. It is common for banks to require directors of companies to provide personal guarantees for the debts of the company.[4] Other advantages of choosing the limited liability company include the ability to grant a floating charge, which is not available to the firm,[5] and easier transfer of ownership through the buying and selling of shares.

The comparison between the advantages and disadvantages of partnerships with those of limited companies must be modified following the passing of the Limited Liability Partnership Act 2000 ("2000 Act"). The adoption of the limited liability partnership ("LLP") as a business format opens the benefit of limited liability to members in an LLP and brings with it other advantages characteristic of a limited company, for example, the ability to grant a floating charge. The law relating to LLPs is considered later in this chapter.[6]

The 2000 Act did not repeal the main pre-existing piece of legislation governing partnerships, the Partnership Act 1890 ("the 1890 Act"), nor the less important Limited Partnership Act 1907 ("the 1907 Act"). The 2000 Act simply created a new type of partnership which the partners may or may not choose to adopt. Those wishing to create a partnership may choose from three types: the 1890 one; the 1907 one; and the 2000 one.

The Scottish and English Law Commissions completed a major review of partnership law on July 31, 2000.[7] This report did not result in legislation.

PARTNERSHIP LEGISLATION

8.1.3 Two of the most important pieces of partnership legislation have already been mentioned: the 1890 Act and the 2000 Act. The latter is commented on in detail below.[8] It is worth providing some background to the former. Lord Reed in an important Scottish case decided in 2006 noted that the 1890 Act was a

---

[2] See 1890 Act s.24(5), which states as a general rule that every partner may take part in the partnership business. Like most of the provisions of this Act, this rule may be excluded by the written partnership agreement.

[3] 1890 Act s.9.

[4] See J. Freeman and M. Godwin, "Incorporating the Micro Business: Perceptions and Misperceptions" in A. Hughes and D.J. Storey (eds), *Finance and the Small Firm* (London: Routledge, 1994), pp.232–281 where they indicate that 54 per cent of respondents taking part in their research said that directors currently provided personal guarantees, principally to banks; cited at para.1.11, *Partnership Law: A Joint Consultation Paper*, 2000. Law Com. Consultation Paper No.159; Scot. Law Com. Discussion Paper No.111.

[5] Although the limited liability partnership created by the Limited Liability Partnership Act 2000 has the ability to grant floating charges: see para.8.6.2.11 below.

[6] See para.8.6.2 below.

[7] *Partnership Law: A Joint Consultation Paper*, 2000. Law Com. Consultation Paper No.159; Scot. Law Com. Discussion Paper No.111. For comment on the proposals see E. Berry, "The Partnership Bill 2003: unnecessary tinkering or much-needed reform?" [2005] J.B.L. 70; J.J. Henning, "Partnership law review: the joint consultation papers and the Limited Liability Partnership Act in brief historical and comparative perspective" [2004] Company Lawyer 163.

[8] See para.8.6.2.2 below.

codifying statute, commenting that it "was not drafted in the manner of most modern statutes".[9] It was not intended to provide an exhaustive statement of the law, but rather a statement of the central principles in a series of general propositions.[10] The provisions of the Act must be applied against the backdrop of case law, both pre- and post-1890. Although it would be wrong to treat the Act as a detailed code containing the answer to every problem, the terms of the Act itself should be the first point of reference for those studying this area of the law.

The Act is divided into four sections: the nature of a partnership; relations of partners to persons dealing with them; relations of partners to one another; and dissolution of partnership, and its consequences. The treatment in this chapter follows the pattern of the Act.

NATURE OF A PARTNERSHIP 8.2

DEFINITION OF A PARTNERSHIP

The 1890 Act defines a partnership as "the relation which subsists between persons carrying on a business in common with a view of profit".[11] Limited companies are excluded from that definition,[12] although a limited company may become an individual partner in a partnership.[13] "Business" is defined as including every trade, occupation, or profession.[14] **8.2.1**

A partnership is a relationship which is contractual in nature, created through agreement.[15] Although in most cases there will be a written document known as the partnership agreement, a partnership can be created through oral agreement. In such cases inferences of the consent necessary to constitute partnership can be made from the facts and circumstances of the case. As Lord Coulsfield explained:

"There is no simple or single test which can be applied in every case so as to establish or negative the existence of a partnership. All the relevant features of the parties' relationship must be examined and a view reached on the basis of all such features."[16]

It is not particularly significant whether the relevant parties describe their relationship as a partnership or not.[17] Recently, Lord Glennie illustrated the factual approach to ascertainment of the existence of a partnership as follows:

"There are certain features which are usually to be found in a partnership. None are present here. There was no firm name, no partnership premises, no partnership employees and no partnership bank account. Nor is there any averment that steps were being taken to establish any of these. There were no partnership accounts or tax returns. None of this is fatal to the contention that there was a partnership, but the lack of any such things points strongly against the likelihood of there being one."[18]

---

[9] *Duncan v MFV Marigold PD145* [2006] CSOH 128; 2006 S.L.T. 975 at [26].

[10] *Duncan v MFV Marigold PD145* [2006] CSOH 128; 2006 S.L.T. 975 at [24], [26]; the drafter of the Act being Frederick Pollock. It is relatively common to refer to the Act as a "partnership code", see, e.g. Lord Reed in *Duncan v MFV Marigold PD145* [2006] CSOH 128; 2006 S.L.T. 975 at [28].

[11] 1890 Act s.1(1).

[12] 1890 Act s.1(2)(a).

[13] A partnership so formed does not, however, avoid the requirement of preparation and publication of accounts, see Partnerships and Unlimited Companies (Accounts) Regulations 1993 (SI 1993/1820).

[14] 1890 Act s.45.

[15] *Pooley v Driver* (1877) 5 Ch.D. 458, per Jessel MR at 471–472. The joint consultation paper indicates that this is part of the common law of England and Scotland and is "so fundamental that it need not be expressed", para.5.18, *Partnership Law: A Joint Consultation Paper*, 2000. Law Com. Consultation Paper No.159; Scot. Law Com. Discussion Paper No.111.

[16] *Dollar Land (Cumbernauld) Ltd v CIN Properties Ltd*, 1996 S.L.T. 186 at 191.

[17] *Inland Revenue Commissioners v Williamson* (1928) 14 T.C. 340, per Lord President Clyde at 340.

[18] *Pine Energy Consultants Ltd v Talisman Energy (UK) Ltd* [2008] CSOH 10 at [28].

Given that the business must be carried on in common, a partnership requires a minimum of two persons. There is no requirement to make an actual profit. All that is required is that the partners carry on business "with a view of profit". Where the entity is a club or a charitable organisation, there will be no intention to make a profit and therefore no partnership.

The partnership may have been formed to carry out one single transaction or purpose. In such a case it is more usual to refer to it as a joint venture rather than a partnership. The partnership legislation applies to joint ventures in the same manner as it does other partnerships. As Lord President Cooper explained:

> "A joint venture is simply a species of the genus partnership, differentiated by its limited purpose and duration (which necessarily affect the extent of the rights and liabilities flowing from the relationship), but in all other essential respects indistinguishable from any other partnership."[19]

Joint ventures being more limited in nature, it may be more difficult to tell whether the parties have reached agreement on all significant points so that one can say with confidence that a joint venture has been created. The normal rules of the law of contract apply, and the parties must be agreed on the essentials of the contract. It is difficult to provide particular guidance on this point, beyond the fact that the essentials of the contract will differ depending upon the nature of the contract, or transaction involved.[20]

The definition contains no reference to the time of commencement of the partnership. This may not necessarily be the moment when the partnership begins trading, but is rather the time when the partners come together to embark on the activity in question.[21] In one case a partnership was formed to run a restaurant business.[22] Activities such as fitting out the premises and purchasing equipment were held to have been partnership activities, even though the restaurant had, at the relevant time, not commenced trading.

The 1890 Act makes use of both the terms "partnership" and "firm". The definition in s.1 tends to suggest that the term "partnership" should be used to describe the actual relation subsisting between the partners, whereas s.4 indicates that the word "firm" should be applied to the collective entity which is the partnership. Usage of these terms in the 1890 Act is, however, inconsistent. This may simply reflect the fact that it is difficult to isolate the two separate meanings when discussing the area as a whole. This chapter seeks, as much as possible, to apply the terms "firm" and "partnership" consistently with usage in the 1890 Act.

The 1890 Act provides guidelines in s.2 to assist with the determination of whether a partnership has been formed. The guidelines, although undoubtedly useful, may not always be relevant to the facts of an individual case.

Guideline 1

"Joint tenancy, tenancy in common, joint property, common ownership or part ownership does not of itself create a partnership . . .".[23] This principle is illustrated in *Sharpe v Carswell*,[24] in which Sharpe's widow sought to obtain compensation for her husband's death aboard a fishing vessel. She argued that Carswell was her husband's employer and therefore that compensation was due under the Workmen's Compensation Act 1906. Carswell argued that because Sharpe had held shares in the fishing boat, Sharpe was a partner and not an employee. It was held that mere ownership of shares did not, without more, render the deceased a partner, and Mrs Sharpe successfully proved her entitlement to compensation under the Act.

---

[19] *Mair v Wood*, 1948 S.C. 83, per Lord President Cooper at 86; and see the recent discussion in *Small v Robert Fleming Tarmac Ltd* CA121/01 Unreported March 27, 2003 OH, Lord Macfadyen.

[20] See the comments of Lord Macfadyen in *Small v Robert Fleming Tarmac Ltd* CA121/01 Unreported at [41], [67], referring to *May & Butcher Ltd v The King* [1934] 2 K.B. 17, per Viscount Dunedin at 21.

[21] *Khan v Miah* [2000] 1 W.L.R. 2123; [2001] 1 All E.R. 20; [2001] All E.R. (Comm) 282.

[22] *Khan v Miah* [2000] 1 W.L.R. 2123; [2001] 1 All E.R. 20; [2001] All E.R. (Comm) 282.

[23] 1890 Act s.2(1).

[24] *Sharpe v Carswell*, 1910 S.C. 391.

Guideline 2

"The sharing of gross returns does not of itself create a partnership . . .".[25] The application of this principle can be seen in *Clark v Jamieson*,[26] a case on very similar facts to *Sharpe v Carswell*.[27] The fact that one person in a fishing business, Clark, was remunerated through a share of gross earnings was not of itself sufficient to establish the existence of a partnership. Importantly, Clark did not contribute to the running capital of the business, nor would he have been liable if the business had made any losses.

Guideline 3

"The receipt by a person of a share in the profits of a business is prima facie evidence that he is a partner in the business, but the receipt of such a share . . . does not in itself make him a partner in the business or liable as such . . .".[28] An individual may receive payments out of the profits of the partnership business for reasons other than his status as a partner. He may be a creditor receiving repayments of a debt in instalments[29] or may have made a loan to the firm the rate of interest of which varies with the firm's profits.[30]

SEPARATE LEGAL PERSONALITY OF THE FIRM

One important difference between Scots and English law, embodied in the 1890 Act, is that in Scots law **8.2.2** a firm has a legal personality which is distinct from that of the partners of whom it is composed.[31] In English law the partnership has no separate legal personality.[32] There are many practical implications of this rule. In Scotland, contracts may be entered into in the name of the firm and the firm can sue and be sued.[33] Although the firm can become a tenant under a lease of heritable property, in practice, the lease is granted to the partners as trustees for the firm.[34]

As already stated, each individual partner is jointly and severally liable for the debts of the firm incurred whilst he is a partner.[35] The obligation of the partner towards the firm is accessory in nature, resembling in this respect a cautionary obligation.[36] A debt due by the firm must first be

---

[25] 1890 Act s.2(2).

[26] *Clark v Jamieson*, 1909 S.C. 132.

[27] *Sharpe v Carswell*, 1910 S.C. 391.

[28] 1890 Act s.2(3).

[29] 1890 Act s.2(3)(a). See *Alna Press Ltd v Trends of Edinburgh*, 1969 S.L.T. (Notes) 91; *Dollar Land (Cumbernauld) Ltd v CIN Properties Ltd*, 1996 S.L.T. 186, per Lord Coulsfield at 195–196. When the case was appealed to the Inner House and House of Lords, partnership issues were not judicially considered: see 1997 S.L.T. 260 IH; 1998 S.L.T. 992 HL.

[30] 1890 Act s.2(3)(d).

[31] 1890 Act s.4(2). This section does not apply in England.

[32] This difference was explored in a recent English appeal to the Supreme Court, *Clyde & Co LLP v Bates van Winkelhof* [2014] UKSC 32. The question before the court was, essentially, whether a member in a limited liability partnership could be treated as an employee for the purposes of s.230(3) of the Employment Rights Act 1996. Lady Hale considered the position prior to the enactment of the Limited Liability Partnerships Act 2000. She acknowledged that, due to the separate legal personality of the Scottish partnership, it might be easier to recognise a Scottish firm's ability to enter into a contract of employment with one of its partners than is the case in English law. It was held that the appellant could be treated as an employee for the purposes of this legislative provision.

[33] Bell, *Commentaries*, II, 508. Where the firm name includes the names of the partners the firm can sue and be sued in its own name: see *Forsyth v Hare and Co* (1834) 13 S. 42. Where the firm uses a descriptive name, the names of three partners (or two if there are only two partners) must be added where the action takes place in the Court of Session: *Antermony Coal Co v Wingate* (1866) 4 M. 1017, per Lord President McNeill at 1018–1019; per Lord Curriehill at 1020; and per Lord Ardmillan at 1022. This latter rule does not apply in the sheriff court; see Act of Sederunt (Sheriff Court Ordinary Cause Rules) 1993 (SI 1993/1956) r.5.7(1). Despite the lack of a separate legal personality in England, in practice the firm is usually entitled to raise and defend court proceedings in its own name.

[34] *Moray Estates Development Co v Butler*, 1999 S.C.L.R. 447.

[35] 1890 Act s.9.

[36] *Mair v Wood*, 1948 S.C. 83, per Lord President Cooper at 86. The obligation of the partner is not entirely analogous to a cautionary obligation. The partner's liability is joint and several whereas co-cautioners would be bound only for a proportionate share of the debt.

constituted against the firm, for example, by obtaining a court decree against the firm, before any of the partners may be found individually liable. Once the debt has been constituted against the firm, any one partner may be liable for the whole amount of the debt, with a right of relief from the other partners and the firm itself. In other words, any individual partner may be called upon to pay the whole amount of the debt. Thereafter, he can require his other partners to repay their shares of the debt to him, in accordance with the proportions agreed in the partnership agreement.[37] In practice, it is possible and indeed common for the firm and the individual partners to be sued in the same action.

Contracts such as partnership involve *delectus personae*. This expression is used to denote the type of contract where one party chooses to contract with another because of the special skill or talents of that other party. The choice of, and reliance on, that party's special skill implies the exclusion of performance of the obligation by any other person.[38] Thus, in theory at least, any change in the membership of a Scottish partnership brings the old firm to an end and creates an entirely new firm. While theoretically the position, this rule would be unworkable in practice, not least because it provides a firm with an easy way to avoid its debts. Not surprisingly, the parties often take the opportunity to amend this position in their written partnership agreement, where it is provided that the separate legal personality of the firm continues notwithstanding a change in the membership of the partnership. Certain provisions of the 1890 Act temper what would otherwise be the inequitable results of this rule.[39] The issue arises most acutely in the context of the liabilities of incoming or retiring partners, dealt with below.[40]

CONTROL OF THE USE OF NAMES

8.2.3 A firm may trade under the name of the existing partners, or under those names with certain minor additions.[41] Should the firm wish to adopt a descriptive name as opposed to one using the partners' surnames, then legislative controls on the use of names apply. Certain names are prohibited under the Act and the use of others is subject to the prior approval of the Secretary of State.[42] Partnerships must include the name of each partner on business documents[43] and an address for each of the partners for service of partnership documents.[44] This information must also be displayed at any place of business of the partnership.[45] Breach of these provisions can result in either civil or criminal sanctions.[46]

RELATIONSHIPS BETWEEN PARTNERS AND THIRD PARTIES

8.3 The 1890 Act contains provisions governing the liability of partners in specific instances of change of membership. These provisions, like many of the other provisions of the Act, provide a "fall back" position only, and may be excluded in a written partnership agreement.

---

[37] If there is no written partnership agreement, the Partnership Act 1890 s.24(1) provides that all partners are entitled to share equally in the firm's profits and must contribute equally towards losses.

[38] W.W. McBryde, *Contract*, 3rd edn (Edinburgh: W. Green, 2007), paras 12–36 to 12–37.

[39] See ss.17, 33, 36.

[40] See paras 8.3.1 and 8.3.2.

[41] The additions are the forenames and initials of the partners and the letter "s" if there is more than one partner sharing the same surname, Companies Act 2006 s.1192(3).

[42] Companies Act 2006 ss.1193–1198.

[43] Companies Act 2006 s.1202.

[44] Companies Act 2006 s.1202. The Act exempts partnerships of over 20 partners from the requirements of s.4(1)(a) subject to certain controls: see Companies Act 2006 s.1203.

[45] Companies Act 2006 s.1204(1).

[46] Companies Act 2006 ss.1205–1206.

LIABILITY OF AN INCOMING PARTNER FOR PRIOR ACTS OF THE FIRM

Where a person is assumed as a new partner in a firm, does he thereby become liable for the debts **8.3.1**
of the firm that pre-date his assumption? This important practical question, not addressed by the 1890
Act, can be answered only with difficulty. Section 17(1) provides that a person who is admitted
as a partner into an existing firm does not thereby become liable to the creditors of the firm for
anything done before he became a partner.[47] That is not, however, the end of the matter. Case law
suggests that this question is resolved through the operation of a presumption. Where a new firm
takes on the whole assets, stock and business of an old firm, it is presumed that it also takes on the
whole liabilities of the old firm.[48] That presumption may, however, be rebutted by evidence to the
contrary. The mere addition of one new partner is not sufficient by itself to rebut this presumption.
In *Heddle's Executrix v Marwick & Hourston's Trustee*, Lord Shand emphasised that this question
must be determined by reference to the facts and circumstances of each individual case.[49] He indicated
that the presumption might be rebutted where a new partner had paid a large sum of capital into
the partnership. His view was borne out in a later case in which the presumption was overturned in
those particular circumstances.[50] More recently, Lord Hodge in *Sim v Howat* preferred an analysis
which did not rely on a presumption, but rather looked at whether the facts gave rise to an inference that
the new firm (including the new partner or partners) had assumed the liabilities of the old firm.[51] In that
case the new partner had made a capital contribution, although it was a relatively small one, the size of
which was determined more as a custom rather than by reference to the value of the firm's business.
Using this consensual analysis, Lord Hodge held nevertheless that the new firm (and therefore all the
partners of the new firm, including the new partner) had assumed the liabilities of the old firm. He
suggested a new conceptual framework based on a binding promise—the new firm promises to pay the
debts of the old firm. He also discussed English law, which adopts a different approach to this
question.

LIABILITY OF A RETIRING PARTNER

The 1890 Act provides that a partner who retires from a firm does not thereby cease to be liable for **8.3.2**
partnership debts or obligations incurred before his retirement.[52] An interesting example of the operation of this rule occurred in *Welsh v Knarston*.[53] A solicitor's firm received instructions in relation to a
client's claim for personal injury compensation. The firm failed to raise an action, and the client's
action became time-barred. After the instructions were received, but before the action became time-
barred, two of the partners left the partnership, thus, in theory, dissolving the partnership. In the subsequent action for negligence by the client against the firm and the partners thereof, the two partners
argued that they were not liable, because, although they had been partners at the time when the instructions were received, they had left the firm prior to the point at which the client's claim had become
time-barred. It was held that each of the partners was under a continuing obligation to raise the action
and that liability survived the dissolution of the partnership.

---

[47] 1890 Act s.17(1).

[48] *Heddle's Executrix v Marwick & Hourston's Trustee* (1888) 15 R. 698.

[49] *Heddle's Executrix v Marwick & Hourston's Trustee* (1888) 15 R. 698.

[50] *Thomson and Balfour v Boag & Son*, 1936 S.C. 2; see, in particular, Lord President Normand at 10, where he approves Lord
Shand's opinion in *Heddle's Executrix v Marwick & Hourston's Trustee* (1888) 15 R. 698. See also *Miller v MacLeod*, 1973 S.C.
172.

[51] *Sim v Howat* [2011] CSOH 115, at [30]. Lord Hodge provides a highly valuable review of the Scottish case law on this
difficult issue. See also further procedure in the same case, [2012] CSOH 171.

[52] 1890 Act s.17(2).

[53] *Welsh v Knarston*, 1972 S.L.T. 96.

AGENCY OF PARTNERS

8.3.3 Partners are agents of the firm, and thus many of the rights and duties which apply between principal and agent apply in a similar manner between the firm and the partners.[54] The partner's role as agent is expanded upon in s.5 of the 1890 Act which defines the partner's authority by reference to the authority which it would be usual for that partner to have in the particular business carried out by the firm[55]: "The acts of every partner who does any act for carrying on in the usual way business of the kind carried on by the firm . . . bind the firm."[56] He will not bind the firm, however, where he is not authorised and the person with whom he is dealing either knows that he has no such authority or does not know or believe him to be a partner.[57]

Where a third party has suffered losses because of negligent advice given by a partner in a firm, it is significant to ask whether the knowledge of that negligent partner can be imputed to the firm. "Employment of a firm is employment of all the partners,"[58] and the negligent partner's knowledge is likely to be imputed to his principal, the firm.[59] This general rule is consistent with the terms of s.16 which provides that notice to any individual partner who habitually acts in the partnership business of any matter relating to partnership affairs operates as a notice to the firm.[60] This general rule applies even if the information given to the individual partner could be described as confidential in nature.[61]

LIABILITY FOR WRONGS

8.3.4 If a partner, by a wrongful act or omission, causes loss or injury to another person who is not a partner, the firm is liable for that wrongful act provided that the wrongful act occurs either when the partner is acting in the course of the business of the firm or the partner has the authority of his co-partners.[62] This rule, embodied in s.10 of the 1890 Act, makes the firm vicariously liable for certain actions of the partner. Some doubt has been caused by the ambiguous wording of s.10. The ambiguity surrounds the type of situations in which the partner will have "the authority of his co-partners". This phrase could mean either that the firm is liable where the general act which the negligent partner was carrying out was authorised by the partnership, or is liable only where the specifically wrongful action was so authorised.[63] If the correct interpretation is the latter of these meanings (which seems unlikely), then the ambit of the firm's vicarious liability will be much narrower.

It is important to note that, in terms of s.10, the firm is only vicariously liable where the person injured is not another partner in the same firm. Thus, in a famous case, one partner in a fishing business was injured when he fell through a hole in the deck caused by the removal of boards in the deck by one of his co-partners. Whilst applying s.10 to find that the firm was not liable, Lord Keith stated that partners act as agents for the partnership: "But as between themselves the partners are really in the position of principals."[64]

---

[54] See *Mair v Wood*, 1948 S.C. 83, per Lord President Cooper at 87. Partners are not agents of one another. In English law a partner cannot be an agent of the firm because the English firm lacks legal personality; see para.2.12, *Partnership Law: A Joint Consultation Paper*, 2000. Law Com. Consultation Paper No.159; Scot. Law Com. Discussion Paper No.111.

[55] See the discussion of implied authority in agency at para.2.3 above.

[56] See s.5

[57] An analogy can be made with apparent authority in agency, discussed at para.2.4.2 above.

[58] *Cleland v Morrison*, 1878–9 6 R. 156, per Lord Gifford at 169.

[59] *Chapelcroft Ltd v Inverdon Egg Producers Ltd*, 1973 S.L.T. (Notes) 37; *Adams v Thorntons WS (No.3)*, 2002 S.C.L.R. 787; 2005 1 S.C. 30 per Lord Penrose at [85].

[60] Except in cases of fraud on the firm committed by or with the consent of that partner; see s.16. The scope of s.16 is not free from doubt, see sheriff principal in *Tait v Brown & McRae*, 1997 S.L.T. (Sh Ct) 63 at 69. It is emphasised in *Lindley & Banks on Partnership*, 18th edn (London: Sweet & Maxwell, 2002), para.12–26 that the information must relate to the partnership; see *Zurich GSG Ltd v Gray & Kellas* [2007] CSOH 91, per Lord Brodie at [17].

[61] *Zurich GSG Ltd v Gray & Kellas* [2007] CSOH 91, per Lord Brodie at [19].

[62] 1890 Act s.10.

[63] See the discussion in C.J. Tyre, "Partnership", *Stair Memorial Encyclopaedia: The Laws of Scotland* (Edinburgh: Butterworths/Law Society of Scotland), Vol.16, para.1043.

[64] *Mair v Wood*, 1948 S.C. 83 at 87; per Lord Keith at 90.

The firm may also be liable to make good losses caused where partnership funds have been misappropriated by a partner.[65] The firm is liable in two types of situations: firstly, where one partner, acting within the scope of his apparent authority receives money or property of a third person and misapplies it[66]; and, secondly, where the firm in the course of its business receives such money or property and it is misapplied by one of more of the partners while it is in the custody of the firm.[67] The reference to apparent authority in the former situation indicates that one should analyse the question from the perspective of the third party, not taking into account any limitations on the partner's authority which have not been communicated to third parties.[68]

RELATIONS OF THE PARTNERS TO ONE ANOTHER

Partners would normally enter into a written partnership agreement which governs their relations *inter* **8.4** *se*. If, however, they have failed to do so, the 1890 Act provides a set of rules as a "fall back" position. Partnership agreements can be amended, although the consent of all of the partners is required for this purpose.[69] If the written agreement includes provisions which should govern a particular situation, it is not possible to prove that an oral variation of the agreement has taken place—variations of a written agreement require to be in writing.[70]

FIDUCIARY DUTIES/REQUIREMENTS OF GOOD FAITH

A partner is subject to stringent duties towards his fellow partners. It is sometimes said that such duties **8.4.1** arise due to the fiduciary nature of the relationship,[71] although a partner could equally be described as being subject to duties of utmost good faith.[72] Many of the duties to be discussed in this section, for example, the duty to account, the duty not to make a secret profit and the duty not to compete with the firm, are fiduciary in nature. The separate issue of the standard of care which individual partners owe primarily to the firm and secondarily to the other partners in the exercise of partnership business is subject to doubt. Older authorities indicate that the standard is the subjective one of the diligence which he would show in the conduct of his own affairs.[73] A Scottish case decided in 2000 suggests that the standard is the lower, more objective, standard of reasonable care only, although the extent of that duty may vary depending on the circumstances of the case.[74]

Many of the more particular aspects of the partner's duties are contained in the 1890 Act. Certain of the duties are owed by an individual partner to the other partners, and others are owed by that individual partner to the firm as a whole.

Duty to account

Under s.28 of the 1890 Act an individual partner owes a duty to render true accounts and full informa- **8.4.1.1** tion of all things affecting the partnership to any partner or his legal representative.[75] This section, with its reference to "all things affecting the partnership" imposes a wide duty. This imposes a duty to

---

[65] 1890 Act s.11. See *New Mining and Exploring Syndicate Ltd v Chalmers and Hunter*, 1912 S.C. 126.

[66] 1890 Act s.11(a).

[67] 1890 Act s.11(b).

[68] See para.2.4.2 above.

[69] 1890 Act s.19.

[70] *Starrett v Pia*, 1968 S.L.T. (Notes) 28.

[71] *Adam v Newbigging* (1888) 13 App Cas 308.

[72] See para.6.5.1 above for the duty of utmost good faith in an insurance contract.

[73] Stair, I, 16, 7 and Erskine, III, 3, 21 referring to Justinian, *Institutes*, III, 25, 9.

[74] *Ross Harper & Murphy v Banks*, 2000 S.L.T. 699, per Lord Hamilton at 702–703.

[75] 1890 Act s.28.

disclose details of any acts which the partner carried out in competition with the partnership[76] or any payment which he has received in contravention of his duties as a partner. The appropriate action for enforcement of this duty is an action of accounting on the part of the firm, which would require the partner to pay to the firm sums made in breach of his duty.[77] The partner may also be liable in damages for breach of duty.[78]

Duty not to make a secret profit

8.4.1.2 This duty, expressed in s.29(1) of the 1890 Act, is owed by the individual partner to the firm as a whole. Again, it is drafted widely, covering benefits "derived from any transaction concerning the partnership, or from any use by him of the partnership property, name, or business connection". The duty also applies to transactions undertaken after dissolution of the partnership through the death of a partner, and before the affairs of the partnership have been wound up.[79]

Duty not to compete with the firm

8.4.1.3 This duty is expressed in s.30 of the 1890 Act, which requires partners acting in a business of the same nature as the firm, without the consent of his partners, to account for and pay over to the firm all profits made by him in that business.[80]

Expulsion of a partner

8.4.1.4 A majority of the partners cannot expel a partner unless a power to do so has been included in the written partnership agreement.[81] Even where such a power exists, the partners are bound to exercise it in accordance with the requirements of good faith, and failure to do so will result in the expulsion having no effect. An illustrative example of this rule can be found in the English case of *Blisset v Daniel*.[82] One of the partners, Blisset, received notice that he had been expelled from the partnership. Although the written partnership agreement did indeed permit the majority to expel another partner, it did not require the partners either to hold a meeting to discuss the expulsion or to give to the expelled partner reasons for the expulsion. Blisset had recently had an argument with another partner, Vaughan, because Vaughan had attempted to foist his son on the partnership as a manager despite the son's evident lack of qualifications. Blisset had objected to the son's appointment. Blisset was expelled by notice, but was given no reasons for the expulsion, nor was a meeting called to discuss the expulsion. It was held that the power to expel must be exercised in good faith and for the good of the partnership as a whole. Because these requirements had not been met in this case, the expulsion was void. In reaching this conclusion it was clearly significant to the court that the partners had persuaded Blisset to sign a set of accounts at a time when it had been agreed that Blisset would be expelled, but when he was unaware of this fact.[83]

If the power to expel is not contained in the written partnership agreement, the only solution for the partners is to dissolve the partnership.

---

[76] Conduct of this type would also be caught by s.30 of the 1890 Act, commented on below at para.8.4.1.3.

[77] *Smith v Barclay*, 1962 S.C. 1.

[78] *Ferguson v Mackay*, 1985 S.L.T. 94.

[79] 1890 Act s.29(2); *Laird v Laird* (1855) 17 D. 984.

[80] *Pillans Bros v Pillans* (1908) 16 S.L.T. 611.

[81] 1890 Act s.25.

[82] *Blisset v Daniel* (1853) 10 Hare. 493.

[83] In these circumstances, the accounts would not have been treated as binding on Blisset; see *Lindley & Banks on Partnership*, 18th edn (2002), para.10–73: "[N]o account will be binding on any partner who may have been induced to sign it by false and fraudulent representations, or in ignorance of material circumstances dishonourably concealed from him by his co-partners"; quoted with approval by Lord Reed in *Montgomery v Cameron & Greig* [2007] CSOH 63 at [28]. See now 19th edn (2010), para.10–75 in the same terms.

MANAGEMENT OF PARTNERSHIP AFFAIRS

The partners are bound by general duties of good faith in relation to the management of the firm. Thus, **8.4.2** where certain partners from two branch offices of a solicitors' firm left the firm, taking with them client files to set up a new firm in competition with the old firm in offices very close to the original branch offices, it was held that the partners had breached their fiduciary duties not to damage the partnership.[84] The court noted, in particular, that they had no right of ownership over the client files, and had severely inconvenienced the partnership by taking such files. The leaving partners were found liable in damages, calculated by reference to the profit made in breach of their partnership duties rather than by reference to the loss suffered by the partnership. This punitive level of damages is characteristic of breaches of fiduciary duty.

The 1890 Act contains rules in s.24 governing the management of partnership affairs which apply where the written partnership agreement is silent. Every partner is entitled to take part in the management of the firm.[85] Importantly, the rules provide that all partners may share equally in the capital and profits of the firm, and must contribute equally to the firm's losses.[86] Thus, if the partners intend that individual partners are to draw different percentages from the profits, then this must be specifically stated in the partnership agreement. In an English Court of Appeal case, Nourse LJ indicated, albeit obiter, that this section created an entitlement for each partner to share equally in the capital of the firm, regardless of the amount of capital individually contributed by that partner either at the commencement of the partnership, or the commencement of his membership as a partner.[87] In his view, however, this presumption could be easily rebutted through proof of an implied agreement that final shares of capital would correspond to original contributions of capital. This slightly unusual result of s.24(1) is often avoided in practice by appropriate drafting in the partnership agreement. Not surprisingly, this section is one of the provisions of the 1890 Act highlighted by the Law Commissions as requiring amendment.[88]

Individual partners have a right to an indemnity from the firm where that partner has made payments or incurred personal liabilities in the ordinary and proper conduct of the business of the firm.[89] This indemnity also extends to acts performed to preserve the business or property of the firm.[90]

Usually, partners are remunerated through a share of profits, and this explains why s.24 of the 1890 Act states that no partner is entitled to remuneration for acting in the partnership business.[91] The exact shares of profits, and shares in which partners contribute to losses, would usually be stipulated in the written partnership agreement. If not, then the default rule in s.24(1) (specifying equal shares) would apply. The "share" of profits to go to an individual may, by agreement, be fixed. Thus, there is a distinction between an equity partner (remunerated through an actual share of profits) and a fixed share partner (remunerated by a fixed amount each year). The 1890 Act contains no reference to fixed share partners—they can only be created in the written partnership agreement. It will not be obvious to those outside the partnership that a fixed share partner is any different from any other partner. He is "held out" to the outside world as a partner, and thus jointly and severally liable with the other partners in the firm for the firm's debts.[92] As a result of s.14 of the 1890 Act, such a partner will be liable to third parties who have given credit to the firm as a result of that partner's representations. The partnership agreement will probably contain an indemnity in favour of the fixed share partner.

---

[84] *Finlayson v Turnbull (No.1)*, 1997 S.L.T. 613.

[85] 1890 Act s.24(5).

[86] 1890 Act s.24(1).

[87] *Popat v Shonchhatra* [1997] 1 W.L.R. 1367, per Nourse LJ at 1372–1373.

[88] See paras 12.16–12.17, *Partnership Law: A Joint Consultation Paper*, 2000. Law Com. Consultation Paper No.159; Scot. Law Com. Discussion Paper No.111.

[89] 1890 Act s.24(2)(a).

[90] 1890 Act s.24(2)(b).

[91] 1890 Act s.24(6).

[92] *Primary Health Care Centres (Broadford) Ltd v Ravangave* [2008] CSOH 14; 2008 Hous. L.R. 24, per Lord Glennie at [15]. See further procedure in the same case [2009] CSOH 46; 2009 S.L.T. 673.

Differences arising as to the ordinary matters connected with partnership business may be decided by a majority of the partnership,[93] provided that all partners are present and able to express a view.[94] Where there is an equal split, case law suggests that those pressing for continuation of the status quo will prevail.[95] There are exceptions to this principle of majority rule, however. Unless this position is changed by agreement, no change in the nature of the partnership business may be made,[96] nor may any partner be introduced, without the consent of all existing partners.[97]

Partners making payments or advances to the firm beyond the amount of capital which it is agreed that he will contribute are entitled to interest on those advances at the rate of 5 per cent.[98] Interest is not payable to individual partners on the amounts of capital which it is agreed that he will contribute until the profits have been ascertained.[99]

PARTNERSHIP PROPERTY

8.4.3 Difficult questions may arise as to whether property is owned either by one or more partners as individuals, or is, in fact, partnership property. This can be an important question, particularly where valuation of a partner's share in the partnership is concerned, either on dissolution of the partnership or on the death of that partner. If the partnership agreement fails to define partnership property, then use can be made of the definition contained in the 1890 Act, namely:

> "All property and rights and interests in property originally brought into the partnership stock or acquired, whether by purchase or otherwise, on account of the firm, or for the purposes and in the course of the partnership business . . .".[100]

The Act further provides that all such property must be "held and applied by the partners exclusively for the purposes of the partnership, and in accordance with the partnership agreement".[101] A further section states that property bought with money belonging to the firm is deemed to have been bought on account of the firm, unless the contrary intention appears.[102]

Because partnership property is owned by the firm as a separate legal person[103] only the firm has an insurable interest in that property for insurance purposes.[104] Thus, partnership property must be insured in the name of the partnership and not in the name of an individual partner or partners.

It may also be important to identify partnership property for diligence purposes. The creditor of a partner as an individual may arrest the partner's share in the partnership in the hands of the firm.[105] The partner's asset is a share in that partnership, and so what is being arrested is an incorporeal right. Case law suggests that specific property cannot be arrested, but rather only the interest of the partner in any surplus assets once realised.[106]

In theory, a partner's share in the partnership is assignable in the same way as any other incorporeal moveable right, namely by assignation followed by intimation to the firm.[107] However, the partnership contract may involve *delectus personae*, in which case an individual partner could not assign his share

---

[93] 1890 Act s.24(8).

[94] *Const v Harris* (1824) Turn. & R. 496, per Lord Chancellor Eldon at 525.

[95] *Donaldson v Williams* (1833) 1 Cr. & M. 345.

[96] 1890 Act s.24(8).

[97] 1890 Act s.24(7).

[98] 1890 Act s.24(3).

[99] 1890 Act s.24(4).

[100] 1890 Act s.20(1).

[101] 1890 Act s.20(1).

[102] 1890 Act s.21. See *McNiven v Peffers* (1868) 7 M. 181; *Davie v Buchanan* (1880) 8 R. 319; *Hardie's Executrix v Wales*, 2003 G.W.D. 13–448.

[103] As explained above at para.8.2.2, the ability of the firm to take a tenancy to heritable property under a lease is complex. These factors are, in effect, limitations on the separate legal personality of the firm.

[104] *Arif v Excess Insurance Group Ltd*, 1986 S.C. 317.

[105] Bell, *Commentaries*, II, 536; Erskine, III 3, 24.

[106] *Parnell v Walker* (1889) 16 R. 917; Erskine, III 3, 24.

[107] cf. *Hill v Lindsay* (1846) 8 D. 472, which suggests that intimation to each partner is required.

in the partnership without the consent of the other partners.[108] Unless the consent of the other partners has been obtained, the assignee is not entitled to interfere in the management or administration of the partnership business, nor require accounts of the partnership transactions to be produced, nor inspect partnership books.[109] His only entitlement is to the share of the profits which would otherwise be due to the assigning partner, and he must accept the account of profits agreed to by the other partners.[110]

DISSOLUTION OF THE PARTNERSHIP

8.5 The word "dissolution" can be used to describe a number of different situations in partnerships. It may, for example, describe the situation where the firm is wound up completely, or where a change in the membership of the partnership terminates the old firm and creates a new firm. In this section dissolution other than by a court is considered first, followed by dissolution by a court.

DISSOLUTION OTHER THAN BY THE COURT **8.5.1**

Rescission of the partnership agreement

8.5.1.1 A right to rescind the partnership agreement arises where one partner has been induced, for example, by fraud or misrepresentation, to enter into the partnership. Section 41 of the 1890 Act refers to three specific rights of the rescinding partner which he may have in addition to any other rights on rescission. Firstly, the rescinding partner has a lien or right of retention over the surplus of partnership assets after satisfaction of the partnership liabilities.[111] This right covers any payment made by the partner into the partnership for the purposes of purchasing a share in the partnership or contributing capital.[112] Secondly, the rescinding partner stands in the place of a creditor of the firm for any payment made by him in respect of partnership liabilities.[113] Thirdly, he has a right to be indemnified by the person guilty of the fraud or making the representation against all debts and liabilities of the firm.[114] As would be the case in other instances of fraudulent or negligent misrepresentation, damages may be available.[115] The right to rescind may still be present where no fraud is involved, but *restitutio in integrum*, as a normal condition of the operation of rescission, must be possible.

Dissolution by notice

8.5.1.2 Where no fixed term was agreed upon for the duration of the partnership the partnership is known as a partnership at will and may be dissolved by notice by one of the partners to all other partners.[116] Where there is a partnership agreement, notice will usually be given in writing, although this is not a requirement of the 1890 Act. It has been held that an intention to dissolve can be implied from the circumstances as a whole, including the actings of the partners.[117] The Act does not specify the amount of

---

[108] See 1890 Act s.24(7); and see para.8.2.2 above.
[109] 1890 Act s.31(1).
[110] 1890 Act s.31(1).
[111] 1890 Act s.41(a).
[112] 1890 Act s.41(a).
[113] 1890 Act s.41(b).
[114] 1890 Act s.41(c).
[115] Damages for fraudulent misrepresentation are, in effect, damages for fraud, on which see J.M. Thomson, *Delictual Liability*, 4th edn (Edinburgh: LexisNexis, 2009), para.2.10. Damages for negligent misrepresentation are available under statute, see Law Reform (Miscellaneous Provisions) (Scotland) Act 1985 s.10. See also *Ferguson v Wilson* (1904) 6 F. 779.
[116] 1890 Act s.26(1).
[117] *Jassal's Executrix v Jassal's Trustees*, 1988 S.L.T. 757.

notice required, or even that it should be a reasonable period.[118] Dissolution is effective as from the date of the notice, or, if the notice is undated, the date of communication of the notice.[119]

Dissolution by expiry of the term

8.5.1.3 A partnership entered into for a specific term will be dissolved on the expiry of that term.[120] Joint ventures will be dissolved once the adventure or undertaking has been completed.[121] Where the partnership was originally entered into for a fixed term, but the partners continue to act as though a partnership were in existence after the expiry of the term, without settling the affairs of the firm or entering into a new agreement, the partnership will become a partnership at will and therefore terminable on notice by one partner to all of the other partners.[122] The rights and duties of the partners under the new partnership will be the same as those which applied under the old partnership so far as these are consistent with the incidents of a partnership at will.[123]

Dissolution by death or bankruptcy

8.5.1.4 The 1890 Act provides that the death or bankruptcy of any partner dissolves the partnership.[124] This provision is, however, subject to the agreement of the parties and the opportunity would almost invariably be taken to amend this default rule in the written partnership agreement. The agreement may, for example, provide that the partners have the option to continue the partnership after the death of one partner.[125] In one unusual case the deceased's personal representatives became partners on the partner's death.[126]

Dissolution by illegality

8.5.1.5 A partnership is dissolved by the happening of any event which makes it unlawful for the business of the firm to be carried on or for the members of the firm to carry it on in partnership.[127] For example, a partnership is dissolved if the outbreak of war renders the partnership agreement illegal. In one case a partnership agreement was rendered illegal by the outbreak of war with Germany because the partners of the firm were an English company and a German company.[128] After the war was over, it was held that the German company was entitled to a share of the profits made by the partnership after dissolution when the English company continued to carry on the business using capital contributed by the German company.

8.5.2 DISSOLUTION BY THE COURT

Permanent incapacity

8.5.2.1 A partner may petition for dissolution of the partnership where one of the other partners is subject to mental incapacity or has become permanently unable to perform his part of the partnership.[129] The

---

[118] Erskine, III, 3, 26; Bell, *Commentaries*, II, 522, 523.

[119] 1890 Act s.32.

[120] 1890 Act s.32(a).

[121] 1890 Act s.32(b).

[122] 1890 Act s.27(1).

[123] 1890 Act s.27(1).

[124] 1890 Act s.33(1).

[125] *WS Gordon & Co Ltd v Thomson Partnership*, 1985 S.L.T. 122.

[126] *Hill v Wylie* (1865) 3 M. 541.

[127] 1890 Act s.34.

[128] *Stevenson & Sons v AG für Cartonnagen-Industrie* [1918] A.C. 239 HL.

[129] 1890 Act s.35(a), (b). In relation to mental incapacity, s.35(a) retains for Scotland the original definition which appeared in the 1890 Act, whereas the definition was amended and updated for England. Given that the Act contains an outdated definition, the partnership agreement should take the opportunity to define the types of mental incapacity which would dissolve the partnership.

petition may be brought on behalf of the partner suffering from mental incapacity. The court may refuse the petition, as happened in one case where the partner suffering from mental incapacity had the option not to participate in the management of the partnership.[130]

Prejudicial conduct

A partner may petition for the dissolution of the partnership on the grounds that another partner has **8.5.2.2** engaged in conduct which, in the opinion of the court, is calculated prejudicially to affect the carrying on of the business.[131]

Breach of contract

The 1890 Act provides that a petition for dissolution can be made where one of the partners "wilfully **8.5.2.3** or persistently commits a breach of the partnership agreement" or conducts himself in such a manner that it would not be reasonably practicable for the remaining partners to carry on the partnership with him.[132] It seems that partners can, in general, be liable to one another for damages for breach of contract.[133] Where that breach is sufficiently serious, it can provide grounds for the dissolution of the partnership. Understandably, the courts are slow to intervene in minor disputes between partners.[134]

Loss

If the partnership can only be carried on at a loss, then this constitutes a ground for dissolution by the **8.5.2.4** court.[135] Raising a petition under this section will probably be relatively straightforward where all partners are agreed that the business can only be carried out at a loss. If this is not the case, then the task of assessing this question falls to the court, which may not find the question easy to answer.

Just and equitable

If a court considers that circumstances have arisen which, in the opinion of the court, render it just and **8.5.2.5** equitable that the partnership be dissolved, then dissolution may be granted by the court.[136] This section tends to be used as a "catch all" ground where the circumstances do not clearly fall within any of the other subsections of s.35.

Where the problem lies in the conduct of one partner alone, then, unless the partnership agreement expressly provides for the expulsion of an individual partner, the court has no power to expel that partner, allowing the remaining partners to continue the business. It must dissolve the partnership as a whole.

PARTNERS' CONTINUING AUTHORITY TO WIND UP PARTNERSHIP AFFAIRS FOLLOWING DISSOLUTION

When a partnership is dissolved, it is no longer a legal person.[137] This being the case, there might be **8.5.3** some doubt as to whether the partners could continue to act as agents in order to complete unfinished

---

[130] *Eadie v MacBean's Curator Bonis* (1885) 12 R. 660.

[131] 1890 Act s.35(c). The standard of behaviour expected of a partner may be high. In *Carmichael v Evans* [1904] 1 Ch. 486, the partnership agreement provided that partners could be expelled for "scandalous conduct detrimental to the partnership business", or for committing "any flagrant breach of the duties of a partner". The court upheld the expulsion of a partner who was convicted of travelling on a train without a ticket, classing the crime committed as one of dishonesty.

[132] 1890 Act s.35(d). See also *Thomson, Petitioner* (1893) 1 S.L.T. 59.

[133] *Gray v Dickson* Unreported August 10, 2007 Perth Sheriff Court at para.8.3.1, relying on *Lindley & Banks on Partnership*, edited by R.C. I'Anson Banks, 17th edn (London: Sweet & Maxwell, 1995), p.691 para.23–197.

[134] *Lindley & Banks on Partnership*, 19th edn (London: Sweet & Maxwell, 2010), para.24–81.

[135] 1890 Act s.35(e).

[136] 1890 Act s.35(f).

[137] Recalling the terms of s.4(2) which provides the Scottish partnership with separate legal personality.

transactions. An agent cannot validly act for a non-existent principal. However, it is an established rule of agency law that agents have a continuing ability to act on behalf of a principal who is "non-existent", for example because he has died or become incapacitated, in order to complete transactions which have been commenced but not completed.[138] This rule of agency law is reflected in s.38 of the 1890 Act, which provides that the authority of each partner continues in order to allow the partners to wind up the affairs of the partnership and complete unfinished transactions, but not otherwise.[139]

The extent of s.38 was analysed by Lord Reed in the important case of *Duncan v MFV Marigold PD145*.[140] This case concerned a partnership which operated a fishing boat. One of the partners died; an event which dissolved the partnership. Although accounts were prepared at the time of his death, this was done without the consent of the surviving partners who continued to operate the boat, providing the deceased's widow with the deceased's share of the profits. Eventually the partnership was wound up. The dispute centred around whether the deceased's estate was due the (higher) sum contained in the cessation accounts, or the (lower) sum representing his share of the partnership on actual winding-up. It was held that the balance due to the estate must (unless otherwise agreed) be ascertained by winding up the affairs of the partnership following the rules expressed in s.44. A cessation account prepared as at the date of dissolution is not (unless otherwise agreed) the measure of the amount due to the estate of a deceased partner.

In his judgment, Lord Reed suggested that the ambit of s.38 is not entirely clear. As a general rule in Scots law, the partners' continuing authority does not extend to engaging the partnership in new transactions.[141] However, certain contracts may be necessary to wind up the affairs of the partnership, for example, a partner must have authority to sell the partnership assets if the affairs of the partnership are to be wound up.[142] Certain English cases which suggest a more extensive power, encompassing the formation of new contracts, are probably not authoritative in Scotland.[143] In any event, it seems that partners can only remain authorised for what Lord Reed described as a "temporary" period.[144] Where partners are involved in the completion of certain contracts on dissolution of the partnership, they continue to operate as agents for the (now dissolved) partnership—they do not become actual parties to the contracts as principals themselves,[145] nor do they act as trustees.[146]

Section 38 was analysed in the context of a petition to the *nobile officium* of the High Court of Justiciary brought in 2008.[147] Partners in a firm had owned and operated a care home which was destroyed by a fire in 2004 in which 14 residents were killed and a further four were injured. The firm had been dissolved by agreement among the partners in 2005. Subsequent to that, the Crown had served an indictment on the three partners of the dissolved firm, that indictment containing 17 charges against the firm for breach of its obligations as employers under the Health and Safety at Work etc. Act 1974. The accused under that indictment was the now dissolved firm, not the partners thereof. The Crown argued, in essence, that the legal personality of the firm continued after dissolution and that it was therefore competent to serve an indictment on the firm in this manner. This argument was rejected, the High Court confirming that the legal personality of the firm did not survive dissolution of the

---

[138] *Pollok v Paterson* December 10, 1811 F.C. 369 at 375; and see para.2.9.6 above.

[139] 1890 Act s.38; although the terms of s.38 reflect the pre-existing Scots common law. See *Duncan v MFV Marigold PD145* [2006] CSOH 128; 2006 S.L.T. 975 at [41].

[140] *Duncan v MFV Marigold PD145* [2006] CSOH 128; 2006 S.L.T. 975 at [26].

[141] See *Duncan v MFV Marigold PD145* [2006] CSOH 128; 2006 S.L.T. 975 at [38], [44], and the references there to the opinions of Lords Reid and Upjohn in *Inland Revenue Commissioners v Graham's Trustees*, 1971 S.C. (HL) 1.

[142] *Duncan v MFV Marigold PD145* [2006] CSOH 128; 2006 S.L.T. 975, per Lord Reed at [41], referring to *Hurst v Bryk* [2002] 1 A.C.185, per Lord Millett at 196.

[143] *Re Bourne* [1906] 1 Ch 113; [1906] 2 Ch 427; *Don King Productions Inc v Warren (No.1)* [2000] Ch. 291. Lord Reed in *Duncan v MFV Marigold PD145* [2006] CSOH 128; 2006 S.L.T. 975 at [66] suggests a more limited ambit to s.38, although he indicates that the matter requires more detailed analysis in a relevant case. The Scottish/English differences are also noted in *Boghani v Nathoo* [2011] EWHC 2101; [2012] Bus. L.R. 429.

[144] *Duncan v MFV Marigold PD145* [2006] CSOH 128; 2006 S.L.T. 975 at [43].

[145] *Inland Revenue Commissioners v Graham's Trustees*, 1971 S.C. (HL) 1, per Lord Reid at 21; approved by Lord Reed in *Duncan v MFV Marigold PD145* [2006] CSOH 128; 2006 S.L.T. 975 at [38].

[146] *Duncan v MFV Marigold PD145* [2006] CSOH 128; 2006 S.L.T. 975 at [67].

[147] *Balmer, Petitioners* [2008] HCJAC 44; 2008 S.L.T. 799.

partnership.[148] It was wrong to interpret the continuing authority of the partners under s.38, which in essence enabled them to wind-up the affairs of the firm, as a continuation of the legal personality of the firm. There was, in effect, no "firm" on which to serve the indictment. The decision was reached through an analysis of the pre-1890 common law, the terms of the 1890 Act, and case law interpreting the latter. This case prompted a Scottish Law Commission consultation[149] and an Act of the Scottish Parliament was eventually passed.[150] Under this statute, it is now possible to prosecute partners of a dissolved firm or hold partners legally responsible where a change in the membership has taken place.[151]

This same issue, i.e. the fact that, on dissolution, the firm ceases to have legal personality, could potentially create problems in the context of leases of heritable property. In practice, the lease is likely to contain a clause providing that it lapses on dissolution of the partnership, or, alternatively, that assignation is permitted prior to dissolution. Even if neither of these clauses is inserted into the lease, the general rule at common law is that the lease will terminate when the partnership is dissolved.[152] In *Lujo Properties Ltd v Green*[153] the tenants under a lease were a firm of solicitors which was dissolved when one of the partners left the partnership. Practically speaking, on dissolution of the partnership, there ceased to be any "tenant" under the lease. The landlords attempted to hold the individual partners liable for the remainder of the rent notwithstanding the dissolution of the partnership. Following *Inland Revenue Commissioners v Graham's Trustees*,[154] it was held that because the lease was assignable, it would revive on assignation to a new tenant. In the absence of such an assignation, the individual partners were held liable under s.38 for the rent due for the unexpired term of the lease.[155]

PARTNERS' RIGHTS IN RESPECT OF APPLICATION OF PARTNERSHIP PROPERTY

On dissolution of the partnership, every partner is entitled to have the property of the partnership **8.5.4** applied in payment of the debts and liabilities of the firm.[156] Surplus assets available after payment of debts and liabilities will be valued so that sums representing each partner's share in such assets can be distributed amongst the partners.[157] Although it would be preferable for the partnership to be wound up by the remaining partners, an individual partner or his representatives is entitled to apply to the court to wind up the business and affairs of the partnership.[158]

The 1890 Act contains provision for repayment of a premium, as opposed to a partner's capital contribution, which a partner paid in order to join the partnership,[159] although payment of such premiums appears to be rare in a modern context.

Particularly difficult problems may arise in connection with the calculation of the individual share payable to a retiring partner or to the representatives of a deceased partner. The method of calculation may be governed by the partnership agreement. The partner's share may be calculated by reference to the amount standing at the individual partner's credit in the balance sheet of the partnership accounts for the previous year. However, valuation of capital assets can be problematic. Difficulties may arise

---

[148] *Balmer, Petitioners* [2008] HCJAC 44; 2008 S.L.T. 799 at [68] and [79], a conclusion which they indicated was consistent with *Inland Revenue Commissioners v Grahams Trustees*, 1971 S.C. (H.L.) 1.

[149] Scottish Law Commission, *Report on the Criminal Liability of Partnerships* (The Stationery Office, 2011), Scot. Law Com. No. 224.

[150] Partnerships (Prosecution) (Scotland) Act 2013.

[151] The terms of s.38 were also amended to make reference to the new Act.

[152] *Inland Revenue Commissioners v Graham's Trustees*, 1971 S.C. (HL) 1.

[153] *Lujo Properties Ltd v Green*, 1997 S.L.T. 225. Lord Reed drew on Lord Penrose's opinion in this case for the purposes of his analysis of the effect of dissolution in *Duncan v MFV Marigold PD145* [2006] CSOH 128; 2006 S.L.T. 975 at [26].

[154] *Inland Revenue Commissioners v Graham's Trustees*, 1971 S.C. (HL) 1.

[155] See also *Moray Estates Development Co v Butler*, 1999 S.L.T. 1338 and *Primary Health Care Centres (Broadford) Ltd v Ravangave* [2008] CSOH 14; 2008 Hous. L.R. 24, per Lord Glennie at [15], where he states that the liability of the partners under the lease following dissolution of the firm is a cautionary one.

[156] 1890 Act s.39.

[157] 1890 Act s.39.

[158] 1890 Act s.39.

[159] 1890 Act s.40.

because the balance sheet may refer to the value of a partnership asset at its date of acquisition by the partnership, rather than its current market value. The court will require to ascertain, as a matter of interpretation of the partnership agreement, whether the partners intended that the assets should be valued at their current market values or at any other value detailed in the accounts. The difficulties surrounding this question can be illustrated by contrasting two cases.

In *Clark v Watson*[160] the partnership agreement provided that, on the death of one partner, all partnership property was to become the property of the remaining partner and that the representatives of the deceased partner were to be paid a sum which would include amounts representing goodwill, a share of the partnership profits up to the date of death, and the capital standing at the credit of the deceased partner in the "accounts" of the partnership. No further definition of the "accounts" of the partnership was contained in the agreement. The heritable property owned by the partnership was entered in previous annual accounts at its original cost plus the cost of renovations and improvements, a value which was far less than its market value at the time of death. It was held that, in view of the lack of specification on which accounts were to be used, a balance sheet should be drawn up detailing the market values of all property at the date of the partner's death. The deceased partner's share would therefore be calculated using current values. This case can, however, be contrasted with *Thom's Executrix v Russel and Aitken*.[161] The partnership agreement in that case provided for payment to the deceased partner's representatives of the "share standing at his credit in the capital of the firm as may be determined by the partnership auditors". "Capital" was interpreted as meaning the book value of the capital, i.e. the value appearing in the accounts or balance sheet. The court could find no basis on which to order revaluation of the assets of the firm to obtain their market values at the date of death. The share payable to the deceased partner's representatives was not, therefore, calculated using up to date market values of the partnership assets. Clearly, much depends on the court's interpretation of the written partnership agreement. To avoid such unpredictable results, careful drafting covering valuation of partnership assets is required.

Section 44, which can be amended in the partnership agreement, sets out a number of rules governing the final distribution of assets. In relation to losses, it provides:

> "Losses, including losses and deficiencies of capital, shall be paid first out of profits, next out of capital, and lastly, if necessary, by the partners individually in the proportion in which they were entitled to share profits."[162]

Thus, losses are borne by the individual partners not in proportion to the percentages of capital which they originally contributed to the partnership, but rather in proportion to the percentages of profits which they were entitled to draw from the partnership.

8.6   LIMITED PARTNERSHIPS AND LIMITED LIABILITY PARTNERSHIPS

THE LIMITED PARTNERSHIPS ACT 1907

8.6.1 The 1907 Act created the first opportunity in the UK for partners to avoid the general rule of joint and several liability for the debts of the firm. The type of partnership created by this Act was not particularly popular and there are many possible reasons for this. It may be because, under the 1907 Act, not all of the partners can avoid joint and several liability. There must be at least one "general partner", who remains liable for all the debts of the firm.[163] Another possible reason is that, within a year of the Act

---

[160] *Clark v Watson*, 1982 S.L.T. 450.
[161] *Thom's Executrix v Russel and Aitken*, 1983 S.L.T. 335.
[162] 1890 Act s.44(a).
[163] Limited Partnerships Act 1907 ("the 1907 Act") s.4(2).

being passed, the private limited company was introduced. The limited company as a business entity fulfilled the need for limited liability.[164] However, the Act remains in force and appears to be here to stay. In a recent joint consultation paper published by the English and Scottish Law Commissions, its amendment rather than repeal was recommended.[165] It remains popular for agricultural tenancies in Scotland and its attractive tax regime has led to its widespread use in the venture capital industry and in property investment.[166]

The general principles of partnership law, embodied mostly in the 1890 Act, apply to partnerships formed under the 1907 Act except as amended by the latter Act.[167] The limited partnership therefore has separate legal personality in Scotland, but not in England.

Definition

The limited partnership[168] comprises both general partners and limited partners. Whereas the general partner or partners are jointly and severally liable for all the debts and obligations of the firm, the limited partner's liability is, of course, limited to the amount of capital which he has contributed to the firm. There must be at least one general partner and one limited partner in existence at any given time.[169] The limited partner is able to contribute capital or property to the partnership,[170] but is not entitled to take part in the management of the firm nor does he have the power to bind the firm.[171] If the limited partner takes part in management, then he becomes liable for the debts and obligations of the partnership incurred during the period when he was involved in management.[172] Thus the limited partnership is attractive to those who would like to finance a firm without being held jointly and severally liable for the firm's debts. **8.6.1.1**

The Act contains an ambiguous exception to the limited partner's prohibition from participation in management. It states that the limited partner is entitled to inspect the books of the firm and "examine into the state and prospects of the partnership business, and may advise with the partners thereon".[173] The exact meaning of the phrase "advise with" remains subject to doubt, but it appears that it does not mean seek to influence or persuade management in the process of running the firm.[174]

The limited partner must not draw any of his capital during the continuation of the partnership.[175] If he does so, he becomes liable for the debts and obligations of the firm up to the amount withdrawn, i.e. he loses his limited liability.[176]

Incorporation

The limited partnership can only be created through registration with the Registrar of Companies.[177] This contrasts with the position under the 1890 Act where a partnership may arise simply as a matter of **8.6.1.2**

---

[164] Companies Act 1907.

[165] Law Commission and Scottish Law Commission, *Limited Partnerships Act 1907: A Joint Consultation Paper* (The Stationery Office, 2001) (the "Joint Consultation Paper"). Law Commission Consultation Paper No.161; Scottish Law Commission Discussion Paper No.118.

[166] Joint Consultation Paper, paras 1.5–1.6 and 4.49; and see, e.g. *Greck v Henderson Asia Pacific Equity Partners (FP) LP* [2008] CSOH 2.

[167] 1907 Act s.7.

[168] The 1907 Act uses the term "limited partnership" to describe the type of partnership created by the Act. This should not be confused with the limited liability partnership, or LLP, created by the Limited Liability Partnership Act 2000, commented on below at para.8.6.2.

[169] 1907 Act s.4(2). A body corporate may be a partner in a limited partnership; see 1907 Act s.4(4).

[170] 1907 Act s.4(3).

[171] 1907 Act s.6(1).

[172] 1907 Act s.6(1).

[173] 1907 Act s.6(1).

[174] See Joint Consultation Paper, para.4.12, citing *Lindley & Banks on Partnership*, 17th edn (1995), para.31–04 fn.17.

[175] 1907 Act s.4(3).

[176] 1907 Act s.4(3).

[177] 1907 Act ss.5, 8, 8A, 13–15.

agreement between the partners, whether express or implied. If the requirements of the 1907 Act in relation to registration are not complied with, then a partnership under the 1890 Act is created.[178]

The Act contains no provision to de-register a limited partnership, and this may mean that the register lists defunct limited partnerships. Curiously, and in contrast to partnerships created under the 1890 Act or the limited liability partnership under the 2000 Act, the choice of a name for a limited partnership is unregulated.[179]

Management

8.6.1.3 The Act provides a set of default provisions governing management of the limited partnership which, like those contained in s.24 of the 1890 Act, may be amended by the express or implied agreement of the partners.[180] The matters covered are the same as those referred to in s.24, although with amendments to reflect the limited partner's lesser importance in management matters. Thus, differences as to ordinary matters concerned with the partnership business are decided by a majority of the general partners,[181] implying that the limited partner could participate if the matter at issue was an extraordinary rather than an ordinary one.[182] It is possible to introduce a new partner without the consent of the limited partner,[183] although the consent of all the general partners to the introduction will still be required.[184] Although the limited partner is not entitled to dissolve the partnership[185] he does have more freedom than a normal partner in certain respects, reflecting his role as an investor rather than a full partner. The other partners are not entitled to dissolve the partnership simply because the limited partner has permitted his share to be charged in some way,[186] and the limited partner may assign his share in the partnership with the consent of the general partners.[187]

Dissolution

8.6.1.4 Whereas the death or bankruptcy of a general partner will dissolve the limited partnership,[188] the death or bankruptcy of a limited partner will not have this effect.[189] The mental incapacity of the limited partner is not a ground for dissolution of the limited partnership unless his share cannot be otherwise ascertained and realised.[190] In the event of the dissolution of the limited partnership, its affairs are wound up by the general partners unless the court otherwise orders.[191]

8.6.2 THE LIMITED LIABILITY PARTNERSHIP ACT 2000

Introduction

8.6.2.1 The 2000 Act introduced a new form of partnership. Unlike partnerships governed by the 1890 Act, **members** of an LLP (this is the correct term for the 2000 Act) are not subject to unlimited personal liability for the firm's debts. Several factors had pointed towards the need for a new type of partnership.

---

[178] 1907 Act s.5.

[179] Apart from the fact that the name must end in "limited partnership" or "LP", see 1907 Act s.8B(2). This lack of regulation was noted by the Law Commissions in their joint consultation, para.3.32.

[180] 1907 Act s.6(5).

[181] 1907 Act s.6(5)(a).

[182] See Joint Consultation Paper, para.4.23.

[183] 1907 Act s.6(5)(d).

[184] This arises by virtue of the 1890 Act s.24(7).

[185] 1907 Act s.6(5)(e).

[186] 1907 Act s.6(5)(c).

[187] 1907 Act s.6(5)(b).

[188] 1890 Act s.33(1).

[189] 1907 Act s.6(2).

[190] 1907 Act s.6(2). Like the equivalent provision under the 1890 Act, this provision has not been amended for Scotland since the passing of the original Act. The terminology used is therefore out of date.

[191] 1907 Act s.6(3).

The consultation documents which preceded the 2000 Act[192] indicated that, in the government's opinion, partnerships imposing unlimited liability were no longer appropriate in a modern context. Unlimited liability was appropriate in the context of small partnerships characterised by agency and good faith. In such partnerships, partners could "keep a close eye" on the standard of work of their fellow partners. That fact justified joint and several liability on the part of all the partners. However, many modern partnerships operate on a global scale with hundreds of partners. Where that is the case, partners cannot perform this supervisory role. Much of the impetus for reform came from the accountancy and other financial professions, concerned at the level of damages awards for professional negligence.[193] Nevertheless, the new LLP is generally applicable and is not limited for use by professional partnerships alone.

The new LLP could be described as a hybrid between a partnership and a company.[194] Certain advantages of the traditional partnership have been retained, broadly, those which relate to internal management, such as the flexibility in management and favourable tax treatment.[195] Externally, i.e. when one considers the LLP from the standpoint of third parties, the LLP is closer to a limited company. The characteristics which an LLP shares with a company include limited liability and the ability to grant floating charges. These new benefits have, however, come at a price. The insolvency regime applicable to companies is applied to LLPs with necessary amendments. Additionally, the LLP is subject to the same relatively stringent administrative requirements as apply to companies in relation to registration, and preparation and registration of annual accounts and an annual return. Thus, in comparison with the traditional partnership, the LLP has no secrecy of financial arrangements and is subject to higher administrative costs.

The governing legislation

The Act came into force on April 6, 2001.[196] The 2000 Act stipulates that the body of partnership law   **8.6.2.2** (found mostly in the 1890 Act and the 1907 Act) will **not** apply to LLPs in the absence of stipulation to the contrary.[197] The effect of the 2000 Act is to introduce a new and different type of partnership in addition to those which are already possible under the 1890 Act and the 1907 Act. Nevertheless, the "flavour" of the 1890 Act can be seen in many of the provisions of the 2000 Act.[198]

The legislation used to introduce the LLP is not user-friendly. The 2000 Act is a relatively short "framework" Act, and the vast majority of the important provisions are found in two sets of regulations: the Limited Liability Partnerships Regulations 2001 which apply to Great Britain[199]; and the Limited Liability Partnerships (Scotland) Regulations 2001[200] which apply to Scotland only.[201] The regulations apply provisions of companies legislation to LLPs by reference. Thus, the substantive provisions cannot be understood by reading the regulations alone. Reference to the companies legislation as a whole is required, read subject to the amendments enacted by the regulations to tailor the companies legislation to LLPs. Section 8.6.2 of this chapter concerning LLPs will not explore the detail of the provisions of company law applied to LLPs. Rather, it is intended to provide a general guide to the area.

---

[192] See DTI Consultation Paper, *Limited Liability Partnerships: A new form of business association for professions*. DTI, 1997. URN 97/597. DTI, *Limited Liability Partnerships: Draft Bill: A consultation document*. DTI, 1998. URN 98/874. DTI, *Limited Liability Partnerships: Draft Regulations: A consultation document*. DTI, 1999. URN 99/1025. DTI, *Limited Liability Partnerships: Regulatory provisions governing relations between members: A consultation paper*. DTI, 2000. URN 00/617. DTI, *Revised Regulatory Default provisions*. DTI, 2000. URN 00/865.

[193] See e.g. *ADT Ltd v BDO Binder Hamlyn* [1996] B.C.C. 808, in which the partners were held jointly and severally liable for an award of £65 million, only £31 million of which was covered by professional indemnity insurance.

[194] As it was most recently by Lord Carnwath in *Clyde & Co v Bates van Winkelhof* [2014] UKSC 32 at [55].

[195] 2000 Act ss.10 and 11.

[196] See useful comment by S. Cross, "Limited Liability Partnerships Act 2000: problems ahead?" [2003] J.B.L. 268.

[197] 2000 Act s.1(5).

[198] See, e.g. the default provisions governing the mutual rights and duties of the partners at Pt VI regs 7 and 8 of the Limited Liability Partnerships Regulations 2001 (SI 2001/1090), or the agency provisions in the 2000 Act s.6.

[199] Limited Liability Partnerships Regulations 2001 (SI 2001/1090) ("the GB Regulations").

[200] Liability Partnerships (Scotland) Regulations 2001 (SSI 2001/128) ("the Scottish Regulations").

[201] The need for a separate set of Scottish Regulations arises due to the fact that certain insolvency matters are devolved to the Scottish Parliament; Scotland Act 1998 ss.28–30 and Sch.5 para.C2.

In November 2007 a consultative document on the application of the Companies Act 2006 to LLPs was produced by the Department for Business Enterprise and Regulatory Reform.[202] This led to the enactment of regulations governing many of the administrative issues relating to LLPs.[203]

Name

8.6.2.3 The same restrictions on the use of names as are applied to companies by the Companies Act 2006 are applied to LLPs.[204] An LLP should not be registered by a name if, in the opinion of the Secretary of State, its use by the LLP would constitute an offence or is offensive,[205] or gives the impression that the LLP is connected with HM Government or with a local authority.[206] The name of an LLP must be followed by "Limited Liability Partnership" or the permitted abbreviations "llp" or "LLP".[207]

A change in the name of the LLP will require the lodging of a form with the Registrar of Companies which is signed by the designated member[208] and submitted together with a fee.[209] The Registrar will then issue a certificate of change of name and the change will be effective from the date of the certificate.[210]

Definition and incorporation

8.6.2.4 The LLP is described in the 2000 Act as a "new form of legal entity"[211] and a "body corporate".[212] It is specifically stated that the LLP has legal personality separate from its members[213] and that is has unlimited capacity.[214] Thus, whilst the separate legal personality of an LLP was an innovation for English law, it was not for Scots law, where 1890 partnerships too have separate legal personality. This status cannot arise until the LLP has been registered, or, using the language of the legislation, incorporated. In other words, unlike an ordinary partnership which may arise simply through the creation of a relationship without registration, an LLP can only be created through registration.

Before an LLP can be incorporated, by virtue of s.2(1)(a), two or more persons associated for carrying on a lawful business with a view to profit must subscribe an incorporation document.[215] The subscribers must complete the relevant form and lodge it with the Registrar of Companies.[216]

This incorporation document contains information such as the name of the LLP,[217] the address of its registered office,[218] and the names and addresses of each of the persons who are to be members of the

---

[202] Department for Business Enterprise and Regulatory Reform, "Application of the Companies Act 2006 to Limited Liability Partnerships: a consultative document", November 2007.

[203] The most important of these are the: (i) Limited Liability Partnership (Accounts and Audit) (Application of Companies Act 2006) Regulations 2008 (SI 2008/1911); (ii) Small Limited Liability Partnerships (Accounts) Regulations 2008 (SI 2008/1912); (iii) Large and Medium Sized Limited Liability Partnerships (Accounts) Regulations 2008 (SI 2008/1913); and (iv) Limited Liability Partnerships (Application of Companies Act 2006) Regulations 2009 (SI 2009/1804).

[204] The Limited Liability Partnerships (Application of Companies Act 2006) Regulations 2009 (SI 2009/1804). See also the Company, Limited Liability Partnerships and Business Names (Miscellaneous Provisions) (Amendment) Regulations 2009 (SI 2009/2404) and the Companies and Business Names (Miscellaneous Provisions) Regulations 2009 (SI 2009/1085).

[205] The Limited Liability Partnerships (Application of Companies Act 2006) Regulations 2009 (SI 2009/1804) reg.8, applying the Companies Act 2006 s.53.

[206] The Limited Liability Partnerships (Application of Companies Act 2006) Regulations 2009 (SI 2009/1804) reg.8, applying the Companies Act 2006 s.54.

[207] 2000 Act Sch.1 Pt I para.2(1).

[208] See para.8.6.2.7 below for the meaning of "designated member".

[209] 2000 Act Sch.1 Pt I paras 4(1), 5.

[210] 2000 Act Sch.1 Pt I para.5(3)(b).

[211] 2000 Act s.1(1).

[212] 2000 Act s.1(2).

[213] 2000 Act s.1(2).

[214] 2000 Act s.1(3).

[215] 2000 Act s.2(1)(a).

[216] If the registered office is located in Scotland, then the form should be lodged with the Registrar in Scotland; 2000 Act s.2(1)(b). The same provisions apply mutatis mutandis for an LLP with its registered office in England.

[217] 2000 Act s.2(2)(b).

[218] 2000 Act s.2(2)(d). The LLP must have a registered office at all times: see 2000 Act Sch.1 Pt II para.9(1).

LLP on incorporation (although such members may be legal persons such as incorporated companies or Scottish partnerships, rather than natural persons).[219] It also identifies the designated and non-designated members.[220] The form is signed by each of the members and also by a solicitor or agent acting for the members in the formation of the LLP, and is submitted by one of those persons to the Registrar together with a registration fee. In addition to the incorporation document, that person must also deliver to the Registrar a statement confirming that the requirements of s.2(1)(a) of the 2000 Act have been complied with, i.e. that the partnership comprises two or more person associated for carrying on lawful business with a view of profit.[221] The LLP agreement itself need not be registered and is therefore not available to the public. Thus, although members of the public have a certain degree of protection, being able to find out the names of the members, secrecy is maintained as regards the internal management of the LLP.

Provided that the incorporation form is in order, the Registrar will issue a certificate of incorporation which bears the date of incorporation, the LLP's registered number and indicates that the LLP is a limited liability partnership.[222] Because the LLP only comes into existence once the Registrar has issued a certificate of incorporation, only once this has occurred may the LLP commence trading.

Despite the fact that the LLP may only be incorporated if it has two members, if membership falls below two, the LLP will continue to exist until it has been dissolved using the relevant winding-up procedures contained in the 2000 Act. If one member alone knowingly continues to trade for more than six months, he becomes jointly and severally liable with the LLP for the debts of the LLP contracted during that period.[223]

It is possible for a partnership originally formed under the 1890 Act to become incorporated as an LLP under the 2000 Act and indeed many of the Scottish law firms have done so. The case of *Re Rogers (Deceased)*[224] is an example of the English courts taking a pragmatic approach to a succession issue involved in this particular situation. In that case a will drawn up by a law firm appointed the partners in that firm (or in any firm which succeeded to it and carried on its practice) as the deceased's executors. The Bristol Probate Registry initially refused to grant probate to two of the partners of the original firm who were now members of the newly formed LLP. In the context of an action for declaration that the LLP was the "firm" which succeeded to the practice of the original firm, Lightman J concluded that the clause of the will could "embrace" the profit-sharing members of the LLP, but not employees or salaried partners of the LLP.[225]

Annual return

The LLP is subject to the same legislation which applies to companies in relation to completing and lodging with the Registrar of Companies an annual return and annual accounts.[226] **8.6.2.5**

Changes in membership

A member may cease to be a member in several ways, i.e. as a matter of agreement between the members, through death or through dissolution of the LLP.[227] He may also cease to be a member by giving "reasonable notice" to the other members.[228] "Reasonable notice" is not defined in the Act, **8.6.2.6**

---

[219] 2000 Act s.2(2)(e).

[220] See para.8.6.2.7 below for the meaning of "designated member".

[221] 2000 Act s.2(1)(c).

[222] 2000 Act s.3.

[223] 2000 Act s.4A.

[224] *Re Rogers (Deceased)* [2006] EWHC 753 (Ch); [2006] 1 W.L.R. 1577.

[225] See J. Morris, "Re Rogers: a solution for LLPs, but a problem for salaried partners?" [2006] P.C.B. 303.

[226] The Limited Liability Partnerships (Accounts and Audit) (Application of Companies Act 2006) Regulations 2008 (SI 2008/1911).

[227] 2000 Act s.4(3).

[228] 2000 Act s.4(3).

although the members may have defined this expression in the written LLP agreement. Any person may, after incorporation of the LLP, become a member by agreement with the existing members.[229]

Where any person becomes or ceases to be a member, notification must be made to the Registrar on the relevant form within 14 days.[230] This form must be signed by the designated member,[231] and by a new member if the change is the appointment of that new member. Any changes in the name or address of an existing member must also be notified to the Registrar within 28 days.[232] Again, the relevant form must be signed by both the member it relates to and a designated member. Failure to comply with these requirements constitutes an offence on the part of the LLP and also on the part of every designated member[233] unless he can show that he took all reasonable steps to ensure that the requirements were complied with.[234]

Designated members

8.6.2.7 On incorporation of the LLP, the incorporation form must indicate which members are designated and which are non-designated members.[235] A designated member is a member who has the same legal responsibilities as the other members, but has additional administrative responsibilities. His duties include ensuring that the LLP complies with the LLP legislation, notifying the Registrar of changes in membership or names and addresses of members, preparing the annual return, appointing an auditor, signing the annual accounts and delivering them to the Registrar, and acting on behalf of the LLP where it is being wound up or dissolved. There must be at least two designated members at any given time.[236] If two designated members are not identified on the incorporation form, then all members of the LLP are automatically designated members.[237] Once a member ceases to be a member of the LLP, his status as a designated member also terminates.[238]

Relationship of members

8.6.2.8 The general rule is that the internal management of the LLP is determined as a matter of agreement between the members.[239] A partnership agreement made prior to the enactment of the 2000 Act may continue to govern a partnership once it becomes an LLP through registration under the 2000 Act.[240] Default provisions govern internal management where the partners have not covered a specific issue in their LLP agreement.[241] Such provisions, contained in the GB regulations, are very similar to those which are contained in the 1890 Act which have already been commented on.[242] Some of these default rules applying to LLPs are fiduciary in nature, for example those which prevent the member from competing with the LLP[243] or require him to account for any benefit he has obtained through the use of the LLP name without the consent of the other members.[244] Recently, Sales J in an English case decided, on the facts of that particular case, that the members did not owe fiduciary duties to one another.[245] This

---

[229] 2000 Act s.4(2).
[230] 2000 Act s.9(1)(a).
[231] For the meaning of "designated member" see para.8.6.2.7 below.
[232] 2000 Act s.9(1)(b).
[233] 2000 Act s.9(4). For the meaning of "designated member" see para.8.6.2.7 below.
[234] 2000 Act s.9(5).
[235] 2000 Act s.8(1).
[236] 2000 Act s.8.
[237] 2000 Act s.8(2).
[238] 2000 Act s.8(6).
[239] 2000 Act s.5(1)(a).
[240] 2000 Act s.5(2).
[241] GB Regulations Pt VI regs 7, 8.
[242] See 1890 Act s.24 and para.8.4 above.
[243] GB Regulations Pt VI reg.7(9).
[244] GB Regulations Pt VI reg.7(10).
[245] *F&C Alternative Investments (Holdings) Ltd v Bathelemy* [2011] EWHC 1731 (Ch); [2011] EWHC 1851 (Ch); [2012] Bus. L.R. 884; [2012] 3 W.L.R. 10; [2011] EWHC 2807 (Ch); [2012] Bus. L.R. 891. Appealed on costs only [2012] EWCA Civ 843; [2013] 1 W.L.R. 548; [2012] 4 All E.R. 1096; [2013] 1 W.L.R. 548.

is a reflection of the fact that s.1(5) of the 2000 Act provides that the mutual rights and duties of the members shall be governed primarily by agreement, and also the fact that the generality of partnership law, including the 1890 Act, does not apply to LLPs. Although the case in question was relatively low level, there is no reason to suspect that it would not be treated as persuasive in Scotland, there being no evidence that it was envisaged that the 2000 Act would apply in a different manner in Scotland and England.

Each of the members is an agent for the LLP[246] and rules which are similar to those contained in the 1890 Act apply in relation to the implied authority of the member.[247]

Liability of individual members for negligence

In order to illustrate the rules on liabilities of members, it is useful to rehearse the position under an **8.6.2.9** 1890 partnership first. In a partnership governed by the 1890 Act, a client who suffers a loss due to the negligent work of a partner has remedies in both contract and delict. His contractual remedy is available primarily against the firm as a separate legal entity, but also against the individual partners who are jointly and severally liable in terms of s.4(2) of the 1890 Act. In other words, if the assets of the firm are insufficient to meet his claim, each partner is individually liable for the whole amount of the debt. If one partner is required to meet the debt in full, he then has a right of relief against the other partners, enabling him to raise an action against them to ensure that the debt is paid in accordance with the shares stipulated in the partnership agreement.[248] A delictual remedy is available against the negligent partner under normal principles of delictual liability for pure economic loss, dependant therefore on proof of an assumption of responsibility by that particular partner.[249]

In the case of LLPs, the client retains his contractual remedy against the LLP as a separate legal entity. This is because the contract exists between that client and the LLP. The client does not, however, have a contractual action against the individual members. Members individually are not jointly and severally liable. The partner simply acts as an agent of the LLP.[250] The lack of joint and several liability on the part of members in an LLP is the most significant difference between partnerships governed by the 1890 Act and those formed under the 2000 Act. In an LLP, the client retains his delictual remedy against the member who has been negligent, provided that a duty of care can be established. This delictual action is therefore the only action available to the client against an individual member of an LLP.

Execution of documents

The Scottish Regulations inserted new provisions into the Requirements of Writing (Scotland) Act **8.6.2.10** 1995 relating to the execution of documents.[251] A document is signed by the LLP if it is signed on its behalf by a member of the LLP.[252] In order to benefit from a statutory presumption as to authenticity of the execution of the document, it must either be subscribed by two members,[253] or subscription by a single member must be witnessed.[254]

---

[246] 2000 Act s.6(1).

[247] 2000 Act s.6(2); and see 1890 Act s.5. See para.8.3.3 above.

[248] Or, if there is no written partnership agreement, by reference to the default rule contained in Partnership Act 1890 s.24(1).

[249] *Hedley Byrne & Co v Heller & Partners* [1964] A.C. 456. On the liability of a company director in this type of situation, see *Williams v Natural Health Foods Ltd* [1998] 1 W.L.R. 830. There are, as yet, no cases on the application of this principle to members of an LLP, but see *Merrett v Babb* [2001] EWCA Civ 214; [2001] Q.B. 1174, and comment by J. Cooke, "Babb and solicitor's negligence: can LLP status provide complete protection from personal liability?" [2006] Professional Negligence 106.

[250] 2000 Act s.6(1). The terms of the legislation which set out the agency relationship are very similar to those contained in the 1890 Act.

[251] See Requirements of Writing (Scotland) Act 1985 Sch.2 para.3A, inserted by the Scottish Regulations Sch.4 para.5.

[252] Requirements of Writing (Scotland) Act 1985 Sch.2 para.3A(5)(a)(1)(a).

[253] Requirements of Writing (Scotland) Act 1985 Sch.2 para.3A(5)(a)(1A).

[254] Requirements of Writing (Scotland) Act 1985 Sch.2 para.3A(5)(a)(1)(b).

Securities and floating charges

8.6.2.11 An LLP has the ability to grant securities and floating charges, which must be registered with the Registrar of Companies in the same way as those granted by companies.[255]

Insolvency

8.6.2.12 As stated above, in return for the benefit of limited liability, LLPs became subject to the more stringent insolvency rules applying to companies. This is achieved through the application to LLPs of the relevant provisions of the Insolvency Act 1986 (with appropriate amendments).[256] Thus, LLPs can enter into voluntary arrangements, or be subject to procedures such as administration, receivership and voluntary and compulsory winding-up.

　　If the LLP is wound up, present and past members who have agreed to be liable to contribute to the assets of the LLP in the event of liquidation will be liable to the extent so agreed.[257] In this respect, an LLP is similar to a company limited by guarantee. Aside from such agreement, an individual member may become liable for the debts of the LLP when it is wound up under what has become known as the "claw back" provisions. A member of an LLP, or any person who has been a member within the period of two years prior to the winding up of the LLP, may be liable to contribute towards claims of creditors if he withdrew any property of the LLP during that period.[258] The form of the withdrawal makes little difference—the provisions apply to withdrawals in the form of shares of profits, salaries, repayment or payment of interest on a loan to the LLP or any other withdrawal.[259] "Property" is also widely defined as any asset of the LLP. The payments made to a fixed share member could be construed as a relevant withdrawal of property, leaving the fixed share partner liable to pay back his payments.

　　In order to achieve such a "claw back", a liquidator, where the LLP is in insolvent liquidation, must apply to the court for an order. The liquidator must prove that, at the time of the withdrawal, the member knew or had reasonable grounds to believe that the LLP was unable to pay its debts,[260] or knew or had reasonable grounds to believe that the LLP would become unable to meet its debts as a result of that withdrawal taken together with any other withdrawals made (or contemplated) at the same time. Therefore, it is not sufficient for the member simply to check that the withdrawal that he is making does not place the LLP in the position of being unable to pay its debts. That member must also check whether any other members have made relevant withdrawals at the same time as his which, collectively, would have this effect on the LLP.

　　If the court is satisfied that these conditions are met it may issue a declaration that the member should contribute to the assets of the LLP in such a manner as it thinks fit. However, the court is not entitled to make such a declaration unless the member knew or ought to have concluded that after each withdrawal there was no reasonable prospect that the LLP would avoid going into insolvent liquidation.

　　The Scottish Regulations apply to LLPs the provisions of the Insolvency Act 1986 and Companies Act 2006 applicable to companies in relation to fraudulent and wrongful trading.[261]

Disqualification

8.6.2.13 Members of LLPs can be disqualified in the same way as directors of companies through the application of the Company Directors' Disqualification Act 1986 to members of LLPs.[262] A member of an LLP

---

[255] Companies Act 1985 s.462 as amended by the Scottish Regulations reg.3 and Sch.1.

[256] See 2000 Act s.14 and Insolvency Act 1986 ss.50–72, as amended by the Scottish Regulations reg.4(1) and Sch.2.

[257] Insolvency Act 1986 s.74, as amended by the GB Regulations reg.5 and Sch.3.

[258] Insolvency Act 1986 s.214A, as amended by the Scottish Regulations reg.4(2) and Sch.3.

[259] Insolvency Act 1986 s.214A(2)(a), as amended by the Scottish Regulations reg.4(2) and Sch.3.

[260] Insolvency Act 1986 s.123(1)(c), as amended by the Scottish Regulations reg.4(2) and Sch.3.

[261] Insolvency Act 1986 ss.212–215, as amended by the Scottish Regulations reg.4(2) and Sch.3.

[262] Company Directors Disqualification Act 1986, as amended by the GB Regulations reg.4(2) and Sch.2 Pt II.

can be disqualified from acting either as a member or as a director of a company. Similarly, a disqualified company director can hold neither role.[263]

Minority protection

Section 4(3) of the 2000 Act provides that any member may cease to be a member in accordance with **8.6.2.14** an agreement with the other members. Thus, as is the case under partnerships governed by the 1890 Act, it is possible for a member to be expelled. As was the case with 1890 partnerships, with LLPs too, a default rule provides that a member cannot be expelled unless a power to do so is contained in the written partnership agreement.[264] A recent English case suggests that where there is no written partnership agreement, the courts will not easily reach the conclusion that a power to expel was orally agreed.[265] Having decided that there was no power to expel, the court did not have to decide whether such power must be exercised in good faith. This is an interesting question given that the generality of partnership law (including, one would assume, authorities such as *Blisset v Daniel*[266]) does not apply to LLPs.[267] The rules under company law relating to minority protection will also apply to members in this type of situation.[268]

---

[263] Company Directors Disqualification Act 1986, as amended by the GB Regulations reg.4(2) and Sch.2 Pt II.

[264] GB Regulations reg.8.

[265] *Eaton v Caulfield* [2011] EWHC 173; [2011] B.C.C. 386.

[266] (1853) 10 Hare 493.

[267] Proudman J seems to suggest, (albeit obliquely, at [25]) that *Blisset v Daniel* might apply to LLPs. His statement is, as explained in the text above, obiter.

[268] Just and equitable winding-up under s.122(1)(g) of the Insolvency Act 1986, becoming s.122(1)(e) as applied to LLPs by Sch.3 to the GB Regulations; or unfairly prejudicial conduct under s.994 of the Companies Act 2006, applied to LLPs by the Limited Liability Partnerships (Application of Companies Act 2006) Regulations 2009 (SI 2009/1804) regs 2 and 48. The operation of both of these sections tends to be excluded by the limited liability partnership agreement in LLPs subject to the 2000 Act, see T. Williams and D. Sutherland, "Partnerships: Limited Thinking", *The Lawyer*, October 22, 2007. For the operation of s.994 to an LLP see *F&C Alternative Investments (Holdings) Ltd v Bathelemy* [2011] EWHC 1731 (Ch); [2011] EWHC 1851 (Ch); [2012] Bus. L.R. 884; [2012] 3 W.L.R. 10; [2011] EWHC 2807 (Ch); [2012] Bus. L.R. 891. Appealed on costs only [2012] EWCA Civ 843; [2013] 1 W.L.R. 548; [2012] 4 All E.R. 1096; [2013] 1 W.L.R. 548.

Chapter 9

Commercial Dispute Resolution

INTRODUCTION

A work of this kind would be incomplete without some indication of the means by which commercial **9.1** disputes are resolved. Since this work has followed the traditional approach of elaborating the rights conferred and obligations imposed on parties by the law, the first thought a reader may have is that parties may resort to the courts whenever disputes arise. Yet disputes may not directly relate to the parties' rights and obligations, or may not do so exclusively, while it is possible for the parties to achieve a rights-based determination of their dispute without involving the courts. Accordingly, while litigation is commonly resorted to, parties may prefer to settle a dispute via arbitration, or seek more consensual means of resolving disputes such as mediation. All will be considered below. It should also be borne in mind that parties may to some extent safeguard themselves against defective performance by the other party through devices such as liquidated damages clauses and retention of title clauses, while the essential principle of Scots contract law that allows a party to withhold performance in response to the other's breach may also offer some recourse.

The previous edition of the book noted that the operation of the dispute resolution "system"[1] was under scrutiny in the form of the Scotttish Civil Justice Review chaired by Lord Justice Clerk Gill (as he was then).[2] Following a consultation paper in November 2007, the Review reported in September 2009. Since then the Scottish Civil Justice Council, charged with keeping the civil justice system under review and making rules for the civil courts, was created by the Scottish Civil Justice Council and Criminal Legal Assistance (Scotland) Act 2013. The Scottish Government issued a consultation paper on legislation to implement the recommendations of the Gill Review in February 2013, *Making Justice Work: the Courts Reform (Scotland) Bill*. The Courts Reform (Scotland) Bill 2014 is before the Scottish Parliament at the time of writing. If it passes in its current form, it will, inter alia, largely consolidate the Sheriff Court Acts of 1907 and 1971; introduce a new "simple procedure" to the sheriff court which will replace summary causes and small claims; reserve all actions where £150,000 or less is sought for the sheriff court, although the possibility will exist that a sheriff can remit such a case to the Court of Session where its importance or difficulty makes this appropriate; and introduce the sheriff appeal court. All appeals from the decisions of sheriffs in civil matters will be made to this court, and it will no longer be possible to appeal directly to the Inner House from the sheriff, although provision is to be made for the sheriff appeal court to refer appeals to the Inner House where they involve complex or novel points of law. It can be appreciated then that certain aspects of the litigation system described below may soon be altered.

9.2   LITIGATION

WHY LITIGATE?

9.2.1 Taking litigation, as the paradigmatic form of legal dispute resolution, as our starting point, the question might be asked why a party might wish to litigate in the first place. The short answer is, of course, that litigation is the primary means provided by the legal system whereby a party might vindicate his rights. Yet, litigation may often be regarded as a last resort. This is due to a variety of factors. Firstly, litigation is public, and matters revealed in litigation, not to say the very fact of litigation itself, can be damaging to the commercial interests of the parties. Secondly, litigation, especially in the adversarial Scottish system, may be harmful to the commercial relationship between the parties in cases where this is an issue of importance. Thirdly, litigation can be immensely protracted. Fourthly, it can also be very costly. Finally, it is designed (as it inevitably must be) to resolve the legal issue between the parties without reference to their wider interests.

JURISDICTION

9.2.2 Assuming that a party decides to litigate, the first issue is whether the court has jurisdiction to entertain his claim. It may be that its jurisdiction has been contractually excluded, as where the parties are bound by an arbitration clause. Such a clause may be ignored by the parties, but if one party pleads its existence, the court is usually compelled (see para.9.3.5) to decline jurisdiction.[3] More fundamentally,

---

[1] H. Genn, *Solving Civil Justice Problems* (Glasgow: Scottish Consumer Council, 2005), suggests that there is no such thing as a civil justice system as civil justice involves a bewildering variety of actors, issues and dispute resolution mechanisms.

[2] This derives from the Scottish Executive Paper, *Modern Laws for a Modern Scotland: A Report on Civil Justice in Scotland* (Edinburgh: Scottish Executive, 2007), which in turn was prompted by the Scottish Consumer Council Report, *The Civil Justice System in Scotland—A Case for Review?* (Glasgow: Scottish Consumer Council, 2005).

[3] *Sanderson v Armour & Co*, 1922 S.C. (HL) 117.

however, the court may not have jurisdiction to begin with. Thus a court may not have jurisdiction because of the nature of the relief sought—certain remedies, e.g. inhibition, may only be sought in the Court of Session—or because of the value of the claim—claims below £5,000 are currently confined to the sheriff court. Alternatively, no Scottish court may have jurisdiction. While it is always possible for parties to invoke the jurisdiction of the Scottish courts in cases where they would not otherwise have jurisdiction,[4] generally there must be a connection between Scotland and the dispute or at least one of the parties. The main ground of jurisdiction is the domicile of the defender,[5] i.e. residence in the case of an individual,[6] the registered office or other official address where central management or control is exercised in the case of a corporation or association.[7] Other situations where the courts might have jurisdiction include where Scotland is the place of performance of the contract,[8] where proceedings relate to moveable property situated in Scotland,[9] where they arise out of the operations of an offshoot of a business or undertaking which is situated in Scotland,[10] or if interdict is sought to restrain a wrong committed in Scotland.[11]

Where the contract is a consumer contract, a consumer domiciled in Scotland may bring proceedings against the other party in Scotland,[12] and (with certain exceptions)[13] may only have proceedings brought against him in Scotland.[14] A consumer contract has a specialised definition in this context. Firstly, it is a contract concluded by a person for a purpose outside his trade or profession,[15] so that a business may sometimes qualify to be regarded as a consumer.[16] Secondly, it must be a contract for a loan repayable in instalments,[17] or a sale of goods by credit,[18] or any other contract concluded with a person who pursues commercial or professional activities in Scotland where the contract falls within the scope of such activities.[19] Finally, transport contracts are excluded.[20]

The issue of the law applicable to the contract has no effect on jurisdiction. Thus if a ground of jurisdiction is established, the Scottish courts will hear a case, even though the contract is governed by a foreign law such as English law.

REMEDIES

It is a characteristic of adjudicatory forms of dispute resolution that remedies may be sought. Most of **9.2.3** the remedies available through litigation are also available through arbitration, albeit that in certain cases the arbitral tribunal may require the assistance of a court to enforce an award against a recalcitrant party. So in both cases, a party may submit a claim for payment or a claim (or counterclaim) for damages, or even ask for an interdict or specific implement. However, whereas it is always open to a party to litigate (unless that right is barred by an agreement to arbitrate), arbitration is not open at the instance of one party unless the parties have bound themselves to arbitrate. Equally, only a court can compulsorily sist a third party to the proceedings, or order arrestment of the defender's funds

---

[4] Civil Jurisdiction and Judgments Act 1982 Sch.8 r.6.
[5] See Sch.8 r.1.
[6] See s.41.
[7] See s.42.
[8] See Sch.8 r.2(b).
[9] See Sch.8 r.2(i).
[10] See Sch.8 r.2(f).
[11] See Sch.8 r.2(j).
[12] See Sch.8 r.3(3)(b).
[13] See Sch.8 r.2(i).
[14] See Sch.8 r.3(4).
[15] See Sch.8 r.3(1).
[16] *Chris Hart (Business Sales) Ltd v Niven*, 1992 S.L.T (Sh Ct) 53.
[17] See Sch.8 r.3(1)(b).
[18] See Sch.8 r.3(1)(a).
[19] See Sch.8 r.3(1)(c).
[20] See Sch.8 r.3(2). This exclusion, however, does not extend to contracts which for an exclusive price provide for a combination of travel and accommodation, i.e. package holiday contracts.

on the dependence of the action, and only the Court of Session can grant inhibition or reduction of a deed.

WHICH COURT?

9.2.4 If the parties have determined on litigation as the means of settling their dispute, the next question is in which court should the pursuer raise the action. The choice will be between the Court of Session and the appropriate sheriff court. The value of the claim may dictate the answer, as the Court of Session cannot entertain any claim which does not exceed £5,000 (although this will rise to £150,000 if the Courts Reform (Scotland) Bill 2014 becomes law), exclusive of interest and expenses, so that such claims must be heard in the sheriff court.[21] By contrast, there is no upper limit on the value of claims which may be heard in either court. So it is entirely possible for claims involving many millions of pounds to be heard in the sheriff court. Whether a pursuer will choose to bring a case in the sheriff court or not will depend on a variety of factors such as his perception of the complexity of the issues and his judgment as to the court best able to handle these, whether he feels counsel should be involved, and considerations of convenience, cost and time. Obviously, if the point is one in relation to which there is likely to be an appeal or a series of appeals—as where a point of fundamental importance is being decided for the first time—the Court of Session might be regarded as more likely to deliver an authoritative answer, while the ladder of appeals from there is shorter than from the sheriff court.

This is not a book on civil procedure, so what follows is a very summary account of how a case might be dealt with in both the sheriff court and the Court of Session.

ORDINARY ACTIONS IN THE SHERIFF COURT

9.2.5 To raise an ordinary action in the sheriff court, the pursuer serves an initial writ on the other party.[22] That party has 21 days from the date of service to respond,[23] failing which the pursuer can request a decree in absence.[24] If the other party does timeously intimate an intention to defend, he has 35 days from the date of service of the writ to lodge written defences with the court.[25] If either party considers that the case lodged for the other side has no real prospect of success, he may apply for a summary decree.[26] Otherwise, the case will call in court for the first time in an options hearing, which will usually occur no earlier than 10 weeks after the expiry of the above mentioned 21 day period,[27] although it may occur earlier if the sheriff so decides or the parties so agree.[28] The writ and any defences may be adjusted at any time up to 14 days before the hearing.[29] An options hearing is so called, because the sheriff has a number of options available, and should select that which should expedite the case.[30] These options include:

- setting a date for a proof, i.e. a hearing at which the parties can lead evidence in support of their respective cases;
- giving the parties further time to adjust their pleadings;
- setting a date for a debate on a point of law which they consider ought to be decided before evidence is led because if it is established it, "would lead to a decree in favour of any party, or

---

[21] The Sheriff Courts (Scotland) Act 1971 (Privative Jurisdiction and Summary Cause) Order 2007 (SSI 2007/507) art.2.

[22] Act of Sederunt (Sheriff Court Ordinary Cause Rules) 1993 (SI 1993/1956) r.3.1.

[23] See r.3.6.(1)(a). The period is 42 days if the defender is not resident or does not have a place of business in Europe: r.3.6.(1)(b). The sheriff may lengthen or shorten these periods on cause shown, but never to a period of less than two days: r.3.6.(2), (3).

[24] See r.7.

[25] See r.9.6.

[26] See r.17.

[27] See r.9.2.

[28] See r.9.2A.

[29] See r.9.8.

[30] See r.9.12.

to limitation of proof to any substantial degree".[31] Thus if for example, the defender argues that the pursuer's case is legally irrelevant, i.e. even if the facts alleged are proved they disclose no cause of action, then there may be some sense in determining this issue in order to decide whether a proof would serve any purpose; and

- setting a date for a proof before answer—this might arise when a point of law has been raised, but the sheriff feels unable to answer it until he has heard the facts, for example the defender may deny supplying goods which suffered from the defect alleged by the pursuer, but plead that even if this were true, the defect in question would not be sufficient to render the goods unsatisfactory. A sheriff may well feel unable to pronounce on the issue of satisfactory quality until the facts are established.

If the case is going to proof, parties will be expected to lodge any production (usually documents) on which they have founded in their pleadings,[32] while there are procedures which enable parties to recover documents or other property held by the other party or by a third party. Naturally, each side may call whichever witnesses it chooses, and such witnesses can be forced to attend and (subject to issues of privilege) to testify, on pain of contempt, although it is possible to admit affidavit evidence. Usually, a good many facts are agreed or admitted, and so need not be the subject of proof. A proof may be spread over a number of days, sometimes separated by significant periods of time. An appeal lies either to the sheriff principal, or directly to the Inner House, and any appeal may ultimately be taken to the Supreme Court. Appeals are not restricted to points of law. The Courts Reform (Scotland) Bill 2014 proposes to create the sheriff appeal court. All appeals from the decisions of sheriffs in civil matters will be made to this court, and it will no longer be possible to appeal directly to the Inner House from the sheriff.

SUMMARY CAUSES IN THE SHERIFF COURT

Introduced in 1976, the summary cause procedure is a streamlined version of that described above, **9.2.6** which is utilised when the amount sought is no more than £5,000, but above £3,000.[33] (The Courts Reform (Scotland) Bill 2014 intends to introduce a new "simple procedure" to the sheriff court which will replace summary causes.) The summons is completed via a pre-printed form, requiring a statement of the details of the claim.[34] If the other party wishes to defend the claim, he must state that defence in his response to the summons.[35] There are no extensive written pleadings, and thus little scope for adjustment of pleadings. Essentially, as long as the broad details of the claim and defence are clear, the issue can proceed to proof. At that stage, the sheriff may dismiss the claim because it is clearly incompetent, or they clearly lack jurisdiction.[36] Otherwise, they must seek to negotiate a settlement between the parties, and only if settlement cannot be achieved will they proceed to try the case.[37] If the sheriff is satisfied that the key facts of the case are in essence agreed, they may decide the case at its first hearing without going to proof.[38] There is no scope for debating a point of law prior to proof. If he so chooses, at the first calling of the case a party may represent himself or be represented by an authorised lay person rather than a solicitor or advocate, while the sheriff may even permit lay representation at the proof.[39] The sheriff may give his decision verbally at the proof or in writing within 28 days thereafter.[40]

---

[31] See r.9.12(3)(c).
[32] See r.21.
[33] The Sheriff Courts (Scotland) Act 1971 (Privative Jurisdiction and Summary Cause) Order 2007 (SSI 2007/507) art.3.
[34] Act of Sederunt (Summary Cause Rules) 2002 (SSI 2002/132) r.4.
[35] See r.8.1.
[36] See r.8.3.1.
[37] See r.8.3.2.
[38] See r.8.3.3(d).
[39] See rr.2, 2A.
[40] See r.8.18.

The streamlined procedure obviously makes the process quicker and less expensive. Other factors also contribute to minimising expense. Thus evidence is not recorded but noted by the sheriff themselves,[41] court dues are lower, as are the fees recoverable as judicial expenses while, although the rules relating to the citing of witnesses and the lodging of productions are essentially the same as in relation to an ordinary action, the modest sums at stake would tend to make parties reluctant to incur significant costs in presenting their cases. An appeal lies on a point of law to the sheriff principal, with a further, very limited, right of appeal to the Inner House, but only if the sheriff principal certifies that the case is suitable for appeal to the Inner House.[42]

SMALL CLAIMS IN THE SHERIFF COURT

9.2.7 In 1988 an even more streamlined form of procedure was introduced, designed to be still more accessible and less expensive than the summary cause procedure. This was the small claims procedure and it operates when no more than £3,000[43] is sought. A small claim is essentially a variant of a summary cause and the procedures are very similar. The new "simple procedure" to be introduced by the Courts Reform (Scotland) Bill 2014 will replace both summary causes and small claims. However, the small claims procedure is premised on the view that the pursuer (and possibly the defender) will represent himself (although legal representation is permitted), so that the sheriff is intended to take a very active role in the conduct of the case. Thus, although the pursuer must still provide the defender with fair notice of his claim,[44] it is the sheriff who is required to identify the issues in the case.[45] Moreover, they are entitled to conduct hearings entirely as they see fit, without regard to the normal rules of evidence and procedure, while the rules specifically state that a hearing "shall be conducted as informally as the circumstances of the claim permit".[46] It is fair to say that not every sheriff is pleased to have this type of freedom.[47] A small claim is initiated in much the same way as a summary cause, but where the pursuer is an individual, the sheriff clerk will themselves arrange for the service of the summons on the defender.[48] If the claim is disputed, the defender so indicates by completing the relevant part of the form and returning it to the sheriff clerk.[49] If no response is lodged by the date indicated on the form, then the pursuer may request a decree.[50] If a timeous response is lodged, disputing the claim, there will then be a hearing. At that hearing the sheriff may dismiss the claim because it is incompetent or they lack jurisdiction.[51] Otherwise, they must seek to negotiate a settlement between the parties, and only if settlement cannot be achieved will they proceed to decide the case.[52] They should, "if possible", reach a decision on the information before them,[53] although it is possible for an evidential hearing to be held if absolutely necessary. Should there have to be such a hearing, the sheriff shall indicate what has to be proved, and what sort of evidence is necessary.[54]

Witnesses may be cited in any hearing, but a party is responsible for the expenses of any witness he calls and for securing the attendance of such witnesses.[55] The small claims procedure takes into account the fact that the prospect of having to pay the other side's expenses if the case is lost deters individuals

---

[41] See r.8.13.
[42] See r.25.
[43] The Small Claims (Scotland) Amendment Order 2007 (SSI 2007/496) amends the Small Claims (Scotland) Order 1988 (SI 1988/1999) under which the ceiling had been £750.
[44] Act of Sederunt (Small Claims Rules) 2002 (SSI 2002/133) r.4.2.
[45] See r.9.2.2(a).
[46] See r.9.3.2.
[47] See Sheriff Nicholson in *Kuklinski v Hassell*, 1993 S.L.T. (Sh Ct) 23.
[48] Sheriff Courts (Scotland) Act 1971 s.36A.
[49] See r.9.1.
[50] See r.8.1.
[51] See r.9.2.1.
[52] See r.9.2.2(b).
[53] See r.9.2.3(c).
[54] See r.9.2.4(b).
[55] See r.17.4.1.

from going to law. Thus a sheriff may not award expenses if a claim does not exceed £200.[56] Otherwise expenses cannot exceed £150 if the claim is £1,500 or less, or exceed 10 per cent of the claim where it is greater than £1,500[57] (unless against a defender who has no real defence).[58] An appeal can be taken to the sheriff principal on a point of law, but no further appeal is possible.

COURT OF SESSION ACTIONS

An ordinary action in the Court of Session is initiated when a summons drawn up in prescribed form is **9.2.8** submitted along with the requisite fee.[59] If the summons meets the requirements of form, it will be signetted, which authorises service on the defender.[60] Once a period of 21 days from the date of service has elapsed, the pursuer can lodge the summons with the court for calling, and must do so within a year and a day of the expiry of the aforementioned period.[61] Once the case appears on the calling list, the defender has three days to intimate to the court that he intends to appear to contest the action.[62] He has seven days from the actual date of calling to lodge written defences in the prescribed form.[63] The pursuer receives a copy of the defences, and he must then lodge the open record within 14 days of the date the defences were lodged (or the period for lodging defences expired).[64] The open record is a document which records the details of the pursuer's case and any defences. There is then a period of eight weeks within which the parties may adjust their pleadings on the open record.[65] At the end of that period the record closes, and within four weeks thereafter the pursuer must lodge the closed record.[66] The options are then that:

- the court fixes a date for a proof;
- the court fixes a date for a proof before answer; or
- the case is scheduled for a debate on a point of law arising from the proceedings.[67]

Where a proof is held, there are of course rules regarding the citation of witnesses and the lodging of productions. An appeal lies to the Inner House (and ultimately to the Supreme Court). Appeals are not restricted to points of law.

COMMERCIAL ACTIONS IN THE COURT OF SESSION AND SHERIFF COURT

As an alternative to ordinary procedure in the Court of Session there exists a special procedure for **9.2.9** commercial actions. A commercial action is an action arising out of or concerned with any transaction or dispute of a commercial or business nature.[68] The relevant practice note[69] made it clear that the dispute need not necessarily be contractual, and provides the following non-exhaustive list of examples: actions related to the construction of a commercial or mercantile document; sale or hire-purchase of goods; the export or import of merchandise; carriage of goods; insurance[70]; banking; financial services; mercantile agency; mercantile usage or custom of trade; building, engineering or construction

---

[56] Sheriff Courts (Scotland) Act 1971 s.36B(1); and see Small Claims (Scotland) Order 1988 (SI 1988/1999) art.4(2).
[57] Sheriff Courts (Scotland) Act 1971 s.36B(1); and Small Claims (Scotland) Order 1988 (SI 1988/1999) art.4(3).
[58] Sheriff Courts (Scotland) Act 1971 s.36B(3).
[59] See Act of Sederunt (Rules of the Court of Session) 1994 (SI 1994/1443) rr.13.1, 13.2.
[60] See r.13.5.
[61] See r.13.7.
[62] See r.17.
[63] See r.18.
[64] See r.22.1.
[65] See r.22.2.
[66] See r.22.3.
[67] See r.22.3.5.
[68] See r.47.1.2.
[69] Practice Note No.6 of 2004.
[70] See *Unipac (Scotland) Ltd v Aegon Insurance Co (UK) Ltd*, 1996 S.L.T. 1197.

contracts; and commercial leases. It continues that some admiralty actions such as those relating to or arising out of bills of lading may be suitable. It has also been held that proceedings relating to insolvency would be regarded as commercial,[71] and actions relating to any of the branches of the law considered in this book would surely be commercial. That being said, a dispute involving a consumer would not be regarded as commercial, and rather surprisingly the court has regarded intellectual property disputes as not suitable for the commercial action procedure.[72]

It is important to realise that "commercial" cases are not automatically assigned to this procedure. It is for the pursuer to elect to invoke it by using the words "commercial action" in the summons.[73] The summons can be less detailed than that employed in an ordinary action as long as it provides details of the orders the pursuer seeks, identifies the parties and the transaction or dispute from which the action arises, provides a summary of the circumstances from which the dispute arises, indicates the legal grounds of the action, and appends any documents founded upon or referred to in the summons.[74] The procedure regarding the service of the summons, the indication of an intention to defend, and the lodging of defences resembles that in an ordinary action. However, the form of defences should reflect the streamlined form of the summons, it being enough if the areas of dispute can be identified from the defences.[75] Again, any documents founded upon or referred to should be appended.[76] The case will first call in court at a preliminary hearing, which will occur within 14 days of the lodging of defences.[77] However, the practice note[78] emphasises that by this stage the parties will fully understand each other's cases, and should have considered whether some or all of the dispute may be amenable to resolution by some other form of dispute resolution. Thus it is presumed that there is a real dispute, which cannot be settled, and that any proof or debate arranged will actually proceed.[79]

A party may apply for the action to be withdrawn from the commercial action procedure at or before this hearing, but not thereafter.[80] (It is also possible at any stage of an ordinary action to apply for it to be treated as a commercial cause.)[81] Whereas in an ordinary action the parties effectively determine how the litigation progresses, the judge in a commercial action is entitled and indeed expected to manage the procedure proactively.[82] Thus they have a wide range of orders at their disposal, and in particular may[83]:

- order either party to provide more detail in the pleadings;
- order the disclosure of witnesses and relevant documents (and the recovery of the latter);
- order to be lodged in process a list of witnesses, any document, any report from a person of skill, any affidavit or any witness statement;
- order the action to proceed to a hearing on the merits without further procedure;
- make any order they think fit for the speedy determination of the action;
- generally make any such order subject to a time limit.

It should be observed that the judge will be a specially selected commercial judge,[84] and that commercial actions can be heard throughout the year, including periods when the court is in vacation.[85]

The emphasis at the preliminary hearing is on clarifying the issues between the parties and thus the best way of proceeding. If the judge decides against proceeding immediately to a hearing on the merits,

---

[71] *Rankin's Trustees v H C Somerville & Russell*, 1999 S.L.T. 166.
[72] *Birt v Celtic Plc* Unreported CA 54/95 CSOH, referred to in Clancy, Murray and Wadia, "*The New Commercial Cause Rules*", 1997 S.L.T. (News) 45.
[73] See r.47.3.1.
[74] See rr.47.3.2, 47.3.3.
[75] See r.47.6.
[76] See r.47.6.
[77] See r.47.8.2.
[78] Practice Note No.6 of 2004, para.11.
[79] See paras 12, 13.
[80] See r.47.9.
[81] See r.47.10; and see para.5 of Practice Note No.6 of 2004.
[82] See r.47.5.
[83] See r.47.11.
[84] See r.47.2.
[85] See r.10.7.

they will fix a date for a procedural hearing in order to decide what procedure is most apt for the determination of the case, and in particular the nature and extent of debate or proof required.[86] At least three days in advance of the procedural hearing, each party must provide advance notice of their proposals for further procedure, and if they propose a debate, they must indicate what should be debated.[87] Advance notice must also be given of the witnesses each party proposes to call and the matters to which they are to speak, and they must lodge any report of a skilled person on which they intend to rely.[88] The procedure generally aims at full advance disclosure of each party's case, and to minimise the time spent on debates. At the hearing, after considering the submissions of the parties, the judge decides whether the case should go to debate or be sent for proof.[89] If the case goes to debate or proof, then the judge, instead of waiting to hear the parties, may direct that written arguments be submitted in advance of the hearing.[90] Moreover, if a proof is ordered, then it is for the judge to decide what needs to be proved and how.[91] And if invited to by the parties, they may dispense with any oral hearing, and determine the matter on the basis of written submissions.[92] With its emphasis on expedition, pro-active case management by the judge, and immense procedural discretion, it can thus be appreciated that the commercial procedure represents a radical departure from traditional Court of Session procedure.

The commercial action procedure is to some degree mirrored in the sheriff court, where a special commercial procedure will be available only if the relevant sheriff principal has so directed.[93] The same sort of transactions are comprehended, although actions relating to consumer credit transactions are specifically excluded.[94] Again, the pursuer must specifically elect for this procedure,[95] although either party may apply to have an ordinary cause transferred to the commercial procedure.[96] By the same token, the sheriff must transfer a commercial action to the ordinary cause procedure if at or before the case management conference (see below), the parties submit a joint motion to that effect, or one party makes such a motion, and the sheriff is of the view that either detailed pleadings are required to enable justice to be done between the parties or other circumstances warrant such an order.[97] Expedition is once more a key objective of the procedure, and the sheriff is empowered to make any order they think fit for the progress of the case.[98] Where the construction of a document is the only matter in the dispute, no pleadings or pleas in law require to be included in the initial writ.[99] Generally the initial writ need only indicate the nature of the dispute, the grounds of action and the remedy sought,[100] while defences must be in the form of answers which allow the extent of the dispute to be identified, and must include the defender's pleas in law.[101] The case management conference is at the centre of any defended action under the commercial procedure. In it the sheriff "shall seek to secure the expeditious resolution of the action."[102] The sheriff generally has the same sort of powers as the judge at the procedural hearing in a commercial action.[103]

---

[86] See r.47.11.3.

[87] See r.47.12.1.

[88] See r.47.12.1.

[89] See r.47.12.2(a). Unlike in an ordinary action, a party may not insist on a debate: *Highland and Universal Properties Ltd v Safeway Properties Ltd*, 1996 S.C. 424.

[90] See r.47.12.2(b).

[91] See r.47.12.2(c), (d), (g), (h).

[92] See r.47.12.2(k).

[93] Act of Sederunt (Sheriff Court Ordinary Cause Rules) 1993 (SI 1993/1956) r.40.1.3. It is currently available in only seven courts, but cases from other sheriffdoms are accepted in Glasgow if the parties agree to prorogate the jurisdiction of Glasgow Sheriff Court. For a study of the operation of the procedure see Elaine Samuel, *Commercial Procedure in Glasgow Sheriff Court* (Edinburgh: Scottish Executive Social Research, 2005)

[94] See r.40.1.2(b).

[95] See r.40.4.

[96] See r.40.5.1.

[97] See r.40.6.1.

[98] See r.40.3.1.

[99] See r.40.7.1.

[100] See Form G1A.

[101] See r.40.9.3.

[102] See r.40.12.1.

[103] See r.40.12.3.

9.3   ARBITRATION

INTRODUCTION TO ARBITRATION

9.3.1 As an alternative to litigation, the parties may seek a binding resolution of their dispute via arbitration, or indeed be obliged to do so because of an arbitration clause in the relevant contract. Arbitration essentially sees the determination of the issue(s) between the parties by a third party—the arbitrator, whose decision takes the form of a formally binding award. The law of arbitration in Scotland is now mainly statutory, governed by the Arbitration (Scotland) Act 2010. The situation is, however, complicated by the fact that, for the moment at least,[104] s.36(3) of the Act leaves open the possibility of parties to arbitration agreements entered into prior to its date of commencement (June 7, 2010) choosing to be governed by the pre-2010 Act law. This will mainly be common law together with a few statutory fragments, but as regards international commercial arbitrations held in Scotland the governing law would be the UNCITRAL Model Law on International Commercial Arbitration (adopted into Scotland by s.66 and Sch.7 of the Law Reform (Miscellaneous Provisions) (Scotland) Act 1990). Moreover, it is possible for parties to a dispute which is neither international nor commercial to invoke the provisions of the Model Law.[105] It would be unwieldy if this work attempted to examine both the 2010 Act and the pre 2010 Act regime (including the Model Law). Accordingly, this chapter will concentrate on the 2010 Act, and readers who wish to know about the pre 2010 Act regime may consult the previous edition of this work.

A few words should be said about the structure of the 2010 Act. It is divided into the Act proper and the Scottish Arbitration Rules contained in Sch.1. The Rules deal mainly with the arbitral procedure and are cast in this form because the framers of the Act thought that parties to arbitrations would be familiar with institutional arbitration rules and would find it helpful if the provisions governing their arbitration adopted this form. Nonetheless, the Rules differ from institutional arbitration rules in that their force derives not from the agreement of the parties, but from the fact that they are statutory provisions. Nonetheless, most of the Rules are default in form and thus yield to the contrary agreement of the parties. The Act in s.9(4) explicitly acknowledges that such contrary agreement may take the form, inter alia, of the adoption of institutional arbitration rules or indeed the adoption of a foreign procedural law. Those of the Rules which are mandatory cannot be modified or disapplied.[106]

WHY ARBITRATE?

9.3.2 If the parties wish a binding resolution of their dispute, but do not want to go to court, then arbitration is the main alternative. It shares some of the advantages and drawbacks of litigation, though this is not invariably the case. So the procedure employed in arbitration can be very flexible indeed, considerably more flexible than even the most radical forms of court procedure described above. Yet many arbitrations simply ape formal court proceedings. Thus, depending on the type of arbitration adopted, arbitration can be considerably more expeditious than court proceedings, or even slower than the most formal proceedings. Equally it can be very inexpensive or (because of the need to meet the costs of employing an arbitrator or arbitrators and support staff, together with the ancillary costs of the arbitral proceedings) significantly more expensive than litigation. It should, however, be noted that one of the founding principles of the Act under s.1(a) is that the object of the arbitration is to resolve disputes "without unnecessary delay or expense". Equally, the tribunal is placed under a duty by the mandatory r.24(1)(c) to conduct the arbitration without unnecessary delay and without incurring unnecessary expense, while

---

[104] As Ministers are empowered by s.36(4) to deprive s.36(3) of effect once the Act the Act has been in operation for 5 years.
[105] See Law Reform (Miscellaneous Provisions) (Scotland) Act 1990 s.66(4).
[106] See s.8 which helpfully lists the mandatory rules. Anyone reading the Act will easily be able to see whether a particular rule is default or mandatory, since it will be headed by the letter "D" or "M". This account will seek to indicate into which category a given rule falls. The provisions of the Act proper are all mandatory.

the mandatory r.25 places the parties under a duty to ensure that the arbitration is conducted without unnecessary delay and without incurring unnecessary expense.

One of the main advantages of arbitration is the ability to choose the arbitrator. Thus the parties may select an individual because of that person's particular knowledge and experience, which they believe will assist them to come to a just decision in the dispute. So while many arbitrators are lawyers, others are drawn from a variety of professions. It is indeed possible to have a tribunal of two or more arbitrators, so that more than one discipline, or more than one legal culture, is represented, the latter being thought to be particularly important in the context of international arbitration. Again, while court proceedings are public, arbitration is private and confidential. It is also the case that if enforcement is sought against a losing party abroad, in a number of states an arbitral award is easier to enforce than a foreign court decree. On the other hand, the powers of an arbitrator are inevitably less extensive than that of a judge, and the assistance of the court may be required to support the arbitration at various points, possibly including the enforcement of the award. Moreover, if the dispute seeks a definitive view on an issue of general importance, such as the correct interpretation of a widely used standard form contract, then it is better to litigate than arbitrate.

WHAT MATTERS MAY BE REFERRED TO ARBITRATION?

The Act does not address this issue, s.30 simply indicating that the Act does not make any dispute arbitrable if it would not otherwise be so. The broad rule of thumb is that, since the foundation of arbitration is agreement, one may refer to arbitration any issue which can be determined by agreement between the parties. Thus while an arbitrator obviously cannot deal with the criminal consequences of fraud, he can be empowered to consider the effect of fraud on the civil relations of the parties.[107] Equally, while the creation and dissolution of a company involves the invocation of state power, and thus can never be within the competence of an arbitrator,[108] since the creation and dissolution of a partnership can be effected by agreement, it is possible to empower an arbitrator to dissolve a firm.[109] In the same way, while only the state can grant a patent, and only a court conclusively rule on whether one has been validly granted,[110] it is open to parties to agree to refer to an arbitrator the question of whether one has infringed the other's patent.[111] The foundation of the arbiter's powers being agreement, the effect of the arbitrator's determination is generally confined to the relations between the parties themselves, and cannot impinge on the rights of third parties. Thus while an arbitrator may decide, as between A and B, whether property has passed under their contract of sale,[112] no arbitrator may actually confer a real right to property. In the particular context of this book, any dispute arising out of the various commercial contracts examined would be arbitrable. As regards bankruptcy, while it is not possible for an arbitrator to make an award of sequestration, the trustee is specifically empowered to refer any claim to arbitration.[113]

9.3.3

THE ARBITRATION AGREEMENT

Apart from statutory arbitrations, where parties are bound by legislation to determine certain types of dispute by arbitration, the basis of arbitration is agreement between the parties that they should

9.3.4

---

[107] *Earl of Kintore v Union Bank of Scotland* (1865) 4 Macq. 465.

[108] See Patten LJ in *Fulham Football Club (1987) Ltd v Richards* [2011] B.C.C. 910 at [73]–[74]. However, at [40] he acknowledged that disputes between shareholders could be arbitrated, while at [61] he accepted that an arbitrator might even be able to give certain forms of relief under s.996 of the Companies Act 2006, where the arbitrator had determined that a shareholder had suffered unfair prejudice under s.994.

[109] See *Hackston v Hackston*, 1956 S.L.T. (Notes) 38.

[110] See Hammerschlag J in *Larkden Pty Ltd v Lloyd Energy Systems Pty Ltd* [2011] N.S.W.S.C. 268 at [64].

[111] See *Dekko v Dingler* (1994) *Revue de l'Arbitrage* 515.

[112] See e.g. *Walker, Grant & Co v Grant* (1838) 1 D 38.

[113] Bankruptcy (Scotland) Act 1985 s.65.

arbitrate. Arbitration is not among those forms of agreement which need to be in writing under the Requirements of Writing (Scotland) Act 1995,[114] and this is not altered by the 2010 Act, although in practice arbitration agreements almost invariably will be in writing. An agreement to arbitrate may take the form of a free standing submission to arbitration once a dispute has arisen, or a clause in the original contract between the parties indicating that disputes between them should be referred to arbitration. In Scotland the courts are reluctant to hold that parties have agreed to arbitrate unless that was clearly their intention. So whereas in England the courts are generally happy to assume that parties who adopt a standard form contract are bound by an arbitration clause therein,[115] that is not the case in Scotland.[116] A fortiori, the Scots courts are reluctant to accept that parties who agree to be bound by the terms of another contract—such as where subcontractors agree to adopt the terms of the main contract—intend to be bound by an arbitration clause in that contract.[117] This position is not altered by the 2010 Act s.4, of which provides that an arbitration agreement is an agreement to submit a present of future dispute to arbitration (including any agreement which provides for arbitration in accordance with arbitration provisions contained in a separate document). This is not so much a provision as a statement of the obvious.

THE EFFECT OF AN ARBITRATION AGREEMENT

9.3.5 The common law position is represented by the statement by Lord Dunedin in *Sanderson v Armour & Co*[118] that "[i]f the parties have contracted to arbitrate to arbitration they must go". Thus at common law, if one party sought to litigate, and the other pleaded the existence of a valid arbitration agreement, then the court would refer the issue to arbitration. This position is largely preserved by the 2010 Act s.10(1), which states that that the court must, on the application of a party to legal proceedings concerning the matter under dispute, sist those proceedings in so far as they concern that matter if:

- an arbitration agreement provides that a dispute on the matter is to be resolved by arbitration (whether immediately or after the exhaustion of other dispute resolution procedures);
- the applicant is a party to the arbitration agreement (or is claiming through or under a party);
- notice of the application has been given to the other parties to the legal proceedings;
- the applicant has not taken any step in the legal proceedings to answer any substantive claim against him, nor otherwise acted since the legal proceedings were brought in a manner indicating a desire to have the dispute resolved by the legal proceedings rather than arbitration; and
- nothing has caused the court to be satisfied that the arbitration agreement concerned is void, inoperative or incapable of being performed.

As regards the last criterion, regard should be had to ss.89 to 91 of the Arbitration Act 1996. Although this is an English Act, these sections apply in Scotland. They have two broad effects. Section 89(1) subjects consumer arbitration agreements to the Unfair Terms in Consumer Contracts Regulations 1999.[119] Section 91(1) then provides that an arbitration agreement will be automatically unfair, and thus not bind the consumer, so far as it relates to a claim for a pecuniary remedy which does not exceed an amount specified by order—currently £5,000.[120] If an agreement is not automatically unfair, it may yet be adjudged unfair under the Regulations. Their broad impact is considered at para.6.12. In the present context they effectively address the situation where an arbitration clause is imposed on a consumer, and

---

[114] See s.1(1).

[115] *Golodetz v Schrier* (1947) 80 Ll. L. Rep. 647.

[116] *McConnell and Reid v Smith*, 1911 S.C. 635.

[117] *Goodwins, Jardine & Co v Brand* (1905) 7 F. 995; *Babcock Rosyth Defence Ltd v Grootcon (United Kingdom) Ltd*, 1998 S.L.T. 1143.

[118] *Sanderson v Armour & Co*, 1922 S.C. (HL) 117 at 126.

[119] (SI 1999/2083).

[120] Unfair Arbitration Agreements (Specified Amounts) Order 1999 (SI 1999/2167). If a claim exceeds £5,000 only because of the addition of VAT, it still falls outside s.91: see Ramsey J in *Mylcrist Builders v Buck* [2009] 2 All E.R. (Comm) 259 at [35].

will not apply where the parties enter into a freestanding arbitration agreement, nor where the parties genuinely agree to insert an arbitration clause into the contract. Where the arbitration clause is not imposed on the consumer, the agreement is very unlikely to be held to be unfair.[121] A consumer is defined under the regulations as a natural person acting for purposes outside his business, if any,[122] but s.90 of the 1996 Act extends the definition in the context of arbitration agreements to embrace legal persons. Thus if a firm or company enters into a normal business contract on the terms dictated by the other party, the regulations do not apply. But if it enters into a contract for non-business purposes, then the regulations potentially apply to any arbitration clause which is not individually negotiated.[123] As regards when an arbitration clause might be unfair, this will usually be the case if before the contract is concluded the clause is not drawn to a consumer's attention and its significance explained.[124] Even then, it will probably still be unfair if it is to the consumer's detriment, such as where the cost of going to arbitration is likely to be significantly greater than litigating.[125] It may, however, be difficult to persuade a court that an arbitration clause in a contract between two businesses is unfair.[126]

This discussion has proceeded on the basis that a consumer can decline to arbitrate where the arbitration agreement is unfair. However, in *Mylcrist Builders* the arbitration had gone ahead without the participation of the consumer, and the company was seeking to enforce the award. Ramsey J held that, since the agreement was not binding on Mrs Buck, the tribunal lacked jurisdiction to make the award, so that enforcement was not possible. That this is the appropriate approach appears to be confirmed by the decision of the European Court of Justice in *Asturcom Telecomunicaciones SL v Rodriguez Nogueira*[127] that, where the consumer had neither appeared in the arbitration nor sought to annul the award, a court which was asked to enforce an award required to consider of its own motion whether the arbitration clause was unfair and refuse enforcement if this was the case, albeit that it also held that an award should stand if the period prescribed by national law for making a challenge had elapsed. The European Court of Justice had previously held in *Mostaza Claro v Centro Movil Milenium SL*[128] that an award cannot stand if the arbitration agreement is void at a consumer's instance under the Unfair Terms in Consumer Contracts Directive, even if the consumer had participated in the arbitration but had failed to raise the issue in the arbitral proceedings.

APPOINTING ARBITRATORS

Assuming that there is a valid arbitration agreement, the first step in referring a dispute to arbitration is **9.3.6** to establish the arbitral tribunal. There are as many ways of doing this as it is possible for human ingenuity to devise. One obvious method would be for the arbitration agreement itself to nominate a particular individual or office holder to act as arbitrator should a dispute arise. Another would be for the agreement to require a particular person or body to nominate an arbitrator. Alternatively, the parties may simply agree on an arbitrator. Or in a two-arbitrator tribunal, it may be contemplated that each party will appoint an arbitrator. Typical modes of constitution of a three-arbitrator tribunal would be for each party to appoint an arbitrator, with the third being appointed by the parties acting together, or perhaps by the other two arbitrators acting together. All such possibilities are countenanced by the law, r.2 of the Act stating that an arbitration agreement need not provide for the appointment of the tribunal, but if it does it may specify who is to form the tribunal, require the parties to appoint the tribunal, permit another person to appoint the tribunal, or provide for the tribunal to be appointed in any other way.

---

[121] See e.g. *Bryen & Langley Ltd v Boston* [2005] B.L.R. 508; especially Rimer J at [44]–[46].
[122] See reg.3(1).
[123] See, e.g. *Heifer International Inc. v Christiansen* [2008] 2 All E.R. (Comm) 831.
[124] See Ramsey J in *Mylcrist Builders v Buck* [2009] 2 All E.R. (Comm) 259 at [51]–[54].
[125] See Ramsey J in *Mylcrist Builders v Buck* [2009] 2 All E.R. (Comm) 259 at [55]–[57].
[126] See *Heifer International Inc. v Christiansen* [2008] 2 All E.R. (Comm) 831.
[127] *Asturcom Telecomunicaciones SL v Rodriguez Nogueira* [2010] 1 C.M.L.R. 29.
[128] *Mostaza Claro v Centro Movil Milenium SL* [2007] 1 C.M.L.R. 22.

However, the real role of the law here is to deal with the situation where the parties have not agreed on the shape of the tribunal or how it should be appointed, or where agreed procedures have failed. The first situation which the law must address is what is to happen when the parties have agreed that any dispute between them is to be arbitrated, but cannot agree how many arbitrators there are to be. Here r.5 states that in such a situation the tribunal is to consist of a sole arbitrator. The rule is default, so the parties may agree on some other default position. Rule 6 then goes on to consider how the tribunal is to be appointed, but as this is also default, the parties may agree something different. If they do not, then if the tribunal is to consist of a sole arbitrator, the parties must jointly appoint an eligible individual within 28 days of either party requesting the other to do so. If there is to be a larger tribunal, then each party must appoint an eligible individual within 28 days of the other(s) requesting it to do so. If there are to be more arbitrators than parties, then the party-appointed arbitrators must jointly appoint the remaining arbitrators.

What if agreed appointing procedures or the default procedures laid down by r.6 break down? In that case the matter is dealt with by the mandatory r.7. This operates on the initial premise that the necessary appointment(s) will be made by an arbitral appointments referee.[129] This novel concept was introduced by the Act. Traditionally, where procedures have broken down, statute has tended to entrust the task of making necessary appointments to the courts. Yet courts have very little experience in making such appointments, while other bodies have considerable experience. Accordingly, s.24(1) of the 2010 Act empowers Ministers, by order, to authorise persons or types of persons to act as an arbitral appointments referee. Although s.24 refers to "persons", it is clear that arbitral appointments referees may be officeholders or institutions.[130] At the same time, the Act acknowledges that a party may not be comfortable with the appointment being made by a referee. Thus the parties may agree that a referee should not act.[131] Otherwise, either party may refer the matter to a referee, giving notice to the other party.[132] The other party may then object to the referring party and the referee within seven days of that notice.[133] If no such objection is made within that period, or the objecting party waives its objections before the end of the period, the referee may make the necessary appointment.[134] Where a referee fails to make an appointment within 21 days of the reference, or the parties have agreed that a referee should not act, or a party has objected to a referee, the Outer House may make the necessary appointment on an application by a party.[135] Before making an appointment the referee or court must, under r.7(8), have regard to the nature and subject matter of the dispute, the terms of the arbitration agreement (in particular any terms relating to the appointment or arbitrators[136]), and the skills, qualifications, knowledge and experience which would make an individual suitable to determine the dispute.

WHO CAN ACT AS AN ARBITRATOR?

9.3.7 The last paragraph spoke of "eligible" individuals being appointed as arbitrators, but who is eligible to act as an arbitrator? Rule 3 states that only an individual may act as an arbitrator, so that it is no longer possible, as was the case at common law, to appoint a firm or an unincorporated body.[137] Rule 4 then provides that an individual is ineligible to act as an arbitrator if aged under 16 or an incapable adult.

---

[129] See r.7(2).

[130] So far authorised to act as referees are the Dean of the Faculty of Advocates the Agricultural Industries Confederation Limited, the Chartered Institute of Arbitrators, the Institution of Civil Engineers, the Law Society of Scotland, the Royal Incorporation of Architects in Scotland, the Royal Institution of Chartered Surveyors and the Scottish Agricultural Arbiters and Valuers Association: see the Arbitral Appointments Referee (Scotland) Order 2010 (SSI 2010/196).

[131] See r.7(2).

[132] See r.7(2)–(3).

[133] See r.7(4).

[134] See r.7(5).

[135] See r.7(6). The court's decision is not open to appeal: see r.7(7).

[136] For example, an agreement that the arbitrator shoud be a lawyer.

[137] See *Bremner v Elder* (1875) 2 R. (H.L.) 136; *Wm Dixon Ltd v James, Heard & Ingram* (1884) 11 R. 739.

Again, this would preclude the possibility, recognised by the common law, of a minor acting as arbitrator.[138] Both these rules are mandatory.

CHALLENGING AND REMOVING ARBITRATORS

An arbitrator can be removed by the parties, by the arbitral tribunal or the Outer House. Since an arbi- **9.3.8** trator's tenure ultimately derives from the agreement of the parties, they can remove an arbitrator at any time for any reason or for none. Equally, the parties can delegate that power to a third party.[139] Moreover, under r.10 a party may object to the tribunal about the appointment of an arbitrator. This can only be done on certain grounds,[140] although since r.10 is a default provision, the parties may extend or narrow those grounds or indeed exclude the rule altogether. The grounds are that the arbitrator:

- is not impartial or independent;
- has not treated the parties fairly[141]; or
- does not have a qualification which the parties agreed (before his appointment) that he must have.

The concept of lack of independence has a special meaning in the context of the 2010 Act, since r.77 states that an arbitrator is not independent if his relationship with any party, his financial or commercial interests, or anything else, gives rise to justifiable doubts about his impartiality. Thus facts such as the arbitrator being related to one of the parties, having some sort of financial interest in the outcome of the dispute, or having behaved in a way that suggests a closed mind or predisposition towards a certain conclusion, will justify an objection. An individual who has been asked to be an arbitrator must without delay disclose to the parties and anyone considering whether to appoint him (e.g. the court) any circumstance known to him which might reasonably be considered relevant in considering whether he is impartial and independent.[142] Someone who has actually been appointed as arbitrator similarly owes a duty of disclosure to the parties in relation to such circumstances which become known to him after his appointment.

It is not unlikely that an arbitrator who is thus challenged may choose to resign, and he would be given the right to do so by the mandatory r.15(1)(c). Otherwise, the tribunal may deal with an objection by confirming or revoking the appointment, while a failure to make a decision within 14 days of the making of a competent rejection sees the appointment automatically revoked.[143] It can be appreciated that, since most arbitral tribunals consist of a single arbitrator, it will usually be that arbitrator who rules on an objection to his own appointment. This might obviously occasion difficulties from time to time, so it is also open to a party under the mandatory r.12 to apply to the Outer House for the removal of an arbitrator. Such an application may be made on a rather wider range of grounds than those on which a challenge may be made. Thus the court may remove an arbitrator if satisfied that:

- the arbitrator is not impartial or independent;
- the arbitrator has not treated the parties fairly;
- the arbitrator does not have a qualification which the parties agreed (before his appointment) that he must have;
- the arbitrator is incapable of acting or that there are justifiable doubts about his ability to act;
- substantial injustice has been or will be caused to that party because the arbitrator has failed to conduct the arbitration in accordance with the parties' agreement or the Rules (in so far as they apply).

---

[138] See *Gordon v Earl of Errol* (1582) Mor. 8915.

[139] See r.11(1)(b).

[140] An objection is additionally only competent if it states the facts on which it is based, is made within 14 days of the objector becoming aware of those facts, and notice of it is given to the other party: r.10(2)(b)–(d).

[141] This would include the arbitrator not treating one of the parties fairly, which is indeed the more likely scenario.

[142] See r.8: a mandatory provision.

[143] See r.10(3)–(4).

This last ground is also the basis on which the court might dismiss the entire tribunal under the mandatory r.13. However, the court may only remove an arbitrator or dismiss the tribunal if certain conditions are met.[144] It can be seen that the first three grounds are also grounds on which an arbitrator might be challenged under r.10, so that the conditions include the condition that the court is satisfied that any available recourse under r.10 has been exhausted.[145]

If any arbitrator ceases to be a member of the tribunal, whether by resignation, becoming ineligible to act as an arbitrator, being removed by the tribunal, the parties, any third party or the court, or by being a member of a tribunal dismissed by the court, r.17(1)(a) directs that the tribunal must be reconstituted in accordance with the procedure used to constitute the original tribunal. Should that procedure fail, r.17(1)(b) provides that the tribunal must be reconstituted in accordance with rr.6 and 7 (see para.9.3.6). Rule 17(2) indicates that it is for the reconstituted tribunal to decide the extent (if any) to which the previous proceedings should stand. Rule 17 is, however, a default provision, so the parties may decide that something quite different should happen in such circumstances, and/or remove the discretion conferred by r.17(2). Rule 18 continues that a provision in an arbitration agreement which indicates that who is to be an arbitrator ceases to have effect when that individual's tenure ends. In other words, if the agreement states that a specific person (or persons) is to act as the arbitrator, it cannot be argued that the arbitration agreement cannot be performed if that person ceases to be an arbitrator. Yet r.18 is also a default provision, so if the parties only wish to arbitrate if a certain individual can act as their arbitrator, they can so agree.

JURISDICTION

9.3.9 Once the tribunal is established, the arbiter can proceed with the reference. Yet a preliminary question may arise as to whether he has jurisdiction to decide the dispute. That leads on to the further question as to who should determine such questions. An allied question is what effect do events which might vitiate a contract have upon the jurisdiction of an arbiter which is derived from a clause in the same contract? There was some common law authority to the effect that if a contract was brought to an end, the same must be true of any arbitration clause it contained.[146] However, that is not the approach taken by the Act, which embraces the concept of the separability of the arbitration agreement. Thus s.5(1) states that an arbitration agreement which forms part or was intended to form part of a contract is to be treated as a separate agreement, while s.5(2) continues that an arbitration agreement is not void, voidable or otherwise unenforceable because the contract of which it forms part is void, voidable or otherwise unenforceable, and s.5(2) concludes that a dispute about the validity of a contract which contains an arbitration agreement may be arbitrated in accordance with that arbitration agreement.

Returning to the issue of who should determine questions of jurisdiction, the Act takes the view that, at least in the first instance, the tribunal should do so. Thus the mandatory r.19 provides that the tribunal may rule on whether there is a valid arbitration agreement, whether the tribunal is properly constituted, and what matters have been submitted to arbitration in accordance with the arbitration agreement. In terms of the mandatory r.20, any party may object to the tribunal on the ground that the tribunal does not have jurisdiction or has exceeded its jurisdiction.[147] Such an objection must be made before, or as soon as reasonably practicable after, the objectionable matter is first raised in the arbitration, although the tribunal may entertain a later objection if it considers that circumstances justify such later objection.[148] It seems to follow that a tribunal cannot consider a late objection if it considers that it is not

---

[144] The other conditions are that the arbitrator or tribunal has been notified of the application for removal or dismissal and given the opportunity to make representations to the court (r.14(1)(a)) and that the court is satisfied that any available recourse to a third party who the parties have empowered to remove an arbitrator or dismiss the tribunal (as is contemplated by certain institutional rules) has been exhausted: r.14(1)(b)(ii). The decision of the Outer House is not subject to appeal, but the tribunal may continue with the arbitration while that decision is pending: r.14(2)–(3).

[145] See r.14(1)(b)(i).

[146] *Municipal Council of Johannesburg v D Stewart & Co*, 1909 S.C. (HL) 53.

[147] See r.20(1).

[148] See r.20(2).

justified. Accordingly, a party who contends that the tribunal lacks jurisdiction cannot wait until the arbitration is well advanced before raising that objection. Such a party might instead attack the award on the basis of lack of jurisdiction, but will probably be regarded as having waived that objection (see para.9.3.14). It is specifically provided that an objection may not be made to the tribunal once it has made its final award.[149] In that case the only recourse would be against the award, but once again there may be no recourse if the party is regarded as having waived its right to contest jurisdiction by not objecting at an appropriate stage. This will not invariably be so, since it may not be evident that a tribunal has exceeded its jurisdiction until the award appears.

A tribunal may either reject or uphold an objection. If it upholds an objection, it must end the arbitration in so far as it relates to a matter over which it has ruled it has no jurisdiction and set aside any provisional or part award made in relation to such a matter.[150] Prima facie, it may rule on an objection as part of its award on the merits, or independently.[151] However, if the parties agree which of these courses it must take, it must proceed accordingly.[152] If the tribunal does have this discretion, the course it takes will tend to depend on how far advanced proceedings are. Thus, while one might ordinarily suppose that it will rule independently on a jurisdictional objection, if it is on the point of making its award, it may prefer to rule on the objection as part of the award. It can be appreciated that, if a tribunal could rule conclusively on objections to its own jurisdiction, obvious possibilities for abuse would exist. Accordingly, a party may appeal to the Outer House within 14 days of such a ruling,[153] with the Outer House's decision on the matter being final.[154] The tribunal may continue the arbitration pending determination of the appeal,[155] and will probably do so if it is convinced the appeal is without merit. It may of course be the case that a party has not objected to the tribunal's jurisdiction because he is convinced that it has no jurisdiction and refuses even to countenance the possibility that it might have by asking it to consider the question. Such a person is protected by s.14(1), which states that a person who is alleged to be a party to an arbitration but who takes no part in the arbitration may question the issue of jurisdiction by court procedings, and the court may grant such remedy, e.g. declarator, interdict, as it thinks appropriate.

It may be added that the Act under r.22 also countenances the possibility of a jurisdictional question being referred directly to the Outer House by a party. This may seem to run contrary to the philosophy that the tribunal itself should initially determine questions of jurisdiction. However, the rule recognises that difficult questions of jurisdiction may arise, which are bound to be appealed to the Outer House whatever view the tribunal takes. Thus there may be merit in bypassing the tribunal and referring the matter straight to the Outer House. This rule is nonetheless a default rule, and so may be excluded by the parties. If the rule is not excluded, any application is still subject to the mandatory r.23. This states[156] that an application is valid only if:

- the parties have agreed it should be made; or
- the tribunal has consented to it being made and the court is satisfied that determining the question is likely to produce substantial savings in expenses[157]; that the application has been made without delay, and there is a good reason why the question should be determined by the court.

The court's determination of the question is final as is its decision as to whether an application is valid.[158] Once more the tribunal may continue the arbitration pending determination of the application.[159]

---

[149] See r.20(2).
[150] See r.20(3).
[151] See r.20(4).
[152] See r.20(4).
[153] See r.21(1). Rule 21 is mandatory.
[154] See r.21(2).
[155] See r.21(3).
[156] See r.23(2).
[157] Presumably by avoiding the need for the tribunal to rule on an objection, followed by an inevitable appeal.
[158] See r.23(4).
[159] See r.23(3).

CONDUCT OF PROCEEDINGS

9.3.10 Just as the parties create the arbitrator's jurisdiction and define its limits through their agreement, so too they can stipulate how they wish the arbitration to be conducted, whether directly or through the invocation of a particular set of arbitral rules. This is reflected in the fact that, under the 2010 Act, only two rules relating to the conduct of the arbitration are mandatory. These are rr.24 and 25, setting out the general duties of, respectively, the arbitral tribunal and the parties. Thus, as already mentioned, r.24(1)(c) imposes on the tribunal a duty to conduct the arbitration without unnecessary delay and without incurring unnecessary expense, while r.25 places the parties under a duty to ensure that the arbitration is so conducted. Rule 24 also states that the tribunal must be impartial and independent and treat the parties fairly, while treating the parties fairly is expressed to include giving each party a reasonable opportunity to put its case and deal with the case of the other party. While these duties cannot be excluded or modified, the extensive provisions of the Act regarding the conduct of the arbitration otherwise yield to the agreement of the parties.

9.3.10.1 Procedure

Yet assuming the parties have reached no agreement on such matters, nor invoked any arbitral rules, the Act has much to say regarding the arbitral proceedings, generally making the tribunal the master of how the arbitration is to be conducted. Thus r.28(1) states that it is for the tribunal to determine the procedure to be followed and the admissibility, relevance, materiality and weight of any evidence. Rule 28(2) then expands upon this by providing that the tribunal may determine:

- When and where the arbitration is to be conducted. Rule 29 separately states that the tribunal may meet and otherwise conduct the arbitration anywhere it chooses in or outwith Scotland. This reflects the fact that while practically all the provisions of the Act only apply where Scotland is the legal seat of the arbitration in terms of s.3, there is a distinction between the seat and where the proceedings are actually conducted. Thus while most arbitrations are likely to be conducted entirely in Scotland, it is possible that certain arbitrations will be conducted partly or entirely outside Scotland. It should also be borne in mind that arbitrations may be conducted entirely by the exchange of documents and/or online, so that there may be no physical proceedings.
- Whether and when the parties are to submit claims or defences, and the extent to which these may be amended.
- Whether any documents or other evidence should be disclosed by or to any party, and if so, when and to whom such disclosures are to be made. It is also the case under r.35 that the tribunal may direct a party to preserve any document or other evidence which that party possesses or controls, or to allow it, an expert or another party (i) to inspect, photograph preserve or take custody of any property the party owns or possesses, which is the subject of the arbitration or as to which any question arises in the arbitration; or (ii) to take samples from or conduct an experiment in such property.
- Whether any questions are to be put to and answered by the parties, and if so what.
- Whether and if so to what extent the tribunal should take the initiative in ascertaining the facts and the law, i.e. the extent to which it should adopt an inquisitorial rather than adversarial approach.
- The extent to which the tribunal is to proceed by way of hearings for the questioning of parties, written or oral argument, presentation or inspection of documents or other evidence, or submission of documents or other evidence. If parties or witnesses are to give evidence, then r.36 allows the tribunal to direct that a party or witness be examined on oath or affirmation, and to administer an oath or affirmation.
- The language to be used in the arbitration and whether a party should supply translations of documents or other evidence. This reflects the fact that one or both of the parties to an arbitration may be foreign, such as where foreign parties agree to arbitrate in Scotland as a neutral venue.
- Whether to apply the rules of evidence used in legal proceedings or any other rules of evidence.

Other powers   9.3.10.2

The tribunal has power under r.32 to appoint a clerk and such other agents, employees and others as it thinks fit to assist it in the conduct of the arbitration. However, the consent of the parties will be required for any appointment in respect of which significant expenses are likely to arise. It will very much depend on circumstances whether the appointment of a legally qualified clerk or other support staff will be sensible. It is also the case that the tribunal is empowered by r.34 to obtain expert opinion on any matter arising in the arbitration, and here the consent of the parties is not required. However, parties must be given a reasonable opportunity to make representations about any written expert opinion and to hear any oral expert opinion and ask questions of the expert.

Representation   9.3.10.3

Under r.33 parties are entitled to be represented in the arbitration by a lawyer or other person as long as they have given advance notice of the representative to the tribunal and other party.

Party failure   9.3.10.4

Where a party delays unnecessarily in submitting or pursuing a claim, and the tribunal considers that there is no good reason for the delay and is satisfied that the delay gives or is likely to give rise to a substantial risk that it will not be possible to resolve the issues in the claim fairly, or has caused or is likely to cause serious prejudice to the other party, r.37(1) directs that the tribunal must end the arbitration and may make such award as it considers appropriate in consequence of the claim. This raises the possibility that a party who makes a claim in an arbitration but fails to pursue it may have that claim dismissed. Rule 37(2) continues that where a party delays unnecessarily in submitting a defence, and the tribunal considers that there is no good reason for the delay, it must continue with the arbitration without treating the delay as an admission. Equally, under r.38 where a party fails to attend a hearing[160] or produce evidence requested by the tribunal, and the tribunal considers that there is no good reason for the failure, it may proceed with the arbitration and make its award on the basis of the evidence (if any) before it. Thus a party who offers no defence, tenders no evidence and does not appear at a hearing will not automatically lose, but is very likely to do so, since the tribunal is entitled to rely on the evidence put forward by the claimant. In terms of r.31, the tribunal is entitled to give such directions to the parties for the purpose of conducting the arbitration as it considers appropriate, and a party must comply with such a direction by the time the tribunal specifies. Should a party fail to comply with a direction or any obligation imposed by the Rules or the agreement of the parties, under r.39(1) the tribunal may order the party to comply. Where a party fails to comply, the tribunal under r.39(2) may, inter alia:

- Direct that the party is not entitled to rely on any allegation or material which was the subject of the order, e.g. where the party has failed to produce evidence, the tribunal may indicate that he may not rely on it.
- Draw adverse inferences from the non-compliance, e.g. assume that the evidence not produced is to the detriment of the party's case.
- Proceed with the arbitration and make the award.

Decision making   9.3.10.5

In r.30 the Act also makes provision for tribunal decision-making where there is more than one arbitrator. If unanimity cannot be reached, then a decision can be reached by majority. If neither unanimity nor majority can be reached, then the chair of the tribunal will make a decision. If there is no chair, then if the tribunal consists of three or more arbitrators the decision will devolve on the last to be appointed, if the tribunal consists of two arbitrators, the decision will devolve on an umpire. Such an umpire is to

---

[160] Having been requested to do so a reasonable period in advance of the hearing.

be appointed by the tribunal, but where the tribunal fails to do so within 14 days of being so requested by a party or arbitrator, any party or arbitrator may request an arbitral appointments referee to make the appointment.

CONFIDENTIALITY AND ANONYMITY

9.3.11 It has never been doubted that arbitral proceedings are private, but various jurisdictions have held different opinions as to whether arbitration attracts obligations of confidentiality. The issue had never arisen in the Scottish courts, but the matter is put beyond doubt by the Act, which addresses the issue in r.26. It should nonetheless be noted that this is a default provision which can be excluded or modified by the parties. Rule 26(1) states that disclosure by the tribunal, any arbitrator or a party of confidential information relating to the arbitration is to be actionable as a breach of an obligation of confidence unless the disclosure:

- is expressly or impliedly authorised by the parties (or can reasonably be considered as having been so authorised;
- is required by the tribunal or otherwise made to assist or enable the tribunal to conduct the arbitration;
- is required in order to comply with any enactment or rule of law;
- is required for the proper performance of the discloser's public functions;
- is required in order to enable any public body or office holder to perform public functions properly;
- can reasonably be considered as needed to protect a party's lawful interests[161];
- is in the public interest;
- is necessary in the interests of justice;
- is made in circumstances in which the discloser would have absolute privilege had the disclosed information been defamatory.

In terms of r.26(4) confidential information means any information relating to the dispute, the arbitral proceedings, the award, or any civil proceedings relating to the arbitration in respect of which an order has been granted under s.15, which information is not and has never been in the public domain. Rule 26(2) directs that the tribunal and the parties must take reasonable steps to prevent unauthorised disclosure of confidential information by any third party involved in the arbitration, e.g. clerks, employees and witnesses. Finally r.26(3) indicates that the tribunal at the outset of the arbitration must inform the parties of the obligations which this rule imposes on them.

Rule 26 mentions s.15. This relates to the separate but related issue of civil proceedings relating to arbitration. Court proceedings are of course public, but this would obviously impinge of the confidential nature of arbitration. Accordingly s.15(1) a party to civil proceedings relating to arbitration (other than proceedings to enforce an award under s.12) may apply to the court for an order prohibiting the disclosure of the identity of a party to the arbitration in any report of the proceedings. Under s.15(2) The court must grant the order unless satisfied that disclosure:

- is required for the proper performance of the discloser's public functions;
- is required in order to enable any public body or office holder to perform public functions properly;
- can reasonably be considered as needed to protect a party's lawful interests;
- would be in the public interest;
- would be necessary in the interests of justice.

The court's determination of an application is not open to an appeal.[162]

---

[161] See *Gray Construction Ltd v Harley Haddow LLP*, 2012 S.L.T. 1035; a case decided at common law.
[162] See s.15(3).

THE COURT AND THE ARBITRATION   9.3.12

It is one of the founding principles of the Act under s.1(c) that courts should not intervention except as provided by the Act. However, it has already been seen that the Outer House may have to become involved in the appointment of the tribunal, or in its dismissal or the removal on an arbitrator. Equally, it may have to deal with a party's objection to an arbitral tribunal's ruling on its own jurisdiction. It will be seen somewhat later that the court may also entertain challenges to arbitral awards. Yet, in the present context, it may be observed that the court has certain powers which it may exercise in support of the arbitration, which powers reflect the fact that the tribunal's jurisdiction is created by the agreement of the parties and so must be limited to the parties, so that it has no power over third parties. Accordingly, in terms of the mandatory r.45(1) the court may, on the application of the tribunal or any party, order a person to attend a hearing in order to give evidence as a witness, or disclose documents or other material evidence to the tribunal.[163] It may be useful for a court otherwise to intervene in support of an arbitration, so r.46 confers a number of other powers on it. In this case, however, the rule is default, reflecting the fact that the parties may prefer that the court should not have some or all of these powers. Accordingly, the parties may exclude r.46 altogether or remove some of the powers it would otherwise confer. Moreover, the court may only take the action sought on an application by a party,[164] while if the arbitration has begun the tribunal must consent to the action unless the court is satisfied that the case is urgent.[165] What are the powers conferred by r.46? Rule 46(1) states that the court has the same power in an arbitration as it has in civil proceedings to:

- appoint a person to safeguard the interests of any party lacking capacity;
- order the sale of any property in dispute in the arbitration;
- make an order securing any amount in dispute in the arbitration;
- make an order under s.1 of the Administration of Justice (Scotland) Act 1972. Section 1(1) of that provision grants the Court of Session and sheriff court the power, "to order the inspection, photographing, preservation, custody and detention of documents and other property (including, where appropriate, land), which appear to the court to be property as to which any question may relevantly arise in existing civil proceedings, or in civil proceedings which are likely to be brought, and to order the production and recovery of any such property, the taking of samples thereof and the carrying out of any experiment thereon or therewith." Section 1(1A) then adds the power to order any person to disclose such information he has as to the identity of any persons who appear to the court to be persons who either might be witnesses in any existing civil proceedings before that court or in civil proceedings which are likely to be brought; or might be defenders in any civil proceedings which appear to the court to be likely to be brought. However, s.1(4) states that the section is subject to the rules regarding privilege, confidentiality of communications and withholding or non-disclosure of information on the grounds of public interest;
- grant warrant for arrestment or inhibition;
- grant interdict or interim interdict;
- grant any other interim or permanent order.

A further power which the court may exercise in support of the arbitration is the power under r.43, on the application by the tribunal or any party to vary any agreed time limit. Once more, since the parties may think it inappropriate that the court should be able thus to override their agreement, this is a default provision. However, if the provision is not excluded, the court may only exercise the power if satisfied that no arbitral process for varying the time limit is available and that someone would suffer a substantial

---

[163] But if the person would have been entitled to refuse to testify or disclose evidence in civil proceedings, the court cannot order him to testify or disclose: r.45(2). *SGL Carbon Fibres Ltd, Petitioners*, 2013 S.L.T. 307; indicates that before the court will exercise its power to disclose documents, the arbitrator must have decided that their disclosure is necessary for the proper determination of the case.

[164] See r.46(2)(a).

[165] See r.46(2)(b).

injustice if no variation was made.[166] It is for the court to determine the extent of any variation[167] and its decision of whether to make a variation (and the extent of any variation) is not subject to appeal.[168]

Under r.41 the court may, on application by any party, determine any point of Scots law arising in the arbitration. This is a controversial provision, since this may be regarded as the ultimate function of the tribunal. Accordingly, it is a default rule. The rule may of course have no application in the first place, since the dispute between the parties may not be governed by Scots law, for example, where foreign parties may have simply chosen Scotland as a neutral arbitral forum. Where the dispute is governed by Scots law, parties may wish to retain the rule, since an award may be challenged on the basis of error of Scots law under r.69, and if a controversial point of Scots law emerges, which is almost bound to generate a r.69 challenge no matter how the tribunal decides it, it may be more sensible to dispose of it at an early stage rather than attacking the award. If the rule is not excluded, the mandatory r.42 adds that such an application is only valid when either:

- the parties have agreed to it being made; or
- the tribunal has consented to it being made, and the court is satisfied that, determining the question is likely to produce a substantial saving in expense, the application was made without delay, and there is a good reason why the question should be determined by the court.

9.3.13 THE AWARD

The ultimate aim of the arbitral process is to produce an award—the equivalent of the judgment of the court in civil proceedings. The Act mentions various types of awards. Thus the tribunal has power to make one or more part awards under the mandatory r.54. A part award will decide some of the issues between the parties, or perhaps only one issue. It may be resorted to when a certain matter or matters is easily disposed of. While a part award disposes of the issue(s) to which it relates once and for all a provisional award grants a remedy only on a provisional basis, and is liable to be overtaken by the final award. While the making of a provisional award may sometimes be very useful, e.g. where one party will clearly be found liable to the other, but the extent of liability is uncertain, it may be useful to order the payment of a modest amount of damages on a provisional basis, especially where the innocent party might otherwise suffer financial hardship. The danger with the making of a provisional award is that a party is awarded a remedy to which he is ultimately found not to be entitled. The power is therefore a controversial one. Consequently, while the tribunal has power to make such awards under r.53, the provision is default and may be excluded. Also default is the power to make draft awards. Rule 55 states that before making an award the tribunal may send a draft to the parties and, if it does so, must consider any representations they make within such period as it specifies. Some would argue that this is a useful means of avoiding errors in the award and thus challenges to the award. Others would say that it simply invites parties to debate the award. It might be noted that the default status of the rule means that the parties may equally agree that a draft award must be issued. Although this is not specifically mentioned by the Act, most awards will be final awards, which conclusively dispose of all the issues before the parties. The form of an award is addressed by r.51, which is a default provision. Thus, although r.51(1) states that the award must be signed by all arbitrators or all those assenting to the award, the parties may insist, for example, that all arbitrators must sign in every case, or that it is sufficient if the presiding arbitrator signs. This is obviously not an issue when there is only a single arbitrator. Rule 51(2) continues that the award must state the seat of the arbitration, i.e. Scotland,[169] when the award is made and when it takes effect, the reasons for the award, and whether any previous provisional or part award has been made and the extent to which it is superseded or confirmed. The award is made by delivering it to each of the parties.[170] In that context it may be added that the mandatory r.56(1)

---

[166] See r.44(2).
[167] See r.44(3).
[168] See r.44(5).
[169] See r.52 adds that an award is treated as made in Scotland even if signed at or delivered to or from another place.
[170] See r.51(3).

provides that the tribunal may refuse to deliver the award to the parties if any fees or expenses for which they are liable under r.60 (see para.9.3.17.1) have not been paid in full. However, on an application by a party the court may order[171]:

- that the tribunal must deliver the award on the applicant paying into the court an amount equal to the fees and expenses demanded, or such lesser amount as may be specified in the order. The court may order the release of the award on payment of a smaller amount than that demanded, when, for example the latter amount seems unreasonably high;
- that the amount paid into the court is to be used to pay the fees and expenses which the court determines as being properly payable; and
- that any balance is to be repaid to the applicant.

The court's decision on such an application is not open to appeal.[172]

What will an award do? Essentially it will uphold or reject the claim (or counterclaim) made by a party, whether in whole or in part. If a claim is entirely rejected, then the award will order nothing, but the matter will then be res judicata. If the tribunal upholds a claim, then it will usually order the payment of a sum of money, whether as a debt or in the form of damages. Indeed, the mandatory r.48 provides that the award may order payment of a sum of money (including a sum in respect of damages), continuing that this sum must be specified in any currency agreement by the parties, or in the absence of such agreement in such currency as the tribunal considers appropriate. The mandatory r.50(1) then provides that the award may order that interest is to be paid on:

- the whole or part of any amount which the award orders to be paid[173] in respect of any period up to the date of the award;
- the whole or part of any amount which is claimed in the arbitration and outstanding when the arbitration began but paid before the award was made, in respect of the period up to the date of payment;
- the outstanding amount of any amount awarded (including arbitration expenses and/or pre-award interest) in respect of the period the date of the award up to the date of payment.

The award may specify the interest rate and the period for which interest is payable (including any rests[174] the tribunal thinks appropriate).[175] An award may make different interest provisions in respect of different amounts,[176] while interest is to be calculated as agreed by the parties or, failing such agreement, in such manner as the tribunal determines.[177] The fact that r.50 is mandatory precludes the parties from excluding the power to award interest, but the parties do control its calculation, and thus can set interest at a negligible rate.

An award need not be confined to ordering the payment of money. Rule 49 states that it may:

- be of a declaratory nature, i.e. simply declare what the rights of the parties are;
- order a party to do or refrain from doing something, i.e. order specific implement or interdict;
- order the rectification or reduction of a deed or other document (other than a decree of court) to the extent permitted by the law governing that deed or other document.

However, r.49 is a default provision, so the parties may decide that the tribunal is not to have some or any of these extra remedies at its disposal. Alternatively they may confer power to grant remedies not mentioned here.

---

[171] See r.56(2)—but by virtue of r.56(3) the court may only make such an order if the applicant has exhausted any available arbitral process of review of the amount of fees and expenses demanded.

[172] See r.56(4).

[173] Or which is payable in terms of an award which merely declares the rights of the parties.

[174] A rest is a period during which interest ceases to be payable.

[175] See r.50(2).

[176] See r.50(3).

[177] See r.50(4).

What considerations should a tribunal take into account in reaching its award? Many awards will see the straightforward application of Scots law to determine the dispute. However, this will not necessarily be so, especially in arbitrations with an international dimension. Thus r.47(1) provides that the tribunal must decide the dispute in accordance with the law chosen by the parties as applicable to the substance of the dispute. If no such choice is made or a purported choice is unlawful, then the tribunal must decide the dispute in accordance with the law determined by the conflict of law rules it considers applicable. It can be seen then that the choice of the parties is the primary determinant of the governing law. Only when they do not make a choice will it fall to the tribunal to do so, and then it will be constrained by conflict of law rules. It might simply decide which system appears to be most closely connected with the dispute, and use the conflict of law rules of that system to ascertain the governing law. Alternatively, it may wish to apply the law of a particular system, and might thus search for a set of conflict of law rules which would suggest that the law of that system should govern the dispute. It would only be if it could not find a set of conflict of law rules which pointed to that conclusion that it could not apply that particular law. The aim of the provision is to have the dispute determined by a particular substantive law, which is emphasised by r.47(2) continuing that "accordingly" the tribunal must not decide the dispute on the basis of general considerations of justice, fairness or equity unless these form part of the law concerned or the parties so agree. Nonetheless, since r.47 is a default provision, the parties may authorise the tribunal to decide the dispute not only on the basis of criteria such as justice, but equally on the basis of non-legal criteria or anational systems of law such as *lex mercatoria*. Rule 47(3) concludes by stating that when deciding the dispute the tribunal must have regard to:

- the provisions of any contract relating to the substance of the dispute;
- the normal commercial or trade usage of any undefined terms in the provisions of such contract;
- any established commercial or trade customs or practice relevant to the substance of the dispute; and
- any other matter which the parties agree is relevant in the circumstances.

Under r.58(1)–(2) the tribunal, either on its own initiative or on an application by a party, may correct a clerical, typographical or other error in the award, arising by accident or omission, or clarify or remove any ambiguity in the award. This is a very useful power, but since the provision is default, the parties may deprive the tribunal of it. A party making an application must at the same time send a copy to the other party,[178] and an application is only valid if made within 28 days of the award or by such later date as the court may specify on an application by the party.[179] Before deciding whether to correct an award, the tribunal must give each of the parties or the non-applicant party a reasonable opportunity to make representations about the proposed correction.[180] A correction can only be made within 28 days of the award when the tribunal proposed the correction, or within 28 days of an application.[181]

9.3.14 CHALLENGING AWARDS

A party may challenge an award before the Outer House on a variety of grounds, but before exploring these it is important to note that a party who appears entitled to challenge an award may in fact be disabled from doing so as a result of having failed to make an objection at the proper time. Thus the mandatory r.76 stipulates that a party who participates in an arbitration without making a timeous objection in relation to a variety of grounds may not raise the objection later before the tribunal or court. Thus a party who believes that the tribunal has no jurisdiction, but who does not raise this issue, cannot ask the tribunal to address the matter when the proceedings are well advanced, nor challenge that jurisdiction before the court, whether in an application to set aside the award or otherwise. It can be seen that this is a provision of general application, not confined to situations where the award is

---

[178] See r.58(3).
[179] See r.58(4). The court's determination is not open to appeal.
[180] See r.58(5).
[181] See r.58(6).

being challenged, but it is convenient to discuss it in the present context. What are the grounds in question? They are that:

- an arbitrator is not eligible to act as such;
- an arbitrator is not impartial and independent;
- an arbitrator has not treated the parties fairly;
- the tribunal does not have jurisdiction;
- the arbitration has not been conducted in accordance with the agreement of the parties or the Rules (in so far as they apply);
- the arbitration has been affected by any other serious irregularity.

What is a timeous objection? An objection is timeous if made as soon as is reasonably practicable after the circumstances giving rise to the ground for objection first arose, or by such later date as may be allowed by the arbitration agreement, the Rules, or the other party. Moreover, the tribunal itself may allow a later objection if it considers that the circumstances justify it. However, r.76 does not apply where a party shows that it did not object timeously because it did not know of the ground of objection and could not have discovered it with reasonable diligence. Thus while a party who seeks to attack an award on the basis that an arbitrator is not impartial will prima facie not be caught by r.76 if he was unaware of the circumstances casting doubt on an arbitrator's impartiality, the rule will still apply if he could easily have found out about those circumstances. Rule 76 deals with a party who participates in an arbitration without objection. Matters are different where a party refuses to participate. Section 14(2) indicates that a person who is alleged to be a party to an arbitration but who takes no part in the arbitration may appeal against an award on the basis of lack of jurisdiction or serious irregularity.

Mechanics of appeal

9.3.14.1

An appeal is only competent where the appellant has exhausted any available arbitral process of appeal or review, including the tribunal's own power to correct an award.[182] An appellant must give notice of any appeal to the other party and the tribunal,[183] while under r.71(4) an appeal must be made no later than 28 days after the latest of the following dates:

- the date when the award is made;
- if the award is subject to correction under r.58, the date on which the tribunal decides whether or not to make that correction; or
- if there has been an arbitral process of appeal or review, the date on which the appellant was informed of the result of that process.

The Outer House[184] may order the tribunal to state its reasons for the award under appeal in sufficient detail to enable it to deal with the appeal properly.[185] It may sometimes be the case that an appeal is made with little prospect of success, and the other party may have to defend the appeal under the risk that he is unable to recover the expenses of so doing. Accordingly, the Outer House[186] may order the appellant (or any applicant for leave to appeal) to provide security for the expenses of the appeal (or application), and dismiss the appeal (or application) if this is not done.[187] However, such an order may not be made only on the ground that the appellant (or applicant) is an individual who resides outwith the UK, or is a body incorporated or formed in a country outwith the UK or managed or controlled from outwith the UK. In other words, while the difficulty in enforcing an award of expenses against a foreign party may influence the decision whether to order the provision of security, the Outer House should not

---

[182] See r.71(2).
[183] See r.71(6).
[184] Or the Inner House in the case of an appeal against the decision of the Outer House.
[185] See r.71(8)(a). And it may also make any order it thinks fit with respect to additional expenses arising from that order: r.71(8)(b).
[186] Or the Inner House in the case of an appeal against the decision of the Outer House.
[187] See r.71(10).

make such an order merely because an appellant is foreign. An even greater concern for a party facing an appeal is that even if the appeal is rejected, the other party will not honour the award. Consequently, the Outer House[188] may order that any amount due under an award under appeal be paid into court or otherwise secured pending its decision on the appeal (or application for leave to appeal) and dismiss the appeal (or application) if this is not done.[189] A further appeal to the Inner House against any decision of the Outer House, whether on a ground of appeal or an issue relating to the making of an appeal, requires the leave of the Outer House, which may be given where it considers that the proposed appeal would raise an important point of principle or practice or that there is some other compelling reason for the Inner House to consider the appeal.[190] The decision of the Outer House on whether to give leave to appeal cannot itself be appealed, while the decision of the Inner House on an appeal cannot be further appealed to the Supreme Court.[191]

9.3.14.2 Grounds of appeal

There are three bases on which an award[192] may be challenged before the Outer House—lack of jurisdiction, serious irregularity and error of Scots law. These are exclusive, since s.13(2) states that an award is not subject to review or appeal except as provided for in Pt 8 of the Rules. The grounds are considered in detail below

9.3.14.2.1 *Jurisdiction*

A jurisdictional appeal may be made under the mandatory r.67 and the Outer House may decide such an appeal by confirming the award, varying it (in whole or in part) any such variation then having effect as part of the award, or setting it aside (in whole or in part).

9.3.14.2.2 *Serious irregularity*

The mandatory r.68 creates the possibility of an appeal to the Outer House on the basis of serious irregularity. In terms of r.68(2) there are various potential categories of serious irregularity, but none will amount to such unless it has caused or will cause substantial injustice to the appellant. In other words, it does not matter if the appellant can bring himself under one of the categories below unless he can also show that this has resulted in a significant difference to the outcome. The categories are;

- the tribunal failing to conduct the arbitration in accordance with the agreement of the parties or the Rules (in so far as they apply);
- the tribunal acting outwith its powers (other than by exceeding its jurisdiction);
- the tribunal failing to deal with all the issues put to it;
- an arbitral appointments referee or other third party empowered by the parties acting outwith his powers;
- uncertainty or ambiguity as to the award's effect;
- the award being contrary to public policy or obtained by fraud or in a way contrary to public policy;
- an arbitrator not having been impartial and independent;
- an arbitrator not having treated the parties fairly;
- an arbitrator having been incapable of acting as such in the arbitration (or there being justifiable doubts about an arbitrator's ability so to act);

---

[188] Or the Inner House in the case of an appeal against the decision of the Outer House.

[189] See r.71(12).

[190] See rr.67(4)–(5), 68(5)–(6), 70(9)–(10), 71(13) (15). An application for leave to appeal must be made no later than 28 days after the decision of the Outer House on the appeal, any such leave expiring seven days after it is granted: r.71(5) (14).

[191] See rr.67(6)–(7), 68(7)–(8), 70(11)–(12), 71(16)–(17).

[192] Including a part award—but no appeal lies against a provisional award: r.71(3). If an appeal has been made against a part award, the tribunal may continue with the rest of the arbitration pending its determination: r.71(7).

- an arbitrator not having a qualification which the parties agreed before his appointment that he must have;
- any other irregularity in the conduct of the arbitration or in the award admitted by the tribunal, or an arbitral appointments referee or other third party empowered by the parties.

It can be appreciated that certain of these categories are more likely to be productive of substantial injustice than others. The Outer House may decide such an appeal by confirming the award, ordering the tribunal to reconsider it (or part of it) or, if it thinks that reconsideration is inappropriate, by setting aside the award (or part of it).[193] It may be seen that setting aside the award is very much the last resort. However, there may be situations where setting aside the award is inevitable, e.g. where it is contrary to public policy. On the other hand, where the issue is that the tribunal failed to deal with all the issues put to it, reconsideration might be expected to be ordered.

Legal error 9.3.14.2.3

It is relatively rare for a legal system to allow for the possibility of an appeal against the award on the basis of an error of law. One reason for this is that the parties have entrusted the determination of their dispute to an arbitral tribunal rather than the court and thus do not contemplate that the court should be able to review the legal correctness of the tribunal's decision. Yet other systems do not share that approach, taking the view that there may be all sorts of reasons why parties have chosen to arbitrate and rejecting the idea that by doing so the parties have impliedly accepted the risk that the tribunal may go seriously wrong in law. Scots law falls into the latter camp. Thus r.69 creates the possibility of a legal error appeal to the Outer House. However, an appeal only lies where there is an error of Scots law, so that the provision does not apply where the substance of the dispute has been settled by reference to the law of some other legal system, e.g. England, or by reference to anational systems or extra-legal principles. Moreover, while rr.67 and 68 are mandatory, the more controversial nature of this ground of appeal is recognised by r.69 being default. Thus the parties may choose to exclude the possibility of an appeal against the award on the basis of an error of Scots law, and r.69(2) states that an agreement to dispense with the need for the tribunal to state its reasons for an award operates as such an exclusion.

If r.69 does apply, the mandatory r.70 specifies a number of conditions for its operation. Thus a legal error appeal may be made only with the agreement of the parties, or the leave of the Outer House.[194] Under r.70(3) such leave may only be given if the Outer House is satisfied that:

- deciding the point will substantially affect a party's rights;
- the tribunal was asked to decide the point; and
- on the basis of the facts found in the award (including any facts treated as established) the tribunal's decision on the point was obviously wrong, or (where the court considers the point to be of general importance) open to serious doubt.

An application for leave is only valid if it identifies the point of law concerned and states why the applicant considers leave should be granted.[195] The Outer House's determination of an application for leave is not open to appeal.[196] If leave is granted, it expires within seven days, so that any appeal can only be made thereafter with the agreement of the parties.[197] As with a serious irregularity appeal, the Outer House may decide a legal error appeal by confirming the award, ordering the tribunal to reconsider it (or part of it), or if it thinks that reconsideration is inappropriate, by setting aside the award (or part of it).[198]

---

[193] See r.68(3).
[194] See r.70(2).
[195] See r.70(4); and the Outer House must determine an application without a hearing unless it is satisfied that a hearing is required: r.70(5).
[196] See r.70(6).
[197] See r.70(7).
[198] See r.70(8).

Under r.72 where a tribunal has been ordered to reconsider its award (or part of it), it must make a new award (or confirm its original award) in the case of a decision by the Outer House by no later than:

- should the decision be appealed, the date falling three months after the appeal (or application for leave to appeal) is dismissed or abandoned;
- if the decision is not appealed, the day falling three months after the decision is made; or
- such other day as the Outer House may specify.

In the case of a decision by the Inner House, the key date is the day falling three months after the decision is made, or such other day as the Inner House may specify.

9.3.15 THE RIGHTS OF ARBITRATORS

9.3.15.1 Remuneration

While at one point the office of arbitrator was presumed to be exercised gratuitously, this has long ceased to be the case. As is discussed at para.9.3.17.1, the parties are under r.60(1) severally liable for the fees and expenses of the arbitrator(s). By virtue of r.60(4), those fees and expenses are to be agreed between the arbitrator(s) and the parties, failing which they will be determined by the Auditor of Court.[199]

However, r.60(6)(b) indicates that r.60 does not affect the power of the Outer House to make an order under r.16. The mandatory r.16 states that where an arbitrator's tenure ends, the Outer House, on an application by any party or the arbitrator concerned, may make such an order as it thinks fit about the arbitrator's entitlement (if any) to fees and expenses[200] and/or the repayment of any fees and expenses already paid to that arbitrator.[201] In terms of r.9 an arbitrator's tenure ends when he becomes ineligible to act as such by becoming an incapable adult; where he is removed by the parties, an authorised third party or the Outer House; where the Outer House dismisses the tribunal of which he forms part; or where he resigns or dies. Some of the situations in which an arbitrator's tenure ends might be regarded as blameworthy, so r.16 allows the Outer House to reflect that fact by restricting the amount of fees and expenses payable and/or ordering him to repay an amount already paid. Yet, although an order under r.16 will normally be made where some element of blame attaches to an arbitrator, this will not necessarily be the case. For example, an arbitrator who has died might already have agreed upon and received a fee for conducting the arbitration. It would be entirely appropriate to seek the repayment of at least part of that fee. The Outer House's determination of an application is not open to appeal.[202] An order under r.16 clearly prevails over the contractual rights of the arbitrator and parties or any determination by the Auditor of Court.

Moreover, r.68(4) states that where a serious irregularity appeal has been made under r.68 on the basis that

- the tribunal has failed to conduct the arbitration in accordance with the Rules or the parties' agreement; or
- an arbitrator has not been impartial and independent; or
- an arbitrator has not treated the parties fairly,

and the Outer House had decided the appeal other than by merely confirming the award, it may make such order as it thinks fit regarding any arbitrator's entitlement (if any) to fees and expenses, and such order may provide for the repayment of fees and expenses already paid. The idea behind this provision is that it will sometimes be appropriate for the court to reduce or even extinguish an arbitrator's

---

[199] If the Auditor has to determine fees and expenses, then unless he decides otherwise, a reasonable amount is to be allowed in relation to all reasonably incurred expenses, while fees are to be determined on the basis of a reasonable commercial rate of charge (r.60(4)).

[200] See r.16(1)(a).

[201] See r.16(1)(b).

[202] See r.16(3).

entitlement to fees and expenses, because the way in which he has conducted the arbitration has led to the award being legitimately challenged. The most obvious situation where that power might be exercised is where the conduct in question has caused the award to be set aside in whole or in part, but it can be appreciated that the power is available even where the award is merely remitted to the tribunal for reconsideration in terms of r.72 (see para.9.3.14.2.3). It may be that the problem has been the behaviour of only one member of the tribunal, as where a particular arbitrator has not been impartial and independent, so that it is possible for the court to deal differently with different members of the tribunal in this context. Since the provision is mandatory, it cannot be qualified or excluded, and it will obviously prevail over the contractual rights of the arbitrator in question and any determination made by the Auditor of Court.

Resignation   9.3.15.2

The mandatory r.15 states that an arbitrator may resign by giving notice to the parties and any other arbitrators if:

- the parties consent to the resignation;
- he has a contractual right to resign in the circumstances;
- his appointment is challenged before the tribunal under r.10 or by the court under r.12;
- the parties, after he is appointed, disapply or modify r.34(1), which allows the tribunal to obtain an expert opinion on any matter arising in the arbitration;
- the Outer House has authorised his resignation, having been satisfied on his application that it is reasonable for him to resign.[203] The Outer House's determination of such an application is final.[204]

If an arbitrator resigns in circumstances other than those described above, the Outer House may, under r.16(1)(a)–(b), make an order reducing his entitlement to fees and expenses, perhaps to zero, and/or may compel him to repay some or all of any fees and expenses he has already received. Indeed, under r.16(1)(c), where an arbitrator has resigned, the Outer House, on an application by any party or the arbitrator concerned, may make such an order as it thinks fit about the arbitrator's liability in respect of acting as an arbitrator. In this context r.16(2) states that the Outer House must, in considering whether to make an order, have particular regard to whether the arbitrator resigned in accordance with r.15. It would be unusual for an arbitrator to make an application in these circumstances, although he might do so if he is anxious to establish that he resigned properly and that no liability should therefore attach to him. Far more likely of course is that a party or perhaps both parties will ask the Outer House to decide that the arbitrator resigned improperly and thus should be liable to the parties. For what should an arbitrator be liable? Presumably he should be liable for any wasted expenses the parties incur which are attributable to the resignation, but the Outer House has a discretion here and may decide to make no order or may order that he bear a restricted liability. The decision of the Outer House is not open to appeal by virtue of r.16(3).

ARBITRAL AND OTHER IMMUNITY   9.3.16

While there is no clear Scottish authority on this issue at common law the mandatory r.73(1) states that neither the tribunal nor any arbitrator is liable for anything done or omitted in the performance or purported performance of the tribunal's functions. By virtue of r.82(1), r.73 also applies to umpires. There are two exceptions under r.73(2). Rule 73 does not apply to any liability arising out of an arbitrator's resignation, an issue which is discussed immediately above. Nor does it apply to any act or omission shown to have been in bad faith. Rule 73(3) extends the r.73 immunity to any clerk to the arbitration or to any agent, employee or other person assisting the tribunal to perform its functions. Moreover, the mandatory r.74(1) states that an arbitral appointments referee or other third party who is asked to

---

[203] See r.15(2).
[204] See r.15(3).

appoint or nominate an arbitrator is not liable for anything done or omitted in the performance or purported performance of that function, unless the act or omission is shown to have been in bad faith. Nor is such a referee or third party liable for the acts or omissions of any arbitrator it nominates or appoints, or of the tribunal of which that arbitrator forms part. Rule 74(1) provides that the rule applies equally to any agent or employee of such a referee or third party.

The mandatory r.75 then states that every person who participates in an arbitration as an expert, witness or legal representative has the same immunity in respect of acts or omissions as that person would have if the arbitration were civil proceedings. What does this mean? Generally, an ordinary witness has absolute immunity in respect of his evidence, in that no civil action may be brought against him on the ground that the things he said or did in the proceedings were said or done either falsely and maliciously or negligently.[205] In court proceedings the immunity covers any statement of the evidence that the witness might give if called to give evidence, e.g. a precognition, and so applies to a potential or prospective witness[206] who may not be called to give evidence.[207] It would also apply to statements made where proceedings are merely in contemplation but have not yet commenced.[208] Presumably such statements should also fall within the scope of r.75. Civil immunity also applies to the early stages of litigation (and so presumably arbitration) where evidence is being collected with a view to the proceedings.[209] In particular it applies to the compilation of expert and technical reports in the course of an investigation with a view to giving evidence.[210] Thus, negligence in the preparation of a report (but not the wrongful fabrication of evidence[211]) is protected as part of the preparation by a potential witness.[212] An expert may perform a dual role, acting firstly as an advisor to a party, and secondly in the capacity as expert witness with all the responsibilities to the court as which that entails.[213] The former role does not attract immunity,[214] while the latter does.

Yet the above account must, however, be read subject to the view of the majority of the Supreme Court in the English case of *Jones v Kaney*[215] that an expert witness is *not* subject to any special immunity, although the case did not attempt to disturb the blanket immunity of ordinary witnesses.[216] Moreover, it addressed only the liability of expert witnesses to the clients who had engaged them, as opposed to "adverse experts" engaged by other parties. However, a Scottish decision of the House of Lords (*Watson v McEwan*[217]) seems to suggest that expert witnesses enjoy the same immunity as other witnesses. While Lord Phillips in *Kaney* looked to distinguish the case on the basis that it was concerned with the expert witness's potential liability for defamation, Lord Hope (dissenting) suggested that it established a more general principle.[218] Lord Hope indeed insisted[219] that *Watson v McEwan* "remains binding in Scotland". Despite that view, it remains possible that the Scots courts will regard *Kaney* as having altered the law on this matter both north and south of the border, since there has never been any suggestion that the two systems differed in their approach to the matter.

---

[205] *Watson v McEwan* (1905) 7 F. (H.L.) 109 at 110; *B v Burns*, 1994 S.L.T. 250 at 252G; *McKie v Strathclyde Police Joint Board*, 2004 S.L.T. 982 at [15]; *Darker v Chief Constable of the West Midlands* [2001] A.C. 435, per Lord Hope at 445H–446B.

[206] *B v Burns*, 1994 S.L.T. 250 at 252G–I.

[207] *Darker v Chief Constable of the West Midlands* [2001] A.C. 435, per Lord Clyde at 458E.

[208] *Darker v Chief Constable of the West Midlands* [2001] A.C. 435, per Lord Hope at 447E.

[209] *Darker v Chief Constable of the West Midlands* [2001] A.C. 435, per Lord Clyde at 458G and Lord Hope at 448B.

[210] *Darker v Chief Constable of the West Midlands* [2001] A.C. 435, per Lord Hope at 448B; *McKie v Strathclyde Police Joint Board*, 2004 S.L.T. 982 at [15].

[211] *Darker v Chief Constable of the West Midlands* [2001] A.C. 435, per Lord Hope at 445–449, Lord McKay at 452, Lord Cooke at 455–456, Lord Clyde at 456–461, Lord Hutton at 471.

[212] *Darker v Chief Constable of the West Midlands* [2001] A.C. 435; per Lord Hutton at 471G–472B; *Evans v London Hospital Medical College* [1981] 1 W.L.R. 184 at 190.

[213] See Lord President Cooper in *Davie v Magistrates of Edinburgh* 1953 S.C. 34 at 40; Cresswell J in *The Ikarian Reefer* [1993] 2 Lloyd's Rep. 68 at 81–82.

[214] *Darker v Chief Constable of the West Midlands* [2001] A.C. 435, per Lord Hope at 448C

[215] *Jones v Kaney* [2011] 2 WLR 823.

[216] See, e.g. Lord Dyson at [101].

[217] *Watson v McEwan* (1905) 7 F. (H.L.) 109.

[218] *Jones v Kaney* [2011] 2 WLR 823. See [136]–[142].

[219] *Jones v Kaney* [2011] 2 WLR 823 at [173].

The third category of individual mentioned by r.75 is a legal representative. Both solicitors and advocates owe a duty of care to their clients and can be sued for giving negligent advice.[220] However, the position regarding their conduct of cases is more complicated. In *Wright v Paton Farrell*[221] Lord President Hamilton noted that at one point it seemed to be the law that advocates enjoyed immunity in respect of their conduct of cases because they held a public office, while solicitors did not because they were employed by their clients.[222] However, in *Rondel v Worsley*[223] Lord Reid had opined that barrister immunity was based on public policy rather than employment status, that there appeared to be no relevant difference between England and Scotland in that respect, and[224] that "public interest does require that a solicitor should not be liable for negligence in carrying out work in litigation which would have been carried out by counsel if counsel had been engaged". Lord President Hamilton observed, that while that view was technically not binding in Scotland, it had been endorsed by a bench of five in *Anderson v HM Advocate*.[225] Yet Lord Osborne[226] noted that, prior to *Rondel v Worsley*, there was extensive authority[227] for the view that "no immunity from suit was recognised in Scots law on the part of solicitors acting alone and without the advice of counsel in relation to in court advocacy". He was further of the opinion[228] that *Rondel v Worsley* had not altered that position, since Lord Reid had only advanced his views tentatively, and there was little real examination of the Scottish position. Moreover, the court in *Anderson v HM Advocate* had simply narrated the views of Lord Reid in *Rondel v Worsley* rather than endorsing them, while any endorsement would in any case have been obiter, since the issue in *Anderson* was whether defective representation could constitute a miscarriage of justice.[229] Lord Johnston expressed no concluded view on the issue, but indicated that he was "not so convinced as" Lord Osborne that "Lord Reid was not amalgamating the roles of solicitor and counsel into one of advocate and certainly there is a certain logic in that approach".

Since *Rondel* was decided the House of Lords in the English case of *Hall (Arthur JS) & Co v Simons*[230] has removed the immunity of a legal representative in respect of conducting both civil and criminal proceedings. All seven of their Lorsdhips agreed that the immunity should be removed in respect of civil proceedings. The minority[231] would have retained the immunity in respect of criminal proceedings. The fact that the minority included Lord Hope clearly carried weight with the First Division in *Wright v Paton Farrell*.[232] The views of the judges in that case are obiter, but favoured declining to follow *Hall* in respect of removing the immunity in respect of criminal proceedings.[233] However, for present purposes the key issue is whether the Scots courts would follow *Hall* in respect of removing the immunity in respect of civil proceedings. The issue did not arise for discussion, but the judges all stressed the reasons why the immunity was particularly important to the effective administration of the system of criminal justice. Most importantly, Lord President Hamilton[234] observed of *Hall* that

> "[t]he fact that their Lordships were unanimously of the view that, in so far as civil proceedings were concerned, advocates' immunity from suit was no longer justified is a telling pointer to a new perception. Counsel . . . urged us not to assume that the same conclusion would or should be reached in relation to civil proceedings in Scotland. It is unnecessary to make that assumption

---

[220] See, e.g. *Hall (Arthur J S) & Co v Simons* [2002] 1 A.C. 615, per Lord Hoffmann at 698D–E, Lord Hobhouse at 741B–C.

[221] *Wright v Paton Farrell*, 2006 S.L.T. 269 at [6]–[11].

[222] See Lord President Inglis in *Batchelor v Pattison and Mackersy* (1876) 3 R. 914 at 918

[223] *Rondel v Worsley* [1969] 1 A.C. 191 at 227.

[224] *Rondel v Worsley* [1969] 1 A.C. 191 at 232.

[225] *Anderson v HM Advocate*, 1996 S.L.T. 155 at 158–159.

[226] *Wright v Paton Farrell*, 2006 S.L.T. 269 at [139].

[227] See, e.g. Lord Campbell in *Purves v Landell* (1845) 4 Bell's App 46 at 61.

[228] *Wright v Paton Farrell*, 2006 S.L.T. 269 at [143].

[229] See *Wright v Paton Farrell*, 2006 S.L.T. 269 at [144].

[230] *Hall (Arthur JS) & Co v Simons* [2002] 1 A.C. 615.

[231] *Hall (Arthur JS) & Co v Simons* [2002] 1 A.C. 615 per Lord Hope at 712A, Lord Hutton at 730C and Lord Hobhouse at 735D.

[232] *Wright v Paton Farrell*, 2006 S.L.T. 269. See especially Lord President Hamilton at [12].

[233] *Wright v Paton Farrell*, 2006 S.L.T. 269. See especially Lord President Hamilton at [32], Lord Osborne at [171] and Lord Johnston at [182].

[234] *Wright v Paton Farrell*, 2006 S.L.T. 269 at [13].

and I do not do so. But, as presently advised, I find it difficult to suppose that the unanimous views of their Lordships on that aspect . . . would not be highly influential on a Scottish court."

The position therefore is somewhat unclear. It was probable that, following *Rondel*, both solicitors and advocates would have immunity in respect of their conduct of civil proceedings, although on one view solicitors have never had that immunity. It is now probable that, following *Hall*, immunity no longer exists. Accordingly, when r.75 speaks of a legal representative having the same immunity as he would enjoy in civil proceedings, it is being misleading.

9.3.17 ARBITRATION EXPENSES

While one might expect the issue of expenses to be dealt with in the discussion of the award, or the rights of arbitrators, the fact that the subject occupies a whole part (Pt 7) of the Rules suggests that it merits separate treatment.

9.3.17.1 **Several liability of parties**

While most of the Rules which regulate expenses are default, the mandatory r.60 makes the parties severally liable to pay to the arbitrators certain fees and expenses. These are:

- the arbitrators' fees and expenses, including their fees for conducting the arbitration, and expenses they incur personally in that endeavour;
- expenses incurred by the tribunal when conducting the arbitration,[235] including

  - the fees and expenses of any clerk, agent, employee or other person appointed by the tribunal to assist it in conducting the arbitration,
  - the fees and expenses of any expert from whom the tribunal obtains an opinion,
  - any expenses in respect of meeting and hearing facilities, and
  - any expenses incurred in determining recoverable arbitration expenses (see para.9.3.17.4).

Several liability is of course separate liability, so that in respect of these fees and expenses the arbitrators may choose to proceed against either party for the whole amount which they are owed, irrespective of the parties' liability as between themselves for such expenses. Thus if the parties have agreed that only one of them will be liable for such expenses, or if the tribunal has ruled to this effect, the arbitrators may still pursue the other party should the ostensibly liable party be unable to pay. The fact that the entire amount has been recovered from one party does not affect the parties' liability as between themselves, as r.60(6)(a) confirms.

Rule 60(2) states that the parties are also severally liable to pay the fees and expenses of any arbitral appointments referee or any other third party to whom the parties give powers in relation to the arbitration. Presumably they are liable to pay such fees and expenses to the referee or third party.

9.3.17.2 **Amount of fees and expenses**

The amount of fees and expenses payable and the terms on which they are payable are prima facie to be agreed by the parties and the arbitrators.[236] In the absence of such an agreement then the amount of fees and expenses payable and the terms on which they are payable are to be determined by the Auditor of the Court of Session.[237] Unless the Auditor decides otherwise, the amount of any fee is to be determined on the basis of a reasonable commercial rate of charge,[238] and the amount of any expenses

---

[235] There may not in fact be any expenses, since although it is obviously possible for the arbitrator(s) to meet the fees and expenses of clerks, experts, etc., and to hire the appropriate facilities, it may be arranged that the parties should provide or hire facilities and/or meet such other fees and expenses directly. Whatever arrangements are made, it would appear that clerks, experts, those who hire out facilities, etc., should they be struggling to receive payment, are not themselves helped by r.60, but must rely on the law of contract to ensure they are paid.

[236] See r.60(3)(a).

[237] See r.60(3)(b).

[238] See r.60(4)(a).

on the basis of a reasonable amount in respect of all reasonably incurred expenses.[239] The Auditor may disallow any expenses that he does not regard as reasonably incurred, and order the repayment of fees or expenses already paid which he considers to be excessive, such order having effect as if it were made by the court.[240] So where, for example, a party has already paid the fees and expenses demanded despite considering them to be excessive, since the tribunal would not otherwise release the award, either party might ask the Auditor to determine the amount of fees and expenses anew. Yet this can only happen where the amount of fees and expenses has not been previously agreed. The Auditor has no power to order the repayment of fees or expenses where the amount thereof was actually agreed, no matter how excessive he considers them to be. Rule 60(6)(b) indicates that r.60 does not affect the power of the Outer House under r.16. This allows the Outer House, on the application of a party or the arbitrator concerned, to make an order relating to the arbitrator's entitlement (if any) to fees and expenses when the arbitrator's tenure ends, e.g. as a result of the arbitrator resigning or being removed by the parties or the court. The Outer House may thus express its disapproval of the arbitrator's behaviour by restricting the amount of fees and expenses payable, and this would prevail over any agreement with the parties and any determination by the Auditor.

Tribunal awarding expenses

9.3.17.3

Rule 62(1) states that the tribunal may make an award allocating the parties' liability between themselves for recoverable (see para.9.3.17.4) arbitration expenses (or any part of those expenses). Yet r.62 is a default rule, so that the parties might exclude it altogether, or vary it in some way. Thus they could remove this power from the tribunal or transfer it to a third party. They might even agree on a basis for the allocation of such liability (but see para.9.3.17.7). By virtue of r.66, such an award may be made together with or separately from an award on the substance of the dispute, and the Rules would apply to an expenses award as they would apply to an award on the substance. If a tribunal chooses not to make an award (or until it does), r.62(3) makes the parties liable for their own expenses, and (as between themselves) liable for an equal share of the expenses for which they are severally liable under r.60.

Where the tribunal does award expenses, r.62(2) directs that it must have regard to the principle that expenses should follow a decision made in favour of a party except where this would be inappropriate in the circumstances. The default nature of the rule means that this provision might be varied, e.g. to give the tribunal complete discretion in how it awards expenses, or to provide an entirely different basis on which expenses should be awarded.

Rule 62(4) concludes by stating that r.62 does not affect the parties' several liability for fees under r.60,[241] nor the liability of any party to any other third party.[242] The former statement is presumably for the avoidance of doubt, since nothing agreed between the parties nor ordered by the tribunal can affect the mandatory several liability imposed by r.60.

Recoverable arbitration expenses

9.3.17.4

A tribunal may award "recoverable arbitration expenses" under r.62, but what does this mean? Essentially, in terms of r.61 such expenses fall into two categories. The first consists of the various fees and expenses for which the parties are liable under r.60. The second consists of the parties' legal and other expenses.[243] However, in relation to this second category it is for the tribunal to determine the amount which is recoverable[244] or arrange for the Auditor of the Court of Session to do so.[245] Moreover, unless the tribunal (or the Auditor) decides otherwise, that amount must be determined on the basis that

---

[239] See r.60(4)(b).
[240] See r.60(5).
[241] See r.62(4)(a).
[242] See r.62(4)(b).
[243] Under r.59(c).
[244] See r.61(2)(a).
[245] See r.61(2)(b).

a reasonable amount is to be allowed in respect of all reasonably incurred expenses,[246] while any doubt as to whether expenses were reasonably incurred or are reasonable in amount is to be resolved in favour of the person liable to pay them.[247] The fact that the Auditor has determined the amount of expenses does not of itself seem to afford a legal basis for their recovery, so that it must be assumed that any such determination will be incorporated into an award. It may be added that r.61 is default and so may be excluded or varied by the parties.

9.3.17.5 Limitation on expenses

Rule 65(1) states that a provisional or part award may cap a party's liability for recoverable expenses at an amount specified in the award, but r.65(2) continues that such an award must be made sufficiently in advance of the expenses to which the cap relates being incurred, or the taking of any steps in the arbitration which are affected by the cap, for the parties to take account of it. There is obviously no point in a final award seeking to impose a cap, since the relevant expenses will already have been incurred. The idea is that the tribunal may impose a ceiling on expenses. Thus while a party is not prevented from spending as much as it likes on the arbitration, if it wins it will not be able to recover more than the capped amount from the other party. This also means that the other party will not be coerced into abandoning the proceedings for fear of incurring an expenses award it could not meet. Rule 65 is a default provision, so the parties may agree to deprive the tribunal of this power.

9.3.17.6 Security for expenses

Rule 64 states that the tribunal may order a party making a claim to provide security for the recoverable arbitration expenses or any part of them.[248] It continues that, if that order is not complied with, the tribunal may make an award dismissing any claim made by that party.[249] However, such an order is not to be made only on the ground that a party is an individual who ordinarily resides outwith the UK,[250] or is a body which is incorporated or formed under the law of a country outwith the UK[251] or which is managed or controlled from outwith the UK.[252] The idea behind this provision is to protect a respondent who fears that it will win the arbitration and be awarded expenses, but be ruined since it will struggle to recover these from the claimant, either because the claimant is of dubious financial stability or has few assets in the UK. It is suggested that being guided by the latter should not offend against the prohibition against making an order on the basis of the claimant's residence, etc. since there is a distinction between making an order simply because the claimant is a foreign national or company, and making an order because the claimant's assets are located in a foreign jurisdiction where an award would be difficult to enforce.

Rule 64 is a default provision. Thus the parties may deprive the tribunal of this power, or subject its exercise to a different set of conditions, or remove the restrictions imposed by r.64(2).

9.3.17.7 Ban on pre-dispute agreements

While, in terms of r.60, the parties cannot alter by agreement their several liability for the arbitrators' fees and expenses and the expenses incurred by the tribunal, they are otherwise free to reach agreement on their liability for expenses as between themselves. That freedom includes the right not to have that latter liability determined by the tribunal. Instead the parties may agree to have it determined by other means, including by simple agreement. Nonetheless, the mandatory r.63 states that any agreement allocating the parties' liability between themselves for any or all of the arbitration expenses has no

---

[246] See r.61(3)(a).
[247] See r.61(3)(b).
[248] See r.64(1)(a).
[249] See r.64(1)(b).
[250] See r.64(2)(a).
[251] See r.64(2)(b)(i).
[252] See r.64(2)(b)(ii).

effect if entered into before the dispute being arbitrated has arisen. This addresses the practice in certain industries of including in arbitration clauses a provision whereby the customer would be liable to meet the entire expenses of any arbitral proceedings whatever their outcome might be. This would clearly act as a considerable disincentive to customers proceeding with the arbitration. While the rule is intended to prevent the abuse of an unequal bargaining position, it will catch any pre-dispute agreement, even if it is less objectionable, e.g. an agreement that expenses will follow success. If the agreement of the parties is struck down by r.63, then the tribunal would have jurisdiction to award expenses under R.61, unless the parties agree differently. Once a dispute has actually arisen, the parties may enter into any agreement they choose regarding their liability for expenses as between themselves—including that one party will be liable for the entire expenses whatever the outcome of the proceedings. At that stage a party would of course have no incentive to agree to such an asymmetrical arrangement.

ENFORCING AN AWARD   9.3.18

It will usually be the case that the party against whom an award is made does not challenge it, but simply acts as it directs. Yet it may happen that such a party, without actually challenging the award, makes no move to abide by it. In such a case, the other party will usually have no option but to apply to the court for the enforcement of the award. The 2010 Act introduces a general enforcement provision in respect of arbitral awards. It governs the enforcement of all arbitration awards whether they are made in Scotland or elsewhere. Nonetheless awards made abroad which are subject to the New York Convention are subject to their own regime under ss.18 to 22 of the Act, while a number of specialist enforcement regimes continue to operate under a variety of other statutes. These will not be considered here. While the Act provides for the enforcement of the awards, it no longer seems open for a party to respond to an action to enforce an award by seeking to have it reduced by exception (*ope exceptionis*), an option available at common law. This is because the possibility is not contemplated by s.12 of the Act, while s.11(2) explicitly rules out any means of court challenge of an award except as provided for by Pt 8 of the Scottish Arbitration Rules. This would also seem to rule out a party raising a petition for suspension of an award.

Section 12(1) of the Act states that the court[253] may, on application by any party, order that a tribunal's award may be enforced as if it were an extract registered decree bearing a warrant for execution granted by the court. This means that the winning party would be able to enforce the award in the same way as a court decree, i.e. proceed immediately to do diligence against the other party's assets. Apart from situations where the court is prohibited from enforcing the award (see below) the use of the word "may" in s.12(1) seems to give the court discretion not to enforce the award. Cases where the court might decline to enforce the award might include the situation where the award deals with issues which are not arbitrable, or where it appears to be illegal or otherwise to offend against public policy.

It also remains possible for an award to be enforced without court action. At common law, if an arbitration agreement was registered for execution in the books of a sheriff court or the Books of Council and Session, then provided the parties agreed,[254] the award may also be so registered. This then allowed summary diligence to be done on the award. Provided the arbitration agreement has been properly registered, s.12(5) of the 2010 Act removes the need for both parties to consent to registration of the award, and instead allows either party to register an award for execution unless they have agreed that this should not happen. While the Requirements of Writing Act 1995 s.6 indicates that it is not competent to register a document for execution unless the document has self-proving status, that provision is impliedly disapplied with regard to arbitral awards by the 2010 Act.

There are a number of situations where the court cannot enforce an award. One is under s.12(3) where it is satisfied that the tribunal lacked jurisdiction to make the award. The court may order enforcement of only part of the award, where that part is within the tribunal's jurisdiction and the remainder is not. However, a party may not wait until the stage of enforcement before raising the issue of jurisdiction, as s.12(4) notes that a party may have lost the right to raise a jurisdictional objection under r.76

---

[253] The Court of Session or the appropriate sheriff court: s.12(8).
[254] See *Baillie v Pollock* (1829) 7 S. 619.

(see para.9.3.14). Thus a party who goes through the arbitral process believing that the tribunal lacks jurisdiction or is exceeding its jurisdiction, but who does not challenge the tribunal's jurisdiction (see para.9.3.14.2.1), cannot then seek to resist enforcement on that basis. It is of course a different matter if the party has refused to engage in the proceedings (see para.9.3.10.4), or if the party had no idea that the tribunal would exceed its jurisdiction until the appearance of the award.

The other situations where an award may not be enforced are laid down by s.12(2). They are where the court is satisfied that the award is:

- the subject of an appeal to the Outer House under any of the grounds laid down by Pt 8 of the Rules (see para.9.3.14.2); or
- the subject of an arbitral process of appeal or review, e.g. an appeal to a second arbitral tribunal or other body;
- the subject of an application to have the award corrected by the tribunal under r.58 (see para.9.3.13),

and that process has not been determined. There appears to be no discretion where the conditions of s.12(2) are met. The court is prohibited from enforcing the award, even where it seems clear that the party who has challenged the award has no prospect of success and has only raised the challenge to give himself a breathing space, during which time he can take action to defeat the ultimate enforcement of the award.

Section 12 does not affect any other right to enforce an award under "any other enactment or rule of law". This means that it remains open for a party to seek enforcement under other regimes, which must obviously include the common law. This will not be addressed here, but is covered at para.9.3.14 of the previous edition of this work.

NON-BINDING FORMS OF DISPUTE RESOLUTION

9.4 As an alternative to litigation or arbitration, the parties may seek to settle their disputes via procedures which do not result in a binding decision being handed down by a third party. There are various forms of such procedures:

9.4.1 NEGOTIATION

Over the years many disputes have been settled by negotiation. This continues to be the case. Negotiations can be carried on directly between the parties or through representatives such as legal advisers. It seems that an agreement to negotiate is not binding.[255]

9.4.2 MEDIATION AND CONCILIATION

While third parties involved in negotiation act directly on behalf of one or other of the parties, other forms of consensual resolution witness a third party playing an independent role. The most common form of such a process is mediation or conciliation. The terms are here employed together as they are often used synonymously, or in so far as they are used to denote different processes there appears to be no consensus as to which term describes which process. The most rudimentary form of mediation/conciliation simply witnesses the third party acting as an intermediary in negotiations between the parties. Another form sees the third party taking a rather more active role, perhaps pointing out the strengths and weaknesses in each party's position, and perhaps indicating to each a position which he thinks the other party might accept. Yet some forms of mediation/conciliation involve the third party in actively exploring with the parties their aims and expectations of the process, suggesting how such aims

---

[255] See *Walford v Miles* [1992] 2 A.C. 128. But note the reservations of Lord Steyn regarding that decision expressed in *Fulfilling the Expectations of Reasonable Men* (1997) 113 Law Quarterly Review 433.

might be best achieved and proactively developing possible lines of solution. In England mediation and conciliation are seen as attracting obligations of confidentiality[256] and as also invoking privilege.[257]

A European Mediation Directive[258] was adopted May 21, 2008, requiring Member States to implement it by May 21, 2011.[259] It was sought to be given effect in Scotland by the Cross-Border Mediation (Scotland) Regulations 2011.[260] They apply only to cross-border disputes, i.e. where at least one party to a dispute is domiciled or habitually resident in a Member State other than that of another party, so that they do not apply to disputes where the parties are all from Scotland or from within the UK. The Scottish regulations do not apply to disputes where mediation began prior to April 6, 2011, and mediation begins when all parties agree to participate in the mediation concerned.[261] A mediator or person involved in the administration of a mediation in a cross-border dispute is not to be compelled in any civil proceedings or arbitration to give evidence or produce any material regarding any information arising out of or in connection with that mediation.[262] However, this privilege does not apply where all the parties agree otherwise,[263] or in the circumstances described in the Directive Article 7.1(a) and (b)[264]; i.e. where outstanding considerations of public policy, especially the best interests of children or the prevention of harm to the physical or psychological integrity of a person, demand otherwise, or in order to ensure the implementation of an agreement resulting from the mediation. Regulations 4 to 9 then extend various prescription and limitation periods and time limits under the Prescription and Limitation (Scotland) Act 1973 and a number of other pieces of legislation. In each case where a period would have expired while mediation was continuing or within eight weeks of it ending, that period will not expire until eight weeks after the end of the mediation. Parts 3 and 4 of the UK Regulations have the same effect in relation to various pieces of legislation which apply across the UK.

Although mediation is as not as well developed as in other jurisdictions, its use in Scotland has been growing, and the process enjoys a degree of official support. The Scottish Mediation Network has been funded by the Scottish Government (and previously the Executive) in order to provide a quality assurance network across all spheres of mediation. Pilot in-court mediation services have operated in several sheriff courts[265] and the Report of the Civil Justice Review (2009) recommended that this be rolled out more generally. The Sheriff Court Rules relating to commercial actions insist that, at the case management conference, the sheriff "shall seek to secure the expeditious resolution of the action",[266] while the sheriff has the power to make any order which he or she "thinks will result in the speedy resolution of the dispute (including the use of alternative dispute resolution)".[267] This probably falls short of a power to order parties to mediate. A consultation by the Sheriff Court Rules Council favoured the creation of a rule which would require parties to consider mediation and other forms of ADR.[268] While this fell short of actually requiring compulsory mediation, it was thought that refusal to participate in such a

---

[256] See *Farm Assist Ltd v Secretary of State for the Environment (No.2)* [2009] EWHC 1102 (TCC).

[257] See *Aird and Aird v Prime Meridian Ltd* [2006] B.L.R. 494; but note *Oceanbulk Shipping & Trading SA v TMT Asia Ltd* [2011] A.C. 662.

[258] Directive 2008/52.

[259] See art.12.

[260] (SSI 2011/234).

[261] See reg.1.

[262] See reg.3(1).

[263] See reg.3(2)(a).

[264] See reg.3(2)(b).

[265] See E. Samuel, *Supporting Court-Users: The In-House Advice and Mediation Projects in Edinburgh Sheriff Court* (Scottish Executive Central Research Unit, 2002); M Ross and D Bain, *In Court Mediation Pilot Projects* (Scottish Government 2010).

[266] Act of Sederunt (Sheriff Court Ordinary Cause Rules) 1993 (SI 1993/1956) r.40.12.(1).

[267] Act of Sederunt (Sheriff Court Ordinary Cause Rules) 1993 (SI 1993/1956 r.40.12.(2)(m). Nothing similar is to be found in the Rules of the Court of Session, although a Practice Note of 2004 states at para.11(1) that parties' legal advisers should have established whether "there is a real dispute, which requires to be resolved by judicial decision rather than other means", and that parties may wish to consider ADR.

[268] Sheriff Court Rules Council, *The Sheriff Court and Alternative Dispute Resolution* (Scottish Executive Justice Department, 2006), paras 2.4–2.5.

process might be reflected in an award of expenses.[269] Certainly, in England courts have on occasion declined to award costs to parties who have unreasonably declined to mediate.[270]

The juridical nature of mediation in Scotland is doubtful. While it would certainly be the case that mediation (or any other ADR process) can yield a binding settlement agreement, it is probably the case that an agreement to mediate is not itself binding. Scots authority on the matter is lacking. English authority traditionally tends to suggest that such agreements are not enforceable.[271] The problem appears to be that it would be difficult to determine whether or not a party had participated in the process in good faith and equally difficult to assess damages arising from breach of the obligation. However, there have been recent suggestions that these do not constitute insurmountable obstacles to enforceability,[272] and other jurisdictions are quite happy to regard such obligations as enforceable.[273]

9.4.3 MED-ARB

Dispute resolution clauses may often involve more than one stage, with the parties initially going to mediation and then to litigation or arbitration if no settlement ensues. This is unobjectionable if the mediator is not involved in the arbitral proceedings. However, med-arb combines elements of mediation and arbitration, as an individual first acts as mediator in the dispute, and then proceeds to arbitrate if mediation has failed. Another variant sees the arbiter actively seeking to promote settlement during the course of proceedings. The obvious concern is that involvement in the mediation process means that the arbitrator is potentially biased, especially if he has been made privy to information which would otherwise be confidential, a possibility acknowledged by Judge Lloyd in *Glencot Development and Design Co Ltd v Ben Barrett & Son (Contractors) Ltd.*[274] Another possibility is that a mediator gains a skewed view of the situation because of a false view communicated by one party. As the other party is not aware of this, he cannot take steps to correct it during the subsequent arbitration process. Certainly, examples exist where courts in other jurisdictions have found awards to be tainted by the appearance of bias following med-arb.[275]

9.4.4 ARB-MED

This is the mirror image of med-arb, and witnesses arbitration occurring prior to mediation. This works because the arbitration award is not published immediately, but will only be revealed if the parties do not reach a settlement through mediation. The theory is that having been through the arbitration process, the parties have a much better sense of the strengths of their respective cases and will thus be more ready to settle. Opinion is divided as to whether the same individual should act as arbitrator and mediator.[276] The advantage is his knowledge of the issues, but the other side of the coin is that the contents of the award may quickly become evident as the mediation process unfolds.

---

[269] *The Sheriff Court and Alternative Dispute Resolution*, para.2.7.

[270] See e.g. *Dunnett v Railtrack Plc (No.2)* [2002] 2 All E.R. 850; C.A. *Halsey v Milton Keynes General NHS Trust* [2004] 1 W.L.R 3002; C.A. indicates the circumstances in which it might be reasonable to decline to mediate. In *PGF II SA v OMFS Co 1 Ltd* [2014] 1 All E.R. 970, the Court of Appeal held that as a general rule, silence in the face of an invitation to participate in ADR was in itself unreasonable, and cost be reflected in an award of costs, regardless of whether there was a good reason for a refusal to engage in ADR.

[271] See *Paul Smith Ltd v H & S International Holdings Ltd* [1991] 2 Lloyd's Rep 127; C.A.

[272] See the views of Longmore LJ in *Petromec Inc v Petroleo Brasileiro SA Petrobras (No.3)* [2006] 1 Lloyd's Rep 121 at [116]–[121].

[273] See *Aiton (Australia) Pty Ltd v Transfield Pty Ltd* [2000] A.D.R.L.J. 342.

[274] *Glencot Development and Design Co Ltd v Ben Barrett & Son (Contractors) Ltd* [2001] B.L.R. 207 at [21]; but see *Mi-Space (UK) Ltd v Lend Lease Constructiion (EMEA) Ltd* [2013] EWHC 2001.

[275] See *Gao Haiyan v Keeneye Holdings Ltd* [2011] HKCFI 240; especially Reyes J at [71]–[77]. The decision was reversed on other grounds at [2011] HKCA 459. And contrast *Acorn Farms Ltd v Schnuriger* [2003] 3 N.Z.L.R. 121.

[276] See H. Brown and A. Marriott, *ADR: Principles and Practice*, 2nd edn (London: Sweet & Maxwell, 2011), paras 19.019–19.020.

NEUTRAL EXPERT/EARLY NEUTRAL EVALUATION 9.4.5

Where a dispute involves complex issues a neutral expert—as opposed to an expert employed by one of the parties—can be employed to analyse the facts in a non-partisan way so that the real issues emerge. The parties are thus aided to settle the case. A variation on this sees a legal expert evaluating the cases so that parties obtain a sense of the likelihood of success, and again may thus be prompted to settle. It is noteworthy that in the Commercial Court in England the presiding judge may, if it appears likely to assist in the resolution of the dispute or certain issues in the dispute, with the agreement of the parties refer such matters to early neutral evaluation. This will be carried out by another judge of the Commercial Court, who will not participate in the case itself should it proceed.[277]

DISPUTE RESOLUTION BOARDS 9.4.6

Such a board is a panel of experts appointed at the beginning of a project. The board sits at regular intervals and hears all the issues that have arisen between the parties during the previous period. The board strives to resolve such issues, but if any issue escalates into an actual dispute, the board will rule on the matter. This ruling may take the form of a recommendation, but may be an actual decision. Such decisions may or may not be binding, but if they are they tend to be provisionally so, since either party may choose not to accept the view of the board and to resort to arbitration or litigation.

EXECUTIVE TRIBUNAL 9.4.7

Sometimes also known as a mini-trial, this involves the representatives (usually lawyers) of the parties to the dispute making within an agreed time-limit a presentation of their respective cases to a panel composed of executives from both sides (who usually have not been involved in the dispute), plus a neutral adviser. The presentations are generally made in an informal way, with any member of the panel free to ask questions. The aims are to identify the strengths and weaknesses of each side's case, and to provide some indication of how actual litigation might develop. In order to expedite matters the parties will have prior to the hearing exchanged key documents, plus witness and expert statements. Following the presentation, the members of the panel seek to achieve a negotiated solution. The role of the neutral may be merely to assist in promoting settlement, but more commonly to provide advice on matters of law and evidence during the presentations and thereafter, if negotiations are deadlocked, to suggest what the likely outcome of litigation would be. The purpose of this would be to encourage the parties to reassess their positions with a view to reaching a settlement.

SUMMARY JURY TRIAL 9.4.8

Sharing some similarities with the executive tribunal, this involves the parties presenting summary versions of their cases to a mock jury, in order to ascertain the reaction of that jury. The theory is that the parties might be helped to achieve a settlement by that reaction, although it might be wondered how realistic a view of the strengths of their cases is obtained by this method.

OMBUDSMEN 9.4.9

Ombudsman schemes are available to consumers in a number of industries, although not all companies participate in the schemes unless obliged to by statute. It is quite common for access to these schemes to be available only to consumers and only after contractual dispute resolution procedures have been resorted to and have failed. Access is usually free or almost free for consumers. Procedures are described as "flexible and informal, and rely heavily on inquisitorial methods".[278] The ombudsman will typically

---

[277] See generally Pt G2 of the *Admiralty and Commercial Courts Guide*, 9th edn (London: Courts and Tribunal Service, 2011).
[278] Office of Fair Trading, *Consumer Redress Mechanisms* (1991), para.4.74.

investigate consumer complaints and seek initially to resolve them via conciliation. If this proves impossible, the ombudsman will issue a decision that will bind the company involved but usually not the consumer. Thus if the latter is dissatisfied with the decision, he is free to pursue other remedies. Generally, in reaching an award an ombudsman will not be confined by the consumer's strict rights and will be entitled to take into account matters such as good practice.[279] So compensation may be awarded if the business behaved questionably, albeit not illegally. There is often an upper limit on the amount that an ombudsman can award the consumer. A specific scheme—the Financial Ombudsman Service—is discussed in rather more detail at the end of Ch.3.

9.4.10 EXPERT DETERMINATION

This is a form of dispute resolution which has grown in popularity over the years. It involves the parties submitting a dispute for determination by an expert in the relevant field. The expert may determine the matter entirely on the basis of his own expertise, but may carry out his own inquiries if necessary. However, this is not in the nature of a judicial enquiry, which is what distinguishes it from arbitration. The aim is to resolve the dispute with finality and maximum expedition. Expert determination has attracted its own distinct jurisprudence in England, and a determination can be challenged on the basis that the expert has failed to abide by his mandate.[280]

9.4.11 WHY RESORT TO ADR?

Leaving aside issues such as counterclaims, in both litigation and arbitration there tends to be a winner and a loser. The dispute between the parties is reduced to a past situation which either did or did not amount to an infringement of a party's legal rights, and for which therefore compensation either is or is not payable. No account is taken of the wider relationship between the parties and their wider interests. This may even mean that a win-lose situation may sometimes become a lose-lose situation. Consider the example of a small software firm which has secured a massive order from a major company. The firm intimates to the company some months before the agreed delivery date that there is no hope of it meeting that date or being able to deliver for a significant period of time. Here is a clear anticipatory breach of contract which would allow the company to rescind and claim damages. Yet let us suppose the firm is on the brink of insolvency. Losing the contract and being sued might put them out of business. The company's claim could be worthless, as any damages awarded would not be practically recoverable, and any resources invested in suing the firm would be thrown away. Indeed, if the company cannot get the very specialised software it requires at the appropriate time, it may risk being unable to fulfil its own contracts, consequently sustaining substantial losses. However, a mediation or negotiation based approach may reveal that a cash-flow problem has meant that the firm has been unable to hire sufficient staff to meet its commitments. An early release of part of the sums payable on completion of the contract allows it to recruit the staff and get back on schedule. In return the company receives a discount and favourable rates in respect of further contracts it negotiates with the firm. Thus a lose-lose situation is transformed into a win-win situation. While real life situations may rarely work out so ideally, this example illustrates the possibilities offered by ADR.

It may also be added that ADR processes are invariably private and confidential. Some are very low cost, or even no cost, although those forms which involve meeting the cost of mediation services might conceivably be more expensive than the more streamlined forms of litigation and arbitration. Equally, while ADR is usually designed to be expeditious, it can be extremely protracted, and of course it should always be remembered that the time and expense invested in such processes is ultimately wasted if no resolution can be reached. Even if a settlement is reached, not all such settlements are binding, so that it is possible that a party might renege. At least litigation and arbitration can guarantee a binding result. It can also be noted that where there is a marked disparity of power, non-adjudicative processes like negotiation and mediation may operate to the detriment of the weaker party, who might well be better served by insisting on their legal rights.

---

[279] See Lewison J in *Bunney v Burns Anderson Plc* [2008] B.L.R. 29 at [22]; Rix LJ in *R v FOS* [2008] B.L.R. 1500 at [80].
[280] See, e.g. Simon Brown LJ in *Veba Oil v Petrotrade Inc.* [2002] 1 Lloyd's Rep. 295 at [26].

INDEX